MW00341905

HUMAN BODY PERCEPTION FROM THE INSIDE OUT

ADVANCES IN VISUAL COGNITION

Series Editors
Gillian Rhodes
Mary A. Peterson

Human Body Perception From the Inside Out
Edited by Günther Knoblich, Ian M. Thornton, Marc Grosjean,
and Maggie Shiffrar

HUMAN BODY PERCEPTION FROM THE INSIDE OUT

Edited by
Günther Knoblich
Ian M. Thornton
Marc Grosjean
Maggie Shiffrar

OXFORD
UNIVERSITY PRESS

2006

OXFORD

UNIVERSITY PRESS

Oxford University Press, Inc., publishes works that further
Oxford University's objective of excellence
in research, scholarship, and education.

Oxford   New York
Auckland   Cape Town   Dar es Salaam   Hong Kong   Karachi
Kuala Lumpur   Madrid   Melbourne   Mexico City   Nairobi
New Delhi   Shanghai   Taipei   Toronto

With offices in
Argentina   Austria   Brazil   Chile   Czech Republic   France   Greece
Guatemala   Hungary   Italy   Japan   Poland   Portugal   Singapore
South Korea   Switzerland   Thailand   Turkey   Ukraine   Vietnam

Copyright © 2006 by Günther Knoblich, Ian M. Thornton, Marc Grosjean, Maggie Shiffrar

Published by Oxford University Press, Inc.
198 Madison Avenue, New York, New York 10016

www.oup.com

Oxford is a registered trademark of Oxford University Press

All rights reserved. No part of this publication may be reproduced,
stored in a retrieval system, or transmitted, in any form or by any means,
electronic, mechanical, photocopying, recording, or otherwise,
without the prior permission of Oxford University Press.

Library of Congress Cataloging-in-Publication Data
Human body perception from the inside out / edited by Günther Knoblich ... [et al.].
    p.   cm.
ISBN-13 978-0-19-517837-1
ISBN 0-19-517837-8
1. Body image.   I. Knoblich, Günther.
BF697.5.B63H86 2005
152.1'88—dc22   2005000609

9 8 7 6 5 4 3 2 1

Printed in the United States of America
on acid-free paper

Contents

Contributors   ix

1 Integrating Perspectives on Human Body Perception   3
    Günther Knoblich, Ian Thornton, Marc Grosjean,
    and Maggie Shiffrar

Section I: Body and Multimodal Perception

2 An Introduction to Body and Multimodal Perception   11
    Marc Grosjean

3 Beyond the Body Schema: Visual, Prosthetic, and Technological
    Contributions to Bodily Perception and Awareness   15
    Nicholas P. Holmes and Charles Spence

4 From "Body in the Brain" to "Body in Space": Sensory
    and Intentional Components of Body Representation   65
    Angelo Maravita

5 Multisensory Representation of Peripersonal Space   89
    Elisabetta Làdavas and Alessandro Farnè

6 A Bayesian View on Multimodal Cue Integration   105
    Marc O. Ernst

Section II: Body Representations

7 Body-Based Views of the World: An Introduction
    to Body Representations   135
    Maggie Shiffrar

8 Body Mereology   147
    Frederique de Vignemont, Manos Tsakiris,
    and Patrick Haggard

9 From Phantom Limb to Phantom Body: Varieties
   of Extracorporeal Awareness   171
   Peter Brugger

10 Covert Imitation: How the Body Schema Acts
   as a Prediction Device   211
   Margaret Wilson

11 Not Just Posturing: Configural Processing of the Human Body   229
   Catherine L. Reed, Valerie E. Stone, and John E. McGoldrick

Section III: Perception of Biological Motion

12 Of Bodies, Brains, and Models: Studying the Perception
   of Biological Motion   261
   Ian M. Thornton

13 Biological Motion: Point-Light Walkers and Beyond   271
   Ian M. Thornton

14 Developing Body Representations: A Review of Infants' Responses
   to Biological-Motion Displays   305
   Jeannine Pinto

15 Computational Principles for the Recognition of Biological
   Movements: Model-Based Versus Feature-Based
   Approaches   323
   Martin A. Giese

16 Evidence for a Network of Brain Areas Involved in Perception
   of Biological Motion   361
   Emily D. Grossman

Section IV: Intention and Action in Body Perception

17 An Introduction to Intention and Action in Body Perception:
   The Body as the Actor's Tool   387
   Günther Knoblich

18 Representational Foundations of Intentional Action   393
   Wolfgang Prinz

19 When the Other Influences the Self: Interference Between Perception
   and Action   413
   Sarah-Jayne Blakemore

20 Representing Intentional Relations and Acting Intentionally
    in Infancy: Current Insights and Open Questions   427
        Chris Moore

Author Index   443

Subject Index   459

Contributors

Sarah-Jayne Blakemore
Institute of Cognitive
   Neuroscience
University College London
17 Queen Square
London WC1N 3AR
United Kingdom
s.blakemore@ucl.ac.uk

Peter Brugger
Department of Neurology
Neuropsychology Unit
University Hospital Zürich
CH-8091 Zürich
Switzerland
peter.brugger@usz.ch

Marc O. Ernst
Max Planck Institute for Human
   Cognitive and Brain Sciences
Spemannstrasse 38
72076 Tübingen
Germany
marc.ernst@tuebingen.mpg.de

Alessandro Farnè
Dipartimento di Psicologia
Università degli Studi
   di Bologna
Viale Berti Pichat, 5
40127, Bologna
Italy
alessandro.farne@unibo.it

Martin A. Giese
ARL, Hertie Center for Clinical
   Brain Research
University Clinic Tübingen
Schaffhausenstr. 113
D-72076 Tübingen
Germany
martin.giese@uni-tuebingen.de

Marc Grosjean
Max Planck Institute for Human
   Cognitive and Brain Sciences
Department of Psychology
Amalienstrasse 33
80799 Munich
Germany
grosjean@cbs.mpg.de

Emily D. Grossman
3151 Social Sciences Plaza
Department of Cognitive
   Sciences
University of California
Irvine, CA 92697-5100
USA
grossman@uci.edu

Patrick Haggard
Institute of Cognitive
   Neuroscience
University College London
17 Queen Square

London WC1N 3AR
United Kingdom
p.haggard@ucl.ac.uk

Nicholas P. Holmes
Department of Experimental
  Psychology
University of Oxford
South Parks Road
Oxford, OX1 3UD
United Kingdom
nicholas.holmes@psy.ox.ac.uk

Günther Knoblich
Department of Psychology
Smith Hall, 101 Warren Street
Rutgers University
Newark, NJ 07102
USA
knoblich@psychology.rutgers.edu

Elisabetta Làdavas
Dipartimento di Psicologia
Università degli Studi di Bologna
Viale Berti Pichat, 5
40127, Bologna
Italy
elisabetta.ladavas@unibo.it

Angelo Maravita
Dipartimento di Psicologia
Università degli Studi di Milano-
  Bicocca
Piazza dell' Ateneo Nuovo, 1
20126, Milano
Italy
angelo.maravita@unimib.it

John E. McGoldrick
Developmental Cognitive
  Neuroscience Program
Department of Psychology
University of Denver

2155 South Race Street
Denver, CO 80208
USA
jmcgoldrick@cambiumlearning.
  com

Chris Moore
Department of Psychology
Dalhousie University
Halifax, Nova Scotia
B3H 4J1
Canada
moore@dal.ca

Jeannine Pinto
Psychology Department
Lafayette College
Easton, PA 18042
USA
pintoj@lafayette.edu

Wolfgang Prinz
Max Planck Institute for Human
  Cognitive and Brain Sciences
Department of Psychology
Amalienstrasse 33
80799 Munich
Germany
prinz@cbs.mpg.de

Catherine L. Reed
Developmental Cognitive
  Neuroscience Program
Department of Psychology
University of Denver
2155 South Race Street
Denver, CO 80208
USA
creed@du.edu

Maggie Shiffrar
Department of Psychology
301 Smith Hall

Rutgers University
Newark, NJ 07102
USA
mag@psychology.rutgers.edu

Charles Spence
Department of Experimental
   Psychology
University of Oxford
South Parks Road
Oxford, OX1 3U
United Kingdom
charles.spence@psy.ox.ac.uk

Valerie E. Stone
Developmental Cognitive
   Neuroscience Program
Department of Psychology
University of Denver
2155 South Race Street
Denver, CO 80208
USA
v.stone@psy.uq.edu.au

Ian M. Thornton
Department of Psychology
University of Wales, Swansea
Singleton Park

Swansea, SA2899
United Kingdom
I.M.Thornton@swansea.ac.uk

Manos Tsakiris
Institute of Cognitive
   Neuroscience
University College London
17 Queen Square
London WC1N 3AR
United Kingdom
e.tsakiris@ucl.ac.uk

Frederique de Vignemont
Institute of Cognitive
   Neuroscience
University College London
17 Queen Square
London WC1N 3AR
United Kingdom
f.vignemont@ucl.ac.uk

Margaret Wilson
Department of Psychology
University of California
Santa Cruz, CA 95064
USA
mlwilson@ucsc.edu

HUMAN BODY PERCEPTION
FROM THE INSIDE OUT

1

Integrating Perspectives on Human Body Perception

Günther Knoblich
Ian Thornton
Marc Grosjean
Maggie Shiffrar

There is but one temple in the universe and that is the body of man.

— Novalis (German lyricist, 1772–1801)

It is in moments of illness that we are compelled to recognize that we live not alone but are chained to a creature of a different kingdom, whole worlds apart, who has no knowledge of us and by whom it is impossible to make ourselves understood: our body.

— Marcel Proust (French novelist, 1871–1922)

It is virtually impossible not to perceive one's own body. When we wake up in the morning, our bodies are the first things we feel and see. As the day goes on we continue to perceive our bodies; in one way or another they are always present, in our perceptual experience, until we fall asleep again at night. Almost equally ubiquitous is the perception of others' bodies, be it those of our partners, children, colleagues, or strangers in real life, on TV, or in projected images.

At first glance, perception of one's own body seems utterly different from perception of other people's bodies. These differences include a differing visual perspective of the body and its parts as well as differences in whether the

3

observer receives proprioceptive information for the observed body. However, a central link among many chapters of this book is that despite these differences, perception of one's own and others' bodies are closely related.

While cognitive psychologists and neuroscientists increasingly focus their attention on the body, such an interest in itself is not new. In one form or another, the body has been central to many of the discourses that shaped cultural history. Scholars, artists, and average people have seen the human body in very different lights over time. For instance, the philosopher Plato considered the body to be the mortal shell of an immortal soul. Ascetics in the Christian religious tradition believed that the body needed to be disciplined in order to engage in soulful prayer. More recently, Proust (quoted in one of the epigraphs above) described the body as a "creature from a different kingdom . . . who has no knowledge of us." However the body has not always aroused denial, disgust, or alienation. Countless visual artists have dedicated their lives to sculpting or drawing the perfect body, and lyricists like Novalis have composed verbal hymns to the body. Today, the body continues to inspire us as we act, dance, and exercise (or, arguably more frequently, watch others act, dance, and exercise). Also, striving for perfection of one's own body, albeit according to questionable "body standards," has become common practice in many cultures.

The focus of early cognitive science on symbolic processing and computer models led to a prevailing view in which the human body was not regarded as a special object. Research from the 1990s and into the twenty-first century, however, has dramatically challenged this assumption and reflects a surge of interest in the "embodied" nature of cognition. As a consequence, human body perception has become an important research topic within several branches of psychology and the neurosciences. Numerous lines of research have started to develop in parallel, each providing its own specific perspective on body perception. Yet, limited cross-talk among these scientific programs has constrained the broader impact of research on body perception. Recent developments, such as the increased interest in perception-action links, can bridge these lines of research and facilitate the development of an integrated view of body perception. The present book is an attempt to pave the way for such an integrated view.

The aim of this book is twofold. The first goal is to provide an accessible state-of-the-art account of the four main research perspectives on body perception. Accordingly, the book is organized into four sections: (1) body and multimodal perception, (2) body representations, (3) perception of biological motion, and (4) intention and action in body perception. The second goal of this book is to highlight the links that exist among these different research lines. To this end, each section begins with an introduction by one of the editors that puts the section in the broader context of human body perception. In addition, references to chapters in different sections are indicated throughout the book.

The first section focuses on body and multimodal perception. This line of research deals with how the integration of information from different sensory modalities both determines and is modulated by the perception of our own body. The main questions that are addressed in this section are: how does vision and its interaction with touch and proprioception contribute to the perceived location and identity of body parts (chapters 3 and 4)? How does multisensory integration differ for events that occur within the space immediately surrounding the body (i.e., peripersonal space) as opposed to outside of it (i.e., extrapersonal space)? In particular, how is multisensory integration within peripersonal space affected by abstract knowledge and self-awareness (chapter 4), and what are the functional properties of this space and the automatic nature of multisensory processing within it (chapter 5)? Moreover, how can the presence of fake limbs or the active use of tools extend peripersonal space beyond the space immediately surrounding the body (chapters 3, 4, and 5)? Finally, what are the computational principles that underlie multisensory integration and, specifically, the relative weighting of information from different sensory modalities (chapter 6)? The various answers provided to these questions lead to the view that the perception of one's own body is based on multimodal representations that act as dynamic points of reference with respect to which multisensory integration occurs.

The second section of this book starts by expanding upon the question of how people represent their own bodies. Clearly, each individual has multiple representations of his or her own body, and each of these representations subserves different systems and goals (chapters 8 and 11). But how do individuals experience their body parts under different conditions (chapters 8 and 9)? How are the relationships between body parts represented (chapter 8)?

The findings from this section indicate that bodies and body parts cannot be understood as complex objects. Instead, they are something wholly different. The complexities of body representations are elaborated further in the study of phantom sensations (chapters 8 and 9). Recent advances have established that neural processes can indeed code for physically absent body parts that are nonetheless experienced (chapter 9). While most researchers have focused on the study of phantoms following amputation, the existence of phantoms for congenitally absent limbs suggests the need for significant shifts in models of body representation. Theories of phantom limb sensations can also be expanded into theories of whole body phantoms (chapter 9). Such an ability to blur the physical distinctions between oneself and other beings suggests that individuals may "project" their own body representations onto the world beyond their own skins.

As inherently social beings, this opens up the possibility that people use their own body representations to represent the bodies of other people (chapters 10 and 11). Support for this idea comes from the finding that the perception of other people's bodies activates the observer's own body representations (chapter 10). Such body-based connections between oneself and others may enable us to anticipate the future actions of other people (chapter 10). If so, such a mechanism could be the foundation for all social action. The last chapter of this section tackles the question of what defines a body (chapter 11). In other words, what collection and arrangement of stimulus properties must be present before I understand that I perceive a body like my own? Studies indicate that bodily orientation and the spatial configuration of limbs are particularly important factors (chapter 11). Such stimulus requirements may ultimately arise from individuals using their own body representations to interpret sensory input (chapter 11).

The theme of the third section is the visual perception of biological—and, in particular, human—motion. The majority of research in this area has involved displays known as Johansson point-light figures (see chapter 13 for a detailed review). In these displays, the human body is reduced to markers placed on the major joints. When shown in motion, such displays convey a clear sense of the underlying action. Research on such biological motion spans many disciplines, including traditional experimental psychology (chapters 13 and 14), neuropsychology, neurophysiology, computational modeling, and neuroimaging (chapters 15 and 16). While understanding the body in motion has given rise to many research directions, there have been three dominant themes. The first concerns the nature of the mechanisms underlying the perception of biological motion (chapters 13, 14, and 15). The second examines the range of information that can be extracted from form-degraded dynamic patterns, for example, the identity, gender, or emotional state of the actor (chapter 12). The third, and most central to the general theme of this book, relates to whether patterns of human motion are in any sense "special" for the visual system (chapters 12, 14, and 16).

The section begins with an overview of the types of stimuli and display manipulations that have been used in experimental studies (chapter 13). Next is the issue of how the visual processing of body motion changes during early development and, in particular, how such developments may co-evolve with increasing motor control of the body (chapter 14). The computational constraints on processing biological motion are then considered, and a neurophysiologically plausible model is described that can account for many psychophysical findings (chapter 15). More generally, chapter 15 also discusses how such theoretical models can be useful additional tools to supplement traditional experimental or analytical methods. Finally, evidence from brain-imaging studies, animal physiology research, and patient data are reviewed, all of which shed light on the brain mechanisms underlying the perception of biological motion (chapter 16). A major theme of this chapter is whether the human brain may have developed network(s) of interconnected regions specifically tuned for the visual interpretation of biological motion.

The last section of this book is dedicated to the role of intention and action in human body perception. The basic idea explored in this section is that the body is the central tool of our mind. We can move our bodies in order to move from one location to another, to grasp and point to objects, or to engage in coordinated actions with others. This raises the question of to what extent the daily experience of intentionally controlling one's body informs and enriches the perception of other intentionally controlled bodies.

The first chapter addresses the representational foundations of intentional action (chapter 18) and looks at the idea that functionally equivalent representations are involved in action control and action perception. This functional equivalence implies that when one perceives another person performing an action, the same representations are activated that one would use to perform the observed action oneself. The second chapter reviews evidence from the neurosciences, which supports the view that the functional equivalence of action production and action perception is implemented in a "mirror system" that involves the pre-motor and the parietal cortex of the human brain (chapter 19). The last chapter introduces the concept of intentional relations, that is, relations between an intentionally acting body and objects that are manipulated by the action (chapter 20). Evidence from early human development suggests that the ability to perceive intentional relations is a crucial prerequisite for understanding others' actions.

Two assumptions recur throughout the four sections of the book, which provide organizing principles that allow one to create links among different lines of research on body perception. The first assumption is that the body should be regarded as a special object of perception. Dedicated sensory systems, in particular the tactile and kinesthetic senses, provide information about one's body that are not directly available for other objects. Importantly, information from these senses is not perceived in isolation but integrated in a flexible and dynamic manner with visual information.

The resulting multisensory codes are combined to form coherent representations that capture the unique structure of the human body. An open question is how flexible such body representations are. The highly adaptive nature of multisensory integration seems to suggest that our brains could adapt to inhabiting a body with a completely different structure. Conversely, neurological syndromes like the experience of phantom limbs suggest that structural body representations are relatively stable, even though sensory input for certain body parts is missing. To summarize, one's own body is a special object of perception, because additional information is available.

Further research illustrates that others' bodies are also special objects of perception, although only visual information about them is available. In particular, there are specific mechanisms to extract body-like forms from perceptual input. Much as for faces, body processing seems to be orientation-specific. Research using point-light displays illustrates that minimal motion information is sufficient to recover structural information about observed bodies. Recent functional-imaging studies suggest that there exist specific brain systems which are dedicated to body processing.

The second recurring assumption in this book is that perception of one's own body and perception of others' bodies are closely related. More specifically, it is postulated that information not directly available for others' bodies can be recovered or simulated using the information available for one's own body. This requires a match of some aspect of the visual information available for others' bodies as well as one's own body. Otherwise, it would be impossible to establish a link between the two. Several possibilities are mentioned. First, there are structural invariants in the relations between different body parts that hold for others' bodies as well as one's own body. Second, bodily movements create characteristic spatiotemporal patterns. In particular, the timing aspect (the rhythm) of these patterns is often relatively invariant for self and other. Third, many bodily movements are carried out intentionally to create certain effects in the environment, for example, to manipulate objects. Typical relationships between body parts and manipulated objects provide a further possibility to achieve a match between self and other.

As soon as such a match is established, the representation of others' bodies and their movements and actions can be enriched using information about one's own body. Using multimodal representations, one can recover proprioceptive information and thus simulate how the other body might feel. Predictive mechanisms normally used to anticipate the consequences of one's own bodily movements become available to anticipate others' bodily movements. Such predictions are not only useful to generate advance information about future events but they can also help to stabilize perception. Both sensory enrichment and movement prediction provide important contributions to the understanding and the interpretation of others' actions. Moreover, they could form an important basis for coordination of one's own and others' bodily movements.

Our hope is that this book will inspire those interested in exploring the cognitive and neuronal bases of human body perception and that it will convince researchers who are not already in the field that body perception is a hot topic that deserves their attention and energy. The chapters collected in this book originated from the talks and discussions given at the symposium The Human Body: Perception From the Inside Out (July 2003, Kloster Irsee, Germany), which was made possible by the generous support of the Max Planck Institute for Human Cognitive and Brain Sciences, Department of Psychology, Munich. We would like to express our gratitude to the Max Planck Society and especially to Professor Dr. Wolfgang Prinz for making this symposium possible. We hope that some of the excitement we felt during the meeting has found its way into the body of this book.

SECTION I

Body and Multimodal Perception

2

An Introduction to Body
and Multimodal Perception

Marc Grosjean

The purpose of this section is to examine how the perception of our own body relies on the integration of information from multiple sensory modalities and how such integration is affected by body perception itself. The interplay between multisensory integration and body perception can be readily illustrated with the following examples. When a person is asked to respond to the tactile stimulation of one of her hands, response speed is slowed by the simultaneous presentation of a visual stimulus close to, as opposed to far away from, her stimulated hand (e.g., Spence, Pavani, Maravita, & Holmes, in press). Moreover, if the vision of the person's arm and hand is replaced with that of a fake limb with an anatomically possible posture, visual stimuli that are now presented far from the person's real hand, but close to the fake hand, can also induce response slowing (i.e., visual-tactile interference; Pavani, Spence, & Driver, 2000). As will be discussed in the chapters that follow, findings such as these demonstrate how the perception of the body and the space around it shapes the way we integrate multisensory information. What is more, they, along with other results, provide a basis for exploring the perceived location, extent, and even identity of body parts.

The way multisensory integration contributes to the perception of the body is addressed in the first three chapters of this section (see also the chapter by de Vignemont, Tsakiris, & Haggard in the next section). In a classification of experimental methods used to study body perception and awareness, Holmes and Spence begin this section by discussing how the perceived location and identity of body parts are determined by visual information and its interaction with tactile and proprioceptive information. They consider, for example, the effect of distorting or displacing people's visual field by having them wear prism glasses. This manipulation is of interest because it induces a conflict between the seen and felt positions of body parts. After some amount of exposure to this conflict, people typically exhibit a form of "visual capture" in that they begin to feel that their body parts are located where they see them (e.g., Hay, Pick, & Ikeda, 1965). Phenomena such as this one reveal the importance of vision in body perception and offer a way of assessing the relative weighting of various sources of information in multisensory integration (an issue that is addressed at length in Ernst's chapter; see below).

Holmes and Spence then go on to examine how the integration of visual and tactile information is affected by the presence of artificial body parts and how representations of the body can incorporate adornments such as clothes. They conclude their chapter with a discussion of the effects of active tool use on multisensory and sensorimotor interactions and the possible integration of tools into bodily representations. In addition to raising a number of new and challenging questions relating to body and multimodal perception, they argue that information pertaining to the body is better understood as being organized via a network of representations subserving different functional specializations, rather than in terms of any single knowledge structure, such as a body schema or body image.

In the next two chapters in this section, Maravita and Làdavas and Farnè elaborate on a number of the issues and findings contained in Holmes and Spence's classification. At the core of both of these chapters lies the idea that representations of the body serve as dynamic points of reference with respect to which multisensory integration takes place. As illustrated with the example provided at the beginning of this chapter, there is compelling behavioral evidence for the idea that the space immediately surrounding the body, known as *peripersonal space*, is characterized by the efficient integration of multimodal events. As reviewed by these authors, the starting point for this line of research comes from the discovery in monkeys of multimodal neurons in various brain areas that respond to tactile stimuli presented at a given body location and visual and/or auditory stimuli presented very close to that location. The critical feature of at least some of these neurons is that their receptive field coordinates are centered on a particular body part, which allows them to represent the space immediately adjacent to it. Based on these findings, a variety of studies involving healthy and brain-damaged humans have tried to characterize how multisensory integration takes place in peripersonal space.

In his chapter, Maravita focuses on how such integration is modulated by intentional actions, abstract knowledge, and self-awareness and on what these modulations tell us about how the body is represented (see also Maravita & Iriki, 2004). For example, he discusses how multisensory integration is affected by the knowledge that what we see when we look into a mirror is an image of ourselves. Indeed, it has been shown that the magnitude of visual-tactile interference obtained when people directly observe a visual stimulus presented close to one of their hands is similar to that obtained when people observe a mirror reflection of the stimulus and one of their hands (e.g., Maravita, Spence, Sergent, & Driver, 2002). This suggests that, based on people's experience with mirrors, far space (around the reflected image of the hand) can be recoded as, and thereby inherit the sensory properties of, near (peripersonal) space. On the basis of these and other findings, Maravita proposes that bodily information should be thought of as being organized with respect to a dynamic representation of the "body in space," rather than in terms of a more static representation of the "body in the brain."

Làdavas and Farnè address a similar set of issues in the next chapter, but with a primary focus on modulations of a phenomenon exhibited by certain right brain–damaged patients: crossmodal extinction. This phenomenon refers to the finding that such patients often fail to notice the presentation of a tactile stimulus to their (contralesional) left hand when it is accompanied by the simultaneous occurrence of a visual stimulus in peripersonal space of the (ipsilesional) right hand (e.g., Làdavas, 2002). Extinction of the stimulus presented to the affected hand is thought to occur because the (normal) representation of the ipsilesional stimulus competes for awareness with the weaker representation of the contralesional stimulus.

By using crossmodal extinction as a signature for the multimodal integration of events in peripersonal space, Làdavas and Farnè discuss the functional properties of this space, the automatic nature of multisensory processing within it, and the degree to which it can be extended beyond the immediate space around the body. A particularly compelling example of how the representation of this space can be dynamically extended concerns the active use of tools (see also the chapters by Holmes and Spence and by Maravita). In one study, Farnè and Làdavas (2000) measured visual-tactile extinction by presenting visual stimuli at the tip of a rake held in the patient's ipsilesional hand. In doing so, they were able to show that the detection of tactile stimuli presented to the contralesional hand was lower immediately after patients had spent some time retrieving objects with the rake than before use of the rake. However, this effect was transient, since they also observed that the amount of crossmodal extinction returned to pre–tool-use levels after a short resting period. As with fake limbs, these results suggest that tools can be, at least temporarily, incorporated into body representations, whereby they extend peripersonal space and modulate multisensory integration within it.

Until now, we have mainly considered the (bodily) conditions under which multisensory integration occurs. In the final chapter of this section, Ernst tackles the issue of characterizing the actual mechanisms that underlie multimodal perception. Starting from the observation that the different senses often provide redundant information about our bodies and the environment, he examines how these sources of information are merged into a robust percept. As the results of his experiments show, visual and haptic size information are combined in a way that is optimal in a statistical sense, as would be predicted from a maximum-likelihood estimation model (e.g., Ernst & Banks, 2002). That is, the variance of the final size estimate of an object that is both seen and felt is less than either of the variances of the individual visual and haptic estimates. Others have shown that this optimal combination of information also arises for visual and proprioceptive information relating to the position of a person's hand (e.g., van Beers, Sittig, & Denier van der Gon, 1999), which points to the importance of this principle for the study of body perception as well.

To account for how perceptual decisions can also be affected by the coupling of signals within and between different modalities, Ernst relies on Bayesian decision theory. In brief, this theory combines maximum-likelihood estimation with prior knowledge of how sensory signals change together. According to this theory, signals that are coupled fuse to some extent during multisensory integration, whereas uncoupled signals do not. Given that visual, tactile, and proprioceptive information pertaining to the body usually change together, this theory provides a basis for understanding why multisensory interference occurs in the space immediately surrounding the body and even all the way to the tip of a tool.

References

Hay, J. C., Pick, H. L., & Ikeda, K. (1965). Visual capture produced by prism spectacles. *Psychonomic Science, 2*, 215–216.

Ernst, M. O., & Banks, M. S. (2002). Humans integrate visual and haptic information in a statistically optimal fashion. *Nature, 415*, 429–433.

Farnè, A., & Làdavas, E. (2000). Dynamic size-change of hand peripersonal space following tool use. *Neuroreport, 8*, 1645–1649.

Làdavas, E. (2002). Functional and dynamic properties of visual peripersonal space. *Trends in Cognitive Sciences, 6*, 17–22.

Maravita, A., & Iriki, A. (2004). Tools for the body (schema). *Trends in Cognitive Sciences, 8*, 79–86.

Maravita, A., Spence, C., Sergent, C., & Driver, J. (2002). Seeing your own touched hands in a mirror modulates cross-modal interactions. *Psychological Science, 13*, 350–355.

Pavani, F., Spence, C., & Driver, J. (2000). Visual capture of touch: Out-of-the-body experiences with rubber gloves. *Psychological Science, 11*, 353–359.

Spence, C., Pavani, F., Maravita, A., & Holmes, N. (in press). Multisensory contributions to the 3-D representation of visuotactile peripersonal space in humans: Evidence from the crossmodal congruency task. *Journal of Physiology* (Paris).

van Beers, R. J., Sittig, A. C., & Denier van der Gon, J. J. (1999). Integration of proprioceptive and visual position-information: An experimentally supported model. *Journal of Neurophysiology, 81*, 1355–1364.

3

Beyond the Body Schema

Visual, Prosthetic, and Technological Contributions to Bodily Perception and Awareness

Nicholas P. Holmes
Charles Spence

1. Introduction

1.1. The Historical Concept of the Body Schema

The concept of the body schema has enjoyed a long and colorful career in the fields of psychology, neuroscience, neuropsychology, and philosophy (Miles, 1957). The inauguration of this concept is often traced back to Head and Holmes (1911–1912), who described both a *postural schema*, underlying our awareness of the position of our body and its parts, particularly the limbs, and a *superficial* or *surface schema*, underlying our capacity to localize stimuli on the skin. However, by the time Head and Holmes described these two schemata, other very similar concepts were already in their third decade of existence. Surveying the ancestry of this family of concepts, Oldfield and Zangwill (1942) traced their source to Munk's writings of 1890. Fifteen years later, Bonnier (1905) argued that his work of 1893 had been the first to express the concept of an organized spatial representation, or "spatial sense," of the body with respect to the world. Despite his insistence, however, most researchers still prefer to cite Head and Holmes (1911–1912) as the discoverers of the body schema.[1]

Since the birth of the concept of the body schema, it has increasingly been used to explain a variety of clinical, behavioral, and experiential phenomena. With its sibling terms of *body image, corporeal awareness, body representation*, and any number of linguistic and theoretical variations upon this theme, several authors have asked whether the concept continues to have any utility

15

(e.g., Kinsbourne, 1995; Poeck & Orgass, 1971). As new bodily experiences, somatic sensorimotor disorders, and experimental manipulations of bodily perception are discovered, accepted, and refined within the medical and scientific communities, the number of phenomena falling under the umbrella of body image/schema disorders and, by implication, the number of functions purportedly performed by the body schemata in the neurologically unimpaired has grown almost exponentially. Head and Holmes's (1911–1912) original definition of the body schema (usually, only the definition of their postural schema is referred to since their superficial schema never achieved such fame) was restricted to proprioceptive information underlying the appreciation of changes in the position and orientation of one's own body parts.

Over the next 85 years, the domain to which the concept of the body schema has been applied has stretched and expanded to include any number of corporeal phenomena—not simply those related to the appreciation of postural change. Berlucchi and Aglioti (1997), in their stimulating review of the phenomena of bodily disorders and recent experimental findings concerning bodily perception, opened the conceptual umbrella wider, perhaps, than anyone else by defining bodily representations as "a mental construct that comprises the sense impressions, perceptions and ideas about the dynamic organization of one's own body and its relation to that of other bodies, [which] is variously termed the body schema, body image and corporeal awareness" (Berlucchi & Aglioti, 1997, p. 560).

In this all-encompassing definition, not only are the various terminologies for different aspects of the body schema(ta) merged into a single definition, but their concept includes "impressions, perceptions, and ideas" rather than being a subset of largely unconscious physiological processes pertaining to proprioception (i.e., to the body schema), and it includes not only the body of the individual him- or herself, but also extends to include the knowledge and perception of all bodies and their relations to our own (i.e., to the body image, according to Campbell's 1995 terminology). Berlucchi and Aglioti's definition of the body schema is wrapped up with that of the definition of the body image, whereas other authors have insisted that these two concepts should be kept quite separate (e.g., Gallagher, 1995).

1.2. Beyond the Body Schema?

Many other definitions of the body schema and/or body image are available, beyond those outlined above. However, rather than attempt to offer our own definition or to review published evidence pertaining to the validity of the concept itself, we aim to avoid this slippery issue here, by concentrating on several aspects of bodily perception and action that emerge in a variety of different experimental methodologies. In the present chapter, we review three broad areas of experimental research: (1) the effects of the manipulation of visual information on the felt location and identity of individual body parts and the extent to which visual and tactile information is integrated under such conditions; (2) how artificial body parts affect the integration of visual and tactile information and how clothes and bodily adornments may become incorporated into bodily representations (for example, clothes may enhance the felt dimensions of the body or body parts); and (3) how the skilled use of a variety of tools may lead to altered multisensory or sensorimotor interactions and the incorporation of such tools into bodily representations. In each case, we shall start with a description of the type of manipulation and provide examples from the experimental literature as to how these various manipulations may be used to study, and hopefully to understand, various aspects of bodily experience. Additionally, wherever possible, we shall make conceptual links among methodological approaches and among human experimental, neuropsychological, neurophysiological, and other domains of study in order to highlight the commonalties (as well as the differences) among them and to use these conceptual links to suggest a variety of new approaches to studying the neural representations of the body and of peripersonal space.

The specific purposes of the present chapter are therefore threefold: (1) to avoid invoking the rather abstract concepts of the body schema, the body image, or a singular body representation and to focus instead on a number of different aspects of bodily experience that may submit to more rigorous experimental investigation.[2] Such aspects include, but are not limited to, the felt location of individual body parts, the relationship between visual and tactile stimuli in personal and extrapersonal space, the attribution of visual and tactile sensations to visible body parts, the identification of or with visible body parts as belonging to oneself, and the incorporation of external objects into normal multisensory and sensorimotor interactions; (2) to provide a classification of the experimental approaches reviewed in the present chapter, particularly regarding the use of tools and other objects, which is an area of much recent interest in our own and in other laboratories; and (3) to suggest new areas of research, particularly regarding the effects of shadows and of clothes and bodily adornments on the perception of and action with the body. Clothes, tools, shadows, and artificial body parts have all been the subject of much speculation as to the extent to which they are incorporated into bodily representations, yet little experimental attention has been devoted to this area until recently. We hope the present review will go some way toward remedying these empirical deficits.

2. Manipulating the Visual Location of Individual Body Parts

By the use of prisms, shadows, mirrors, and video monitors, we can displace the visual location or projection of the body artificially with varying degrees of abstraction from natural viewing conditions. In these ways, the visual image of our hands, for example, can be displaced to appear in another portion of space, or visual feedback concerning their movements can be delayed so that they appear at another (subsequent) instant in time. These methods introduce conflicts between the visually specified positions, movements, or orientations of the body and its parts, on the one hand, and the information provided by proprioception, touch, balance, and audition on the other. Given that, in many situations, visual information dominates over information from the other senses, particularly with respect to spatial localization (Battaglia et al., 2003), one might ask: to what extent can the brain be "fooled" by the visually specified position of the body?

2.1. Prismatic Displacement of the Entire Visual Field

When prisms, and even ordinary prescription lenses, are placed in front of the eyes, the visual field is distorted in a manner dependent on the optical characteristics of the prisms or lenses. In order to adjust to such distortions and to allow effective sensorimotor integration and control to occur, recalibration of sensory and/or motor representations or reference frames is required. This recalibration might take a variety of forms: the topographic representation of the visual field could be shifted or rotated; the egocentric midline could be rotated or shifted; and/or the gain of oculomotor and other motor control functions could be adjusted to compensate for the optical distortion. The particular form that this recalibration takes has been shown to depend on a variety of factors, for example, whether active pointing toward a target is performed during prism exposure; whether the arm is visible during exposure; whether the head is restrained; and whether the recalibration is measured in terms of shifts in visual, auditory, or somatic/egocentric reference points (see Harris, 1965, for an early review). The following discussion will focus specifically on changes in the *felt location* of visible body parts induced by prismatic displacement.

2.1.1. Behavioral Studies

Through the use of distorting prisms, the felt location of parts of the body can be modified, a phenomenon often termed the *visual capture* of felt body position, referring to the effect of viewing your arm, for example, in a different position than that in which it feels to be (through proprioceptive and somatosensory inputs; Hay, Pick, & Ikeda, 1965). With exposure to this conflict between the seen and felt position of your arm, the felt position seems to recalibrate toward that of the seen position—we *feel* our body parts to be where we *see* them. Various factors modulate the extent of this visual capture of body-part position, such as the allocation of attention to either visual or proprioceptive cues (Kelso, Cook, Olson, & Epstein, 1975; see also Shimojo, 1987) or the performance of localization or target-pointing tasks (Warren & Schmitt, 1978). The *attended modality*, or the modality most relevant for performance of a particular task, tended in each case to show less recalibration than the *unattended,* or less task-relevant, modality.

When visual capture is measured immediately after participants experience *passive* movements of their arms, the recalibration of felt arm location toward the seen location has been shown to be larger than when visual capture is measured immediately after participants make *active* movements (Welch, Widawski, Harrington, & Warren, 1979). Interestingly, these effects of active and passive movements on the relative weighting of visual and propriocep-tive information in the visual capture of felt location are the opposite to those reported by Welch et al. for "prism adaptation" (the correction of pointing errors under prismatic visual displacement), suggesting that independent processes contribute to the changes in the felt location of body parts, on the one hand, and target-pointing adaptation, on the other.

A more recent manipulation of the relative weighting of visual and pro-prioceptive information in the production of visual capture was performed by Mon-Williams, Wann, Jenkinson, and Rushton (1997). They measured par-ticipants' errors in pointing either to a target on a table in front of them or in matching the positions of their two index fingertips, when one was above the table and the other below. The participants viewed the table, the target, and one of their hands through adjustable prisms, which produced a variety of possi-ble displacements of the visual field (10 displacements to the left and 10 to the right), and found that in all conditions, the matched position of the unseen finger was biased toward the visually specified location of either the target or the seen hand. The participants were then tested in a dimly lit room under similar conditions, where targets and finger positions were highlighted by illuminated LEDs and the participants' upper hands were visible. In this sit-uation, only the target-pointing task showed a strong visual bias, whereas the positions of the two fingers were matched with much greater accuracy, thus displaying little visual capture. This latter effect suggests that, depending on the information that is available to the participants and the reliability of that information (for example, visual information may be very reliable under good lighting conditions but less so under conditions of near-darkness), the con-tributions of visual and proprioceptive information to felt body-part location (and to subsequent effects on visuomotor behavior) is weighted differently (cf. Alais & Burr, 2004; Battaglia et al., 2003; see also Ernst & Banks, 2002; chapter 6; and van Beers, Sittig, & Denier van der Gon, 1999).

2.1.2. Neurophysiological and Neuropsychological Studies

The experimental dissociation and adaptive recalibration of the seen and felt locations of body parts has relevance to the neuropsychological phenomenon of supernumerary limbs, which occur in cases of paralysis of the body following lesions to the spinal cord (Ohry, Gur, & Zeilig, 1989), head injury (Rogers & Franzen, 1992), right-hemisphere stroke (Halligan & Marshall, 1995; Halligan, Marshall, & Wade, 1993; Hari, Hänninen, Mäkinen, Jousmäki, Seppä, & Salonen, 1998; Sellal, Renaseau-Leclerc, & Labrecque, 1996), or biparietal infarctions (Vuilleumier, Reverdin, & Landis, 1997). Illusory supernumerary or phantom limbs have also been induced in paraplegic patients by vestibular stimulation (Le Chapelain, Beis, Paysant, & André, 2001). Patients with supernumerary limbs typically complain of *feeling*, for example, a "third" arm or an extra set of legs in addition to *seeing* the normal set of two arms and two legs. In these cases, it seems that there is a vivid dissociation between the seen and felt locations of body parts and that this dissociation does not lead to capture of visual or proprioceptive information by its counterpart in the other sensory modality. This failure to capture the arm or leg position may thus lead to the feeling of supernumerary limbs. Similar effects can be brought about by pressure-cuff ischemia of the limbs in normal participants (Gross & Melzack, 1978), suggesting that a disruption of proprioceptive input from the limbs may give rise to this phenomenon. Further experimental means of inducing supernumerary or phantom limbs in both amputees and in normal healthy participants will shed much light on the neural contributory processes (see especially chapter 9).

Shimojo (1987) provided a direct link between supernumerary limbs and visual capture when normal participants in his study were asked to describe the felt location of a finger when it was viewed directly through one eye and simultaneously through a refracting prism with the other eye. This manipulation produced two visual images of the participants' hands—visual supernumerary limbs. When participants moved their fingers while viewing their double images, they reported that *only one image* at any one time would capture the felt location of their hands, but that this felt location could switch between the two images depending, for example, on the location of visual fixation and, more particularly, on which image was endogenously attended to. The findings of this experiment suggest that, whatever mechanism is responsible for the visual capture of felt body position in normal humans, it may be damaged in patients with supernumerary limbs. This mechanism binds visual and proprioceptive information, weighting each modality according to the reliability of the information and the experimental context. Normally, this mechanism supports only one felt location at a time for each body part, which may or may not be an accurate representation of the limb's true position. When damaged, however, this mechanism gives rise to the phenomenological possibility of supernumerary limbs.

2.2. Shadows of the Body

For most of our waking life, the shadow (or shadows) of our body follows every move we make and throws itself at our feet with concern neither for what lies beneath nor for the obstacles in its path. It is ever-present, so long as sufficient light is available; it shrinks and stretches as overhead illumination looms and recedes respectively; it even duplicates itself when multiple light sources are available, as on a floodlit football field. Given the near-omnipresence of our shadow throughout life, surprisingly little experimental work has addressed the status of the body's shadow with respect to the neural representation of the body itself.[3]

2.2.1. Behavioral Studies

Pavani and Castiello (2004) studied the effect of seeing a shadow of one's own arm on the association between visual stimuli presented away from the body (in peripersonal space) and vibrotactile stimuli presented to the fingers of the hand that either cast or did not cast the shadow. Participants in their experiment made speeded judgments concerning the elevation of a vibrotactile target presented to their thumb or forefinger on the left or right hand while trying to ignore simultaneous visual distractor stimuli presented randomly from either above or below a central fixation point. The visual distractors were therefore either "congruent" or "incongruent" with respect to the relevant vibrotactile target stimulus (and the required response). Additionally, one of the participants' hands was back-lit, casting a shadow of that hand such that the shadow "reached" toward the central distractor lights: the shadow of one hand "held" the visual distractors just as the participants' hands held the vibrotactile targets (see Figure 3.1).

Using this visuotactile crossmodal congruency paradigm, Pavani and Castiello (2004) found that the effect of the visual distractors on vibrotactile RTs was significantly larger for the hand whose shadow reached toward the visual distractors than for the hand not currently casting the shadow. In two control experiments, participants either wore a glove on the hand which cast a polygonal-shape shadow (to ascertain that the visual appearance of the shadow cast by the hand was responsible for the enhanced congruency effect) or a hand-shaped outline was drawn on the table next to the distractors. Both control experiments failed to show any enhanced crossmodal congruency effects for the distractors that were connected to the hand in these ways (see also Igarashi, Kitagawa, & Ichihara, 2003). Pavani and Castiello's experiment, perhaps the first to examine the effect of shadows on the multisensory perception of the body and of peripersonal space, suggested that one effect of our shadows is to bind extrapersonal visual events to simultaneously occurring tactile events. This shadow-associated binding might enable somewhat faster reactions to threatening situations. For instance, when we are walking along on a sunny day, gazing at our feet or at the uneven ground ahead, the sight of an object (or its shadow) approaching the shadow of our own body may provide information relevant to an upcoming collision, or worse, to predators. Any slight advantage

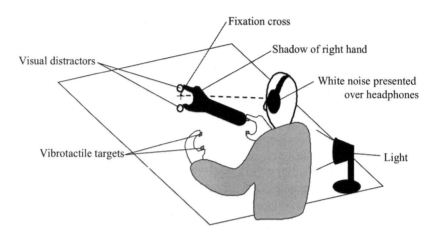

Figure 3.1. The use of shadows to study visuotactile integration in normal participants. Participants held their hands over a table such that the projection of the shadow of one of their hands reached toward two visual distractor stimuli presented away from the body. Participants made localization judgments on one of four vibrotactile targets presented directly to the thumb and forefinger of both hands. The effect of the visual distractors on simultaneous vibrotactile discrimination performance was greatest for the hand that projected the shadow toward the distractors (redrawn from Pavani & Castiello, 2004).

in perceiving the world in relation to our body, even in relation to its shadow, is likely to pay off in a world of rapidly moving and potentially harmful objects.

The study of shadows therefore seems likely to provide a fruitful area for future research with respect to the perception and the neural representation of the body. The earlier report by Shimojo (1987) reviewed above claimed, albeit anecdotally, that visual capture of arm position still occurred, though to a lesser extent, when the visual image of the arm was degraded or replaced with just its shadow. Many of the various experimental techniques discussed in this chapter could be applied to the study of shadows and might shed further light on their perceptual effects, for instance, to address questions such as: does exposure to the movements of one's shadow during prism adaptation target-pointing tasks result in the same kind of recalibration that follows visual exposure to the arm itself? Does viewing an enlarged shadow of a body part enhance the spatial resolution of tactile perception for that body part (see Kennett, Taylor-Clarke, & Haggard, 2001)? How else can distorting one's shadow affect corporeal perceptions? Are the spatial and temporal constraints of self-recognition (see below) equally applicable to shadows of the body as to the body itself? Are there neuropsychological patients with selective deficits for recognition of their own shadows? Do shadows behave more like visual supernumerary limbs or like limbs displaced by prisms or mirrors? Do they extend peripersonal space in a manner similar to that of mirrors or of tools (discussed below)? Do we have a sense of "ownership" of our shadows? Do we react with pain and avoidance responses when our shadows are "threatened"? Answers to these intriguing questions will have to await further empirical study.

2.3. Mirror Reflections and Self-Recognition

Mirrors present visual situations that are one step abstracted from that of prisms and lenses. While what we see in the mirror is light reflected from objects, light that is always obedient to the laws of optics, those objects may not be within direct view of our eyes or within reach of our limbs. In fact, the very purpose of mirrors is to allow us to see those objects not in our direct view: with mirrors, we can see around corners and behind our heads; in the mirror, we can even see our own eyes. Mirrors introduce the possibility of seeing our own bodies as if they were the bodies of others, or rather, seeing our *own* body (but left-right reversed) as if from another person's perspective. While viewing our body in the mirror, every movement we make is reflected back to us instantaneously, and the visual properties of that reflected image of our body mimic exactly the temporal and spatial patterning of our physical body.

Viewing our body in the mirror introduces various peculiarities as compared to how our body appears to us directly, for example, we can approach and recede from our own body in the mirror; we see our body reduced in size and at a distance; we can see parts of our body otherwise invisible to us or without making the usual orienting movements (see Gregory, 1996, for extended discussion on the significance of mirrors). Mirrors can alter the view we have of our body quite drastically, yet after some experience, we are able to recognize ourselves in the mirror immediately and can perform all manner of operations with almost no effort at all. The capacity to adapt to a mirror-reversed visual representation of ourselves for the performance of self-directed and other movements must rely on significant plasticity in the sensorimotor system. This capacity might, for instance, require the generation and maintenance of mirror-reversed visuomotor programs, which are activated when the cognitive and sensorimotor context suggests that what you see before you is a mirror image of yourself, rather than a direct image of someone else. This context-dependent activation of stored sensorimotor programs could be instantiated in the cerebellum (e.g., Wolpert, Miall, & Kawato, 1998) and might provide a fast and powerful mechanism to transform or remap external visual stimuli as they pertain not to the external world, but to our own body.

While mirrors have been used for a long time to distort and displace vision of one's own body (e.g., Burnett, 1904; Jackson & Zangwill, 1952), there has been a recent resurgence of interest in their empirical usage (e.g., Franz & Packman, 2004; Holmes, Crozier, & Spence, 2004; Holmes & Spence, in press;

Holmes, Snijders, & Spence, 2005; Ro, Wallace, Hagedorn, Farnè, & Pienkos, 2004). In the following section, we review several applications of mirrors in studying multisensory representations of the body.

2.3.1. Behavioral Studies

The *identification* with one's mirror-reflected body has recently been studied by examining the effects of mirror reflections with the crossmodal congruency task (Maravita, Spence, Sergent, & Driver, 2002; see also chapter 4). The results of these experiments suggest that visual stimuli presented near our body, but viewed in a mirror as if presented from extrapersonal space (as retinal, eye, and head position information would suggest), are referred or related more strongly to concurrent vibrotactile stimulation than visual stimuli in equivalent retinal locations but viewed through the mirror (i.e., when the mirror was transparent).[4] The crossmodal congruency task may therefore provide an experimental index for the process of identification with the body's mirror-reflected image.

We have also recently used mirrors to examine the visual capture of the felt location of individual body parts (see Figure 3.2; Holmes, Crozier, & Spence, 2004; Holmes & Spence, in press; Holmes et al., 2005). In these studies, based on the mirror-box techniques of Ramachandran and colleagues (Ramachandran & Rogers-Ramachandran, 1996; Ramachandran, Rogers-Ramachandran, & Cobb, 1995), participants viewed their left arms in a mirror positioned along the sagittal plane and made reaching movements to a target with their unseen right arms. When the visually specified position of the (virtual) right arm was the same as the proprioceptively specified position of the (real) right arm, subsequent unseen reaching movements made with the right arm to the target were accurate (i.e., they landed within 1–2 cm of the target). When the visually and proprioceptively specified arm positions were in conflict, however, reaching accuracy deteriorated significantly (to as far as 6–10 cm away from the target) and was linearly related to the size of the visual-proprioceptive conflict (i.e., reaching errors were 30–40% of the difference between visually and proprioceptively specified initial arm positions (Holmes, Crozier, & Spence, 2004). In follow-up experiments (Holmes & Spence, in press), we showed that this visual capture effect increased with the duration of visual exposure to the conflict situation prior to reaching and was larger for reaching movements made following active, visuomotor experience of the multisensory conflict than for passive visual exposure alone.

Several other researchers have used mirrors to examine the effect of visual manipulations on simultaneous somatosensory or sensorimotor perception or behavior. An early experiment by Nielsen (1963) examined whether the identification with, and visual control of, one's hand could be manipulated by using a mirror. Unlike in Maravita, Spence, Sergent, and Driver's (2002)

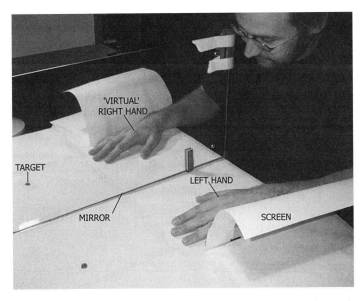

Figure 3.2. The use of a mirror to study the visual capture of felt body-part location and the visual recalibration of proprioception. One of the authors, N. P. H., is shown viewing his left hand reflected in a mirror positioned along the midsagittal plane, producing the impression of viewing his right hand (*virtual right hand*). After a period of exposure (typically around 6–10 seconds of passive visual or active visuomotor viewing) to this situation, participants in this experiment reported feeling that the mirror reflection of their left hand felt as if it were their right hand. When participants subsequently made reaching movements with their unseen right hand to a target, their reaching accuracy was significantly affected (compared to a no-mirror or no-hand control condition) by the visually specified position of their apparent right arm and hand. The left hand was placed behind a screen in some control conditions, while the mirror was occluded by a large screen in others (see Holmes et al., 2004; Holmes & Spence, submitted).

experiment, however, participants in Nielsen's study were not aware that any mirrors were involved in the experiment. Nielsen's participants viewed their hands through a rectangular aperture and were asked to draw smoothly along a straight line away from their bodies with a pencil, trying to keep as close as possible to the line at all times (see Figure 3.3). In the crucial experimental conditions, the participant's view of his or her hand was exchanged, by means of a mirror, with a view of the experimenter's hand in an identical position, wearing an identical glove to those the participants wore and holding an identical pencil. Participants later reported that they had been unaware of the change in the identity of the hand. In the mirror condition, after a few trials of drawing straight lines, the experimenter started to draw curved lines that deviated from the straight, and most of the participants adjusted their drawing in a direction opposite to the experimenter's line in an attempt to correct for their perceived deviation. Accompanying this aberrant drawing, participants

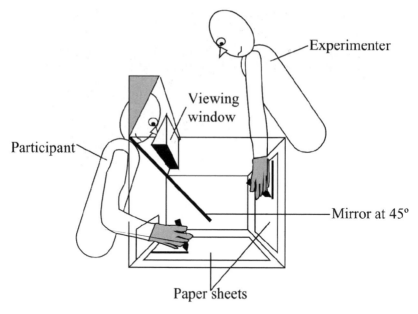

Figure 3.3. The use of a mirror to study the identification with, and control of, one's arm and hand while drawing. Participants viewed either their own right hand or, as shown in the figure, a mirror reflection of the experimenter's left hand while drawing smoothly along a straight line. Participants were not told that they would be viewing the experimenter's hand at any point. Surprisingly, when viewing the experimenter's hand drawing curved rather than straight lines, they felt as if they had lost control of their *own* hand rather than that they were not viewing their own hand (redrawn from Nielsen, 1963).

reported feeling some sort of external force, like a magnet was manipulating their movements. Surprisingly, most participants still claimed that the hand they were viewing was their own and that the lines they saw in front of them were their own drawings, but they reported that their movements had become less voluntary than usual. It seems, therefore, that once a participant has identified with, or felt a sense of ownership of, a hand they see in front of them (albeit viewed through an aperture), they are willing to accept it as part of their own bodies, but feel that the control, accuracy, and authorship of their own *movements* were lost to some degree. It is interesting to note that participants resolved the discrepancy in terms of losing *control* of their own bodies rather than in terms of losing the sense of *identification* with the aberrant body part (see also Sullivan, 1969).

The behavioral research outlined above has begun to disentangle various aspects of our experiences of viewing our body in a mirror. Areas of specific interest include, but are not limited to, the following: (1) to what extent is the identification with the mirror image as belonging to the bodily self necessary for distant visual stimuli to be remapped as near stimuli or to be associated with the body in multisensory interactions? (2) what visual factors contribute to this process of identification? (3) are identification with a seen body part, visual capture of felt body-part location, and the visual recalibration of proprioceptive information independent and dissociable components or merely different aspects of the same underlying psychological and/or neurological mechanism? (4) to what extent can these findings using the mirror-box technique be related to the older experimental literature on prism adaptation? Are the underlying mechanisms the same? Answers to these questions will no doubt require further research, but we suggest that an examination of the interrelations among different experimental techniques and how they relate to findings concerning certain aspects of bodily experience, for example those listed above, will greatly facilitate such research.

2.3.2. Neurophysiological and Neuropsychological Studies

In a study of a patient exhibiting crossmodal extinction, Maravita, Spence, Clarke, Husain, and Driver (2000) found that their patient's visuotactile extinction was modulated by vision of the patient's own hands in a mirror. *Visuotactile extinction* is a disorder whereby patients are able to detect visual or tactile stimuli presented to either side of their bodies in isolation. However, when two stimuli are presented simultaneously to different sides, the stimulus presented on the left is often "extinguished" by the stimulus on the right (most reported cases are of patients suffering from right-hemisphere brain damage). Although this deficit was first demonstrated with simultaneous stimuli presented in the same modality, patients have also been found to exhibit left *tactile* extinction upon simultaneous presentation of a right *visual* stimulus (e.g., di Pellegrino, Làdavas, & Farnè, 1997; Làdavas, 2002; Mattingley, Driver, Beschin, & Robertson, 1997). For some patients, this crossmodal extinction is worse when the visual stimulus is presented close to their right hands (e.g., within 20 cm) compared to when it is presented far from their hands (e.g., more than 40 cm away). This dissociation between crossmodal extinction for near and far space allowed Maravita and colleagues to examine the effects of viewing oneself in a mirror on the magnitude of any crossmodal extinction reported. When viewed in a mirror, a far visual stimulus may in fact be the reflection of a near visual stimulus. Maravita et al.'s patient showed the expected modulation of crossmodal extinction. Visual stimuli applied near the hands, but seen only via the mirror reflection, resulted in increased crossmodal extinction compared to when the patient viewed a pair of gloved rubber hands "holding" the visual stimuli behind the now-transparent mirror (see also chapters 4 and 5).

The use of mirrors to examine visuotactile and sensorimotor processing related to participants' identification with the mirror image of a body part as being a part of their own body may fruitfully be compared with the effects of observing the actions of *another* person on the participants' *own* sensorimotor behavior. It is in this context that "mirror neurons" are most relevant. In the ventral premotor cortex of macaque monkeys, a population of neurons has been shown to respond preferentially both to the observation of a specific action performed by another individual (another macaque or even a human experimenter) and to the performance of that action by the monkey itself (Rizzolatti, Fadiga, Gallese, & Fogassi, 1996). These mirror neurons seem to represent a link between the observation and the production of actions—in short, for imitation (see also chapters 10 and 19). Reed and Farah (1995; see also chapter 11) argued that the body schema represented the positions and movements of both the body of the individual him- or herself and that of other people when observed visually (and, we might suggest, perhaps when touched, heard, or even smelled?). Such a system for the recognition of other people (or members of the same species) might also provide at least part of the neuro-physiological basis for self-recognition and/or the visual guidance of movements in the mirror. Viewing one's own movements in a mirror provides a form of reafferent feedback that may be used to correct and to guide movements toward targets seen in the mirror. In order to complete the necessary sensorimotor transformation of mirror images into movements, identification with the body in the mirror and specific mirror-reversed coordinate transformations need to occur. That specific neural mechanisms may exist for either or both of these functions is suggested, first, by the limited number of species that are able to recognize themselves in the mirror (Gallup, 1970; Itakura, 1987a, 1987b) and, second, by the existence of mirror agnosia and mirror ataxia in human neuropsychological patients (Binkofski, Buccino, Dohle, Seitz, & Freund, 1999; Ramachandran, Altschuler, & Hillyer, 1997; Sathian, Greenspan, & Wolf, 2000). Patients with mirror ataxia are unable to guide the movements of their hands to targets when those targets are viewed in a mirror, yet they remain able to reach toward targets when the targets are viewed directly, suggesting that the lesions they sustained have selectively impaired the ability to make mirror-image transformations for the explicit purpose of the visual guidance of reaching movements.

2.4. Televisual Display of Body Parts

Perhaps the method that gives the experimenter the greatest control over the presentation of visual feedback pertaining to the body for experimental purposes is using a television screen or monitor. By capturing the image of a participant's body part in a camera and playing it back to him on a television screen, it becomes possible to dissociate both the spatial and temporal factors pertaining to the visual appearance of that body part from its location and movement as specified by the other senses: proprioception, touch, and (occasionally) audition. When presented on screen, the visual characteristics of the body are constrained far less by reality than for other optical manipulations. There are no necessary or lawful relationships among the position, movement, size, orientation, or color of the body as seen on screen and the body as it would be seen directly. The experimenter may control all of these factors, and this ability gives televisual manipulations a distinct advantage over the use of prisms, lenses, and mirrors in investigating certain aspects of bodily representations. It becomes possible to examine, for example, the effects of delays in visual feedback following voluntary movements on identification with a body part in the monitor (e.g., Daprati, Franck, Georgieff, Proust, Pacherie, Dalery, & Jeannerod, 1997).

Several disadvantages with the use of televisual display should also be mentioned, though. First, the quality of the on-screen image and the unavoidable small time delays in electronic processing (at least one frame of the monitor's output, or around 70 ms for video encoding and decoding; Marescaux, Leroy, Gagner, Rubino, Mutter, Vix, Butner, & Smith, 2001) may make the presentation less realistic when compared to naturalistic or optically displaced viewing. Second, the two-dimensional visual presentation of body parts may limit the kinds of neural systems that are engaged by the stimuli. For example, neurons in the macaque premotor cortex, which encode the positions of three-dimensional objects approaching the body in peripersonal space, do not respond to the two-dimensional projected images commonly used to stimulate visual receptive fields (RFs; Graziano, Hu, & Gross, 1997; see also Jarvelainen, Schürmann, Avikainen, & Hari, 2001, for related results in humans; and Rizzolatti et al., 1996, for similar properties of mirror neurons). These limitations may have the consequence that the behavioral findings generated by the use of televisual methods of visual presentation may apply only to the specific context of viewing your own body parts on the television— something that is obviously quite uncommon in everyday life. Nevertheless, there can be no doubt that this relatively modern invention will continue to offer insights into the multisensory representations of the body in the brain.

2.4.1. Behavioral Studies

In order to dissociate the effects of visual perception of a body part from the effects of orienting toward that body part on any advantages in tactile information processing (as assessed by simple detection RTs), Tipper, Phillips, Dancer, Lloyd, Howard, and McGlone (2001) presented black-and-white images of parts of their participants' own bodies on a monitor positioned in front of them. Tactile targets were presented to the participants' cheeks and necks, and simple detection RTs were recorded while participants viewed different parts of their bodies on the video monitor. Tipper and colleagues found that viewing a body site speeded detection of tactile targets applied to that body site as compared to viewing an alternative body site (e.g., tactile stimulation of the face while viewing video feedback of the neck). This finding conforms well to an earlier study by this group (Tipper, Lloyd, Shorland, Dancer, Howard, & McGlone, 1998), where visual and proprioceptive information were dissociated for vision specifically of the participants' hands. In their second experiment, Tipper et al. (2001) used a color monitor and three fixed cameras, which provided a random presentation of one of three body parts on a trial-by-trial basis. The participants were instructed to attend to one of the body sites throughout each block of trials. When viewing an image of a particular body site on any given trial, detection latencies for tactile targets were significantly shorter only for stimuli presented to the same body part as viewed on the monitor. The use of video monitors in these experiments allowed the dissociation of visual and proprioceptive effects in the behavioral advantages gained by orienting toward a particular body site. A previous study using simple detection RTs (Honoré, Bordeaud'hui, & Sparrow, 1989) had also shown a small RT advantage when the participants' gaze was toward the site of tactile stimulation, as compared to when their gaze was directed away from the stimulation (in each case, on the left or right ankle). These studies seem to point to a common finding: that increasing the information available to a participant concerning upcoming potential somatosensory target stimuli, whether by proprioceptive, visual, or perhaps more abstract, symbolic, or cognitive means, can facilitate detection of those targets. Further experiments of this nature could examine the effects of providing other kinds of information regarding the stimulated body parts, for example, nonpredictive verbal cues, line drawings, shadows, or artificial body parts, on the detection and discrimination of and responses to body part–specific tactile (or visual) stimulation.

Apart from studying the facilitation of tactile detection RTs, video monitors have also been used to study the perceived *identity* of a viewed body part under various experimental conditions. Daprati et al. (1997) studied the ability of different subgroups of schizophrenic patients to identify movements of their own hand as compared to vision of an experimenter's hand performing a similar action or a different action. Vision of the participant's right arm was provided by means of a mirror and a closed-circuit television system, which superimposed images of either the participant's or the experimenter's (identically gloved) hand over the actual position of the participant's hands. When compared to a group of normal control participants, the schizophrenic group made significantly more misattribution errors in discriminating their own movements from those of the experimenter. The increase in errors only occurred when participants observed the experimenter's hand performing the *same* movement as they themselves produced and not when they viewed their own movements on screen nor when they viewed the experimenter performing a *different* movement than their own. This technique was particularly useful in manipulating, on a trial-to-trial basis, the identity of the hand seen in front of the participant in relation to the movements made by the participant.

This technique has also been used to examine the effects of the spatial coincidence of the visually presented hands with the participant's own hands (van den Bos & Jeannerod, 2002; see also Knoblich, 2002). In a forced-choice paradigm, normal human participants were better at identifying their own gloved hand (presented adjacent to an image of the experimenter's hand on the screen) when they performed a movement compared to performing no movements. Participants were also more likely to attribute a movement to themselves when the hand they viewed on screen was in anatomical alignment with their own hand. Similarly, Franck, Farrer, Georgieff, Marie-Cardine, Daléry, d'Amato, and Jeannerod (2001) manipulated both the spatial and temporal aspects of visual feedback of self-generated movements by presenting participants (both normal controls and schizophrenic patients) with a synthesized virtual image of a hand, which moved in response to the participants' hand movements in three conditions. Simulated movements were either congruent with the participants' own movements, delayed by between 0 and 500 ms, or deviated in their movement direction by between 0° and 40° from the paths of the participants' actual movements. Franck and coworkers found that normal participants agreed that the movement they saw matched their own hand movements when the virtual image movement was delayed by up to 100 ms or deviated by up to 5°. Beyond these thresholds, however, the proportion of movements rated as matching the participant's own rapidly decreased, approaching zero for delays greater than 400 ms and for angular deviations greater than 30–40°. The temporal and spatial distortions required for the schizophrenic groups to reach the same level of performance were larger in each case than for the normal control participants.

It would be interesting to use this televisual presentation method in a study such as that of Nielsen (1963). One could ask to what extent visual feedback can be manipulated *after* a participant has identified with his or her limb without destroying that feeling of identification. The angle of deviation of movements or the temporal delay in feedback could be changed gradually during a block of line-drawing trials. One could measure the participants' sensitivity to deviations before and after identification with the limb as their own. In effect, identification with the limb would become an experimental variable. Based on the research reviewed here, one might predict that both the temporal and spatial deviations required to produce a "disownership" or misidentification of the viewed limb would be greater following identification with a body part as compared to before. Designing an objective measure of "identification" would be a crucial first step in this regard.

2.4.2. Neurophysiological and Neuropsychological Studies

The use of televisual equipment to study the identification with body parts and the recognition of self-generated actions has already been applied to a variety of clinical groups. As noted earlier, Daprati et al. (1997) and Franck et al. (2001) compared the self-attribution of observed movements in different subgroups of schizophrenic patients and in normal controls. Similar studies have also been performed in patients with apraxia resulting from lesions of the left parietal cortex (Sirigu, Daprati, Pradat-Diehl, Franck, & Jeannerod, 1999) and in a patient suffering from large sensory fiber polyneuropathy, resulting in complete loss of touch, vibration, pressure, and kinesthesis (Farrer, Franck, Paillard, & Jeannerod, 2003). These patients were significantly impaired in recognizing their own movements, or rather, they made more mistakes in attributing to themselves the observed movements of the experimenter. In comparison, two patients with motor and premotor cortical lesions (Sirigu et al., 1999) were as good as, or better than, the normal controls on these movement-attribution tasks. The selective deficits in apraxic and deafferented patients suggest that self-attribution of movement relies on the ability to integrate or compare visually perceived movements with proprioceptive afferent information arising from the patients' own movements, rather than simply on the perception or generation of movements per se. Understanding how various neuropsychological and psychiatric patient subpopulations perform on these tasks will offer insight into the neural mechanisms involved in these self-identification and self-attribution processes.

From a single-cell neurophysiological perspective, televisual display of the body or body parts of experimental animals has not been developed as greatly as for human participants. The approach was utilized recently by Iriki, Tanaka, Obayashi, and Iwamura (2001), who trained Japanese macaque monkeys to view their arms and hands on a video monitor while they reached for pieces of food (also visible on the monitor). A screen occluded direct vision of the monkeys' hands, but a small window allowed direct view when opened. Iriki and colleagues recorded the activity of neurons in the postcentral bank of the primary somatosensory cortex (Brodmann's areas 2 and 5) and found that most cells responded to the visual presentation of a small piece of food in the space near the hands when viewed directly (i.e., through the small window). When viewing the food and hand indirectly via the video monitor, 27% of the neurons continued to respond to the presentation of the food. The further use of this technique to study somatosensory and visual activity of neurons in the posterior parietal and premotor cortices while experimental animals learn to use distorted or displaced visual information to view their own body parts (e.g., Bossum, 1964, 1965; Clower, Hoffman, Votaw, Faber, Woods &

Alexander, 1996) may provide insights into the neural bases for much of the work on self-recognition and of visual, proprioceptive, and somatosensory interactions under situations of intermodal conflict.

Several important issues arising from Iriki et al.'s (2001) experiments need further investigation, such as the different roles of neural activity relating to somatosensory, visual, attentional, and motor factors and the spatial control and nature of the effective visual stimuli. One particularly interesting issue for the present purposes concerns the fact that while the neurons studied by Iriki et al. (2001) were activated by two-dimensional visual stimuli presented on a television screen, neurons representing peripersonal space in the premotor cortex do not respond to such stimuli (see Graziano et al., 1997; Holmes & Spence, 2004, for discussion of these issues). Although the use of such neurophysiological techniques on great apes such as chimpanzees is probably not justified ethically, some closely related behavioral studies have been performed (Menzel, Savage-Rumbaugh, & Lawson, 1985; see also Eddy, Gallup, & Povinelli, 1996), and further explorations of the behavioral capacities of the higher primates will be of great importance in this area.

3. Prosthetic Manipulations of the Body

In this section, we consider those experimental manipulations of the body that introduce *artificial* substitutes for, or extensions of, body parts and examine how that may affect the visual capture of proprioception, the identification with seen body parts, or the incorporation of objects into sensorimotor and multisensory interactions. First, we examine the effect of clothing and other objects continuously in contact with our bodies in relation to the perception or representation of the body itself. This "clothing effect" has not, as far as we are aware, been studied experimentally in any great detail, yet several recent neurophysiological and neuropsychological findings suggest that the effect of clothing on the representations of the body in the brain may be of great interest. Second, we examine the substitution of real body parts with artificial simulacra. Unlike in the visual manipulations discussed earlier, where the body parts observed by the participants were real and belonged to the viewer (though optically displaced), the body parts in the experiments described below were artificial, and the participants were often aware of this fact. Yet still, the brain was to an extent fooled by the presentation of these fake body parts. The behavioral and clinical studies we review below may be of great relevance to the design of prostheses for amputees and their use in rehabilitation. Understanding the extent to which artificial extensions of the body are incorporated into the brain's neural representation of the body itself may be an important first step toward this end (for a variety of views, see Gallagher, 1995; Melzack, 1990; Rabischong, 1993; Riddoch, 1941).

3.1. The Clothing Effect

> A corset ... is filled by the body, not at one point merely, but throughout its whole extent; on every occasion of contact with this stiff case the tension and firmness of its framework is felt exactly as if both properties belonged to our body. ... With every tight girdle, every bracelet, there is to some extent a recurrence of this feeling; the first pair of trousers fastened by braces fill the boy with pride in the manly vigour of his existence, even though the ideal of his wishes remains the steel suit of armour. (Lotze, 1854/1885, p. 595)

This entertaining quotation from Lotze summarizes the effect that clothes have on our perception of the extent and capabilities of our bodies. Clothes have many biological, social, and cultural purposes, such as for protection, modesty, and decoration (Flügel, 1930), but clothes also enhance the physical size of the body (at least in appearance), and it has been suggested that clothes and jewelry, when "worn-in," become as much a part of the body as the physical body itself. Head and Holmes (1911–1912, p. 188) are often quoted in this regard for their comment that "a woman's power of localization may extend to the feather in her hat." Flaccus (1906), writing several years before Head and Holmes, had already fleshed out the ideas of Lotze concerning this incorporation of foreign articles into the brain's representation of the body, as illustrated by the following passage: "the incorporation of originally unrelated objects into the 'Me' as a system of presented elements is one of the commonplaces of psychology. Our clothing ... is ordinarily felt as an integral part of ourselves" (Flaccus, 1906, p. 69). In one sense, then, clothes are "our extended skin" (McLuhan, 1964/2001). To what extent has empirical study provided support for this view?

In the brief review presented below, we suggest that, although perhaps not immediately obvious, clothing and other inanimate objects continuously in contact with the body may have a great bearing on those aspects of bodily experience considered in this chapter. If one accepts that tools can become extensions of the body (discussed below), then the effects of clothing must be even more related to the body itself than are the tools we pick up, use temporarily, and discard at will. It seems that we are typically less aware of our clothing than of the pencils, cutlery, and other tools that we use throughout the day, yet the sensorimotor and biomechanical consequences of a pair of shoes, for example, are equally if not more important for the brain than those of a pencil held between our fingers. During the first few days of breaking in a new pair of shoes, it is probably true to say that a significant part of the process is due to the body's skeletomuscular and neural adaptation to the new shoes. For an illustration of this, try wearing someone else's well-worn shoes for a while—you may still find you have to break them in.

3.1.1. Neurophysiological
and Neuropsychological Studies

Despite the intuitive nature of the idea, little empirical work has addressed the incorporation of clothes into bodily representations. There are anecdotal examples of jewelry and other bodily adornments persisting in the phantom sensations of those with amputated arms or hands (e.g., Melzack, 1992), but Aglioti, Smania, Manfredi, and Berlucchi (1996) carried out perhaps the first experimental study of this incorporation phenomenon. They studied a patient who had suffered a stroke in the right cerebral hemisphere, resulting in sensory and motor deficits on the left side of the body, including extrapersonal and personal neglect and denial of ownership of the left hand. When this patient was asked to describe the ring on her left hand, she could do so perfectly well, but only for the superficial characteristics of the ring. Intriguingly, the ring was disowned along with the left arm, and no autobiographical memories concerning the ring could be retrieved. When the experimenters transferred the ring onto the right hand, however, the patient could describe the ring in detail, and in addition, the autobiographical memories concerning the ring were available to the patient. This finding was replicated with another of the patient's rings and her watch but could not be replicated with objects that did not belong to the patient or those that were not related to the left hand (e.g., a ring that did not belong to her or earrings which did). From this result, one might predict that whatever bodily factors contribute to the spectrum of neglect and denial disorders, those same impairments ought to be found when tested, not using the body itself as the object, but using the clothing and other artificial appendages temporarily or semipermanently connected to the body.

A recent neurophysiological example may be of relevance to the effects of clothing on neural representations of the body. While recording from within the polysensory zone of the precentral gyrus in macaque monkeys, Graziano, Alisharan, Hu, and Gross (2002) reported finding neurons that appeared to show activity related to the *habituation* to objects associated with the body. This "clothing effect" consisted in the lack of, or the reduction in, response in several neurons with tactile RFs on the arms, when the RFs were stimulated by contact with the chair to which the primate had become accustomed. Neurons in the polysensory precentral gyrus are thought to encode the positions of objects in peripersonal space with respect to individual body parts and/or the specific defensive movements required to avoid impact with these objects (Graziano, Taylor, & Moore, 2002). It seems that such neurons responded vigorously only to those objects that were novel, unexpected, or threatening. Once the animal was comfortable with the presence of the chair, this zone of the precentral gyrus was no longer "interested" in tactile stimuli resulting from contact with it. Another group of researchers, recording from neurons in the medial bank of the intraparietal sulcus, also found a dissociation between touches delivered to the body by an object or by other parts of the monkey's body (Iwamura, Tanaka, Hikosaka, & Sakamoto, 1995). However, in this case, only contact between parts of the body itself and the somatosensory RF under study elicited a reduction in neural firing, as compared to touches delivered by other objects, including the primate's chair.

Graziano et al.'s (2002) result might be one empirical analogue of the incorporation of clothes and other objects commonly associated with the body into the brain's multisensory representations of the body and/or the space around the body and is deserving of further study. Alternatively, however, this reduction in neural firing may simply represent a form of habituation to familiar, and therefore probably safe, objects that are often in contact with the body. It would be of importance to know the developmental time scale of such effects: what kind and what length of experience with an external object is required for the development of this habituation or clothing effect? This neurophysiological approach might also be brought to bear upon the following suggestion, made by several authors (Flaccus, 1906; Flügel, 1930; Riddoch, 1941): once a familiar incorporated object, such as a tool, prosthesis, or article of clothing, becomes unwieldy or painful, then the body may "reject" or "dismember" the artificial enhancement from the phenomenal body. Under this view, the integration of the corporeal and the artificial therefore depends upon the absence of pain, discomfort, or uncoordination associated with the use of the extracorporeal appendage. It would be interesting to know how, for example, would the neurons recorded by Graziano et al. (2002) respond if the chair to which the monkey had become habituated suddenly gave the animal a small electric shock? Would the cells then respond when the tactile RF was subsequently touched by the chair, and if so, for how long would they continue to respond in the absence of such aversive stimulation?

The possibility that the brain comes to represent physical objects attached to, or often in association with, the body as parts of the body itself perhaps seems implausible at first thought. However, consider the case of fingernails and teeth in humans or of feathers, antlers, hooves, and tusks in other animals. Weber (1846) and Gibson (1966) both pointed out that, while there are no somatosensory receptors in our fingernails, at the ends of our teeth, or in the horns of an antelope, we and presumably other animals can still use what sensory information is available from the sensitive roots of these otherwise insensate structures to perceive objects in contact with them and thereby to perceive the dental or keratinous members themselves. This process, sometimes referred to as "eccentric projection" or "distal attribution" (e.g., Epstein, Hughes, Schneider, & Bach-y-Rita, 1986; Loomis, 1993; Lotze, 1854/1885), is at least logically similar to that of the incorporation of insensate objects into the brain's body representations or to the extension of the body or of peripersonal space by tools and prostheses (for an intriguing firsthand account of the incorporation of *internal* prostheses into a patient's conscious body image, see Money & Sollod, 1978). This logical similarity suggests that it may be a matter of extended sensorimotor or conjoint multisensory experience or of a rigid physical coupling between the body and its horny or technological appendages that determine the extent to which objects are thus incorporated.

3.2. The Virtual Body Effect

Several of the experimental manipulations discussed so far have involved changing the perceived location of a body part by mirrors, prisms, or televisual means. In some of these experiments, participants were aware that they were being placed under conditions of sensory conflict, and in others, they were not. In the case of many of the following studies of the "virtual body effect" or the "rubber hand illusion," participants were fully aware of the manipulations at hand, yet still the experimenter was able to fool the senses of his or her participants, inducing illusions and measurable perceptual effects in otherwise implausible conditions (for examples where participants were unaware of such manipulations, see Tastevin, 1937; Welch, 1972).

3.2.1. Behavioral Studies

The rubber hand illusion, reported by Botvinick and Cohen (1998; see also the fake-finger illusion in Tastevin, 1937), involved the presentation of a fake, realistically appearing hand in front of normal human participants, while hiding the participant's own right hand from view.[5] The experimenters then began to brush both the participant's right hand (hidden out of sight) and the rubber hand in full view of the participant, with similar brushstrokes being made on the two hands. After a short while, the majority of participants began to feel that they were feeling the brushstrokes not in the location of their real hand, but where they *saw* the rubber hand to be located. They attributed the touches seen delivered to a fake hand to their own body, based on the simultaneous felt touches delivered to their real hand. Many people spontaneously reported that they felt as if the rubber hand they were viewing were their real hand. Most important, participants were subsequently asked to reach, with their eyes closed and their hand under the table, toward the index finger of their left hand. Botvinick and Cohen found that the errors participants made in reaching toward their own hands (a finger-position matching task, similar to that used by Mon-Williams et al., 1997) was correlated with the percentage of time during the brushing exposure period that the participants reported feeling the illusion (though see Holmes et al., 2005, for an alternative view). Acquiring objective measurements of the effects of such illusions is important both to avoid the potential charge of subjective biases in the reporting or conduct of such experiments (e.g., Orne, 1962; Rosenthal, 1967) and also to ascertain the extent to which subjective impressions about the positions of body parts are accompanied by observable changes in sensorimotor coordination. If it is the case, for example, that *every* change in one's subjective impression of body position or movement (i.e., *conscious body image*, according to some definitions) is accompanied by some measurable change in posture or sensorimotor coordination (i.e., unconscious body schema), then the body image and body schema (Gallagher, 1995) might not be empirically dissociable in neurologically intact participants. This would suggest that only when brain damage occurs can the hypothetical body image and body schema be disentangled experimentally.

Using a different paradigm, Pavani, Spence, and Driver (2000) examined the effect of the *orientation* of a pair of rubber hands on the extent to which visual and tactile stimuli interact in the crossmodal congruency task in normal human participants. Two rubber hands were positioned on a platform, each "holding" a pair of visual distractors (see Figure 3.4). The participants' hands were out of view below the platform and held a pair of foam cubes containing vibrotactile stimulators. Both the participants and the rubber hands wore blue rubber gloves to minimize superficial visual cues concerning hand identity. The crucial experimental manipulation was the orientation of the fake hands with respect to the participants' own hands. When the fake hands were aligned in an anatomically plausible position (i.e., directly above, parallel to, and pointing the same way as the participants' arms, as in Figure 3.4), the effect of the visual distractors on simultaneous vibrotactile RTs was significantly larger than when the fake hands were presented in an anatomically implausible posture (i.e., with the rubber hands at 90° to the longitudinal axis of the real arms). This suggests that the extent to which the participants "identified" with the fake hands and/or the extent to which they attributed visual stimuli to their own hands modulated the magnitude of the visuotactile interactions. This modulation occurred despite the fact that participants were fully informed of the experimental manipulations and despite the task (discriminating vibrotactile elevation) and the stimuli remaining identical across the two experimental conditions.

Other behavioral studies of this phenomenon have asked how similar must the visually presented stimulus be to the participant's own body in order for the attribution or capture effects to occur. Austen and coworkers found that even the presentation of green, hairy, "alien" hands in front of the participants modulated the extent to which visual stimuli and tactile stimuli interacted in the crossmodal congruency task. Over a number of studies, Austen and colleagues (Austen, Soto-Faraco, Enns, & Kingstone, 2004) showed that the presence, appearance, position, and posture (palm up or palm down) of the fake hands all had varying modulatory effects on the magnitude of the crossmodal congruency effects. It seems that the similarity of the fake hands to the

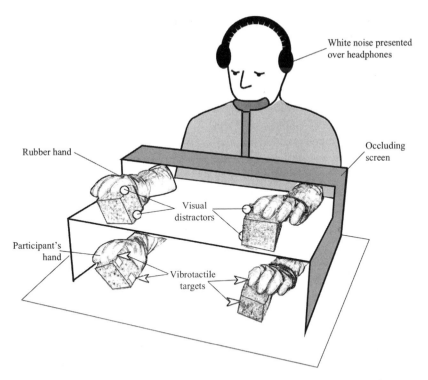

Figure 3.4. The use of rubber hands to study the attribution of visual and tactile stimuli to artificial body parts (see Pavani et al., 2000). Participants held two cubes containing two vibrotactile stimulators on each side in upper and lower locations. Rubber hands "holding" visual distractors were placed on top of an occluding screen, which prevented direct view of the participants' own hands. Visuotactile interference was greatest when the rubber arms were placed in spatial alignment with the participants' own hands, as shown in the figure (redrawn from Pavani et al., 2000).

participants' real hands, across a number of stimulus dimensions, enhances the effect of visual distractors on simultaneous tactile decisions (see also Holmes et al., 2005).

The plasticity of the virtual body effect was recently tested to the extreme by Armel and Ramachandran (2003), who used both a rubber hand and a *table* in replicating the experiment of Botvinick and Cohen (1998). In three experiments, when participants received synchronous touches to a visible rubber hand and their own hidden hand, they rated the extent to which the seen hand was *felt* to be their own significantly higher than when the two stroking stimuli were applied asynchronously (replicating the finding of Botvinick & Cohen, 1998). In another experiment, Armel and Ramachandran removed the rubber hand and stroked the table, or else placed the rubber hand out of reach of the participants' hands. Repeating the synchronous stroking under these conditions reduced the participants' subjective ratings of hand ownership in the prototypical fake hand conditions; however, they were still significantly higher than their respective control conditions. As an objective measure of the incorporation of the fake hand or table into the body image, the skin conductance response (SCR) was measured following a sudden and potentially painful movement made by the experimenter (bending back the fingers of the rubber hand by 90° in the two rubber hand experiments, or ripping a piece of tape off the table in the table experiment). Mean SCR measurements were correlated with those of the intensity ratings, suggesting that this measure of autonomic arousal in response to potential bodily harm might be an objective measure of these incorporation phenomena. It would be important for future studies in this regard to use computer-controlled delivery of the potentially painful movements, in order to test these SCR effects at finer spatial and temporal scales and to remove the possibility of any experimenter-induced effects.

3.2.2. Neurophysiological and Neuropsychological Studies

Further empirical work on the virtual body or rubber hand effect has highlighted some commonalties across a variety of behavioral and neuroscientific disciplines. Recording from single neurons in alert macaque monkeys, Graziano (1999) studied the responses of premotor cortical neurons to both three-dimensional visual stimuli approaching a particular body part and to somatosensory or proprioceptive stimulation of the same body part. Graziano found that when the monkey's arm was hidden from view, the *selectivity* of the responses to visual stimuli decreased (i.e., the extent to which visual stimuli activated these neurons as a function of the position of the arm: the proprioceptive RF), suggesting a role for the *seen* position of the arm in these neural responses, but did not disappear altogether (suggesting a complementary role for proprioceptive information). Inspired, perhaps, by the rubber-hand findings of Botvinick and Cohen a year earlier, the responses of these cells were then tested with a detached, stuffed monkey's arm lying above the hidden real arm. The neurons' sensitivity to arm position when only the stuffed arm was visible was higher than when no arm was visible, but not as high as when the real arm was visible: the visual appearance of an arm, either the monkey's own or a similar arm, modulated the responses of these visuotactile neurons. Similar effects were found when neurons in Brodmann's area 5 were examined (Graziano, Cooke, & Taylor, 2000). Several neurons tested were even sensitive to the left/right identity of the visually presented arm, firing with higher frequency, for example, when a stuffed right arm was presented on the right side of the body, as compared to the presentation of a stuffed left arm on the right side, regardless of whether the arm was oriented prone or supine. Area 5 neurons show primarily somatosensory and proprioceptive responses, often responding preferentially to particular postures of particular body parts, while systematic or overt visual responses are not often found in this area. However, area 5 postural neurons *are* sensitive to body part–specific visual information, since the activity of a group of these cells was modulated by the appearance, specifically the position and orientation, of a stuffed monkey's arm when the monkey's own arm was hidden. Following these results, one might predict that the rubber-hand illusion in human participants may be attenuated by the presentation of a hand that is incompatible or incongruent with the concurrent stimulation (for example, a left rubber hand situated on the right side, during tactile stimulation of the participants' right hand). Furthermore, it would be of interest to know if the rubber-hand illusion can still be produced using such gross anatomical discrepancies as visual stimulation of a rubber hand paired with tactile stimulation of the participant's unseen leg.

In addition to behavioral and neurophysiological studies of the fake body part phenomenon, certain neuropsychological patients have been examined either in similar experimental circumstances or have been found to display symptoms potentially related to these phenomena following brain damage. For instance, Farnè, Pavani, Meneghello, and Làdavas (2000) examined 10 patients with tactile extinction following brain damage to the right hemisphere using a crossmodal extinction task. They found that *visual* stimuli presented near the visible *right* hand reduced the number of simultaneous *left tactile* stimuli detected (i.e., crossmodal extinction). The new finding in Farnè et al.'s study was that when a rubber hand was positioned on the right side (with the patients' right arms behind their backs), detection of left tactile stimuli also decreased significantly, but only when the rubber hand was in an anatomically realistic orientation.

Rorden, Heutink, Greenfield, and Robertson (1999) reported a patient suffering from a build-up of pressure in his right cerebral cortex due to a cyst. Just as for the patient reported by Halligan, Hunt, Marshall, and Wade (1996), this patient could detect tactile stimuli applied to his left hand only, or at least more often, when he could *see* the stimuli being applied. Rorden et al. asked their patient to place his hands underneath a table, while he received a series of brief tactile stimuli to his left hand delivered by a solenoid. At the same time, and on all trials, a yellow LED flashed briefly above the table either attached to the experimenter's hand (which was oriented at 180° with respect to the patient's hand) or attached to a rubber hand (which was aligned with the patient's own unseen left hand). Detection of randomly presented left tactile stimuli significantly improved in the aligned rubber-hand condition compared to the misaligned experimenter's-arm condition. In each condition, the false-alarm rate was 4%, suggesting that the patient was not simply more likely to respond when the rubber hand was in a congruent position. Rorden et al. concluded that it was not the position of visual stimuli that enhanced the patient's tactile detection, but rather the association of the visual stimulus with an aligned limb or, more specifically, that the attribution of both the visual and tactile stimuli to the patient's limb resulted in improved tactile detection.

Finally, the phenomena of the rubber-hand illusion and of the (mis)attribution of visual stimuli to one's own body or to the extinction of simultaneous tactile stimuli may have some important connection with certain phenomena experienced in the condition of somatoparaphrenia. Following brain damage, or as a symptom of a psychotic disturbance, certain patients claim that parts of their bodies do not belong to them (e.g., Bottini, Bisiach, Sterzi, & Vallar, 2002; Halligan, Marshall, & Wade, 1995; Nightingale, 1982; Sacks, 1986; see also Moss & Turnbull, 1996, for an account of misoplegia, or hatred for a limb) and as a consequence develop peculiar delusions or rationalizations concerning their "alien" body parts. The occurrence of this disorder of bodily perception is rare, and its presentation is often complicated by psychiatric disturbance and symptoms of neglect and anosognosia. Despite these caveats, however, it is tempting to suggest that the misattribution to another individual of one's own body parts or of stimuli applied to those body parts is in some way similar to the illusory attribution of visual and tactile stimuli to visible rubber hands in normal individuals (for a possible example of the converse of this misattribution, see Bradshaw & Mattingley, 2001). At what level, if at all, are these phenomena related? Can the experimental methods described here be applied to study the neural and cognitive processes that contribute to the generation of bizarre delusions of body ownership observed in somatoparaphrenia or anosognosia? Once again, we must await further research for definitive answers to these intriguing questions.

4. Extending the Body With Tools

The use of tools, from toothbrushes to cattle prods, represents a major family of achievements in the evolution of sensorimotor skill, and this is reflected in the limited number of animal species that manufacture and/or use tools as part of their everyday lives. The number of species, particularly of primates, that have been observed to use tools in the wild is steadily growing, but the technological gap between humans and other animals is undeniably vast. Humans use tools in almost every sphere of their lives and at almost every time of day; from the morning toothbrush and tea spoon, to the pencil, scissors, and ruler at the office; from the wrench and chisel in the workshop, to the needle, knife, and broom in the home; and from the pool cue in the pub, to the baseball bat and hockey stick on the sports field.

In recent years, the connection among tools, the multisensory representations of peripersonal space, and the hypothetical body schema has come into sharp focus, following the advent of a number of methodological approaches to studying the effects of tool use on these neural representations. In this section, we survey these approaches, provide a classification of different kinds of tool, and suggest how they may differ in the effects they have on neural representations of space and of the body. Unlike the concept of the "body schema," which remains at best ill defined and at worst conceptually meaningless (Kinsbourne, 1995; Poeck & Orgass, 1971), "tool use," as a collection of explicit behaviors involving interactions between physical objects and the body, may submit to a more rigorous definition and classification. We hope that such a classification might also help to shed light on the underlying neural processes that permit the use of a variety of tools.

4.1. Tools as Physical Intermediaries Between the Body and the Environment

One of the most useful definitions of *tool use* is that provided by Benjamin Beck in 1980. He cataloged the available published examples of the use and manufacture of tools by animals and arrived at the following definition (which he admitted was not yet complete, even after 15 years of trying):

> [T]ool use is the external employment of an unattached environmental object to alter more efficiently the form, position, or condition of another object, another organism, or the user itself when the user holds or carries the tool during or just prior to use and is responsible for the proper and effective orientation of the tool. (Beck, 1980, p. 10)

We understand *tool use* to mean this deliberate and purposeful manipulation of an independent, (usually) hand-held object in order to act upon another object to achieve a behavioral goal. Since the explosion of computer usage and virtual technologies since the 1980s, we suggest that this definition should be refined to include only *physical* interactions with other objects, mediated by tools, and to exclude, for example, *electronic* or *optical* interactions with objects, such as the use of a computer mouse to move an onscreen cursor, of a laser to point at a screen, of a telesurgical device, or of any action that is not directly and physically mediated by the hand and tool combined.[6] This stronger definition is necessary, we suggest, to draw a clear distinction between the behaviors involved (and the putative neural systems implicated) in the use of objects as conventional tools and the other manipulations discussed here. For example, Làdavas (2002, p. 22) suggested that mirrors are "tools" in an analogous way to that of physical objects held in the hand, at least in terms of their effects on the neural representation of peripersonal space. While the idea that mirrors are tools is not unreasonable in itself—the forms and varieties of human technology are arguably limitless—it may be preferable to make clear distinctions when interpreting the behavioral effects of such diverse experimental manipulations. Under Beck's (1980) definition, a mirror would only be a tool if it were held in the hand before or during usage and if the reference to "alteration of an object's position" is intended to include the virtual alteration of position by means of reflectance. While Beck may not have dealt specifically with the issue of mirrors, we feel that mirrors should not be classified as tools.

As far as we are aware, tools first became of relevance to the neuropsychological field when Liepmann (1905) brought attention to the selective deficits that some brain-damaged patients displayed in relation to the perception of tools and their usage of them (ideomotor and ideational apraxia). Such patients can, for example, name a tool and describe its function, but are unable to grasp and use the tool properly. Other patients show the reverse deficit, and some show an inability to use a tool (e.g., a hammer) unless the target of the tool's action is present (see Goldenberg & Hagmann, 1998; Hayakawa, Yamadori, Fujii, Suzuki, & Tobita, 2000). Parallel to this descriptive and experimental literature on apraxia, the idea that the skillful use of tools affects the brain's representations of the body has gained popularity. Head and Holmes (1911–1912) are often cited as the originators of this idea, but a cursory dip into a variety of sources once again provides a number of related earlier examples. For instance, Samuel Butler, in his satirical novel *Erewhon* (1872/1926), described machines as "extra-corporal limbs... supplementary limbs" (1926, p. 266), while the concept of "eccentric projection," the referral of sensations beyond the limits of the body and neural tissues, probably originated in the early psychophysical speculations of Fechner and Weber (e.g., Weber, 1846/1996), was taken up by Lotze (1854/1885), and discussed critically by James (1890). Philosophers enjoy this idea of the bodily incorporation of familiar objects as well (for a sociological perspective, see McLuhan, 1964/2001). Gilbert Ryle (1949/1963, p. 180) suggested that "mechanical auxiliaries to the body, such as motor-cars and walking sticks" are referred to in normal speech as part of the bodily self (for example, we might prefer to say "I crashed into the wall" instead of "My car crashed into the wall"), while even parts of the bodily self, such as the hair ("I cut my hair" is usually preferred to "I cut myself"), are not given this pride of place in the category of "me" but are consigned instead to that of "mine." Polanyi (1958/1973, pp. 55–58) drew notice to the importance of "subsidiary" versus "focal" awareness or attention when using our bodies and tools to perform skilled actions. With unfamiliar objects, he suggested, our attention is focused on the objects themselves, while we have only a subsidiary awareness of our bodies during object manipulation. In contrast, once objects become familiar to us, and we have become skillful in their use, our focal attention is directed to the *goal* of the use of those objects, while our subsidiary awareness extends both to the body and the tool combined. This philosophical distinction is similar (at least in how it relates the body to tools) to the neurophysiological distinction drawn by Johnson and Grafton (2002) concerning acting *on* objects versus acting *with* them (see also chapter 4 in this volume on the importance of action in representations of peripersonal space).

4.1.1. Behavioral Studies

Clearly, the idea of the incorporation of tools into corporeal representations is popular and intriguing and is deserving of both philosophical and empirical investigation. Here, we concern ourselves only with the question: What empirical work, beyond the work on apraxia and the neuropsychological deficits in the use of objects and tools, has been brought to bear on the effects of tools on neural representations of the body and of peripersonal space? The recent resurgence of interest in tools and the body was stimulated in part by a study reported by Iriki, Tanaka, and Iwamura (1996). This group of researchers suggested that, when we use a tool, the neural representation of the body in the post-central gyrus and the visual (or rather, multisensory) space surrounding the body is "extended" at the level of the visual RFs of single neurons. Their work on macaque monkeys trained to use tools has galvanized members of the cognitive neuroscience community to apply an empirical approach to understanding tool use in humans. It was a full 6 years after their study, however, before visuotactile behavioral analogues of this putative effect were published.

Maravita, Spence, Kennett, and Driver (2002) used the crossmodal congruency task to examine the extent to which visual stimuli associated with tools (toy golf clubs modified for experimental purposes) interacted with the processing of simultaneous vibrotactile stimuli (see Figure 3.5 and chapter 4). The crucial behavioral manipulation in their experiments was for participants to cross and uncross the tips of the tools actively after every fourth trial of the crossmodal congruency task. Maravita et al. found that when the tools were actively crossed over the midline, the typical spatial contingencies of the crossmodal congruency effect were reversed: visual and tactile stimuli presented on the same tool interacted more than bimodal stimuli presented on the same side of space. This finding suggested that one effect of active tool use is to associate visual stimuli presented at the tip of a tool with simultaneous somatosensory stimulation of the hand that holds the tool. This effect has been interpreted as evidence of the extension of peripersonal space by the use of tools, as first suggested by Iriki et al. (1996), although other explanations are possible and need to be investigated further (see Holmes & Spence, 2004; Holmes, Calvert, & Spence, 2004; Holmes, Sanabria, Calvert, & Spence, 2005). For example, the influence of tool movement preparation, multisensory spatial attention, stimulus-response compatibility, and response priming and selection on these multisensory behavioral effects are important issues that need to be resolved (e.g., see Creem & Proffitt, 2001; Handy, Grafton, Shroff, Ketay, & Gazzaniga, 2003; Riggio, Gawryszewski, & Umiltà, 1986; Tucker & Ellis, 1998; Yamamoto & Kitazawa, 2001).

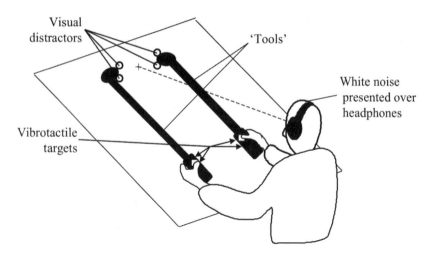

Figure 3.5. The use of tools to study the interaction of extrapersonal visual stimuli with vibrotactile stimuli. Participants held two plastic tools, each containing two vibrotactile stimulators in upper and lower elevations. Visual distractors presented at the end of actively used tools interacted significantly more with vibrotactile stimuli on the same tool than on the opposite tool. This same-tool effect occurs whether the tools are held straight (as shown in the figure) or with the tips of the tools crossed over into the opposite hemispace (redrawn from Maravita, Spence, Kennett, & Driver, 2002; see also Holmes et al., submitted).

4.1.2. Neurophysiological and Neuropsychological Studies

Separate from the impairments in using tools shown by patients with ideomotor and ideational apraxia, neuropsychological patients have provided another opportunity to examine the effects of tool use on multisensory interactions in extrapersonal space and to investigate potential ways of alleviating these patients' deficits. Modeling their research on the experiments of Iriki et al. (1996), Farnè and Làdavas (2000) asked patients with tactile extinction following right-brain damage to repeatedly retrieve an object (a small red, plastic fish) from the top of a table with a small rake (40 cm long). After 5 minutes of this tool-use practice, the patients were tested in a standard crossmodal extinction paradigm (see Làdavas, 2002; chapter 5). Farnè and Làdavas observed that, immediately after using the tool, the percentage of left tactile stimuli detected was significantly lower than the baseline level. This result would appear to be in line with the suggestion of Iriki et al. (1996) that tool use extends the boundary between peripersonal and extrapersonal space.

Further work on this aspect of tool use has shown that, for these effects of tool use to occur, there must be a continuous, physical linkage between the patients' hands and the visual test stimuli (Maravita, Husain, Clarke, & Driver, 2001; see also chapter 4). Additionally, Maravita, Clarke, Husain, and Driver

(2002) used a tool to *improve* the detection of tactile stimuli in the crossmodal extinction paradigm. Rather than reaching toward the visual stimulus with the tool held in the unimpaired right hand, the patient in this experiment held the tool in the impaired left hand, to which the tactile stimuli were presented. The logic of this experiment was that if visual stimuli presented at the end of a tool "activated" a neural representation of the hand holding the tool (as is suggested in several of the studies discussed above), then this should have the effect of enhancing the multisensory representation of the impaired hand when that hand is used to hold the tool. This is just what was demonstrated: the use of a tool by the impaired hand increased the proportion of detected stimuli applied to that hand.

In the related neuropsychological syndrome of left visuospatial neglect, tool use has also been included as an experimental variable. Certain patients with unilateral spatial neglect show a more severe neglect for peripersonal space than for extrapersonal space (Halligan & Marshall, 1991), in that, when they perform line bisections near their body, the errors they make are more severe than for equivalent bisections carried out farther from the body (e.g., 1 meter away, using a laser pointer). Berti and Frassinetti (2000) asked a patient with left neglect for near space to bisect lines near to and far from his body, using his finger, a stick, or a laser pen to indicate the halfway point on the horizontal lines. When lines were bisected in near space with the hand or in far space with a stick, the patient made average bisection errors of 24–29% to the right of the line's midpoint. When bisecting lines in far space with a laser pointer, however, the mean rightward error was only 9%. This effect was interpreted in terms of the stick (a tool) causing a remapping of far space as near space (i.e., extending peripersonal space), thus impairing the performance of the patient, whose neglect was worse for near space. The opposite effect (i.e., tool use improving performance) has also been demonstrated for a patient whose neglect was more severe for stimuli in far space (Frassinetti, Rossi, & Làdavas, 2001).

In summary, the evidence is now mounting on the effects of manipulating tools, which serve as functional extensions of the body, on the integration of multisensory stimuli near to and far from the body (see chapter 4; Maravita & Iriki, 2004; Maravita, Spence, & Driver, 2003; see also Handy et al., 2003; and Johnson-Frey, 2004, for other cognitive neuroscientific approaches to tool use). These effects primarily involve remapping, or linking *distal visual* stimuli to simultaneous *proximal tactile* stimuli. It is not yet clear at what level of processing this remapping takes place. There is some doubt, for example, whether the visuotactile representation of peripersonal space is literally extended by active tool use (Holmes & Spence, 2004; Holmes, Calvert, & Spence, 2004), or whether instead some other system (or systems) is (are) modulated during tool use, for example, that of motor preparation, or the capture or allocation of visual, spatial, or multisensory attention, or whether all of these factors play important roles. Research in the next few years should clarify some of the basic conceptual and experimental issues concerning the effect of tool use on the neural representations of the body and of peripersonal space.

4.2. Pointing Tools: Computer Mice, Flashlights, and Laser Pointers

Physical objects held in the hand and used to point to parts of the visual world are here labeled as *pointing tools*. The most commonly used of such tools (at least in the modern office) is the computer mouse. A physical object (the mouse) is moved across a surface, and this movement is transduced by electrical or optical sensors and converted into the movement of a cursor across the screen of the computer to which the mouse is connected (whether physically or electromagnetically). Similarly, with laser pointers and flashlights, a physical object is held in the hand and moved around to highlight a particular part of the visual scene. There may be justification for a further subclassification within this category of tools, based upon the spatial relations between the position and movement of the pointing object and that of the point highlighted in space. With the computer mouse, there is an arbitrary relationship between the position and movement of the mouse, on the one hand, and that of the computer cursor, on the other. Furthermore, the movements of both the pointing device and the cursor on screen are constrained to movements within a two-dimensional plane. When a computer mouse is rotated by 180°, the computer cursor then moves in the opposite direction compared to before the rotation, while the initial position of the cursor is unaffected by the rotation alone. When the same transformations are applied to a flashlight or a laser pen, however, both the position in and movement through space of the light spot are rigidly coupled to that of the pointing device itself. Based on this rigid coupling of the object and its optical effect on the world, one might be more inclined to define laser pointers and flashlights as "tools" than to do so for computer mice. As we shall see below, neuropsychological studies suggest that the use of laser pointers and sticks (i.e., tools proper) have quite different effects on various clinical measures of neglect and crossmodal extinction.

4.2.1. Behavioral Studies

The arbitrary spatial relationship between the position and movement of the computer mouse and that of the cursor has been used very productively to study the learning and retention of new visuomotor programs. Tamada, Miyauchi, Imamizu, Yoshioka, and Kawato (1999) studied the connectivity of the cerebellum and several parts of the cerebral cortex in a tool-use learning task. This task involved learning to use a computer mouse in which the position of the cursor was rotated with respect to that of the mouse, such that each movement was diverted from its normal path by around 75°. At first, participants found this difficult, but with some practice, they were able to track a randomly moving visual target on screen, aiming to minimize the positional error of the cursor with respect to the target. In a more detailed study, the same group examined the cerebellar activity correlated with the improvements in visuomotor tracking performance as participants learned to use such a rotated mouse (Imamizu, Kuroda, Miyauchi, Yoshioka, & Kawato, 2003; Imamizu, Miyauchi, Tamada, Sasaki, Takino, Pütz, Yoshioka, & Kawato, 2000). These later studies suggested that the cerebellum, in particular the evolutionarily more recent lateral cerebellum, was involved with both the creation and maintenance of internal models of tools and the cognitive aspects of tool use. This construction of internal models of external objects is very similar to the idea of the incorporation of tools into the neural representation(s), or the motor or sensory schemata, of the body.

Such cerebellar activity probably represents a very important part of the process of the adaptation of the body and brain to external objects. An important question to clarify in these rotated-mouse studies, however, is to what extent the activity measured, and by implication the internal model generated, is related to the *tool object* itself and to what extent does it relate simply to the *body*? To make this question clearer, would the same cerebellar activation be found if participants simply moved their hands to track a visual target in the absence of a mouse? A sensor could be attached to the participant's forefinger to measure its position and to translate that to a position of the cursor. Indeed, just such an experiment was carried out and detailed in an earlier report by the same group with similar behavioral results (Imamizu, Uno, & Kawato, 1995), implying that these results apply more to the understanding of visuomotor coordination of the body than to the use of tools per se. Indeed, other similar studies by the same researchers have interpreted their results in terms of "visuomotor learning" (Imamizu et al., 1995; Miall, Imamizu, & Miyauchi, 2000), suggesting that the role of the mouse itself in these studies is not clear. Furthermore, with the use of mouse touch-pads, where no grasping of a mouse object is even required, the distinction between "tool use" and "visuomotor learning" becomes even more blurred (see, for example, Balslev, Nielsen, Law, & Paulson, 2003).

4.2.2. Neurophysiological and Neuropsychological Studies

The only studies to use laser pointers to investigate the neural representation of extrapersonal space, as far as we are aware, have been performed with neuropsychological patients. In relation to the effects of active tool use on the body (reviewed earlier), the use of laser pointers has been used as a condition to compare with using tools proper. Halligan and Marshall (1991) studied a patient with visuospatial neglect, as evidenced by large rightward errors in a line bisection task. They asked their patient to bisect lines in near space by using both a pencil and a laser pen and in far space by using the laser pen and throwing a dart (the patient was a skilled darts player). The patient's performance was much better when line bisections were carried out in far space than in near space, even when measured with the dart-throwing measure. In this patient, therefore, the laser pen did not seem to extend peripersonal (near) space. Similarly, Frassinetti et al. (2001) studied a patient who bisected lines in near and far space with both a stick and a laser pointer. As expected, this patient, whose neglect was worse for far space than for near space, showed an improvement in far space only when the stick was used to bisect the lines: neglect for far space was not modulated by using a laser pointer. Several other studies back up these findings that there is little effect of the use of laser pointers on the representation(s) of extrapersonal space (Berti & Frassinetti, 2000; Berti, Smania, & Allport, 2001). Finally, one patient showed a different dissociation between near and far space and the use of sticks and laser pointers, which has muddied the water for interpreting these tool-use studies. In this patient, neglect was worse for near space regardless of the bisection method (i.e., stick or laser) *and* worse when using the stick, regardless of the distance (i.e., near or far) from the body (Pegna, Petit, Caldara-Schnetzer, Khateb, Sztajzel, & Landis, 2001). The extent to which the above patients' deficits for sensorimotor and multisensory interactions in peripersonal and extrapersonal space depend upon the difficulty of the motor task, as well as the effects of tool use per se, is an important question for future research (see also chapter 5).

4.3. Detached Tools: Telesurgical and Robotic Devices

Some modern examples of tools cannot be assimilated into the standard view of tools as we defined it earlier. These are devices where, while the human operator holds one part of the tool in his or her hand and while the target object is a real, physical object, with which the functional part of the tool interacts in the performance of some behavioral goal, there is no rigid, physical linkage between the user and the target object. Beck's (1980) definition of tool use does include *throwing* objects to hit targets, but in this case there is a continuous physical linkage across space and time that connects the thrower or dropper to the target via the continued existence and movement of the missile. The most prominent example of a tool that requires no physical linkage between user and target (other than the imperceptible linkage provided by electromagnetic energy) is a telesurgical device. In telesurgery, or any other form of remote manipulation of robotic devices, the user manipulates a scalpel, joystick, or other user interface; the movements of the interface are then converted into electrical signals, which are subsequently used to control a robotic device at a distance from the user. Since the movements are encoded electronically, the user and the robot do not necessarily need to be in the same room. Indeed, the separation of the surgeon from the patient, for example, is limited only by the speed of electrical processing and transmission, the mechanical operation, and the ability of the surgeon to adapt to the inevitable temporal delays caused by these processes (see Held & Durlach, 1993; Marescaux et al., 2001). This fact makes the methods of televised presentation reviewed earlier an ideal means by which to study the effects of teleoperation on corporeal representations. The development of this technology will be of great importance in medicine, allowing, for example, specialist surgeons to perform and/or direct operations on one continent, while the patient lies anesthetized in another.

Important for our definition of the *detached tool* is that the user of such a tool should actually *feel* the (simulated) interaction of the functional part of the tool with its target object. Such interaction can be provided by force feedback through the joystick or scalpel. Vital for operating on human tissue, the surgeon requires an acute sensitivity for the pressure applied to the body by the scalpel, the density of the tissue under the knife, and the presence of obstacles that may impede progress or harm the patient if mistakenly damaged. Investigation of the various factors that influence the surgeon's (or other teleoperator user's) sense of direct connection with the target objects—the feeling of *presence* or *telepresence* at the distal end of the teleoperator system (Held & Durlach, 1993; Loomis, 1993; Minsky, 1980)—will undoubtedly improve the control of teleoperated devices and their use, for example, in surgery, planetary exploration, or bomb disposal. Such factors include, but are probably not limited to, the resolution and field of view of visual displays; the consistency between the information provided across sensory modalities; the extent to which the user is aware of the teleoperator system itself; and, perhaps most important, the time delays between the production of movements and the generation of their sensory consequences (Held & Durlach, 1993). Overall, the goal of remote manipulation is to provide a wide range of realistic and tightly coupled sensorimotor interactions, albeit through a virtual or, rather, a detached world perceived and acted upon remotely. The closer these machines mimic the operations of the human brain and body, the more likely our interactions with them will be effortless and natural. The creation of such "anthropomorphic" machines might lead to new insights about how the brain represents the body and its relation to the world in its more natural, technologically unadorned state.

5. Summary and Conclusions

In this review, we have provided an overview of a wide variety of methods for studying the brain's representations of the body and their relation to multisensory and sensorimotor interactions in personal, peripersonal, and extrapersonal space. We have focused on the contributions of visual information, on the effects of artificial body parts and clothes, and on the effects of the use of a variety of tools on sensorimotor and multisensory interactions relating to the body. In reviewing this research, we have tried to highlight certain commonalties among the methods, particularly those regarding certain aspects of bodily perception and awareness. We suggest that focusing on these individual aspects of bodily experience may provide a more fruitful framework for understanding the body and the brain than invoking the abstract concepts of a body schema, body image, or any singular body representation. The brain contains numerous representations of the body at many levels of neural processing and in many cortical and subcortical regions. The functional or phenomenological outcomes of these integrated, distributed neural networks may provide better targets for experimental or theoretical work than any single "homuncular" body representation.

The scope of the various approaches reviewed in the present chapter covers a number of academic disciplines, from engineering and computing, to neurophysiology and neuropsychology, to psychophysics and the phenomenology of bodily perception. What these various approaches have in common is the attempt to understand how the brain constructs representations of both the body that supports it and the world which contains it; and furthermore, how such an understanding might aid in the design of human-computer interfaces, neural prostheses, replacement body parts, and navigation or rehabilitation aids for the blind and those with sensorimotor impairments. In the remainder of this chapter, we shall try to draw a few links among some of the methodologies discussed and briefly highlight some important recent developments.

The methodological classification we have provided (see Table 3.1) should be viewed as only a first step toward defining and distinguishing the various conceptual and experimental approaches to studying various aspects of the multisensory representations of the body. Doubtless there will be some overlap between methods, particularly as technology progresses and further sensorimotor manipulations fall within the realm of the possible. For example, Perkowitz (1999) reported that new computer mouse devices have been developed that provide active somatosensory feedback during interaction with your desktop computer: Imagine feeling the weight of a large, "heavy" computer file as it is dragged to the trash folder, or receiving tactile alerting signals as you click "delete" on the menu bar. Such tactile feedback could go some way to bridging the gap between our definitions of the *detached tool* and the *pointing tool* described earlier. It is almost certainly a question of degree as to what richness or complexity of tactile feedback from a hand-held device is sufficient to engender the same form of incorporation of the device as would be expected during telesurgery, for example, where immersion and presence are essential for the safe and effective usage of the equipment.

Table 3.1 A taxonomy of bodily manipulations. *Spatial*: possible spatial manipulations of the body, including *displacement* of the visual position of the body or a body part or sensations in those parts; *rotation* of the relation between movements of the body and of the mouse pointer; and *reversal* of the visual image of the body. *Distortion* of the visual form of the body. *Temporal*: possible temporal manipulations of visual feedback of the body, including *delays* in feedback of the visual image; and *synchrony* between visual and tactile information. The effects of exposure duration, learning, and so on could be studied in all of the techniques reviewed here. *Capture*: does this manipulation lead to visual capture of the felt location of body parts? *Attribution*: does this manipulation lead to the attribution of visible tactile or visual stimulation of a nonbody object (such as a rubber arm) displaced from the body or body part to the body itself (e.g., "feeling" the touches to a rubber arm)? *Identification*: does this method lead to the feeling that a visible body part is one's own body part (i.e., body or body-part ownership)? *Depersonalization*: can this method be used to *dissociate* the felt ownership of part of the body from the rest of the body? *Incorporation*: does this method lead to the incorporation of external objects, stimuli, or space into perceptual or motor representations of the body? In these latter four categories, for some cases where specific experiments have not, to our knowledge, been carried out, we have made a yes or no judgment as a starting hypothesis. Question marks (?) highlight specific areas for future research. *Clinical relevance*: to which clinical disorders or therapeutic interventions might the method be of relevance? *References*: behavioral studies are given preference, while clinical and neurophysiological studies are cited when no relevant behavioral studies exist.

Manipulation	Spatial	Temporal	Visual Capture	Attribution	Identification	Depersonalization	Incorporation	Clinical Relevance	References
Prisms (wedge)	Displace	—	Yes	Yes	Yes	No	—	Supernumerary limb; unilateral neglect	Hay et al., 1965; Mon-Williams et al., 1997; Shimojo, 1987
Shadows	Displace Distort	—	No	Yes	?	?	—	?	Pavani & Castiello, 2003; Shimojo, 1987
Mirrors (*distorting)	Displace Reverse Distort*	—	Yes	Yes	Yes	Yes	—	Mirror ataxia/agnosia; anorexia; dysmorphophobia	Burnett, 1904; Holmes et al., 2004; Jackson & Zangwill, 1952; Maravita, Spence, Sergent, & Driver, 2002; Nielsen, 1963
Video monitors	Displace Distort Reversal	Delay	Yes	Yes	Yes	Yes	—	Schizophrenia; apraxia	Daprati et al., 1997; Tipper et al., 1998, 2001; van den Bos & Jeannerod, 2002

continued

Table 3.1 (continued)

Manipulation	Spatial	Temporal	Visual Capture	Attribution	Identification	Depersonalization	Incorporation	Clinical Relevance	References
Clothing/ prostheses	Distort	——	Yes	Yes	Yes	No	Yes	Phantom limb; deafferentation	Aglioti et al., 1996; Graziano et al., 2002
Virtual body/ rubber arm/hand	Displace	Synchrony	Yes	Yes	Yes	Yes	Yes	Supernumerary limb; somatoparaphrenia	Botvinick & Cohen, 1998; Pavani et al., 2000; Tastevin, 1937
Tools	Distort Displace	——	No	?	No	No	Yes	Apraxia; neglect	Holmes et al., 2004; Maravita, Spence, Kennett, & Driver, 2002
Pointing tools Mouse	Rotate	Delay	No	No	No	No	No	Optic ataxia?	Imamizu et al., 2000, 2003; Miall et al., 2000
Laser/ Flashlight	——	——	No	No	No	No	No	Optic ataxia?	Frassinetti et al., 2001; Halligan & Marshall, 1991
Detached tools	Displace	Delay	?	?	No	No	Yes	Telesurgery	Held & Durlach, 1993; Marescaux et al., 2001
Mental tools	Displace	Delay	?	?	?	?	?	Paralysis	Carmena et al., 2003; Nicolelis, 2001

Another point of correspondence among the methodologies might lie in comparisons of the processes of visual capture, on the one hand, and identification with or of the attribution of sensations to visible body parts on the other (see Table 3.1). In order to identify with a particular body part, or with its prosthetic substitute (in the form of a fake hand, for example), is the process of visual-proprioceptive realignment a necessary precondition or a consequence of identification itself? Are these independent processes: one underlying our ability to adapt automatically to sensory realignment and sensorimotor perturbations, the other providing a basis for self-recognition and the awareness of our own actions? Perhaps one process is dependent on the other, or perhaps the two are aspects of the same underlying process or set of processes (see Holmes, Snijders, & Spence, 2005, for an attempt to resolve this issue)? This is similar to the question of the distinction between the (unconscious) body schema and the (potentially conscious) body image: is one wholly dependent on the other in unimpaired participants, or can they be dissociated experimentally? There may also be grounds for a distinction between those experimental manipulations that attempt to introduce some form of incorporation of objects or body parts not belonging to the participant (e.g., Botvinick & Cohen, 1998) and those studies that aim to achieve what is perhaps the opposite of this: the depersonalization of parts of the participants' bodies (e.g., Jackson & Zangwill, 1952).

In parallel with the study of the body experimentally, a vast clinical literature has amassed, detailing the various disorders of corporeal awareness that result from a variety of brain lesions, particularly those involving the parietal lobes. To what extent can neuropsychological and neuropsychiatric distinctions among disorders of the body be mapped onto the conceptual and methodological categories discussed here? Is the experience of supernumerary or phantom limbs, for instance, analogous to the dissociation of seen and felt body-part position induced by prismatic displacement or mirror reflection? Similarly, does the experimental technique of tendon vibration (e.g., Lackner, 1988) produce an experience more similar to that of supernumerary limbs than that offered by prisms? How does disownership, denial, neglect, unconcern, or hatred for a particular body part relate to processes of bodily perception and action in unimpaired experimental participants? How do disorders in the perception of body *shape* (for example, in anorexia, dysmorphophobia, and hypnagogic, epileptic, and migraine illusions; Leker, Karni, & River, 1996; Podoll & Robinson, 2000) relate to the normal perception of distorted images of the body in mirrors, shadows, and television monitors (e.g., Taylor-Clarke, Jacobsen, & Haggard, 2004), or to the effects of anesthesia on the perception of the body in normal human participants (e.g., Gandevia & Phegan, 1999)?

Finally, to what extent can the brain support a representation of the body that is either extended or detached in relation to its normal corporeal boundaries? Concerning the extended body, we have in mind the situation of the skilled acrobat who walks on stilts, physically extending her legs by several meters. Taken to the extreme, could the brain support an integrated sensori-motor representation of an extended body with six legs and a metallic exo-skeleton (see the account of the performance artist Stelarc in Geary, 2002)? In the notion of the detached body, we are thinking of a situation where the brain alone is used to control a machine, perhaps in close connection with the body, but able nonetheless to operate independently of the body itself and of bodily adornments. Such a possibility is quickly being realized by Nicolelis and colleagues, who trained macaque monkeys to operate remote devices directly via the neural activity in frontal and parietal sensorimotor areas (Carmena, Lebedev, Crist, O'Doherty, Santucci, Dimitrov, Patil, Henriquez, & Nicolelis, 2003; Nicolelis, 2001; Wessberg, Stambaugh, Kralik, Beck, Laubach, Chapin, Kim, Biggs, Srinivasan, & Nicolelis, 2000). After some training, the monkeys no longer needed to make overt movements themselves, but instead could control the robot simply by "thought" alone—one presumes by producing normal motor commands but suppressing the actual bodily movements—a situation akin to motor imagery in humans (Jeannerod & Frak, 1999). This raises the possibility of direct neural control of machines in the same way that the neurally and physically unimpaired have immediate control over their own bodies. Suddenly, the once remote possibility of brains detached from bodies, yet still in dominion over them—a favorite thought-experiment of the phi-losopher and armchair psychologist (see the amusing tale in Dennett, 1978)—comes almost within grasping distance. The implications such a development will have for our theories of the embodied mind, body image, and body schema are perhaps best left for future reviewers to examine.

Notes

1. This may, of course, simply reflect a bias toward citing English-language articles.

2. The term *neural representation(s) of the body* (or similar terms) in the present chapter, wherever used, is intended to apply as broadly as possible to any neural sys-tem(s) that is (are) involved in processing information related to the body, from all submodalities of somatosensation to multisensory and sensorimotor information and the neural processing thereof. In using such terms, we do not mean to refer to any single neural representation, nor to any single brain area that processes a singular body rep-resentation, nor to any single process, model, map, or schema. At the present stage, we simply wish to draw together a number of different experimental approaches relating to visual and proprioceptive interactions in bodily perception and to highlight various commonalties and differences among them, relating this to relevant neuroscientific and neuropsychological findings where possible.

3. The realistic simulation of shadows may be of great importance in enhancing various virtual-reality environments, providing further justification for the increased study of body shadows and their effects on perception and action.

4. In this regard, the apparently enhanced effect of the visual distractors when viewed through a mirror could, alternatively, be due to a *decreased* congruency effect attributable

to viewing the targets through a transparent occluder compared to viewing them in a mirror. The effect of occluders and of direct vision of the hand during the crossmodal congruency task is being investigated further in our laboratory.

5. The effects are likely to be greater when both rubber and hidden hands are of the same side of the body, based on evidence from several single units in the macaque posterior parietal cortex (Brodmann's area 5), which seem to distinguish between left and right arms (Graziano et al., 2000).

6. Beck's (1980) definition, incidentally, *does* include objects such as sticks, stones, and even feces, which are thrown or released in order to strike another object or animal.

References

Aglioti, S. A., Smania, N., Manfredi, M., & Berlucchi, G. (1996). Disownership of left hand and objects related to it in a patient with right brain damage. *Neuroreport, 8*, 293–296.

Alais, D., & Burr, D. (2004). The ventriloquist effect results from near-optimal bimodal integration. *Current Biology, 14*, 257–262.

Armel, K. C., & Ramachandran, V. S. (2003). Projecting sensations to external objects: Evidence from skin conductance response. *Proceedings of the Royal Society of London, B: Biological Sciences, 270*, 1499–1506.

Austen, E. L., Soto-Faraco, S., Enns, J. T., & Kingstone, A. F. (2004). Mislocalizations of touch to a fake hand. *Cognitive, Affective, and Behavioral Neuroscience, 4*, 170–181.

Balslev, D., Nielsen, F. Å., Law, I., & Paulson, O. B. (2003). *Tool proprioception at your fingertips: Somatosensory representations for tool location.* Paper presented at the International Multisensory Research Forum, June 14–17, 2003, Hamilton, Canada.

Battaglia, P. W., Jacobs, R. A., & Aslin, R. N. (2003). Bayesian integration of visual and auditory signals for spatial localization. *Journal of the Optical Society of America, A, 20*, 1391–1397.

Beck, B. B. (1980). *Animal tool behavior: The use and manufacture of tools by primates.* New York: Garland.

Berlucchi, G., & Aglioti, S. A. (1997). The body in the brain: Neural bases of corporeal awareness. *Trends in Neurosciences, 20*, 560–564.

Berti, A., & Frassinetti, F. (2000). When far becomes near: Remapping of space by tool-use. *Journal of Cognitive Neuroscience, 12*, 415–420.

Berti, A., Smania, N., & Allport, A. (2001). Coding of near and far space in neglect patients. *NeuroImage, 14*, 98–102.

Binkofski, F., Buccino, G., Dohle, C., Seitz, R. J., & Freund, H. (1999). Mirror agnosia and mirror ataxia constitute different parietal lobe disorders. *Annals of Neurology, 46*, 51–61.

Bonnier, P. (1905). L'Aschématie. *Revue Neurologique, 13*, 605–609.

Bossum, J. (1964). Mechanisms of prism adaptation in normal monkeys. *Psychonomic Science, 1*, 377–378.

Bossum, J. (1965). The effect of brain lesions on prism-adaptation in monkey. *Psychonomic Science, 2*, 45–46.

Bottini, G., Bisiach, E., Sterzi, R., & Vallar, G. (2002). Feeling touches in someone else's hand. *Neuroreport, 13*, 249–252.

Botvinick, M. M., & Cohen, J. (1998). Rubber hands "feel" touch that eyes see. *Nature, 391*, 756.

Bradshaw, J. L., & Mattingley, J. B. (2001). Allodynia: A sensory analogue of motor mirror neurons in a hyperaesthetic patient reporting instantaneous discomfort to another's perceived sudden minor injury? *Journal of Neurology, Neurosurgery and Psychiatry, 70,* 135–136.

Burnett, C. T. (1904). Studies in the influence of abnormal position upon the motor impulse. *Psychological Review, 11,* 370–394.

Butler, S. (1872/1926). *Erewhon.* London: Cape.

Campbell, J. (1995). The body image and self-consciousness. In J. L. Bermúdez, A. J. Marcel, & N. Eilan (Eds.), *The body and the self* (pp. 29–42). Cambridge, MA: MIT Press.

Carmena, J. M., Lebedev, M. A., Crist, R. E., O'Doherty, J. E., Santucci, D. M., Dimitrov, D. F., Patil, P. G., Henriquez, C. S., & Nicolelis, M. A. L. (2003). Learning to control a brain-machine interface for reaching and grasping by primates. *Public Library of Science, 1,* 1–15.

Clower, D. M., Hoffman, J. M., Votaw, J. R., Faber, T. L., Woods, R. P., & Alexander, G. E. (1996). Role of posterior parietal cortex in the recalibration of visually guided reaching. *Nature, 383,* 618–621.

Creem, S. H., & Proffitt, D. R. (2001). Grasping objects by their handles: A necessary interaction between cognition and action. *Journal of Experimental Psychology: Human Perception and Performance, 27,* 218–228.

Daprati, E., Franck, N., Georgieff, N., Proust, J., Pacherie, E., Dalery, J., & Jeannerod, M. (1997). Looking for the agent: An investigation into consciousness of action and self-consciousness in schizophrenic patients. *Cognition, 65,* 71–86.

Dennett, D. C. (1978). *Brainstorms.* Brighton, England: Harvester.

di Pellegrino, G., Làdavas, E., & Farnè, A. (1997). Seeing where your hands are. *Nature, 388,* 730.

Eddy, T. J., Gallup, G. G., & Povinelli, D. J. (1996). Age differences in the ability of chimpanzees to distinguish mirror-images of self from video images of others. *Journal of Comparative Psychology, 110,* 38–44.

Epstein, W., Hughes, B., Schneider, S., & Bach-y-Rita, P. (1986). Is there anything out there? A study of distal attribution in response to vibrotactile stimulation. *Perception, 15,* 275–284.

Ernst, M. O., & Banks, M. S. (2002). Humans integrate visual and haptic information in a statistically optimal fashion. *Nature, 412,* 429–433

Farnè, A., & Làdavas, E. (2000). Dynamic size-change of hand peripersonal space following tool use. *Neuroreport, 11,* 1645–1649.

Farnè, A., Pavani, F., Meneghello, F., & Làdavas, E. (2000). Left tactile extinction following visual stimulation of a rubber hand. *Brain, 123,* 2350–2360.

Farrer, C., Franck, N., Paillard, J., & Jeannerod, M. (2003). The role of proprioception in action recognition. *Consciousness and Cognition, 12,* 609–619.

Flaccus, L. W. (1906). Remarks on the psychology of clothes. *Pedagogical Seminary, 13,* 61–83.

Flügel, J. C. (1930). *The psychology of clothes.* London: Woolf.

Franck, N., Farrer, C., Georgieff, N., Marie-Cardine, M., Daléry, J., d'Amato, T., & Jeannerod, M. (2001). Defective recognition of one's own actions in patients with schizophrenia. *American Journal of Psychiatry, 158,* 454–459.

Franz, E. A., & Packman, T. (2004). Fooling the brain into thinking it sees both hands moving enhances bimanual spatial coupling. *Experimental Brain Research, 157,* 174–180.

Frassinetti, F., Rossi, M., & Làdavas, E. (2001). Passive limb movements improve visual neglect. *Neuropsychologia, 39*, 725–733.

Gallagher, S. (1995). Body schema and intentionality. In J. L. Bermúdez, A. J. Marcel, & N. Eilan (Eds.), *The body and the self* (pp. 225–244). Cambridge, MA: MIT Press.

Gallup, G. G. (1970). Chimpanzees: Self-recognition. *Science, 167*, 86–87.

Gandevia, S. C., & Phegan, C.M.L. (1999). Perceptual distortions of the body image due to local anaesthesia and other changes in peripheral input. *Journal of Physiology (London), 514*, 609–616.

Geary, J. (2002). *The body electric: An anatomy of the new bionic sciences.* London: Weidenfeld & Nicolson.

Gibson, J. J. (1966). *The senses considered as perceptual systems.* New York: Allen and Unwin.

Goldenberg, G., & Hagmann, S. (1998). Tool use and mechanical problem solving in apraxia. *Neuropsychologia, 36*, 581–589.

Graziano, M. S. A. (1999). Where is my arm? The relative role of vision and proprioception in the neuronal representation of limb position. *Proceedings of the National Academy of Sciences, USA, 96*, 10418–10421.

Graziano, M. S. A., Alisharan, S. E., Hu, X. T., & Gross, C. G. (2002). The clothing effect: Tactile neurons in the precentral gyrus do not respond to the touch of the familiar primate chair. *Proceedings of the National Academy of Sciences, USA, 99*, 11930–11933.

Graziano, M. S. A., Cooke, D. F., & Taylor, C. S. R. (2000). Coding the location of the arm by sight. *Science, 290*, 1782–1786.

Graziano, M. S. A., Hu, X. T., & Gross, C. G. (1997). Visuospatial properties of ventral premotor cortex. *Journal of Neurophysiology, 77*, 2268–2292.

Graziano, M. S. A., Taylor, C. S., & Moore, T. (2002). Complex movements evoked by microstimulation of precentral cortex. *Neuron, 34*, 841–851.

Gregory, R. L. (1996). *Mirrors in mind.* New York: Freeman.

Gross, Y., & Melzack, R. (1978). Body image: Dissociation of real and perceived limbs by pressure-cuff ischemia. *Experimental Neurology, 61*, 680–688.

Halligan, P. W., Hunt, M., Marshall, J. C., & Wade, D. T. (1996). When seeing is feeling: Acquired synaesthesia or phantom touch? *Neurocase, 2*, 21–29.

Halligan, P. W., & Marshall, J. C. (1991). Left neglect for near but not far space in man. *Nature, 350*, 498–500.

Halligan, P. W., & Marshall, J. C. (1995). Supernumerary phantom limb after right hemisphere stroke. *Journal of Neurology, Neurosurgery and Psychiatry, 59*, 341–342.

Halligan, P. W., Marshall, J. C., & Wade, D. T. (1993). Three arms: A case study of supernumerary phantom limb after right hemisphere stroke. *Journal of Neurology, Neurosurgery and Psychiatry, 56*, 159–166.

Halligan, P. W., Marshall, J. C., & Wade, D. T. (1995). Unilateral somatoparaphrenia after right hemisphere stroke: A case description. *Cortex, 31*, 173–182.

Handy, T. C., Grafton, S. T., Shroff, N. M., Ketay, S., & Gazzaniga, M. S. (2003). Graspable objects grab attention when the potential for action is recognized. *Nature Neuroscience, 6*, 421–427.

Hari, R., Hänninen, R., Mäkinen, T., Jousmäki, V., Forss, N., Seppä, M., & Salonen, O. (1998). Three hands: Fragmentation of human bodily awareness. *Neuroscience Letters, 240*, 131–134.

Harris, C. S. (1965). Perceptual adaptation to inverted, reversed and displaced vision. *Psychological Review, 72*, 419–444.

Hay, J. C., Pick, H. L., & Ikeda, K. (1965). Visual capture produced by prism spectacles. *Psychonomic Science, 2,* 215–216.

Hayakawa, Y., Yamadori, A., Fujii, T., Suzuki, K., & Tobita, M. (2000). Apraxia of single tool use. *European Neurology, 43,* 76–81.

Head, H., & Holmes, G. (1911–1912). Sensory disturbances from cerebral lesions. *Brain, 34,* 102–254.

Held, R., & Durlach, N. (1993). Telepresence, time delay and adaptation. In S. R Ellis, M. K. Kaiser, & A. J. Grunwald (Eds.), *Pictorial communication in virtual and real environments* (pp. 232–246). London: Taylor & Francis.

Holmes, N. P., Calvert, G. A., & Spence, C. (2004). Extending or projecting peripersonal space with tools? Multisensory interactions highlight only the distal and proximal ends of tools. *Neuroscience Letters, 372,* 62–67.

Holmes, N. P., Crozier, G., & Spence, C. (2004). When mirrors lie: "Visual capture" of arm position impairs reaching performance. *Cognitive, Affective, and Behavioral Neuroscience, 4,* 193–200.

Holmes, N. P., Sanabria, D., Calvert, G. A., & Spence, C. (2005). One tool or two? Using a single tool induces spatial biases in visual-tactile interactions. Manuscript submitted for publication.

Holmes, N. P., & Spence, C. (2004). The body schema and the multisensory representation(s) of peripersonal space. *Cognitive Processing, 5,* 94–105.

Holmes, N. P., & Spence, C. (2004). Visual capture of arm position in a mirror: Spatial and temporal factors. *Experimental Brain Research,* in press.

Holmes, N. P., Snijders, H. J., & Spence, C. (2005). Reaching with alien limbs: Visual exposure to prosthetic hands in a mirror biases proprioception without accompanying illusions of ownership. Manuscript submitted for publication.

Honoré, J., Bordeaud'hui, M., & Sparrow, L. (1989). Reduction of cutaneous reaction time by directing eyes toward the source of stimulation. *Neuropsychologia, 27,* 367–371.

Igarashi, Y., Kitagawa, N., & Ichihara, S. (2003). *The effect of hand picture on tactile discrimination.* Poster presented at the International Multisensory Research Forum, June 14–17, 2003, Hamilton, Canada.

Imamizu, H., Kuroda, T., Miyauchi, S., Yoshioka, T., & Kawato, M. I. (2003). Modular organization of internal models of tools in the human cerebellum. *Proceedings of the National Academy of Sciences, USA, 100,* 5461–5466.

Imamizu, H., Miyauchi, S., Tamada, T., Sasaki, K., Takino, R., Pütz, B., Yoshioka, T., & Kawato, M. I. (2000). Human cerebellar activity reflecting an acquired internal model of a new tool. *Nature, 403,* 192–195.

Imamizu, H., Uno, Y., & Kawato, M. I. (1995). Internal representations of the motor apparatus: Implications from generalization in visuomotor learning. *Journal of Experimental Psychology: Human Perception and Performance, 21,* 1174–1198.

Iriki, A., Tanaka, M., & Iwamura, Y. (1996). Coding of modified body schema during tool use by macaque postcentral neurons. *Neuroreport, 7,* 2325–2330.

Iriki, A., Tanaka, M., Obayashi, S., & Iwamura, Y. (2001). Self-images in the video monitor coded by monkey intraparietal neurons. *Neuroscience Research, 40,* 163–175.

Itakura, S. (1987a). Mirror guided behavior in Japanese monkeys (*Macaca fuscata fuscata*). *Primates, 28,* 149–161.

Itakura, S. (1987b). Use of a mirror to direct their responses in Japanese monkeys (*Macaca fuscata fuscata*). *Primates, 28,* 343–352.

Iwamura, Y., Tanaka, M., Hikosaka, O., & Sakamoto, M. (1995). Postcentral neurons of alert monkeys activated by the contact of the hand with objects other than the monkey's own body. *Neuroscience Letters, 186*, 127–130.

Jackson, C. V., & Zangwill, O. L. (1952). Experimental finger dyspraxia. *Quarterly Journal of Experimental Psychology, 4*, 1–10.

James, W. (1890). *The principles of psychology*. Dover: Holt.

Jarvelainen, J., Schürmann, M., Avikainen, S., & Hari, R. (2001). Stronger reactivity of the human primary motor cortex during observation of live rather than video motor acts. *Neuroreport, 12*, 3493–3495.

Jeannerod, M., & Frak, V. (1999). Mental imaging of motor activity in humans. *Current Opinion in Neurobiology, 9*, 735–739.

Johnson, S. H., & Grafton, S. T. (2003). From "acting on" to "acting with": The functional anatomy of object-oriented action schemata. *Progress in Brain Research, 142*, 127–139.

Johnson-Frey, S. H. (2004). The neural bases of complex tool use in humans. *Trends in Cognitive Sciences, 8*, 71–78.

Kelso, J. A. S., Cook, E., Olson, M. E., & Epstein, W. (1975). Allocation of attention and the locus of adaptation to displaced vision. *Journal of Experimental Psychology: Human Perception and Performance, 1*, 237–245.

Kennett, S., Taylor-Clarke, M., & Haggard, P. (2001). Noninformative vision improves the spatial resolution of touch in humans. *Current Biology, 11*, 1188–1191.

Kinsbourne, M. (1995). Awareness of one's own body: An attentional theory of its nature, development, and brain basis. In J. L. Bermúdez, A. J. Marcel, & N. Eilan (Eds.), *The body and the self* (pp. 205–223). Cambridge, MA: MIT Press.

Knoblich, G. (2002). Self-recognition: Body and action. *Trends in Cognitive Sciences, 6*, 447–449.

Lackner, J. R. (1988). Some proprioceptive influences on the perceptual representation of body shape and orientation. *Brain, 111*, 281–297.

Làdavas, E. (2002). Functional and dynamic properties of visual peripersonal space. *Trends in Cognitive Sciences, 6*, 17–22.

Le Chapelain, L., Beis, J., Paysant, J., & André, J. M. (2001). Vestibular caloric stimulation evokes phantom limb illusions in patients with paraplegia. *Spinal Cord, 39*, 85–87.

Leker, R. R., Karni, A., & River, Y. (1996). Microsomatoagnosia: Whole body schema illusion as part of an epileptic aura. *Acta Neurologica Scandinavica, 94*, 383–385.

Liepmann, H. M. O. (1905). Die linke Hemisphäre und das Handeln. *Münchener Medicinische Wochenschrift, 49*, 2322–2326.

Loomis, J. M. (1993). Distal attribution and presence. *Presence, 1*, 113–119.

Lotze, R. H. (1854/1885). *Microcosmus: An essay concerning man and his relation to the world*. Edinburgh: Clark.

Maravita, A., Clarke, K., Husain, M., & Driver, J. (2002). Active tool-use with contralesional hand can reduce crossmodal extinction of touch on that hand. *Neurocase, 8*, 411–416.

Maravita, A., Husain, M., Clarke, K., & Driver, J. (2001). Reaching with a tool extends visual-tactile interactions into far space: Evidence from cross-modal extinction. *Neuropsychologia, 39*, 580–585.

Maravita, A., & Iriki, A. (2004). Tools for the body (schema). *Trends in Cognitive Sciences, 8*, 79–86.

Maravita, A., Spence, C., Clarke, K., Husain, M., & Driver, J. (2000). Vision and touch through the looking glass in a case of crossmodal extinction. *Neuroreport, 11,* 3521–3526.

Maravita, A., Spence, C., & Driver, J. (2003). Multisensory integration and the body schema: Close to hand and within reach. *Current Biology, 13,* 531–539.

Maravita, A., Spence, C., Kennett, S., & Driver, J. (2002). Tool-use changes multimodal spatial interactions between vision and touch in normal humans. *Cognition, 83,* 25–34.

Maravita, A., Spence, C., Sergent, C., & Driver, J. (2002). Seeing your own touched hands in a mirror modulates cross-modal interactions. *Psychological Science, 13,* 350–355.

Marescaux, J., Leroy, J., Gagner, M., Rubino, F., Mutter, D., Vix, M., Butner, S. E., & Smith, M. K. (2001). Transatlantic robot-assisted telesurgery. *Nature, 413,* 379–380.

Mattingley, J. B., Driver, J., Beschin, N., & Robertson, I. H. (1997). Attentional competition between modalities: Extinction between touch and vision after right hemisphere damage. *Neuropsychologia, 35,* 867–880.

McLuhan, M. (1964/2001). *Understanding media: The extensions of man.* London: Routledge & Kegan Paul.

Melzack, R. (1990). Phantom limbs and the concept of a neuromatrix. *Trends in Neurosciences, 13,* 88–92.

Melzack, R. (1992). Phantom limbs. *Scientific American, 266,* 120–126.

Menzel, E. W., Savage-Rumbaugh, E. S., & Lawson, J. (1985). Chimpanzee (*Pan troglodytes*) spatial problem solving with the use of mirrors and televised equivalents of mirrors. *Journal of Comparative Psychology, 99,* 211–217.

Miall, R. C., Imamizu, H., & Miyauchi, S. (2000). Activation of the cerebellum in co-ordinated eye and hand tracking movements: An fMRI study. *Experimental Brain Research, 135,* 22–33.

Miles, T. R. (1957). On the difference between men and machines. *British Journal for the Philosophy of Science, 7,* 277–292.

Minsky, M. (1980). Telepresence. *OMNI, 2,* 44–52.

Money, J., & Sollod, R. (1978). Body image, plastic surgery (prosthetic testes) and Kallmann's syndrome. *British Journal of Medical Psychology, 51,* 91–94.

Mon-Williams, M., Wann, J. P., Jenkinson, M., & Rushton, K. (1997). Synaesthesia in the normal limb. *Proceedings of the Royal Society of London, B: Biological Sciences, 264,* 1007–1010.

Moss, A. D., & Turnbull, O. H. (1996). Hatred of the hemiparetic limbs (misoplegia) in a ten year old child. *Journal of Neurology, Neurosurgery and Psychiatry, 61,* 210–211.

Nicolelis, M. A. L. (2001). Actions from thoughts. *Nature, 409,* 403–407.

Nielsen, T. I. (1963). Volition: A new experimental approach. *Scandinavian Journal of Psychology, 4,* 225–230.

Nightingale, S. (1982). Somatoparaphrenia: A case report. *Cortex, 18,* 463–467.

Ohry, A., Gur, S., & Zeilig, G. (1989). "Duplicate limbs" sensation in acute traumatic quadriplegia. *Paraplegia, 27,* 257–260.

Oldfield, R. C., & Zangwill, O. L. (1942). Head's concept of the schema and its application in contemporary British psychology. Part I: Head's concept of the schema. *British Journal of Psychology, 32,* 267–286.

Orne, M. T. (1962). On the social psychology of the psychological experiment: With particular reference to demand characteristics and their implications. *American Psychology, 17,* 776–783.

Pavani, F., & Castiello, U. (2004). Binding personal and extrapersonal space through body shadows. *Nature Neuroscience, 7,* 14–16.

Pavani, F., Spence, C., & Driver, J. (2000). Visual capture of touch: Out-of-the-body experiences with rubber gloves. *Psychological Science, 11,* 353–359.

Pegna, A. J., Petit, L., Caldara-Schnetzer, A., Khateb, A., Sztajzel, R., & Landis, T. (2001). So near yet so far: Neglect in far or near space depends on tool use. *Annals of Neurology, 50,* 820–822.

Perkowitz, S. (1999). Feeling is believing. *New Scientist, 163,* 34.

Podoll, K., & Robinson, D. (2000). Macrosomatognosia and microsomatognosia in migraine art. *Acta Neurologica Scandinavica, 101,* 413–416.

Poeck, K., & Orgass, B. (1971). The concept of the body schema: A critical review and some experimental results. *Cortex, 7,* 254–277.

Polanyi, M. (1958/1973). *Personal knowledge: Toward a post-critical philosophy.* London: Routledge & Kegan Paul.

Rabischong, P. (1993). Human prehension and its prosthetic substitution. In A. Berthelet & J. Chavaillon (Eds.), *The use of tools by human and nonhuman primates* (pp. 68–77). Oxford: Clarendon.

Ramachandran, V. S., Altschuler, E. L., & Hillyer, S. (1997). Mirror agnosia. *Proceedings of the Royal Society of London, B: Biological Sciences, 264,* 645–647.

Ramachandran, V. S., & Rogers-Ramachandran, D. (1996). Synaesthesia in phantom limbs induced with mirrors. *Proceedings of the Royal Society of London, B: Biological Sciences, 263,* 377–386.

Ramachandran, V. S., Rogers-Ramachandran, D., & Cobb, S. (1995). Touching the phantom limb. *Nature, 377,* 489–490.

Reed, C. L., & Farah, M. J. (1995). The psychological reality of the body schema: A test with normal participants. *Journal of Experimental Psychology: Human Perception and Performance, 21,* 334–343.

Riddoch, G. (1941). Phantom limbs and body shape. *Brain, 64,* 197–222.

Riggio, L., Gawryszewski, L. D. G., & Umiltà, C. (1986). What is crossed in the crossed-hand effects? *Acta Psychologica, 62,* 89–100.

Rizzolatti, G., Fadiga, L., Gallese, V., & Fogassi, L. (1996). Premotor cortex and the recognition of motor actions. *Cognitive Brain Research, 3,* 131–141.

Ro, T., Wallace, R., Hagedorn, J. C., Farnè, A., & Pienkos, E. (2004). Visual enhancing of tactile perception in posterior parietal cortex. *Journal of Cognitive Neuroscience, 16,* 24–30.

Rogers, M. J., & Franzen, M. D. (1992). Delusional reduplication following closed-head injury. *Brain Injury, 6,* 469–476.

Rorden, C. R., Heutink, J., Greenfield, E., & Robertson, I. H. (1999). When a rubber hand "feels" what the real hand cannot. *Neuroreport, 10,* 135–138.

Rosenthal, R. (1967). Covert communication in the psychological experiment. *Psychological Bulletin, 67,* 356–367.

Ryle, G. (1949/1963). *The concept of mind.* Harmondsworth, England: Penguin.

Sacks, O. (1986). The man who fell out of bed. In O. Sacks, *The man who mistook his wife for a hat* (pp. 53–55). London: Picador.

Sathian, K., Greenspan, A. I., & Wolf, S. L. (2000). Doing it with mirrors: A case study of a novel approach to neurorehabilitation. *Neurorehabilitation and Neural Repair, 14,* 73–76.

Sellal, F., Renaseau-Leclerc, C., & Labrecque, R. (1996). The man with 6 arms: An analysis of supernumerary phantom limbs after right hemisphere stroke. *Revue Neurologique, 152,* 190–195.

Shimojo, S. (1987). Attention-dependent visual capture in double vision. *Perception, 16*, 445–447.

Sirigu, A., Daprati, E., Pradat-Diehl, P., Franck, N., & Jeannerod, M. (1999). Perception of self-generated movement following left parietal lesion. *Brain, 122*, 1867–1874.

Sullivan, R. (1969). Experimentally induced somatagnosia. *Archives of General Psychiatry, 20*, 71–77.

Tamada, T., Miyauchi, S., Imamizu, H., Yoshioka, T., & Kawato, M. I. (1999). Cerebro-cerebellar functional connectivity revealed by the laterality index in tool-use learning. *Neuroreport, 10*, 325–331.

Tastevin, J. (1937). En partent de l'experience d'Aristotle: Les déplacements artificiels des parties du corps ne sont pas suivis par le sentiment de ces parties ni pas les sensations qu'on peut y produire. *L'Encephale, 32*, 57–84, 140–158.

Taylor-Clarke, M., Jacobsen, P., & Haggard P. (2004). Keeping the world a constant size: Object constancy in human touch. *Nature Neuroscience, 7*, 219–220.

Tipper, S. P., Lloyd, D. M., Shorland, B., Dancer, C., Howard, L. A., & McGlone, F. P. (1998). Vision influences tactile perception without proprioceptive orienting. *Neuroreport, 9*, 1741–1744.

Tipper, S. P., Phillips, N., Dancer, C., Lloyd, D. M., Howard, L. A., & McGlone, F. P. (2001). Vision influences tactile perception at body sites that cannot be viewed directly. *Experimental Brain Research, 139*, 160–167.

Tucker, M., & Ellis, R. (1998). On the relations between seen objects and components of potential actions. *Journal of Experimental Psychology: Human Perception and Performance, 24*, 830–846.

van Beers, R. J., Sittig, A. C., & Denier van der Gon, J. J. (1999). Integration of proprioceptive and visual position-information: An experimentally supported model. *Journal of Neurophysiology, 81*, 1355–1364.

van den Bos, E., & Jeannerod, M. (2002). Sense of body and sense of action both contribute to self-recognition. *Cognition, 85*, 177–187.

Vuilleumier, P., Reverdin, A., & Landis, T. (1997). Four legs: Illusory reduplication of the lower limbs after bilateral parietal lobe damage. *Archives of Neurology, 54*, 1543–1547.

Warren, D. H., & Schmitt, T. L. (1978). On the plasticity of visual-proprioceptive bias effects. *Journal of Experimental Psychology: Human Perception and Performance, 4*, 302–310.

Weber, E. H. (1846/1996). Tastsinn und Gemeingefühl. In H. E. Ross & D. J. Murray (Eds.), *E. H. Weber on the tactile senses* (pp. 141–148). Hove, UK: Earlbaum Taylor and Francis.

Welch, R. B. (1972). The effect of experienced limb identity upon adaptation to simulated displacement of the visual field. *Perception & Psychophysics, 12*, 453–456.

Welch, R. B., Widawski, M. H., Harrington, J., & Warren, D. H. (1979). An examination of the relationship between visual capture and prism adaptation. *Perception & Psychophysics, 25*, 126–132.

Wessberg, J., Stambaugh, C. R., Kralik, J. D., Beck, P. D., Laubach, M., Chapin, J. K., Kim, J., Biggs, S. J., Srinivasan, M. A., & Nicolelis, M. A. L. (2000). Real-time prediction of hand trajectory by ensembles of cortical neurons in primates. *Nature, 408*, 361–365.

Wolpert, D. M., Miall, R. C., & Kawato, M. I. (1998). Internal models in the cerebellum. *Trends in Cognitive Sciences, 2*, 338–347.

Yamamoto, S., & Kitazawa, S. (2001). Sensation at the tips of invisible tools. *Nature Neuroscience, 4*, 979–980.

4

From "Body in the Brain" to "Body in Space"

Sensory and Intentional Components of Body Representation

Angelo Maravita

1. Body Representation

Our body is many things. From a sensory perspective the body is the physical space where all somatosensory input is coded. From a motor point of view, the body is the effector through which each one of us can interact with objects in external (extrapersonal) space.

How the body is represented in the brain is a fascinating issue which has been explored by philosophers and scientists from different viewpoints. Early neurological literature proposed the term *coenesthesia* to indicate a sense of the body created by a multitude of deep proprioceptive input (Brissaud, 1895; Deny & Camus, 1905). This concept had a great conceptual and clinical appeal and was gradually elaborated by referring to complex "images" (Münk, 1890, cited in Poeck & Orgass, 1971) of body parts present in the cerebral cortex. Through experimental ablation of cortical areas in dogs, Münk proposed that such images were held in the frontoparietal, sensorimotor cortex since early childhood (Münk, 1890, cited in Poeck & Orgass, 1971). The term *schema* was subsequently introduced by the French neurologist Bonnier (1905) to indicate an internal representation of the body which had a specific importance in the spatial orientation and localization of our body with respect to objects in external space. Disturbances of such a schema, mainly due to peripheral, vestibular syndromes, led to a variety of clinical disorders; in particular the loss of it was named *aschematia* (see Vallar & Papagno, 2002, for a critical review of a number of Bonnier's case studies). A larger diffusion of the term *body schema* was reached with the work of Head and Holmes

(1911). In a detailed description of the neurology of the sensory systems, they gave their detailed account of what a central body schema is. Sensations coming from the periphery reach the somatosensory cortex via the thalamus and produce cortical activations which are specific for each type of sensation (thermal, tactile, and so on). One of the specific characteristics of the cortex, according to Head and Holmes, is that of comparing each new sensation with other ones. In particular, in regard to proprioceptive stimulation (i.e., the position sense), the authors wrote:

> At any moment we can become conscious of the position of any part of our bodies, and although such postural recognition is not constantly in the central field of attention, it always forms the measure against which we judge subsequent changes. . . . Not uncommonly a patient with a cortical lesion can recognise that some movement has occurred, but is unable to discover its direction or amplitude. (Head & Holmes, 1911, p. 186)

Then Head and Holmes also famously defined the term *schema*:

> For . . . [the] combined standard against which all subsequent changes of posture are measured before they enter into consciousness, we propose the word schema. . . . Every new posture or movement is recorded on this plastic schema, and the activity of the cortex brings every fresh group of sensations evoked by altered posture into relation with it. (p. 187)

Although no precise attempt to indicate a putative localization of body schema(s) in the cortex was made, which was subsequently favored by the diffusion of detailed anatomical notions about the functions of the human cortex in vivo (e.g., Penfield, 1955; Penfield & Faulk, 1955), the importance of the "sensory" cortex (possibly primary plus "associative" regions) for keeping this constantly updated schema of the body was clearly underlined by these authors.

Furthermore, the main, unconscious construct of the body schema was also completed by another aspect of body knowledge, which was the relative ability to locate stimuli on the body surface. These two faculties (or schemata) were likely to hold different neural substrates as shown by Head and Holmes's Patient Hn (case 14) who, after brain damage "never failed to locate the stimulated spot correctly, although he could not tell the position of his hand" (Head & Holmes, 1911, p. 187). In more recent times, many fascinating case studies have also reported the opposite clinical picture, that is, the inability of patients to locate the spot of a stimulation on their body surface in the syndrome called *autotopagnosia* (see, e.g., De Renzi & Faglioni, 1963; Semenza & Goodglass, 1985).

The conceptual and terminological distinction between a body schema, a mainly unconscious, automatically updated representation of the body, and a *body image*, a more explicit knowledge about the shape and location of different sites of our body surface, is a matter of debate even today (for discussion about this distinction see Gallagher, 1998; and chapter 3).

In summary, the influential view about the body schema present at the beginning of the twentieth century was that of an online representation of the actual posture of the body, which was continuously updated by subsequent movements, accompanied by a more conscious knowledge about the surface and shape of the body.

These ideas were then gradually refined by considering automatic, multisensory, and conscious elements as critical determinants of the "body schema" (see Schilder, 1935). The concept of a body in the brain was then related to different aspects of bodily knowledge and bodily awareness and their disruption following damage to the central nervous system or limb amputation (e.g., Berlucchi & Aglioti, 1997; Coslett, 1998; Critchley, 1953; Cumming, 1988; Gross, Webb, & Melzack, 1974; Maravita, Spence, & Driver, 2003; Vallar & Papagno, 2002).

Suggestive clues to the existence of a representation of the body in the brain come from the rich literature on phantom limbs (Mitchell, 1871). Typically, this term refers to the persistent perception of a part of the body which is no longer present due to amputation (for reviews, see Berlucchi & Aglioti, 1997; Ramachandran & Hirstein, 1998). The persisting sense of an amputated limb suggests that body representation may be partially independent from current sensory input. Furthermore, since phantom sensations have been reported even in children with congenital aplasia (Weinstein & Seresen, 1961), it has been suggested that a representation of the body in the brain may already exist in the brain from birth or very early developmental stages, independently from any previous somatosensory input (e.g., Melzack, 1990). However such a representation, albeit innate, is likely to be very plastic. A rich literature on long- and short-term plasticity shows that cortical sensory and motor maps are extremely plastic and, for example, they can change their size as a consequence of peripheral deafferentation (for a review, see Kaas, 2000). Furthermore, although phantoms are observed in children with congenitally absent limbs, the incidence of phantom sensations increases proportionally with the age of the person at amputation (Melzack, Israel, Lacroix, & Schultz, 1997; Simmel, 1962). This body of evidence suggests a role for experience, even possibly through the observation of other conspecifics, for the development of a body representation (see discussion in Brugger et al., 2000; and chapter 9).

In this chapter, the idea of a "body in the brain" will be referred to as *body representation*. Critical to this term is, first, the reference to a putative neural network that holds a representation of our own body structure (see discussion in Berlucchi & Aglioti, 1997). This network is likely to be quite distributed. According to Melzack (1990), the parietal and insular cortex and limbic structures are likely to be involved. Recent clinical studies have stressed the importance of the temporoparietal junction for many neurological symptoms involving distorted body representation, such as autoscopy or out-of-the-body experiences (Blanke, Landis, Spinelli, & Seeck, 2004; see also chapter 9 for a discussion of this and similar neurological disorders), while imaging studies have shown the importance of lateral occipitotemporal areas for the coding of images of body parts (Downing, Jiang, Shuman, & Kanwisher, 2001) and of frontoparietal areas for the coding of touch across postural changes (e.g., Lloyd et al., 2003; Valenza et al., 2004). Besides a predetermined innate structure, the representation of the body is certainly plastic and is highly shaped by experience. An appropriate reference to this view is provided by Melzack who, while elaborating on his idea of a *neuromatrix*, wrote:

> The concept of a neuromatrix may seem radical, but it may be visualized as a Hebbian "cell assembly" whose synaptic connections are genetically laid down ... and in which synaptic competition due to input results in ... the eventual neural-synaptic architecture unique for the individual body. (Melzack, 1990, p. 91; see also Berlucchi & Aglioti, 1997, for further discussion of this view of body representation)

In this chapter, this concept of body representation will be discussed by referring to some of its critical determinants, as gathered from recent experimental evidence in animals and humans. More than trying to provide a new, general definition of body knowledge, the purpose of this chapter is to show how this representation is constructed by the efficient integration of multisensory input, how intentional action is a critical determinant to its plasticity (and ultimately one of the main reasons that a representation of the body exists), and how body awareness and the complex of beliefs and knowledge about our bodies and the environment are strictly linked to the concept of body representation (see also chapter 3 for a discussion about the definition of body representation).

First, it will be discussed how body representation originates from the efficient integration of somatic sensations (touch and proprioception) with sensations originating from other sensory modalities (typically vision). This process critically determines the relationship between our body and extrapersonal space.

Second, it will be discussed how body representation may be related to motor preparation and execution. On the one hand, the way our body is shaped critically influences our range of actions. On the other hand, however, action may plastically alter body representation, as shown by the changes in multisensory integration between bodily and extrapersonal stimuli induced by the intentional use of long tools, which can efficiently extend our action space.

Third, the role that abstract knowledge about a particular perceptual situation, as well as self-awareness and the complex of personal beliefs about our own body in determining our conscious experience of body integrity, perception, and action will be discussed.

2. Multisensory Aspects of Body Representation

It is becoming increasingly clear that body representation results from the integration of input originating from different sensory modalities. Proprioceptive inputs are surely important to determine the position of different body segments in relationship to each other and to external space (Roll, Roll, & Velay, 1991). However information about body shape and posture also comes from other sensory modalities, such as vision and touch. The subjective perception of one's own body, for example, may be distorted in the absence of vision. Congenitally blind children may overrepresent some parts of their bodies (e.g., the limbs) when they are asked to reproduce models of their own bodies with plasticine (Kinsbourne & Lempert, 1989). Interestingly, the overrepresentation of the limbs suggests the importance of intentional actions toward stimuli in external space for body representation.

Critical evidence for the multisensory construction of body representation comes from experimental paradigms whereby different modalities create a conflict between the seen and felt position of body segments. For example, the vision of a false limb in a posture different from (although mechanically compatible with) that of a real but invisible limb may be gradually incorporated in the subject's body representation so that the felt position of the real limb approaches that of the seen fake limb. This "virtual body effect" (Austen, Soto-Faraco, Pinel, & Kingstone, 2001) can be indirectly inferred by studying the effect of observing a fake, alien arm on somatosensory perception. For example, it is well known that visual stimuli can interfere with somatosensory stimuli delivered at the hand, more when they are presented *close* to the stimulated hand than when they are presented *far* away from the hand (Spence, Pavani, Maravita, & Holmes, in press; chapter 3). In other words, visual-tactile interference is stronger for stimuli within near, or peripersonal space, than far space (e.g., Làdavas, 2002; chapter 5; Maravita et al., 2003). In recent experiments it has been shown that visual-tactile interference from stimuli farther away from the hand can be enhanced when the visual stimuli are delivered close to a fake hand (Farnè & Làdavas 2000; Pavani, Spence, & Driver, 2000). Interestingly, this effect occurs only when the alien arm holds a posture that is anatomically possible for the observer. Furthermore, when vision of a fake limb is accompanied by visible tactile stimulation of such a limb, synchronous with touches to the real, invisible limb, the feeling of perceptual displacement of one's own real limb toward the fake one is even greater and is often spontaneously reported, with surprise, by some subjects (Armel & Ramachandran, 2003; Botvinick & Cohen, 1998). These experiments suggest that vision of a fake limb can alter the perceived position of the participant's arm and of any tactile stimulus delivered to it, even if the participant knows that the observed limb is a fake one.

Also, the conflict between tactile and proprioceptive information may produce surprising alterations of body representation, as shown by Lackner and colleagues (Lackner, 1988). A vibration delivered to the arm biceps, while it remains still, may induce the illusory feeling of a forearm extension (i.e., the angle between the upper arm and forearm is felt to be larger than it really is). If this proprioceptive illusion is induced while the participant's hand is touching her head or nose, this induces a strong conflict between the illusory feeling that her own forearm is extending and the tactile input that the finger of the same arm is still touching the body. The resulting subjective experience is that the touched body part is distorted or dislocated. Some subjects reported that their noses, touched by the illusorily extending forearms, were elongated (hence the common reference to this illusion as the "Pinocchio illusion") or duplicated, while other subjects reported that their necks were tilting backward.

At a single-neuron level, conflicts between vision and proprioception may modulate cellular discharge. Graziano and colleagues showed that neurons in the premotor cortex may discharge not only in response to visual stimuli near (typically, approaching) the animal's hand, but also to stimuli approaching a stuffed, dummy monkey arm, while the monkey's real arm was hidden from view. Critically, for some such neurons, the visual response was stronger when the seen posture of the dummy arm coincided with that of the real arm (Graziano, 1999). Similarly, neurons in parietal area 5 can significantly increase their tonic discharge when a dummy arm is presented which holds a similar posture to that of the real monkey's arm, which is hidden from direct view (Graziano, Cooke, & Taylor, 2000).

These data support the view that body representation is constructed through the integration of inputs, relative to body parts, that arise from different sensory modalities. As we mentioned above, somatosensory stimuli to the body are efficiently integrated with visual stimuli coming from extrapersonal space. Further results from electrophysiological recordings clearly show that some brain areas are capable of integrating visual and somatosensory responses. Among them, in the macaque monkey, around 50% of the neurons in the ventral premotor cortex (area F4) (Fogassi et al., 1996), 70% of neurons in the ventral intraparietal (VIP) area (Duhamel, Colby, & Goldberg, 1998), 20–30% of neurons in the posterior parietal cortex (area 7b) (Leinonen, Hyvarinen, Nyman, & Linnankoski, 1979; Graziano & Gross, 1994), and 24% of cells in the putamen (Graziano & Gross, 1994) show both visual (vRF) and tactile (tRF) receptive fields, meaning that they discharge in response to both visual and tactile stimuli. The majority of neurons in areas F4, 7b, and the putamen, and around one half of VIP neurons prefer visual stimulation in *spatial proximity* with the body (peripersonal space) (e.g., Graziano & Gross,

1994; Rizzolatti, Scandolara, Matelli, & Gentilucci, 1981). Critically, each one of these cells code a region of *peripersonal* visual space which is spatially aligned to the preferred somatosensory receptive field of that cell. For example, VIP neurons with somatosensory receptive fields on the right upper face will respond to stimuli presented to the right upper quadrant of the visual field (Duhamel, Colby, & Goldberg, 1998) or a premotor neuron with a tactile receptive field on the arm or hand will discharge in response to visual stimuli approaching that body part. These cells constitute a functional network of bimodal neurons subserving a common representation of the body surface and the visual space near the body.

Another critical finding is that the spatial selectivity of visual responses for some such multisensory neurons in area F4, VIP, and putamen is not merely retinotopic. For instance, in some neurons with a tRF on the arm, the corresponding vRF may shift along with the arm if it is moved in space (5% of tested bimodal neurons in the putamen [Graziano & Gross, 1994] and 86% in the ventral premotor cortex [Graziano, Yap, & Gross, 1994]). Also, shifting gaze position while the spatial location of the visual stimulus is kept constant does not affect (or minimally affects) the firing rate of most neurons in the ventral premotor cortex (Fogassi et al., 1996; Gentilucci, Scandolara, Pigarev, & Rizzolatti, 1983; Graziano, Yap, & Gross, 1994; Rizzolatti, Fadiga, Fogassi, & Gallese, 1997) and of a subset of neurons in area VIP that respond to visual stimuli very close (ultranear stimuli; Colby, Duhamel, & Goldberg, 1993) to the body (Duhamel, Colby, & Goldberg, 1998). This system may be critical for coding space in coordinates centered on the body, thus putting each body part in strict spatial relationship to any visual event that may occur nearby.

Taking into account the above experimental evidence, body representation should not be considered simply as a static picture, or map, of one's own skin surface, but more as a dynamic representation of the *body in space*, whereby the body is a critical reference point for the representation of the external space adjacent to it (Maravita et al., 2003). In this respect, not only the sensory modalities typically linked to the construction of the body schema but also the visual modality concurs in determining a complex representation of the body and its peripersonal space (see review in Graziano & Botvinick, 2002; also see Lloyd, Shore, Spence, & Calvert, 2003; Macaluso, Frith, & Driver, 2002, for recent neuroimaging data on crossmodal integration between vibrotactile and peripersonal visual stimuli, relative to eye or hand position).

3. Intentional Aspects of Body Representation

Once this multisensory link between somatic and peripersonal space has been established, the functional relevance of such a link may be looked for. This may be a critical determinant to any concept of body representation if, following

Elian, Marcel, and Bermudez (1996), "one of the features distinguishing our relation to our own bodies from our relations to other physical objects is the fact that we can act directly with our bodies" (p. 21).

The main reason that multisensory integration with peripersonal space is particularly efficient, as we have discussed in the previous section, is likely to be that in this particular region of space we may reach for objects of interest, or we may be reached by interesting—or dangerous—visual objects (see, e.g., Cooke, Taylor, Moore, & Graziano, 2003). In recent years, single-neuron recordings in the monkey brain have changed the vision of a "purely perceptual" construction of a body map in the brain toward a more multicomponent, action-oriented one. In this view, multiple frontoparietal networks integrate information from discrete regions of the body surface and external space in a way that is functionally relevant to specific actions performed by different body parts (e.g., Colby, 1998; Graziano & Gross, 1998a; Jeannerod, Arbib, Rizzolatti, & Sakata, 1995; Rizzolatti et al., 1997; Rizzolatti, Luppino, & Matelli, 1998). Thus, specific regions of the posterior parietal cortex, where sensory input relative to specific body regions converge from different sensory modalities, are strictly linked to premotor areas where specific motor plans can be programmed (e.g., reaching versus grasping; see review in Rizzolatti et al., 1998). In an extreme view, visual attention to extrapersonal stimuli basically consists of motor preparation toward such stimuli (Rizzolatti, 1983). The space around the body, in this view, becomes functionally relevant to the actions to be performed there. At a single-cell level, for example, the extension of the visual receptive field of ventral premotor neurons may expand radially, depending on the speed of an approaching visual stimulus. In an elegant experiment, Fogassi et al. (1996) recorded from bimodal neurons in ventral premotor area F4 of the macaque, while objects approached the monkey's face by means of a robotic arm. Neurons discharged to the visual stimulus as soon as it entered their visual receptive field. Critically, however, the visual receptive field expanded radially when the speed of the approaching stimulus increased. This evidence was interpreted as suggesting that the visual stimuli approaching the body are coded depending on possible actions (grasping, avoidance) to be performed upon them. Motor preparation necessary to code for actions clearly needs to be much faster as the speed of the approaching stimulus increases. As a consequence, the visual response of premotor neurons starts earlier when the speed of the approaching visual stimulus increases (Fogassi et al., 1996). This explanation in terms of motor programming was preferred to more "perceptual" ones (earlier increase of firing rate due to increased saliency of faster-approaching stimuli, or a simple computation of the time-to-contact by such premotor neurons) also considering that the visual response of neurons in this area usually requires the presentation of three-dimensional stimuli, which are typically able to trigger grasping or avoidance actions (see discussion in Fogassi et al., 1996).

Further clues on the motor-intentional determinants of body representation may come from the recent literature on the effect of tool use on sensory-motor integration in humans and animals (see Maravita & Iriki, 2004, for a review). This literature takes its inspiration from the idea that any tool which is used by the body to act in space may gradually become included in the body representation itself as if it were a physical extension of it. In this view, the neurological literature describes the process of inclusion of extracorporeal objects in the body schema (Critchley, 1979; Head & Holmes, 1911) as well as the pathological denial of the ownership of extracorporeal objects, like a wedding ring, which are in contact with body parts whose ownership is denied following brain damage (Aglioti, Smania, Manfredi, & Berlucchi, 1996).

These behavioral reports have recently been followed by a number of experiments trying to establish whether the use of tools has some consequence on the neural representation of the body in the monkey brain. Iriki has recently found that neurons in the anterior bank of the intraparietal sulcus of the monkey brain respond to tactile stimuli delivered to the arm or shoulder, but also to visual stimuli delivered close to the same body parts (however see Holmes & Spence, in press; and chapter 3 about methodological issues relative to Iriki's experiments). However the visual receptive field of some such neurons is not static, but can be enlarged dynamically if the animals are trained (Ishibashi, Hihara, & Iriki, 2000) to use long tools to retrieve small bits of apple out of hand's reach (Iriki, Tanaka, & Iwamura, 1996). In other words, when the rake becomes a functional extension of the arm, the spatial properties of neurons coding for visuotactile peripersonal space around the hand extends to more distal visual space, which is now reachable by the tool tip. Once the tip of the tool becomes a distal probe of the hand in space, that is, it can be used to act in far space, responses to visual stimuli around the tip increase as if the hand itself were moved closer to the stimuli.

In humans, several experimental reports suggest that responses to stimuli at the tip of a long tool may present a similar pattern as those elicited by stimuli adjacent to the body. For example, temporal order judgments of asynchronous touches may be similarly disrupted both when subjects cross their hands or when they cross two sticks, wielded by either hand, the tips of which are vibrated (Yamamoto & Kitazawa, 2001). Similarly, the above-mentioned crossmodal interference typically found between tactile stimuli at the hands and visual stimuli near them (see Spence et al., in press, for a review of this effect studied with the crossmodal congruency paradigm, plus chapter 3) can be present also for visual stimuli in far space when these are presented close to the tips of long tools held by the tactually stimulated hands, as recently shown by Maravita and colleagues (Maravita, Spence, Kennett, & Driver, 2002). These authors showed that when participants held two long tools uncrossed, the visual distractor at the tip of one tool interfered more strongly with vibrotactile targets delivered to the hand on the same side than with those delivered on the contralateral hand. This effect of spatial contingency is typically found with the crossmodal congruency paradigm with visual stimuli presented directly near the hands (Spence et al., in press). However when the tools were crossed, so that each set of distractors rested in the opposite side of space as the hand wielding the tool to which they were connected, the typical spatial contingency of the interference reversed. Now tactile judgment on each hand was more severely disrupted by distractors on the opposite side of space (yet linked to that hand by the tool) than by distractors on the same side in external space (yet linked to the opposite hand via the tool). Such a reversal of the pattern of interference was achieved after prolonged, active use of the tools (i.e., crossing and uncrossing the tools every few trials for around 60 minutes), thus suggesting that the intentional use of the tools may have played a major role in its occurrence (see details of the experiments in Maravita, Spence, Kennett, & Driver, 2002; and also chapter 3 for further related crossmodal results in normal subjects).

Further evidence for the extension of multimodal integration from peripersonal space to the tip of actively used tools comes from the literature on brain-damaged patients suffering from neglect or extinction. Patients with neglect may be unaware of visual, tactile, or auditory stimuli presented on the side of space opposite to the location of a brain lesion. Also, when such patients are asked to indicate the midpoint of a drawn line, their subjective midpoint appears to be shifted farther toward the ipsilesional side as compared to the true, objective midpoint (Bisiach & Vallar, 2000). Berti and Frassinetti (2000) studied a patient with unilateral visual neglect, whose bias in line bisection was selectively present in near, but not far, space. Critically, in this patient, neglect became manifest also in far space when she used a long stick, as opposed to a laser pointer, to physically reach lines to bisect in far space (Figure 4.1a). The authors concluded that the physical reaching of the object in far space enabled that space to acquire perceptual properties similar to those of near space, thus showing an increased amount of neglect (see also Pegna et al., 2001, for related results).

Similar evidence has been found by studying patients with crossmodal extinction, who are unaware of tactile stimuli delivered to the hand contralateral to the side of a brain lesion (typically, the left hand following a right-hemisphere lesion), when they are presented with a simultaneous visual stimulus close to the hand ipsilateral (typically, the right one) to the lesion (di Pellegrino, Làdavas, & Farnè 1997). Furthermore, it has been observed that crossmodal extinction is stronger for visual stimuli close to, compared to far away from, the ipsilesional hand (di Pellegrino et al., 1997). In other words the spatial proximity of the visual stimulus to the ipsilesional hand is important to elicit extinction of a contralesional touch. However, extinction can become stronger even in response to far visual stimuli, once these stimuli are reached by a tool that is actively wielded with the ipsilesional hand (Farnè & Làdavas 2000;

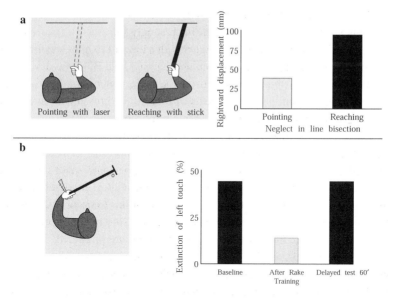

Figure 4.1. Projection of peripersonal space to the tip of a tool: Evidence from neglect and extinction patients. (a) Schematic drawing of the experiment performed by Berti and Frassinetti (2001). *Left panel* (pointing condition): the patient performs bisections of lines in far space, out of hand's reach, by means of a laser pointer (depicted as a red dotted bar). The *middle panel* depicts the patient performing line bisections using a long stick (reaching condition), depicted as a black bar. *Right panel*: results of the average rightward displacement on line bisection in the two conditions. The rightward bias, typically observed in neglect, is nearly absent in the pointing condition, while it is stronger and of similar amount to that showed by the patient in near space (not shown), when far space becomes reachable with the stick. This suggests that properties which are typical of near, peripersonal space can be projected to far space, when we can reach it with a tool. (b) Effect of tool use on crossmodal extinction. A patient shows extinction of left vibrotactile stimuli (yellow symbol) when simultaneous right visual stimuli (red circle) are presented. After the patient is trained to use a rake (depicted in black in the figure) to reach for far objects with his left hand, extinction decreases, as shown by the graph in the right panel. The rake, after it has been used for a while, is likely to link the two stimuli in a common, bimodal representation, thus reducing their competition. The right column of the graph shows that extinction goes back to the pretraining level after some time away from the training (redrawn from Maravita, Clarke, Husain, & Driver, 2002). *See color insert.*

Maravita, Husain, Clarke, & Driver, 2001; see also Làdavas, 2002, and Maravita & Iriki, 2004, for review). With a conceptually similar logic, albeit with the opposite result on extinction, Maravita and colleagues (Maravita, Clarke, Husain, & Driver, 2002) showed that visual stimuli delivered in the ipsilesional, right space, which typically produced strong extinction of left touches in their patient B. V., had a reduced detrimental effect on the perception of contralesional touches (i.e., a reduction of extinction was observed), when the patient reached the source of such right visual stimuli with the tip of a rake wielded with his left hand (see Figure 4.1b). Interestingly the amount (as well as the duration) of the improvement was higher with a longer (20 minutes) than with a shorter (10 minutes) preliminary training, during which B. V. was asked to use the rake to collect objects scattered on the table, out of hand's reach. This finding suggests that the above effects of tool use on crossmodal interactions are dependent to some extent on the amount of tool use.

This body of evidence on the effect of tool use in animals and normal and brain-damaged human subjects suggests that once the tools are actively wielded, the perceptual properties typical of peripersonal space and, in particular, the crossmodal visual-tactile integration and/or interference are extended to the tip of the tool. Critically, in order for this to occur, the tool has to be intentionally used to reach for (Maravita et al., 2001) or act upon (Farnè & Làdavas, 2000) the far visual space where stimuli are presented.

This intentional use of tools may be a clue to the existence of an intentional component of body representation, or plasticity of body representation, if one thinks that only through the intentional use of, for example, a rake may this object become somewhat included in our body representation and its tip thus may efficiently act as a functional probe of our body into far space (cf. Critchley, 1979; Iriki et al., 1996; Maravita & Iriki, 2004). To quote again Head and Holmes (1911):

> It is to . . . these [body] "schemata" that we owe the power of projecting our recognition of posture . . . beyond the limits of our own bodies to the end of some instrument held in the hand. Without them we could not probe with a stick, nor use a spoon unless our eyes were fixed upon the plate. Anything which participates in the conscious movement of our bodies . . . becomes part of these schemata: A woman's power of localization may extend to the feather in her hat. (p. 188)

It is interesting to note that the relative importance of prolonged use of an extrapersonal object to incorporate it into our body representation may depend on the type of object used and on the type of task to be performed with it. While pointing with a stick may produce a somewhat quicker incorporation (e.g., Berti & Frassinetti, 2000; Maravita et al., 2001), more complex or skilled tool use may require longer training (Farnè & Làdavas, 2000; Maravita, Clarke, et al., 2002; Maravita, Spence, Kennett, & Driver, 2002). Furthermore, the nature of such incorporation may be different depending on the type of actions performed with a tool. While retrieving distant objects with a rake (the task typically used in experiments with monkeys [Iriki, Tanaka, & Iwamura, 1996] and in some experiments with human subjects [Farnè & Làdavas, 2000; Maravita, Clarke, Husain, & Driver, 2002]) may possibly expand peripersonal space properties to the tip of the tool, including the space between the hand and the tool, pointing tasks may simply transfer such properties to the tip of the tool (see discussion in chapter 3). This functional extension of the wielding hand to the tip of a tool may be definitely more conceptual than merely physical in the case of virtual tools like computer mice or telesurgery devices where a surgeon may operate on a patient lying miles away, as well as in virtual-reality environments or immersive video games (Loomis, 1992; Obayashi, Tanaka, & Iriki, 2000; see also Maravita & Iriki, 2004). In such cases, a strict functional link between the body and the tip of the tool is likely to be created even in the absence of precise somatosensory input coming from the objects upon which the tool is physically acting. Nonetheless, the precise correspondence among intended actions, observed movements of the tool/cursor, and the effects of such movements might be enough to create the link.

4. Contributions of Abstract Knowledge and Self-Awareness to Body Representation

The representation that we have of our own body at any given moment is modulated not only by primary sensory input, but also by some more abstract knowledge and interpretation of any afference coming from our body and the extracorporeal environment. In conditions of conflict between vision and touch, like in the illusion described by Botvinick and Cohen (1998) reported earlier, subjects may startle when they realize that their own hands are being "felt" at the position of the seen fake hands. Thus, although there might be conflicting sensory input coming from different sensory modalities, which may even create some erroneous sensory experiences, our "knowledge" of the body and of the general conditions of stimulation remain stable. The extent to which this stable representation of the body may temporarily be disrupted by sensory conflict may depend on our experience with a particular situation. One example of a daily sensory conflict concerning our body is the situation of observing oneself reflected in a mirror. When we observe our own face in a mirror, we never experience ourselves to be at the position of the observed image (which is projected on the retina as if it were at double the distance between our eyes and the mirror; Gregory, 1998). Our knowledge about our own body structure and about mirror reflections is enough to avoid startling ourselves any time we comb our hair in front of a mirror.

This observation is supported by experimental data showing that body parts observed in a mirror are attributed to near, personal space and not to far space, as the visual image observed in the mirror would suggest. An intriguing aspect of observing one's own mirror reflection is that the seen image has the same optical properties as distant visual information (being projected as if it had a source that lies "through the looking glass"), and yet such distant visual information can relate to touches felt at the body surface. This arises, for example, any time we see the distant mirror reflection of the comb running through our hair, for which the actual location is peripersonal while the visual image suggests an extrapersonal or distant object. In a series of experiments, it has been shown that the interference of visual distractors presented near the hand on the localization of tactile targets at the hand (cf. Spence et al., in press; and chapter 3) is of a similar magnitude when visual distractors and the hands are observed directly or when they are observed as a mirror reflection (Maravita, Spence, Sergent, & Driver, 2002). Since, as mentioned above, this interference effect is typically stronger when visual distractors are presented near the stimulated body part (peripersonal visual space) than far away from it (far space; Spence et al., in press), the above evidence suggests that the visual space around the mirror reflection of one's own hand, and consequently the reflection of the hand itself, has sensory properties (i.e., has a similar representation) more akin to near peripersonal than to far extrapersonal space (see discussion in Maravita et al., 2003). A neurological case study (Maravita, Spence, Clarke, Husain, & Driver, 2000) examined the effect of mirrors on crossmodal visual-tactile extinction (Figure 4.2). These authors studied a right brain–damaged patient showing extinction of left touch by right visual stimuli. As often observed in similar patients and as discussed above, extinction of tactile stimuli on the left hand was reduced for stimuli farther away than closer to the right hand (di Pellegrino et al., 1997). However, when apparently distant visual stimuli seen in the mirror were actually the mirror reflection of visual stimuli close to the right hand (but hidden from the patient's direct view), their disruptive effect on the perception of left touches during bilateral stimulations increased again. This evidence suggests that, in the mirror situation, right visual stimuli were correctly interpreted as originating from near, peripersonal space, where their effect on the extinction of left touches was greater.

Although subjects are known to shift the locus of perceived tactile stimuli into external objects in some conflicting perceptual situations (e.g., Armel & Ramachandran, 2003; Botvinick & Cohen, 1998), in situations like the one mentioned above, one does not usually "feel" him- or herself as projected inside the mirror. However, sensory remapping of visual stimuli reflected in the mirror seems to occur automatically. Although, in principle, one could hypothesize that it is the tactile stimulus that is relocated at the apparent far distance of the observed visual stimulus (where the visual-tactile integration could thus occur), as suggested by the mirror, it seems more likely that reflected visual images originating from stimuli located in near space are recoded to their true position in peripersonal space (thus increasing their interactions with tactile stimuli), given our familiarity with observing ourselves in reflecting surfaces.

A logically related observation to the above experiments with mirrors has been recently published by Pavani and Castiello (2004). These authors have shown that visual distractors presented at the location of a shadow cast by the hand at some distance from the body produce a similar amount of crossmodal

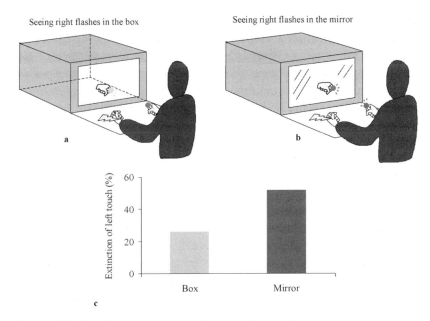

Figure 4.2. Recoding of visual stimuli reflected in a mirror to peripersonal space: Evidence from crossmodal extinction. A patient with crossmodal extinction receives vibrotactile stimuli on the left hand (yellow symbol) and visual LED flashes on the right side (green or red circle). (a) Schematic sketch of the box condition. The patient observes the contents of the box, including a fake hand holding an LED that generates the visual stimulus (note that in the real experimental setting, direct view of the hands was prevented by an opaque panel). (b) In the mirror condition, the patient sees the mirror reflection of his own right hand, together with a reflection of the nearby LEDs (held in his hand). The positions of the visible mirror reflections in this condition exactly matched those of the equivalent items inside the box in the box condition. (c) The graph shows the amount of extinction for the box and mirror conditions. Extinction increases in the mirror condition, producing a comparable effect of directly observing the visual stimulus in contact with the right hand (not shown). This suggests that mirror reflections of objects near the body, although suggesting a visual stimulus far in space, "through the looking glass," are automatically recoded as near objects (redrawn from Maravita, Spence, Sergent, & Driver, 2002). *See color insert.*

interference on a tactile-elevation judgment task performed at the hand to that produced by the same visual distractors presented close to the hand itself (see Spence et al., in press; and chapter 3 for discussion about this interference paradigm). This result suggests that the brain automatically codes shadows cast by the body as strictly related to the body itself. In this way the space location where the shadow is cast, albeit far from the body, is treated as peripersonal, thus producing a similar amount of visual-tactile interference as that produced by the space immediately adjacent to the body.

There are other instances where our own body parts may be related to visual stimuli seen at a distance from our bodies. For example, in a video monitor, we may observe our own hand, which may actually be resting on the table, displaced anywhere in space. However, the knowledge that we hold about the physical structure of our body is enough to prevent us from feeling "disembodied" and from attributing the image of that particular hand to ourselves. An intriguing perceptual consequence of this was observed by Tipper and colleagues (Tipper et al., 1998; Tipper et al., 2001). These authors showed that reaction time to a tactile stimulus is enhanced when the stimulated body part is visible in a video monitor. This effect is specific for the stimulated body part, since the enhancement does not occur when the monitor provides visual feedback from a body region different from the stimulated one. Also the enhancement produced by visual feedback is larger for body parts normally accessible to vision either directly, like the hand, or indirectly via a mirror, like the face, than when looking at body sites which are not normally visible to oneself, like the neck (Tipper et al., 2001).

Logically related evidence has been provided at the single-neuron level in the monkey. When animals were trained to observe their own hand in a video monitor while retrieving bits of food, the response of a small subset of bimodal neurons (see above) to a visual stimulus approaching the video image of the hand in the monitor increased (Iriki, Tanaka, Obayashi, & Iwamura, 2001) in a similar way as when the hand was in direct view. Iriki and colleagues interpreted these findings as evidence that these neurons (and possibly the animal itself) could be trained to "recognize" the seen hand in the monitor as their own. As a consequence, the space adjacent to the video image of the hand acquired similar perceptual properties to those of the space around the monkey's real hand. In support of this view, Iriki and coworkers reported that when the image of a spider or snake was approached to the hand in the monitor, the animal immediately retracted the hand in a similar fashion to when a similar visual scene was observed directly.

The correct interpretation of what we see in a mirror when we observe the reflection of our own body is likely to depend upon complex perceptual, abstract, but even intentional components. Surely our feeling of personal belonging for mirror reflections of our own body parts is greatly enhanced when movements of those body parts generate congruent movements of the corresponding mirror reflection. This mutual correspondence between self-movements and vision may not be enough to recognize one's own body parts in pathological conditions. Schizophrenics, for example, may critically lack a sense of agency and be unable to recognize whether movements observed in a monitor are executed by themselves or by an experimenter (Daprati et al., 1997).

The conflicting situation of discriminating one's own from an alien hand moving in a video monitor may also induce many errors in the case of reduced awareness of one's own body following brain damage (Daprati, Sirigu, Pradat-Diehl, Franck, & Jeannerod, 2000). This evidence suggests that body representation and body awareness are critically linked. In some instances, the sense of one's own body can be critically disrupted. Apart from the extreme and unusual complete loss of awareness of one's body (Deny & Camus, 1905), more frequent clinical conditions may be reported of patients losing awareness of the contralesional parts of their body. Patients, for example, may have the feeling that the contralesional arms do not belong to themselves but to someone else, or that these are actually prosthetic devices. Patients may also deny motor deficits of the contralesional limbs and state that they can move them perfectly even when they are completely paralyzed (e.g., Bisiach & Vallar, 2000; Feinberg, Roane, & Ali, 2000). Critchley listed all of the syndromes that typically follow parietal lesions, including unilateral neglect and all of the pseudopsychiatric delusions concerning the contralesional side of the body (somatoparaphrenia) under the label of "disturbances of the body image" (Critchley, 1953).

Clues in favor of a disruption of body representation in neglect come from an experiment conducted by Coslett (1998). In this experiment, patients with unilateral spatial neglect for the left side were less accurate when judging whether displayed drawings depicted right or left hands (cf. Parsons, 1987). Since this task requires observers to match the seen drawing of a hand to a mental representation of their own hands, the author proposed that, in neglect patients, the three-dimensional representation of the body (body schema) was defective on the left side. In such instances, however, the impairment of attentional orienting to the contralesional side of the body, and in particular to the contralesional limbs, might be critical (Kinsbourne, 1995). In this view, the unawareness of the contralesional side of the body may be viewed in the context of a more general inattention for the contralesional extrapersonal space, which may be ameliorated by external interventions, like caloric vestibular stimulation, to a similar extent (Bisiach, Rusconi, & Vallar, 1991).

An important role of personal beliefs for body representation has been shown by a study by Bottini and colleagues (Bottini, Bisiach, Sterzi, & Vallar, 2002). A patient with left unilateral neglect denied the ownership of her left arm, which she attributed to her niece. When tactually stimulated on that arm, the patient did not report any sensation. However when the examiner agreed with the patient that the arm, which was again tactually stimulated, was indeed her niece's, the patient started reporting the stimuli. This evidence nicely suggests that the disrupted representation of the contralesional side of the patient's body could be modulated by acting on the overt beliefs that the patient had about her own body representation.

5. Conclusion

The representation of the body in the brain is a complex construct. The different aspects of body representation discussed in this chapter do not account for a localized representation of the body in the brain nor for a simple mechanism underlying it. Moreover, they do suggest that a representation of the body at different levels, both conscious and unconscious, is present in the brain at any given time. However, more than giving a unitary definition of what body representation is, or is not, this chapter has focused on the analysis of experimental results providing insightful information about some critical determinants of body representation.

First, it has been discussed how the body is critically immersed in a multisensory space, which constantly provides a high number of stimuli that are analyzed by different sensory modalities and integrated with those coming from the body itself in a unitary representation (see Maravita et al., 2003).

Second, the importance of intentional actions toward extrapersonal space as main determinants of body representation and its plasticity has been underlined (e.g., Maravita & Iriki, 2004).

Finally, we have discussed instances in which the representation of our body in space is influenced by our abstract knowledge about the surrounding environment (such as, for example, when dealing with mirror reflections or virtual reality), by lack of body awareness, and by personal beliefs about our body integrity and functions, as shown by the dramatic reports of somatoparaphrenic patients following right-hemisphere damage (e.g., Bottini et al., 2002).

Surely it is of extreme interest to assess the extent to which any of these determinants of body representation are conscious or unconscious. Different levels of conscious representation might be assumed depending on whether we refer to body schema or to body image, although this difference is still a matter of discussion (for a detailed discussion of this difference, see Gallagher, 1998). Many changes in our body posture are normally unconscious. The original concept of body schema corresponded to that of an unconscious and "automatically" updated proprioceptive construction (see Head & Holmes, 1911). This unconscious construction of a proprioceptively based representation may follow the evidence that much of our motor activity is performed without consciously attending to our moving muscles or body segments. Indeed any movement (moving an arm to reach for an object or putting a foot forward to proceed in walking) is followed by a series of postural adjustments of which we are completely unaware and which are often part of deeply learned motor patterns. Furthermore, while acting in everyday life, we typically attend to the goals of our actions (e.g., objects to reach), while we only rarely focus on any proprioceptive input itself (O'Shaughnessy, 1996).

Even the seemingly conscious aspects of body representation may not be completely conscious. The ability to point toward a determined part of our body without the aid of vision may be critically determined by some implicit construction of our body representation. Patients who show personal neglect are unable to point to the contralesional side of their bodies (Bisiach, Perani, Vallar, & Berti, 1986). However this evidence may not simply indicate a destruction of a putative map relative to the contralesional side of the body but may suggest the disruption of complex factors related to attentional orienting (e.g., Kinsbourne, 1995; see also the interesting early proposal by Head & Holmes, 1911, of the necessary role of attention in bringing to consciousness any proprioceptive input or postural change) or of the knowledge and the complex of beliefs about our body structure (Bottini et al., 2002). Furthermore, the simple notion that we have moved a part of our body as a consequence of an intentional command may be disrupted if the automatic and unconscious processes responsible for matching the planned movement and the sensory feedback from the executed movement fails. Surprisingly, for example, brain-damaged patients may state that they can perfectly move a paralyzed limb (Feinberg et al., 2000) or, by contrast, involuntarily and unconsciously execute a motor command that they are simply trying to imagine (Schwoebel, Boronat, & Coslett, 2002).

Many of the above issues are still to be explored, and clinical and behavioral observations raise more and more intriguing questions. Going to more philosophical grounds, even the relationship between a sense of ownership of our body parts and self-awareness is still a matter of fascinating debate (for a discussion, see Elian, Marcel, & Bermudez, 1996).

The approaches of the modern discipline of cognitive neuroscience are progressively adding more insight into the mechanisms of body representation. In particular the approach that considers body representation not only as a body in the brain but progressively more and more as a body in space, or even a body in action space, is particularly fascinating and promising.

Acknowledgments I am grateful to Peter Brugger, Nicholas Holmes, and Charles Spence for their helpful and insightful comments on this chapter.

References

Aglioti, S., Smania, N., Manfredi, M., & Berlucchi, G. (1996). Disownership of left hand and objects related to it in a patient with right brain damage. *Neuroreport, 8*, 293–296.

Armel, K. C., & Ramachandran, V. S. (2003). Projecting sensations to external objects: Evidence from skin conductance response. *Proceedings of the Royal Society of London, B: Biological Sciences, 270*, 1499–1506.

Austen, E. L., Soto-Faraco, S., Pinel, J. P. J., & Kingstone, A. F. (2001). Virtual body effect: Factors influencing visual-tactile integration. *Abstract of the Psychonomic Society, 6*, 2.

Berlucchi, G., & Aglioti, S. (1997). The body in the brain: Neural bases of corporeal awareness. *Trends in Neurosciences, 20*, 560–564.

Berti, A., & Frassinetti, F. (2000). When far becomes near: Re-mapping of space by tool use. *Journal of Cognitive Neuroscience, 12*, 415–420.

Bisiach, E., Perani, D., Vallar, G., & Berti, A. (1986). Unilateral neglect: Personal and extra-personal. *Neuropsychologia, 24*, 759–767.

Bisiach, E., Rusconi, M., & Vallar, G. (1991). Remission of somatoparaphrenic delusion through vestibular stimulation. *Neuropsychologia, 29*, 1029–1031.

Bisiach, E., & Vallar, G. (2000). Unilateral neglect in humans. In F. Boller & J. Grafman (Eds.), *Handbook of neuropsychology* (2d ed., pp. 459–502). Amsterdam: Elsevier.

Blanke, O., Landis, T., Spinelli, L., & Seeck, M. (2004). Out-of-body experience and autoscopy of neurological origin. *Brain, 127*, 243–258.

Bonnier, P. (1905). L'Aschématie. *Revue Neurologique, 13*, 605–609.

Bottini, G., Bisiach, E., Sterzi, R., & Vallar, G. (2002). Feeling touches in someone else's hand. *Neuroreport, 13*, 249–252.

Botvinick, M., & Cohen, J. (1998). Rubber hands "feel" touch that eyes see. *Nature, 391*, 756.

Brissaud, E. (1895). *Leçons sur les maladies nerveuses*. Paris: Masson.

Brugger, P., Kollias, S. S., Muri, R. M., Crelier, G., Hepp-Reymond, M. C., & Regard, M. (2000). Beyond re-membering: Phantom sensations of congenitally absent limbs. *Proceedings of the National Academy of Science, USA, 97*, 6167–6172.

Colby, C. L. (1998). Action-oriented spatial reference frames in cortex. *Neuron, 20*, 15–24.

Colby, C. L., Duhamel, J.-R., & Goldberg, M. E. (1993). Ventral intraparietal area of the macaque: Anatomic location and visual response properties. *Journal of Neurophysiology, 69*, 902–914.

Cooke, D. F., Taylor, C. S., Moore, T., & Graziano, M. S. (2003). Complex movements evoked by microstimulation of the ventral intraparietal area. *Proceedings of the National Academy of Science, USA, 100*, 6163–6168.

Coslett, H. B. (1998). Evidence for a disturbance of the body schema in neglect. *Brain and Cognition, 37*, 527–544.

Critchley, M. (1953). Disorders of the body-image. In M. Critchley (Ed.), *The parietal lobes* (pp. 225–255). New York: Hafner.

Critchley, M. (1979). *The divine banquet of the brain and other essays*. New York: Raven.

Cumming, W. J. (1988). The neurobiology of the body schema. *British Journal of Psychiatry*, Suppl. 2, 7–11.

Daprati, E., Franck, N., Georgieff, N., Proust, J., Pacherie, E., Dalery, J., & Jeannerod, M. (1997). Looking for the agent: An investigation into consciousness of action and self-consciousness in schizophrenic patients. *Cognition, 65*, 71–86.

Daprati, E., Sirigu, A., Pradat-Diehl, P., Franck, N., & Jeannerod, M. (2000). Recognition of self-produced movement in a case of severe neglect. *Neurocase, 6*, 477–486.

Deny, G., & Camus, P. (1905). Sur une forme d'hypocondrie aberrante due à la perte de la conscience du corps. *Revue Neurologique, 9*, 461–467.

De Renzi, E., & Faglioni, P. (1963). Autotopoagnosia. *Archives of Psychology Neurology and Psychiatry, 24*, 1–34.

di Pellegrino, G., Làdavas, E., & Farnè, A. (1997). Seeing where your hands are. *Nature, 388*, 730.

Downing, P. E., Jiang, Y., Shuman, M., & Kanwisher, N. (2001). A cortical area selective for visual processing of the human body. *Science, 293*, 2470–2473.

Duhamel, J.-R., Colby, C. L., & Goldberg, M. E. (1998). Ventral intraparietal area of the macaque: Congruent visual and somatic response properties. *Journal of Neurophysiology, 79*, 126–136.

Elian, N., Marcel, A., & Bermudez, J. L. (1996). Self-consciousness and the body: An interdisciplinary introduction. In J. L. Bermudez, A. Marcel, & N. Elian (Eds.), *The body and the self* (pp. 1–28). Cambridge, MA: MIT Press.

Farnè, A., & Làdavas, E. (2000). Dynamic size-change of hand peripersonal space following tool use. *Neuroreport, 11*, 1645–1649.

Feinberg, T. E., Roane, D. M., & Ali, J. (2000). Illusory limb movements in anosognosia for hemiplegia. *Journal of Neurology, Neurosurgery and Psychiatry, 68*, 511–513.

Fogassi, L., Gallese, V., Fadiga, L., Luppino, G., Matelli, M., & Rizzolatti, G. (1996). Coding of peripersonal space in inferior premotor cortex (area F4). *Journal of Neurophysiology, 76*, 141–157.

Gallagher, S. (1998). Body schema and intentionality. In N. Elian (Ed.), *The body and the self* (pp. 225–244). Cambridge, MA: MIT Press.

Gentilucci, M., Scandolara, C., Pigarev, I. N., & Rizzolatti, G. (1983). Visual responses in the postarcuate cortex (area 6) of the monkey that are independent of eye position. *Experimental Brain Research, 50*, 464–468.

Graziano, M. S. (1999). Where is my arm? The relative role of vision and proprioception in the neuronal representation of limb position. *Proceedings of the National Academy of Science, USA, 96*, 10418–10421.

Graziano, M. S., Cooke, D. F., & Taylor, C. S. (2000). Coding the location of the arm by sight. *Science, 290*, 1782–1786.

Graziano, M. S., & Gross, C. G. (1994). The representation of extrapersonal space: A possible role for bimodal, visual-tactile neurons. In M. S. Gazzaniga (Ed.), *The cognitive neurosciences* (pp. 1021–1034). Cambridge, MA: MIT Press.

Graziano, M. S., & Gross, C. G. (1998). Spatial maps for the control of movement. *Current Opinion in Neurobiology, 8*, 195–201.

Graziano, M. S., Yap, G. S., & Gross, C. G. (1994). Coding of visual space by premotor neurons. *Science, 266*, 1054–1057.

Graziano, M. S. A., & Botvinick, M. M. (2002). How the brain represents the body: Insights from neurophysiology and psychology. In B. Hommel (Ed.), *Common mechanisms in perception and action: Attention and performance XIX* (pp. 136–157). Oxford: Oxford University Press.

Gregory, R. (1998). *Mirrors in mind.* London: Penguin.

Gross, Y., Webb, R., & Melzack, R. (1974). Central and peripheral contributions to localization of body parts: Evidence for a central body schema. *Experimental Neurology, 44*, 346–362.

Head, H., & Holmes, G. (1911). Sensory disturbances from cerebral lesions. *Brain, 34*, 102–254.

Holmes, N., & Spence, C. (in press). The body schema and the multisensory representation(s) of peripersonal space. *Cognitive Processing.*

Iriki, A., Tanaka, M., & Iwamura, Y. (1996). Coding of modified body schema during tool use by macaque postcentral neurons. *Neuroreport, 7*, 2325–2330.

Iriki, A., Tanaka, M., Obayashi, S., & Iwamura, Y. (2001). Self-images in the video monitor coded by monkey intraparietal neurons. *Neuroscience Research, 40*, 163–173.

Ishibashi, H., Hihara, S., & Iriki, A. (2000). Acquisition and development of monkey tool-use: Behavioural and kinematic analyses. *Canadian Journal of Physiological Pharmacology, 78*, 1–9.

Jeannerod, M., Arbib, M. A., Rizzolatti, G., & Sakata, H. (1995). Grasping objects: The cortical mechanisms of visuomotor transformation. *Trends in Neurosciences, 18*, 314–320.

Kaas, J. (2000). The reorganisation of sensory and motor maps after injury in adult mammals. In M. S. Gazzaniga (Ed.), *The cognitive neurosciences* (pp. 223–236). Cambridge, MA: MIT Press.

Kinsbourne, M. (1995). Awareness of one's own body: An attentional theory of its nature, development and brain basis. In N. Elian (Ed.), *The body and the self* (pp. 205–223). Cambridge, MA: MIT Press.

Kinsbourne, M., & Lempert, H. (1989). Human figure representation in blind children. *Journal of General Psychology, 102*, 33–37.

Lackner, J. R. (1988). Some proprioceptive influences in the perceptual representation of body shape and orientation. *Brain, 111*, 281–297.

Làdavas, E. (2002). Functional and dynamic properties of visual peripersonal space. *Trends in Cognitive Sciences, 6*, 17–22.

Leinonen, L., Hyvarinen, J., Nyman, G., & Linnankoski, I. (1979). I. Functional properties of neurons in lateral part of associative area 7 in awake monkeys. *Experimental Brain Research, 34*, 299–320.

Lloyd, D. M., Shore, D. I., Spence, C., & Calvert, G. A. (2003). Multisensory representation of limb position in human premotor cortex. *Nature Neuroscience, 6*, 17–18.

Loomis, J. (1992). Distal attribution and presence. *Presence, 1*, 113–119.

Macaluso, E., Frith, C. D., & Driver, J. (2002). Crossmodal spatial influences of touch on extrastriate visual areas take current gaze direction into account. *Neuron, 34*, 647–658.

Maravita, A., Clarke, K., Husain, M., & Driver, J. (2002). Active tool-use with contralesional hand can reduce crossmodal extinction of touch on that hand. *Neurocase, 8*, 411–416.

Maravita, A., Husain, M., Clarke, K., & Driver, J. (2001). Reaching with a tool extends visual-tactile interactions into far space: Evidence from cross-modal extinction. *Neuropsychologia, 39*, 580–585.

Maravita, A., & Iriki, A. (2004). Tools for the body (schema). *Trends in Cognitive Sciences, 8*, 79–86.

Maravita, A., Spence, C., Clarke, K., Husain, M., & Driver, J. (2000). Vision and touch through the looking glass in a case of crossmodal extinction. *Neuroreport, 11*, 3521–3526.

Maravita, A., Spence, C., & Driver, J. (2003). Multisensory integration and the body schema: Close to hand and within reach. *Current Biology, 13*, 531–539.

Maravita, A., Spence, C., Kennett, S., & Driver, J. (2002). Tool-use changes multimodal spatial interactions between vision and touch in normal humans. *Cognition, 83*, B25–34.

Maravita, A., Spence, C., Sergent, C., & Driver, J. (2002). Seeing your own touched hands in a mirror modulates cross-modal interactions. *Psychological Science, 13*, 350–355.

Melzack, R. (1990). Phantom limbs and the concept of a neuromatrix. *Trends in Neurosciences, 13*, 88–92.

Melzack, R., Israel, R., Lacroix, R., & Schultz, G. (1997). Phantom limbs in people with congenital limb deficiency or amputation in early childhood. *Brain, 120*, 1603–1620.

Mitchell, S. W. (1871). Phantom limbs. *Lippincott's Magazine, 8*, 563–569.

Münk, H. (1890). *Uber die Functionen der Grosshirnrinde* (2d ed.). Berlin: Hirschwald.

Obayashi, S., Tanaka, M., & Iriki, A. (2000). Subjective image of invisible hand coded by monkey intraparietal neurons. *Neuroreport, 11*, 3499–3505.

O'Shaughnessy, B. (1996). Proprioception and the body image. In N. Elian (Ed.), *The body and the self* (pp. 175–203). Cambridge, MA: MIT Press.

Parsons, L. M. (1987). Imagined spatial transformation of one's body. *Journal of Experimental Psychology: General, 116*, 172–191.

Pavani, F., & Castiello, U. (2004). Binding personal and extrapersonal space through body shadows. *Nature Neuroscience, 7*, 14–16.

Pavani, F., Spence, C., & Driver, J. (2000). Visual capture of touch: Out-of-the-body experiences with rubber gloves. *Psychological Science, 11*, 353–359.

Pegna, A. J., Petit, L., Caldara-Schnetzer, A. S., Khateb, A., Annoni, J. M., Sztajzel, R., & Landis, T. (2001). So near yet so far: Neglect in far or near space depends on tool use. *Annals of Neurology, 50*, 820–822.

Penfield, W. (1955). The twenty-ninth Maudsley lecture: The role of the temporal cortex in certain psychical phenomena. *Journal of Mental Science, 101*, 451–465.

Penfield, W., & Faulk, M. E., Jr. (1955). The insula: Further observations on its function. *Brain, 78*, 445–470.

Poeck, K., & Orgass, B. (1971). The concept of the body schema: A critical review and some experimental results. *Cortex, 7*, 254–277.

Ramachandran, V. S., & Hirstein, W. (1998). The perception of phantom limbs: The D. O. Hebb lecture. *Brain, 121*, 1603–1630.

Rizzolatti, G. (1983). Mechanisms of selective attention in mammals. In D. J. Ingle (Ed.), *Advances in vertebrate neuroethology* (pp. 261–297). London: Plenum.

Rizzolatti, G., Fadiga, L., Fogassi, L., & Gallese, V. (1997). The space around us. *Science, 277*, 190–191.

Rizzolatti, G., Luppino, G., & Matelli, M. (1998). The organization of the cortical motor system: New concepts. *Electroencephalography and Clinical Neurophysiology, 106*, 283–296.

Rizzolatti, G., Scandolara, C., Matelli, M., & Gentilucci, M. (1981). Afferent properties of periarcuate neurons in macaque monkeys. II: Visual responses. *Behavioral Brain Research, 2*, 147–163.

Roll, P., Roll, R., & Velay, J.-L. (1991). Proprioception as a link between body space and extra-personal space. In J. Paillard (Ed.), *Brain and space* (pp. 112–132). New York: Oxford University Press.

Schilder, P. (1935). *The image and appearance of the human body: Studies in the constructive energies of the psyche.* London: Kegan Paul, Trench, Trubner.

Schwoebel, J., Boronat, C., & Coslett, H. B. (2002). The man who executed "imagined" movements: Evidence for dissociable components of the body schema. *Brain and Cognition, 50*, 1–16.

Semenza, C., & Goodglass, H. (1985). Localization of body parts in brain injured subjects. *Neuropsychologia, 23*, 161–175.

Simmel, M. L. (1962). Phantom experiences following amputation in childhood. *Journal of Neurology Neurosurgery and Psychiatry, 25*, 69–78.

Spence, C., Pavani, F., Maravita, A., & Holmes, N. (in press). Multisensory contributions to the 3-D representation of visuotactile peripersonal space in humans: Evidence from the crossmodal congruency task. *Journal of Physiology.*

Tipper, S. P., Lloyd, D., Shorland, B., Dancer, C., Howard, L. A., & McGlone, F. (1998). Vision influences tactile perception without proprioceptive orienting. *Neuroreport, 9*, 1741–1744.

Tipper, S. P., Phillips, N., Dancer, C., Lloyd, D., Howard, L. A., & McGlone, F. (2001). Vision influences tactile perception at body sites that cannot be viewed directly. *Experimental Brain Research, 139*, 160–167.

Valenza, N., Seghier, M. L., Schwartz, S., Lazeyras, F., & Vuilleumier, P. (2004). Tactile awareness and limb position in neglect: Functional magnetic resonance imaging. *Annals of Neurology, 55*, 139–143.

Vallar, G., & Papagno, C. (2002). Pierre Bonnier's (1905) case of bodily "aschematie." In C. Code, C. W. Wallesch, A. Joannette, & A. Roch Lecours (Eds.), *Classic cases in neuropsychology* (Vol. 2, pp. 147–170). Hove, UK: Psychology Press.

Weinstein, S., & Seresen, E. A. (1961). Phantoms in case of congenital absence of the limbs. *Neurology, 11,* 905–911.

Yamamoto, S., & Kitazawa, S. (2001). Sensation at the tips of invisible tools. *Nature Neuroscience, 4,* 979–980.

5

Multisensory Representation of Peripersonal Space

Elisabetta Làdavas
Alessandro Farnè

1. Introduction

Humans can represent visual objects in nearby (peripersonal) space through multisensory (visual-auditory-tactile) integrative processes, as indicated by the large body of evidence that has been recently accumulated (Spence & Driver, 2004). In nonhuman primates, multisensory integration at the single-neuron level is a frequent feature of spatial representation, especially in the coding of near peripersonal space, that is, the sector of space that closely surrounds the animal's body parts (Duhamel et al., 1991, 1998; Graziano & Gross, 1995, 1998; Hyvarinen & Poranen, 1974; Rizzolatti et al., 1981, 1998). Since the 1990s, neuropsychological and neurophysiological research has provided comparative support to the notion that multisensory coding of near peripersonal space in both species shares several similarities at a functional and, to some extent, at a neuroanatomical level (Bremmer, Schlack, Duhamel, et al., 2001; Bremmer, Schlack, Shah, et al., 2001; Calvert, Spence, & Stein, 2004; Làdavas, 2002; Macaluso, Driver, & Frith, 2003; Weiss et al., 2003).

In monkeys, several brain structures, such as the putamen and parietal areas 7b and VIP, as well as premotor areas (F2 and F4, following Rizzolatti and colleagues' nomenclature), are crucially involved in representing the space immediately adjacent to the animal's body. A relatively high proportion of neurons contained in these structures are multimodal, as they display tactile, visual, and/or auditory receptive fields (RFs), in quite a good spatial register, that respond to tactile, visual, and/or auditory stimuli. The multisensory response is evoked whenever a visual (or auditory) object is displayed near the body part (e.g., head or hand) where the tactile RF is located. However, visual and auditory RFs have a limited extension in depth, which is confined to the space immediately

89

surrounding the monkey's body (within a few centimeters). Their visually and auditorily evoked activity show gradients of response, such that the neuronal discharge decreases as the distance between visual or auditory stimuli and the cutaneous RF increases. In addition, vision-related activity seems to operate in coordinates that are centered on body parts; that is, visual RFs move in space according to the position of the associated tactile RF located on a given body part, when it is moved. Moreover, the position of the visual RFs of multimodal neurons does not change when the monkey gazes in different directions. Therefore, the somatotopic organization of multimodal receptive fields gives rise to multisensory maps of the space immediately adjacent to the animal's body.

2. Neuropsychological Evidence of Peripersonal Space Representation in Humans

Here we report behavioral findings providing evidence in favor of the existence, in humans, of sensory integration systems representing space through the multisensory processing of tactile and visual events. In particular, these findings show that multimodal integration may take place in a privileged manner within a limited sector of space closely surrounding the body surface, that is, in near peripersonal space. They also show that, conversely, the strength of such an integration is markedly reduced when sensory events originate from outside this limited sector of space, that is, in far peripersonal space.

On the basis of the neurophysiological findings reported above, we asked whether the space immediately surrounding the body (hereinafter, near peripersonal space) can be represented in the human brain through multisensory processes that are similar to those described in monkeys. We addressed this question by testing patients with visuotactile crossmodal extinction. This term refers to a clinical sign, whereby some patients with right-brain damage (RBD) fail to report a tactile stimulus delivered to their contralesional left hand when a concurrent visual stimulus is presented to their ipsilesional right hand (di Pellegrino et al., 1997; Mattingley et al., 1997). Most interestingly, recent studies from our laboratory revealed that the severity of this phenomenon is nicely modulated by the physical distance between visual stimuli and a patient's ipsilesional hand. In a typical situation, a visual stimulus is presented either near (about 5 cm) or far (about 40 cm) from the patient's ipsilesional hand. In the former case, when the visual stimulus is presented within near peripersonal space, crossmodal extinction is usually found in a very severe form, most of the contralesional touches being missed by the patients. By contrast, when the same visual stimulus is presented in far peripersonal space, crossmodal extinction is usually much weaker, with several contralesional touches being reported correctly.

In this respect, it has been frequently found that the degree of crossmodal extinction obtained by visually stimulating the near peripersonal space of the right hand (perihand space) is comparably severe to that obtained by touching the right hand (Làdavas, di Pellegrino, et al., 1998; Làdavas, Zeloni, & Farnè, 1998; Làdavas & Farnè, 2004a, 2004b). In other words, physically touching or visually stimulating the right perihand space may have almost identical consequences on the left somatosensory accuracy. This sharply contrasts with the consequences produced on left tactile perception by presenting the same visual stimulus far away from the right hand, which leads to a much higher left somatosensory accuracy. In sum, one of the main findings that has emerged from studies conducted up to now on multisensory processing in extinction patients is that crossmodal extinction is tightly linked to the visually (or auditorily) stimulated area: relatively mild crossmodal extinction can be obtained when visual (or auditory) stimuli are displayed in far peripersonal space, and comparatively more severe crossmodal extinction emerges when visual (or auditory) stimuli come from the immediate proximity of the patient's right hand, that is, in near peripersonal space. A similar pattern of performance is observed when crossmodal extinction is assessed at the level of the patient's face, by presenting visual stimuli and tactile stimuli onto the ipsilesional and contralesional hemiface, respectively (Làdavas, Zeloni, & Farnè, 1998). The functional characteristics of crossmodal extinction between different body parts (face and hand) is currently under examination in our laboratory.

Although a precise definition of peripersonal space extent is not yet available, studies from our and other laboratories (see chapters 3 and 4) have pointed out that maximal multisensory processing can be obtained by very proximal stimulation of the hand (within 5 cm), whereas a significant drop in multisensory integration effects is observed following farther stimulation (about 40 cm away from the hand; see Figure 5.1). Therefore, near and far peripersonal space can be functionally distinguished on the basis of the patient's performance.

In keeping with our hypothesis, the prevalence of visuotactile extinction in the space closely surrounding the patient's body constitutes neuropsychological evidence that the human brain represents visual peripersonal space through a multisensory system. Owing to such multisensory integration processes, proximal visual stimulation of the ipsilesional hand would highly activate its somatosensory representation, which, in extinction patients, would benefit from the unbalanced competition between ipsi- and contralesional spatial representations. In extinction patients, as a consequence of the ipsilesionally biased competition, the concurrent activation of the somatosensory representation of the contralesional hand, elicited by a tactile stimulus, and of the ipsilesional hand, through proximal visual stimulation, would ultimately produce a severe extinction of tactile stimuli delivered to the contralesional hand because of its comparatively weaker representation. By contrast, the visual stimulation of the ipsilesional hand in far peripersonal space (e.g., farther away and above it) would weakly activate the somatosensory representation

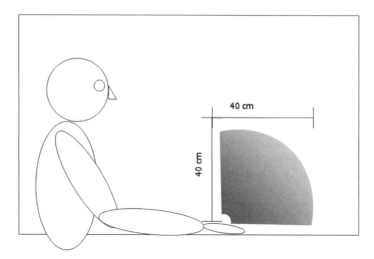

Figure 5.1. Schematic illustration exemplifying the limited sector of space (blue) surrounding the ipsilesional hand that can be considered as near peripersonal space as operationally defined on the basis of patients' performance. Patients' ability to perceive touches delivered to the left contralesional hand (not shown) is significantly worse when visual stimuli are concurrently delivered closer to the hand surface (darker blue) rather than farther from the same hand (lighter blue). Color fading represents the lack of a sharp border of near peripersonal space, although significant improvement in touch detection is usually observed when visual stimuli are presented about 40 cm away from the ipsilesional hand. *See color insert.*

of the right hand. By reducing the ipsilesional competitive advantage, this would produce a milder form of crossmodal visuotactile extinction, as actually observed.

Moreover, we showed that the perception of contralesional tactile stimuli not only can be interfered with, but it is also favored by the simultaneous presentation of a visual stimulus, depending on the spatial arrangement (congruent or not) of visual and tactile stimuli with respect to the contralesional affected side of the body. In particular, spatially incongruent visuotactile presentations (i.e., ipsilesional visual stimulus and contralesional tactile stimulus) exacerbate the pathological phenomenon; that is, presenting a visual stimulus in the opposite side relative to the left (affected) hand results in a reduced perception of touches delivered to that hand. On the contrary, spatially congruent visuotactile presentation reduces the symptom; that is, presenting a visual stimulus to the same contralesional side enhances the perception of tactile events on that hand (Làdavas, di Pellegrino, et al., 1998). Finally, both the reduction and enhancement of left tactile perception are most effectively obtained following visual stimulation of near peripersonal space, compared to far peripersonal space (for a further discussion of the role of spatial and temporal discrepancies on multisensory integration, see chapter 6).

Overall, the near-far modulation of the severity of crossmodal extinction is highly consistent with the functional properties of multisensory processing described in monkeys (Graziano et al., 1997), thus favoring the idea that human and nonhuman primates might share similar cerebral mechanisms for the multisensory representation of near peripersonal space.

3. Functional Properties of Visual Peripersonal Space

In the monkey, not only vision (or audition) and touch, but also proprioception converge to feed multimodal neurons, conveying relevant information about arm (or head) position in space. Indeed, some of these neurons also respond to peripersonal visual stimuli when the vision of the arm is prevented (Graziano et al., 1994). However, when proprioception is the only source of information about arm position, the responsiveness of multimodal cells to proximal visual stimulation is comparatively reduced or extinguished (Graziano, 1999; Graziano et al., 2000; MacKay & Crammond, 1987), thus implying that visual cues about the position of a given body part are more important than proprioceptive cues.

In agreement with the higher activation observed in the monkey's multimodal cells when visual and proprioceptive cues are both available, a neuropsychological study by Làdavas and colleagues (Làdavas et al., 2000) showed that, in humans, proprioception alone is not sufficient to effectively activate the representation of the perihand space. In particular, whenever the vision of the hand was prevented, crossmodal extinction was no longer modulated by the distance of the visual stimulus from the patient's ipsilesional hand (i.e., near versus far). Therefore, when hand position is specified only on the basis of proprioceptive cues, crossmodal extinction is not maximal in near peripersonal space. This might be related to the relatively fast adaptation of proprioceptive signals, whose role in sensory integration may rapidly decay (Obayashi et al., 2000), thus showing that the visual information about the hand position is additionally needed to obtain crossmodal effects differentially distributed between far and near peripersonal space.

Other studies have further shown that visual information about hand location is not only necessary, but also sufficient for the integrated processing of visual-tactile input to occur in peripersonal space. In this respect, neurophysiological findings have shown that when the monkey's real arm is hidden from view, but a realistic fake arm is visible at the same location or at a different location from the monkey's own arm, multimodal neurons in Area 5 are modulated by the sight of a fake arm (Graziano et al., 2000). Similar evidence has been provided in humans by Farnè and colleagues (Farnè et al., 2000). Visual-tactile extinction was assessed in a group of RBD patients by displaying visual stimuli either near or far from their ipsilesional (real) hands, as well as near rubber hands that could be visually aligned or misaligned with the patients' ipsilesional shoulders. In the latter conditions, visual stimuli were thus presented far from the patients' ipsilesional hands (placed behind their backs).

The findings showed that a strong crossmodal extinction was induced by a visual stimulus presented near a seen rubber hand, its severity being comparable to that obtained by presenting the same visual stimulus near the patient's real hand. Critically, crossmodal extinction was markedly reduced when the same rubber hand was misaligned with respect to the subject's shoulder. Besides extending the notion of visual dominance over proprioception to the cognitive processes that are responsible for the multisensory coding of near peripersonal space, these results also demonstrate a sort of reluctance of the visual-tactile system to "accept" discrepant information provided by proprioception and vision.

Most notably, this impenetrability seems to emerge despite the subjects' conscious awareness concerning the actual discrepancy between the senses. Indeed, both visual arrangements of the rubber hands (compatible and incompatible) were incongruent compared to the sensed position of the patients' right hands, which were located behind their backs.

4. Automatic Multisensory Processing of Nearby Space

In the light of the above reported findings, we further hypothesized that proximal visual stimuli may be processed as being near the body independent of their actual possibility of touching it, thus being resistant to more cognitive, top-down processing. In other words, we verified whether multisensory coding of nearby visual objects in humans is mandatory, taking place whether or not a visual object can physically touch the body (Farnè et al., 2003). This would imply, as a corollary, that multisensory coding of nearby space occurs whether or not the objects are physically reachable. To verify this hypothesis, the crossmodal visuotactile extinction was examined in a group of RBD patients by displaying a visual stimulus either near or far from their right hands, which could be screened or not by a transparent piece of Plexiglas (Figure 5.2).

The results showed that the typical near-far modulation of crossmodal extinction was present both when the screen was present and when it was absent. Indeed, patients were explicitly aware that the transparent barrier would prevent any possibility for the visual stimulus to get into physical contact with their own right hands. In contrast, the Plexiglas did not block either visual or proprioceptive cues, which provided congruent inputs relative to the spatial proximity of the hand and the visual stimulus (see Figure 5.2). Therefore, these findings confirm that visuotactile integration processes can occur automatically, along a bottom-up flow of information that is not necessarily affected by top-down regulation of sensory processing.

Why should the processing of nearby space resist top-down influences? An answer to this question might be the possible evolutionary advantage in

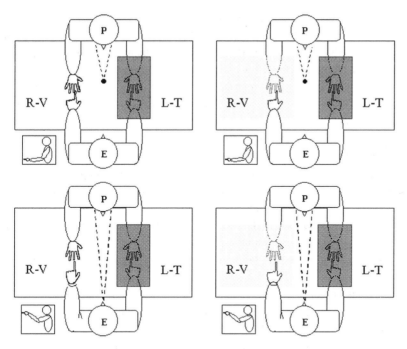

Figure 5.2. Schematic illustration of the crossmodal visual-tactile conditions and the experimental setting with the patient (P) and examiner (E) relative positions, viewed from above. The visual stimulus (V; wiggling of the experimenter's index finger) could be located near (*top row*) or far from the patient's right (R) hand, located below (*bottom row*) the visual stimulus. Tactile (T; mechanical stimuli provided through synthetic probes) stimulation was delivered to the patient's left (L) hand, which was screened from view by opaque cardboard shields (blue rectangles). Note that in one set of conditions (*right column*), a transparent Plexiglas barrier (yellow rectangles) was inserted between the patient's hand and the visual stimulus, whereas no barrier was used in the other set of conditions (*left column*). From Farnè, Demattè, & Làdavas, 2003. Reprinted with permission. *See color insert.*

facilitating the preparation and execution of appropriate motor responses to nearby objects provided by the multisensory processing of space. In the monkey, this possibility is supported by the fact that both inward and outward movements of the head and arm are partly mediated by multisensory neurons that, by acting as multisensory-motor interfaces, can control movements on the basis of both cutaneous and visual information, responding to an object when the skin has not (yet) been touched. Such a multimodal control can combine information concerning the position of a visual stimulus relative to the head, hand, or both, which can be relevant even for relatively simple actions, such as avoiding an object approaching the face or the hand, reaching to grasp an object, or bringing food to the mouth.

This information is most likely provided by bimodal visuotactile neurons, as regions of the premotor cortex coding head movements, mouth grasping, and coordinated hand-mouth actions are reciprocally connected with area VIP (Rizzolatti et al., 1998). Furthermore, Fogassi and colleagues (Fogassi et al., 1996) have found that visual RFs of visuotactile neurons in Area F4 expand as the velocity of an approaching visual object increases, a functional characteristic that seems quite appropriate for preparing actions toward nearby stimuli. The nature of the action (approach-escape) and its actual execution might partly depend upon the characteristics of the visual stimulus (attractive-repulsive) and the ongoing degree of voluntary motor control (Blakemore et al., 1998, 1999, 2002).

Recently, the idea that multisensory-motor interfaces might code complex avoidance (hand withdrawal) or defensive (protecting the head with the hand) reactions received some preliminary support (Cooke & Graziano, 2003; Cooke et al., 2003; Graziano et al., 2001). In the light of such a possible protective function, it would be certainly advantageous that the multisensory coding of peripersonal space is fast and mainly outside the control of top-down mechanisms.

Related evidence supporting this view can be found in human studies favoring a bottom-up control of visually driven withdrawal reactions. Pathologically exaggerated withdrawal reflexes have been reported in a patient with a right parietal lesion by Denny-Brown and colleagues (Denny-Brown et al., 1952; Mori & Yamadori, 1989). When approached by the experimenter's hand, the patient's hand was involuntarily moved away, as if to avoid the examiner's hand. The automatic nature of this reaction has been underlined by Hoogenraad and colleagues (Hoogenraad, Ramos, & van Gijn, 1994). They reported a patient who, following a right parietal lobe infarction, presented a dense hemianesthesia and hemiplegia for the left hand with the eyes closed. With eyes open, however, visual stimuli induced withdrawal and pain in the numb arm. This brisk hand reflex, "as if it had been stung," was consistently evoked whenever the patient's left hand was approached by the experimenter, but not when the contact could not be visually anticipated or when the patient himself approached his left arm with the right hand. Embarrassed by the inability to avoid withdrawal movements of his left arm, the patient tied it to his belt. As the authors suggested, this phenomenon might be related to the anticipatory activity of bimodal neurons (cf. MacKay & Crammond, 1987).

5. Is Peripersonal Space Extension Fixed in Space?

Besides the static near-far aspect of multisensory coding, other important questions about such a multimodal representation of near peripersonal space in humans concern its possible dynamic properties. As an example, one might wonder whether its extension is fixed in space or can be modified and, if the latter is the case, by what kind of experience? Is visual sensory information about our body sufficient to induce plastic changes on peripersonal space, or is some kind of visuomotor activity necessary to produce such a remapping?

In the case of the animal literature, some of these questions have already found an answer. Several recent studies have examined whether the near peripersonal space of monkeys' hands, and especially its spatial location and size, can be modified following different kinds of sensorimotor experience. So far, the use of tools as extensions of personal space and the monitor-based online control of hand motor actions are the two types of manipulations that have been shown to modulate the spatial extent of peripersonal space representation (Iriki, Tanaka, & Iwamura, 1996; Iriki, Tanaka, Obayashi, & Iwamura, 2001; Obayashi et al., 2000).

In particular, a recoding of relatively far visual stimuli as nearer ones has been documented in monkey single-cell studies after active tool use. In these studies, a rake-shaped tool was used by the animal to reach objects located outside its reaching distance, which was thus physically extended by the rake. Following a few minutes of use of the rake (to retrieve distant food pellets) the visual RFs of some parietal bimodal neurons had expanded their size. This fast expansion along the tool axis, which seemed to incorporate the tool into the hand's peripersonal space representation, was followed by a fast back contraction to the pre–tool-use dimension after a short rest in using the tool, even if the monkey was still passively holding the rake (Iriki et al., 1996).

By investigating crossmodal extinction in a group of RBD patients, Farnè and Làdavas (2000) documented in humans a similar remapping of far space as near space (Figure 5.3). In this study, the severity of visual-tactile extinction was assessed by displaying visual stimuli at the distal edge of a 38 cm-long rake, passively held in the patient's right hand. The patient's performance was evaluated before tool use, after a short period (5 minutes) of tool use, after a short period ($\pm$ 10 minutes) of rest, as well as immediately after manual pointing that did not involve the use of the rake. As shown in Figure 5.4, stronger crossmodal extinction was found immediately after the patients used the rake to retrieve distant objects (post-tool immediate), compared to the pre–tool-use level, thus suggesting an expansion of near peripersonal space of the hand. This increase in size lasted for a few minutes, and a short resting period was enough for crossmodal extinction to regain the pre–tool-use level, thus suggesting a fast back contraction of the initially expanded perihand space (Figure 5.4, post-tool delayed).

These findings first suggested that the expansion of the area surrounding the hand (where visuotactile integration is maximal) is highly dependent upon the purposeful use of the tool aimed at physically interacting with objects located outside the hand-reaching space. Since crossmodal extinction did not vary if hand movements were executed without the tool (Figure 5.4, post-pointing immediate), it can also be excluded that perihand expansion results from directional ocular or hand motor activity. Further neuropsychological evidence of expansion of perihand space in humans has been reported by other authors (see chapter 4) and yielded similar results (Berti & Frassinetti, 2000; Maravita et al., 2001; Pegna et al., 2001).

6. The Determinants of Peripersonal Space Plasticity

Besides tool use, animal and human studies have provided additional converging evidence that remapping of far space as near space can be obtained through visual control of the image of a hand, either via monitor or mirror (Iriki et al., 2001; Maravita et al., 2000; Maravita & Iriki, 2004; Maravita, Spence, &

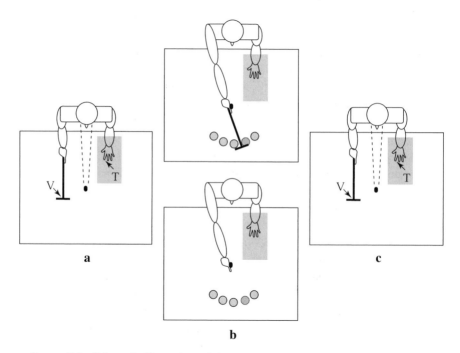

Figure 5.3. Schematic illustration of the experimental set-up (viewed from above) used to assess the variation in the size of peripersonal space representation area following tool use, through changes in the amount of crossmodal extinction. Patients passively held a rake (T-shaped black line), in their right hands. Their left hands were screened from view (gray rectangle), while their right hands and the rake were visible. Visual stimuli (V) were presented at the distal edge of the rake, whereas unseen tactile stimuli (T) were delivered to the patients' left hands (as indicated by arrows). Crossmodal extinction was assessed before (a) and after (c) the patients were engaged in two different tasks concerning the same distant objects. Red plastic tokens were located (one at a time) in one (red circle) of five possible locations (gray circles represent the alternative positions). The patients had to retrieve the object with the rake (b *top*), or just point their index fingers toward it (b *bottom*). From Farnè and Làdavas, 2000. Reprinted with permission. *See color insert.*

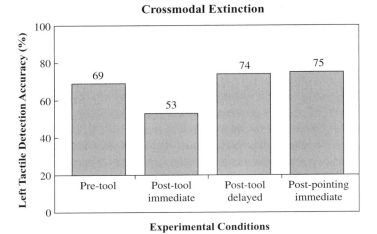

Figure 5.4. Mean detection accuracy (in percentages) of tactile stimuli delivered to the left hand as a function of the experimental conditions. From Farnè and Làdavas, 2000. Reprinted with permission.

Driver, 2003). However, we were particularly interested in the way in which the representation of perihand space can be expanded by means of the use of tools. This is because tools enable human beings, as well as other animals, to act on objects that would otherwise not be reachable by hands (Johnson-Frey, 2003), enormously widening their sphere of influence and, furthermore, opening rehabilitating perspectives (Ackroyd et al., 2002; Maravita et al., 2002). Indeed, the notion that tool use can change space perception raises several questions about the crucial determinants of perihand space extension. First of all, is a passive change of the corporeal visual appearance (the tool in the hand) sufficient, or is some goal-directed activity needed? Is there a (linear) relationship between the length of a tool and the increase of perihand space size? Also, does such an increase depend upon the absolute length of the tool or the length of the tool that can be effectively used to act on objects?

We recently addressed these questions (Farnè, Bonifazi, & Làdavas, in press; Farnè, Iriki, & Làdavas, 2005). In particular, we investigated whether a prolonged but passive exposure to a hand-held tool can increase the perihand space representation. We also verified whether a short tool (30 cm long) would increase perihand space to a lesser extent than a longer one (60 cm long). Finally, to investigate whether perihand space increase depends upon the physical or operative length of the tool, we dissociated within the same tool the physical aspect from its functional properties. In particular, we devised a hybrid tool that was physically equivalent to the long one (60 cm of absolute length), but whose functionally effective part (the tines) was only 30 cm away from the hand, being thus equivalent to the shorter tool (30 cm long). The results showed that crossmodal extinction, as assessed 60 cm away from the patient's ipsilesional hand, did not increase after a 5-minute period of *passive* exposure to a 60 cm-long tool. Instead, crossmodal extinction assessed at an equally far distance increased after an equally long period of *use* of an equally long tool.

These findings imply that the phenomenon of tool incorporation into the multisensory perihand space cannot be obtained just by passive perceptual assimilation of a bigger corporeal configuration constituted by the hand and tool ensemble. Such a physical enlargement of the body space would not modify the "body schema" (Head & Holmes, 1911–1912) in an effective way (see also Bermudez, Marcel, & Eilan, 1995; Gallagher, 1986). In sharp contrast, the body schema seems to be clearly altered by a purposeful utilization of a tool. Indeed, immediately after the use of the same 60 cm-long tool to retrieve distant objects, crossmodal extinction significantly increased compared to the situation of passive exposure reported above, thus confirming that the multisensory perihand area can expand along the tool axis toward the distal edge of the rake.

Concerning the second question, we found that the severity of crossmodal extinction was modulated by the length of the tool used to retrieve distant objects. Indeed, when visual-tactile extinction was measured at the far location (60 cm), the use of the short tool (30 cm) produced weaker effects than the use of a longer one (60 cm). Although weaker, the amount of crossmodal extinction obtained at the same 60 cm far location after the use of the short (30 cm) tool was still significantly larger than that obtained after the passive tool exposure. These results have two major implications. On the one side, they show that perihand space extension is directly and differentially modulated by tool length. On the other side, they reveal that the size increase induced by tool use is not strictly coincident with the length of the tool, but includes portions of space located beyond the distal edge of the tool. In this additional portion, however, the strength of multisensory integration is weaker. Thus, the distal border of the elongated area is not sharply limited to the tool tip, but extends (fading) beyond it.

Concerning our third question, we found that the differential amount of crossmodal extinction obtained with different tools was determined by the operative length of the tool and not by its absolute length. Indeed, crossmodal extinction observed (at the same far location) after the use of the hybrid tool (physically 60 cm long, but operationally 30 cm long) was weaker than that induced by the use of the 60 cm-long tool. Conversely, crossmodal effects induced by use of a regular 30 cm-long tool and the hybrid tool were comparable. As motor activity was similar in the use of both rakes, the crucial difference between the 60 cm-long tool and the hybrid tool was the location of the functional part of the rake (the tines). Therefore, these findings demonstrate that perihand space elongation depends upon the *functionally effective* length of the tool, that is, the distance at which the operative part of the tool is located with respect to the hand, being dissociated from its global physical appearance.

7. Conclusion

In conclusion, the neuropsychological findings we reviewed in this chapter, together with those derived from neurophysiological studies, converge in shedding light on the brain mechanisms responsible for coding space through multisensory processing (see also Farnè & Làdavas, 2002). They particularly underline the main parameters through which crossmodal interaction can be selectively modulated. Crossmodal interaction appears to be systematically influenced by the distance between a stimulus and the body and by the availability of visual versus proprioceptive information. Further, multisensory processing involved in representing peripersonal space is characterized by a high degree of relatively fast functional plasticity, such that crossmodal space representation can be shaped by using tools to purposefully interact with the environment, with a seemingly very flexible and finely tuned sensitivity to the functional characteristics of the tool being used. All of these characteristics may be part of a relevant evolutionary adaptive role played by multisensory processing.

References

Ackroyd, K., Riddoch, M. J., Humphreys, G. W., Nightingale, S., & Townsend S. (2002). Widening the sphere of influence: Using a tool to extend extrapersonal visual space in a patient with severe neglect. *Neurocase, 8*, 1–12.

Bermudez, J. L., Marcel, A. J., & Eilan, N. (1995). *The body and the self.* Cambridge, MA: MIT Press.

Berti, A., & Frassinetti F. (2000). When far becomes near: Remapping of space by tool use. *Journal of Cognitive Neuroscience, 3*, 415–420.

Blakemore, S.-J., Frith, C. D., & Wolpert, D. M. (1999). Spatio-temporal prediction modulates the perception of self-produced stimuli. *Journal of Cognitive Neuroscience, 11*, 551–559.

Blakemore, S.-J., Wolpert, D. M., & Frith, C. D. (1998). Central cancellation of self-produced tickle sensation. *Nature Neuroscience, 1*, 635–640.

Blakemore, S.-J., Wolpert, D. M., & Frith, C. D. (2002). Abnormalities in the awareness of action. *Trends in Cognitive Sciences, 6*, 237–242.

Bremmer, F., Schlack, A., Duhamel, J. R., Graf, W., & Fink, G. R. (2001). Space coding in primate posterior parietal cortex. *NeuroImage, 14*, S46-S51.

Bremmer, F., Schlack, A., Shah, N. J. Z. O., Kubischik, M., Hoffmann, K. P., Zilles, K., & Fink, G. R. (2001). Polymodal motion processing in posterior parietal and premotor cortex: A human fMRI study strongly implies equivalencies between humans and monkeys. *Neuron, 29*, 287–296.

Calvert, G., Spence, C., & Stein, B. (2004). *The handbook of multisensory processes.* Cambridge, MA: MIT Press.

Cooke, D. F., & Graziano, M. S. A. (2003). Defensive movements evoked by air puff in monkeys. *Journal of Neurophysiology, 90*, 3317–3329.

Cooke, D. F., Taylor, C. S. R., Moore, T., & Graziano, M. S. A. (2003). Complex movements evoked by microstimulation of the ventral intraparietal area. *Proceedings of the National Academy of Sciences, 100*, 6163–6168.

Denny-Brown, D., Meyers, J. S., & Horenstein, S. (1952). The significance of perceptual rivalry resulting from parietal lesions. *Brain, 75*, 433–471.

di Pellegrino, G., Làdavas, E., & Farnè, A. (1997). Seeing where your hands are. *Nature, 338*, 730.

Duhamel, J. R., Colby, C. L., & Goldberg, M. E. (1991). Congruent representation of visual and somatosensory space in single neurons of monkey ventral intra-parietal area (VIP). In J. Paillard (Ed.), *Brain and space* (pp. 223–236). New York: Oxford University Press.

Duhamel, J. R., Colby, C. L., & Goldberg M. E. (1998). Ventral intraparietal area of the macaque: Congruent visual and somatic response properties. *Journal of Neurophysiology, 79*, 126–136.

Farnè, A., Bonifazi, S., & Làdavas, E. (in press). The role played by tool-use and tool-length on the plastic elongation of peri-hand space: A single case study. *Cognitive Neuropsychology.*

Farnè, A., Demattè, M. L., & Làdavas E. (2003). Beyond the window: Multisensory representation of peripersonal space across a transparent barrier. *International Journal of Psychophysiology, 50*, 51–61.

Farnè, A., Iriki, A., & Làdavas, E. (2005). Shaping multisensory actionspace with tools: Evidence from patients with cross-modal extinction. *Neuropsychologia, 43*, 238–248.

Farnè, A., & Làdavas, E. (2000). Dynamic size-change of hand peripersonal space following tool use. *Neuroreport, 8*, 1645–1649.

Farnè, A., & Làdavas, E. (2002). Auditory peripersonal space in humans. *Journal of Cognitive Neuroscience, 14*, 1030–1043.

Farnè, A., Pavani, F., Meneghello, F., & Làdavas, E. (2000). Left tactile extinction following visual stimulation of a rubber hand. *Brain, 123*, 2350–2360.

Fogassi, L., Gallese, V., Fadiga, L., Luppino, G., Matelli, M., & Rizzolatti, G. (1996). Coding of peripersonal space in inferior premotor cortex (area F4). *Journal of Neurophysiology, 76*, 141–157.

Gallagher, S. (1986). Body image and body schema: A conceptual clarification. *Journal of Mind and Behavior, 7*, 541–554.

Graziano, M. S. A. (1999). Where is my arm? The relative role of vision and proprioception in the neuronal representation of limb position. *Proceedings of the National Academy of Science, 96*, 10418–10421.

Graziano, M. S. A., Cooke, D. F., & Taylor, S. R. (2000). Coding the location of the arm by sight. *Science, 290*, 1782–1786.

Graziano, M. S. A., & Gross, C. G. (1995). The representation of extrapersonal space: A possible role for bimodal, visuo-tactile neurons. In M. S. Gazzaniga (Ed.), *The cognitive neuroscience. The cognitive neurosciences* (pp. 1021–1034). Cambridge, MA: MIT Press.

Graziano, M. S. A., & Gross C. G. (1998). Visual responses with and without fixation: Neurons in premotor cortex encode spatial locations independently of eye position. *Experimental Brain Research, 118*, 373–380.

Graziano, M. S. A., Hu, X. T., & Gross, C. G. (1997). Visuospatial properties of ventral premotor cortex. *Journal of Neurophysiology, 77*, 2268–2292.

Graziano, M. S. A., Taylor, C. S. R., & Moore, T. (2001). Complex movements evoked by microstimulation of precentral cortex. *Neuron, 34*, 841–851.

Graziano, M. S. A., Yap, G. S., & Gross, C. G. (1994). Coding visual space by premotor neurons. *Science, 266*, 1054–1057.

Head, H., & Holmes, G. (1911–1912). Sensory disturbances from cerebral lesions. *Brain, 34*, 102–254.

Hoogenraad, T. U., Ramos, L. M. P., & van Gijn, J. (1994). Visually induced central pain and arm withdrawal after right parietal lobe infarction. *Journal of Neurology, Neurosurgery and Psychiatry, 57*, 850–852.

Hyvarinen, J., & Poranen, A. (1974). Function of the parietal associative area 7 as revealed from cellular discharges in alert monkeys. *Brain, 97*, 673–692.

Iriki, A., Tanaka, M., & Iwamura, Y. (1996). Coding of modified body schema during tool use by macaque postcentral neurons. *Neuroreport, 7*, 2325–2330.

Iriki, A., Tanaka, M., Obayashi, S., & Iwamura, Y. (2001). Self-images in the video monitor coded by monkey intraparietal neurons. *Neuroscience Research, 40*, 163–173.

Johnson-Frey, S. H. (2003). What's so special about human tool use? *Neuron, 39*, 201–204.

Làdavas, E. (2002). Functional and dynamic properties of visual peripersonal space in humans. *Trends in Cognitive Sciences, 6*, 17–22.

Làdavas, E., di Pellegrino, G., Farnè, A., & Zeloni G. (1998). Neuropsychological evidence of an integrated visuo-tactile representation of peripersonal space in humans. *Journal of Cognitive Neuroscience, 10*, 581–589.

Làdavas, E., & Farnè, A. (2004a). Neuropsychological evidence on integrated multisensory representation of space in humans. In G. Calvert, C. Spence, & B. Stein (Eds.), *The handbook of multisensory processes* (pp. 799–818). Cambridge, MA: MIT Press.

Làdavas, E., & Farnè, A. (2004b). Neuropsychological evidence for multimodal representations of space near specific body parts. In C. Spence & J. Driver (Eds.), *Crossmodal space and crossmodal attention* (pp. 69–98). New York: Oxford University Press.

Làdavas, E., Farnè, A., Zeloni, G., & di Pellegrino, G. (2000). Seeing or not seeing where your hands are. *Experimental Brain Research, 131*, 458–467.

Làdavas, E., Zeloni, G., & Farnè, A. (1998). Visual peripersonal space centred on the face in humans. *Brain, 121*, 2317–2326.

Macaluso, E., Driver, J., & Frith, C. D. (2003). Multimodal spatial representations engaged in human parietal cortex during both saccadic and manual spatial orienting. *Current Biology, 13*, 990–999.

MacKay, W. A., & Crammond, D. J. (1987). Neuronal correlates in posterior parietal lobe of the expectation of events. *Behavioral Brain Research, 24*, 167–179.

Maravita, A., Clarke, K., Husain, M., & Driver, J. (2002). Active tool use with the contralesional hand can reduce cross-modal extinction of touch on that hand. *Neurocase, 8*, 411–416.

Maravita, A., Husain, M., Clarke, K., & Driver, J. (2001). Reaching with the tool extends visual-tactile interactions into far space: Evidence from cross-modal extinction. *Neuropsychologia, 39*, 580–585.

Maravita, A., & Iriki, A. (2004). Tools for the body (schema). *Trends in Cognitive Sciences, 8*, 79–86.

Maravita, A., Spence, C., Clarke, K., Husain, M., & Driver, J. (2000). Vision and touch through the looking glass in a case of crossmodal extinction. *Neuroreport, 169*, 3521–3526.

Maravita, A., Spence, C., & Driver, J. (2003). Multisensory integration and the body schema: Close to hand and within reach. *Current Biology, 13*, 531–539.

Mattingley, J. B., Driver, J., Beschin, N., & Robertson I. H. (1997). Attentional competition between modalities: Extinction between touch and vision after right hemisphere damage. *Neuropsychologia, 35*, 867–880.

Mori, E., & Yamadori, A. (1989). Rejection behaviour: A human homologue of the abnormal behaviour of Denny-Brown and Chambers' monkey with bilateral parietal ablation. *Journal of Neurology Neurosurgery and Psychiatry, 52*, 1260–1266.

Obayashi, S., Tanaka, M., & Iriki, A. (2000). Subjective image of invisible hand coded by monkey intraparietal neurons. *Neuroreport, 11*, 3499–3505.

Pegna, A. J., Petit, L., Caldara-Schnetzer, A. S., Khateb, A., Annoni, J. M., Sztajzel, R., & Landis, T. (2001). So near yet so far: Neglect in far or near space depends on tool use. *Annals of Neurology, 50*, 820–822.

Rizzolatti, G., Luppino, G., & Matelli, M. (1998). The organization of the cortical motor system: New concepts. *Electroencephalography and Clinical Neurophysiology, 106*, 283–296.

Rizzolatti, G., Scandolara, C., Matelli, M., & Gentilucci, M. (1981). Afferent properties of periarcuate neurons in macaque monkeys. II: Visual responses. *Behavioral Brain Research, 2*, 147–163.

Spence, C., & Driver, J. (Eds.). (2004). *Crossmodal space and crossmodal attention.* New York: Oxford University Press.

Weiss, P., Marshall, J. C., Zilles, K., & Fink, G. R. (2003). Are action and perception in near and far space additive or interactive factors? *NeuroImage, 18*, 837–846.

6

A Bayesian View on Multimodal Cue Integration

Marc O. Ernst

1. Introduction

We perceive our own body and the world surrounding us via multiple sources of sensory information derived from several modalities, including vision, touch, and audition. To enable interactions with the environment, this information has to converge into a coherent and unambiguous multimodal percept of the body and the world. But how does the brain come up with such a unique percept? In this chapter, I review a model that in the statistical sense describes an optimal integration mechanism. The benefit of integrating sensory information comes from a reduction in variance of the final perceptual estimate. Furthermore, I point out how this integration scheme can be incorporated into a larger framework using Bayesian decision theory (BDT).

To illustrate the problem of sensory integration, imagine driving a nail into wood using a hammer. The position of the nail in space can be seen, but may also be derived from an estimate of the arm posture, while holding the nail in one hand. That is, vision and the estimate of body posture both provide information about the nail's position in space. Slight discrepancies in the representation of information between the estimates naturally arise due to the fact that the process of sensory estimation is inherently noisy. This results in an interesting situation: the observer either has to decide which information to trust in a given situation (vision or the body sense) or it has to find a way to best combine the discrepant information and come up with an optimal decision (or action).

However, having more than one (redundant) estimate available can be an advantage: the accuracy with which an environmental property can be judged increases with the number of individual perceptual estimates available. In the hammer example, the position in space can be estimated more reliably using both estimates (vision and the sense of the body's posture from somatosensory information) instead of only one. That is, to accurately hit the nail with the hammer it is best to integrate the position information from the two estimates into one common representation (for a more detailed discussion on the integration of sensory information into a body image, see chapter 4). One could speculate that this may be one reason it is better for you to hold the nail yourself, instead of having someone else hold it for you while hitting it with the hammer.

Not all information derived from different sensory modalities is redundant. In the majority of cases, information derived from the different modalities will be complementary in nature, such as when feeling an object's weight while seeing its color. Naturally, different combination rules have to be applied for combining such complementary information into a stable percept (for a recent review, see Ernst & Bülthoff, 2004). Here, I concentrate on the integration mechanisms for redundant sensory information, such as the spatial position of the hand or the size of an object that can be seen and felt simultaneously.

2. The Probabilistic Nature of Sensory Estimation

The problem of sensory combination can be understood using signal detection theory (Green & Swets, 1988). Perception is a probabilistic process. If one estimates an environmental property, such as an object's size, the estimate will have some variance associated with it. As a result, if the same environmental property is estimated consecutively 100 times, all 100 perceptual estimates may vary slightly. Figure 6.1 shows schematically the probability density distribution for estimating an object's size s. In the simplest case this probability density distribution has a Gaussian shape and is unbiased. This distribution is then defined by its mean $\bar{S}$, which for an unbiased estimator corresponds to the object's size s and its standard deviation σ:

$$\hat{S} = N(\bar{S}, \sigma). \tag{1}$$

If the reliability r is defined as the inverse of the variance σ^2

$$r = \frac{1}{\sigma^2} \tag{2}$$

then the larger the variance of the associated distribution, the less reliable is the associated perceptual estimate.

For experimentally estimating the variance of a sensory signal, classical psychophysical discrimination paradigms, such as a 2-interval forced-choice (2-IFC) task, can be used. Subjects performing this task must compare, for example, the sizes of two objects—standard S_0 with comparison S—presented sequentially. If the difference in size between the two intervals $(S - S_0)$ is large, subjects will

A)

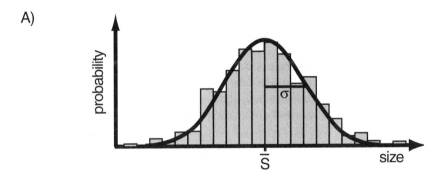

B)

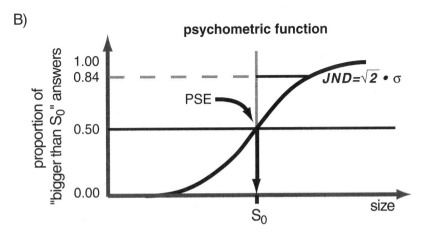

Figure 6.1. (A) Schematic illustration of the probability density function for the estimation of an object's size s. The histogram indicates the distribution of answers derived from the size-estimation process. The fitted curve has a Gaussian shape (with standard deviation σ and mean $\bar{S}$) and indicates the probability density function. (B) Schematic drawing of a psychometric function derived using a 2-interval forced-choice task given the probability density function for estimating the object's size from A. The just-noticeable difference (*JND*) derived at the 0.84 point corresponds to $JND = \sqrt{2} \cdot \sigma$. *PSE* is the point of subjective equality.

have no problem discriminating them, and consequently they will make only few errors. With decreasing size differences, however, the error rate will rise. If the probability density functions for S and S_0 are Gaussian with identical variance σ^2, the resulting psychometric function is a cumulative Gaussian (see Figure 6.1). The just-noticeable difference (*JND*), defined at the 84% level (the difference between the 50% and the 84% points), provides an estimate

$$JND = \sqrt{2}\sigma \tag{3}$$

for the variability of the underlying Gaussian distribution.

3. Combining Redundant Signals

"Redundant signals" may to some degree sound like a waste of information. But actually this is not necessarily so. There are two major advantages in having redundant information available: the first is that the system is more robust, because when one estimate is not available at a given time (or its information is degraded), the other estimate can substitute for it. The second advantage is that the final estimate becomes potentially more reliable compared with the reliability of the individual estimates feeding into the combined percept.

What is the statistically optimal strategy for combining redundant sensory information? Figure 6.2 shows the probability density distributions (the likelihood functions) for two independent estimates, each of which is derived from a stimulus in a different modality. In the example discussed here, it is a size estimate that is derived from a visual and a haptic size stimulus ($\hat{S}_V$ and $\hat{S}_H$). According to the maximum-likelihood estimation (MLE) scheme (Landy et al., 1995), the integrated estimate $\hat{S}_{VH}$ is a weighted average across the individual sensory signals with weights w_i that sum up to unity (the index i refers to the individual modalities $i = 1 \ldots j \ldots N$; Cochran, 1937):

$$\hat{S} = \sum_i w_i \hat{S}_i \quad \text{where} \quad \sum_i w_i = 1. \tag{4}$$

Optimally, weights are chosen to be proportional to the reliability of a given signal. That is, if the visual modality provides the more reliable information in a given situation, this signal is given higher weight.

$$w_j = \frac{r_j}{\sum_i r_i}. \tag{5}$$

In the example shown in Figure 6.2, the variance associated with the visual size estimate is four times less than the variance associated with the haptic size estimate. That is, the visual information is four times more reliable. Therefore, the combined estimate (the weighted sum) is closer to the visual than to the haptic estimate (in the example here, the visual weight is 0.8 according to Equation 5). Under other circumstances, where the haptic modality provides the more reliable estimate, the situation is reversed.

The variance of the combined estimate will be less than that of either of the individual estimates feeding into the combination process. That is, the reliability improves when information is combined. According to the MLE principle, the reliability of the combined estimate is the sum of the reliabilities of the individual estimates:

$$r = \sum_i r_i. \tag{6}$$

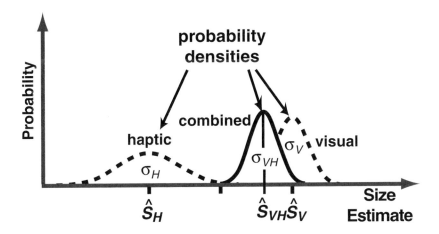

Figure 6.2. Schematic drawing of the likelihood functions of the individual visual and haptic size estimates and of the combined visual-haptic size estimate, which is a weighted average according to the MLE integration rule. The variance associated with the visual-haptic distribution is less than either of the two individual estimates. From Ernst and Banks, 2002. Reprinted with permission.

One can show that the MLE integration scheme is statistically optimal in that it provides the most reliable unbiased sensory estimate, given that the individual estimates are Gaussian distributed and that these noise distributions are independent. However, even if the noise distributions of the individual estimates show a correlation, one can still benefit from the combination of sensory information, and the combined estimate will be more reliable than each individual estimate alone (Oruç, Maloney, & Landy, 2003).

In a recent study, we showed that humans integrate visual and haptic information in such a statistically optimal fashion (Ernst & Banks, 2002). Others have demonstrated that this finding of optimality holds not only for the integration across vision and touch, but also for the integration of information across and within other sensory modalities, such as vision and audition (Alais & Burr, 2004; Hillis, Watt, Landy, & Banks, 2004; Knill & Saunders, 2003). Further, the MLE scheme holds also for the integration of sources of sensory information that include the body sense. This was recently shown by van Beers, Sittig, and Denier van der Gon (1998, 1999). They investigated how proprioceptive information about the position of the hand in space integrates with visual information and found the MLE model qualitatively confirmed. That is, perceptual information about one's own body seems to be no different from information derived from the other sensory modalities as far as the integration mechanism is concerned. Thus, maximum-likelihood estimation is an effective and widely used strategy utilized by the perceptual system.

In the Ernst and Banks (2002) study, subjects had to discriminate the sizes of two objects presented sequentially in a 2-IFC task. The objects either could only be seen, could only be felt, or could be both seen and felt simultaneously. The visual stimulus was a random-dot stereogram portraying a bar of given size. The haptic stimulus was generated using two haptic force-feedback devices (PHANTOM™ from SensAble Inc.; see Figure 6.3 for details). To vary the reliability of the visual stimulus, we added noise to the depth of the dots that formed the random-dot pattern (0%, 67%, 133%, and 200% depth noise relative to the depth that the bar was raised from the background plane).

To determine the reliability of each sensory modality alone, we conducted within-modal visual-only and haptic-only discrimination experiments. The reliabilities can be deduced from the *JND* measurements using Equations 2 and 3. The within-modal reliabilities can then be used to come up with predictions for crossmodal performance. Two kinds of predictions can be made

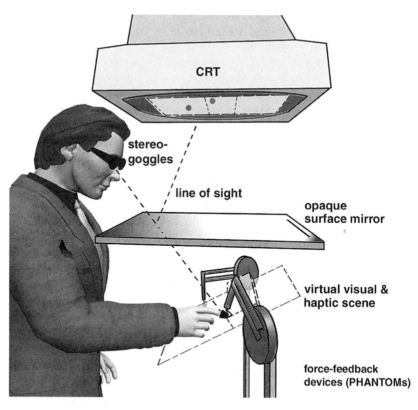

Figure 6.3. In the visual-haptic set-up, observers view the reflection of the visual stimulus binocularly in a mirror using stereo goggles. The haptic stimulus is presented using two PHANTOM™ force-feedback devices, one each for the index finger and thumb. With this set-up, the visual and the haptic virtual scenes can be independently manipulated. From Ernst and Bülthoff, 2004. Reprinted with permission. *See color insert.*

that, if confirmed experimentally, would demonstrate optimal integration behavior. On the one hand, we can make predictions for the weights of the
signals (using Equations 2, 3, and 5); experimentally we can derive the visual
and haptic weights from measurements of the point of subjective equality
(*PSE*) in a crossmodal experiment. On the other hand, we can make predictions for the variance of the combined percept (using Equations 2, 3, and 6).
Combined variance can be determined experimentally from the crossmodal
JNDs. It is important to note that these predictions have no free parameter and
are merely based on the within-modal *JNDs*.

To determine whether combined visual-haptic performance is statistically
optimal according to the MLE model, we again used a 2-IFC discrimination
task. In the standard interval, we now introduced a small discrepancy between
visual and haptic size information ($\Delta = \pm 3$ mm and ± 6 mm). Using the
comparison stimulus, which was varied in size between 45 mm and 65 mm
and which contained no size discrepancy between visual and haptic information, we determined the size that was perceived equally in the comparison
stimulus and the standard stimulus (the *PSE*). This perceived size (and so the
PSE) directly depends on the weights of the individual signals. Given the four
different noise levels and the within-modal visual-only and haptic-only discrimination data (JND_V and JND_H) we can calculate the relative visual reliabilities to be 0.78 for 0% noise, 0.75 for 67% noise, 0.48 for 133% noise, and
0.16 for 200% noise. These relative visual reliabilities are predictions for the
visual weights. As can be seen in Figure 6.4, predicted *PSE*s correspond well
with the empirically determined *PSE*s ("perceived size" as determined by the
50% point of the psychometric functions). In the no-noise condition, the *PSE*
is close to the visual standard, demonstrating a high visual weight. In the 200%
noise condition, the *PSE* is close to the haptic standard, demonstrating a low
visual but a high haptic weight. With added noise to the visual display, there is
a smooth transition from visual dominance to haptic dominance.

A correct prediction of weights (and *PSE*s) is a first hint that information is
combined optimally. However, there are different strategies that would give the
same result. For example, this may be a switching strategy in which the observer bases her answers on the estimate of one or the other modality at a time
but switches answers between the modalities in proportion to their relative
reliabilities (Ernst & Bülthoff, 2004; Landy & Kojima, 2001). Even though
such a strategy would provide the same weights as are predicted from the
MLE model, in using such a strategy, the combined *JNDs* could never become
lower than the *JNDs* for each individual estimate alone. Therefore, a stronger
test of statistical optimality is to show that crossmodal visual-haptic estimates
become more reliable when combined; that is, they have a lower *JND*. Predictions for combined visual-haptic *JNDs* can be derived from the within-
modal *JNDs* using Equation 6. Experimentally, we determined the combined
visual-haptic *JNDs* from the crossmodal psychometric functions. As can be

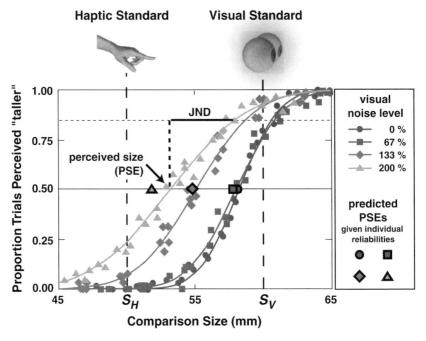

Figure 6.4. Visual-haptic size-discrimination performance determined with a 2-interval forced-choice task (Ernst & Banks, 2002). We manipulated the relative reliabilities of the individual signals by adding noise to the visual display (0%, 67%, 133%, and 200%). With these different relative reliabilities, we measured four discrimination curves. When the relative visual reliability decreases with added noise, the perceived size as indicated by the *PSE* is more and more determined by the haptic size estimate (haptic standard) and less by the visual size estimate (visual standard). This demonstrates the weighting behavior adopted by the brain and the smooth change from visual dominance (red circles) to haptic dominance (orange triangles). As indicated in the figure, the *PSEs* predicted from the individual visual and haptic discrimination performance (symbols with black outlines) correspond well with the empirically determined *PSEs* in the combined visual-haptic discrimination task. Four naïve subjects participated. From Ernst and Bülthoff, 2004. Reprinted with permission. *See color insert.*

seen in Figure 6.5, the predicted and empirical *JND*s correspond well. This demonstrates that humans actually combine visual and haptic size information in a fashion that is indistinguishable from statistical optimality (Ernst & Banks, 2002).

4. Benefits and Potential Costs
of Integrating Information

As demonstrated above, integrating sensory information has the potential benefit of reducing the variance of the associated sensory estimate and increasing its reliability. However, integrating sensory information may also come at a

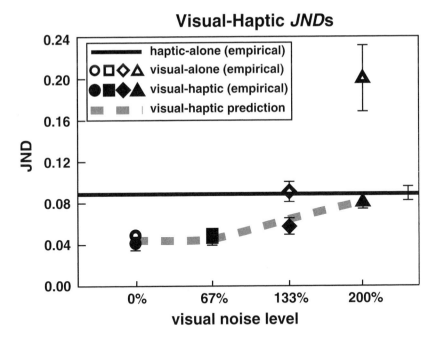

Figure 6.5. Size-discrimination thresholds (*JND*s) for visual-alone, haptic-alone, and visual-haptic combined comparisons. For the visual stimulus, we used four different noise levels (see text). The reliability of the haptic stimulus was not altered. From the individual visual-alone and haptic-alone *JND*s we derived predictions for the combined visual-haptic performance using Equation 6 (dashed line). Predicted and empirically determined visual-haptic *JND*s correspond well for all four visual noise levels (Ernst & Banks, 2002). Error bars denote the standard error of the mean across subjects ($n = 4$). From Ernst and Banks, 2002. Reprinted with permission.

cost. The brain potentially may lose access to the individual input signals feeding the integrated percept. That is, by jointly presenting visual and haptic information, as we have done in the experiment presented above, it may be impossible for the brain to independently access the individual sensory information without it being influenced by the other signal. If the brain loses access to the individual estimates, we should be able to observe metameric behavior. That is, there may be different physical stimuli that lead to exactly the same perceptual experience, indiscriminable from one another. Such metameric behavior is demonstrated in Figure 6.6, right panel.

Figure 6.6 is a schematic diagram that shows the expected discrimination performance, first if the two cues are completely independent (left panel), and second if the two cues are fused into a single percept (right panel). With two independent cues, that is, the percept of each cue is unbiased when presented in combination, the likelihood functions are radial symmetric in a *JND* normalized cue_1&cue_2 space (for simplicity, we here assume that the noise distributions of the signals are Gaussian with constant σ and that there is no correlation between the noise distributions of the cues; cf. Figure 6.11). With that, there is no direction in the cue_1&cue_2 discrimination space that is particularly special. Given an optimal decision rule that takes both independent cues into account (statistical benefit; Graham, 1989), discrimination performance for discriminating a cue_1&cue_2 stimulus from the standard is equal in all directions. Therefore, in the independent-cue case, discrimination thresholds around the standard object will form a circle in the cue_1&cue_2 space.

The situation is different if two cues are not independent but instead are fused into a single percept (Hillis, Ernst, Banks, & Landy, 2002). To be optimal the fusion rule is to form the weighted average between the cues (Equation 4; $cue_{12} = w_1\Delta cue_1 + w_2\Delta cue_2$). That is, if two cues are totally fused at the perceptual level, the same percept will result whether they both indicate a medium value or if they differ radically from one another but average to a medium value. Hence a high value on one cue can always be compensated for by a low value on the other cue. In other words, fusion is equivalent to averaging a two-dimensional stimulus (cue_1-dimension and cue_2-dimension) onto a single, fused dimension. This fused dimension is the positive diagonal in Figure 6.6, right panel, where the cue_1 signal maps onto the cue_2 signal. If,

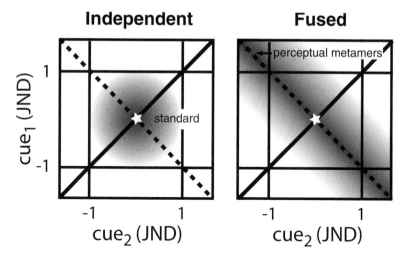

Figure 6.6. Schematic drawing of predictions for discrimination performance for independent cues (*left*) and for completely fused cues (*right*). Plotted is the hypothetical discrimination performance of a two-cue stimulus (cue_1, cue_2) from the standard stimulus (white star; $cue_{1,0}$, $cue_{2,0}$). The cue_1&cue_2 discrimination space is shown in units of *JND*. The gray shading is coding for discrimination performance (ranging from dark being nondiscriminable to white being perfectly discriminable). As indicated, if the two cues (cue_1 and cue_2) are independent, there is no explicit direction in this discrimination space and the discrimination contour is a circle around the standard object. If the cues are fused, however, using the weighted averaging rule (e.g., the MLE model), objects along the negative diagonal (dashed line in right panel) are not discriminable, i.e., they are perceptual metamers with respect to the standard object.

for example, cue_1 and cue_2 were visual and haptic sizes, respectively, the positive diagonal is the line where visual and haptic sizes are equal, that is, it is the common-size axis.

If cues are fused, it should be obvious that also discrimination performance will be affected. Along the fused dimension (e.g., along the common-size axis in the visual-haptic example) discrimination will remain possible. However, for stimuli not along this dimension, discrimination performance will drop, and it will be impossible to discriminate stimuli that were averaged to exactly the same value—i.e., that are perceptual metamers. Stimuli that form the same average fall along one particular direction ($\Delta cue_1/\Delta cue_2$) in this discrimination space. This direction is $\Delta cue_1/\Delta cue_2 = -w_2/w_1$ (Hillis et al., 2002). In Figure 6.6, right panel, where cues are plotted in *JND* units, all objects lying on the negative diagonal have the same average and therefore form perceptual metamers with respect to the standard object. Objects lying on lines parallel to the negative diagonal form a different set of perceptual metamers.

With this in mind, one can now also imagine that discrimination performance may not fall in one of the two categories illustrated in Figure 6.6, but actually may lie somewhere in between. That is, discrimination performance may not be circular around the standard, and it also may not be a single diagonal stripe in discrimination space. Instead, discrimination performance might form an ellipse elongated in the direction that is determined by the weight of the signals ($\Delta cue_1/\Delta cue_2 = -w_2/w_1$)—the same direction that indicates metameric behavior in the fused case. The magnitude of the elongation of the discrimination ellipse is a reflection of the degree to which the original information feeding into the combination process is accessible and so defines the "strength of coupling" between the signals.

We investigated such discrimination performance for two different sets of stimuli using a 3-interval oddity task (Hillis et al., 2002). In a crossmodal experiment, we investigated visual-haptic discrimination performance for object size (Figure 6.7, left panel). In a within-modal experiment we investigated slant discrimination performance (Figure 6.7, right panel). The slant was defined by two visual cues: binocular disparity and texture. Depending on the set of signals used, we found different strengths of coupling between the signals, that is, we found strong coupling for signals derived from within the visual modality (disparity and texture signals to slant) and weaker coupling for visual and haptic signals to size. This can be seen in Figure 6.7: in both cases, the discrimination thresholds form an elliptical shape—even though in the disparity-texture condition this ellipse is somewhat distorted. This is due to the fact that the reliability of disparity-defined and texture-defined slant changes with slant rather than remaining constant. The MLE model for complete fusion predicts the deformation in the data as can be seen from the green prediction lines (for details, see Hillis et al., 2002). The single-cue *JNDs* (red lines), the predicted constraint lines for fused performance (green lines), and the

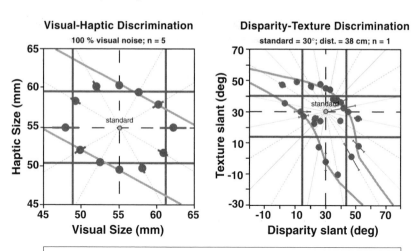

Figure 6.7. Discrimination performance for visual and haptic size discrimination (*left panel*) and for binocular disparity and texture-slant discrimination (*right panel*). In red are the single-cue *JND*s for discriminating each individual cue from the standard (green circle). The pairs of red horizontal constraint lines correspond to the *JND*s for haptic size discrimination and texture-slant discrimination, respectively. The pairs of red vertical constraint lines correspond to the *JND*s for visual size discrimination and disparity-slant discrimination, respectively. In green, we plotted the discrimination predictions (*JND*s for discrimination from standard) when assuming the MLE model for integration (i.e., complete fusion of the signals). Discrimination performance in the direction of the green constraint lines indicates metameric behavior. In purple are plotted the discrimination thresholds in the different directions for combined cue performance (Hillis et al., 2002). *See color insert.*

discrimination data can be seen in Figure 6.7. The elongation of the discrimination ellipse is clearly more pronounced in the disparity-texture experiment than in the visual-haptic experiment. That is, we clearly observed metameric behavior in the disparity-texture condition, where discrimination performance for the combined stimuli in the upper left and the lower right quadrants of the figure is worse than single-cue discrimination performance (single-cue *JND*s are indicated by the red lines). Metameric behavior is less pronounced in the visual-haptic condition. However, in both conditions, performance is not truly metameric over a wide range. In conclusion, there seems to be a stronger coupling (interaction) between the within-modal disparity-texture signals than between the crossmodal visual-haptic signals.

How can the different levels of interaction that determine the strength of coupling between the two sets of cues be understood? As described above, in cases of complete fusion, the system loses access to the individual estimates. If for some reason, however, the system needs to retain access to the individual estimates, it makes sense that the system does not fuse the signals completely. One obvious candidate for when it is necessary to retain access to the individual estimates is if the mapping between signals is not fixed, but changes in response to a constant conflict between signals. Without some degree of access to the individual estimates, it would be impossible to detect conflicts between signals and so it would be impossible for the system to change the mapping between signals in order to overcome the conflict.

Starting with Helmholtz (1867), there is a huge literature on visuomotor and visual-haptic adaptation, demonstrating the enormously rapid and flexible plasticity of the human visuomotor system (for a review, see Welch, 1978; see also chapter 3). This clearly indicates that there are often situations in which the mapping between the visual and haptic cues changes. Therefore, in the visual-haptic case, it makes sense that the system by and large maintains access to the individual signals.

There is also adaptation for signals within vision. Adams, Banks, and van Ee (2001), for example, observed an adaptation effect after wearing special magnifying glasses for a number of days, and they demonstrated that this adaptation effect is the consequence of recalibration of the relationship between disparity and perceived slant (i.e., a change in mapping). This is reasonable because certainly during growth the relationship between binocular signals, which depend on the interocular distance, and other monocular signals changes, and the system needs to adjust for that. However, compared with crossmodal visual-haptic adaptation, which can happen within seconds and after only a few exposures to the conflict, within-visual adaptation seems to be much slower, sometimes taking days or weeks.

The mapping between the different signals can fluctuate on different time scales. For adapting the mapping between signals quickly, a reliable estimate of the conflict is needed; for adapting slowly, each estimate of the conflict does not need to be very precise—only the average over many observations must yield a reliable conflict estimate. Strong coupling between signals, which introduces a strong perceptual bias, yields a less-reliable estimate of possible conflicts than does weak coupling between signals. If the relationship between signals derived from the same object or event is never changing (the mapping is constant), the system does not need to retain access to the individual estimates, and the signals can be completely fused. Because the mapping between the disparity and texture signals does not change quickly (Adams, Banks, & van Ee, 2001), we can infer that for disparity and texture cues to slant it is not so critical to retain reliable access to the individual estimates, and therefore there can be strong coupling between the disparity-texture signals. The reverse is true for visual-haptic size signals.

In conclusion, it seems that the necessity for changes in the mapping and how quickly they should occur determines the strength of coupling. In the following section, I aim to explain this strength of coupling using a Bayesian prior.

5. The Strength of Coupling and Bayesian Decision Theory

In the previous sections I have demonstrated that humans integrate visual and haptic information in a statistically optimal fashion. I have also shown that complete fusion between visual and haptic signals does not occur; rather there seems to be only some weaker coupling between the signals. Is that a contradiction, or is there a common explanation? I will try to answer this question using Bayesian decision theory (BDT).

To better understand the integration mechanisms, it is useful to examine more closely the strength of coupling between the sensory signals. Therefore, I present next an experiment that directly analyzes the extent to which the individual signals are accessible when provided with a combined visual-haptic stimulus. Determining the accessibility of the individual signals in combination can be done using a mixed design in which a combined visual-haptic stimulus is compared to either a visual-only or a haptic-only stimulus. When the comparison stimulus is visual-only, subjects are instructed to ignore the haptic component of the combined stimulus and vice versa. Visual-only and haptic-only trials were randomly intermixed. By introducing a small discrepancy between the visual and haptic information in the combined stimulus, one can estimate which signal has the higher weight. If the brain retains access to the individual visual and haptic information, then when compared to the visual-only stimulus, there should be no influence of the haptic modality (i.e., a visual weight of one) and vice versa (i.e., a visual weight of zero when the combined stimulus is compared to the haptic-only stimulus). On the other hand, if in combination, visual and haptic information is completely fused (i.e., not accessible independently), comparing the combined stimulus to either the visual-only or the haptic-only stimulus should provide identical results (i.e., the relative weight of the signals should be identical in both conditions).

The results of such an experiment can be seen in Figure 6.8. For this experiment we used a 2-IFC task to measure discrimination performance. Subjects compared a combined visual-haptic stimulus to either a visual-only stimulus (solid line) or a haptic-only stimulus (dashed line). We determined the relative visual weights from the *PSEs* of these psychometric functions (for details of the methods, see Ernst & Banks, 2002). For each of the two conditions we derived weights for four different reliability levels. As in the previous experiment (Figure 6.4), we varied the reliability of the signals by adding noise to the random-dot pattern that constituted the visual display (0%, 67%, 133%, and 200% visual noise). The stimulus was exactly the same as described above and by Ernst and Banks (2002).

Independence of signals predicts a visual weight of zero if compared to the haptic-only (H) stimulus and a visual weight of one when compared to the visual-only (V) stimulus. Complete fusion of signals predicts that the visual

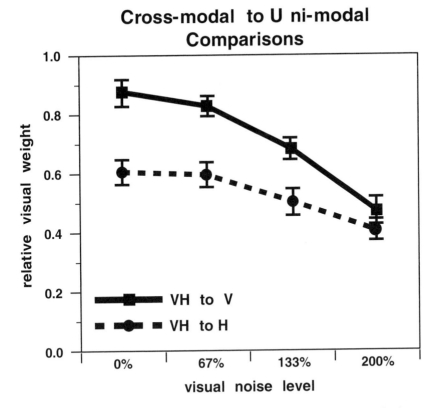

Figure 6.8. Crossmodal to unimodal comparisons. The weights are determined using a 2-IFC size-discrimination task with a stimulus similar to that used in Ernst and Banks (2002). The solid line indicates visual weights that were determined from a condition where the combined visual-haptic stimulus (VH) was compared to a visual-only stimulus (V). The dashed line indicates visual weights that were obtained from a condition where the combined visual-haptic stimulus (VH) was compared to a haptic-only stimulus (H). Trials from both conditions were randomly intermixed. We determined weights in both conditions for four different noise levels to alter the relative reliability of the signals. The noise was added to the visual display only. Error bars denote the standard error of the mean across subjects (n = 4). From Ernst and Banks, 2002. Reprinted with permission.

weights in the two conditions should be identical. Neither prediction was confirmed. Instead we found relative visual weights that were in between these two predictions. The relative visual weights differed between the two conditions. Vision was weighted more heavily when the combined stimulus was compared to the visual modality, and the haptic modality was weighted more heavily when the combined stimulus was compared to the haptic modality. Such a result was obtained across all four noise levels (Figure 6.8). That is, it seems that we have no direct access to the original haptic or visual information feeding into the combination process, but instead this information is altered (biased) by the accompanying modality. In other words, subjects cannot ignore the task-irrelevant stimulus even when they are instructed to fully attend to only one of the two sensory signals and to ignore the other. It is probably worth noting that there are several studies now showing that this form of sensory integration is not modulated by attention (e.g., Bertelson, Vroomen, De Gelder, & Driver, 2000; Vroomen, Bertelson, & De Gelder, 2001).

If the visual-haptic signals are not completely fused into a unified percept and they are also not independent, in which case the percept would be unbiased, what is the percept that is associated with the visual-haptic stimulus? From the VH-to-V experiment, we can conclude how much the visual size percept is biased by the presence of the haptic component in the combined visual-haptic stimulus. Conversely, from the VH-to-H experiment, we can conclude how much the haptic-size percept is biased by the presence of the visual component in the combined visual-haptic stimulus. The visual and haptic biases correspond to the weights (*PSEs*) determined in the VH-to-V and VH-to-H experiments, respectively. No visual bias would mean that visual weight is $w_V = 1$ in the VH-to-V experiment; no haptic bias would mean that visual weight is $w_V = 0$ in the VH-to-H experiment (independence). As indicated previously, a bias in the percept that would indicate complete fusion would result in identical weights in the two experiments (VH-to-V and VH-to-H).

To illustrate the percept associated with a visual-haptic stimulus, the results from Figure 6.8 are replotted in Figure 6.9 in a two-dimensional visual-haptic space. Haptic size is plotted on the ordinate, visual size on the abscissa. In general, a visual-haptic stimulus (unfilled circle) results in a size percept (filled circle) that is biased in vision and in touch relative to the physical size of the stimulus ($S_{V,0}$, $S_{H,0}$). Quantifying these biases (weights) requires a visual-haptic stimulus that is off the identity line. The identity line for which the visual and haptic sizes are equal is the positive diagonal in Figure 6.9.

The bias corresponds to a relative size shift between stimulus and percept ΔS and depends on the weights. The visual size shift with weights determined in the VH-to-V experiment corresponds to

$$\Delta S_V = (1 - w_V) \cdot (S_{V,0} - S_{H,0}); \tag{7}$$

the haptic size shift with weights determined in the VH-to-H experiment corresponds to

$$\Delta S_H = w_V \cdot (S_{V,0} - S_{H,0}). \tag{8}$$

In Figure 6.9, I plot these biases for the four visual-noise conditions: on the abscissa there is the visual size shift, on the ordinate the haptic size shift. The dashed arrow indicates the overall bias from physical to perceived size of the visual-haptic stimulus. The length of this arrow (in relation to the distance

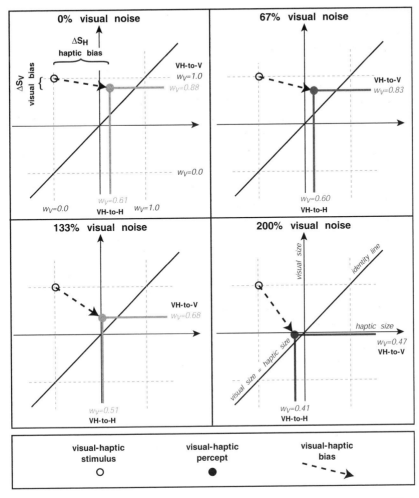

Figure 6.9. Visual-haptic percepts (filled circles) in relation to the stimuli (unfilled circles) that gave rise to them. The four panels show the results for four different noise levels. The abscissa indicates the visual size, the ordinate the haptic size of the object. Visual sizes were compared in the VH-to-V condition, haptic sizes in the VH-to-H condition. From this, the visually and haptically perceived sizes were determined using *PSE*s (weights). The difference between physical and perceived size (the visual-haptic bias; dashed arrow) directly depends on the weights of the signals (see Equations 8 and 9). *See color insert.*

between stimulus and identity line) is an indication for the strength of coupling between the visual and haptic signals. The more pronounced the bias, the longer the arrow, the stronger the coupling. If the estimates were independent, perceived size would be identical to physical size and so the length of the arrow would be zero. If the visual and haptic signals were fused completely, the percept would lie on the identity line (positive diagonal) corresponding to a maximal bias and the maximal possible length of the arrow. As can also be seen in Figure 6.9, the actual results fall in between independence and complete fusion.

The direction of the bias (orientation of the arrow) should correspond to the relative reliabilities of the visual and haptic signals, that is, the optimal combined visual-haptic weights. If the visual information is more reliable than the haptic information, there is a stronger haptic than visual bias, so that the orientation of the arrow is closer to horizontal (Figure 6.9, upper two panels). Conversely, if the haptic information is more reliable than the visual information, there is a stronger visual than haptic bias, so that the orientation of the arrow is closer to vertical (Figure 6.9, lower right panel). Equal reliabilities of the signals should correspond to a bias along the negative diagonal (Figure 6.9, lower left panel). As can be seen in Figure 6.9, the directions of the biases for all different noise levels correspond well to the relative reliabilities of the visual and haptic signals (cf. Figure 6.5); that is, the direction of bias corresponds well to the optimal combined visual-haptic weights.

To bring all of the findings discussed above together, BDT seems to be an appropriate common framework (Figure 6.10). Bayesian inference provides a formal way to model uncertainty about the world by combining existing knowledge (the prior) with observational, sensory evidence (the likelihood function) to infer the most probable interpretation of the environment (the posterior; Kersten & Yuille, 2003; Kersten, Mamassian, & Yuille, 2004; Knill & Richards, 1996; Mamassian, Landy, & Maloney, 2002; Yuille & Bülthoff, 1996). Bayes' Rule states that the posterior probability $p(W|I)$ is proportional to the product of the likelihood function $p(I|W)$ and prior probability distribution $p(W)$: $p(W|I) \propto p(I|W) \times p(W)$. In general, the Bayesian framework can be used to construct "ideal observer" models as a standard for comparison with human performance. This framework has recently seen much success in describing observers' perception and performance in a variety of visual (Adams & Mamassian, 2004; Knill, 1998; Saunders & Knill, 2001; Weiss, Simoncelli, & Adelson, 2002;), visual-haptic (Adams, Graf, & Ernst, 2004; Ernst & Banks, 2002; Hillis et al., 2002), visual-auditory (Alais & Burr, 2004), and visuomotor (Körding & Wolpert, 2004) coordination tasks.

The first step in BDT is to construct the posterior. After combining the prior and the likelihood function into the posterior distribution using Bayes' Rule, to perform an action or to come to a decision, the second step is to define the goal for the task using gain/loss functions (Figure 6.10; Mamassian et al., 2002; Schrater & Kersten, 2000). That humans can behave very close to optimally when making decisions or actions was demonstrated by Trommershäuser, Maloney, and Landy (2003). They showed that statistical decision theory can be used to accurately explain pointing behavior under risk using different cost functions. A complete Bayesian model has to consider all three parts that make up BDT: sensory estimation, prior knowledge, and a decision-making process (e.g., Ernst & Bülthoff, 2004; Kersten, 1999; Mamassian et al., 2002).

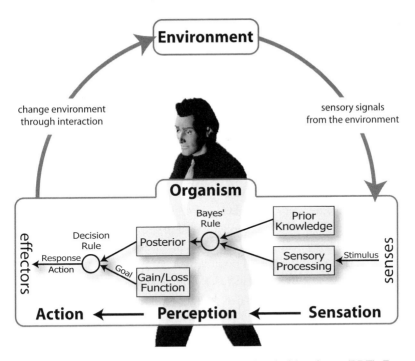

Figure 6.10. Perception/action loop including Bayesian decision theory (BDT). From Ernst and Bülthoff, 2004. Reprinted with permission. *See color insert.*

To model multimodal cue integration using a Bayesian approach, a prior is necessary to describe the interactions between the signals. A robust system that behaves plastically to body changes or to modifications in the environment often has to adapt the mapping between its signals. As suggested above, the ease of adapting the mapping depends on the strength of coupling between the signals (i.e., their interaction): weak coupling allows for more vigorous changes than does strong coupling. However, not all mappings between two signals are equally likely. For example, if the signals are visual and haptic sizes, the changes in the mapping that naturally occur are in the order of a few millimeters only. As a result, there is a probability distribution representing the mappings that naturally occur. In the following, I will show that a Bayesian prior that corresponds to the probability distribution for the different mappings between two signals can be used to model the observed sensory interactions.

Such a prior, which codes for the mapping between two signals, is aligned along the identity line. In the simplest case, spread of the prior will be Gaussian distributed (see Figure 6.11, middle column). The standard deviation of this distribution determines the influence of the prior. That is, the sensory signal (the likelihood function) is biased more if the prior is represented by a narrow (Figure 6.11C–G) than a wide (Figure 6.11B) distribution. If the prior is completely flat, that is, the standard deviation approaches infinity, the posterior is equal to the likelihood distribution, and the bias is negligible (Figure 6.11A).

The likelihood function associated with a sensory signal represents the sensory information available to the system. It is determined by a mean and its variance (Figure 6.11, left column). The smaller the variance associated with a sensory signal, the more reliable is the sensory information. The posterior, which is proportional to the product of likelihood and prior, determines the percept (the maximum a posteriori, or MAP estimate). That is, both the likelihood and the prior affect the percept. The strength of the bias depends on the relation between the two distributions. If the likelihood is very reliable, it can be less biased by a prior. And vice versa: if the prior is given by a narrowly tuned distribution, it will bias the likelihood more. If the prior is reduced to a delta function (variance approaches zero), the Bayesian scheme discussed here corresponds to the MLE model discussed earlier in the chapter.

The influence of the prior therefore determines the strength of coupling between the signals and the degree to which the signals interact. Hence, we call this prior the *coupling prior*, and it relates to the probability for knowing the mapping between sensory signals. If the mapping is known for sure, signals can be fused; on the contrary, if the mapping is unknown, signals should be kept separate.

Given the priors used in the examples shown in Figure 6.11 (all aligned along the identity line), the direction of the bias is only determined by the

---

Figure 6.11. Schematic illustration of several examples demonstrating sensory combinations with a Bayesian prior. In the *left column*, there are the likelihood distributions indicating the sensory information available. In the *middle column* are the priors that relate to the probability distributions for the mappings between the sensory signals. The multimodal percept is based on the posterior (*right column*). According to Bayes' Rule, the posterior is proportional to the product of likelihood and prior. The relationship between likelihood and prior, therefore, determines the degree of coupling between the signals. (A) The prior is flat so that the likelihood equals the posterior. This indicates independence between the signals. (B) The prior is aligned along the identity line and is moderately spread. The cues therefore show some moderate interaction (coupling). (C) The prior is tuned very sharply (delta function). This situation corresponds to complete fusion. (D) and (E) Only the relative variances of the two signal estimates determine the direction of bias. This corresponds to the weighting of the signals. (C, D, and E correspond to the MLE model discussed earlier in this chapter.) (F) In all cases discussed previously, it was assumed that the noise distributions of the two signals are independent. If they are correlated, the likelihood ellipse is rotated in the cue$_1$&cue$_2$ space. This slightly changes the weighting between the signals (see Oruç et al., 2003). (G) If there is a positive correlation (ρ_{12}) between the noise distributions of the cues and the reliabilities differ substantially so that $\rho_{12} > \sqrt{r_1/r_2}$, the weight for cue$_1$ will become negative and the weight for cue$_2$ will be bigger than 1 (the sum of the weights must be 1; see Oruç et al., 2003). In this example, the direction of bias is therefore above vertical.

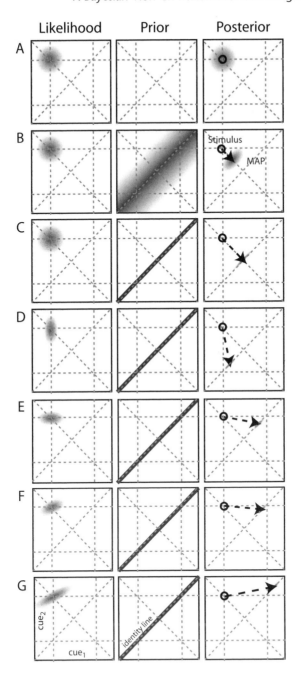

relative reliabilities between the two sensory signals (cues). The relative reliabilities of the signals therefore define the direction in which the perceptual estimate is biased by the coupling prior (Figure 6.11C–E). In the visual-haptic example discussed above, if the visual estimate is more reliable than the haptic estimate, the bias is closer to the visual modality, and vice versa. This corresponds to the weighting of the sensory signals. Thus, both the weighting of the signals, that is, the direction in which the percept is biased by the prior, as well as the strength of coupling between the signals can be explained using this Bayesian approach.

In the experiment shown in Figure 6.9, the strength of coupling increased slightly with added visual noise in the four noise conditions (i.e., the more noise that was added, the closer the combined percept is to the identity line). This effect can also be explained with the Bayesian framework. The variance of the associated sensory estimate (likelihood function) increases with added noise. Therefore, with a likelihood function that is less salient, the coupling prior can become more influential.

Introducing the coupling prior can thus explain the results of the two experiments that were presented in Figures 6.7 and 6.8. These experiments demonstrated that there is no complete fusion but some weaker coupling between the sensory signals. In the first experiment (Figures 6.4 and 6.5), however, we found that subjects integrate information in a statistically optimal fashion. Does this mean there was complete fusion in this first experiment? The combined visual-haptic stimulus was identical in all three of these experiments. Therefore, it can be assumed that the percept of this stimulus was so as well. The only difference between these experiments was the decision that had to be made with respect to the combined stimulus. In Experiment 1, we used a 2-IFC task in which the combined visual-haptic stimulus was compared to different versions of the same visual-haptic stimulus, and the subjects' task was to discriminate size. In Experiment 2, we used a 3-interval oddity task, in which each interval contained a visual-haptic stimulus. Two of the intervals were identical, and the stimulus in the odd interval differed in either visual and/or haptic size. The subjects' task was to discriminate the odd visual-haptic stimulus. Experiment 3 was virtually identical to Experiment 1 using again a 2-IFC task. The only difference was that subjects were to do size discrimination between a visual-haptic stimulus and a visual-only or haptic-only comparison stimulus. The difference between the experiments is the task—i.e., the decision or action to be taken upon the identical visual-haptic percept. Therefore, the apparent different experimental results (optimal integration versus incomplete fusion) seem to be related to differences in the task at the decisional level and not to the differences in the percept of the visual-haptic stimulus per se.

Exploiting BDT, these differences in experimental results can be subsumed in the gain/loss functions (cf. Figure 6.10, second step). If the goal of the perceptual system is to come up with the optimal (most reliable) decision, it is not necessary that the signals have to be completely fused. In contrast, the system may perform optimally because the decision process is optimal and takes the reliability of the individual sensory estimates into account (not implying that the decisions or actions have to be conscious). Using BDT, the decision (action) process can be modeled using gain/loss functions. Gain/loss functions define the goal of the task and thus are task dependent.

Using a 2-IFC task as in the first experiment, it cannot be distinguished whether the sensory signals are optimally integrated into a fused percept or whether subjects come up with an optimal decision that integrates the information available by taking the reliabilities of the individual sensory signals into account. In both cases, subjects' answers would have the lowest variance possible. Integration of signals (meaning, optimal use of sensory information) could be performed on either of these two levels—the perceptual level describing the coupling between the signals (task independent) and the decisional level comprising the goal of the task (task dependent). If the signals were completely (mandatorily) fused, the percept should not be separable any more by using another task. Residuals of the individual visual and haptic signals, however, were found in Experiments 2 and 3. Here we found incomplete fusion. Thus, to combine the findings of all three experiments, I here assume that multisensory cue combination is a two-step process. In the first step, the signals are perceptually coupled. This coupling is task independent and can be described with the coupling prior. In the second step, the goal of the task is defined. This goal is defined using gain/loss functions. This second step may also be optimal. That is, even holding a weak coupling prior, performance can still be optimal. Therefore, BDT with an optimal decision stage together with a coupling prior unites all of the experimental findings presented. Thus, Bayesian decision theory constitutes a comprehensive framework for characterizing sensory integration.

6. Concluding Remarks

Multiple sensory signals derived from several modalities can provide redundant sensory information about one's own body and the environment. This chapter has been a review of mechanisms that may be exploited by the perceptual system to integrate such redundant sensory information into a coherent percept in order to come to an optimal decision or action.

Three experiments on visual-haptic combination of size information were discussed. The first experiment demonstrated that humans integrate visual and haptic size information in a statistically optimal fashion by maximally reducing the variance of the final perceptual decision. However, as demonstrated by the results of the second experiment, this does not necessarily imply that the sensory size signals are mandatorily fused into a unified percept. Instead, we found a weaker form of interaction between the size information from vision and touch. The degree of interaction between the sensory signals was taken as a definition for the strength of coupling between the signals. We indirectly determined the actually perceived visual and haptic sizes associated with the visual-haptic stimulus in the third experiment. The perceived size of the visual-haptic stimulus was in fact in between the sizes predicted from either complete fusion or independence of the signals.

Bayesian decision theory offers an excellent basis for modeling these findings using a common framework. To account for the sensory interactions, that is, the coupling between the signals, a Bayesian prior was introduced. This coupling prior represents the probability distribution of naturally occurring mappings between the sensory signals, that is, it codes for the certainty of knowing the mapping between signals. If the mapping almost never changes, the prior is represented by a very narrow distribution, and signals can be fused completely. If the mapping constantly changes, however, the distribution is more spread, and signals are fused less vigorously, but may still interact. If there is no mapping between signals (they carry no redundant information), the coupling prior will be flat, and the signals do not interact, that is, the signals will be independent.

Why does the mapping between signals change? In order to be robust against changes in the environment or changes occurring to the body, our perceptual and perceptual-motor system has to be very flexible. The system can compensate for such changes through the process of adaptation, which corresponds to a change in mapping between signals. For example, human beings are very skilled at using tools. Using a tool often requires a mapping from visual coordinates to the coordinates of the tool's end. Thus, using tools can be seen as an extension of the body that requires adaptation (see chapters 4 and 5). Fusing signals mandatorily so that the system loses access to the incoming information would prevent such adaptation from happening, because the discrepancy between the signals could not be detected. Without the discrepancy being detected, the error signal necessary for adaptation (the re-mapping of signals) is missing. A reliable error signal allows for quick adaptation; adaptation to an unreliable error signal should be slow. Therefore, whenever quick adaptation is necessary (e.g., for the remapping of vision to body sense during tool use—plasticity of peripersonal space) signals should not be tightly coupled, maintaining the chance to reliably detect an error signal; on the contrary, when adaptation can occur on a longer time frame (as argued for the disparity-texture example from Experiment 2), coupling can be stronger and so the signals are fused more completely.

Integration of signals is only reasonable if they are derived from the same object or event; unrelated signals should be kept separate. For example, we have recently shown that sensory integration breaks down with signals that are not in temporal synchrony (Bresciani, Ernst, Drewing, Bouyer, Maury, & Kheddar,

2004) or that come from largely different locations in space (Gepshtein, Burge, Banks, & Ernst, 2004). In order to know which signals derived from the different modalities belong together, the correspondence problem has to be solved. Signals are likely to originate from the same object or event if they are derived roughly at the same time, from roughly the same location in space. The likelihood of correspondence increases with the number of concordant attributes, where each attribute is one dimension in a hyperdimensional multimodal space. The coupling prior that is responsible for integration to occur is maximally tuned at the origin when all multisensory attributes agree. If one or more attributes contain a discrepancy between the sensory signals, for example, when signals are derived at different locations but at the same time, the coupling prior should become more flat. With a completely flat prior, there is no interaction, and the signals are independent. This concept of correspondence would therefore predict that integration of sensory signals only occurs when the conflict between sensory attributes is small. As an example, consider the integration of visual and somatosensory information. Such signals concerning the spatial position of the body should only be integrated if not in conflict. That is, visual-somatosensory interactions should decrease (integration should break down) outside of peripersonal space where visual-somatosensory spatial conflicts become large. Experiments conducted by Làdavas and Farnè (chapter 5) confirm this prediction (see also chapters 3 and 4).

In the beginning of this chapter, I introduced an integration model based on the maximum-likelihood estimate (MLE). Later, I switched to a Bayesian model that combines the likelihood with a prior. How do those two models relate to each other? The MLE model was formulated in a one-dimensional space (e.g., the space of physical size), and it can describe sensory integration in this one-dimensional space. Once we realized that the visual and haptic signals are not completely fused, the problem of sensory integration became two-dimensional (e.g., visual size being one, haptic size being the other dimension). For describing such a two-dimensional situation, the MLE model was not appropriate any more. I therefore switched to the Bayesian model in which the prior is responsible for the interactions occurring between the sensory signals. Independence could be modeled with a flat prior (the standard deviation σ of the Gaussian prior approaches infinity), or the complete fusion with a prior that corresponds to a delta function (the standard deviation σ of the Gaussian prior approaches zero). Complete fusion corresponds to a reduction from two to one dimensions and can be described with a prior representing a delta function. Therefore, the MLE model corresponds to the Bayesian model with a coupling prior that is a delta function (Figure 6.11C–E). In general, compared to the MLE model, the Bayesian model is more comprehensive because by using a prior with an intermediate standard deviation σ it can also describe interactions that are in between complete fusion and independence.

We have shown that sensory signals are not necessarily completely fused into a unified percept, yet subjects can perform in a close to optimal fashion when asked to report the combined percept (Experiment 1). In order to perform optimally under such conditions, the nervous system has to know the reliability of the sensory signals and take them into account when making decisions or actions. Using BDT, this implies that both stages—the sensory combination stage exploiting the Bayesian prior as well as the decision stage—have to be optimal. Naturally, this does not necessarily imply that the actor is consciously aware of her decisions or actions.

As a conclusion, I have proposed that a Bayesian model that uses a coupling prior for describing sensory interactions is a convenient theoretical framework for understanding multimodal cue integration as a continuous process between independence and complete fusion.

Acknowledgments This work was supported by the Max Planck Society and by the Fifth Framework IST Program of the EU (IST-2001–38040, TOUCH-HapSys). Thanks to Michael Landy, Knut Drewing, and Johannes Burge for helpful comments on this chapter.

References

Adams, W. J., Banks, M. S., & van Ee, R. (2001). Adaptation to three-dimensional distortions in human vision. *Nature Neuroscience, 4,* 1063–1064.

Adams, W. J., Graf, E. W., & Ernst, M. O. (2004). Experience can change the "light-from-above" prior. *Nature Neuroscience, 7,* 1057–1058.

Adams, W. J., & Mamassian, P. (2004). Bayesian combination of ambiguous shape cues. *Journal of Vision, 4,* 921–929.

Alais, D., & Burr, D. (2004). The ventriloquist effect results from near optimal crossmodal integration. *Current Biology, 14,* 257–262.

Bertelson, P., Vroomen, J., De Gelder, B., & Driver, J. (2000). The ventriloquist effect does not depend on the direction of deliberate visual attention. *Perception & Psychophysics, 62,* 321–332.

Bresciani, J.-P., Ernst, M. O., Drewing, K., Bouyer, G., Maury, V., & Kheddar, A. (2005). Feeling what you hear: Auditory signals can modulate tactile tap perception. *Experimental Brain Research, 162,* 172–180.

Cochran, W. G. (1937). Problems arising in the analysis of a series of similar experiments. *Journal of the Royal Statistical Society, 4*(Suppl.), 102–118.

Ernst, M. O., & Banks, M. S. (2002). Humans integrate visual and haptic information in a statistically optimal fashion. *Nature, 415,* 429–433.

Ernst, M. O., & Bülthoff, H. H. (2004). Merging the senses into a robust percept. *Trends in Cognitive Sciences, 8,* 162–169.

Gepshtein, S., Burge, J., Banks, M. S., & Ernst, M. O. Optimal combination of vision and touch has a limited spatial range. Manuscript submitted for publication. Graham, N. (1989). *Visual pattern analyzers.* New York: Oxford University Press.

Green, D. M., & Swets, J. A. (1988). *Signal detection theory and psychophysics.* Los Altos, CA: Peninsula.

Helmholtz, H. von. (1867). *Handbuch der physiologischen Optic, Vol. 3.* Leipzig: Voss.

Hillis, J. M., Ernst, M. O., Banks, M. S., & Landy, M. S. (2002). Combining sensory information: Mandatory fusion within, but not between, senses. *Science, 298*, 1627–1630.

Hillis, J. M., Watt, S., Landy, M. S., & Banks, M. S. (2004). Slant from texture and disparity cues: Effects of base slant and distance. Manuscript in preparation.

Kersten, D. (1999). High-level vision as statistical inference. In M. S. Gazzaniga (Ed.), *The new cognitive neurosciences* (2nd ed., pp. 353–363). Cambridge, MA: MIT Press.

Kersten D., Mamassian, P., & Yuille, A. (2004). Object perception as Bayesian inference. *Annual Review of Psychology, 44*, 271–304.

Kersten, D., & Yuille, A. L. (2003). Bayesian models of object perception. *Current Opinion in Neurobiology, 13*, 150–158.

Knill, D., & Richards, W. (1996). *Perception as Bayesian inference.* Cambridge: Cambridge University Press.

Knill, D. C. (1998). Discriminating surface slant from texture: Comparing human and ideal observers. *Vision Research, 38*, 1683–1711.

Knill, D. C., & Saunders, J. A. (2003). Do humans optimally integrate stereo and texture information for judgments of surface slant? *Vision Research, 43*, 2539–2558.

Körding, K. P., & Wolpert, D. M. (2004). Bayesian integration of sensorimotor learning. *Nature, 427*, 244–247.

Landy, M. S., & Kojima, H. (2001). Ideal cue combination for localizing texture defined edges. *Journal of the Optical Society of America, A, 18*, 2307–2320.

Landy, M. S., Maloney, L. T., Johnston, E. B., & Young, M. J. (1995). Measurement and modeling of depth cue combination: In defense of weak fusion. *Vision Research, 35*, 389–412.

Mamassian, P., Landy, M., & Maloney, L. T. (2002). Bayesian modelling of visual perception. In P. N. Rao, B. A. Olshausen, & M. S. Lewicki (Eds.), *Probabilistic models of the brain* (pp. 13–36). Cambridge, MA: MIT Press.

Oruç, I., Maloney, T. M., & Landy, M. S. (2003). Weighted linear cue combination with possibly correlated error. *Vision Research, 43*, 2451–2468.

Saunders, J. A., & Knill, D. C. (2001). Perception of 3D surface orientation from skew symmetry. *Vision Research, 41*, 3163–3183.

Schrater, P. R., & Kersten, D. (2000). How optimal depth cue integration depends on the task. *International Journal of Computer Vision, 40*, 71–89.

van Beers, R. J., Sittig, A. C., & Denier van der Gon, J. J. (1998). The precision of proprioceptive position sense. *Experimental Brain Research, 122*, 367–377.

van Beers, R. J., Sittig, A. C., & Denier van der Gon, J. J. (1999). Integration of proprioceptive and visual position information: An experimentally supported model. *Journal of Neurophysiology 81*, 1355–1364.

Vroomen, J., Bertelson, P., & De Gelder, B. (2001). The ventriloquist effect does not depend on the direction of automatic visual attention. *Perception & Psychophysics, 63*, 651–659.

Weiss, Y., Simoncelli, E. P., & Adelson, E. H. (2002). Motion illusions as optimal percepts. *Nature Neuroscience, 5*, 598–604.

Welch, R. B. (1978). *Perceptual modification: Adapting to altered sensory environments.* New York: Academic Press.

Yuille, A. L., & Bülthoff, H. H. (1996). Bayesian theory and psychophysics. In D. Knill & W. Richards (Eds.), *Perception as Bayesian inference* (pp. 123–161).Cambridge: Cambridge University Press.

SECTION II

Body Representations

7

Body-Based Views
of the World
An Introduction to Body Representations

Maggie Shiffrar

1. Introduction

The goal of this section is to introduce research findings and conclusions regarding the interface between the perception of one's own body and the perception of other people's bodies. The unifying concept that makes this interface possible is the body schema. Although body representations are discussed thoroughly in the chapters that follow, we can begin with a general definition of the *body schema* as an internal, multimodal representation of the relative locations of an individual's own body parts. As the following chapters make clear, there is no single body representation. Instead, individuals have multiple body representations that serve different systems and goals (see chapters 8 and 11).

As the first two chapters in this section demonstrate, body representations assist individuals in the organization and perception of information from their own bodies. Additionally, the last two chapters in this section demonstrate that body representations assist individuals in their perceptions of other people's bodies. Thus, this section is organized so as to reflect the functional duality of body representations.

One of the most compelling early pieces of evidence that individuals use their own body schema to interpret the actions of others comes from Reed and Farah (1995). In this study, participants were asked to view and to compare two sequentially presented postures of another person. Participants were also asked to move their limbs while performing the comparative task. Performance in the perceptual memory task was found to depend upon participant movement. Specifically, when participants moved their arms, their memory for other people's arm postures selectively improved. When participants moved their legs, their memory for other people's leg postures selectively improved. Importantly, participant movement had no impact on memory for the positions of inanimate control figures. Thus, what we do with our own bodies selectively impacts how we perceive and remember the bodies of others. More recent findings indicate that this effect extends to other perceptual-motor comparisons (e.g., Jacobs & Shiffrar, 2004) and is bidirectional in that what we see also influences how we move (see chapter 19).

The psychological implications of this bodily convergence of self-other analyses are profound and extensive. An example of this can be found in the recent political scandal of prisoner abuse at the Abu Gharib prison in Iraq. Numerous internal and external reports suggest that although written descriptions of prisoner abuse had been in circulation for several months, officials did not recognize their severity or significance until photographs of those abuses were made available. Independent of the surrounding political issues, the existence of such a phenomenon still leaves us with a core question. Why is it that written descriptions of bodily abuse do not carry the same psychological punch as visual depictions? This question can be understood through the findings discussed in this section. If observers automatically map the perceived bodily information from other people onto their own body representations, as suggested by a number of the findings in this section, then their psychological connections with other people become inherently embodied. It follows that seeing photographs of other people being physically hurt and humiliated automatically taps related physical experiences of bodily pain and suffering in the observer (Carr et al., 2003; cf. Singer et al., 2004). As a result, pictures of other people's bodies give rise to physical and empathic responses in a way that no text can produce. As the following chapters demonstrate, we're just not built to relate to words in the same way that we relate to images of people. Instead, we experience the world through our own bodies.

2. Representing One's Own Physical Body

In the first chapter in this section, "Body Mereology," de Vignemont, Tsakiris, and Haggard tackle three core questions concerning the perception of one's own body. First, how are parts of the body related to one another and to the body as a whole? Second, how is the variety of sensory and motor cues integrated in the formation of multimodal body representations? Lastly, how do we come to understand stimuli as pieces of our own body?

As de Vignemont and his colleagues discuss, body mereology refers to the relations between one part of the body and another and between one part and the body as a whole. Their approach to this issue focuses on how individuals experience their own bodies. That is, how do I come to experience my right hand as such? Their analysis suggests that body parts are defined at a functional, cognitive level. Since actions structure the organization and segmentation of the body into functional units, body mereology differs profoundly from object mereology.

Such uniqueness of the human body is a thread that runs through many of the chapters in this book, including those by Wilson and by Reed and her colleagues. Since successful action requires input from both the motor and sensory systems (e.g., Cole, 1995), de Vignemont and his colleagues suggest that representations of the body depend upon action-defined interactions between different body parts and between different sensory and motor modalities. Furthermore, the existence of multiple simultaneous representations of the body is supported by the finding that body parts are related to one another in qualitatively different ways. Specifically, in somatosensory mereology, the parts of the body are organized as an undifferentiated tactile sheet. In motor mereology, the body is segmented at the joints. Both mereologies coexist.

Such conclusions imply that body parts cannot be represented or understood in isolation. Support for this premise comes from these authors' discussion of phantom sensations. A *phantom limb* refers to the felt experience of an absent limb. Theories of limb and whole body phantoms are discussed in Brugger's chapter. In the de Vignemont et al. chapter, the phenomena of phantom sensations and personal neglect are used to emphasize the point that the organization of bodily representations is an inherently dynamic process that takes the whole body into account.

The flip side of missing body parts is adding body parts. While the experience of extra, or supernumerary, limbs is rare, studies of everyday tool use suggest that brain mechanisms can readily incorporate new elements into body representations. This important issue is addressed further in chapters 4 and 5 and provides additional support for the flexible nature of body representations.

Having established the plastic nature of body representations, de Vignemont and his colleagues turn to the rubber-hand illusion to examine the multimodal nature of body representations. In any task that requires a fusion of sensory information from different modalities, a critical issue is how that information is combined. Fusion is especially tricky when different sources of information have differing degrees of reliability. The rubber-hand illusion, first studied by Botvinick and Cohen (1998), is used as a test for the comparison of visual, tactile, and proprioceptive inputs to body representations. Briefly, to produce this illusion, a rubber hand is placed next to an individual's unseen real hand. When the rubber hand is in the same orientation as the individual's unseen hand, and both hands are touched simultaneously, a participant will often report that the rubber hand feels as if it is his own hand. Such a phenomenon suggests that vision, namely, seeing the fake hand, can capture or control the interpretation of tactile and proprioceptive information. Yet, bodily experience cannot be reduced to the sum of its inputs. Indeed, de Vignemont and colleagues describe recent results supporting the premise that body representations serve as top-down modulators that shape coherent bodily interpretations from disparate sensory inputs.

3. Representing a Phantom Body

The complexity of body representations is further elaborated in Brugger's chapter on phantom sensations. As Brugger explains, for many years, scientists did not take seriously reports of phantom sensations, that is, the experience of feeling body parts that do not exist. Early studies often interpreted phantom experiences in terms of religious or ghostly causes. However, advances in brain imaging and behavioral techniques have created a renaissance in the scientific study of phantom sensations. The majority of this research has focused on the experience of phantom limbs following limb amputation. This work has had a significant impact on fundamental neuroscientific tenets concerning the extent of cortical plasticity and the flexibility of body representations.

Brugger's chapter also challenges the idea that body awareness can be understood as an all-or-nothing phenomenon. For example, approximately half of the individuals with phantom limbs experience something known as *obstacle shunning*. This phenomenon refers to a decreased awareness of one's phantom when that phantom limb occupies the same space as a physical object. To prevent such experiences, some individuals report moving their phantom limbs to avoid colliding with physical objects. Such reports suggest that constraints on the movement of physical limbs somehow spill over to the experience of phantom limbs. Furthermore, it suggests that bodily awareness varies significantly across individuals and across conditions. For example, Brugger explains that individuals experiencing an extra limb following brain damage often describe their phantoms as real. Conversely, individuals experiencing a phantom after limb loss describe their phantoms as felt illusions.

For some time, the experience of phantom sensations was understood as reflecting a bodily memory for a now-missing limb (e.g., Ramachandran & Hirstein, 1998). Brugger points out that such conclusions ignore the existence of phantoms that do not follow amputation, such as the experience of phantom limbs in individuals born without the corresponding physical limbs. Obviously, phantom sensations in these individuals cannot be ascribed to changes in body structure. Instead, phantoms must originate from more-complex interactions between physical bodies and their representations.

Indeed, Brugger et al.'s (2000) article in the *Proceedings of the National Academy of Sciences* goes a long way in describing the neural mechanisms associated with phantoms of congenitally absent limbs and thus in challenging earlier theories of phantom sensation. In an extensive case study, Brugger and his colleagues conducted behavioral and imaging studies with A. Z., a woman born without forearms and legs but who experienced vivid phantoms of these never-present limbs. In one study, they replicated Parsons's (1987) mental imagery task in which participants are asked to report whether a depicted hand or foot corresponds to the left or right half of the body. Reaction time data with body parts and with objects differ systematically (Parsons, 1987). This difference has been attributed to motor system activation during body, but not object, perception (Parsons et al., 1995). Specifically, Parsons and his colleagues suggested that (normally bodied) individuals performed the mental rotation task with hand stimuli by mentally modeling a reach. Brugger and his colleagues asked whether A. Z. might spontaneously perform such a mental reach with her phantom hands. If so, A. Z. should produce a pattern of reaction time data similar to that produced by subjects with physical hands. Conversely (dare we say, on the other hand), since A. Z. had no motor experience reaching with physical hands, she might perform mental imagery tasks with hand stimuli in the same way that normally handed individuals perform mental imagery with objects. The results indicated that A. Z.'s reaction time data followed the same pattern as those from normally handed individuals. Brain-imaging results provided further support for the idea that A. Z. used some of the same neural machinery to move and perceive her phantom limbs as normally developed individuals use to move and imagine their physical limbs. Such results suggest that body representations have an innate component and/or that visual experience of other people's intact bodies is sufficient for the development of at least some aspects of whole body representations.

Brugger's article then turns to the issue of whole body phantoms, that is, the perception of a complete other at a nearby spatial location or the perception of oneself from an out-of-body perspective. It is posited that the perception of an additional self or another person might result from errors in the localization of representations of postural and kinesthetic information. Out-of-body experiences are understood as a breakdown of the integration of proprioceptive, tactile, and visual inputs from one's own body with simultaneous difficulties in the differentiation of personal and extrapersonal space.

Such an approach to the understanding of whole body phantoms suggests that individuals may use their own body representations to create some understanding of other people. In clinical cases, such outward projection of bodily information can cause major life disturbances, such as the young man who jumped out of a window, risking death, in an attempt to rid himself of his perceived body double (Brugger et al., 1994). However, as Brugger notes, under normal conditions, the outward focus of some components of one's own body schema can have faciliatory, prosocial consequences. This idea is extended in the subsequent chapter by Wilson.

4. Representing Other People's Bodies

Previous chapters have outlined the reasons that body representations can be understood as organizers of motor and sensory information from an individual's own body. Wilson's chapter on covert imitation turns our focus away from the internal self and onto the outside social world. The crux of her argument is that individuals use their own body representations to predict, understand, and imitate the actions of other people.

Wilson describes and interconnects significant evidence from a variety of laboratories that supports the hypothesis that imitable stimuli hold a special status in perceptual analyses. Across a number of distinct domains, individuals have been found to imitate the actions, both subtle and obvious, of other people. This imitation appears to be largely unconscious and spontaneous. When we see someone smile, we can't help but smile a bit ourselves (e.g., Wallbott, 1991). Similarly, as the aforementioned example of the Abu Gharib prison scandal suggests, when we see another person in pain, we feel our own pain (Carr et al., 2003). Thus, Wilson concludes that the presentation of imitable stimuli is associated with activation of the observer's own action-planning and body-representation mechanisms. This conclusion is supported by the findings of researchers of mirror neurons, that is, neurons selectively responsive to the observation and production of the same goal-oriented action. Furthermore, human-imaging data indicate that when observers perceive a movement trajectory that they are physically capable of imitating, activation of body-representation and action-planning centers results. Conversely, when observers perceive human movement trajectories that they cannot imitate, no such activation is found (Stevens et al., 2000). These findings support Wilson's argument that perception of truly imitative actions is indeed associated with activation of the observer's own body representation. Nonetheless, Wilson points out that spontaneous imitation is not always in the observer's best interest. Consistent with this, activity in the neural connections between what we see and what we do can be modulated by our conscious intentions (Decety et al., 1997).

Wilson outlines a number of the potential advantages of such attunement to imitative stimuli. First, it can be used to increase perceptual sensitivity to the actions of others. Indeed, if motoric and body schema mechanisms are able to send disambiguating information to visual processes during the analysis of imitable action, but not or less so during the analysis of non-imitable action, then the perceptual analysis of other people's actions should be selectively enriched. Numerous studies support this conclusion. For example, when stimulus identification requires the integration of visual motion information over space and time, perception of imitable human actions is significantly enhanced relative to perception of comparable nonhuman objects in motion and of non-imitable human actions (Shiffrar, Lichtey, & Heptulla Chatterjee,

1997; Shiffrar & Pinto, 2002). Consistent with Wilson's premise, when observers are asked to interpret point-light displays of humans and animals (see chapter 13), recognition performance with human stimuli is much greater than with animal stimuli (Jacobs, Chouchourelou, & Shiffrar, 2005). Furthermore, motor abilities impact perceptual abilities since athletes are more accurate than nonathletes in their percepts of point-light displays of physically challenging actions (Jacobs et al., 2005). Thus, individual differences in the types of actions that observers can imitate are tightly associated with individual variations in action perception. Lastly, out of all possible stimuli, one's own actions are most imitable. It follows from Wilson's argument that observers should therefore demonstrate the greatest perceptual sensitivity to their own actions. Wilson reviews a number of studies that suggest just that. For example, Knoblich and his colleagues (e.g., Knoblich & Flach, 2001) have shown that observers are better able to predict the outcomes of their own actions than the outcomes of other people's actions. Furthermore, Loula and her colleagues (2004) reported that observers demonstrate greater visual sensitivity to their own actions than to the actions of their friends or those of strangers. Thus, Wilson builds a solid foundation for the thesis that the perception of other people is based upon the embodied self.

Wilson then elaborates on the theme of perceptual emulation of imitable stimuli as a means to better anticipate the future actions of other people, such as their next step (Verfaillie, De Troy, & Van Rensbergen, 1994). Wilson focuses her argument on conversational turn taking. Speakers demonstrate exquisitely timed coordination in their conversational turn taking. Conversations usually flow smoothly between speakers without noticeable pauses or regular switching intervals. Since no temporal gaps consistently separate one person's speech from another's, listeners must somehow prepare to speak before the current speaker has finished. How could this happen? Wilson describes how a listener's ability to anticipate the behavior of a speaker could solve this dilemma. That is, a listener's own motor-planning system may play a key role in her ability to converse interactively. Again, such an ability to generalize from current to future actions only holds true for physically possible, and hence imitable, future actions (Kourtzi & Shiffrar, 1999).

5. Defining Other People's Bodies

In the final chapter of this section, Reed, Stone, and McGoldrick examine the central question of what defines a body as human. Previous studies have addressed this issue by comparing perception of the human body with perception of inanimate objects (e.g., Shiffrar et al., 1997). Such comparisons, while a sensible starting place, leave numerous factors uncontrolled. Human bodies and inanimate objects differ along a wide variety of dimensions, including shape, intentionality, and musculature, that might ultimately define performance differences in psychophysical tasks involving bodies and objects.

To overcome such pitfalls, Reed and her colleagues begin with an analysis of face-perception research. It is an odd fact that face-perception research and body-perception research are largely conducted in parallel as if faces and bodies are not attached. Providing a much needed remedy to this disconnect, Reed and colleagues provide an overview of the features and processes underlying face perception. These include the argument that specific brain mechanisms, such as the fusiform face area in the ventral temporal cortex, are involved in the perception of faces (Kanwisher, 2000). Furthermore, face perception can be selectively or disproportionately disrupted as a result of brain damage and stimulus manipulation. Lastly, human observers individuate faces and objects at different categorical levels. Taken together, such a convergence of findings suggests that the visual perception of faces differs significantly from the visual perception of objects.

The next step in the argument by Reed and colleagues is to look for similarities and differences between face perception and body perception. Like faces, identifiable neural mechanisms are thought to contribute selectively to the visual analysis of bodies (see chapter 16). Again, as with faces, body perception can be selectively disrupted with certain types of brain damage and through a variety of stimulus manipulations. Thus, bodies and faces are perceived in analogous ways.

Previous researchers have argued that the perception of faces depends upon holistic or configural processes. Reed and her colleagues illustrate how "configural processing" can be defined in different ways and how the use of different definitions can significantly alter one's conclusions. A critical factor in our understanding of configural processes is stimulus orientation. Upright and inverted faces are analyzed differently because inversion appears to disrupt both metric and configural analyses of facial parts.

To identify further the similarities and differences between face perception and body perception, these authors describe recent evidence that upright and inverted body postures are perceived differently, as opposed to upright and inverted houses (Reed, Stone, Bozova, & Tanaka, 2003). Furthermore, this inversion effect is found only for whole-body analyses and not for analyses of individual body parts or scrambled body parts (Reed, Stone, Grubb, & McGoldrick, 2004), and it extends to analyses of moving bodies (Pinto & Shiffrar, 1999). Lastly, under some conditions, faces and bodies are perceived differently and are differentially affected by various masks, suggesting that the perception of faces and bodies involves both overlapping and distinct processes.

But where does such configural processing come from? Reed and her colleagues examine two possibilities. The first is that configural processing arises from visual expertise. If you have sufficient experience in viewing a particular class of object (e.g., dogs), your perceptual analysis eventually shifts from parts-based to configural (e.g., Tanaka & Gauthier, 1997). The second possibility is that *embodiment*, that is, the motor, proprioceptive, and kinesthetic experiences associated with living in a body and face, gives rise to configural processing of faces and bodies. Reed and colleagues conducted a test of these two explanations in which subjects judged familiar and rare postures of people and dogs (see Figure 11.6). Their results support the importance of embodiment in the development of configural processes. Reed and colleagues conclude their chapter by positing that configural processing ultimately arises from observers using their own body representations to interpret the visual world. This conclusion meshes well with that of Wilson's chapter in that perceptual analyses are thought to involve a kind of projection of the observer's own bodily representation.

In sum, the results and ideas discussed in these chapters form a strong perspective on how people see their world. To the extent that features of perceived stimuli resemble information contained within the observer's own bodily representations, perceptual processes shift. In this shift, perceptual processes increasingly incorporate additional sources of information about the human body in general and the observer's own body in specific. By projecting information from our own bodies into the perceived world, we become more socially attuned beings. Indeed, the developmental research findings of Meltzoff and Moore (e.g., 2002) and others suggest that we come into this world ready and able to perform such egocentric body matching. When taken together, the research discussed in this section suggests that we can be understood as embodied beings optimized for the organization and analysis of like-me information. The end result of this perceptual-motor system is a body-based view of the world.

References

Botvinick, M., & Cohen, J. (1998). Rubber hands "feel" touch that eyes see. *Nature, 391,* 756.

Brugger, P., Agosti, R., Regard, M., Wieser, H.-G., & Landis, T. (1994). Heautoscopy, epilepsy and suicide. *Journal of Neurology, Neurosurgery, and Psychiatry, 57,* 838–839.

Brugger, P., Kollias, S. S., Müri, R. M., Crelier, G., Hepp-Reymond, M. C., & Regard, M. (2000). Beyond re-membering: Phantom sensations of congenitally absent limbs. *Proceedings of the National Academy of Sciences, USA, 97,* 6167–6172.

Carr, L., Iacoboni, M., Dubeau, M. C., Mazziotta, J. C., & Lenzi, G. L. (2003). Neural mechanisms of empathy in humans: A relay from neural systems for imitation to limbic areas. *Proceedings of the National Academy of Sciences, USA, 100,* 5497–5502.

Cole, J. (1995). *Pride and a daily marathon.* Cambridge, MA: MIT Press.

Decety, J., Grezes, J., Costes, N., Perani, D., Jeannerod, M., Procyk, E., Grassi, F., & Fazio, F. (1997). Brain activity during observation of actions: Influence of action content and subject's strategy. *Brain, 120,* 1763–1777.

Jacobs, A., Chouchourelou, A., & Shiffrar, M. (2005). Is it "biological" motion? Manuscript under review.

Jacobs, A., Pinto, J., & Shiffrar, M. (2004). Frequency, context, and the visual perception of human movement, *Journal of Experimental Psychology: Human Perception & Performance, 30*, 822–835.

Jacobs, A., & Shiffrar, M. (2005). Walking perception by walking observers. *Journal of Experimental Psychology: Human Perception & Performance, 31*, 157–169.

Kanwisher, N. (2000). Domain specificity in face perception. *Nature Neuroscience, 3*, 759–763.

Knoblich, G., & Flach, R. (2001). Predicting the effects of actions: Interactions of perception and action. *Psychological Science, 12*, 467–472.

Kourtzi, Z., & Shiffrar, M. (1999). Dynamic representations of human body movement. *Perception, 28*, 49–62.

Loula, F., Prasad, S., Harber, K., & Shiffrar, M. (2005). Recognizing people from their movements. *Journal of Experimental Psychology: Human Perception & Performance, 31*, 210–220.

Meltzoff, A. N., & Moore, M. K. (2002). Imitation, memory, and the representation of persons. *Infant Behavior & Development, 25*, 39–61.

Parsons, L. M. (1987). Imagined spatial transformation of one's body. *Journal of Experimental Psychology: General, 116*, 172–191.

Parsons, L. M., Fox, P. T., Downs, J. H., Glass, T., Hirsch, T. B., Martin, C. C., Jerabek, P. A., & Lancaster, J. L. (1995). Use of implicit motor imagery for visual shape discrimination as revealed by PET. *Nature, 375*, 54–58.

Pinto, J., & Shiffrar, M. (1999). Subconfigurations of the human form in the perception of biological motion displays. *Acta Psychologica: Special Issue on Object Perception & Memory, 102*, 293–318.

Ramachandran, V. S., & Hirstein, W. (1998). The perception of phantom limbs. *Brain, 121*, 1603–1630.

Reed, C. L., & Farah, M. J. (1995). The psychological reality of the body schema: A test with normal participants. *Journal of Experimental Psychology: Human Perception and Performance, 21*, 334–343.

Reed, C. L., Stone, V., Bozova, S., & Tanaka, J. (2003). The body inversion effect. *Psychological Science, 14*, 302–308.

Reed, C. L., Stone, V. E., Grubb, J., & McGoldrick, J. E. (2004). Turning configural processing upside down: Part- and whole body postures. Manuscript in preparation.

Shiffrar, M., Lichtey, L., & Heptulla Chatterjee, S. (1997). The perception of biological motion cross apertures. *Perception & Psychophysics, 59*, 51–59.

Shiffrar, M., & Pinto, J. (2002). The visual analysis of bodily motion. In W. Prinz & B. Hommel (Eds.), *Common mechanisms in perception and action: Attention and Performance, Vol. 19* (pp. 381–399). Oxford: Oxford University Press.

Singer, T., Seymour, B., O'Doherty, J., Kaube, H., Dolan, R., & Frith, R. J. (2004). Empathy for pain involves the affective but not sensory components of pain. *Science, 303*, 1157–1162.

Stevens, J. A., Fonlupt, P., Shiffrar, M., & Decety, J. (2000). New aspects of motion perception: Selective neural encoding of apparent human movements. *Neuroreport, 11*, 109–115.

Tanaka, J. W., & Gauthier, I. (1997). Expertise in object and face recognition. In R. L. Goldstone, P. G. Schyns, & D. L. Medin (Eds.), *Psychology of learning and motivation series. Vol. 36: Perceptual mechanisms of learning* (pp. 83–125). San Diego, CA: Academic Press.

Verfaillie, K., De Troy, A., & Van Rensbergen, J. (1994). Transsaccadic integration of biological motion. *Journal of Experimental Psychology: Learning, Memory, & Cognition, 20*, 649–670.

Wallbott, H. G. (1991). Recognition of emotion from facial expression via imitation? Some indirect evidence for an old theory. *British Journal of Social Psychology, 30*, 207–219.

8

Body Mereology

Frederique de Vignemont
Manos Tsakiris
Patrick Haggard

Introduction: Parts, Body, and the Self

The body is made up of parts. This basic assumption is central in most neuroscientific studies of bodily sensation, body representation, and motor action. Yet, the assumption has rarely been considered explicitly. We may indeed ask how the body is internally segmented and how body parts can be defined. That is, how can we sketch the mereology of the body? *Mereology* (from the Greek *meros*, meaning "part") is the theory of parthood relations, of the relations of part to whole and the relations of part to part within a whole. Traditionally, it addresses the metaphysical question of the relation between constitution and identity: is the sameness of parts *necessary* for identity? One of the most famous examples is the story of the cat Tibbles, who loses his tail. If a cat survives the annihilation of its tail, then the cat *with* tail (before the accident) and the cat *without* tail (after the accident) are numerically the same in spite of their having different proper parts (Wiggins, 1980). Therefore, the cat cannot be identified to the corresponding amount of feline tissue, even if it is constituted by it. As Wiggins (1968, p. 90) said, "No man is the same as his forearm."

In this chapter, we will not raise the metaphysical issue of personal identity, even if, as with Tibbles, we will mention the possibility of deletion of body parts. Rather, we are interested in the epistemological and phenomenological dimensions of the mereology of the body. Is somesthetic experience linked to body parts, or to the body as a whole? How are those parts to be described, and how do they relate to each other? Can the way I experience my body as a whole be reduced to the way I feel each of my body parts?

The body that we experience cannot be fully reduced to a bundle of tissues and organs. As Merleau-Ponty (1945) noticed, the body is an object that never leaves us. While we can perceive an object from different perspectives or cease

147

to perceive it, we experience "the feeling of the same old body always there" (James, 1890, p. 242). The amount of information received on one's own body is quantitatively superior to what one can receive from any external object: not only can one see or touch one's own body, one also always receives a continuous flow of proprioceptive and somesthetic inputs. The embodied self is thus constructed from sensory inputs, but still cannot be reduced to the representation of coextended limbs. In addition to simply pooling information from different senses, body representations also synthesize the various signals into an integrated meaningful experience by establishing consistent relationships between body parts and the whole.

The simplest scientific approach to bodily experience is a reductive one. We begin by assuming that the phenomenology of the perceiving and acting body is not a primitive fact, but can be analyzed. We approach this analysis by considering how the phenomenology of the body can be broken down into a phenomenology of body parts. This approach allows us to investigate the "embodied self" by reviewing how recent experimental data address three intimately related questions about body mereology: (1) What is the relation between the body parts and the body as a whole? (2) How are the various sources of information from different body parts combined to form a coherent body representation? (3) What is the relation between the body and the self?

1. The Mereological Organization of the Body

We can perform actions without having first to direct attention to the position of our limbs. One might therefore assume that the continuous flow of information about our body that we use in action is always present to consciousness: we would always be aware of the body in all its details (O'Shaughnessy, 1980). However, many experiments have shown that actions are often performed outside the conscious field (Jeannerod, 1997) and do not require conscious representation of body position. For instance, Castiello, Paulignan, and Jeannerod (1991) showed that an unexpected target jump becomes available to consciousness 200 ms after the sensorimotor adjustment. It has also been demonstrated that we tend to adhere to the goal and not to the way it has been achieved (Fourneret & Jeannerod, 1998). In fact, it seems that the body remains most of the time at the margin of consciousness as an undifferentiated whole (Gurwitsch, 1985; O'Shaughnessy, 1995).

On the other hand, we can also allocate specific attention to one part of the body, either voluntarily or because we are attracted by the saliency of a bodily sensation. Itches, pains, and other bodily sensations can seem very focal indeed, popping out compellingly from the background experience of the body. This focality suggests that the localization of bodily sensations shows special characteristics. Bodily sensations appear to be encoded in a specialized somatotopic frame of reference, which we call *body space*. Body space is characterized by the fact that it is quite distinct from external spatial locations. Body space can be interpreted as the mental map of the spatial disposition of body parts and of the relationship between the various parts of the body and the whole. It has to be distinguished from external objective space: a painful body part can move relatively to the external spatial framework without the pain itself moving within the body space. For instance, the pain in my thumb is not felt in my mouth just because my thumb is in my mouth (Block, 1983).

Merleau-Ponty (1945, p. 98) notices, "The outline of my body is a frontier which ordinary spatial relations do not cross." Consequently, we can ask about its internal mereological organization: how is the body segmented into parts?

1.1. Differentiation of Body Parts

One of the main problems of mereology is to define the relevant parts of the object. We single out the handle of the cup as a proper part because of its functional role, but we could as well decide to isolate another part on purely spatial criteria such as the base of the cup. The same problem thus arises for the body: how to differentiate the relevant body parts? Representations of the body can be segmented at different levels: sensorimotor, visuospatial, and semantic (Sirigu et al., 1991). We suggest that body parts could be analyzed in either of two different ways: through qualitative topology and quantitative geometry. *Topology* means differentiating the whole body into categorically distinct parts (e.g., arm, finger). *Geometry* means differentiating the body into zones with metric properties such as extent. In this section, we begin by showing that topological mereology of the body differs according to whether sensory or motor aspects of the body are considered. We next consider the mental representation of geometric relations among body parts.

1.1.1. Somatosensory Mereology

The body surface may be viewed as an undifferentiated tactile sheet, without categorical divisions corresponding to anatomical body parts. The connectivity between neurons in the cerebral cortex is responsible for imposing an ordered structure on this undifferentiated sheet. The different adjacent regions of the tactile sheet compete with each other to "own" cortical representation, by an ongoing process of lateral inhibition between cortical neurons, limiting the spread of excitation among adjacent neurons, thereby functionally isolating cells that are anatomically near each other. A structured map arises because specific patterns of lateral inhibition emerge during sensory experience. Indeed, primary somatosensory representations do generally follow the natural anatomical divisions of body parts, having receptive fields confined to single fingers or limbs (Blankenburg et al., 2003; Penfield & Rasmussen, 1950). Penfield and Boldrey (1937) described the somatotopical organization of SI, which associates cortical areas to a part of the body surface, resulting in the metaphor of a "homunculus." However, this body part–based organization does not imply that the body is naturally differentiated into categorical parts at the level of primary representation. The structure of the homunculus is not a necessary property of the network wiring, but the result of plastic changes in tactile input altering the inhibitory competition between neurons. Differentiation into distinct body parts at the primary somatosensory level may be a reflection of how our bodies have been used, rather than a natural unit of neural representation.

It is only at a more cognitive level that the body space is properly differentiated into distinct body parts. The criteria of such differentiation are not fixed and may vary according to the function of the body representation. Again, the brain's differentiation of somatosensory input into body-part categories is not innate, but may reflect the pattern of sensory inputs generated by our interactions with the environment. Mereological organization of the body representation should thus be influenced by tactile experience. Indeed, paired associative stimulation of adjacent digits produces confusions between the trained digits in identification tasks (Braun et al., 2000) and an increasing overlap between their cortical representations (Schweizer et al., 2001). Neuropsychological conditions, such as finger agnosia, suggest that poor differentiation of adjacent body parts can occur at a more cognitive level without deficit in primary sensation. For example, Kinsbourne and Warrington (1962) suggested that the ring and middle digits lose their separate identities in finger agnosia. Their representations become functionally fused. A similar line of argument may explain the errors made by autotopagnosic patients in pointing to body parts (Ogden, 1985; Sirigu et al., 1991). Patients may point either toward the contiguous body part (the wrist, rather than the hand) or to the contralateral body part (right hand rather than left hand) (Semenza, 1988).

We suggest that differentiation of the body into parts may reflect a competitive process of mutual inhibition occurring at the cognitive level of body representation. This could, for example, be a more abstract version of the competitive inhibition process between receptive fields known to exist in primary somatosensory representation. Nevertheless, this differentiation does not preclude, but rather highlights, the mutual relationship between parts that constitutes the body as a whole. Studies show indeed that the overall spatial configuration between the limbs plays a central role in body representation. The inversion of body parts affects the recognition of the body, while it does not influence the recognition of physical objects (see chapter 11). Interestingly, the inversion effect can be elicited only if the biomechanical posture is motorically possible (Reed et al., 2003). This result points out the importance of a motor representation of the body.

1.1.2. Motor Mereology

Any object may be broken down into its constituent parts based on spatial information. However, our own body is a unique object because we can move it voluntarily. Therefore, body mereology may differ from other objects because our voluntary actions may provide an organizing principle for segmenting the body into parts. Interestingly, a motor mereology begins with a different spatial object from a somatosensory mereology. We have already described the so-matosensory body surface as an undifferentiated sheet. In contrast, the starting point of motor mereology would be the set of muscles that one can voluntarily move. This is a group of different objects, rather than a continuous sensory organ. Furthermore, intentional actions impose an additional functional orga-nization because of the sets of body parts that work together in intentional movements. For example, when I move my forearm, my hand and fingers follow. In contrast, if someone touches my forearm, this usually does not tell me anything about the sensation in my hand and fingers. Accordingly, the repre-sentations in the primary somatosensory cortex (SI) and primary motor cortex (MI) have quite different organizing principles. Although both have compa-rable gross somatotopy, fine somatotopy differs sharply between the two areas. While the receptive field of each neuron of SI corresponds to a small well-defined part of the cutaneous surface (Blankenburg et al., 2003), MI represen-tations of the different body parts strongly overlap. MI seems to be organized for representing muscle groups and patterns of movement rather than individual muscles (Lemon, 1988). Furthermore, accumulating evidence suggests that somatotopical organization in SI allows for additive activation, such that the corresponding cortical volume of the movement of three fingers is the sum of the volumes for the individual fingers moved alone (Hlustik et al., 2001). This does not seem to be the case in MI, "where the 'sum of the parts' is qualitatively different than the sum found for SI. . . . MI and SI share a common somatotopic principle but the somatotopy in SI is more discrete and segregated, in contrast to the more integrated and overlapping somatotopy in MI" (Hlustik et al., 2001, p. 319).

The pattern of activation in MI suggests that the control of any finger movement recruits a population of neurons distributed throughout MI, rather than a segregated population that would map point-to-point distinct move-ments based on a somatotopic organization (Schieber & Hibbard, 1993).

A more conceptual way of thinking about body representation may suggest that action plays an important role in imposing categorical structure on body space. In particular, we act around our joints, and these become body-part boundaries. While there seem to be no specific natural boundaries for the somatosensory body, we may suggest that the joints constitute the landmarks for segmenting the acting body:

Individual body parts are paradigmatically identified in terms of hinges. The forearm, for example, is the volume between the elbow and the wrist.... Using hinges provides a nonarbitrary way of segmenting the body that accords pretty closely with how we classify body parts in everyday thought and speech. (Bermudez, 1998, p. 156)

The topological mereology of the body seems immediately present even in primary representations for action, while in the somatosensory system, mereology seems to emerge only at a more cognitive level.

1.1.3. The Size of Body Parts

Body mereology has qualitative and quantitative aspects. While *body topology* concerns the boundaries between body parts, *body geometry* refers to metric

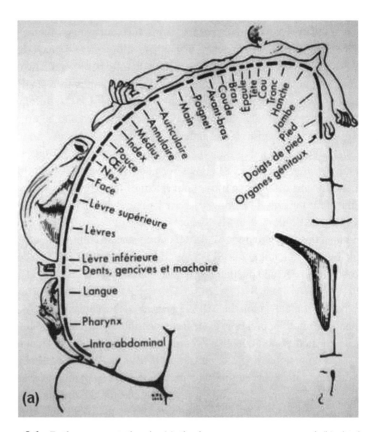

Figure 8.1. Body representation in (a) the human motor cortex and (b) the human somatosensory cortex. Adapted from Penfield and Rasmussen, 1950. Used with the permission of the Gale Group.

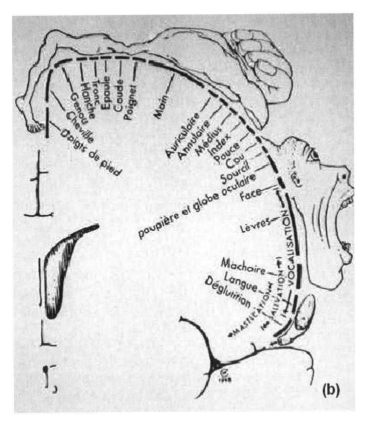

Figure 8.1. Continued.

relations, such as the relative size of body parts. Information about body-part size is essential for planning and control of action; for example, if I want to switch on the light, I need to know the length of my arm in order to decide whether I can reach the switch without getting up from my chair. The afferent somatosensory and proprioceptive systems do not provide any direct information about body-part size. Moreover, the body maps in the primary somatosensory cortex are highly distorted: physically small areas of skin, such as the fingertips, have much larger cortical territories than do large body parts, such as the upper arm or back. Several studies suggest that the perceived size of body parts reflects mutual interactions between these underlying neural representations.

First, Gandevia and Phegan (1999) suggested that the perceived size of body parts may be modulated by afferent inputs. These authors asked subjects to draw their lips and thumb at their currently perceived sizes, while either of these body parts was temporarily anesthetized. The lip and the thumb were chosen because they are represented in a common region of the primary somatosensory cortex. Anesthesia increased the perceived size of the anesthetized body part and had a similar but smaller effect on the other, nonanesthetized part. The transfer from the anesthetized to the nonanesthetized part was attributed to the shared cortical representation of the hand and face. This result suggests that the cognitive representation of the body is driven by integration over regions of the primary cortical map.

Taylor-Clarke et al. (2004) investigated how the tactile perception of a stimulus depends on the body part that is touched. Subjects compared the distance between two points touched on the index finger with a second distance presented on the forearm. Subjects perceived tactile distances on the finger as larger than identical distances on the forearm, presumably due to the relative imbalance of the cortical territories of these body parts. However, this effect was significantly reduced after subjects merely *viewed* a distorted image of their bodies in which the hands were reduced and shown at the end of enlarged forearms. A visual representation of the volumetric size of body parts provided the spatial information required to interpret tactile stimuli. This result suggests that the neural representation of tactile information local to each body part depends on an internal body model in which the size of each part is represented. This body model is driven at least partly by vision and defines the mereological composition of the body.

Lackner (1988) showed that the internal body model also receives proprioceptive inputs. He induced illusory perception of the size of body parts by vibrating the tendons of arm muscles. Such vibrations induce illusory arm movements. Subjects were required to grasp their noses during the vibration. Subjects reported that they experienced their noses as elongating by as much as 30 cm. This "Pinocchio illusion" constitutes the solution of a sensorimotor conflict: the vibration gives the illusion of arm extension, but the fact that the hand maintains contact with the nose means that the nose is also moving. Since the head and the body are stationary, the combined sensory input is interpreted as the nose elongating. Body parts are thus represented in their mutual mereological relationship, and the representation of the body cannot be reduced to independent representations of each body part. Therefore, the configuration of the whole body is "inferred" from the various inputs, rather than directly perceived. The body scheme results from the interactions among the different body parts and the different sensory modalities.

Taken together, all of these studies suggest that the geometric mereology of the body is fundamentally a product of multisensory integration. The spatial representation of the body depends on the integration of tactile, proprioceptive, and visual inputs. Vision may play a special structuring role by imposing a metric organization based on bounded body parts on a relatively continuous sensory sheet.

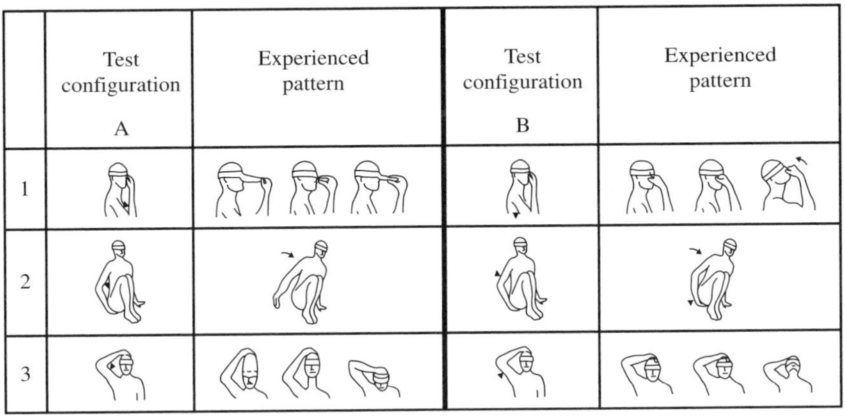

Test configuration A	Experienced pattern	Test configuration B	Experienced pattern
1			
2			
3			

Figure 8.2. The Pinocchio illusion. Experimental configurations and results with (A) biceps brachii vibration and (B) triceps brachii vibration. From Lackner, 1998. Used with the permission of Oxford University Press Journals.

1.2. Addition and Deletion

Illusions of body-part size show that body space does not constitute a complete and accurate display of the body in our mind. Furthermore, the borders of body space do not always coincide with the actual limits of the physical body. Several kinds of neuroscientific data clarify the body concept by describing the neural mechanisms and psychological consequences of deletion and addition of body parts.

1.2.1. Deletion

Amputation provides the most obvious example of body-part physical deletion. It is accompanied by major cortical reorganization giving rise to *phantom* sensations, which feel as though they originate in the absent body part. Thus, light touch on the face area contralateral to the amputation elicits somatotopically mapped sensations on the phantom limb (Ramachandran & Rogers-Ramachandran, 1996). This effect is thought to arise because cortical regions previously representing the amputated body part become responsive to stimuli on the face after amputation, yet the subjective sensation correlated with the neural activity retains the feel of the phantom (Ramachandran & Hirstein, 1998). Studies of rapid reorganization of tactile neurons following amputation in animals suggest that these sensations arise because cortical neurons representing the body receive afferent inputs from several body parts. A process of lateral inhibition between inputs ensures that the neuron responds to a single body region, while the other latent inputs are suppressed. When the body part containing the receptive field of a given neuron is deleted, this inhibitory process becomes imbalanced, and these latent connections are unmasked. Thus, neurons that represented a finger become responsive to stimulation of adjacent body parts, such as the other fingers and palm, within minutes of finger amputation (Merzenich et al., 1984).

Such experiments have clear implications for body mereology, because they show that the differentiation of the whole body into constituent parts reflects a dynamic process of neural competition between representations in the somatosensory system. Differentiation of body parts may be partly innately encoded. Indeed, aplasic patients born with a limb missing still feel the presence of a phantom body part (see chapter 9), implying an innate structured body representation. Interestingly, the phenomenon of phantom limbs can be understood only if we take into account the body as a whole. Indeed, we cannot explain the existence of the phantom limb if we consider it independently from other parts of the body: where can it come from, as there is no sensory information from the absent limb? However, the change induced by amputation is not only local, since the neural representation of other regions of the body reorganizes to invade the relevant area of the cortex. Body parts should thus not be understood in isolation, but always on the background of their relationships with other body parts.

While phantom limbs result from the physical deletion of body parts, personal neglect reflects the mental deletion of body parts. Patients forget the existence of one side of their body or even deny the ownership of one of their limbs. Indeed, somatosensory information does not automatically suffice for feeling a sense of ownership toward the body that one directly perceives. For instance, Bottini et al. (2002) reported the case of F. B., an asomatognosic patient who was unable to report touches delivered on her left hand and who attributed the hand to her niece. The examiner slightly touched one of her hands after warning F. B. that he was going to touch (a) her right hand, (b) her left hand, or (c) her niece's hand. The examiner asked her to report whether she felt a tactile sensation while she was blindfolded. The results showed that she was unable to report any tactile sensation on her "alien" hand in condition (b), but that her tactile anesthesia completely recovered in condition (c). In other words, she could feel the touch only on her so-called niece's hand. Consequently, the mental boundaries of one's own body are not only fixed by proprioceptive inputs, but result rather from more complex phenomena, which we will investigate in the second part of this chapter.

1.2.2. Addition

What would happen to the neural and psychological representation of the body if a body part were added rather than removed? This question at first seems silly. Although body parts change considerably in size and slightly in shape with normal lifespan development and disease, their number, differentiation, and identity do not normally change. However, experimental neuroscience, neurology, and neuropsychiatry all suggest that the brain's mereology of the body is sufficiently plastic to incorporate and subsume new body parts. Here, we briefly review the addition of body elements in somatoparaphrenic delusions involving supernumerary limbs, in tool use, and in anosognosia.

The neurological phenomenon of a *supernumerary limb* can be interpreted in terms of failure to inhibit a mechanism that maintains body space. In one form of this rare condition, the patient reports the presence of an additional arm. The supernumerary arm typically has the correct anatomical parts, though its size may be unusual and change over time. Interestingly, the arm is often experienced as attached to the body at the midline (Boisson & Luaute, 2004). Hari et al. (1998) described a patient with frontal and callosal lesions who experienced ghost supernumerary limbs in the location previously occupied by the left arm or leg. Subsequent fMRI comparisons between periods when the additional limb was and was not experienced showed an increased activity in the supplementary motor area during the delusion (McGonigle et al., 2002). The authors speculated that the delusion arose because the lesion had produced a fractionation between the normally coherent efferent and afferent representations of the body. As a result, the efferent and afferent signals gave rise to two separate bodily percepts, rather than a single integrated whole. These results suggest that a specific neural mechanism maintains a coherent representation of body parts by integrating several sensory and motor inputs. In the next section of this chapter, we describe studies of the rubber-hand illusion in normal subjects, which seems to rely on a similar mechanism.

Tool use is a characteristic feature of many animals and is often taken as a hallmark of intelligence. Several recent studies suggest that neural representations of the body may be altered when using a tool to extend the subject's reaching space (see Maravita & Iriki, 2004; also see chapter 4). Studies of bimodal neurons in the monkey parietal cortex have focused on the spatial relation between visual and tactile receptive fields. Tactile receptive fields on the hand gradually displaced their visual receptive field from an initial position near the hand toward the tip of the tool, as a function of tool learning (Iriki et al., 1996). In human subjects with unilateral lesions, active use of a tool improved the crossmodal links between visual stimuli at the tool tip and tactile events at the hand (Farnè & Làdavas, 2000; Maravita et al., 2002). Mereologically, the tool appears to become a new segment of the limb within the cognitive body representation. Alternatively, the tool may become incorporated into the representation of an existing segment, with an appropriate adjustment to segment length. These neural changes may underlie the anecdotal observation that a person using a tool experiences tactile sensations located at the tool tip.

A recent neuropsychological study reinforces the idea of a specific brain process associated with the addition of elements to body representations. Aglioti et al. (1996) reported the case of a patient who denied ownership of her

Table 8.1 Somatosensory and motor mereology

	Somatosensory Mereology	Motor Mereology
Physical origin	Skin	Muscle and joints
Primary cortical area	SI	MI
Internal structure	Continuous somatotopy	Integrated and overlapping somatotopy
Segmenting principle	No intrinsic segmentation	Action
Landmarks for body segmentation	None	Joints
Structuring principle	Contiguity	Coherence
Organization	Spatial	Functional
Confusion of body parts	Autotopagnosia	Motor neglect
Addition of body parts	Supernumerary limbs	Tool use
Deletion of body parts	Phantom sensations	Phantom movements

left hand following a right-hemisphere lesion. She likewise denied ownership of a ring worn on her left hand. When the same ring was worn on the unaffected right hand, she correctly recognized it as belonging to her. The ring attached to the body was processed in the same way as the hand to which it was attached, by the brain processes responsible for creating a coherent sense of the body. That is, the ring was incorporated into the mental representation of the hand on which it was worn. These data suggest that body representations are flexible and can dynamically include new components under proper conditions, which we will investigate in the next section. Such cases also demonstrate an intriguing link between sensorimotor representation of body parts and the sense of self, which has been discussed elsewhere (Haggard et al., 2003).

In summary, the mental map of the body is characterized both by its internal organization and by its borders. Body mereology addresses two main questions: (1) how do we differentiate the body into parts (segmenting process)? (2) how are the body parts organized (structuring process)? The answers vary according to the somatosensory mereology and the motor mereology.

2. Multisensory Body Mereology

The phenomena of addition and deletion of body parts would remain a mystery if we described the brain as a passive receptor of sensory information. Body representations do not merely reflect peripheral inputs, but are the result of an active process of integration of afferent information (vision, proprioception, and touch) and efferent signals. The consistency among several sources of information provides a strong cue for individuating body parts. More particularly, visual information plays an important role in the addition of body parts. Indeed, somatosensory perception is often quite local and provides little information about the relation between body parts, while vision carries global information about the body as a whole and has the capacity to link together the different body parts. Multisensory integration can thus provide a window into the investigation of bodily synthesis.

In this section, we use a specific example of multisensory integration, the so-called rubber-hand illusion, to illustrate how the mind constructs a synthesis of the body as a whole using sensory inputs from specific body parts. This section therefore emphasizes the importance of the holistic aspect of body representation in the integration of body parts. This corresponds to the key mereological question of how the whole relates to the sum of the parts. We will suggest that body parts are individuated on the basis of multisensory matching. Furthermore, we will distinguish two kinds of mechanisms involved in the self-attribution of body parts: a bottom-up process based on Bayesian correlation and a top-down process based on the synthetic representation of the body as a whole.

2.1. The Body as a "Common Sensible"

The body space is what Aristotle called a *common sensible*, that is, a property represented by different modalities. The multisensory nature of the body has usually been neglected by the philosophical tradition, which has focused more on contrasting the body with other physical objects or with the bodies of other people (Anscombe, 1959; Merleau-Ponty, 1945). The multisensory nature of the body has been considered only to emphasize the private inner knowledge that we have for our own bodies. Internal perception such as nociception and proprioception may even be considered as the primitive core of self-consciousness (Bermudez, 1998). However, this approach ignores the fact that our knowledge of our bodies typically results from the integration of multimodal information.

Several studies show the importance of the interactions among vision, touch, and proprioception (Driver & Spence, 1998). Indeed, visual information alters tactile sensation, and tactile stimulation orients visual attention. The sight of body parts increases temporal and spatial tactile sensitivity: visual information about your hand can reduce tactile target detection time and improve tactile spatial resolution (Kennett et al., 2002). The crossmodal effect can be so strong that vision of the hand being touched may elicit a tactile sensation, even if no real touch occurs (Halligan et al., 1997).

These crossmodal effects may rely on two kinds of neural mechanisms. Electrophysiological studies in the monkey have shown in the premotor and the parietal cortex the existence of bimodal neurons that combine visual and somesthetic signals (Duhamel et al., 1997; Graziano, Cooke, & Taylor, 2000). Furthermore, recent experiments suggest that back projections from multimodal areas to unimodal areas may also play a role (Macaluso, Frith & Driver, 2000; Taylor-Clarke, Kennett, & Haggard, 2002). In brief, hetero-modal areas integrate the different sources of information, but the perceptual consequences of these interactions could be also realized in the so-called unimodal areas (Calvert et al., 1998). Thus, primary areas may be unimodal in terms of their afferent information, yet they may be affected by other kinds of signals.

Therefore, despite the fact that all sensory modalities do not always provide the same representation of the body, we tend to maintain consistency by the resolution of sensory conflicts, and we experience a single unified body representation. How is such integration possible? The main problem is to understand how the relevant elements needed to bind as a single entity are selected and segregated (Treisman, 1998). In other words, how do I avoid combining together proprioceptive information from my own hand and visual information from your hand or even from the table? According to Ramachandran, there is no active binding process. Mere conjunction between sensory inputs is sufficient to integrate any object within the body. However, we will argue from the high consistency of body representations that this is not the case.

In order to be integrated, the different kinds of information have to be considered as being from a common source. Then the question is to understand how this source is individuated. We may draw a parallel with selective attention: what is the nature of the underlying units of attention? Traditional models, such as Posner's, characterize attention in spatial terms: we code one stimulus at a time selected on the basis of its location and by excluding stimuli from other locations. In contrast, recent models emphasize the role of discrete objects: we attend to independent individuals that we can track over time, rather than to spatial regions of the visual field (Scholl, 2001). If we apply the distinction between space-based and object-based attention to the problem of multimodal body representations, we may sketch two hypotheses. According to the first one, it is sufficient to assign a common spatiotemporal source to somesthetic and visual information (Armel & Ramachandran, 2003). We will defend instead a second hypothesis that a cognitive body representation modulates the integration of visual and somesthetic information.

2.2. Self-Attribution of a Rubber Hand

The rubber-hand illusion (RHI), originally reported by Botvinick and Cohen (1998), can serve as an experimental paradigm which can address the relationship between multisensory mereology and the body. This claim is supported by the fact that the constituting elements of the illusion involve visual and tactile events, and the integration of these percepts produces strong phenomenological and behavioral responses that are body related.

In the original experiment (Botvinick & Cohen, 1998), subjects sat with their left arms resting on a table, hidden behind a screen. They were asked to fixate on a rubber hand presented in front of them, and the experimenter stroked with two paintbrushes both the subject's hand and the fake hand simultaneously. After the stimulation period, subjects reported:

a. They felt as if the rubber hand were their own hand.
b. It was as if subjects were feeling the touch of the paintbrush in the location where they saw the rubber hand touched.
c. They did *not* feel as if their (real) hand were drifting toward the rubber hand.

Surprisingly, and contrary to the introspective evidence (see point c above), when subjects were asked to indicate the felt position of their own hands after the stimulation period, they perceived their hands to be closer to the rubber hand than it really was. That was true only when the two hands were synchronously stimulated and not when both hands were asynchronously stimulated. According to Botvinick and Cohen, "[T]he effect reveals a three-way interaction between vision, touch and proprioception, and may supply evidence concerning the basis of bodily self-identification" (Botvinick & Cohen, 1998, p. 756). In other words, vision captured the tactile sensations, and this intersensory match led to proprioceptive alteration. This result seems to suggest that "intermodal matching can be sufficient for *self-attribution*" (p. 756; italics added). This conclusion can be justified by the fact that proprioception is generally thought to be the sense of the self par excellence (Bermudez, 1998).

Armel and Ramachandran (2003) stimulated the subject's hand and a rubber hand synchronously or asynchronously. After the stimulation, they "injured" the fake hand and measured skin-conductance responses (SCRs) from the subject's unstimulated hand. SCRs were stronger after synchronous stimulation compared to asynchronous stimulation between the real and fake hands. Even more surprisingly, differences between synchronous and asynchronous conditions were also significant when subjects were looking not at a fake hand, but at the table being stroked. The authors concluded that this illusion ("it feels like the fake hand/table is my hand"; p. 1504) is the result of Bayesian perceptual learning, and they observed that "the brain's remarkable capacity for extracting statistical correlations in sensory input is most apparent in the table condition" (p. 1505). That would suggest that the RHI is simply the result of an association between synchronous visuotactile events, a purely bottom-up mechanism, and that *any* object can become part of *me*, simply because strong statistical correlations between different sensory modalities are both necessary and sufficient conditions for "deceiving our brains."

On this view, psychological concepts such as embodiment and selfhood are unnecessary, because purely Bayesian principles of statistical correlation are sufficient to extend the body representation, which can include "body parts" even as implausible as tables (Armel & Ramachandran, 2003). Another hypothesis derived from this Bayesian account of the RHI is that proprioceptive drifts should be significantly larger only for the stimulated body part and smaller or even absent for unstimulated body parts. We tested this hypothesis in two experiments, in which contrary to the experiment by Botvinick and Cohen, we stimulated only one (Experiment 1) or two (Experiment 2) fingers and not the whole hand (Tsakiris & Haggard, 2005).

In Experiment 1, subjects viewed a rubber hand being stroked by a paintbrush on either the index or the little finger. The subject was always stroked with a similar paintbrush on the same finger as the rubber hand was stroked. However, the rubber hand and the subject's hand were stroked either synchronously, in the experimental condition, or asynchronously, in the control condition. We obtained judgments for the felt position of the index finger or for the little finger in different blocks. Participants judged the felt position of their finger(s) by indicating a number on a ruler that was presented in front of them and at the same gaze depth as the rubber hand. During judgment, both the rubber hand and the participant's hand were out of view. We used the proprioceptive drift as a convenient, continuous, and quantitative measure of self-attribution. Proprioception is intimately related to the sense of bodily self (Bermudez, 1998), but it is not a direct measure of self-attribution per se. The results showed that only the stimulated finger was perceived as significantly drifted toward the rubber hand (see Figure 8.3a).

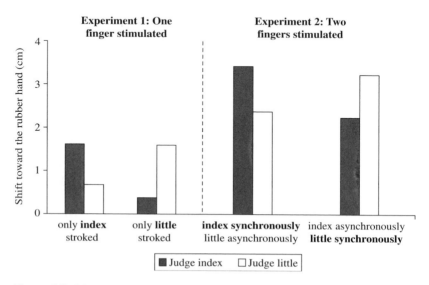

Figure 8.3. Mean perceptual shifts across conditions for Experiments 1 and 2. To isolate the part of the positional drift due to visual-tactile integration and obtain a true measure of the RHI, we subtracted the judgment errors obtained in the asynchronous conditions from the judgment errors obtained in the synchronous conditions.

This effect was further replicated in Experiment 2, in which both the index and the little fingers were stimulated across all conditions, but the pattern of stimulation was manipulated independently on each finger. This manipulation guaranteed that each finger received equal amounts of stimulation in each condition. Our first analysis focused on the differences in the perceived position of index versus little finger, in the condition where index was stroked synchronously/little asynchronously compared to the condition where little finger was stroked synchronously/index asynchronously. The analysis replicated the finding of the previous experiment, because only the finger that was synchronously stimulated was perceived to be significantly closer to the rubber hand (see Figure 8.3b), suggesting that synchronous visual and tactile correlation is a necessary condition for the build-up of the illusion. These data confirm the Bayesian hypothesis because the proprioceptive drifts were localized to the stimulated finger(s).

However, as part of Experiment 2, we also stimulated both the index and the little fingers synchronously or asynchronously with respect to the rubber fingers, and then obtained judgments for the felt position of the middle finger, which was never stimulated. By comparing the perceived position of the middle finger when both the little and index fingers were stimulated asynchronously to the condition when both fingers were stimulated synchronously, we showed that synchronous stimulation caused the unstimulated middle finger to drift just as much as the little and index fingers, which were stimulated. This finding suggests that there is a spreading gradient of the RHI to unstimulated fingers. Therefore, the localized proprioceptive drift is not absolute. A cognitive, mereological representation of the arrangement of fingers may explain the observed spreading of the effect to the unstimulated middle finger. A purely Bayesian account cannot explain why the middle finger drifted at all in the absence of any stimulation. If the RHI can extend to body parts that are not stimulated, is it also possible to have synchronous stimulation without inducing the RHI? If so, local multisensory integration would then be neither necessary nor sufficient for bodily synthesis.

The finding of an RHI effect for an unstimulated finger suggests that factors other than local multisensory integration may be sufficient for self-attribution. We suggest that coherence with a cognitive body representation may be one such factor. To test this hypothesis, we manipulated the felt and seen hand identities. In Experiment 3, we stimulated the middle finger of the subjects' left hands, while they were looking at a left or a right rubber hand being stimulated on the middle finger. As shown in Figure 8.4a, we found large proprioceptive drifts when subjects were looking at a congruent rubber hand identity and almost no drifts when they were looking at the middle finger of an incongruent rubber hand identity. The fact that we observed a negative effect (i.e., no drift) in the presence of stimulation suggests that mere statistical correlation between visual and tactile events is not sufficient for the induce-

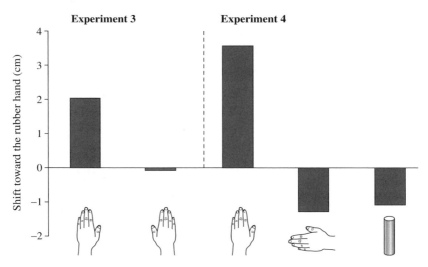

Figure 8.4. Mean perceptual shifts across conditions for Experiments 3 and 4. In Experiment 3, subjects judged the perceived position of the stimulated middle finger. In Experiment 4, subjects judged the perceived position of the stimulated index finger.

ment of the RHI, as measured by proprioceptive drift. These data suggest that the need for compatibility between the felt and seen sensation goes beyond the level of spatial and temporal congruency. We suggest that body representations play a modulatory top-down role in this process of body-related multisensory integration.

In Experiment 4, we further investigated the role of such body representations. First we asked whether the RHI would occur if the rubber hand were in an incongruent posture (e.g., rotated by $-90°$) with respect to the subject's own hand. Second, we asked whether a neutral object (e.g., a wooden stick) would induce similar effects. The results showed that the subjects mislocalized the position of their own hands *only* when the rubber hand was in a congruent posture (see Figure 8.4b). In other words, synchronous stimulation between the subject's hand and a rubber hand at an incongruent posture or a neutral object did not elicit the RHI, at least as it is measured by proprioceptive drift. These findings imply that mere correlation between visual and tactile percepts is not a *sufficient* condition for self-attribution of a rubber hand or any other object, at least not when the subject's body configuration is not respected.

Overall, the results obtained in these experiments argue against a purely Bayesian interpretation of the relationship between intermodal matching and self-attribution. First, a neutral object did not elicit any significant difference in the perceived position of the subjects' hands. Even when this neutral object was replaced by a rubber hand, the synchronicity of visual and tactile events did not suffice for the inducement of the RHI, because of the incongruence between the rubber hand and the subjects' own hands at a level that goes beyond synchronous stimulation. Hand posture and hand identity have been identified as two kinds of body-space influence that modulate the visuotactile integration underlying the RHI (see also Pavani, Spence, & Driver, 2000; Rorden et al., 1999). Graziano and colleagues made similar observations during the recording of bimodal neurons in parietal area 5 (Graziano, Cooke, & Taylor, 2000). These bimodal neurons of the monkey brain were sensitive to the position of the fake arm when fake and real hands were stroked synchronously, but *only* when the fake arm was aligned with the monkey's body. Such findings provide support for an active role of body representations in the processes underlying the RHI. It seems that attribution requires a plausible and congruent visual object to bind with a body part, with respect to the general body-space configuration.

At first sight, the localized effects in Experiments 1 and 2 provide support for the Bayesian approach, because stronger statistical correlations are expected for the stimulated finger(s). Nevertheless, two of our findings challenge a strict Bayesian account. First, the unstimulated middle finger drifted to an equivalent extent when two fingers were stimulated synchronously (Experiment 2). The experience of ownership of the rubber hand was global. In other words, participants did not feel as if only the stimulated finger was their own finger, but they felt as if the whole rubber hand was part of them. Second, a synchronously stimulated middle finger did not drift when subjects were looking at an incongruent rubber-hand identity (Experiment 3). A purely bottom-up account cannot explain either of these effects.

However, the RHI is a purely passive experience, and to that extent it lacks ecological validity. Intermodal matching in real life occurs within a dynamic and active interaction between the agent and the environment, during which multimodal sensory and motor signals need to be integrated, but also differentiated on the basis of their origin. A recent experiment on self-recognition shows that efferent information clearly contributes to the ability to match proprioceptive and visual representations of a remote bodily effect (Tsakiris et al., in press). Subjects experienced a passive extension of their right index fingers, either as an effect of a movement of their own left hands (self-generated action) or as imposed externally by the experimenter (externally generated action). The visual feedback was manipulated so that subjects could see either their own right hands (view-own-hand condition) or someone else's right hand (view-other's-hand condition) undergoing an equivalent passive extension of their index fingers. Self-recognition was significantly more accurate when the passive displacement of the right hand was self-generated, even though there was congruent visuoproprioceptive feedback across conditions and despite the fact that it was the affected right hands and not the acting left hands that the subjects were watching. In the absence of efferent information, congruent visual and proprioceptive feedback, as is the case in the RHI, led to a misattribution of the moving hand.

Taken overall, such results favor an interplay between bottom-up and top-down influences in the process of bodily synthesis. Even though intermodal matching seems to be a prerequisite for self-identification and self-attribution, the RHI suggests that our sense of our bodies is more than the sum of the correlated visual and tactile percepts. Therefore, multisensory percepts are not integrated in a simple additive manner, but instead respect a set of conditions that guarantee the functional and phenomenological coherence of the experienced body. This set of background conditions constitutes a cognitive model or representation of the body and its part relations. The involvement of this model may explain the specific and vivid phenomenology that characterizes the multisensory integration of bodily information in the RHI.

Conclusion: The Body and the Self

Mereology raises the following questions: how do humans differentiate the parts of the body? What is the relationship between the hand and the body? How does one know that the hand belongs to the body? We have investigated the principles of body mereology governing segmenting, structuring, and grouping. From a phenomenological point of view, bodily experiences display a unity and a consistency that have to be explained in the context of the body as an integrated agent in interaction with the world.

The mereology of the sensing body begins with an undifferentiated somatosensory sheet. Here, relationships among the body parts are based on spatial contiguity in a cortical map. The body parts do not seem to be explicitly differentiated in a categorical way. Body part *categories* seem to arise only at a higher, cognitive level of representation. In several cases, vision of body parts may play an important role in providing this structure. Finally, the geometric mereology of the body has been studied by judgments of body-part size. These studies suggest that the spatial arrangement of body parts is a fusion or interpretation of available multisensory information from across the whole body. The phenomena of phantom limbs and supernumerary limbs illustrate the plasticity of the sensing body as well as the relationships among the body parts: what one feels in one body part may depend on what one feels in another.

In contrast, voluntary action seems to presuppose a perfectly segmented and consistent representation of the body. If one decides to lift an arm, one must be able to distinguish the arm from other body parts. Action thus plays a dual role. First, it structures or segments the mental representation of the body into functional units of movements defined by the joints. Second, action groups disparate body parts together, for example, when all of one's fingers work together to grasp a glass in a coordinated grip. We suggest that phenomenal experience of the acting body therefore represents body parts in a more global way than do experiences of the sensory body. Consequently, the mereology of the sensing body and the mereology of the acting body provide different ways of differentiating and grouping body parts. Efferent mereology may be more consistent than afferent mereology. However, in both cases, body parts are not represented in isolation, but are interpreted in their interactions with other body parts as well as with the body as a whole.

We have thus suggested that somatosensory mereology is based on spatial contiguity, while motor mereology is based on the functional coherence of body movements during intentional actions. In contrast, it seems that multisensory mereology is intimately related to the sense of ownership of body parts. Indeed, body parts are experienced not only as parts of the body, but also as parts of *one's own* body. Therefore, we may ask how one self-attributes body parts. More particularly, is the sense of ownership the cause or the result of the multisensory synthesis of bodily information? We think that this is a modern neuroscientific instance of the old contrast between Humean and Kantian views of the self. According to Hume, we are confronted with a "bundle" of bodily experiences. The sense of ownership results from their synthesis into a consistent representation of the body as a whole. The results of Botvinick and Cohen (1998) and Armel and Ramachandran (2003) agree with this view. These authors argue that intermodal matching is a sufficient condition for the sense of ownership. Developmental psychology also suggests that multimodal integration is at the source of the recognition of one's own body (Rochat, 1998). However, we have presented data from the rubber-hand illusion suggesting that it is not in fact sufficient. We do not self-attribute a piece of wood or the contralateral hand, at least on the basis of the quantitative measures used in our study. Furthermore, if the embodied self is merely the result of bodily synthesis, what role does it play? It would be purely epiphenomenal.

In contrast, according to the Kantian hypothesis, self-attribution is a prerequisite of multimodal integration: I self-attribute bodily experiences ("I see my hand" and "I feel my hand") *before* combining them into a unified experience of the multisensory body. One thus avoids mistakenly combining the tactile perception of one's own hand with the visual experience of someone else's hand. Self-consciousness would thus constitute a prior necessary condition of body synthesis. On this view, the RHI should never occur at all, since I know that the rubber hand is not part of me. Therefore, I should be unable to include it in an integrated multisensory bodily experience. More important, the Kantian view leaves open the source of self-consciousness: if the embodied self does not result from the multisensory integration of bodily information, where does it come from?

We suggest that neither of these classical theories of the self is consistent with modern neuroscientific and psychophysical data on bodily sensation. Consequently, we would like to suggest a third hypothesis: the sense of ownership arises from the integration of afferent and also efferent sources of information.

However, this integration process is also modulated by a synthetic cognitive model of the body as a whole.

References

Aglioti, S., Smania, N., Manfredi, M., & Berlucchi, G. (1996). Disownership of left hand and objects related to it in a patient with right brain damage. *Neuroreport, 8*, 293–296.

Anscombe, G. E. M. (1959). *Intention.* Oxford: Blackwell.

Armel, K. C., & Ramachandran, V. S. (2003). Projecting sensations to external objects: Evidence from skin conductance response. *Proceedings of the Royal Society of London, Series B, 270*, 1499–1506.

Bermudez, J. L. (1998). *The paradox of self-consciousness.* Cambridge, MA: MIT Press.

Blankenburg, F., Ruben, J., Meyer, R., Schwiemann, J., & Villringer, A. (2003). Evidence for a rostral-to-caudal somatotopic organization in human primary somatosensory cortex with mirror-reversal in areas 3b and 1. *Cerebral Cortex, 13*, 987–993.

Block, N. (1983). Mental pictures and cognitive science. *Philosophical Review, 92*, 499–541.

Boisson, D., & Luaute, J. (2004). Les somatoparaphrénies. *Annales Médico Psychologiques, 162*, 55–59.

Bottini, G., Bisiach, E., Sterzi, R., & Vallar, G. (2002). Feeling touches in someone else's hand. *Neuroreport, 13*, 249–252.

Botvinick, M., & Cohen, J. (1998). Rubber hands "feel" touch that eyes see. *Nature, 391*, 756.

Braun, C., Schweizer, R., Elbert, T., Birbaumer, N., & Taub, E. (2000). Differential activation in somatosensory cortex for different discrimination tasks. *Journal of Neuroscience, 20*, 446–450.

Calvert, G. A., Brammer, M. J., & Iversen, S. D. (1998). Crossmodal identification. *Trends in Cognitive Sciences, 2*, 247–253.

Castiello, U., Paulignan, Y., & Jeannerod, M. (1991). Temporal dissociation of motor responses and subjective awareness. A study in normal subjects. *Brain, 114*, 2639–2655.

Driver, J., & Spence, C. (1998). Attention and the cross-modal construction of space. *Trends in Cognitive Sciences, 2*, 254–262.

Duhamel, J. R., Bremmer, F., BenHamed, S., & Graf, W. (1997). Spatial invariance of visual receptive fields in parietal cortex neurons. *Nature, 389*(6653), 845–848.

Farnè, A., & Làdavas, E. (2000). Dynamic size-change of hand peripersonal space following tool use. *Neuroreport, 11*, 1645–1649.

Fourneret, P., & Jeannerod, M. (1998). Limited conscious monitoring of motor performance in normal subjects. *Neuropsychologia, 36*, 1133–1140.

Gandevia, S. C., & Phegan, C. M. (1999). Perceptual distortions of the human body image produced by local anaesthesia, pain and cutaneous stimulation. *Journal of Physiology, 514*, 609–616.

Graziano, M. S., Cooke, D. F., & Taylor, C. S. (2000). Coding the location of the arm by sight. *Science, 290*(5497), 1782–1786.

Gurwitsch, A. (1985). *Marginal consciousness.* Athens: Ohio University Press.

Haggard, P., Taylor-Clarke, M., & Kennett, S. (2003). Tactile perception, cortical representation and the bodily self. *Current Biology, 13*, R170–173.

Halligan, P. W., Marshall, J. C., Hunt, M., & Wade, D. T. (1997). Somatosensory assessment: Can seeing produce feeling? *Journal of Neurology, 244*, 199–203.

Hari, R., Hanninen, R., Makinen, T., Jousmaki, V., Forss, N., Seppa, M., & Salonen, O. (1998). Three hands: Fragmentation of human bodily awareness. *Neuroscience Letters, 240*, 131–134.

Hlustik, P., Solodkin, A., Gullapalli, R. P., Noll, D. C., & Small, S. L. (2001). Somatotopy in human primary motor and somatosensory hand representations revisited. *Cerebral Cortex, 11*, 312–321.

Iriki, A., Tanaka, M., & Iwamura, Y. (1996). Coding of modified body schema during tool use by macaque postcentral neurons. *Neuroreport, 7*, 2325–2330.

James, W. (1890). *The principles of psychology, Vol. 1.* New York: Holt.

Jeannerod, M. (1997). *The cognitive neuroscience of action.* Oxford: Blackwell.

Kennett, S., Spence, C., & Driver, J. (2002). Visuo-tactile links in covert exogenous spatial attention remap across changes in unseen hand posture. *Perception and Psychophysics, 64*, 1083–1094.

Kinsbourne, M., & Warrington, E. (1962). A study of finger agnosia. *Brain, 85*, 47–66.

Lackner, J. R. (1988). Some proprioceptive influences on the perceptual representation of body shape and orientation. *Brain, 111*, 281–297.

Lemon, R. (1988). The output map of the primate motor cortex. *Trends in Neurosciences, 11*, 501–506.

Macaluso, E., Frith, C., & Driver, J. (2000). Selective spatial attention in vision and touch: Unimodal and multimodal mechanisms revealed by PET. *Journal of Neurophysiology, 83*, 3062–3075.

Maravita, A., Clarke, K., Husain, M., & Driver, J. (2002). Active tool use with the contralesional hand can reduce cross-modal extinction of touch on that hand. *Neurocase, 8*, 411–416.

Maravita, A., & Iriki, A. (2004). Tools for the body (schema). *Trends in Cognitive Sciences, 8*, 79–86.

McGonigle, D. J., Hanninen, R., Salenius, S., Hari, R., Frackowiak, R. S., & Frith, C. D. (2002). Whose arm is it anyway? An fMRI case study of supernumerary phantom limb. *Brain, 125*, 1265–1274.

Merleau-Ponty, M. (1945). *Phénoménologie de la perception.* Paris: Gallimard.

Merzenich, M. M., Nelson, R. J., Stryker, M. P., Cynader, M. S., Schoppmann, A., & Zook, J. M. (1984). Somatosensory cortical map changes following digit amputation in adult monkeys. *Journal of Comparative Neurology, 224*, 591–605.

Ogden, J. A. (1985). Autotopagnosia: Occurrence in a patient without nominal aphasia and with an intact ability to point to parts of animals and objects. *Brain, 108*, 1009–1022.

O'Shaughnessy, B. (1980). *The will: Dual aspect theory.* Cambridge: Cambridge University Press.

O'Shaughnessy, B. (1995). Proprioception and the body image. In J. L. Bermudez, A. Marcel, and N. Eilan (Eds.), *The body and the self* (pp. 175–205). Cambridge, MA: MIT Press.

Pavani, F., Spence, C., & Driver, J. (2000). Visual capture of touch: Out-of-the-body experiences with rubber gloves. *Psychological Science, 11*, 353–359.

Penfield, W., & Boldrey, E. (1937). Somatic motor and sensory representation in the cerebral cortex of man as studied by electrical stimulation. *Brain, 60*, 339–448.

Penfield, W., & Rasmussen, T. (1950). *The cerebral cortex of man.* New York: Macmillan.

Ramachandran, V. S., & Hirstein, W. (1998). The perception of phantom limbs. *Brain, 121*, 1603–1630.

Ramachandran, V. S., & Rogers-Ramachandran, D. (1996). Synaesthesia in phantom limbs induced with mirrors. *Proceedings of the Royal Society of London, 263*, 377–386.

Reed, C. L., Stone, V. E., Bozova, S., & Tanaka, J. (2003). The body-inversion effect. *Psychological Science, 14*, 302–308.

Rochat, P. (1998). Self perception and action in infancy. *Experimental Brain Research, 123*, 102–109.

Rorden, C., Heutink, J., Greenfield, E., & Robertson, I. H. (1999). When a rubber hand "feels" what the real hand cannot. *Neuroreport, 10*, 135–138.

Schieber, M. H., & Hibbard, L. S. (1993). How somatotopic is the motor cortex hand area? *Science, 261*(5120), 489–492.

Scholl, B. J. (2001). Objects and attention: The state of the art. *Cognition, 80*, 1–46.

Schweizer, R., Braun, C., Fromm, C., Wilms, A., & Birbaumer, N. (2001). The distribution of mislocalizations across fingers demonstrates training-induced neuroplastic changes in somatosensory cortex. *Experimental Brain Research, 139*, 435–442.

Semenza, C. (1988). Impairment in localization of body parts following brain damage. *Cortex, 24*, 443–449.

Sirigu, A., Grafman, J., Bressler, K., & Sunderland, T. (1991). Multiple representations contribute to body knowledge processing. Evidence from a case of autotopagnosia. *Brain, 114*, 629–642.

Taylor-Clarke, M., Jacobsen, P., & Haggard, P. (2004). Keeping the world a constant size: Object constancy in human touch. *Nature Neuroscience, 7*, 219–220.

Taylor-Clarke, M., Kennett, S., & Haggard, P. (2002). Vision modulates somatosensory cortical processing. *Current Biology, 12*, 233–236.

Treisman, A. (1998). Feature binding, attention and object perception. *Philosophical Transactions of the Royal Society of London, B, 353*(1373), 1295–1306.

Tsakiris, M., & Haggard, P. (2005). The rubber hand illusion re-visited: Visuo-tactile integration and self-attribution. *Journal of Experimental Psychology: Human Perception and Performance, 31*, 80–91.

Tsakiris, M., Haggard, P., Franck, N., Mainy, N., & Sirigu, A. (In press). A specific role for efferent information in a self-recognition task. *Cognition*.

Wiggins, D. (1968). On being in the same place at the same time. *Philosophical Review, 77*, 90–95.

Wiggins, D. (1980). *Sameness and substance*. Oxford: Blackwell.

9

From Phantom Limb
to Phantom Body
Varieties of Extracorporeal Awareness

Peter Brugger

Corporeal awareness refers to the experience of having a body. While this may appear self-evident given our constant daily experience of embodiment, the neuronal processes mediating this experience are nonetheless highly manifold and complex. Corporeal awareness relies on perceptual functions (e.g., tactile, proprioceptive, gravitational, visual) and on motor programs for bodily action. Yet, it also comprises a sense of the self as the object of sensory stimulation and as the agent of motor intentions and executions. Moreover, identifying with a body implies knowledge of its borders. Thus, the study of corporeal awareness includes investigations of the many functionally organized spaces for each distinct sensory and motor representation that surrounds our body. In the past, various terms have been used to capture some of the heterogeneous functions that guarantee a continuous sense of embodiment. Some of the more frequently used terms are body schema, body image, body self, somesthesis, coaenesthesia, and somatognosia. Critchley (1955/1979) complained about the fact that these terms were employed more or less interchangeably despite the fact that they had originally been introduced to designate specific facets of bodily perception and representation. He therefore proposed the deliberately less definitive term *corporeal awareness* as an all-encompassing descriptor of the experience of having a body.

The present chapter provides a phenomenological account of those borderlands of corporeal awareness in which subjects experience a discrepancy between the spatial extents of their physical and phenomenal bodies. Such discrepancies may occur at the level of single limbs but also at the level of the entire body. This chapter begins with brief reviews of selected clinical and experimental findings pertaining to various manifestations of the phantom-limb phenomenon. This is followed by a discussion of what is referred to as the *hemiphantom* or *phantom half-body*, that is, the experience of a deafferented/deefferented half of one's body as an entity living a life on its own. Finally, an overview will be presented of a peculiar class of reduplicative disorders known as *autoscopic phenomena* in which one's entire body is experienced as a phantom.

While research on limb phantoms has enjoyed increasing popularity since the 1980s, investigations of whole-body phantoms are still largely a matter of clinical descriptions. However, experimental paradigms that have proven useful in elucidating the neuropsychological mechanisms underlying phantom-limb experiences can be adapted for the systematic study of phantom bodies. Also, the neuropsychology of spatial and conceptual perspective taking and of the experience of agency over one's actions should be considered for the interpretation of the psychological content of autoscopic experiences.

1. Phantom Body Parts

1.1. Amputation Phantoms

An *amputation phantom* is the persistent experience of the postural and motor aspects of a limb after its physical loss. The reluctance of the medical community to consider amputees' reports about such phantom limbs is reflected in the history of the subject. Riddoch (1941, p. 197) noted that the subjective survival of a limb "must be as old as survival from amputation." Early accounts of phantom limbs can be traced back at least to the 10th century. These accounts were intermingled with religiously motivated resurrection fantasies (Price & Twombly, 1978) to such a degree that it is difficult to separate keen introspective report from folk psychological interpretation. Later theories (see Finger & Hustwit, 2003; Halligan, 2002, for historical overviews) about the origins of phantom sensations can conveniently be dichotomized according to whether they focus more on peripheral or central processes. The essence of peripheral theories is pathetically captured in the words of Gallinek (1939, p. 420): "peripheral stimuli are the blood which the sensory ghost must drink in order to be awakened to its phantom existence." Such stimuli include random firings of axon terminals in the stump and irritations by scar tissue and neuromas (see, e.g., Katz, 1992). Later theories emphasized involvement of the central nervous system at the level of the spinal cord (Cronholm, 1951). A quarter of a century ago, peripheral and spinal factors were still considered by some authors as sufficient to explain the genesis of phantom sensations (see especially Carlen et al., 1978, who even ridiculed any postulate of a cortical involvement). However, subcortical and cortical reorganization had much earlier been described as essential concomitants of limb amputation. Specifically, it was argued that changes in the corporeal awareness of a lost hand in response to

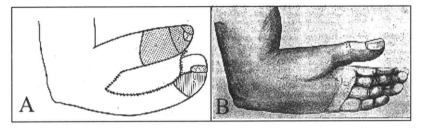

Figure 9.1. (A) Surgical reshaping of the forearm of a hand amputee into a tongue-like tool (Krukenberg hand). Shaded areas correspond to fields with systematic referral of touch to the phantom hand. (B) An artist's drawing of a patient's description of the reshaping of a phantom hand, previously felt in the space distal to the stump, within 12 to 24 hours after kineplastic surgery. The radial part of the arm was felt as a huge thumb opposing the four fingers felt within the ulnear part of the arm. This observation illustrates the tight interplay of peripheral and central factors in the genesis of phantom sensations. Adapted with permission from Brücke (1950, Figures 1 and 2).

reshaping of the forearm stump would constitute a "wholistic reaction of the sensory cortex and cortico-thalamic system" to the new functional properties of the arm (Brücke, 1950, p. 154; Figure 9.1; see Kallio, 1952, for an alternative, mostly peripheral interpretation of similar observations).

Since the 1980s, the literature on the cerebral correlates of amputation phantoms has grown exponentially. Along with prior animal research (Kaas et al., 1983; Pons et al., 1991), these studies helped to revise an axiom within the neurosciences, that is, the claim that the adult human brain is largely resistant to functional reorganization. A variety of behavioral and neuroimaging techniques have been used to monitor the cortical and subcortical reorganizational processes following limb amputation in humans (see Ramachandran & Hirstein, 1998, for review). Flor et al. (1995), using magnetic source imaging, described shifts in the cortical hand area (contralateral to amputation) in the magnitude of centimeters that correlated almost perfectly with a subject's rated severity of phantom limb pain.

However, referred-sensation studies have shown that nonpainful phantom sensations can serve as markers of plastic changes during deafferentation. *Referred sensations* are sensations localized to a phantom body part after stimulation (usually tactile) of a remote site on the subject's body known as the *trigger zone* (Aglioti et al., 1997). The most common trigger zone for upper-limb amputees is the subject's face (see also chapter 8). Clinically, these sensations have been extensively documented (e.g., Cronholm, 1951; Henderson & Smyth, 1948). Ramachandran et al. (1992) described representations of upper-limb phantoms, apparently somatotopically organized, on the face, chest, and axilla of several amputees. These and later authors interpreted the regular correspondence between the face as a trigger zone and the phantom hand as the site of referral as evidence for an "invasion" of the deafferented hand area into the neighboring postcentral area of face representation (see Clarke et al., 1996, for an inverse relationship between trigger and referral zones in a patient with intact hands but surgical deafferentation of the cheek). The exact neurophysiological mechanisms underlying these remapping phenomena are still unclear. The most commonly discussed mechanisms are axonal sprouting (intracortical and/or thalamocortical) and the unmasking of existing synaptic connections (see Kew et al., 1997, for discussion). However, the correspondence pattern between trigger zones and sites of referral does not appear to be stable over time and can change drastically within months (e.g., Halligan, Marshall, & Wade, 1994; Halligan, Marshall, Wade, et al., 1993). Thus, while there was great initial enthusiasm about and emphasis on the apparent somatotopy of referred sensations (Ramachandran et al., 1992), later investigations showed that trigger and reference zones could be located in body parts represented in clearly nonadjacent cortical areas (e.g., Grüsser et al., 2004; Knecht et al., 1996, 1998). Such findings suggest a possible subcortical mediation of sensory referral. For a crossmodal analogue of referred sensations, see Cacace et al. (1999).

Dynamic aspects of phantom limbs have been captured in many experiments. For example, the reality of virtual movements, or the voluntary movement with one's phantom limb, has been elegantly demonstrated in simple behavioral experiments (e.g., Franz & Ramachandran, 1998). Several neuroimaging studies have attempted to shed some light on the functional neuroanatomy of voluntary movements of amputation phantoms (e.g., Ersland et al., 1996; Lotze et al., 2001; Roux et al., 2003). These studies have shown that phantom movement sensations are associated with activations of primary and secondary sensorimotor cortical areas, even decades after the loss of a limb.

Corporeal awareness on the level of single limbs is shaped by interactions with the visual modality. For example, the phenomenon of *obstacle shunning* refers to the diminished awareness of a phantom limb during the observation of a physical object invading the space that the phantom appears to occupy (Jalavisto, 1950). Scattered observations and systematic explorations of shunning behavior (e.g., Abbatucci, 1894; Katz, 1920; Poeck, 1963; Riechert, 1934; Simmel, 1956) have revealed three major findings: (1) there are large interindividual differences in the degree of shunning as roughly 50% of amputees do not show any pronounced obstacle shunning; (2) among the physical objects used to test for shunning behavior, the human body appears to play a special role (with little data on the specificity of the amputee's own compared to other people's bodies); and (3) pronounced shunning tendencies may elicit unique phantom limb movements, that is, movements specific to the experimental situation (e.g., a wall-approaching test) and not usually experienced in everyday life. One example is the "bending" of a phantom limb beyond regular joint constraints to avoid "contact" with solid matter (Poeck, 1963).

More recent experimentation on visual-somesthetic interactions has concentrated on the visual observation of one's own limb, specifically, the one contralateral to the amputated extremity. Critically, the spared extremity is observed in a mirror placed vertically in the parasagittal plane to thus match the purely somesthetic phantom percept with respect to handedness and perceived location in space (e.g., Ramachandran et al., 1995; Ramachandran & Rogers-Ramachandran, 1996). Under these conditions, observed touch applied to the real limb may also be felt in the phantom (but see Hunter et al., 2003). Observed movements of the existing limb may be felt as mirror movements in the phantom, a principle that has found therapeutic applications beyond the treatment of phantom-limb pain (Altschuler et al., 1999; Ramachandran et al., 1999).

In view of these empirical studies, it would appear that what was labeled a "sensory ghost" by Mitchell in 1866 (the term *phantom limb* was also coined in this work) has completely lost its ghostly character. It is important to note, however, that we still continue to be haunted by considerable misconceptions. First, the literature on phantom limbs is heavily biased toward the analysis of cases after amputation. Second, at least in the popular mind, "phantom sensation" is implicitly equated with "phantom pain." Figure 9.2 illustrates this point with data from 172 people who provided spontaneous associations to the

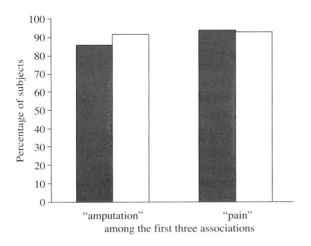

Figure 9.2. Stereotypes in spontaneous associations to the term *phantom* as used in medicine. Medically trained individuals (gray bars; $n = 84$) and laypeople alike (light bars; $n = 88$) show strong biases for association with the terms *amputation* and *pain*. These popular stereotypes are paralleled by an overrepresentation of reports on *painful* phantom sensations after amputation in the scientific literature.

term *phantom* as a medical term. Overall, these subjects wrote down an average of 5.8 associations to the term *phantom* in the allotted 60 seconds. Subjects were categorized as either "medically trained" or "laypersons." The medically trained subjects comprised general practitioners, neurology residents, and qualified nursing staff, as well as 48 fourth-year medical students. Laypersons had, for the most part, academic training in fields other than medicine and psychology. No differences were apparent between women's ($n = 87$) and men's ($n = 85$) associations. The population stereotypes somewhat anecdotally communicated in Figure 9.2 were similar for medically trained and untrained subjects. Clearly, amputation and pain are tightly associated with the medical term *phantom*.

Similar biases can be found in the medical literature. A search for the keyword "phantom sensations"[1] (December 2003) in the Web-of-Science for the publication years 1945 to 2003 produced 58 entries, more than 50% accompanied by the keyword "amputation" and more than 60% by "pain." The fact that amputation phantoms form just one of many different types of phantom-limb manifestations should become evident in this chapter. The overemphasis of pain among the many sensory qualities of phantom limbs (e.g., posture, temperature, weight, kinesthesis) can probably be explained by the fact that amputees usually complain about painful phantom sensations spontaneously, but mention painless phantom sensations only after specific inquiry (Egyd & Janke, 1967). Also, if present, phantom pain is a most distressing condition for which, judged by evidence-based medical criteria, no reliable therapeutic intervention can currently be offered (Stremmel et al., 2002). However, estimates of the prevalence of phantom-limb pain after amputation vary between around 80% (Houghton et al., 1994; Sherman et al., 1984) to less than 0.5% (Kolb, 1952, p. 586). In any case, both the tendencies to regard "phantom limb" as synonymous with "amputation phantom" and "phantom sensation" as synonymous with "phantom pain" hamper the recognition of a conceptual similarity between the phantom limb and phantom body.

1.2. Phantoms After Spinal-Cord Injury

Limb phantoms are also experienced after spinal-cord injury and may be defined as the phenomenal persistence of postural and, optionally, kinesthetic information about the deafferented and deefferented limbs. Lower limbs are thus affected in paraplegic patients (Conomy, 1973; Figure 9.3) while upper limbs are affected after brachial plexus lesions (Mayer-Gross, 1929), and both lower and upper limbs are affected in tetraplegia (Davis, 1975; Ohry et al., 1989). Important early contributions to general phenomenology and individual differences in corporeal awareness after spinal-cord injury can be found in Becker (1949), Bors (1951), Melzack and Loeser (1978), and Riddoch (1941).

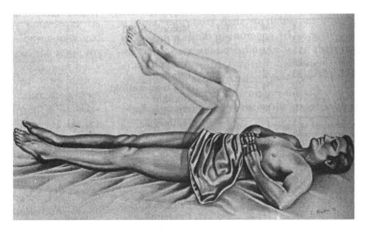

Figure 9.3. Phantom legs in a patient with spastic paraplegia (sensorimotor impairment at the T-7 level) acquired in a motorcycle accident. Note that the phantom legs mimic the posture of the real legs shortly before injury. This patient failed to "get the legs back down to where they really were" (Conomy, 1973, p. 844). More typically, other patients with phantoms after spinal-cord injury can easily abolish the phantom-limb percept by looking at their real limbs. Reproduced from Conomy (1973, Figure 1) with the permission of Lippincott-Raven Publishers.

A recent population-based study found the prevalence of phantoms after spinal-cord injury comparable to that reported in amputees (Siddall & McClelland, 1999). Yet, "spinal phantoms" often escape the attention of the clinician because they are not specifically inquired about and are usually less vivid and not as persistent as amputation phantoms (Bors, 1951). Furthermore, spinal phantom sensations are often confounded with residual sensations, such as pain and paresthesias (Burke & Woodward, 1976). Finally, loss of consciousness during the trauma appears to decrease the chance that phantom limb experiences will be reported (Ettlin et al., 1980).

Most important with respect to the modification of corporeal awareness by crossmodal sensory integration is the observation that phantom leg sensations in paraplegia are frequently "suppressed" by visual feedback from looking at one's own paralyzed limbs (e.g., Conomy, 1973). Yet, occasionally, the view of one's existing limb does not suppress the compelling nature of somatic phantom sensations. In a case reported by Reichert and Sewekow (2002), a patient with a phantom arm after resection of an intraspinal tumor could feel his phantom in superposition with objects. This absence of obstacle shunning occurred despite the fact that the patient could clearly see both of his arms. It is possible that the spatial separation between the physical arm and the phantom arm may have prevented the suppression of phantom sensations by visual information.

Neuroimaging studies in paraplegic patients have documented large-scale reorganization of those cortical areas devoted to sensorimotor control. These changes are associated not only with the deafferented and deefferented lower limbs but also with the unaffected upper limbs (Bruehlmeier et al., 1998; Curt et al., 2002; Turner et al., 2001). Importantly, a recent fMRI study of paraplegic patients' motor imagery of the lower limbs showed high correlations between activations specifically in primary and secondary motor areas and the rated vividness of phantom foot movements (Alkadhi et al., 2005). Visual observation of simulated hand movements may enhance motor imagery–induced cortical activity in some patients with phantoms after brachial plexus avulsion and may lead to a reduction of phantom limb pain (Giraux & Sirigu, 2003).

As in the literature on amputation phantoms, the issue of referred sensations has received special attention. While most reports found a referral of stimuli applied to normesthetic parts of the body to phantoms or deafferented body parts (e.g., Bors, 1979; Srinivasan et al., 1998), referral in an opposite direction does also occur (e.g., Nathan, 1956). An fMRI study of referred sensations after spinal-cord injury (Moore et al., 2000) provided clear evidence for a coactivation of regions widely separated from one another, both on the body surface and as representational loci within the postcentral gyrus.

1.3. Supernumerary Phantoms After Brain Damage

Given that the critical factor for the genesis of a phantom limb is a partial or full deafferentation and/or deefferentation of the corresponding real limb *at any level of sensorimotor integration*, phantoms are also experienced after damage to subcortical or cortical brain regions. The term *supernumerary phantom* thus refers to the awareness of having an "extra limb" in addition to the regular set of two arms and two legs.[2] In the medical literature of the early 20th century, such awareness was referred to as "pseudo(poly)melia" or a "reduplication of body parts" (see Weinstein et al., 1954, for a review of this early literature). Although the etiology of brain damage is commonly a vascular incident or a space-occupying lesion (Donnet et al., 1997; Halligan, Marshall, & Wade, 1993; Miyazawa et al., 2004; Sellal et al., 1996; Vuilleumier, Reverdin, et al., 1997), supernumerary phantoms have also been described after traumatic brain injury (Rogers & Franzen, 1992), during the course of a demyelating disease (Mayeux & Benson, 1979), or as an epileptic manifestation (Hécaen & de Ajuriaguerra, 1952; Riddoch, 1941). Typically, postural and movement qualities are reported whereas painful sensations are rather exceptional (e.g., Canavero et al., 1999). Movements of and tactile stimuli applied to a real limb can occasionally be transferred to the phantom (Hari et al., 1998; Figure 9.4A).

The key difference between supernumerary phantoms after brain damage and phantoms after the loss of a limb or its disconnection at the spinal level concerns the patient's insight into the reality of the phenomenon. As "real" as the latter may feel, they are always recognized as illusory percepts. In contrast,

(A)

(B)

Figure 9.4. (A) Experience of supernumerary "ghost limbs" in a patient with a bifrontal and anterior callosal lesion (drawing by the patient). While the *posture* of the phantom hand mimicked the one of the left hand with a time lag of up to one minute, its *movements* copied those of the right hand. Tactile stimuli to either left or right hand were transferred also to the other two hands, such as the patient would feel carrying three bags, or having three dogs on a lead, when in actuality only one object was present. Reproduced from Hari et al. (1998, Fig. 2), with permission from Elsevier. (B) The Australian artist Stelarc during a 1982 "Handwriting" performance. His project "Third Hand" involved the incorporation of an artificial supernumerary hand whose movements were controlled by abdominal and leg muscles. Avant-garde in the domain of art, Stelarc's experimentation could also contribute to the evolution of our scientific understanding of corporeal awareness. Photograph by K. Oki, with permission by Stelarc.

the experience of a supernumerary phantom is often commented on in delusional ways (Ehrenwald, 1930; Roth, 1944). As a rule, the more a patient's
awareness of the physical limb contralateral to brain damage is compromised
(up to the degree of complete "aschematia"; Bonnier, 1905), the more its
phantom existence is experienced as the only reality that counts.

The designation of a supernumerary phantom limb as a "spare" limb (Grossi
et al., 2002; Worthington & Beevers, 1996) or as "one I grew for protection"
(Weinstein et al., 1954, p. 50) is indicative of some degree of anosognosia, that
is, the denial of a sensorimotor hemisyndrome. Such an interpretation can be
comforting to the patient. However, when in addition to the loss of pure motor
control over the physical limb, one also loses one's sense of agency over the
phantom, an individual's experience may be rather negative. Such emotionally
distressing phantoms have much in common with an "alien" or "anarchic"
limb (Marchetti & Della Salla, 1998) that may engage in self-destructive behavior, particularly after right-hemisphere damage (see Brugger, 2001, for further references). In these cases, the transition to somatoparaphrenic delusions
(see below) becomes blurred.

Among the experimental studies conducted with patients experiencing supernumerary phantoms, the one by Hari et al. (1998; see Figure 9.4A) is significant. These authors reported a stroke patient who experienced a left "ghost
arm" that vanished when the patient either looked at or moved the real left arm.
An fMRI study showed that the phantom percept was accompanied by an
activation of right-hemisphere motor areas, previously implicated in the preparation of motor actions in normal subjects (McGonigle et al., 2002). This
patient did not provide a delusional interpretation of her supernumerary phantom; had she done so, the functional neuroanatomy of her ghostly limb would
certainly have looked different. Specifically, the implication of cortical networks mediating motor intentions and the agency over bodily action would have
been predicted (e.g., Blakemore et al., 2002; Spence et al., 1997). A unique
approach to the phenomenology of supernumerary phantoms was offered by the
Australian performance artist Stelarc (1995). In his project "The Third Hand,"
he extended his body with an additional hand, attached to his right arm and
rendered functional by amplified EMG signals of his abdominal and leg muscles. This arrangement allowed him to write a word simultaneously with three
hands (Figure 9.4B). Stelarc's introspective report of how he gained control over
and agency of his artificial supernumerary limb is not only revealing for the
interpretation of cases in which such functions are lost after brain damage, but is
also relevant to research on the brain's assimilation of tools and prostheses (Iriki
et al., 1996; Lotze et al., 1999; Maravita et al., 2001; Weiss et al., 1999). For a
brief review of further experimental approaches to supernumerary phantom
body parts, both limbs and nonlimb parts, see Brugger (2003a).

One more difference between phantoms after brain damage and "lower-
level" phantoms concerns crossmodal aspects. While amputation phantoms

and phantoms after spinal-cord injury are almost never *seen* by mentally healthy amputees or paraplegics, some patients with supernumerary phantoms have reported both visual and postural-kinesthetic awareness of their "extra" limb (e.g., Critchley, 1953, pp. 244–245; Halligan & Marshall, 1995; Halligan, Marshall, & Wade, 1993; Todd & Dewhurst, 1955, p. 54). The patient of Miyazawa et al. (2004) who felt a supernumerary set of left upper and lower extremities (after left thalamic hemorrhage without anosognosia), could clearly see arms and legs but not hands and feet. This "spilling over" of corporeal awareness into the visual domain is unique to cases in which the deafferentation occurred on a highly integrated level. It should be noted, however, that visualization of amputation phantoms was reported in the early literature (e.g., Menninger-Lerchenthal, 1948; Price, 1976; Reny, 1899). These observations may be indicative of the powerful top-down effects of belief systems on lower-level sensory functions. Indeed, they give testimony to relatively neglected interactions between neuropsychological mechanisms and factors hitherto considered purely "social psychological" (see Brugger, 2001).

1.4. Phantoms of Congenitally Absent Limbs

Another type of phantom is known as *congenital phantom limb* or *aplasic phantom limb*. These terms refer to the corporeal awareness of a limb that has been missing since birth, that is, in congenital limb aplasia. While the number of case reports of congenital phantoms is impressively large, there remains a relative paucity of experimental investigations. This underrepresentation of empirical research within the huge literature on phantom limbs may explain the absence of a generally accepted theory of congenital phantoms. In fact, the genuineness of congenital phantoms is not unequivocally appreciated. Some authors are still inclined to dismiss the possibility of phantom awareness of a limb that has never physically developed (e.g., Flor et al., 1998; Montoya et al., 1998; Skoyles, 1990). In this context, reference to Pick (1915) is usually provided. This author authoritatively stated that congenital phantoms could not exist because the respective limb "had never been part of the body scheme" (p. 260). Among the speculations offered to account for congenital phantom limbs are the following:

Speculation 1: Stump Characteristics

In many persons reporting congenital phantoms, absence of proximal limb structures is accompanied by at least some rudimentary preservation of distal body parts ("intercalary aplasia"; O'Rahilly, 1951). Based on an analysis of such cases, it was suggested that phantom sensations comprised kinesthetic illusions resulting from an abnormally enhanced motility of these distal body parts (Simmel, 1961). This idea may make sense in the context of a very particular subset of limb dysplasia. Obviously, however, it cannot explain the occurrence of phantoms for limbs missing in their entirety nor the highly specific features of distal phantom parts, such as entire sets of properly arranged fingers. Furthermore, phantom temperature sensations in a limb absent since birth (Lacroix et al., 1992) can hardly be encompassed by abnormally represented movement information for residual body parts.

Speculation 2: Spared Representation of the Contralateral, Intact Limb

Early case reports of congenital phantoms frequently involved persons missing only one limb (see Scatena, 1990; Vetter & Weinstein, 1967, for comprehensive reviews). Accordingly, the phantom sensations of these individuals were interpreted as transpositions of sensorimotor maps from the intact limb of one hemisphere to the other (e.g., Burchard, 1965; Grouios, 1996). The core idea here was most clearly summarized by Grouios (1996) in his introduction of the case of a 12-year-old boy born without his right forearm (5 cm above the elbow). The child experienced phantom fingers of his missing hand. Grouios (1996) concluded:

> It seems that the upper and lower limbs in people with congenital limb deficiency are linked in the brain as a result of frequent co-activation. Hence, sensory input of the left upper limb, for example, projects not only to the somatosensory cortex of the right cerebral hemisphere but— by identified or unidentified commissural pathways—to mirror-symmetrical points in the left cerebral hemisphere. It thus contributes to a weak formation of the cortical representation of the right upper limb. (pp. 503–504)

It is most evident that, as convincing as such a theory may appear for cases of *unilateral* limb absence, it fails to account for the situation where *both* upper and/or *both* lower limbs are missing. Such cases are not unique (e.g., Brugger et al., 2000; Poeck, 1964; Saadah & Melzack, 1994; Weinstein & Sersen, 1961), and their theoretical importance was recognized early on (Valentin, 1836, p. 643). Importantly, the phantom sensations reported by persons with bilateral limb aplasia are not qualitatively different from those described after unilateral defect.[3]

Speculation 3: Hand-Mouth Coordination

Behavioral and ultrasonic data on the thumb-sucking behavior of human fetuses have demonstrated a functional link between hand movements and anticipatory mouth opening. Based on these data, Gallagher et al. (1998) proposed that an innate motor schema of hand-mouth coordination may be responsible for phantoms of congenitally absent limbs. In the absence of a hand, the cortical area involved in face representation may invade the cortical areas involved in hand representation. "Activation of the expanded face-representing neural map may also reactivate the indigenous limb-representing neurons and thus cause the phantom experience" (Gallagher et al., 1998, p. 59). As thoughtful as these reflections are in the struggle to explain the genesis of upper-limb congenital phantoms, they obviously cannot be used to explain the formation of phantoms of feet and legs that have never physically developed. Indeed, as if anticipating such a critique, Gallagher and colleagues (1998) included only cases of upper-limb phantoms in their tabular overview of previously published cases of congenital phantoms.

To test the various predictions outlined above, we recently presented the case of A. Z., a 44-year-old woman born without forearms and legs (Brugger et al., 2000; Figure 9.5A). For as long as A. Z. can remember, she has experienced phantom forearms including hands and fingers. The symmetric bilateral absence of her upper extremities ruled out the possibility that representations of an intact limb were responsible for the genesis of her phantom hands. Since her conically shaped upper stumps were free of any appendages (i.e., rudimentary fingers), we could also reject Simmel's (1961) proposal that congenital phantom limbs reflect the increased mobility of distal appendages. Finally, the fact that A. Z. reported a distinct awareness of phantom legs and feet, including first and fifth toes (Figure 9.5A), cannot be explained by referring to an innate schema for hand-mouth motor interactions (Gallagher et al., 1998). In contrast, behavioral data indicated an intact postural representation of hands. Specifically, A. Z.'s performance in hand/foot laterality tasks (which require a speeded motor decision as to whether pictures of a hand or foot display a left or a right limb) showed a reaction time pattern that replicated the pattern produced by subjects born with intact bodies (e.g., Parsons, 1987). Most convincing was a regular "medial-lateral gradient" for palm views of left and right hands (Funk, 2001; Figure 9.5B). The significant reaction time advantage for medially over laterally oriented hands indicated that A. Z.'s visual recognition of hands was constrained by biomechanical joint constraints in the same way as that of normal subjects (Parsons, 1994) and that of persons born with only one upper extremity but no phantom sensations of the missing limb (Funk & Brugger, 2002). When A. Z. performed self-paced movements with her phantom fingers while lying in an MR scanner, phantom finger movements consistently activated cortical areas similar to those described in comparable studies with amputees (e.g., Ersland et al., 1996), without however involving the primary sensorimotor cortex (Figure 9.5C). Finally, transcranial magnetic stimulation (TMS) over the sensorimotor cortex, but also at premotor and parietal stimulation sites, elicited specific phantom hand and finger sensations (Brugger et al., 2000).

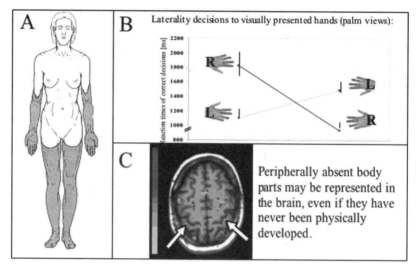

Figure 9.5. (A) A. Z., a 44-year-old woman born without forearms and legs but with vivid phantoms (shaded areas) of most missing body parts. Drawing by Peter Roth, Zürich. (B) A. Z.'s reaction-time pattern to visually presented hands ("a left or a right hand?") was constrained by the awkwardness of displayed postures, despite the fact that her brain has never received any information about hand posture. Data reproduced from Funk (2001) with the permission of the author. (C) Rhythmic movements of the right phantom fingers activated the premotor and parietal cortex bilaterally but not the primary sensorimotor areas for hand representation (arrows). Modified from Figure 3 in Brugger et al. (2000). *See color insert.*

On first consideration, the results obtained with A. Z. appear to constitute unequivocal evidence for an innate representation of the human body or at least its extremities. Melzack (1990; Melzack et al., 1997) proposed the concept of a *neuromatrix*, or a neural network integrating different components of corporeal awareness across modalities and extending throughout selective areas of the whole brain while mainly comprising the posterior parietal lobes and thalamocortical and limbic loops. According to his view, the rough spatial distribution of the neuromatrix is genetically prewired while the specific synaptic connections are later modulated by sensory experience (see Abramson & Feibel, 1981; Mikorey 1952; Poeck, 1964, 1969; and Weinstein & Sersen, 1961, for earlier related proposals). We have noted, however (Brugger et al., 2000, 2001) that there still remains the theoretical possibility that a somatic (postural and kinesthetic) limb representation could have been built up by the regular visual observation of other people moving their limbs. We are currently exploring the functionality of A. Z.'s "mirror system" (Buccino et al., 2001; Rizzolatti et al., 2001) and wish to compare it with that of people born with a similarly incomplete body, but with an "amelic corporeal awareness," that is, no history of phantom sensations (see Funk et al., in press, for preliminary findings).

2. The Phantom Half-Body: Personification in Somatoparaphrenia

Among the agnosias, anosognosia undoubtedly provides the most challenging puzzle to behavioral neurologists. Patients with this disorder fail to recognize those symptoms of an illness that are most obvious to any third person. In the narrow sense, anosognosia refers to the nonrecognition, or even active denial, of hemiplegia, that is, the paralysis of one half of the body (Babinski, 1914). Almost always associated with a neglect of the contralesional side of space, anosognosia is a typical parietal lobe disorder (Ramachandran, 1995), more frequently observed after right-sided than left-sided lesions. Several hypotheses have been proposed to account for anosognosia for sensorimotor hemi-syndromes (for an overview, see Vuilleumier, 2004), but none can fully explain the diversity of symptoms displayed by different patients.

One condition frequently associated with anosognosia is *somatopara-phrenia* (Gerstmann, 1942), that is, the delusional rejection of the ownership of the disabled side of the individual's own body (commonly, the left side). Somatoparaphrenia involves a productive elaboration that reflects a breakdown in the distinction between oneself and others (Boisson & Luauté, 2004; Paulig et al., 2000). It is this awareness, distorted as it may be, of one side of one's body that we here conceptualize as a *phantom half-body*. Patients may conceive of their paralyzed limbs as belonging to the examiner, a family member, or some unknown human being. Some reports describe a restriction of the disownership to a single limb, mostly the hand, but it is unclear how far this "restriction" actually results from the structure of the interview itself.

In any case, somatoparaphrenia has also been labeled a *personification anosognosia* (Juba, 1949), and this label points out a key link among super-numerary phantom limbs, phantom half-bodies, and the reduplications of one's entire body. Specifically, each of the above conditions can be described as a gradually increasing personification of one's own body parts. Indeed, the split-off, paralyzed half-body is sometimes designated as a "hemiplegic twin"; yet, hemiplegia is not a necessary condition for the experience of one's hemibody as a phantom. Benedek and von Angyal (1939) described a patient with only a mild hypoesthesia, that is, an impaired tactile sense, of the left side of his body. Nevertheless, this patient denied ownership of his left side. He referred to it as "his brother" for whom he felt pity because he appeared to be paralyzed. This tendency to attribute one's own deficits to other people, whether real or imaginary, was termed *transitivism* by Wernicke (1900). Transitivistic reactions demonstrate that a deficit in one's own corporeal awareness may be well recognized at an implicit level, without evoking, however, an overt emotional concern about one's own state of health. In the place of pity for "the other," anger may be expressed if, for instance, patients complain about having to eat and breathe for themselves as well as for the one lying beneath (Ley & Stauder, 1950; von Stockert, 1944). Such "residual identification" with the part of the body that is claimed to be someone else is also evident in the patients' frequent emphases that the illusory person looks similar to themselves, is a family member, carries a similar name, or has the same occupation.

Published attempts to experimentally manipulate a patient's experience of somatoparaphrenia are relatively rare. It is known that the delusional interpretation, along with anosognosia proper, may temporarily be abolished by caloric vestibular stimulation (Ramachandran, 1995; Rode et al., 1992). This procedure activates the vestibular cortex contralateral to the stimulated ear and arguably restores sensory and attentional functions (Bottini et al., 1994), especially those of the right hemisphere (Dieterich et al., 2003). On the other hand, somatoparaphrenic delusions about left-sided limbs can be extended to involve also the right side of the body when that right side is experimentally rendered "paralyzed" by transient immobilization (Guthrie & Grossman, 1952). The influence of visual self-observation on claims about limb disownership was investigated by Verret and Lapresle (1978). These authors introduced the case of a woman with anosognosia who claimed that her medical doctor was continuously lying along her left side, and she was concerned about his frequent touching her body with his hand. When this doctor showed her his two hands, she was prepared to believe that he had three hands rather than acknowledge that something was wrong with her own left hand. These authors showed that their patient's delusion was dependent on visual perception of her own body. When this was prevented, she immediately recognized her left side as belonging to herself. Interestingly, visual observation of herself in a mirror (while direct view of her own body was still shielded) also restored self-recognition, ruling out the possibility that the personification of her left side could have been conceived of as a "filling-in" process in the course of a severe left-sided neglect. In another patient with somatoparaphrenia and neglect, Daprati et al. (2000) found no influence of visual observation of one's own moving hand on ownership judgments.

An important contribution to the mechanism of "incorporation" of non-body parts into corporeal awareness was provided by Aglioti et al. (1996). In a patient with somatoparaphrenia, claims about disownership of the left hand spread to several rings she still wore on that hand. Temporarily moved over to her right hand, the same rings were immediately recognized. Other objects, never previously associated with the left hand, were normally commented on when placed on the left hand. In a review of this work (Berlucchi & Aglioti, 1997, p. 561; italics added) the authors concluded that "somatoparaphrenia suppresses both the *me* and the *mine* experiences of the disowned body part and related paraphernalia." They further emphasized the importance of their case for the understanding of an "extended corporeal awareness," that is, one that includes inanimate objects such as tools, vehicles, prostheses, and so on.[4]

It is also worth noting that one clinical feature sometimes associated with somatoparaphrenia, exosomesthesia (Roth, 1944; Shapiro et al., 1952), provides another, more vague example of extended body boundaries. Exosomesthesia refers to the feeling of touch localized in objects in peripersonal space and is possibly related to the phenomenon of "extracorporeal phantom tics" as reported in a different context (Karp & Hallett, 1996).[5] An intriguing dissociation between tactile sensitivity and ownership of a body part was described by Bottini et al. (2002). The authors applied tactile stimulation to the hands of a blindfolded stroke patient with anosognosia whose somatoparaphrenic delusion involved the personification of her left side as her niece. Each touch stimulus was announced as being applied to (1) the patient's right hand, (2) the patient's left hand, or (3) the niece's hand. Right-hand stimuli were recognized 100% correctly, left-hand stimuli with 0% accuracy *as long as attention was directed to the paralyzed hand*, but left-hand stimuli were recognized 80% correctly after directing the patient's attention to a delusion-compatible representation of the same body part. This finding shows that top-down expectations may temporarily boost tactile sensitivity in a hypoesthesic region of the body. At the same time, it elegantly proves that spared tactile sensitivity in a body part does not necessarily lead to a sense of ownership for this particular part.

More systematic experimental studies comparing patients' interpretations of supernumerary phantoms with somatoparaphrenic delusions are needed to justify the conceptualization of somatoparaphrenia as the experience of a "phantom hemibody." As yet, such a notion rests primarily on clinical grounds. Especially in the German and French neurological literature of the first half of the 20th century, the phantom half-body was placed somewhere halfway between the supernumerary phantom limb and the various phantoms of the entire body, to which we now proceed.

3. Whole-Body Phantoms: Autoscopic Phenomena

Autoscopic phenomena involve the visualization of one's entire body in extracorporeal space or the feeling that "another body" (by inference, one's own) is lying, standing, or walking close by. This class of phenomena can thus be conceived of as a duplicative experience of one's own body. The duplication may be restricted to the visual modality, in which case an image of one's own body is seen as if one watched oneself in a mirror (autoscopic hallucination). Phenomenologically more similar to the experience of phantom body parts is the "feeling of a presence," a mere somesthetic illusion that lacks visual features and must be viewed as an extension of corporeal awareness into extracorporeal space. Visual and somesthetic senses merge in what is usually referred to as a *doppelgänger experience*, or heautoscopy. *Heautoscopy* is defined as an experience in which one sees another person who is clearly identified as one's own self and whose body is also felt to be a duplication of one's own (see section 3.3 and Figure 9.6B). A similar merging of visual and bodily duplication occurs in an out-of-body experience (OBE). The difference between heautoscopy and an OBE is the following: in heautoscopy, the person reports an encounter with another embodied self, while in OBE one experiences a shift in spatial perspective, that is, a detachment from one's own body, which is then viewed as if from a location in extracorporeal space. This shift in spatial perspective may be accompanied by a shift in psychological perspective, that is, a shift in the experienced relationship between the two selves. With the study of doppelgängers and OBEs (for variants of autoscopic phenomena not considered in the present chapter, see Brugger et al., 1997), we enter a subfield of neuropsychology that pushes the use of the prefix "neuro" to its limits. Historically, these experiences belonged to the domain of parapsychology, a field that has provided valuable phenomenological accounts but whose theoretical models assumed a physical separation of body and mind in a literal sense and has thus remained out of the main body of scientific inquiry (Brugger, 2003b).

3.1. Phantom Bodies: The Feeling of a Presence

The *feeling of a presence* is the vivid experience that some invisible being occupies a precisely "felt" location in near extrapersonal space. The phenomenon is also known as *Anwesenheit* (Thompson, 1982), *concrete awareness* (*leibhafte Bewusstheit*; Jaspers, 1913), and *false proximate awareness* (Koehler & Sauer, 1984). An elderly patient of Critchley's (1953, p. 242) with bilateral cortical atrophy reported that she "would wake in the night with the very intense feeling that somebody was in the room—a person she knew; indeed, with whom she was very familiar. Sometimes, she was at a loss to decide who this could be, but on many occasions, it would dawn on her that this person was none other than herself."

Another of Critchley's patients experienced the purely somesthetic bodily reduplication as an aura of a migraine attack (Critchley, 1986, p. 203; see Lippman, 1953; and Podoll & Robinson, 2001, for similar cases): "They are both 'me' and 'I.' They are about a foot apart, the 'new' body being always on the right side. Yet I've never seen him with my eyes, though I feel his presence very intensely."

Although identification with one's own body or self is rarely reported as explicitly as in Critchley's cases, several phenomenological features justify the conceptualization of the felt presence as an extension of one's own corporeal awareness into extracorporeal space: (1) as in phantom limbs, the spatial localization of the felt being is commonly precise, despite the lack of confirmation of any presence by the visual modality; (2) there is a synchrony of movements such that the invisible being walks along with the patient and often imitates arm and leg movements, either simultaneously or with a time lag (as in Hari et al.'s 1998 case of a supernumerary phantom arm); (3) in cases of focal brain lesions, the parietal lobes are most frequently affected while visual areas are usually spared; (4) after unilateral parietal lobe lesions, the phantom presence is confined to the contralesional space. If strictly lateralized presences are reported after *bilateral* lesions, the right side of space is more often mentioned (Brugger et al., 1996); and (5) as in cases of a personification of one's phantom half-body (see above), a transitivistic function of "alien" felt presences is sometimes obvious (Bychowski, 1943). Thus, exhausted mountaineers frequently overcome hopeless situations by caring for "the other," who climbs with them and whose presence is felt compellingly enough to be offered food (e.g., Smythe, 1934).

Together, these observations suggest that the feeling of a presence rests on postural and kinesthetic representations of one's own body that are falsely localized in extrapersonal space. Ownership over these nonvisual components of corporeal awareness does not need to be acknowledged, not even by those persons who explicitly note distinct changes in bodily awareness during the experience (such as sensorimotor weaknesses or feelings of depersonalization; Brugger et al., 1999). The illusion must thus be considered an invisible, purely "somesthetic *doppelgänger*" (Grüsser & Landis, 1991). For auditory variants of the illusion in the presence of temporal lobe dysfunction, see Gloning, Gloning, and Hoff (1957, case 2) and Blanke et al. (2003).

3.2. Visual Doppelgänger (Autoscopy)

In contrast to the feeling of a presence, autoscopic hallucinations lack any somesthetic component. Originally labeled "mirror hallucinations" (*hallucinations spéculaires*; Féré, 1891; Nouet, 1923), they involve the seeing of one's own body or only one's face as if reflected in a mirror (Zamboni et al., 2005). Unfortunately, most modern reviews of autoscopic phenomena (e.g., Dening & Berrios, 1994; Devinsky et al., 1989; Leischner, 1961) intermingle autoscopic hallucinations and multimodal doppelgänger experiences. Yet, in the French neurologic literature of the turn of the 19th century, the unimodal visual character of autoscopic hallucinations was clearly recognized (Sollier, 1903). This visual variant of autoscopic phenomena is the only one that occurs exclusively after overt brain damage. Occipital areas are primarily involved as the visual symptoms that often accompany autoscopic hallucinations (e.g., light flashes, colored photisms) are typically of elementary nature and thus indicative of low-level visual processing deficiencies. Correspondingly, autoscopic

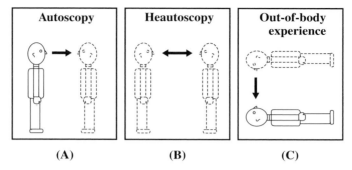

Autoscopy	Heautoscopy	Out-of-body experience
(A)	**(B)**	**(C)**

Figure 9.6. Three types of autoscopic phenomena. (A) In an autoscopic hallucination, the patient (*left*) sees himself as reflected in a mirror. Corporeal awareness is not transferred to the hallucinated image, and the perspective is clearly body-centered. (B) Heautoscopy, or "seeing one's self," implies the existence of two selves. Corporeal awareness spreads to the doppelgänger, and the perspective may shift between ego-centric and alter-ego-centered. (C) In an out-of-body experience, the observing self appears to perceive the body from a location in extracorporeal space (often, but not necessarily, from a vantage point). Modified from Figure 5 of Blanke et al. (2004).

hallucinations, such as the appearance of one's face or body against a background, are most frequently seen after visual cortex damage with occasional simultaneous impairment of the temporal lobes (Maximov, 1973). Involvement of the "extra-striate body area" (Downing et al., 2001) in the lateral occipitotemporal cortex seems likely. If the image of oneself is lateralized, it is usually to the left visual field (Brugger et al., 1997), reflecting, perhaps, the dominance of the right hemisphere in the recognition of one's own face (e.g., Kircher et al., 2001; see Keenan et al., 1999, for review). Consistent with the absence of aspects of corporeal awareness, other than visual representation, in an autoscopic hallucination, is the point in phenomenal space on which the observer's perspective rests. This perspective is always body-centered, that is, the patient describes the hallucination as observed from a regular within-body perspective (Figure 9.6A).

3.3. From Seeing to Being One's Own Doppelgänger: Heautoscopy and Out-of-Body Experiences

Heautoscopy means "seeing one's self" and thus implies the existence of *two* selves, one who observes and one who is observed. Unlike in autoscopic hallucinations, visual aspects of bodily reduplication do not predominate. On the contrary, one's doppelgänger is typically described as a pale, foggy, ghostlike, and transparent figure. More important are feelings of psychological affinity toward one's double. As in the feeling of a presence, the doppelgänger is experienced as a space-occupying entity, which is, however, always recognized as "another me," even if the visual features do not match one's own ("dissimilar heautoscopy": Grotstein, 1983; Sollier, 1903; "heterosexual heautoscopy": Carp, 1952; Letailleur et al., 1958). Increasing ownership over the one encountered in extrapersonal space, that is, the doppelgänger, is paralleled by increasing feelings of depersonalization and a sense of "hollowness" of or detachment from one's real body. In many instances, patients are at a loss to decide where in space to localize the "real me," within the boundaries of the physical body or beyond (Figure 9.6B).

As is evident from this unstable perspective, the transition between heautoscopy (*seeing* a doppelgänger) and an OBE (*being* the doppelgänger) is necessarily blurred. The defining feature of an OBE is the illusory perception of one's own body *from outside* (Figure 9.6C). The term *doppelgänger* is never used in a person's description of an OBE. A proposed mechanism common to both types of autoscopic reduplication is the deficient integration (1) of proprioceptive, tactile, and visual aspects of corporeal awareness, and (2) of information pertaining to personal and extrapersonal space (Blanke et al., 2002, 2004). Implication of the temporoparietal junction, reportedly mediating these integrative functions (e.g., Làdavas, 2002), is in fact suggested in a majority of clinical case reports on autoscopic phenomena (Blanke et al., 2004; Menninger-Lerchenthal, 1946).

It must be noted, however, that heautoscopy and in particular OBEs are also reported by apparently healthy persons. Repeated occurrence of OBEs may be interpreted by the subject as a "paranormal" ability. Nevertheless, a subsequent diagnosis of a neurological disease such as temporal lobe epilepsy (Vuilleumier, Despland, et al., 1997) or multiple sclerosis (Zurfluh, 1983) suggests that these experiences may have to be interpreted as the first manifestations of the disorder. Often, heautoscopy and OBEs occur in the same person, and frequent alternation between the two variants is reported within a single episode of bodily reduplication, especially in the course of a seizure disorder (Kamiya & Okamoto, 1982; Lunn, 1970). We have documented a dramatic case of repeated rapid perspective changes (heautoscopy versus OBE) in a patient with complex-partial seizures (Brugger et al., 1994):

This 21 year old man had been suffering from seizures since age 15. They originated in the left mesio-basal region that contained a tumor. After having stopped anticonvulsive medication against the advice of his doctors, he woke up one morning and, to his amazement, saw himself still lying in bed. As he was anxious to get to work, he tried to wake up the body in the bed first verbally, then by aggressive attempts to shake the body and even jumping on it. The localization of the observing self switched repeatedly from the one being upright to the one passively lying in bed. While being the supine one, he felt completely awake, though paralyzed and increasingly scared by the attacks of "the other me." In order to stop the "intolerable feeling of being divided in two" he finally jumped out of a window of his third floor appartment [*sic*]. A large bush saved his life.

The issue of perspective taking may provide a springboard for the fusion of physiological and psychological theories of autoscopic phenomena. The physiology of the maintenance of and shifts in first-person perspective is no longer beyond our grasp (see Vogeley & Fink, 2003, for review). Indeed, there is reason to believe that the ability to shift one's spatial perspective may be a prerequisite for higher-order transformations in perspective related to imitation and empathy (Gallese, 2001; Hatfield et al., 1994; Ruby & Decety, 2003).

In autoscopic phenomena, the shifts in spatial perspective illustrated in Figure 9.6 are systematically related to changes in the subject's psychological perspective toward the phantom double. During autoscopic hallucinations, maintenance of a body-centered perspective is unshakable. The visual doppelgänger is observed with amazement but never elicits confusion about "being in two places at once." In contrast, the unstable spatial perspective experienced during heautoscopy is frequently perceived as threatening and may be accompanied by self-destructive behaviors (Carp, 1952; Maack & Mullen, 1983; Wigan, 1884). Finally, the subjectively unequivocal spatial detachment from one's own body in an OBE is almost always paralleled by an emotionally detached attitude toward a serious illness or a life-threatening danger. The role of denial in OBEs has been repeatedly emphasized (Ehrenwald, 1974; Menz, 1984), and transitivistic reactions are the rule. Subjects during an OBE in the course of a near-death experience (Greyson, 2000) are subjectively convinced that it is their *bodies* that face danger, not their selves. The description of an OBE during a near-drowning, taken from the belletristic literature, may illustrate this point:

In his mind, Findlayson had already escaped from the boat, and was circling high in the air to find a rest for the sole of his foot. His body—he was really sorry for its gross helplessness—lay in the stern, the water rushing about its knees. "How very ridiculous!" he said to himself..., "The poor beast is going to be drowned.... I am on shore already. Why doesn't it come along?" (Kipling, 1893/2003, "The Bridge Builders," p. 19)

One phenomenological detail common to both heautoscopy and OBEs concerns the illusory perception of nonbody parts during bodily reduplication. While this issue has received some attention in the older literature, its treatment is underrepresented in more recent work. Gurewitsch (1933) mocked Menninger-Lerchenthal's (1932) analysis of Goethe's heautoscopic experience, in which he saw himself sitting on a horse. Gurewitsch argued that, according to Menninger-Lerchenthal's view of the doppelgänger as an externalized body schema, Goethe would have reduplicated not only his own body schema, but also that of the horse. Menninger-Lerchenthal (1935, pp. 164–166) rejected the validity of this critique, pointing out that, for a person on horseback, the horse transiently becomes a part of his own body schema. In fact, the reduplication of body-related paraphernalia such as clothes, tools, or vehicles is the rule both in heautoscopy and OBEs and is reminiscent of the incorporation of hand-related paraphernalia in amputation phantoms and their reduplication in cases of supernumerary phantom arms (Hari et al., 1998; see Figure 9.4A). The view, from an apparent out-of-body location, of environmental objects beyond grasping space poses a different problem. There are many indications, especially from scattered observations in the parapsychological literature, that vision in an OBE involves the synesthetic integration of auditory environmental cues, much like the phenomenal visual experience of patients who deny their cortical blindness (Goldenberg et al., 1995). For the role of the vestibular system in shaping complex visual phenomenology, see Skworzoff (1931) and Blanke et al. (2004).

4. Research Perspectives

Encounters with a phantom of one's own body and self or experiences of oneself as a phantom are incomparably more complex than are sensations of a single phantom limb. To equate a (supernumerary) phantom arm with "an autoscopic double of the real arm" (Todd & Dewhurst, 1955, p. 54) or the heautoscopic doppelgänger with a "phantom of the entire body" (Mikorey, 1952) and an OBE with a "generalized version of the phantom limb experience" (Metzinger, 2003, p. 488) may be considered oversimplifications, if not mere metaphors. After all, whole-body amputations do not occur, nor are patients reporting autoscopic reduplications in a state of complete bilateral deafferentation/deefferentation (but see Bilikiewicz, 1969; and Wisdom, 1953, for thought-provoking speculations). Yet, from a phenomenological perspective, subjects' descriptions of the perceived lawfulness of out-of-body states are highly reminiscent of those of subjects describing out-of-limb experiences.

One example concerns the phenomenon of obstacle shunning, repeatedly mentioned above in connection with phantom limbs. If, during an OBE, subjects walk around in a virtual environment, their reactions to contact with solid matter vary greatly. Some report being unable to "penetrate" (imagined) obstacles; others easily pass through furniture and walls (Figure 9.7A); while still others do so only with considerable reluctance (e.g., Bruce, 1999; Leaning, 1928; Monroe, 1971).[6] It would be unwise to disregard such meticulous descriptions just because most of them originate from the parapsychological literature. Taking phenomenology seriously does not imply accepting paranormal interpretations. It rather opens up the possibility of investigating phenomena that have retained a "ghostly" character solely because they have not yet been subject to experimental scrutiny.

The case of obstacle shunning is a neat illustration of the modifications of corporeal awareness by "intuitive physics," that is, top-down influences by knowledge about the behavior of physical objects. Paradigms to quantify the strength of such interactions between perception and knowledge exist. Most elegant is a method introduced by Shiffrar and Freyd (1990), who showed that visual apparent motion of body parts is influenced by the depiction of a solid object along with two rapidly alternating pictures of a limb at slightly different locations (Figure 9.7B). As long as the temporal interval between the two pictures is brief (typically <300 ms), the apparent motion trajectories of the body part pass right through the solid object. However, with longer inter-stimulus intervals, obstacle shunning manifests itself as an adjustment of these trajectories such that the path of apparent motion becomes curved and thus avoids the location of the solid object. This methodology should be applied to

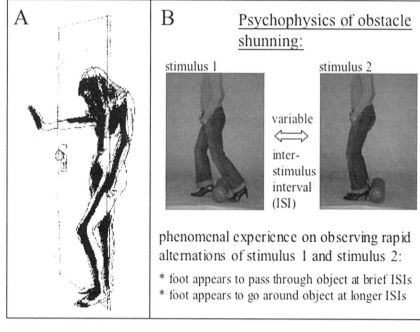

Figure 9.7. (A) During an out-of-body experience, some individuals report an ability, others an inability, to "penetrate" solid matter. The decreased ability to maintain corporeal awareness at a position in space seen or imagined to be occupied by a solid object is reminiscent of obstacle shunning in amputees (see section 1.1). (B) Solidity constraints in the perception of apparent motion of the human body (Shiffrar & Freyd, 1990). Individual differences in obstacle shunning may reflect individual differences in the susceptibility to visual-somesthetic interactions. Reproduced from Vieira (1986, Figure 262), with the permission of the author.

subjects with phantom limbs or phantom bodies who vary in their shunning behavior. We would predict stronger solidity constraints in those subjects who report shunning behavior in their spontaneous phantom experiences as compared to subjects who do not. Such a finding would provide a plausible basis to a phenomenon as yet considered too bizarre to be investigated.

Unjustified neglect of phenomenological detail is not restricted to reports from parapsychological sources. The neurological literature on hemiphantoms and phantoms of the entire body is replete with clinical observations whose meaningfulness for a neuropsychological understanding of corporeal awareness could only be appreciated after further experimentation. Among the relatively low-level somesthetic aspects of such phantoms, we mention a consistent bias, not present for amputation phantoms, for a more salient representation of the upper parts of the body. In fact, meaningful interactions with one's hemiphantom in somatoparaphrenia are more often reported for the "action dominant" upper limbs. Consistent with this, in autoscopic phenomena, visualization is sometimes restricted to head, arms, and chest (Blanke et al., 2004; Conrad, 1953; Genner, 1947; but see Blanke et al., 2002).

Interestingly, work with healthy subjects has produced evidence for a similar relative overrepresentation of the upper extremities. Reed and Farah (1995) explored the perception of changes in another person's limb positions as influenced by simultaneous movements of the observer's own limbs. Changes in arm positions were easier to detect than those in leg positions. The pattern of results further suggested that information about one's own body is used in a mandatory way when judging another person's visually perceived body posture (for additional discussion, see chapters 7 and 11). Reed and Farah's work is thus an early contribution to a growing body of literature on the intimate relationships of action observation and action execution (see Gallese & Goldman, 1998; Rizzolatti et al., 2001, for overviews). The system matching these two processes should be one central focus of future research concerning the variability of individual phantom experiences. Potential contributions of this system to the genesis of phantoms could be of particular theoretical importance in the discussion of innate components of corporeal awareness, both for body parts (see above) and for entire bodies (e.g., Ring & Cooper, 1999).

Among the "higher-order" phenomena of phantom experiences are those pertaining to the distinction between self and nonself. While phantoms after peripheral or spinal deafferentation are always considered an integral part of one's own body and self (except in cases of psychotic elaboration; Gallinek, 1939; Stip & Perreault, 1993), this distinction may get blurred in the face of hemi- or whole-body phantoms. Maintenance of a body-centered perspective appears to prevent one's reduplicated body from taking an autonomous role and thus becoming out of control of one's own intentions (Brugger, 2002). This clinical observation is consistent with a view of a continuum from motor to conceptual cognition (Amorim, 2003; Ruby & Decety, 2003). The psychological content of autoscopic reduplications may thus be shaped by a patient's awareness, more or less compromised, of the true source of own action plans. On the one hand, currently popular experimental designs to investigate agency attributions in normal subjects or selected patient groups (e.g., Farrer & Frith, 2002; Knoblich, 2003; see Blakemore & Decety, 2001; and Wegner, 2002, for overviews) should be applied also to patients with autoscopic phenomena. On the other hand, once-popular but apparently forgotten clinical concepts, such as that of transitivism should be revived. Intriguingly simple experiments have shown that the projection of one's own disturbances of corporeal awareness onto other people depends on the alignment of one's own body axis with that of others (Gloning, Hift, et al., 1957), an observation highly relevant to transitivistic own-body projections onto merely hallucinated bodies (Schilder, 1919).

Certainly, in addition to promoting studies with special populations, more efforts should be undertaken to refine the methods to evoke phantom sensations in healthy subjects. These comprise the provocation of a transient limb deafferentation, for example, by intravenous regional or by pressure-cuff-induced anesthesia (e.g., Brasil-Neto et al., 1992; Gross & Melzack, 1978; Melzack & Bromage, 1973) and the application of vibratory stimulation (Craske, 1977; Jones, 1988; see also chapter 8 for discussion). The latter technique allows the transient dissociation of objectively realized and subjectively felt positions of one's limbs by tendon vibration. Clever elaborations of this basic technique have been introduced to elicit the experience of various nonlimb phantoms. Most famous is the "Pinocchio illusion," i.e., the experience of a phantom nose (Lackner, 1988; for the use of tendon vibration to produce a phantom of one's entire body, see Lackner, 1992).

Both phantoms of paraplegic patients and vibration-induced phantoms in healthy subjects typically disappear upon looking at the real limb. Little is known about the precise nature of this visual-somesthetic interaction. It is known, however, that vision and somatosensation are highly cooperative senses (e.g., Newport et al., 2001; see also chapters 3, 4, and 5). Although under certain conditions, vision will "capture" proprioception, under other conditions the brain is more inclined to believe proprioceptive information rather than vision (e.g., Mon-Williams et al., 1997; Wann & Ibrahim, 1992). Understanding the processes that regulate these shifts in visual-proprioceptive dominance is especially important for a better understanding of transitions from seeing to being one's own doppelgänger. As *feeling* a phantom hand can be induced by watching the mirror image of one's existing hand (Ramachandran et al., 1995), continuous observation of an online image of one's entire body can produce an effect of whole-body visual capture (Stratton, 1899), just as the person immersed in a virtual-reality environment actually *feels* herself to be at the place where her own body is seen (Rheingold, 1991, p. 264).

Notes

1. The keyword *phantom* alone would have included also articles using the term in a completely different meaning. These include the definition of a dummy used for demonstrations during medical training or for simulation purposes. In our 1-minute experiment, subjects who produced associations to this type of phantom (medical students, exclusively) were not considered for the analyses.

2. According to this definition, phantom limbs after spinal-cord injury would also appear to belong to the category of "supernumerary phantoms." Traditionally, however, the term is reserved for the awareness of extra limbs after brain lesions (Brugger, 2003a).

3. In direct opposition to this "bilateral representation" hypothesis (Grouios, 1996), Kinsbourne (1995) proposed an attentional model of congenital phantoms that views intact representations of one spared limb as *inhibitory* to the genesis of phantom sensations. This made him overestimate the actual incidence of bilateral (as opposed to unilateral) limb aplasia (p. 217).

4. It should be noted here that individual patients' reactions to the sight of paraphernalia vary greatly. One patient of Sandifer (1946) accused his doctor of wearing his (the patient's) ring when urged to look at his left hand, which he claimed to be the doctor's. Confabulative "incorporation" of a nurse's arm, including her wristwatch, was reported by Critchley (1953, p. 239). On the other hand, mere visual observation of a scar on the left, subjectively disowned arm could restore ownership for a patient discussed by Juba (1949, case 2).

5. An equivalent of exosomesthesia can be produced in normal subjects who watch an examiner touch a rubber hand aligned with their own hand, which is similarly touched but remains concealed from vision (Botvinick & Cohen, 1998; Pavani et al., 2000; chapter 8). The taps thus delivered are felt "out there" in an apparent out-of-body location. This rubber-hand effect has generated significant secondary research, in particular in connection with clinical disorders involving unilateral somatosensory deficits (Farnè et al., 2000; Rorden et al., 1999).

6. This latter author reports the absence of shunning behavior during an OBE. Trajectories of phantom body motion were nevertheless constrained by higher-order conceptual knowledge about physical objects: "I went out into the corridor, and I just went through the door (force of habit I suppose, for my exit might just as well have been through the wall, because I did not open the door at all but just went through)" (Leaning, 1928, p. 27).

Acknowledgments   Part of the work described in this chapter was supported by Swiss National Science Foundation grant no. 3100–67168.01.

References

Abbatucci, J. (1894). *Etude psychologique sur les hallucinations des amputés.* Unpublished doctoral thesis, University of Bordeaux.

Abramson, A. S., & Feibel, A. (1981). The phantom phenomenon: Its use and disuse. *Bulletin of the New York Academy of Medicine, 57*, 99–112.

Aglioti, S., Smania, N., Atzei, A., & Berlucchi, G. (1997). Spatio-temporal properties of the pattern of evoked phantom sensations in a left index amputee patient. *Behavioral Neuroscience, 111*, 867–872.

Aglioti, S., Smania, N., Manfredi, M., & Berlucchi, G. (1996). Disownership of left hand and objects related to it in a patient with right brain damage. *Neuroreport, 8*, 293–296.

Alkadhi, H., Brugger, P., Hotz Boendermaker, S., Crelier, G., Curt, A., Hepp-Reymond, M.-C., & Kollias, S. S. (2005). What disconnection tells about motor imagery: Evidence from paraplegic patients. *Cerebral Cortex, 15*, 131–140.

Altschuler, E. L., Wisdom, S. B., Stone, L., Foster, C., Galasko, D., Llewellyn, D. M. E., & Ramachandran, V. S. (1999). Rehabilitation of hemiparesis after stroke with a mirror. *Lancet, 353*, 2035–2036.

Amorim, M.-A. (2003). "What is my avatar seeing?" The coordination of "out-of-body" and "embodied" perspectives for scene recognition across views. *Visual Cognition, 10*, 157–199.

Babinski, M. J. (1914). Contribution à l'étude des troubles mentaux dans l'hémiplégie organique cérébrale (anosognosie). *Revue Neurologique, 27*, 845–848.

Becker, H. (1949). Über Störungen des Körperbildes und über Phantomerlebnisse bei Rückenmarksverletzten. *Archiv für Psychiatrie und Zeitschrift für die gesamte Neurologie, 182*, 97–139.

Benedek, L., & von Angyal, L. (1939). Über Körperschemastörungen bei Psychosen teils unter experimentellen Bedingungen. *Monatsschrift für Psychiatrie und Neurologie, 101*, 26–84.

Berlucchi, G., & Aglioti, S. (1997). The body in the brain: Neural bases of corporeal awareness. *Trends in Neuroscience, 20*, 560–564.

Bilikiewicz, T. (1969). Total somatectomy and its psychopathological consequences. *Polish Medical Journal, 8*, 481–493.

Blakemore, S.-J., & Decety, J. (2001). From the perception of action to the understanding of intention. *Nature Reviews Neuroscience, 2*, 561–567.

Blakemore, S.-J., Wolpert, D. M., & Frith, C. D. (2002). Abnormalities in the awareness of action. *Trends in Cognitive Sciences, 6*, 237–242.

Blanke, O., Ortigue, S., Coeytaux, A., Martory, M. D., & Landis, T. (2003). Hearing of a presence. *Neurocase, 9*, 329–339.

Blanke, O., Ortigue, S., Landis, T., & Seeck, M. (2002). Stimulating illusory own-body perceptions. *Nature, 419*(6904), 269–270.

Blanke, O., Landis, T., Spinelli, L., & Seeck, M. (2004). Out-of-body experience and autoscopy of neurological origin. *Brain, 127*, 243–258.

Boisson, D., & Luauté, J. (2004). Les somatoparaphrénies. *Annales Médico Psychologiques, 162*, 55–59.

Bonnier, P. (1905). L'aschématie. *Revue Neurologique, 54*, 605–609.

Bors, E. (1951). Phantom limbs of patients with spinal cord injury. *Archives of Neurology and Psychiatry, 66*, 610–631.

Bors, E. (1979). Extinction and synesthesia in patients with spinal cord injuries. *Paraplegia, 17*, 21–31.

Bottini, G., Bisiach, E., Sterzi, R., & Vallar, G. (2002). Feeling touches in someone else's hand. *Neuroreport, 13*, 249–252.

Bottini, G., Sterzi, R., Paulesu, E., Vallar, G., Cappa, S. F., Erminio, F., Passingham, R. E., Frith, C. D., & Frackowiak, R. S. (1994). Identification of the central vestibular projections in man: A positron emission tomography activation study. *Experimental Brain Research, 99*, 164–169.

Botvinick, M., & Cohen, J. (1998). Rubber hands "feel" touch that eyes see. *Nature, 391*, 756.

Brasil-Neto, J. P., Cohen, L. G., Pascual-Leone, A., Jabir, F. K., Wall, R. T., & Hallett, M. (1992). Rapid reversible modulation of human motor outputs after transient deafferentation of the forearm: A study with transcranial magnetic stimulation. *Neurology, 42*, 1302–1306.

Bruce, R. (1999). *Astral dynamics: A new approach to out-of-body experiences.* Charlottesville, VA: Hampton Roads.

Brücke, H. (1950). Über die Umorganisation des Körperschemas nach plastisch-chirurgischen Eingriffen. *Wiener Klinische Wochenschrift, 62,* 152–154.

Bruehlmeier, M., Dietz, V., Leenders, K. L., Roelcke, U., Missimer, J., & Curt, A. (1998). How does the human brain deal with a spinal cord injury? *European Journal of Neuroscience, 10,* 3918–3922.

Brugger, P. (2001). From haunted brain to haunted science: A cognitive neuroscience view of paranormal and pseudoscientific thought. In R. Lange & J. Houran (Eds.), *Hauntings and poltergeists: Multidisciplinary perspectives* (pp. 195–213). Jefferson, NC: McFarland.

Brugger, P. (2002). Reflective mirrors: Perspective-taking in autoscopic phenomena. *Cognitive Neuropsychiatry, 7,* 179–194.

Brugger, P. (2003a). Supernumerary phantoms: A comment on Grossi et al.'s (2002) spare thoughts on spare limbs. *Perceptual and Motor Skills, 97,* 3–10.

Brugger, P. (2003b). Neuropsychiatrie und Parapsychologie autoskopischer Phänomene. *Nervenarzt, 74,* 293–295.

Brugger, P., Agosti, R., Regard, M., Wieser, H.-G., & Landis, T. (1994). Heautoscopy, epilepsy and suicide. *Journal of Neurology, Neurosurgery, and Psychiatry, 57,* 838–839.

Brugger, P., Kollias, S. S., Müri, R. M., Crelier, G., Hepp-Reymond, M.-C., & Regard, M. (2000). Beyond re-membering: Phantom sensations of congenitally absent limbs. *Proceedings of the National Academy of Sciences, USA, 97,* 6167–6172.

Brugger, P., Regard, M., & Landis, T. (1996). Unilaterally felt "presences": The neuropsychiatry of one's invisible Doppelgänger. *Neuropsychiatry, Neuropsychology, and Behavioral Neurology, 9,* 114–122.

Brugger, P., Regard, M., & Landis, T. (1997). Illusory reduplication of one's own body: Phenomenology and classification of autoscopic phenomena. *Cognitive Neuropsychiatry, 2,* 19–38.

Brugger, P., Regard, M., Landis, T., & Oelz, O. (1999). Hallucinatory experiences in extreme-altitude climbers. *Neuropsychiatry, Neuropsychology, and Behavioral Neurology, 12,* 67–71.

Brugger, P., Regard, M., & Shiffrar, M. (2001). Hand movement observation in a person born without hands: Is body scheme innate? *Journal of Neurology, Neurosurgery, and Psychiatry, 70,* 276.

Buccino, G., Binkofski, F., Fink, G. R., Fadiga, L., Fogassi, L., Gallese, V., Seitz, R. J., Zilles, K., Rizzolatti, G., & Freund, H.-J. (2001). Action observation activates premotor and parietal areas in a somatotopic manner: An fMRI study. *European Journal of Neuroscience, 13,* 400–404.

Burchard, J. M. (1965). Zur Frage nach der Natur von Phantomerlebnissen bei angeborener Gliedmassenverstümmelung. *Archiv für Psychiatrie und Zeitschrift für die gesamte Neurologie, 207,* 360–377.

Burke, D. C., & Woodward, J. M. (1976). Pain and phantom sensations in spinal paralysis. In P. J. Vinken & G. W. Bruyn (Eds.), *Handbook of clinical neurology, Vol. 26* (pp. 489–499). Amsterdam: North Holland.

Bychowski, G. (1943). Disorders in the body image in the clinical pictures of psychoses. *Journal of Nervous and Mental Disease, 97,* 310–335.

Cacace, A. T., Cousins, J. P., Parnes, S. M., McFarland, D. J., Semenoff, D., Holmes, T., Davenport, C., Stegbauer, K., & Lovely, T. J. (1999). Cutaneous-evoked tinnitus.

II: Review of neuroanatomical, physiological and functional imaging studies. *Audiology and Neuro-Otology, 4*, 258–268.

Canavero, S., Bonicalzi, V., Castellano, G., Perozzo, P., & Massa-Micon, B. (1999). Painful supernumerary phantom arm following motor cortex stimulation for central poststroke pain. *Journal of Neurosurgery, 91*, 121–123.

Carlen, P. L., Wall, P. D., Nadvorna, H., & Steinbach, T. (1978). Phantom limbs and related phenomena in recent traumatic amputations. *Neurology, 28*, 211–217.

Carp, E. (1952). Troubles de l'image du corps. *Acta Neurologica et Psychiatrica Belgica, 52*, 461–475.

Clarke, S., Regli, L., Janzer, R. C., Assal, G., & de Tribolet, N. (1996). Phantom face: Conscious correlate of neural reorganization after removal of primary sensory neurons. *Neuroreport, 7*, 2853–2857.

Conomy, J. P. (1973). Disorders of body image after spinal cord injury. *Neurology, 23*, 842–850.

Conrad, K. (1953). Über ein eigenartiges Spiegelphantom: Heautoskopisches Phänomen als Dauerzustand bei Hypophysentumor. *Nervenarzt, 24*, 265–270.

Craske, B. (1977). Perception of impossible limb positions induced by tendon vibration. *Science, 196*, 71–73.

Critchley, M. (1953). *The parietal lobes*. London: Hafner.

Critchley, M. (1955/1979). *The divine banquet of the brain and other essays*. New York: Raven.

Critchley, M. (1986). *The citadel of the senses and other essays*. New York: Raven.

Cronholm, B. (1951). *Phantom limbs in amputees*. Stockholm: Ivar Haeggströms.

Curt, A., Alkadhi, H., Crelier, R. G., Hotz Boendermaker, S., Hepp-Reymond, M.-C., & Kollias, S. S. (2002). Changes of non-affected upper limb representation in paraplegic patients as assessed by fMRI. *Brain, 125*, 2567–2578.

Daprati, E., Sirigu, A., Pradat-Diehl, P., Franck, N., & Jeannerod, M. (2000). Recognition of self-produced movement in a case of severe neglect. *Neurocase, 6*, 477–486.

Davis, A. (1975). Pain and suffering after spinal cord injury. *Clinical Orthopaedics, 112*, 76–80.

Dening, T. R., & Berrios, G. E. (1994). Autoscopic phenomena. *British Journal of Psychiatry, 165*, 808–817.

Devinsky, O., Feldmann, E., Burrowes, K., & Bromfield, E. (1989). Autoscopic phenomena with seizures. *Archives of Neurology, 46*, 1080–1088.

Dieterich, M., Bense, S., Lutz, S., Drzezga, A., Stephan, T., Bartenstein, P., & Brandt, T. (2003). Dominance for vestibular cortical function in the non-dominant hemisphere. *Cerebral Cortex, 13*, 994–1007.

Donnet, A., Schmitt, A., Poncet, M., Graziani, N., & Grisoli, F. (1997). Hallucinations de membres surnuméraires, héminégligence gauche et hypersexualité dans un cas d'hématome capsulo-lenticulaire droit. *Revue Neurologique, 153*, 587–590.

Downing, P. E., Jiang, Y., Shuman, M., & Kanwisher, N. (2001). A cortical area selective for visual processing of the human body. *Science, 293*, 2470–2473.

Egyd, B., & Janke, M. (1967). Erfahrungen mit der Phantomgymnastik bei der Rehabilitation Amputierter. *Beiträge zur Orthopädie und Traumatologie, 14*, 521–529.

Ehrenwald, H. (1930). Verändertes Erleben des Körperbildes mit konsekutiver Wahnbildung bei linksseitiger Hemiplegie. *Monatsschrift für Psychiatrie und Neurologie, 75*, 89–97.

Ehrenwald, J. (1974). Out-of-the-body experiences and denial of death. *Journal of Nervous and Mental Disease, 159*, 227–233.

Ersland, L., Rosen, G., Lundervold, A., Smievoll, A. I., Tillung, T., Sundberg, H., & Hugdahl, K. (1996). Phantom limb imaginary fingertapping causes primary motor cortex activation: An fMRI study. *Neuroreport, 8*, 207–210.

Ettlin, T. M., Seiler, W., & Kaeser, H. E. (1980). Phantom and amputation illusions in paraplegic patients. *European Neurology, 19*, 12–19.

Farnè, A., Pavani, F., Menghello, F., & Làdavas, E. (2000). Left tactile extinction following visual stimulation of a rubber hand. *Brain, 123*, 2350–2360.

Farrer, C., & Frith, C. D. (2002). Experiencing oneself vs. another person as being the cause of an action: The neural correlates of the experience of agency. *NeuroImage, 15*, 596–603.

Féré, C. (1891). Note sur les hallucinations autoscopiques ou spéculaires et sur les hallucinations altruistes. *Comptes Rendus de la Societée de Biologie, 43*, 451–453.

Finger, S., & Hustwit, M. P. (2003). Five early accounts of phantom limb in context: Paré, Descartes, Lemos, Bell, and Mitchell. *Neurosurgery, 52*, 675–686.

Flor, H., Elbert, T., Knecht, S., Wienbruch, C., Pantev, C., Birbaumer, N., Larbig, W., & Taub, E. (1995). Phantom-limb pain as a perceptual correlate of cortical reorganization following arm amputation. *Nature, 375*, 482–484.

Flor, H., Elbert, T., Mühlnickel, W., Pantev, C., Wienbruch, C., & Taub, E. (1998). Cortical reorganization and phantom phenomena in congenital and traumatic upper-extremity amputees. *Experimental Brain Research, 119*, 205–212.

Franz, E. A., & Ramachandran, V. S. (1998). Bimanual coupling in amputees with phantom limbs. *Nature Neuroscience, 1*, 443–444.

Funk, M. (2001). *Mentale Rotation von Händen und körperfremden Objekten: Untersuchungen mit Kindern und Erwachsenen mit und ohne kongenitalem Handmangel.* Unpublished master's thesis, University of Zurich.

Funk, M., & Brugger, P. (2002). Visual recognition of hands by persons born with only one hand. *Cortex, 38*, 860–863.

Funk, M., Shiffrar, M., & Brugger, P. (in press). Hand movement observation by individuals born without hands: Phantom limb experience constrains visual limb perception. *Experimental Brain Research.*

Gallagher, S., Butterworth, G. E., Lew, A., & Cole, J. (1998). Hand-mouth coordination, congenital absence of limb, and evidence for innate body schemas. *Brain and Cognition, 38*, 53–65.

Gallese, V. (2001). The "shared manifold" hypothesis. From mirror neurons to empathy. *Journal of Consciousness Studies, 8*, 33–50.

Gallese, V., & Goldman, A. (1998). Mirror neurons and the simulation theory of mind-reading. *Trends in Cognitive Sciences, 2*, 493–501.

Gallinek, A. (1939). The phantom limb: Its origins and its relationship to the hallucination of psychotic states. *American Journal of Psychiatry, 96*, 413–422.

Genner, T. (1947). Das Sehen des eigenen Spiegelbildes als epileptisches Äquivalent. *Wiener Klinische Wochenschrift, 59*, 656–658.

Gerstmann, J. (1942). Problem of imperception of disease and of impaired body territories with organic lesions. Relation to body scheme and its disorders. *Archives of Neurology and Psychiatry, 48*, 890–913.

Giraux, P., & Sirigu, A. (2003). Illusory movements of the paralyzed limb restore motor cortex activity. *NeuroImage, 20*, S107–S111.

Gloning, I., Gloning, K., & Hoff, H. (1957). Die Halluzinationen in der Hirnpathologie. *Wiener Zeitschrift für Nervenheilkunde, 14*, 289–310.

Gloning, I., Hift, S., Pateisky, K., & Tschabitscher, H. (1957). Körperschemastörung im Bereich der Augenregion. *Wiener Zeitschrift für Nervenheilkunde, 13*, 84–99.

Goldenberg, G., Müllbacher, W., & Nowak, A. (1995). Imagery without perception: A case study of anosognosia for cortical blindness. *Neuropsychologia, 33,* 1373–1382.

Greyson, B. (2000). Dissociation in people who have near-death experiences: Out of their bodies or out of their minds? *Lancet, 355,* 460–463.

Gross, Y., & Melzack, R. (1978). Dissociation of real and perceived limbs by pressure-cuff ischemia. *Experimental Neurology, 61,* 680–688.

Grossi, D., Di Cesare, G., & Tamburro, R. P. (2002). On the syndrome of the "spare limb": One case. *Perceptual and Motor Skills, 94,* 476–478.

Grotstein, J. S. (1983). Autoscopy: The experience of oneself as a double. *Hillside Journal of Clinical Psychiatry, 5,* 259–304.

Grouios, G. (1996). Phantom limb perceptuomotor "memories" in a congenital limb child. *Medical Science Research, 24,* 503–504.

Grüsser, O.-J., & Landis, T. (1991). Visual agnosia and other disturbances of visual perception and cognition. In J. Cronly-Dillon (Ed.), *Vision and visual dysfunction, Vol. 12* (pp. 297–303). London: Macmillan.

Grüsser, S. M., Mühlnickel, W., Schaefer, M., Villringer, K., Christmann, C., Koeppe, C., & Flor, H. (2004). Remote activation of referred phantom sensation and cortical reorganization in human upper extremity amputees. *Experimental Brain Research, 154,* 97–102.

Gurewitsch, M. (1933). Weitere Beiträge zur Lehre vom interparietalen Syndrom bei Geisteskrankheiten. *Zeitschrift für die gesamte Neurologie und Psychiatrie, 146,* 126–144.

Guthrie, T. C., & Grossman, E. M. (1952). A study of the syndromes of denial. *Archives of Neurology and Psychiatry, 68,* 362–371.

Halligan, P. W. (2002). Phantom limbs: The body in mind. *Cognitive Neuropsychiatry, 7,* 251–268.

Halligan, P. W., & Marshall, J. C. (1995). Supernumerary phantom limb after right hemisphere stroke. *Journal of Neurology, Neurosurgery, and Psychiatry, 59,* 341–342.

Halligan, P. W., Marshall, J. C., & Wade, D. T. (1993). Three arms: A case study of supernumerary phantom limb after right hemisphere stroke. *Journal of Neurology, Neurosurgery, and Psychiatry, 56,* 159–166.

Halligan, P. W., Marshall, J. C., & Wade, D. T. (1994). Sensory disorganization and perceptual plasticity after limb amputation: A follow-up study. *Neuroreport, 5,* 1341–1345.

Halligan, P. W., Marshall, J. C., Wade, D. T., Davey, J., & Morrison, D. (1993). Thumb in cheek? Sensory reorganization and perceptual plasticity after limb amputation. *Neuroreport, 4,* 233–236.

Hari, R., Hänninen, R., Mäkinen, T., Jousmäki, V., Forss, N., Seppä, M., & Salonen, O. (1998). Three hands: Fragmentation of human bodily awareness. *Neuroscience Letters, 240,* 131–134.

Hatfield, E., Cacioppo, J. T., & Rapson, R. L. (1994). *Emotional contagion.* Cambridge: Cambridge University Press.

Hécaen, H., & de Ajuriaguerra, J. (1952). *Méconnaissances et hallucinations corporelles.* Paris: Masson.

Henderson, W. F., & Smyth, G. E. (1948). Phantom limbs. *Journal of Neurology, Neurosurgery, and Psychiatry, 11,* 88–112.

Houghton, A. D., Nicolls, G., Houghton, A. L., Saadah, E., & McColl, L. (1994). Phantom pain: Natural history and association with rehabilitation. *Annals of the Royal College of Surgeons of England, 76,* 22–25.

Hunter, J. P., Katz, J., & Davis, K. D. (2003). The effect of tactile and visual sensory inputs on phantom limb awareness. *Brain, 126*, 579–589.

Iriki, A., Tanaka, M., & Iwamura, Y. (1996). Coding of modified body schema during tool use by macaque postcentral neurons. *Neuroreport, 7*, 2325–2330.

Jalavisto, E. (1950). Adaptation in the phantom limb phenomenon as influenced by the age of the amputees. *Journal of Gerontology, 5*, 339–342.

Jaspers, K. (1913). Über leibhaftige Bewusstheiten (Bewusstheitstäuschungen), ein psychopathologisches Elementarsymptom. *Zeitschrift für Pathopsychologie, 2*, 150–161.

Jones, L. A. (1988). Motor illusions: What do they reveal about proprioception? *Psychological Bulletin, 103*, 72–86.

Juba, A. (1949). Beitrag zur Struktur der ein- und doppelseitigen Körperschemastörungen: Fingeragnosie, atypische Anosognosien. *Monatsschrift für Psychiatrie und Neurologie, 118*, 11–29.

Kaas, J. H., Merzenich, M. M., & Killakey, H. P. (1983). The reorganization of somatosensory cortex following peripheral nerve damage in adult and developing mammals. *Annual Review of Neuroscience, 6*, 325–356.

Kallio, K. E. (1952). Phantom limb of forearm stump cleft by kineplastic surgery. *Journal International de Chirurgie, 12*, 110–119.

Kamiya, S., & Okamoto, S. (1982). Double consciousness in epileptics: A clinical picture and minor hemisphere specialization. In H. Akimotot, H. Kazamatsuri, M. Seino, & A. Ward (Eds.), *Advances in epileptology: 13th epilepsy international symposium* (pp. 397–401). New York: Raven.

Karp, B. I., & Hallett, M. (1996). Extracorporeal "phantom" tics in Tourette's syndrome. *Neurology, 46*, 38–40.

Katz, D. (1920). Psychologische Versuche mit Amputierten. *Zeitschrift für Psychologie und Physiologie der Sinnesorgane, 85*, 83–117.

Katz, J. (1992). Psychophysiological contributions to phantom limbs. *Canadian Journal of Psychiatry, 37*, 282–298.

Keenan, J. P., McCutcheon, B., Freund, S., Gallup, Jr., G. G., Sanders, G., & Pascual-Leone, A. (1999). Left hand advantage in a self-face recognition task. *Neuropsychologia, 37*, 1421–1425.

Kew, J. J. M., Halligan, P. W., Marshall, J. C., Passingham, R. E., Rothwell, J. C., Ridding, M. C., Marsden, C. D., & Brooks, D. J. (1997). Abnormal access of axial vibrotactile input to deafferented somatosensory cortex in human upper limb amputees. *Journal of Neurophysiology, 77*, 2753–2764.

Kinsbourne, M. (1995). Awareness of one's own body: An attentional theory of its nature, development and brain basis. In J. J. Bermudez, A. Marcel, & N. Eilan (Eds.), *The body and the self* (pp. 205–223). Cambridge, MA: MIT Press.

Kipling, R. (1893/2003). The bridge-builders. In R. Kipling, *The day's work* (pp. 4–33). Hazleton: Pennsylvania State University.

Kircher, T. T. J., Senior, C., Phillips, M. L., Rabe-Hesketh, S., Benson, P. J., Bullmore, E. T., Brammer, M., Simmons, A., Bartels, M., & David, A. S. (2001). Recognizing one's own face. *Cognition, 78*, B1–B15.

Knecht, S., Hennigsen, H., Elbert, T., Flor, H., Höhling, C., Pantev, C., & Taub, E. (1996). Reorganization and perceptual changes after amputation. *Brain, 119*, 1213–1219.

Knecht, S., Hennigsen, H., Höhling, C., Elbert, T., Flor, H., Pantev, C., & Taub, E. (1998). Plasticity of plasticity? Changes in the pattern of perceptual correlates of reorganization after amputation. *Brain, 121*, 717–724.

Knoblich, G. (2003). Wahrnehmung eigener Handlungen und ihrer Konsequenzen. *Psychologische Rundschau, 54*, 80–92.

Koehler, K., & Sauer, H. (1984). Jasper's sense of presence in the light of Huber's basic symptoms and DSM-III. *Comprehensive Psychiatry, 25*, 183–191.

Kolb, L. C. (1952). The psychology of the amputee: A study of phantom phenomena, body image and pain. *Collected Papers of the Mayo Clinic, 44*, 586–590.

Lackner, J. R. (1988). Some proprioceptive influences on the perceptual representation of body shape and orientation. *Brain, 111*, 281–297.

Lackner, J. R. (1992). Multimodal and motor influences on orientation: Implications for adapting to weightlessness and virtual environments. *Journal of Vestibular Research, 2*, 307–322.

Lacroix, R., Melzack, R., Smith, D., & Mitchell, N. (1992). Multiple phantom limbs in a child. *Cortex, 28*, 503–507.

Làdavas, E. (2002). Functional and dynamic properties of visual peripersonal space. *Trends in Cognitive Sciences, 6*, 17–22.

Leaning, F. E. (1928). Ex-corporeal consciousness. *British Journal of Psychical Research, 2*, 24–28, 51–56.

Leischner, A. (1961). Die autoskopischen Halluzinationen (Heautoskopie). *Fortschritte der Neurologie und Psychiatrie, 29*, 550–585.

Letailleur, M., Morin, J., & LeBorgne, Y. (1958). Héautoscopie hétérosexuelle et schizophrénie: Etude d'une observation. *Annales Médico-Psychologiques, 116*, 451–461.

Ley, H., & Stauder, K. H. (1950). Zur Neurologie und Psychopathologie des Morbus Bang. Zugleich ein Beitrag zum Phänomen der sogenannten "Ichverdoppelung." *Archiv für Psychiatrie und Zeitschrift für Neurologie, 183*, 564–580.

Lippman, C. W. (1953). Hallucinations of physical duality in migraine. *Journal of Nervous and Mental Disease, 117*, 345–350.

Lotze, M., Flor, H., Grodd, W., Larbig, W., & Birbaumer, N. (2001). Phantom movements and pain: An fMRI study in upper limb amputees. *Brain, 124*, 2268–2277.

Lotze, M., Grodd, W., Birbaumer, N., Erb, M., Huse, E., & Flor, H. (1999). Does use of a myoelectric prosthesis prevent cortical reorganization and phantom limb pain? *Nature Neuroscience, 2*, 501–502.

Lunn, V. (1970). Autoscopic phenomena. *Acta Psychiatrica Scandiniavica, 46*(Suppl. 219), 118–125.

Maack, L. H., & Mullen, P. E. (1983). The doppelgänger, disintegration and death: A case report. *Psychological Medicine, 13*, 651–654.

Maravita, A., Husain, M., Clarke, K., & Driver, J. (2001). Reaching with a tool extends visual-tactile interactions into far space: Evidence from cross-modal extinction. *Neuropsychologia, 39*, 580–585.

Marchetti, C., & Della Salla, S. (1998). Disentangling the alien and anarchic hand. *Cognitive Neuropsychiatry, 3*, 191–208.

Maximov, K. (1973). Epilepsie occipitale avec hallucinations héautoscopiques. *Acta Neurologica Belgica, 73*, 320–323.

Mayer-Gross, W. (1929). Ein Fall von Phantomarm nach Plexuszerreissung. *Nervenarzt, 2*, 65–72.

Mayeux, R., & Benson, D. F. (1979). Phantom limb and multiple sclerosis. *Neurology, 29*, 724–726.

McGonigle, D. J., Hänninen, R., Salenius, S., Hari, R., Frackowiak, R. S. J., & Frith, C. D. (2002). Whose arm is it anyway? An fMRI case study of supernumerary phantom limb. *Brain, 125*, 1265–1274.

Melzack, R. (1990). Phantom limbs and the concept of a neuromatrix. *Trends in Neuroscience, 13*, 88–92.

Melzack, R., & Bromage, P. R. (1973). Experimental phantom limbs. *Experimental Neurology, 39*, 261–269.

Melzack, R., Israel, R., Lacroix, R., & Schultz, G. (1997). Phantom limbs in people with congenital limb deficiency or amputation in early childhood. *Brain, 120*, 1603–1620.

Melzack, R., & Loeser, J. D. (1978). Phantom body pain in paraplegics: Evidence for a central "pattern generating mechanism" for pain. *Pain, 4*, 195–210.

Menninger-Lerchenthal, E. (1932). Eine Halluzination Goethes. *Zeitschrift für Neurologie, 140*, 486–495.

Menninger-Lerchenthal, E. (1935). Das Truggebilde der eigenen Gestalt. Heautoskopie, Doppelgänger. *Abhandlungen aus der Neurologie, Psychiatrie, Psychologie und ihren Grenzgebieten, 74*, 1–196.

Menninger-Lerchenthal, E. (1946). Der eigene Doppelgänger. *Beiheft zur Schweizerischen Zeitschrift für Psychologie und ihre Anwendungen, 11*, 1–95.

Menninger-Lerchenthal, E. (1948). Das Phantomglied. *Wiener Klinische Wochenschrift, 60*, 265–267.

Menz, R. (1984). The denial of death and the out-of-the body experience. *Journal of Religion and Health, 23*, 317–329.

Metzinger, T. (2003). *Being no one: The self-model theory of subjectivity.* Cambridge, MA: MIT Press.

Mikorey, M. (1952). *Phantome und Doppelgänger.* Munich: Lehmanns.

Mitchell, S. W. (1866). The case of George Dedlow. *Atlantic Monthly, 18*, 1–11.

Miyazawa, N., Hayashi, M., Komiya, K., & Akiyama, I. (2004). Supernumerary phantom limbs associated with left hemisphere stroke: Case report and review of the literature. *Neurosurgery, 54*, 228–231.

Monroe, R. A. (1971). *Journeys out of the body.* Garden City, NY: Doubleday.

Montoya, P., Ritter, K., Huse, E., Larbig, W., Braun, C., Töpfner, S., Lutzenberger, W., Grodd, W., Flor, H., & Birbaumer, N. (1998). The cortical somatotopic map and phantom phenomena in subjects with congenital limb atrophy and traumatic amputees with phantom limb pain. *European Journal of Neuroscience, 10*, 1095–1102.

Mon-Williams, M., Wann, J. P., Jenkinson, M., & Rushton, K. (1997). Synaesthesia in the normal limb. *Proceedings of the Royal Society of London, B, 264*, 1007–1010.

Moore, C. I., Stern, C. E., Dunbar, C., Kostyk, S. K., Gehi, A., & Corkin, S. (2000). Referred phantom sensations and cortical reorganization after spinal cord injury in humans. *Proceedings of the National Academy of Sciences, USA, 97*, 14703–14708.

Nathan, P. W. (1956). Reference of sensation at the spinal level. *Journal of Neurology, Neurosurgery, and Psychiatry, 19*, 88–100.

Newport, R., Hindle, J. V., & Jackson, S. R. (2001). Links between vision and somatosensation: Vision can improve the felt position of the unseen hand. *Current Biology, 11*, 975–980.

Nouet, H. (1923). Hallucination spéculaire et traumatism cranien. *Encéphale, 18*, 327–329.

Ohry, A., Gur, S., & Zeilig, G. (1989). "Duplicate limbs" sensation in acute traumatic quadriplegia. *Paraplegia, 27*, 257–260.

O'Rahilly, R. (1951). Morphological patterns in limb deficiencies and duplications. *American Journal of Anatomy, 89*, 135–193.

Parsons, L. M. (1987). Imagined spatial transformation of one's body. *Journal of Experimental Psychology: General, 116*, 172–191.

Parsons, L. M. (1994). Temporal and kinematic properties of motor behavior reflected in mentally simulated actions. *Journal of Experimental Psychology: Human Perception and Performance, 20*, 709–730.

Paulig, M., Weber, M., & Garbelotto, S. (2000). Somatoparaphrenie. Eine "Positiv-Variante" der Anosognosie für Hemiplegie. *Nervenarzt, 71*, 123–129.

Pavani, F., Spence, C., & Driver, J. (2000). Visual capture of touch: Out-of-the-body experiences with rubber gloves. *Psychological Science, 11*, 353–359.

Pick, A. (1915). Zur Pathologie des Bewusstseins vom eigenen Körper. *Neurologisches Centralblatt, 34*, 257–265.

Podoll, K., & Robinson, D. (2001). The idea of a presence as aura symptom in migraine. *Neurology, Psychiatry, and Brain Research, 9*, 71–74.

Poeck, K. (1963). Zur Psychophysiologie der Phantomerlebnisse. *Nervenarzt, 34*, 241–256.

Poeck, K. (1964). Phantoms following amputation in early childhood and in congenital absence of limbs. *Cortex, 1*, 269–275.

Poeck, K. (1969). Phantome nach Amputation und bei angeborenem Gliedmassenmangel. *Deutsche Medizinische Wochenschrift, 94*, 2367–2374.

Pons, T. P., Garraghty, P. E., Ommaya, A. K., Kaas, J. H., Taub, E., & Mishkin, M. (1991). Massive cortical reorganization after sensory deafferentation in adult macaques. *Science, 252*, 1857–1860.

Price, D. B. (1976). Miraculous restoration of lost body parts: Relationship to the phantom limb phenomenon and to limb-burial superstitions and practices. In W. D. Hand (Ed.), *American folk medicine: A symposium* (pp. 49–71). Berkeley: University of California Press.

Price, D. B., & Twombly, S. J. (1978). *The phantom limb phenomenon: A medical, folkloric and historical study.* Washington, DC: Georgetown University Press.

Ramachandran, V. S. (1995). Anosognosia in parietal lobe syndrome. *Consciousness and Cognition, 4*, 22–51.

Ramachandran, V. S., Altschuler, E. L., Stone, L., Al-Aboudi, M., Schwartz, E., & Siva, N. (1999). Can mirrors alleviate visual hemineglect? *Medical Hypotheses, 52*, 303–305.

Ramachandran, V. S., & Hirstein, W. (1998). The perception of phantom limbs: The D. O. Hebb lecture. *Brain, 121*, 1603–1630.

Ramachandran, V. S., & Rogers-Ramachandran, D. (1996). Synaesthesia in phantom limbs induced with mirrors. *Proceedings of the Royal Society of London, B, 263*, 377–386.

Ramachandran, V. S., Rogers-Ramachandran, D., & Cobb, S. (1995). Touching the phantom limb. *Nature, 377*, 489–490.

Ramachandran, V. S., Stewart, M., & Rogers-Ramachandran, D. C. (1992). Perceptual correlates of massive cortical reorganization. *Neuroreport, 3*, 583–586.

Reed, C. L., & Farah, M. J. (1995). The psychological reality of the body schema. A test with normal participants. *Journal of Experimental Psychology: Human Perception and Performance, 21*, 334–343.

Reichert, K., & Sewekow, K. (2002). Der Mann mit den drei Armen. Phantomgliederleben bei einem intramedullären Ependymom. *Nervenarzt, 73*, 548–551.

Reny, F.-A. (1899). *Contribution à l'étude des membres fantômes.* Unpublished doctoral thesis, University of Nancy.

Rheingold, H. (1991). *Virtual reality.* New York: Simon and Schuster.

Riddoch, G. (1941). Phantom limbs and body shape. *Brain, 64*, 197–222.

Riechert, T. (1934). Beobachtungen an einem Phantomarm. *Nervenarzt, 7*, 506–511.

Ring, K., & Cooper, S. (1999). *Mindsight: Near-death and out-of-body experiences in the blind.* Palo Alto, CA: William James Center for Consciousness Studies.

Rizzolatti, G., Fogassi, L., & Gallese, V. (2001). Neurophysiological mechanisms underlying the understanding and imitation of action. *Nature Reviews Neuroscience, 2*, 661–670.

Rode, G., Charles, N., Perenin, M.-T., Vighetto, A., Trillet, M., & Aimard, G. (1992). Partial remission of hemiplegia and somatoparaphrenia through vestibular stimulation in a case of unilateral neglect. *Cortex, 28*, 203–208.

Rogers, M. J. C., & Franzen, M. D. (1992). Delusional reduplication following closed-head injury. *Brain Injury, 6*, 469–476.

Rorden, C., Heutink, J., Greenfield, E., & Robertson, I. H. (1999). When a rubber hand "feels" what the real hand cannot. *Neuroreport, 10*, 135–138.

Roth, N. (1944). Unusual types of anosognosia and their relation to the body image. *Journal of Nervous and Mental Disease, 100*, 35–43.

Roux, F.-E., Lotterie, J.-A., Cassol, E., Lazorthes, Y., Sol, J.-C., & Berry, I. (2003). Cortical areas involved in virtual movement of phantom limbs: Comparison with normal subjects. *Neurosurgery, 53*, 1342–1353.

Ruby, P., & Decety, J. (2003). What you believe versus what you think they believe: A neuroimaging study of conceptual perspective taking. *European Journal of Neuroscience, 17*, 2475–2480.

Saadah, E. S. M., & Melzack, R. (1994). Phantom limb experiences in congenital limb-deficient adults. *Cortex, 30*, 479–485.

Sandifer, P. H. (1946). Anosognosia and disorders of body scheme. *Brain, 69*, 122–137.

Scatena, P. (1990). Phantom representations of congenitally absent limbs. *Perceptual and Motor Skills, 70*, 1227–1232.

Schilder, P. (1919). Projektion eigener Körperdefekte in Trugwahrnehmungen. *Neurologisches Centralblatt, 38*, 300–302.

Sellal, F., Renaseau-Leclerc, C., & Labrecque, R. (1996). L'homme à six bras: Un examen de membres fantômes surnuméraires après ramollissement sylvien droit. *Revue Neurologique, 152*, 190–195.

Shapiro, M. F., Fink, M., & Bender, M. B. (1952). Exosomesthesia or displacement of cutaneous sensation into extrapersonal space. *Archives of Neurology and Psychiatry, 68*, 481–490.

Sherman, R. A., Sherman, C. J., & Parker, L. (1984). Chronic phantom and stump pain among American veterans: Results of a survey. *Pain, 18*, 83–95.

Shiffrar, M., & Freyd, J. J. (1990). Apparent motion of the human body. *Psychological Science, 1*, 257–264.

Siddall, P. J., & McClelland, J. (1999). Non-painful sensory phenomena after spinal cord injury. *Journal of Neurology, Neurosurgery, and Psychiatry, 66*, 617–622.

Simmel, M. L. (1956). On phantom limbs. *Archives of Neurology and Psychiatry, 75*, 637–647.

Simmel, M. L. (1961). The absence of phantoms for congenitally missing limbs. *American Journal of Psychology, 74*, 467–470.

Skoyles, J. R. (1990). Is there a genetic component to body schema? *Trends in Neuroscience, 13*, 409.

Skworzoff, K. (1931). Doppelgänger-Halluzinationen bei Kranken mit Funktionsstörungen des Labyrinths. *Zeitschrift für die gesamte Neurologie und Psychiatrie, 133*, 762–766.

Smythe, F. S. (1934). *Everest 1933.* London: Hodder and Stoughton.

Sollier, P. (1903). *Les phénomènes d'autoscopie.* Paris: Alcan.

Spence, S. A., Brooks, D. J., Hirsch, S. R., Liddle, P. F., Meehan, J., & Grasby, P. M. (1997). A PET study of voluntary movement in schizophrenic patients experiencing passivity phenomena (delusions of alien control). *Brain, 120,* 1997–2011.

Srinivasan, A. V., Velmurugendran, U. C., Nadu, T., Rogers-Ramachandran, D., & Ramachandran, V. S. (1998). Allesthesia and extinction of referred sensations after brachial plexus avulsion. *Neurology, 50*(Suppl. 4), A256.

Stelarc. (1995). Towards the post-human: From psycho-body to cyber-system. *Architectural Design, 65,* 90–96.

Stip, E., & Perreault, M. C. (1993). Phantom limb in schizophrenia and the central hypothesis. *Canadian Journal of Psychiatry, 38,* 151–152.

Stratton, G. M. (1899). The spatial harmony of touch and sight. *Mind, 8,* 492–505.

Stremmel, C., Sitti, R., & Eder, S. (2002). Phantomschmerzen nach Major-Amputationen. *Deutsche Medizinische Wochenschrift, 127,* 2015–2020.

Thompson, C. (1982). Anwesenheit: Psychopathology and clinical associations. *British Journal of Psychiatry, 141,* 628–630.

Todd, J., & Dewhurst, K. (1955). The double: Its psychopathology and psychophysiology. *Journal of Nervous and Mental Disease, 122,* 47–55.

Turner, J. A., Lee, J. S., Martinez, O., Medlin, A. L., Schandler, S. L., & Cohen, M. J. (2001). Somatotopy of the motor cortex after long-term spinal cord injury or amputation. *IEEE Transactions on Neural Systems and Rehabilitation Engineering, 9,* 154–160.

Valentin, G. (1836). Ueber die subjectiven Gefühle von Personen, welche mit mangelhaften Extremitäten geboren sind. *Repertorium für Anatomie und Physiologie, 1,* 328–337.

Verret, J. M., & Lapresle, J. (1978). Syndrome d'Anton-Babinki avec reconnaissance du membre supérieur gauche lors de sa vision dans un miroir. *Revue Neurologique, 134,* 709–713.

Vetter, R. J., & Weinstein, S. (1967). The history of the phantom in congenitally absent limbs. *Neuropsychologia, 5,* 335–338.

Vieira, W. (1986). *Projeciologia: Panorama das expêriencias da consciência for a do corpo humano.* Rio de Janeiro: Author.

Vogeley, K., & Fink, G. R. (2003). Neural correlates of the first-person-perspective. *Trends in Cognitive Sciences, 7,* 38–42.

von Stockert, F.-G. (1944). Zur Psychopathologie der typhösen Erkrankungen, gleichzeitig ein Beitrag zum Phänomen der Ichverdoppelung. *Nervenarzt, 17,* 234–239.

Vuilleumier, P. (2004). Anosognosia: The neurology of beliefs and uncertainties. *Cortex, 40,* 9–17.

Vuilleumier, P., Despland, P. A., Assal, G., & Regli, F. (1997). Voyages astraux et hors du corps: Héautoscopie, extase et hallucinations expérientielles d'origine épileptique. *Revue Neurologique, 153,* 115–119.

Vuilleumier, P., Reverdin, A., & Landis, T. (1997). Four legs. Illusory reduplication of the lower limbs after bilateral parietal lobe damage. *Archives of Neurology, 54,* 1543–1547.

Wann, J. P., & Ibrahim, S. (1992). Does proprioception drift? *Experimental Brain Research, 91,* 162–166.

Wegner, D. M. (2002). *The illusion of conscious will.* Cambridge, MA: Bradford.

Weinstein, E. A., Kahn, R. L., Malitz, S., & Rozanski, J. (1954). Delusional reduplication of parts of the body. *Brain, 77,* 45–60.

Weinstein, S., & Sersen, E. A. (1961). Phantoms in cases of congenital absence of limbs. *Neurology, 11*, 905–911.

Weiss, T., Miltner, W. H. R., Adler, T., Brückner, L., & Taub, E. (1999). Decrease in phantom limb pain associated with prosthesis-induced increased use of an amputation stump in humans. *Neuroscience Letters, 272*, 131–134.

Wernicke, C. (1900). *Grundriss der Psychiatrie in klinischen Vorlesungen.* Leipzig: Thieme.

Wigan, A. L. (1884). *A new view of insanity.* London: Longmans, Brown, Green and Longmans.

Wisdom, J. O. (1953). The concept of "phantom-body." *Proceedings of the XIth International Congress of Philosophy, 7*, 175–179.

Worthington, A., & Beevers, L. (1996). Two arms, three hands: A supernumerary phantom phenomenon after right middle cerebral artery stroke. *Neurocase, 2*, 135–140.

Zamboni, G., Budriesi, C., & Nichelli, P. (2005). "Seeing oneself": A case of autoscopy. *Neurocase, 11*, 212–215.

Zurfluh, W. (1983). *Quellen der Nacht.* Interlaken: Ansata.

10

Covert Imitation

How the Body Schema Acts as a Prediction Device

Margaret Wilson

The body schema can interact with perception, cognition, and behavior in a variety of ways. In some cases, the body schema is used as a representational device in service of higher cognitive functions. Examples include covert articulation in working memory, mentally counting on one's fingers to assist with internal calculations, and mentally rotating one's hand or one's whole body during a spatial reasoning task. In other cases, the body schema provides a bridge between perception and action, treating perceived objects as things to be manipulated with the body. This has been explored in the literatures on perception-for-action and the "how" system of visual processing. In still other cases, the body schema again interfaces with perception, but does something rather different with the input. Instead of planning interactive or manipulative behaviors, the body schema may encode the stimulus essentially by *copying* it. This may occur in particular with stimuli that, in some relevant way, match our own bodies. When we see other people sitting, standing, and moving, we are perceiving a stimulus that is isomorphic to the body that we ourselves inhabit and cause to move.

This chapter explores the cognitive consequences of that isomorphism. I propose that, unlike perception-action links that generate object-appropriate interactive behaviors, perceived human movements activate the body schema for *perceptual* reasons. In particular, I argue that the body schema acts as a prediction device, allowing more robust perceptual processing than would otherwise be possible. I conclude by applying this account to a particular case, namely, the tracking of another person's speech behavior when taking turns in a conversation.

1. Imitable Stimuli Are Different

A growing body of evidence shows that the human brain accords a special status to perceptual stimuli that are imitable—that is, stimuli which can be copied by the observer's own body. Such stimuli of course include the visually perceived body postures, actions, and facial expressions of other people, but also include auditory stimuli, such as vocal noises, and, more particularly, language. Unlike the vast majority of nonhuman stimuli that we perceive in our daily lives, this particular category of stimuli can be mapped onto and re-produced by the observer's body.

The structural similarity between an imitable stimulus and the observer's own body suggests that, at a minimum, the two may be represented in the brain in commensurable terms. That is, both are arguably represented in terms of the body's parts and relationships between parts and the three-dimensional movement patterns that such a structure can produce. This claim in fact has a parallel in the speech perception literature, in the form of gestural theories of speech perception. According to this general class of theories, heard speech sounds are represented not in terms of their acoustic properties but in terms of the articulatory gestures of the vocal tract that produced them. Because of this, mental representations of perceived phonemes are commensurable with rep-resentations of phoneme production (e.g., Browman & Goldstein, 1992; Fowler, Brown, Sabadini, & Weihing, 2003; Studdart-Kennedy, 2002).

Emerging data suggest that an even stronger claim can be made regarding the relationship of perceived bodies and one's own body. It appears that imitable stimuli actually activate the perceiver's own body schema. Such stimuli generate imitative motoric representations in the brain—that is, representations of how our own bodies would perform analogous movements (for reviews, see Rizzolatti, Craighero, & Fadiga, 2002; Wilson, 2001). In short, the brain engages in covert imitation, routinely and automatically. The evidence for this claim comes from a variety of fields, ranging from neuropsychology to social psychology.

In monkeys, for example, a population of neurons dubbed *mirror neurons* has been identified in the premotor cortex. These neurons fire both when the monkey plans a movement, but also when the monkey merely observes a stimulus that suggests that movement (Clark, Tremblay, & Ste-Marie, 2003; di Pellegrino, Fadiga, Fogassi, Gallese, & Rizzolatti, 1992; Fadiga, Fogassi, Pavesi, & Rizzolatti, 1995; Gallese, Fadiga, Fogassi, & Rizzolatti, 1996; Hari, Forss, Avikainen, Kirveskari, Salenius, & Rizzolatti, 1998; Maeda, Kleiner-Fisman, & Pascual-Leone, 2002; for review see Fogassi & Gallese, 2002). These neurons reinforce the distinction made at the beginning of this chapter between manipulative uses of the body schema and imitative uses of the body schema. Some of these neurons (the *broadly congruent* mirror neurons) rep-resent relationships between objects and actions, while others (the *strictly congruent* mirror neurons) represent imitations of a perceived conspecific.

Although these neurons appear to be restricted primarily to grasping movements of the hand or mouth, their existence suggests a possible evolutionary basis for more sophisticated covert imitation abilities in humans. Indeed, neurological work in humans has recently shown that observing finger, hand, arm, mouth, or foot movements performed by another can produce related motor activation in the observer. The activities that can produce such activation are not restricted to simple movements, but can include linguistic mouth movements (Fadiga, Craighero, Buccino, & Rizzolatti, 2002; Watkins, Strafella, & Paus, 2003) and, for observers who are piano players, patterns of piano notes (Haueisen & Knösche, 2001).

These neurological findings confirm and build upon what has already been learned from behavioral evidence, that imitation of others' actions seems to have a special status in the human cognitive system. The path from perception to imitative action appears to be privileged or "greased," making imitation an easy, automatic, and sometimes involuntary reaction to perceiving others. This tendency to imitate has long been known in the field of social psychology, where it is referred to as *emotional contagion* or the *chameleon effect* (Chartrand & Bargh, 1999; Hatfield, Cacioppo, & Rapson, 1994). Unconscious mimicry of others in social situations occurs for facial expressions, hand gestures, body postures, speech patterns, and breathing patterns (Bavelas, Black, Lemery, & Mullett, 1986; Bernieri, 1988; Boker & Rotondo, 2002; Chartrand & Bargh, 1999; Dimberg, Thunberg, & Elmehed, 2000; Goldinger, 1998; McFarland, 2001; Neumann & Strack, 2000; Paccalin & Jeannerod, 2000; Rotondo & Boker, 2002; Shockley, Santana, & Fowler, 2003; Surakka & Hietanen, 1998; Wallbott, 1991; Zajonc, Pietromonaco, & Bargh, 1982).

Sometimes this mimicry appears to be driven by effortful task demands. For example, Wallbott (1991) reported that when subjects were asked to identify emotional facial expressions, and a videotape was taken of the subject's own face during the task, the particular facial expression being considered on any given trial could be identified from the subject's own facial expression. Similarly, Zajonc, Pietromonaco, and Bargh (1982) showed that subjects spontaneously mimicked the expressions of faces they were instructed to memorize. Furthermore, disrupting this mimicry—by having the subjects chew gum—interfered with their memory. In the domain of speech, Neumann and Strack (2000) found that people imitate tone of voice as well as content when repeating what they have just heard. In further support of this idea that activating one's own bodily representations assists with tasks such as recognizing and categorizing others' actions, Adolphs, Damasio, Tranel, Cooper, and Damasio (2000) reported a study of 108 focal brain lesion patients, showing that recognition of emotional facial expressions relies on the somatosensory cortex in the right hemisphere. This suggests that recognition of emotions depends in part on running a simulation of the body sensations involved in experiencing that emotion oneself.

In addition, though, some cases of mimicry appear to occur spontaneously, in ways unrelated to the person's primary task or goal. For example, Bernieri (1988) reported that, in student-teacher pairs, there was more postural similarity between pairs that were interacting than between pairs where each person was interacting with someone else. Similarly, Chartrand and Bargh (1999) found that subjects imitated the actions of a confederate, like foot shaking and nose rubbing. They also found that when the confederate imitated the subject, it led to increased liking of the confederate. People also copy the breathing patterns of others, for example, when watching a person walk or run (Paccalin & Jeannerod, 2000) or when listening to a conversational partner (McFarland, 2001). Furthermore, imitation is a type of response that appears to emerge very early in life, possibly even from birth (Field, Woodson, Greenberg, & Cohen, 1982; Meltzoff & Moore, 1977, 1995; but see Heyes, 2001, for critique; also see chapters 4 and 9 for further discussion of the issue of innateness versus plasticity of the body schema).

Even in more-artificial laboratory settings, imitation appears to be a fast and automatic process, resulting in more-rapid reaction times than arbitrary stimulus-response mappings (see Prinz, 2002, for review). In this sense, imitation can be viewed as a special case of stimulus-response compatibility, where greater physical similarity between a stimulus and the required response results in faster reaction times than pairings with less similarity. Thus, people are faster to perform a finger movement in response to seeing the same finger movement (that is, to imitate) than they are to perform the same finger movement in response to an arbitrarily assigned stimulus (Brass, Bekkering, Wohlschläger, & Prinz, 2000). Similar results occur for pronouncing a syllable in response to hearing that same syllable (Fowler, Brown, Sabadini, & Weihing, 2003; Porter & Castellanos, 1980; Porter & Lubker, 1980).

Taken together, these various findings indicate that there is a strong connection between the perceived postures and movements of other people's bodies and one's own body schema—the mental representation of how one's own body would form those postures and movements. This connection sometimes results in overt, often unconscious, imitation, but even when no overt imitation occurs there appears to be covert imitation, the activation of representations for movement that do not reach the level of overt execution.

It is worth noting here that not all reactions to perceiving others are imitative. Many human activities require monitoring the behavior of others while engaging in quite different behaviors ourselves. Some examples are cooperative, as in ballroom dancing, and some are competitive, as in football. In addition, we may sometimes generate nonimitative motoric reactions even with passive viewing. In Prinz's (1987) example of watching someone in a movie nearly fall off a cliff, the motor involvement of the observer will be aimed at trying not to fall—by cringing sideways in one's movie seat, perhaps. This will occur regardless of the motor behavior of the movie character (who, for example, might be unaware of the danger or might be considering suicide).

There are two possible ways to reconcile these cases with the data discussed above. One possibility is that covert imitation occurs unless there is a competing agenda. On this account, covert imitation would primarily be activated under conditions of relatively uninvolved observation. When, instead, one is an active participant in a rapid, ongoing, interactive event, covert imitation would be superseded. (Watching someone walk off a cliff may be a special case, in which, having stepped into the other's shoes and engaged the body schema, one then can't help engaging in self-preserving movements.)

A second possibility is that multiple motoric representations can coexist. Such a state of affairs would certainly be useful, given that so much of our experience with conspecifics is interactive. This possibility is given credence by accounts which suggest the existence of multiple models for motor control (Wolpert & Kawato, 1998). In this case, "the" body schema might in fact be a confederation of multiple representations, held together by their common contribution to a sense of corporeal awareness (see chapter 9), but called upon in an ad hoc fashion by specific task demands. Thus, simulating what another person *is* doing, what another person *ought* to do, and what you yourself *intend* to do may be just various possibilities for multiple motor-based representations of the situation.

This still leaves unanswered, though, the question of why covert imitation is *ever* triggered, let alone as frequently as the above data suggest. What is the purpose of such mental activation, which does not have as its goal the preparation of useful behaviors?

2. Why Covert Imitation?

As noted above, actual explicit imitation does sometimes occur, but it is usually for subtle actions, such as placing the body in a particular posture or responding to others' facial expressions. For actions that are of larger scale and more goal-oriented, imitation does not occur so regularly and indeed would often be inappropriate. We do not start clearing away plates with the waiter in a restaurant, nor do we get up and pace around the stage when someone else is lecturing, nor do we kiss strangers whom we have just seen kissing each other. Yet the neurological evidence suggests that even in these cases imitative motor programs are generated—they just aren't executed, and indeed neurological effort may be needed to actively inhibit such execution (Baldissera, Cavallari, Craighero, & Fadiga, 2001; Brass, Derrfuss, Matthes-von Cramon, & von Cramon, 2003). This raises the question: what is the purpose of this covert imitation, if it does not usually result in overt behavior? Why would the brain put resources into such an activity? A variety of possibilities have been proposed in the literature, and it is possible that many or even all of these are functions served by covert imitation.

One possibility is that covert imitation does indeed exist for the purpose of facilitating overt imitation, for those relatively rare but important occasions when imitating others is the appropriate response (e.g., Iacoboni, Woods, Brass, Bekkering, Mazziotta, & Rizzolatti, 1999; Rizzolatti, Fogassi, & Gallese, 2001). Among humans, imitation serves a variety of important social functions. These include observational learning, where individuals learn new skills, behaviors, and cultural norms from those around them without being actively taught (e.g., Blandin, Lhuisset, & Proteau, 1999), and interpersonal bonding, where imitation of body postures, emotional expressions, and activities can signal affiliation and liking between the two individuals (e.g., Chartrand & Bargh, 1999; Lakin & Chartrand, 2003). Thus, the evolutionary importance of overt imitation may justify the investment of neural resources even when overt imitation does not occur.

It has also been suggested that covert imitation plays a role in interpreting other people's actions (Arbib & Rizzolatti, 1996; Gallese & Goldman, 1998; Kohler, Keysers, Umiltà, Fogassi, Gallese, & Rizzolatti, 2002; Rizzolatti, Fogassi, & Gallese, 2001, 2002; Rizzolatti & Luppino, 2001). This can be taken to mean categorizing actions, for example, understanding various instances of eating as all being instances of the same type of action; or it can be taken more broadly to mean understanding the intentions and goals behind actions, leading ultimately to understanding others' mental states (e.g., Gallese & Goldman, 1998). Thus, a conspecific's hand moving across one's visual field while the fingers close is not just seen as a visual movement sequence but is understood to be an act of grasping and furthermore may be interpreted as an intention to steal food. Covert imitation could make this possible if the observer's brain not only reproduces the motoric patterns of an action, but also reproduces the sensory consequences that normally accompany the action, such as the feeling of the hand closing around an object (e.g., Blakemore & Decety, 2001; Hesslow, 2002; Knoblich & Jordan, 2002; Rizzolatti, Craighero, & Fadiga, 2002; cf. Hommel, Müsseler, Aschersleben, & Prinz, 2001). Thus, the observer may be able to access the reasons for performing that action—in other words, the intention of the actor.

Further, it has been suggested that this ability to understand the intent of others' actions via modeling with one's own body may underlie more sophisticated social cognition abilities, such as empathy and theory of mind. By putting oneself in the other's shoes, one gains an insight into not only the activities of the other, but perhaps also the mental states and emotions of that other. Thus, what originated as modeling others for selfish reasons—understanding others' actions so as not to be outwitted by them—may have had the further consequence of making it possible to "feel for" another person.

But the possible uses of covert imitation do not end here. It has been suggested that the homology of brain location between Broca's area and the site of the mirror neurons in monkeys may indicate that the linkage between the self's and others' action for grasping was a precursor to language, which also involves an identity mapping between self-produced and other-produced forms (Miklósi, 1999; Studdart-Kennedy, 2002). And from yet a different perspective, it has been suggested that efficient maintenance of information in working memory depends on the ability to do rapid cycling between quasi-perceptual and quasi-motoric versions of the same represented information (Wilson, 2001).

In short, the brain is an opportunist, and it is likely that once the connection between input and output forms of imitable stimuli was established, that connection came to be exploited for a variety of cognitive purposes. The proposal advanced here, though, is that of another possible function of covert imitation, one which perhaps may be a strong candidate for why such a connection arose in the first place. This is the possibility that covert imitation serves a specifically *perceptual* function. Top-down filling-in of information that is absent from the physical stimulus, but is highly probable based on past experience, is one of the essential functions of a perceptual system that needs to provide sufficiently robust information about the world to maximize survival potential. A special case of such top-down filling-in may be that which occurs when the stimulus is imitable—that is, when the stimulus is a conspecific moving and behaving in the environment. Such stimuli may form a special class not only because perceptually completing and anticipating their movements under imperfect perceptual conditions may be of particular importance to the perceiver, but also because extra resources for performing such perceptual completion and anticipation may be already built in. These extra resources consist of the perceiver's representation of her own body. If mapping a conspecific's perceived body onto one's own body schema results in information feeding back downward to affect the ongoing perception itself, a particularly robust ability to visually represent others' actions may result.

3. Keeping Up With the World in Real Time

One of the demands placed on a system that must not only perceive the external world but then also interact with that world is the demand of keeping up with the world in real time. The nature of this problem has been highlighted, for example, in the literature on motor control, where the neural transmission time to receive and interpret incoming sensory information (for example, visual and kinesthetic feedback of the exact trajectory of one's hand) is simply too slow to be effective for the fine-tuning of motor commands during actual execution (see

Desmurget & Grafton, 2000, for review). The same problem exists for perceiving and reacting to other kinds of events in the world that are not self-generated: catching a moving target, grabbing food away from a rival, avoiding a punch thrown by an enemy. The limits imposed by neural transmission time mean that we are continually receiving information about the world that is a few hundred milliseconds out of date.

The way out of this impasse is to mentally simulate the world in real time. Such mental simulation, if accurately initialized by bottom-up sensory information and if well calibrated to the principles that make actions in the world proceed as they do, should be able to provide immediate, moment-by-moment predictions of how an ongoing external event is unfolding. Thus, responses can be initiated without waiting for final confirmation from actual sensory input and can be executed in time to appropriately interface with the external event. This concept of a real-time simulation of a currently ongoing external event is borrowed from the fields of engineering and robotics and is variously called a *forward-model* or an *emulator* (for reviews, see Desmurget & Grafton, 2000; Grush, in press; Miall & Reckless, 2002; Wolpert & Flanagan, 2001).

The concept of an emulator has been explored most thoroughly in the literature on motor control, but here we will focus on its possible role in perception. A perceptual emulator would act as a source of top-down information to help with interpretation of the incoming perceptual signal. Just as in other cases of top-down influence, the prediction generated by an emulator would be treated as a hypothesis or best guess of what is going on. This best guess would be used to fill in missing information and disambiguate under conditions of uncertainty, as well as to create expectations of the immediately upcoming future to be verified by the incoming signal. When a stimulus disappears, as behind an occluder, an emulator would be able to continue tracking its motion slightly beyond the point where it disappeared.

Perceptual anticipation of this kind is in fact a well-known phenomenon. Movement or implied movement results in mental extrapolation of the trajectory beyond what was actually perceived, a phenomenon known as *representational momentum* (Finke & Freyd, 1985; Freyd & Finke, 1984). For example, when an object is shown in three successive positions, implying movement in a particular direction, subjects are more likely to say that a probe location differs from the final object location when the probe is shifted backward along the object's trajectory than when it is shifted forward. In other words, subjects have a difficult time rejecting a forward-shifted probe as being different from what they actually saw.

It has been suggested that representational momentum might actually be an artifact of a lower-level process, such as eye movements, and indeed, in cases of smooth motion of an object, representational momentum can be eliminated by preventing eye movements (Kerzel, 2002b; Kerzel, Jordan, & Müsseler, 2001). However, with implied motion and apparent motion, representational momentum occurs even without eye movements (Kerzel, 2003). These findings indicate that representational momentum is in fact a representational effect and not an artifact of eye gaze. Indeed, representational momentum occurs even for certain entirely static stimuli, such as a rocket ship or a spring released from compression (Freyd, 1983; Freyd, Pantzer, & Cheng, 1988; Reed & Vinson, 1996). Furthermore, areas of the brain that process visual motion are activated by static stimuli that imply motion and by moving stimuli that become occluded (Kourtzi & Kanwisher, 2000; Olson, Gatenby, Leung, Skudlarski, & Gore, 2003; Senior et al., 2000), and disruption of these brain areas by transcranial magnetic stimulation eliminates representational momentum (Senior, Ward, & David, 2002). In short, the findings of representational momentum suggest that the perceptual system extrapolates movement beyond what is actually perceived.

This perceptual extrapolation is not a unique phenomenon, but is merely one of a whole category of filling-in or completion effects that characterize perception. Examples that involve static patterns include *illusory contours*, where a compelling perception of an edge is experienced based on surrounding stimuli that merely imply that edge; *amodal completion*, where a partially occluded object looks like a whole object that is only partly visible, rather than like a cut-off object exactly abutting another object; and *boundary extension*, where objects and scenes are remembered immediately after as containing more information than was actually present. Other completion effects involve patterns that extend over time. In these cases, the perceptual system fills in missing information after the fact. The primary example in this case is apparent motion, where two alternately presented stimuli are perceived as a single object moving back and forth.

In all of these cases, incomplete perceptual patterns are perceived as more complete than they really are. That is, our perceptual experience incorporates information that is not physically present but that is highly probable or expected, either based on prior experience with similar patterns or based on principles such as geometric simplicity (cf. Shepard, 1994). The only difference between these phenomena and perceptual prediction is that the former involves the completion of patterns that are static or already finished, while the latter involves the completion of patterns that have not yet finished unfolding over time.

Arguably, perceptual prediction is also a variant of one of the oldest known phenomena of psychology: classical conditioning. Because of its historical ties to behaviorism, classical conditioning is usually described in terms of direct links between a stimulus and a behavior. Today, however, our main concern is not with behaviors themselves but with the underlying mechanisms that cause behaviors. If the findings of classical conditioning were not so thoroughly familiar, they would stand out as a strong indication that animals and humans anticipate immediately upcoming events that adhere to previously experienced patterns. The dog salivates because it expects food; the rabbit winces because it expects a puff of air in its eye. While the animal may not have explicit knowledge of what is to come, it seems incontrovertible that the animal can "feel it coming"—in other words, that the animal is engaging in perceptual prediction.

4. Perceptual Prediction for Human Movements

Because of the biomechanics of the human body, many actions require preparatory movements—the arm pulling back before throwing a punch, the legs bending before a jump, the face and torso convulsing before a burst of laughter. A perceiver who can "see" where a movement is heading has enormous advantages, both physically and socially.

However, in order to be successful, an emulator must internalize principles or regularities of the external system that allow predictability. This suggests that emulating perceptual events will be sharply limited in certain ways. Two types of cases clearly lend themselves to emulation. The first is movement trajectories that follow simple geometric principles, such as linear translation, rotation, smooth arcs, and so on. The second case is movement patterns that are stereotypic and highly familiar, such as a ball bouncing, a snowball or water balloon bursting on impact, a line of dominoes falling, or a wave breaking. Together, these two categories of movement buy us a lot. However, there still remain a large number of events in the real world that do not lend themselves to perceptual prediction. Indeed, a study by Kerzel (2002a) has shown that when both direction and final position of the inducing stimuli are varied randomly to disrupt predictability, representational momentum is absent. By and large, any event that is nonuniform and nonstereotypic will not be a good candidate for emulation. The jointed structure of the human body means that human movement is not uniform, in any simple geometric sense, and the diversity and creativity of human activity means that human movement is often nonstereotypic.

Yet, it has been shown that perceptual prediction does occur for perceived human body movement. For example, Verfaillie, De Troy, and Van Rensbergen (1994) asked subjects to watch a point-light walker and to try to detect changes that occurred between eye fixations. The eye is temporarily blind during saccades, so a change that is timed, through eye-tracking technology, to occur during a saccade can only be detected by comparing presaccade and postsaccade information. Subjects were able to detect certain kinds of changes, such as rotation of the Figure in depth, but had difficulty detecting other kinds of changes, such as translation of the entire Figure sideways. It would appear from this that configural changes are more noticeable than changes in location of the Figure as a whole. And yet subjects were poor at detecting a change of configuration when it depicted the Figure in a posture that the walker would be taking in the immediately upcoming future. Just as in the cases of representational momentum described earlier, subjects had difficulty rejecting the changed display because their perceptual representation had been updated to reflect the immediate future of the perceived action. A similar conclusion comes from a study using computer-generated human Figures (Verfaillie & Daems, 2002). Subjects were shown sequences of body postures that implied movement. Subsequently, subjects were faster to respond to new postures that would have immediately followed from the sequences shown previously than they were when responding to unrelated postures or postures that would have immediately preceded the sequences.

These results imply that perceptual prediction does occur for the complex, jointed movement of the human body. This further suggests that the human perceptual system incorporates an emulator, in the sense defined earlier, that is isomorphic to the human body. While it is possible that such an emulator is hard-wired into the perceptual system or learned in purely perceptual terms, an equally plausible hypothesis is that the emulator draws on body-schematic knowledge derived from the observer's representation of his own body. This hypothesis gains some support, albeit indirect, from the evidence reviewed above regarding the ubiquity of covert imitation, indicating a tight connection between perceptual (third-person) and motor (first-person) representations of the human body.

Further, there is additional evidence accumulating for this hypothesis that is more direct. For example, recent evidence shows that mirror neurons can project a partially perceived motion a short way into the future, as when a grasping motion is initiated in view of the observer but completed behind an occluding screen (Umiltà et al., 2001). This suggests that mirror neurons function not only to reason backward to the intentions behind an action (a form of "retrodiction") but also can reason forward to fill in the upcoming trajectory of the movement.

Further evidence comes from the literature on apparent motion (a form of perceptual filling-in, as discussed earlier), which shows distinct characteristics for human versus nonhuman stimuli. For apparent motion of the human body, viewers often report seeing trajectories that obey the biomechanical constraints of the human body, even when these trajectories are not the most direct path (Shiffrar & Freyd, 1990, 1993). This preference for possible over impossible paths does not occur for nonhuman objects. Furthermore, it has been shown that areas of the brain related to representing the body and planning movement are activated when subjects perceive these biomechanically possible paths during the human apparent-motion task (Stevens, Fonlupt, Shiffrar, & Decety, 2000). This suggests that body schema resources are used for filling-in when one perceives biomechanically possible human movement.

Finally, it has been shown that perceptual prediction for human movement is best when we are viewing ourselves—that is, when viewing the movement of a body whose motor programs are maximally similar to our own. Knoblich, Flach, and colleagues (Knoblich & Flach, 2001; Knoblich, Seigerschmidt, Flach, & Prinz, 2002) have shown that subjects are better at guessing the endpoint of an action when viewing a videotape of themselves than when viewing a videotape of another person. This is true for large-scale movements, such as throwing darts, and small-scale movements, such as handwriting. In short, it appears that perceptual prediction exploits motoric knowledge as well as purely perceptual knowledge. (Naturally, this suggests that predictability in real-world situations is limited by the fact that other people do not move their bodies exactly as the perceiver does. Indeed, for the fine-scale and personally idiosyncratic movements of handwriting, predictability of others' movements was close to zero. However, the high degree of precision obtainable when observing oneself may be more than is usually needed. That is, perceptual prediction based on one's own body schema may be sufficiently accurate for most situations.) By adding biomechanical knowledge based on one's own body schema to the process of emulating others' movements, increased robustness, accuracy, and duration of the model may be achieved.

5. The Case of Turn-Taking

The remainder of this chapter will briefly apply this proposal to one particular case of human interaction: turn-taking in conversation. One of the remarkable features of turn-taking is the smoothness and accuracy of the coordination between speakers; yet the cognitive mechanisms that underlie this ability have been surprisingly understudied in cognitive science. The proposal advanced here is that perceptual emulation of one's conversational partner, of the sort described above, enables the normal operation of turn-taking.

Turn-taking appears to be a fundamental fact of human conversation, occurring cross-culturally and occurring even when the sensorimotor substrate of conversation is either impaired or radically different from the norm, as in those with Parkinson's disease or those who use tactile sign language. Turn-taking is essential to the normal operation of conversational pragmatics. Conversational participants are socially attuned to phenomena such as interruptions, pauses before responding, relevance of a turn to the previous turn, and so on, all of which are dependent upon the underlying normalcy of turn-taking.

Unlike more formal types of speech exchange, such as occur in ceremonies, debates, and so on, conversation is distinguished by the complete lack of any a priori agreement as to who will speak when. One of the curious features of conversation, then, is the precision with which participants manage and organize turn-taking. Turn transitions are typically very smooth, often involving no gap or overlap that can be detected by the unaided human ear. Even more startling, it has been shown that conversational participants are attuned to one another's timing even after a speech act has ended: brief silences tend to be broken at cyclically regular intervals, rather than at any random moment after the previous utterance has ended (Wilson & Zimmerman, 1986). These surprising phenomena demand an explanation and, furthermore, an explanation at a cognitive level to account for how individual participants can produce behavior this finely synchronized with the perceived behavior of others.

There have been various proposals as to the types of cues that speakers and listeners use to detect that a turn is ending, to indicate the desire to take the floor, or to indicate willingness or unwillingness to yield the floor. These cues include semantic, syntactic, prosodic, and nonverbal cues. Notice, however, that knowing *that* a turn is ending is not sufficient for knowing, with a high degree of precision, *when* a turn is ending. This ability to anticipate an upcoming turn-ending as it approaches seems to be crucial for explaining the timing of turn-taking. That timing is far too precise to be explained on the basis of stimulus and reaction. By the time a speaker's utterance actually ends, the next speaker's vocal apparatus must already be in gear preparing for the immediately forthcoming speech. Thus, anticipation of the time course of the final moments of a turn as they unfold appears to be key to explaining turn-taking.

Based on these observations, perceptual prediction appears to be a necessary component of normal conversational turn-taking. And, as previously argued, activation of the perceiver's own body schema seems to be the most parsimonious way to explain perceptual prediction for complex imitable events such as human action. In short, this line of argument yields the proposal that conversational turn-taking relies on covert imitation in order to perceptually emulate one's conversational partner.

This proposal may sound at first as though it commits itself to a strong version of the motor theory of speech perception. However, it is more accurate to say that this proposal commits itself to a motor theory of talk-in-interaction. The claim is not that motor activity is generally necessary for perceiving or understanding speech, but that motor activity plays a role in the moments immediately surrounding a turn-transition, when coordination with one's conversational partner becomes essential.

6. Concluding Remarks

More generally, one may ask whether the ideas put forward in this chapter imply a "motor theory of conspecific perception." Again, the answer is that motor activation is clearly not essential for perception. We can perceive many complex events that we cannot model motorically, such as the workings of machinery and the movements of animals with very different body structures from our own. Likewise, there is no reason to believe that we would be incapable of perceiving human movement without the involvement of motoric resources. The claim, instead, is that motoric resources add robustness and predictive power to perceptual emulation, enhancing the information that can be extracted from the perceptual signal. Such motoric involvement may be particularly useful for specific task demands, such as computationally demanding transformations like the mental rotation of body parts (e.g., Parsons & Fox, 1998; Parsons et al., 1995), or online, timing-dependent coordination of one's own actions with another's actions. However, unless competing demands (e.g., divided attention or perhaps conflicting motor planning) mitigate against such involvement, motorically based emulation may be an effortless, automatic, and routine part of the perception of conspecifics.

References

Adolphs, R., Damasio, H., Tranel, D., Cooper, G., & Damasio, A. (2000). A role for somatosensory cortices in the visual recognition of emotion as revealed by three-dimensional lesion mapping. *Journal of Neuroscience, 20,* 2683–2690.

Arbib, M. A., & Rizzolatti, G. (1996). Neural expectations: A possible evolutionary path from manual skills to language. *Communication & Cognition, 29,* 393–424.

Baldissera, F., Cavallari, P., Craighero, L., & Fadiga, L. (2001). Modulation of spinal excitability during observation of hand actions in humans. *European Journal of Neuroscience, 13,* 190–194.

Bavelas, J. B., Black, A., Lemery, C. R., & Mullett, J. (1986). "I show how you feel": Motor mimicry as a communicative act. *Journal of Personality and Social psychology, 50,* 322–329.

Bernieri, F. (1988). Coordinated movement and rapport in teacher-student interactions. *Journal of Nonverbal Behavior, 12,* 120–138.

Blakemore, S.-J., & Decety, J. (2001). From the perception of action to the understanding of intention. *Nature Reviews Neuroscience, 2,* 561–567.

Blandin, Y., Lhuisset, L., & Proteau, L. (1999). Cognitive processes underlying observational learning of motor skills. *Quarterly Journal of Experimental Psychology, 52A,* 957–979.

Boker, S. M., & Rotondo, J. L. (2002). Symmetry building and symmetry breaking in synchronized movement. In M. I. Stamenov & V. Gallese (Eds.), *Mirror neurons and the evolution of brain and language* (pp. 163–171). Philadelphia: Benjamins.

Brass, M., Bekkering, H., Wohlschläger, A., & Prinz, W. (2000). Compatibility between observed and executed finger movements: Comparing symbolic, spatial, and imitative cues. *Brain and Cognition, 44,* 124–143.

Brass, M., Derrfuss, J., Matthes-von Cramon, G., & von Cramon, D. Y. (2003). Imitative response tendencies in patients with frontal brain lesions. *Neuropsychology, 17,* 265–271.

Browman, C. P., & Goldstein, L. (1992). Articulatory phonology: An overview. *Phonetica, 49,* 155–180.

Chartrand, T. L., & Bargh, J. A. (1999). The chameleon effect: The perception-behavior link and social interaction. *Journal of Personality & Social Psychology, 76,* 893–910.

Clark, S., Tremblay, F., & Ste-Marie, D. (2003). Differential modulation of corticospinal excitability during observation, mental imagery and imitation of hand actions. *Neuropsychologia, 42,* 105–112.

Desmurget, M., & Grafton, S. (2000). Forward modeling allows feedback control for fast reaching movements. *Trends in Cognitive Sciences, 4*, 423–431.

Dimberg, U., Thunberg, M., & Elmehed, K. (2000). Unconscious facial reactions to emotional facial expressions. *Psychological Science, 11*, 86–89.

di Pellegrino, G., Fadiga, L., Fogassi, L., Gallese, V., & Rizzolatti, G. (1992). Understanding motor events: A neurophysiological study. *Experimental Brain Research, 91*, 176–180.

Fadiga, L., Craighero, L., Buccino, G., & Rizzolatti, G. (2002). Speech listening specifically modulates the excitability of tongue muscles: A TMS study. *European Journal of Neuroscience, 15*, 399–402.

Fadiga L., Fogassi L., Pavesi G., & Rizzolatti G. (1995). Motor facilitation during action observation: A magnetic stimulation study. *Journal of Neurophysiology, 73*, 2608–2611.

Field, T., Woodson, R., Greenberg, R., & Cohen, D. (1982). Discrimination and imitation of facial expression by neonates. *Science, 218*, 179–181.

Finke, R. A., & Freyd, J. J. (1985). Transformations of visual memory induced by implied motions of pattern elements. *Journal of Experimental Psychology: Learning, Memory, & Cognition, 11*, 780–794.

Fogassi, L., & Gallese, V. (2002). The neural correlates of action understanding. In M. I. Stamenov & V. Gallese (Eds.), *Mirror neurons and the evolution of brain and language* (pp. 13–35). Philadelphia: Benjamins.

Fowler, C. A., Brown, J. M., Sabadini, L., & Weihing, J. (2003). Rapid access to speech gestures in perception: Evidence from choice and simple response time tasks. *Journal of Memory and Language, 49*, 396–413.

Freyd, J. J. (1983). The mental representation of movement when static stimuli are viewed. *Perception & Psychophysics, 33*, 575–581.

Freyd, J. J., & Finke, R. A. (1984). Representational momentum. *Journal of Experimental Psychology: Learning, Memory, & Cognition, 10*, 126–132.

Freyd, J. J., Pantzer, T. M., & Cheng, J. L. (1988). Representing statics as forces in equilibrium. *Journal of Experimental Psychology: General, 117*, 395–407.

Gallese, V., Fadiga, L., Fogassi, L., & Rizzolatti, G. (1996). Action recognition in the premotor cortex. *Brain, 119*, 593–609.

Gallese, V., & Goldman, A. (1998). Mirror neurons and the simulation theory of mind-reading. *Trends in Cognitive Sciences, 2*, 493–501.

Goldinger, S. D. (1998). Echoes of echoes? An episodic theory of lexical access. *Psychological Review, 105*, 251–279.

Grush, R. (in press). The emulation theory of representation: Motor control, imagery, and perception. *Behavioral and Brain Sciences*.

Hari, R., Forss, N., Avikainen, S., Kirveskari, E., Salenius, S., & Rizzolatti, G. (1998). Activation of human primary motor cortex during action observation: A neuromagnetic study. *Proceedings of the National Academy of Sciences, USA, 95*, 15061–15065.

Hatfield, E., Cacioppo, J. T., & Rapson, R. L. (1994). *Emotional contagion*. Cambridge: Cambridge University Press.

Haueisen, J., & Knösche, T. R. (2001). Involuntary motor activity in pianists evoked by music perception. *Journal of Cognitive Neuroscience, 13*, 786–792.

Hesslow, G. (2002). Conscious thought as simulation of behavior and perception. *Trends in Cognitive Sciences, 6*, 242–247.

Heyes, C. (2001). Causes and consequences of imitation. *Trends in Cognitive Sciences, 5*, 253–261.

Hommel, B., Müsseler, J., Aschersleben, G., & Prinz, W. (2001). The theory of event coding (TEC): A framework for perception and action planning. *Behavioral and Brain Sciences, 24*, 849–937.

Iacoboni, M., Woods, R. P., Brass, M., Bekkering, H., Mazziotta, J. C., & Rizzolatti, G. (1999). Cortical mechanisms of human imitation. *Science, 286*, 2526–2528.

Kerzel, D. (2002a). A matter of design: No representational momentum without predictability. *Visual Cognition, 9*, 66–80.

Kerzel, D. (2002b). The locus of "memory displacement" is at least partially perceptual: Effects of velocity, expectation, friction, memory averaging, and weight. *Perception & Psychophysics, 64*, 680–692.

Kerzel, D. (2003). Attention maintains mental extrapolation of target position: Irrelevant distractors eliminate forward displacement after implied motion. *Cognition, 88*, 109–131.

Kerzel, D., Jordan, J. S., & Müsseler, J. (2001). The role of perception in the mislocalization of the final position of a moving target. *Journal of Experimental Psychology: Human Perception and Performance, 27*, 829–840.

Knoblich, G., & Flach, R. (2001). Predicting the effects of actions: Interactions of perception and action. *Psychological Science, 12*, 467–472.

Knoblich, G., & Jordan, J. S. (2002). The mirror system and joint action. In M. I. Stamenov & V. Gallese (Eds.), *Mirror neurons and the evolution of brain and language* (pp. 115–124). Philadelphia: Benjamins.

Knoblich, G., Seigerschmidt, E., Flach, R., & Prinz, W. (2002). Authorship effects in the prediction of handwriting strokes: Evidence for action simulation during action perception. *Quarterly Journal of Experimental Psychology, 55A*, 1027–1046.

Kohler, E., Keysers, C., Umiltà, M. A., Fogassi, L., Gallese, V., & Rizzolatti, G. (2002). Hearing sounds, understanding actions: Action representation in mirror neurons. *Science, 297*, 846–848.

Kourtzi, Z., & Kanwisher, N. (2000). Activation in human MT/MST by static images with implied motion. *Journal of Cognitive Neuroscience, 12*, 48–55.

Lakin, J. L., & Chartrand, T. L. (2003). Using nonconscious behavioral mimicry to create affiliation and rapport. *Psychological Science, 14*, 334–339.

Maeda, F., Kleiner-Fisman, G., & Pascual-Leone, A. (2002). Motor facilitation while observing hand actions: Specificity of the effect and role of observer's orientation. *Journal of Neurophysiology, 87*, 1329–1335.

McFarland, D. H. (2001). Respiratory markers of conversational interaction. *Journal of Speech, Language, and Hearing Research, 44*, 128–143.

Meltzoff, A. N., & Moore, M. K. (1977). Imitation of facial and manual gestures by human neonates. *Science, 198*, 75–78.

Meltzoff, A. N., & Moore, M. K. (1995). Infants' understanding of people and things: From body imitation to folk psychology. In J. L. Bermudez, A. Marcel, & N. Eilan (Eds.), *The body and the self* (pp. 43–69). Cambridge, MA: MIT Press.

Miall, R. C., & Reckless, G. Z. (2002). The cerebellum and the timing of coordinated eye and hand tracking. *Brain and Cognition, 48*, 212–226.

Miklósi, A. (1999). From grasping to speech: Imitation might provide a missing link. *Trends in Neuroscience, 22*, 151–152.

Neumann, R., & Strack, F. (2000). "Mood contagion": The automatic transfer of mood between persons. *Journal of Personality and Social Psychology, 79*, 211–223.

Olson, I. R., Gatenby, J. C., Leung, H.-C., Skudlarski, P., & Gore, J. C. (2003). Neuronal representation of occluded objects in the human brain. *Neuropsychologia, 42*, 95–104.

Paccalin, C., & Jeannerod, M. (2000). Changes in breathing during observation of effortful actions. *Brain Research, 862,* 194–200.

Parsons, L. M., & Fox, P. T. (1998). The neural basis of implicit movements used in recognising hand shape. *Cognitive Neuropsychology, 15,* 583–615.

Parsons, L. M., Fox, P. T., Downs, J. H., Glass, T., Hirsch, T. B., Martin, C. C., Jerabek, P. A., & Lancaster, J. L. (1995). Use of implicit motor imagery for visual shape discrimination as revealed by PET. *Nature, 375,* 54–58.

Porter, R., & Castellanos, F. (1980). Speech production measures of speech perception: Rapid shadowing of VCV syllables. *Journal of the Acoustical Society of America, 67,* 1349–1356.

Porter, R., & Lubker, J. (1980). Rapid reproduction of vowel-vowel sequences: Evidence for a fast and direct acoustic-motoric linkage. *Journal of Speech and Hearing Research, 23,* 593–602.

Prinz, W. (1987). Ideo-motor action. In H. Heuer & A. F. Sanders (Eds.), *Perspectives on perception and action* (pp. 47–76). Hillsdale, NJ: Erlbaum.

Prinz, W. (2002). Experimental approaches to imitation. In A. Meltzoff & W. Prinz (Eds.), *The imitative mind: Development, evolution, and brain bases* (pp. 143–162). New York: Cambridge University Press.

Reed, C. L., & Vinson, N. G. (1996). Conceptual effects on representational momentum. *Journal of Experimental Psychology: Human Perception and Performance, 22,* 839–850.

Rizzolatti, G., Craighero, L., & Fadiga, L. (2002). The mirror system in humans. In M. I. Stamenov & V. Gallese (Eds.), *Mirror neurons and the evolution of brain and language* (pp. 37–59). Philadelphia: Benjamins.

Rizzolatti, G., Fogassi, L., & Gallese, V. (2001). Neurophysiological mechanisms underlying the understanding and imitation of action. *Nature Reviews Neuroscience, 2,* 661–670.

Rizzolatti, G., Fogassi, L., & Gallese, V. (2002). Motor and cognitive functions of the ventral premotor cortex. *Current Opinion in Neurobiology, 12,* 149–154.

Rizzolatti, G., & Luppino, G. (2001). The cortical motor system. *Neuron, 31,* 889–901.

Rotondo, J. L., & Boker, S. M. (2002). Behavioral synchronization in human conversational interaction. In M. I. Stamenov & V. Gallese (Eds.), *Mirror neurons and the evolution of brain and language* (pp. 151–162). Philadelphia: Benjamins.

Senior, C., Barnes, J., Giampietro, V., Simmons, A., Bullmore, E. T., Brammer, M., & David, A. S. (2000). The functional neuroanatomy of implicit-motion perception or "representational momentum." *Current Biology, 10,* 16–22.

Senior, C., Ward, J., & David, A. S. (2002). Representational momentum and the brain: An investigation into the functional necessity of V5/MT. *Visual Cognition, 9,* 81–92.

Shepard, R. N. (1994). Perceptual-cognitive universals as reflections of the world. *Psychonomic Bulletin & Review, 1,* 2–28.

Shiffrar, M., & Freyd, J. J. (1990). Apparent motion of the human body. *Psychological Science, 1,* 257–264.

Shiffrar, M., & Freyd, J. J. (1993). Timing and apparent motion path choice with human body photographs. *Psychological Science, 4,* 379–384.

Shockley, K., Santana, M.-V., & Fowler, C. A. (2003). Mutual interpersonal postural constraints are involved in cooperative conversation. *Journal of Experimental Psychology: Human Perception & Performance, 29,* 326–332.

Stevens, J. A., Fonlupt, P., Shiffrar, M., & Decety, J. (2000). New aspects of motion perception: Selective neural encoding of apparent human movements. *Neuroreport, 11,* 109–115.

Studdart-Kennedy, M. (2002). Mirror neurons, vocal imitation, and the evolution of particulate speech. In M. I. Stamenov & V. Gallese (Eds.), *Mirror neurons and the evolution of brain and language* (pp. 207–227). Philadelphia: Benjamins.

Surakka, V., & Hietanen, J. K. (1998). Facial and emotional reactions to Duchenne and non-Duchenne smiles. *International Journal of Psychophysiology, 29,* 23–33.

Umiltà, M. A., Kohler, E., Gallese, V., Fogassi, L., Fadiga, L., Keysers, C., & Rizzolatti, G. (2001). I know what you are doing: A neurophysiological study. *Neuron, 31,* 155–165.

Verfaillie, K., & Daems, A. (2002). Representing and anticipating human actions in vision. *Visual Cognition, 9,* 217–232.

Verfaillie, K., De Troy, A., & Van Rensbergen, J. (1994). Transsaccadic integration of biological motion. *Journal of Experimental Psychology: Learning, Memory, & Cognition, 20,* 649–670.

Wallbott, H. G. (1991). Recognition of emotion from facial expression via imitation? Some indirect evidence for an old theory. *British Journal of Social Psychology, 30,* 207–219.

Watkins, K. E., Strafella, A. P., & Paus, T. (2003). Seeing and hearing speech excites the motor system involved in speech production. *Neuropsychologia, 41,* 989–994.

Wilson, M. (2001). Perceiving imitatible stimuli: Consequences of isomorphism between input and output. *Psychological Bulletin, 127,* 543–553.

Wilson, T. P., & Zimmerman, D. H. (1986). The structure of silence between turns in two-party conversation. *Discourse Processes, 9,* 375–390.

Wolpert, D. M., & Flanagan, J. R. (2001). Motor prediction. *Current Biology, 11,* R729–R732.

Wolpert, D. M., & Kawato, M. (1998). Multiple paired forward and inverse models for motor control. *Neural Networks, 11,* 1317–1329.

Zajonc, R. B., Pietromonaco, P., & Bargh, J. A. (1982). Independence and interaction of affect and cognition. In M. S. Clark & S. T. Fiske (Eds.), *Affect and cognition: The seventeenth annual Carnegie symposium on cognition* (pp. 211–227). Hillsdale, NJ: Erlbaum.

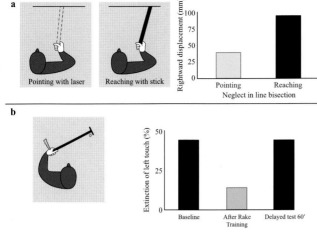

FIGURE 4.1 Projection of peripersonal space to the tip of a tool: Evidence from neglect and extinction patients. (a) Schematic drawing of the experiment performed by Berti and Frassinetti (2001). *Left panel* (pointing condition): the patient performs bisections of lines in far space, out of hand's reach, by means of a laser pointer (depicted as a red dotted bar). The *middle panel* depicts the patient performing line bisections using a long stick (reaching condition), depicted as a black bar. *Right panel*: results of the average rightward displacement on line bisection in the two conditions. The rightward bias, typically observed in neglect, is nearly absent in the pointing condition, while it is stronger and of similar amount to that showed by the patient in near space (not shown), when far space becomes reachable with the stick. This suggests that properties which are typical of near, peripersonal space can be projected to far space, when we can reach it with a tool. (b) Effect of tool use on crossmodal extinction. A patient shows extinction of left vibrotactile stimuli (yellow symbol) when simultaneous right visual stimuli (red circle) are presented. After the patient is trained to use a rake (depicted in black in the figure) to reach for far objects with his left hand, extinction decreases, as shown by the graph in the right panel. The rake, after it has been used for a while, is likely to link the two stimuli in a common, bimodal representation, thus reducing their competition. The right column of the graph shows that extinction goes back to the pretraining level after some time away from the training (redrawn from Maravita, Clarke, Husain, & Driver, 2002).

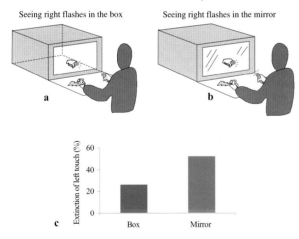

FIGURE 4.2 Recoding of visual stimuli reflected in a mirror to peripersonal space: Evidence from crossmodal extinction. A patient with crossmodal extinction receives vibrotactile stimuli on the left hand (yellow symbol) and visual LED flashes on the right side (green or red circle). (a) Schematic sketch of the box condition. The patient observes the contents of the box, including a fake hand holding an LED that generates the visual stimulus (note that in the real experimental setting, direct view of the hands was prevented by an opaque panel). (b) In the mirror condition, the patient sees the mirror reflection of his own right hand, together with a reflection of the nearby LEDs (held in his hand). The positions of the visible mirror reflections in this condition exactly matched those of the equivalent items inside the box in the box condition. (c) The graph shows the amount of extinction for the box and mirror conditions. Extinction increases in the mirror condition, producing a comparable effect of directly observing the visual stimulus in contact with the right hand (not shown). This suggests that mirror reflections of objects near the body, although suggesting a visual stimulus far in space, "through the looking glass," are automatically recoded as near objects (redrawn from Maravita, Spence, Sergent, & Driver, 2002).

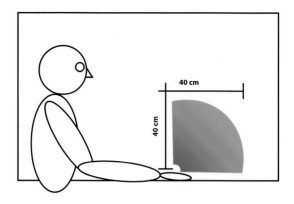

FIGURE 5.1 Schematic illustration exemplifying the limited sector of space (blue) surrounding the ipsilesional hand that can be considered as near peripersonal space as operationally defined on the basis of patients' performance. Patients' ability to perceive touches delivered to the left contralesional hand (not shown) is significantly worse when visual stimuli are concurrently delivered closer to the hand surface (darker blue) rather than farther from the same hand (lighter blue). Color fading represents the lack of a sharp border of near peripersonal space, although significant improvement in touch detection is usually observed when visual stimuli are presented about 40 cm away from the ipsilesional hand.

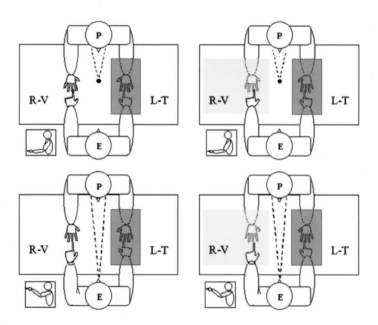

FIGURE 5.2 Schematic illustration of the crossmodal visual-tactile conditions and the experimental setting with the patient (P) and examiner (E) relative positions, viewed from above. The visual stimulus (V; wiggling of the experimenter's index finger) could be located near (*top row*) or far from the patient's right (R) hand, located below (*bottom row*) the visual stimulus. Tactile (T; mechanical stimuli provided through synthetic probes) stimulation was delivered to the patient's left (L) hand, which was screened from view by opaque cardboard shields (blue rectangles). Note that in one set of conditions (*right column*), a transparent Plexiglas barrier (yellow rectangles) was inserted between the patient's hand and the visual stimulus, whereas no barrier was used in the other set of conditions (*left column*). From Farnè, Demattè, & Làdavas, 2003. Reprinted with permission.

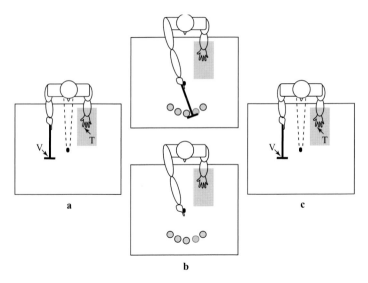

FIGURE 5.3 Schematic illustration of the experimental set-up (viewed from above) used to assess the variation in the size of peripersonal space representation area following tool use, through changes in the amount of crossmodal extinction. Patients passively held a rake (T-shaped black line), in their right hands. Their left hands were screened from view (gray rectangle), while their right hands and the rake were visible. Visual stimuli (V) were presented at the distal edge of the rake, whereas unseen tactile stimuli (T) were delivered to the patients' left hands (as indicated by arrows). Crossmodal extinction was assessed before (a) and after (c) the patients were engaged in two different tasks concerning the same distant objects. Red plastic tokens were located (one at a time) in one (red circle) of five possible locations (gray circles represent the alternative positions). The patients had to retrieve the object with the rake (b *top*), or just point their index fingers toward it (b *bottom*). From Farnè and Làdavas, 2000. Reprinted with permission.

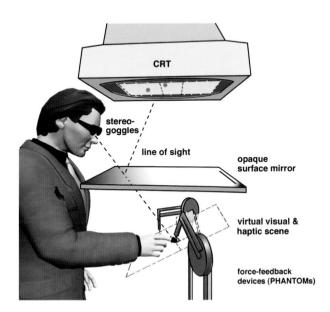

FIGURE 6.3 In the visual-haptic set-up, observers view the reflection of the visual stimulus binocularly in a mirror using stereo goggles. The haptic stimulus is presented using two PHANTOM™ force-feedback devices, one each for the index finger and thumb. With this set-up, the visual and the haptic virtual scenes can be independently manipulated. From Ernst and Bülthoff, 2004. Reprinted with permission.

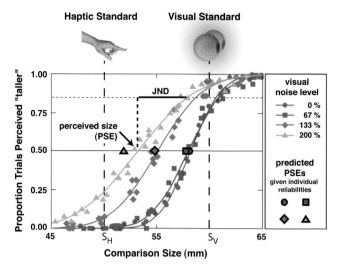

FIGURE 6.4 Visual-haptic size-discrimination performance determined with a 2-interval forced-choice task (Ernst & Banks, 2002). We manipulated the relative reliabilities of the individual signals by adding noise to the visual display (0%, 67%, 133%, and 200%). With these different relative reliabilities, we measured four discrimination curves. When the relative visual reliability decreases with added noise, the perceived size as indicated by the *PSE* is more and more determined by the haptic size estimate (haptic standard) and less by the visual size estimate (visual standard). This demonstrates the weighting behavior adopted by the brain and the smooth change from visual dominance (red circles) to haptic dominance (orange triangles). As indicated in the figure, the *PSE*s predicted from the individual visual and haptic discrimination performance (symbols with black outlines) correspond well with the empirically determined *PSE*s in the combined visual-haptic discrimination task. Four naïve subjects participated. From Ernst and Bülthoff, 2004. Reprinted with permission.

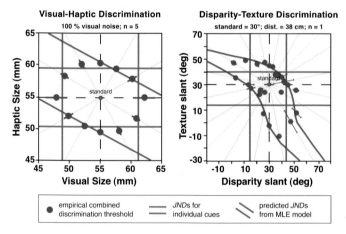

FIGURE 6.7 Discrimination performance for visual and haptic size discrimination (*left panel*) and for binocular disparity and texture-slant discrimination (*right panel*). In red are the single-cue *JND*s for discriminating each individual cue from the standard (green circle). The pairs of red horizontal constraint lines correspond to the *JND*s for haptic size discrimination and texture-slant discrimination, respectively. The pairs of red vertical constraint lines correspond to the *JND*s for visual size discrimination and disparity-slant discrimination, respectively. In green, we plotted the discrimination predictions (*JND*s for discrimination from standard) when assuming the MLE model for integration (i.e., complete fusion of the signals). Discrimination performance in the direction of the green constraint lines indicates metameric behavior. In purple are plotted the discrimination thresholds in the different directions for combined cue performance (Hillis et al., 2002).

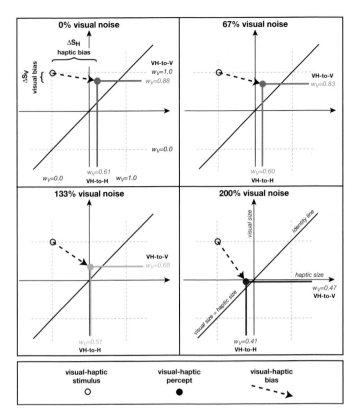

FIGURE 6.9 Visual-haptic percepts (filled circles) in relation to the stimuli (unfilled circles) that gave rise to them. The four panels show the results for four different noise levels. The abscissa indicates the visual size, the ordinate the haptic size of the object. Visual sizes were compared in the VH-to-V condition, haptic sizes in the VH-to-H condition. From this, the visually and haptically perceived sizes were determined using *PSEs* (weights). The difference between physical and perceived size (the visual-haptic bias; dashed arrow) directly depends on the weights of the signals (see Equations 8 and 9).

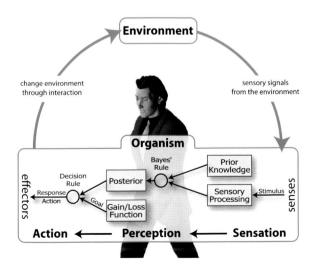

FIGURE 6.10 Perception/action loop including Bayesian decision theory (BDT). From Ernst and Bülthoff, 2004. Reprinted with permission.

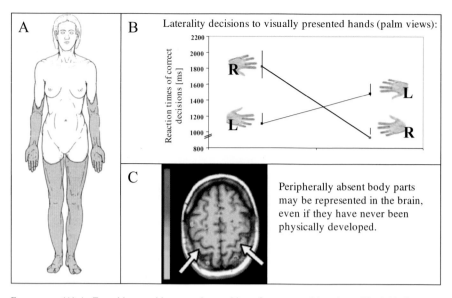

FIGURE 9.5 (A) A. Z., a 44-year-old woman born without forearms and legs but with vivid phantoms (shaded areas) of most missing body parts. Drawing by Peter Roth, Zürich. (B) A. Z.'s reaction-time pattern to visually presented hands ("a left or a right hand?") was constrained by the awkwardness of displayed postures, despite the fact that her brain has never received any information about hand posture. Data reproduced from Funk (2001) with the permission of the author. (C) Rhythmic movements of the right phantom fingers activated the premotor and parietal cortex bilaterally but not the primary sensorimotor areas for hand representation (arrows). Modified from Figure 3 in Brugger et al. (2000).

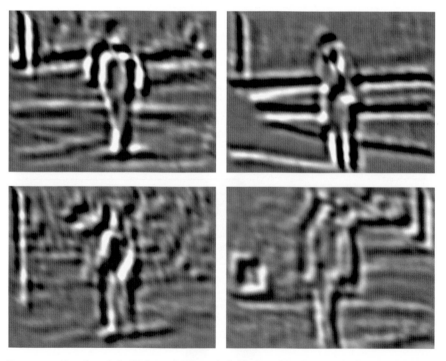

FIGURE 13.3 Four degraded still shots of different individuals walking in the park. The *upper right* and *lower left* images are female, the others male. While some sense of body shape can still be obtained from these images, it was only when in motion that gender categorization was above chance.

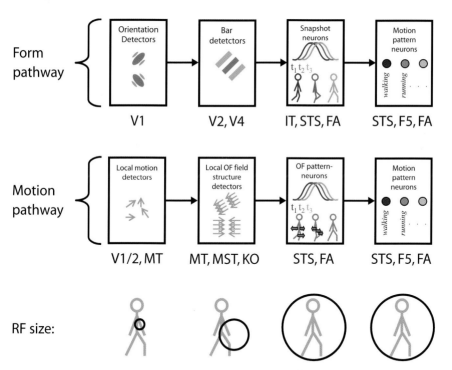

FIGURE 15.1 Overview of the model with two pathways for the processing of form and optic flow information. Abbreviations indicate potentially corresponding areas in the monkey and human cortex. Approximate sizes of the receptive fields compared to a walker stimulus are indicated below. In the cortex, the two pathways converge at the level of the superior temporal sulcus (STS) (further abbreviations: IT: inferotemporal cortex; FA: fusiform and occipital face area; F5: premotor cortex). Modified from Giese (2004) with kind permission of Springer Science and Business Media.

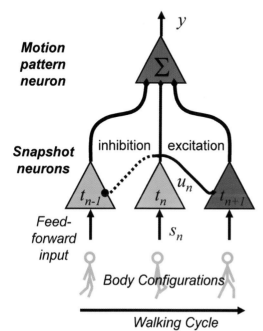

FIGURE 15.2 Asymmetric recurrent connections between the neurons result in responses that are strongly sequence-selective. The snapshot neurons that encode the body shape at time t_n activate neurons encoding immediately subsequent configurations (e.g., at $t_n + 1$) and inhibit the other snapshot neurons. The outputs of the snapshot neurons (and the optic flow pattern neurons) encoding the same motion patterns are summed and temporally smoothed by the corresponding motion pattern neurons. Modified from Giese (2004) with kind permission of Springer Science and Business Media.

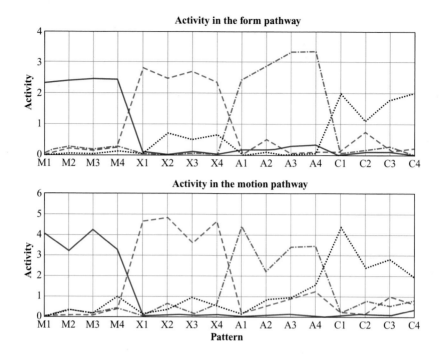

FIGURE 15.3 Activity of motion pattern neurons of the two pathways (motion and form) after training with the gaits of four actors (M, X, A, and C). Different line styles indicate different motion pattern neurons.

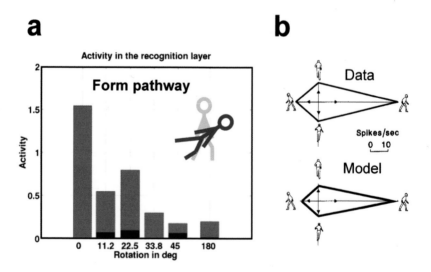

FIGURE 15.4 View dependence of the neural activity of motion pattern neurons in the form pathway. (a) Activation of a motion pattern neuron trained with walking strongly decreases when the test view (gray stick figure) is rotated against the training view (dark stick figure). (b) Similar view dependence is observed if walkers are rotated in depth. The *upper panel* shows the activity of a biological movement–selective neuron in area TPO in the STS for different directions of walking (adapted from Perrett et al., 1985). The *lower panel* shows the dependence of the (normalized) activity of a motion pattern neuron (form pathway).

11

Not Just Posturing
Configural Processing of the Human Body

Catherine L. Reed
Valerie E. Stone
John E. McGoldrick

Introduction

Artists have long understood the power of manipulating visual representations of the human body. German artist Georg Baselitz is known for his provocative, upside-down human figures (Figure 11.1). He inverted his figures to minimize the emotional and meaningful aspects of the human body and to compel viewers to focus on the abstract structure of the composition. As he explained it, "An object painted upside down is suitable for painting because it is unsuitable as an object." The transformation of a human body into an abstract form via inversion suggests that the human visual-object recognition system has specific processes that give rise to our perception of human bodies and their actions. In this chapter, we will learn from the artist and try to understand what perceptual and cognitive processes underlie human body perception.

Human bodies perform important functions in the world that allow us to communicate, share social experiences, and create physical changes in our environment. Bodies and their postures convey information about the identity, age, gender, intentions, and emotional states of other people as well as our-selves. However, cognitive neuroscience tends to be bodiless—most re-searchers acknowledge the body, but they typically do not give it any special status over other types of animate and inanimate objects (e.g., Biederman, 1987; Caramazza & Shelton, 1998; Marr, 1982; McBeath, Morikawa, & Kaiser, 1992). As a result, relatively little research outside of this book ad-dresses what information is contained within human body representations or elucidates the mechanisms used to process body-related information.

Figure 11.1. *Male Nude (Self-Portrait)* (1975) by Georg Baselitz. Oil and charcoal on canvas. Printed with the permission of the North Carolina Museum of Art.

The primate brain contains multiple representations of the body (e.g., Blanke, Landis, Spinelli, & Seeck, 2004; Colby & Duhamel, 1996; Ehrsson, Geyer, & Naito, 2003; Hlushchuk, Forss, & Hari, 2004; Oram & Perrett, 1996; Penfield & Jasper, 1954; Taylor-Clarke, Jacobsen, & Haggard, 2004; chapter 8; also see chapter 4 for a review). This suggests that the body is an important contributor to perceptual and cognitive functions. However, little is known, or at least agreed upon, regarding how these body representations may contribute to cognition. Here we review studies of static and dynamic human body recognition to define properties of human body representations and the role that they play in perception and cognition. We suggest that the human body holds a unique status in our minds and brains because its functional representation inherently includes both visual structure and action (Slaughter & Heron, 2004). In other words, the body representation may be where form and action meet (e.g., Kourtzi & Kanwisher, 2000b; Pinto & Shiffrar, 1999; Shiffrar, 1994).

"Special" Objects

To investigate body-specific representation and processing, one place to start is to compare the human body with a class of objects that is also considered "special" and that shares a number of structural and functional commonalties, such as human faces (Slaughter, Stone, & Reed, 2004). First, we consider what is special about faces and then relate this to body postures.

Evidence from neuroimaging studies, from prosopagnosia, and from behavioral studies of phenomena such as recognition of inverted stimuli has shown that the brain may treat faces differently than other objects (see Kanwisher, Downing, Epstein, & Kourtzi, 2001, for a review). Patients with prosopagnosia have a selective deficit in face recognition that does not necessarily extend to other objects (e.g., Damasio, Damasio, & Van Hoesen, 1982; Farah, 1990). In neurologically intact participants, several behavioral effects show that faces are processed differently from other objects; for example, faces are disproportionately more difficult to recognize inverted than upright compared to other objects, and scrambling (i.e., changing the relative position of the parts) affects familiar face recognition more than other object recognition (Baenninger, 1994; Donnelly, Humphreys, & Sawyer, 1994; Scapinello & Yarmey, 1970; Yin, 1969).

In general, objects are easily distinguished from each other by distinctive features (e.g., color, size, specific part shapes). However, what distinguishes faces from other objects is the categorical level at which one typically recognizes the particular exemplar of the object (Damasio et al., 1982; Rosch, Mervis, Gray, Johnson, & Boyes-Braem, 1976; Tanaka & Gauthier, 1997). For example, when one sees a common object, typically one recognizes it at a basic level; when one sees a picture of a bicycle or a cup, one recognizes it as a bike or as a cup, respectively, without identifying which bike or which cup. However, when one sees a person next to a bike, one recognizes that person as Barbara or Katie, at the subbasic, exemplar level. Further, to distinguish between two faces one needs to know more than which parts are present (e.g., eyes, nose, and mouth) (see Figure 11.2, top panel). Instead, individual face recognition demands that the general spatial arrangement of features be preserved (e.g., the eyes are above the nose) and that very fine distinctions be made based on the hierarchical placement, relative shape, and distance

Figure 11.2. *Top*: How do we distinguish between two faces? *Bottom*: How do we distinguish between two body postures?

between these parts (e.g., how far are the eyes above the nose)—in other words, their *configuration* (Leder & Bruce, 2000). Thus, the visual system may recognize faces differently from other objects because faces have certain abstract properties: (a) almost all faces share the same set of parts, and (b) individual faces are distinguished by subtle differences in the appearance and relative position of those parts. This implies that the visual system uses a different processing mechanism for faces than for other objects; this mechanism is termed *configural processing*.

Nonetheless, faces may not be the only class of stimuli that elicit specialized processing from the visual system. Just as in the face-processing literature, single-cell, neuropsychological, and neuroimaging studies provide evidence that bodies are processed differently from other nonhuman objects. Recordings from a subpopulation of neurons in the superior temporal sulcus of the macaque monkey were found to be selectively sensitive to whole-body stimuli relative to control stimuli, such as the head alone (Wachsmuth, Oram, & Perrett, 1994). Evidence for separate neural substrates for human body representations also comes from patients suffering from autotopagnosia. These patients are unable to locate a body part in the context of a whole body despite relatively intact object recognition and spatial ability. They can recognize and name body parts individually, demonstrating that the problem is not with knowledge about the parts themselves, their perception, or linguistic capabilities. The deficit appears to be specific to the body and is not a more general impairment in locating parts of complex objects (Ogden, 1985). Finally, recent neuroimaging studies (Downing, Jiang, Shuman, & Kanwisher, 2001; Grossman & Blake, 2001, 2002; see chapter 16) provide evidence that a specific region of the visual cortex—the right lateral occipitotemporal cortex— may be specialized for detecting human bodies, separate from both faces and other nonhuman objects (e.g., houses, tools). These studies did not investigate whether this area was selectively activated for differences in human body postures.

Behavioral studies also show differences between the processing of bodies and objects. For example, when viewing apparent motion displays in which two images alternate back and forth between two locations, people typically perceive objects as following the shortest path of apparent motion. However, when viewing human bodies in two different body postures, they perceive body parts as following longer, anatomically plausible paths rather than the shortest path (Shiffrar & Freyd, 1993). Reed and Farah (1995) found that the movement of a person's own body influenced memory for a model's body posture, but did not influence memory for the positions of analogous abstract block objects. In addition, body postures are demonstrated to be recognized differently from other nonface objects in that inverted body postures are disproportionately more difficult to recognize than upright body postures compared to other objects (Reed, Stone, Bozova, & Tanaka, 2003). In sum, body representations appear to differ from those of other objects.

Because faces and bodies co-occur in visual experience and share many abstract visual properties, there may be analogous cognitive processes used for recognizing both types of stimuli. Like faces, most bodies share the same set of parts, but they can vary in their configuration. Body postures differ from each other in the relative position of those parts. Consider how one recognizes that two body postures are the same or different (see Figure 11.2, bottom panel). To distinguish between two postures, one needs to know more than what parts are present (e.g., arms, legs, torso) or even their relative spatial arrangement (e.g., the head is above the arms). Like faces, individual body-posture recognition requires very fine distinctions to be made based on the relative shape and position of these parts. Further, when we see a body posture, we typically recognize it not so much as a human body at the basic level, but instead as an exemplar-level posture that conveys specific information about a person's emotional state, attentional direction, or action intentions (e.g., run or punch). Thus, the similarities that are involved in distinguishing between two faces and two body postures suggest that body postures may be recognized via configural processing. Body shape may also convey information about a person's individual identity, with subtle configural differences in body shape allowing individual recognition. Both individuals and body postures may be recognizable at the individual exemplar level by using configural information.

The characteristics of face and human body recognition coincide well with the idea that two types of systems exist within visual object recognition processing. These systems are not distinguished by content—i.e., face versus object—but instead by a more general definition of domain: *feature-based* versus *configural* processing (Carey, 1992; Leder & Bruce, 2000; Tanaka & Gauthier, 1997). Many researchers have proposed that faces are "unique" because they are recognized using different processes from most other objects. However, some differences between face and object processing that were thought to support the uniqueness of face processing have been found to apply to nonface objects that either share certain abstract properties with faces or are viewed by highly experienced viewers (e.g., dogs, birds, computer-generated "Greebles") (Carey, 1992; Diamond & Carey, 1986; Gauthier & Tarr, 1997; Reed, Nyberg, Stone, & Grubb, 2004; see Tanaka & Gauthier, 1997, for review). Some researchers have suggested that what viewer expertise does is change recognition processing from part-based to configural (Carey, 1992; Diamond & Carey, 1986; Tanaka & Gauthier, 1997). Given that we recognize specific faces and body postures more than most other objects in our physical environment, it would make sense that we would be expert face and body processors and that we would process both faces and bodies configurally.

Configural Processing

Above we distinguished between processing based on object type (i.e., faces, nonfaces) and processing based on certain abstract stimulus properties (i.e., feature-based versus configural). Although researchers now discuss the "special processing" used for faces in terms of a more general algorithm for configural processing (e.g., Leder & Bruce, 2000; Tanaka & Gauthier, 1997), there are different ways to define configural processing. It has been a contentious concept in the object-recognition literature, so some precise definition and operationalization of the concept may help to clarify the various meanings of *configural*.

Relative Position of Parts or Features

The broadest conceptualization of configural processing refers to the relative spatial positions of individual features or what Carey and colleagues (1992; Diamond & Carey, 1986) describe as first-order relational properties among parts. In terms of the face, first-order spatial relations refer to the relative positions of the nose, eyes, and mouth in two-dimensional "face space." More precisely, it may be defined as the relative positions in coordinate space of constituent parts of an object, such as the placement of the eyes above the nose. Certainly, scrambled faces are much more difficult to recognize than normal faces, and this difference between the recognition of scrambled and intact stimuli is significantly larger for faces than for other objects (Baenninger, 1994; Donnelly, Humphreys, & Sawyer, 1994). However, all normal faces share the same relative position of parts and yet are easily distinguished. Thus, the crucial aspect of facial configuration on which face identity recognition depends must be defined differently (Carey, 1992).

Exact Distances Between Features

Other studies point to a definition of configural processing that depends on the exact distances between parts or features (e.g., Carey, 1992). When the relative positions of face parts are the same, but the exact distances between parts of the face vary, face recognition is affected. In caricatures, distances between parts of the face are altered to exaggerate certain features. Caricatures are better recognized than a normal face (Carey, 1992; Rhodes, Brennan, & Carey, 1987; Rhodes, Byatt, Tremewan, & Kennedy, 1997). Freire, Lee, and Symons (2000) also explored the importance of metric distance and varied the configuration of face stimuli by moving the eyes, nose, or mouth up or down or by moving the eyes closer together or farther apart. They found that these configural changes also affected recognition.

Holistic Representations

Parts of a face are recognized more easily in the context of the whole configuration of the face than in isolation (Tanaka & Farah, 1993; see Gauthier & Tarr, 2002, for a review of holistic-processing conceptions). Farah, Tanaka, and colleagues have interpreted *holistic processing* to mean that face features, spatial relationships between these features, and respective distances between features are not explicitly represented, but are embedded in a complex pattern for which recognition involves a type of template matching. That is, configural processing may depend on representations of the whole object and may not be elicited by object parts or more local relations among subsets of parts.

Together, these various conceptions of configural processing can be aggregated to construct a configural-processing continuum (e.g., Carey, 1992; Diamond & Carey, 1986; Leder & Bruce, 2000; Reed, Stone, Grubb, & McGoldrick, in press; Tanaka & Farah, 1993). Figure 11.3 graphically illustrates the configural-processing continuum. Objects such as houses that are recognized using key features (e.g., color, size, specific part shapes) and only rough spatial relationships (Biederman, 1987) are at recognition-by-parts end of the continuum. Faces, recognized using more-detailed spatial information about the hierarchical position of the relative parts to each other in addition to the precise positions of those parts, are at the other end. The face end of the continuum is often described as "holistic." Objects recognized using non-holistic configural processing would lie in between.

In the face-recognition literature, the inversion paradigm has been used extensively to investigate the configural processing of faces. Observers compare two successively presented stimuli that are either both upright or both inverted, and determine whether they are the same or different (Figure 11.4). An inversion effect refers to the finding that upside-down stimuli are disproportionately slower to be recognized and more difficult to recognize than upright stimuli. The strongest inversion effect is typically found for faces. In contrast to faces, the recognition of other, mono-oriented, familiar objects, such as houses and outdoor scenes, does not typically produce strong inversion

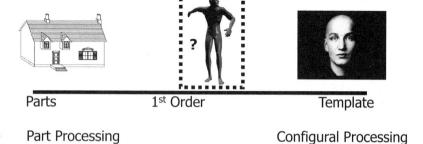

Parts   1st Order   Template

Part Processing   Configural Processing

Figure 11.3. The configural-processing continuum from part-based or feature-based processing to holistic processing. Houses are considered to be a class of objects recognized on the basis of their parts and features. Faces are considered to be a class of objects recognized on the basis of the holistic configuration of their features. What kind of processing is used by the visual system to recognize the human body?

effects. The face inversion effect is generally interpreted as an indicator of configural processing for faces (Freire, Lee, & Symons, 2000; Scapinello & Yarmey, 1970; Tanaka & Gauthier, 1997; Yin, 1969). However, as we have just seen, "configural" could refer to several different types of information, so it is important to specify which *type* of configural processing is disrupted by inversion. The inversion manipulation clearly alters the spatial relations among the parts (i.e., the coordinates of parts) in face space while preserving the exact relative distances. Thus, the section of object space in which a part lies must also be important for configural processing. Evidence to further support the link between configural processing and the face inversion effect comes from studies that manipulate configural information and examine subsequent mediations of the inversion effect. Freire, Lee, and Symons (2000) gave participants a recognition task with upright and inverted faces that either had small changes in the metric distances between the features or different sets of features in the same spatial locations, and they found that the metric changes were the most difficult to recognize upside-down.

Recognition of parts within the whole in upright and inverted faces has been investigated by asking participants first to learn the names of faces and of isolated face parts, for example, Joe's face or Joe's nose (Tanaka & Farah, 1993). At test, participants were asked to recognize the learned versus a novel part (e.g., Which nose is Joe's nose?). The recognition tests showed parts in isolation or in the context of a whole face and included upright and inverted stimuli. Face parts were better recognized upright in whole faces. When the recognition test stimuli were inverted, the whole versus part recognition advantage disappeared for inverted faces. Young, Hellawell, and Hay (1987) showed participants upright and inverted composite faces constructed by combining the top and bottom halves of different faces and found that identifying parts within the whole was difficult for upright faces, consistent with holistic processing, but that individual parts were easily identified in the inverted faces. Thus, some operationalizations of "configural" interact with the inversion effect. Inverting a face does not just disrupt the coordinates of parts in face space, but also disrupts holistic processing and the ability to detect small changes in metric distances.

What might configural processing mean for body postures? Body postures can vary from each other by subtle differences in the relative position of body parts (e.g., hands on hips versus hands at sides) (see Figure 11.2, bottom panel). Coupling the inversion paradigm with systematic manipulations of body, face, and house stimuli, we documented the importance of configural processing for static human body postures. Reed, Stone, Bozova, and Tanaka (2003) compared the recognition of upright and inverted faces, houses, and body postures, using a standard inversion paradigm in which two stimuli were compared sequentially (Figure 11.4). Participants were significantly slower and less accurate at recognizing upside-down body postures than upright body postures.

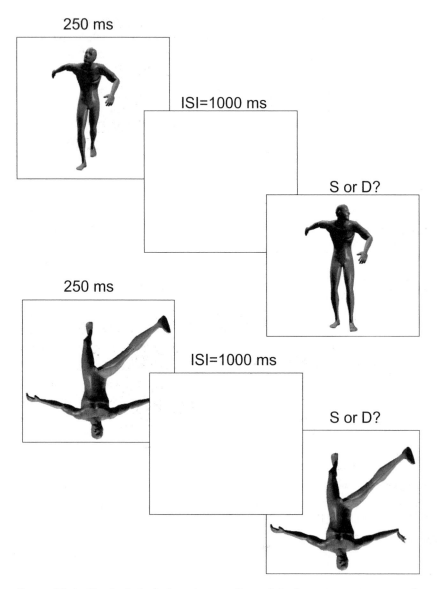

Figure 11.4. The basic body-inversion paradigm. A body posture was presented, followed by a blank screen, and then a target was presented. Participants determined whether the two stimuli were the same or different. The *top panel* illustrates an upright "different" trial. The *bottom panel* illustrates an inverted "same" trial.

Moreover, the size of the inversion effect was of comparable magnitude to that found for faces. In contrast, no inversion effect was found for houses.

Nonetheless, the body inversion effect per se does not tell us which aspects of body representation elicit configural processing. To determine what characteristics of the human body contribute to configural processing, a recent study (Reed, Stone, et al., in press) manipulated the type of configural information available in the body stimulus as has been done in the face-recognition literature (e.g., Leder & Bruce, 2000). Using the inversion effect as an indicator of configural processing, testing began at the recognition-by-features end of the continuum. Participants were asked to determine whether two individual body parts (i.e., an isolated arm, leg, or head) were in the same posture (Figure 11.5a). Their performance was compared to complete body postures as well as to analogous house stimuli. Although arms, legs, and heads have readily visible local configuration information, no inversion effects were found for isolated body parts or for the house stimuli. Inversion effects were found only for complete bodies.

The first-order part of the continuum was examined next. To disrupt relative spatial locations of body parts, scrambled body stimuli were constructed (Figure 11.5b) in which body parts were attached to the trunk in different locations (e.g., an arm was located off the neck). These scrambled body postures did not elicit configural processing either. It appears that specific spatial relations between parts are critical in the sense that the location of one body part constrains the location of another.

Last, the holistic end of the continuum was investigated. Body postures were compared with faces because faces are thought to be processed holistically (e.g., Farah, Wilson, Drain, & Tanaka, 1998; Tanaka & Farah, 1993). To disrupt holistic processing, half-body postures and half-faces were constructed that did not contain complete body or face information, respectively (Figure 11.5c). The comparison of half-stimuli to whole stimuli was useful because half-stimuli preserved the presence of some of the parts, some of their shapes, and some of the part hierarchy from the whole-body stimuli, but did not include all of the information required for a template (i.e., the whole body or face). In addition, there were two types of half-stimuli. One type depicted body stimuli that were divided into upper and lower regions. The other type depicted body stimuli that were divided into left and right regions. The two different types of half-stimuli allowed us to determine if the presence of some body parts were more important for configural processing than were others. The results showed inversion effects for both half- and whole-body stimuli, suggesting that complete template information (i.e., an identical match) was not necessary for the configural processing of the human body. Similar effects were found for faces.

The half-stimuli were examined further to distinguish whether specific features (e.g., the eyes or the arms) or whether the spatial relations of specific parts (e.g., the eyes over the nose over the mouth or the head over the arms over the legs) were driving the inversion effect. The two types of half-stimuli were examined separately. Surprisingly, inversion effects were found only for the vertically divided bodies and faces. Bodies and faces are essentially symmetrical along the vertical axis so the existence of similar parts on the

a) Body Parts:

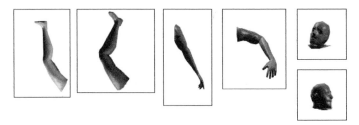

b) Scrambled Bodies:

c) Half Bodies:

Figure 11.5. Manipulations of configural body-posture information: (a) body parts in isolation; (b) scrambled body parts; and (c) half-body parts.

missing side can be inferred from the given side. The basic spatial relations of parts, or their structural hierarchy, can also be inferred. Thus, it appears that the structural hierarchy of parts is critical for eliciting configural processing on both body postures and faces.

The above research shows that both faces and body postures are recognized using configural processes. The face and body inversion effects are affected by similar stimulus manipulations. It is tempting to conclude that the visual system processes face and body-posture stimuli in the same way. However, there may be multiple levels of processing for visual recognition. Although faces and body postures may share some configural processing at a certain stage, processing of the two stimulus categories may not be same all the way through the system. Two studies have explored potential differences between face and body recognition at the holistic end of the configural-processing spectrum by using other paradigms than the inversion paradigm. In the original face study, Tanaka and Farah (1993) proposed that faces may be re-presented as a complex template-type face pattern in which the individual parts are embedded but not explicitly represented. If this were true, then a face part should be recognized better when it is presented in the context of a whole face relative to when it is presented by itself in isolation. Indeed, this is what they found. In addition, Seitz (2002) asked participants to view a whole body or face during a 5-second inspection period and, following a 500-ms inter-stimulus interval (ISI), to determine which of two alternatives in a recognition-test display matched the original. The recognition test presented either face or body parts in isolation or within the context of the whole face or body. She found that participants were better at recognizing both face and body parts within the context of the whole face or body. Seitz concluded that bodies as well as faces were recognized holistically.

However, McGoldrick (2004) conducted a slightly different study that more closely replicated Tanaka and Farah (1993) with body parts and body postures by including both upright and inverted test stimuli. In his study, participants learned the names of isolated face and body parts (e.g., Joe's face or Joe's arms). In an initial self-paced learning session, participants learned to asso-ciate a person's name with a particular face or body part. Participants then were given a two-alternative forced-choice recognition test to answer the on-screen question regarding which one was a previously learned part (e.g., Which arm is Joe's arm?). The recognition tests included upright and inverted isolated parts and upright and inverted whole faces and bodies. He hypothe-sized that if body postures were processed holistically, then like faces, upright body parts should be recognized better in the context of the whole body. Further, the critical test of the holistic processing hypothesis is that the whole-versus-part recognition advantage should disappear for inverted body postures. McGoldrick replicated Tanaka and Farah's (1993) face results as well as Seitz's results in that body parts and face parts were better recognized upright in whole bodies and faces. Nonetheless, the inversion effect was different for faces and bodies. When the recognition test stimuli were inverted, the whole versus part recognition advantage remained for inverted bodies, but disappeared for inverted faces. These results suggest that body postures are processed configurally, but not necessarily holistically. Thus, the recognition of faces and bodies involves some distinct processes.

In a second study, McGoldrick (2004) pursued potential holistic configural-processing differences between faces and body postures by creating a body-posture version of a masking study conducted by Farah et al. (1998). Participants performed a sequential same/different matching task in which an upright face, an inverted face, an upright body, or an inverted body was presented briefly. A pattern mask followed the initial stimulus and then participants determined if a second target of the same type and orientation matched it. The critical manipulation was whether the intervening mask was either a *whole mask* (a novel but complete stimulus object, such as a whole face, house, or word) or a *part mask* consisting of parts of the stimulus (a scrambled face or body in which the parts were rearranged but positioned where other parts would normally exist). If upright faces and body postures were recognized as undifferentiated wholes, so that part representation played a relatively small role in their recognition, then a part mask should have impaired performance less than a whole mask. There should be no difference between masks for inverted stimuli because the configural spatial relations are disrupted, and the pattern is no longer recognized as a face or body posture and thus can be easier to ignore. McGoldrick replicated the results of Farah et al. (1998) for faces: whole masks but not part masks disrupted upright face recognition only, and a face inversion effect was found. In contrast, the body postures produced an inversion effect, but there was no difference between part and whole masking. It appears that manipulations of the spatial relations in masks that disrupt face recognition do not have the same disruptive effect on body-posture recognition. Thus, body postures do not appear to be recognized like faces in a holistic, undifferentiated manner.

In summary, comparisons between the recognition of faces and of bodies tell us that body postures are recognized using configural information about spatial relations between parts and about the relationship of parts to the body hierarchy. However, despite many similarities in processing, there are processing differences between faces and bodies. One source of this difference may be in the differing abilities of the face and body to move. Faces have limited degrees of freedom in terms of how the facial features can move, but human body limbs have many movement possibilities. In the above masking experiment by McGoldrick (2003), it is possible that the most effective kind of mask was not used to disrupt holistic processing in the body conditions. Instead of static masks, dynamic body masks may have been more effective. If action and ability to move are critical components of body representation, as suggested by de

Vignemont et al. (see chapter 8) and Wilson (see chapter 10), then stimuli that engage the visual motion-perception system and the motor system may be important contributors to the configural processing of body postures.

Configural Processing for Biological Motion Displays

The integration of body structure with body movement is ubiquitous in our visual world. We are constantly moving and performing actions. We watch other people do the same. Even static images of objects in motion imply motion, especially pictures of human bodies in motion, and permit us to make predictions about that motion (e.g., Kourtzi & Kanwisher, 2000a, 2000b; Kourtzi & Shiffrar, 1999). The ability to recognize configurations of body parts may be even more important for the recognition of moving bodies than for static bodies. In this section we will consider how configural processing is used for the visual recognition of moving bodies in biological motion displays. Configural processing is critical for these point-light walker displays because the visual system must put together many moving points of light to create integrated representations of the body and movement. The importance of motion in visual object recognition has long been recognized in the phenomena of biological motion. More recently there has been a greater focus and appreciation of the importance of body representations for biological motion (see chapters 14 and 16).

For biological-motion paradigms, researchers create point-light displays of a moving human figure. Often the human figure is walking. Typically, discrete light elements are attached to the major joints of an otherwise invisible person. Although no explicit contours, textures, or colors indicate the presence of a human figure, the visual system is able to extract the structure of a human body from the motion of these elements within 200 ms (Johansson, 1973, 1976). In these paradigms, observers typically judge the presence or absence of a human form or identify some aspect of the action that the point-light figure is performing. Observers' exquisite sensitivity to detecting human motion within these impoverished visual displays can be disrupted by changing the relation among the light points (e.g., observers fail to detect a human body when the point lights are placed off the major body joints). This suggests that the visual system performs a global analysis that relies on the biomechanically constrained configuration of the lights. A configural representation of the body and how its parts relate to the whole-body hierarchy in terms of structure and biomechanics constrains the possible interpretations of the point-light movements.

Inversion effects for biological motion are well documented for both adults and children (Bertenthal & Pinto, 1994; Grossman & Blake, 2001, 2002; Pavlova & Sokolov, 2000; chapters 14 and 16). The spontaneous recognition of point-light walkers is greater for upright orientations relative to inverted orientations (e.g., Pavlova & Sokolov, 2000, 2003; Shipley, 2003). More specifically, observers are less likely to detect (Bertenthal & Pinto, 1994), organize (Shiffrar, Lichtey, & Heptulla Chatterjee, 1997), or identify (Sumi, 1984) these displays when they are presented upside-down. This decreased ability to perceive biological motion occurs even though both the upright and inverted displays of human locomotion have the same hierarchical structure, the same rigid relationships, and the same oscillatory motion trajectories (Pinto & Shiffrar, 1999). When human figure or form space is altered by inversion, it disrupts human motion space as well. In sum, the above findings suggest that both static and dynamic human body information is processed configurally, as indexed by inversion effects. This unique processing mechanism may be used to a greater extent to recognize human bodies and their actions than to recognize other inanimate objects and their movements.

Researchers have proposed that the visual system performs a global integration of motion signals over time and space to create a representation of body configuration. It is reasonable to postulate that this global analysis aids configural-processing mechanisms so that all of the light points can be processed together rapidly and accurately to create a body representation. Just as we can ask with static body postures and faces, "What kind of configural information contributes to recognition?" we can also ask for biological-motion displays, "What kind of configural information is necessary to perceive a dynamic body?" Point-light displays of human locomotion have been used to address whether or not local changes in configuration are crucial. Simultaneous masking has been used to reveal the visual system's sensitivity for both the detection and identification of biological motion. In this paradigm, observers viewed displays containing point-light human Figures that were masked by superimposed moving point-lights created from scrambled point-light walker elements (Bertenthal & Pinto, 1994). Bertenthal and Pinto (1994) theorized that if recognition relied on the perception of the local elements, then the addition of this visual noise should interfere with the perception of biological motion. Despite the masking, they found that human figures could be identified. These results suggest that the lights consistent with the body and its motion were processed as an integrated representation.

To explicitly investigate what kind of configural information about human structure and locomotion contributes to the perception of dynamic bodies, Pinto and Shiffrar (1999) used this simultaneous-masking paradigm in conjunction with the inversion paradigm. They used point-light stimulus manipulations that were consistent with those used to investigate the configural processing of faces and static bodies. First, they assessed the detection and identification of biological motion under conditions where limb extremities, central body components, and joints were missing. Then they assessed biological motion in which the limb organization was scrambled. Last, they assessed biological motion in which only partial body information was available. Consistent with the findings for faces and static bodies, they found that local body-part motion information was not sufficient to indicate human form. Further, scrambling limb organization disrupted body perception. The disruption of the limb organization relative to the trunk seemed to eliminate the important structural characteristics of the human form in motion that are necessary for its recognition. Finally, partial body information was not always sufficient to produce the impression of a dynamic body. The perception of a human figure in motion was dependent upon visual information explicating the organizing features of the human body structure, namely, limb symmetry and hierarchical organization of the limbs around the principle axis of the torso. Although information from the entire body was not necessary for the perception of human motion, subconfigurations that maintained the symmetry and principal axes of the body and its movement were necessary. Thus, it appears that the visual system does not decompose biological-motion displays into their constituent parts. Rather, integration occurs for displays that include light points that convey the hierarchical structural and biomechanical properties of the human body.

In sum, the similarities between the visual recognition of static and dynamic bodies are striking. Disrupting similar stimulus properties for static body postures and point-light walkers has detrimental effects on human body processing and recognition. The recognition of both static and dynamic body stimuli requires information about the structural hierarchy of the body within which body parts are organized. In other words, for both static and dynamic displays, enough visual information must be provided so that the general structural organization of the body can be reconstructed.

Configural Processing, Expertise, and Embodied Representations

The above research emphasizes the human visual system's sensitivity to the human body and its ability to use configural processing to make fine distinctions between postures and movements. From what sources does this configural processing arise? The literature on expertise in object recognition suggests that configural processing arises from extensive experience in viewing a particular class of objects. Configural processing is said to increase the visual system's sensitivity to fine distinctions between highly similar exemplars within a class of objects. Faces and bodies complicate the issue of pure viewing experience because humans have "embodied" internal experience of both faces and bodies, distinguishing them from other object classes in yet another dimension. Our ability to move and use our faces and bodies for functional purposes may influence the visual recognition of other faces and bodies. This interaction between visual and motor systems is suggested by neurophysiological evidence with humans and monkeys, which has revealed a class of "mirror" neurons that are active when a motor action is both performed and observed (see Gallese & Goldman, 1998, for a review; Rizzolatti, Fadiga, Gallese, & Fogassi, 1996). The ability both to see and to move our faces and bodies produces another type of expertise other than pure perceptual expertise. As a result, faces and bodies may more strongly evoke configural processing relative to other objects.

To what extent is the configural processing used to recognize human bodies different from the configural processing used to recognize other classes of objects to which we have considerable exposure? One possibility is that human observers have human body-specific mechanisms and representations that are socially relevant and are used to recognize and produce actions (Reed, 2002; Wilson, 2001). Another possibility is that human observers are configural-processing experts when it comes to recognizing human forms because of our overwhelming visual exposure to them.

These two possibilities can be reformulated into two types of expertise: perceptual expertise and embodiment. *Perceptual expertise* refers to the amount of visual experience an observer has with a particular class of objects. This is the type of expertise studied by Tanaka, Gauthier, Curran, and their colleagues (e.g., Gauthier, Curran, Curby, & Collins, 2003; Tanaka & Gauthier, 1997). They argue that the purpose of configural processing is to aid in the fast and accurate recognition of closely spaced, highly similar exemplars within a class of objects. They have demonstrated that objects that are recognized via their parts by novices can be recognized configurally by experts. Thus, visual exposure can account for differences in object processing. In this view of configural processing, there is nothing special about faces, or any other object, other than the number of experiences we have had trying to recognize them.

Alternatively, one may argue that a different type of expertise, *embodiment*, is specific to the human body. Although vertebrate bodies are broadly similar to the human body, the specific ways in which the human body can move are different from those of other animals. Experiences of the body's configural constraints can be coopted for visual perception so that both the visual system and the motor system are involved in representing the locations of one's own as well as another's body parts in space (Reed & Farah, 1995; Wilson, 2001). In other words, visual sensitivity to the configural properties of the human body may be a function of being able to physically produce them (Prinz, 1997).

By investigating configural recognition processes used for human bodies and comparing them to other animal bodies, these sources of expertise can be disentangled. It can be determined how much visual recognition of human body postures relies upon perceptual expertise and how much might rely on the fact that human viewers have bodies and thus have privileged access to their motoric abilities. A recent study used inversion effects to compare the recognition of upright and inverted human and canine static body postures in common and rare postures (Reed, Nyberg, et al., 2004). Both are animate objects with biomechanical constraints and hierarchical relations among parts. To operationalize perceptual expertise, visual exposure of the body postures was varied, because common postures for humans and canines are viewed more than rare postures. To operationalize embodiment expertise, human and canine body postures were compared. The human versus canine manipulation determined whether the inversion effects were specific to human forms. The familiarity of posture manipulation addressed whether viewing frequency alone could account for the inversion effects (Figure 11.6). The results showed that human figures produced significantly larger inversion effects than did the canine figures. Common postures were recognized better than rare postures. Pair-wise comparisons for each condition revealed that both common and rare human body postures produced inversion effects; however, only the common canine postures produced significant inversion effects. When dog owners were

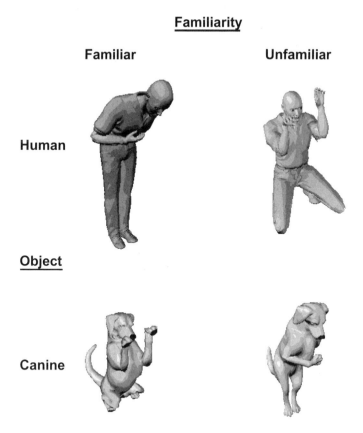

Figure 11.6. Examples of familiar and unfamiliar human body postures and canine body postures.

compared to non-owners, dog owners showed an overall effect of viewing frequency but no difference in the presence or size of the inversion effect for the canine conditions.

In sum, these results suggest that expertise and configural processing appear to involve more than purely perceptual experiences. Our fast and accurate recognition of human body postures via configural processing may be based on body-specific knowledge and representations as well.

However, the lack of significant interactions among object type, viewing frequency, and orientation suggests something else. The lack of large differences between familiar and unfamiliar canine positions suggests that despite differences in the biomechanics between canines and humans, viewers may have been using the knowledge and experience of how their own bodies operated to interpret the canine postures. More generally, we may use our own body representations to interpret the visual world when correspondences between our physical forms and other objects are clearly visible. In other words, we may use our extensive expertise at perceiving and interacting with our own human bodies to facilitate the interpretation of other objects in our visual environment, at least to the extent that we can map our bodies onto those perceptual objects.

Supporting this idea, Cohen's (2002) biological-motion study tested experts and novices for their perception of upright and inverted human and animal point-light displays. Only familiar types of motion were used for humans and animals. Consistent with Reed, Nyberg, et al.'s (2004) results for humans and canines, inversion effects were found for animal as well as human displays, suggesting that both types of stimuli can be processed configurally. A second experiment tested the detection of upright and inverted humans, dogs, and seals by expert dog and seal trainers, respectively. Contrary to what would be expected by a viewing-exposure theory of expertise, Cohen found no expertise differences. These findings are consistent with the static body posture research: although perceptual expertise is associated with increased discriminability in general, expertise was not closely related to the inversion effect. One interpretation for why expertise may not influence the perception of animal biological motion may be that both animal experts and novices used their own bodies' representations to help interpret the presence of biological motion in point-light animal displays. Finer-level discriminations among the perceptions of different types of animals may have been obscured by the present not present response.

These studies of static and dynamic body perception suggest that our visual object recognition processes may be influenced by how our bodies can be mapped onto or interact with perceptual objects. A study by Reed, McGoldrick, Shackelford, and Fidopiastis (2004) found that the body's ability to move and to perform actions upon other objects constrained the cognitive representations of other objects as well as the human body. Participants were given a picture of a complete body, bear, or bicycle and a set of cards in which the object was divided into multiple pieces (Figure 11.7). For each object, the task was to put similar object parts together. In the initial condition, participants were allowed to make as many piles or categories as needed. In the following conditions, participants were asked to make two, three, or four piles. From this sorting, dissimilarity data were analyzed using multidimensional scaling (MDS) techniques to create a conceptual space. Parts that were commonly grouped together and were viewed as being similar were placed closer together in the MDS solution than parts that were never grouped together and were viewed as being dissimilar. The results indicated that people categorized all three objects and their parts on both visual (what parts looked like, where they were located) and functional (what parts do) characteristics. However, the human body was sorted differently from the other objects. It was sorted primarily on the basis of parts that shared functional properties or by action-generating parts (e.g., legs, arms, and head). Interestingly, the bear and the bicycle were sorted based on the degree to which humans interacted with them. For example, the MDS analysis revealed that the bicycle appeared to be categorized from a rider-based viewpoint, as if the participant were sitting on the bicycle (e.g., visible parts versus nonvisible parts, parts used for propulsion versus parts used for structural support). In contrast to bicycles, most of us have little experience interacting with bears, and the MDS analysis reflected this. Participants tended to use primarily visual properties to categorize the parts of the bear. Bear parts were grouped into left, right, upper, and lower portions of the bear.

In sum, our expertise and experience with our own bodies may permit the visual system to recognize other perceptual objects configurally. If how we interact with objects is part of the mental representation, then this may facilitate perception and action. Further, the extent to which humans are able to create correspondences between their own bodies and perceptual objects may influence the visual system's ability to employ configural-processing mechanisms.

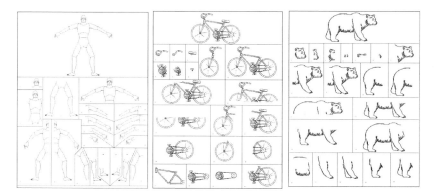

Figure 11.7. Human body, bike, and bear stimuli were divided into various combinations of their parts. Participants sorted parts that went together into the same piles.

Common Spatial Body Representations for Static and Dynamic Human Bodies

Comparing the recognition of static and dynamic human bodies reveals striking similarities in the configural-processing mechanisms used to recognize them and the experimental manipulations used to disrupt their recognition. These similarities are surprising because the visual information in static body postures is very different from that in biological-motion displays. In static body postures, the structure of the human form is explicitly represented, but its motion or represented action must be inferred. In contrast, biological-motion displays explicitly represent biologically constrained visual motion, but the physical structure of the body must be inferred. These processing similarities, despite the information differences, suggest that both types of human body stimuli may rely on common, long-term, spatial body representations, or body representational systems, that are multimodal and used for the self and others. One term that has been associated with this kind of body representation is the *body schema* (e.g., chapter 4; Reed, 2002; Slaughter & Heron, 2004).

The integration of human form and motion inputs in the body schema is consistent with other psychological and neuropsychological research as well as our own personal experiences. Reed and colleagues (Reed & Farah, 1995; Reed & McGoldrick, 2004) developed a dual-task paradigm to investigate the integration of visual information about another person's body position with proprioceptive information about one's own body position. The primary task required participants to determine if two sequentially viewed body positions were the same or different. Before each trial, participants were cued to focus on either the arm or the leg positions. The concurrent secondary task required participants to move either their arms or their legs into a nonrepetitive sequence of postures that did not match the body posture of the primary task. These studies showed that participants' memories for another person's body position could be affected by the participants' own movements. In Reed and Farah (1995), memory for arm or leg positions was relatively facilitated, or improved, if the participant moved the same body part as the one to which they were attending in the primary task (i.e., movement of the arms improved memory for arm position). In addition, this facilitation effect was specific to human body postures because when inanimate Lego objects replaced human body postures in the primary task, participants' movements had no effect on their memories for object position.

In one experiment of a second study, Reed and McGoldrick (2004) used a similar paradigm to demonstrate that the relative facilitation effect for body position memory was dependent upon actual participant motion. The primary task was similar to that used in Reed and Farah (1995). However, the secondary task was replaced with a body-related, visual task. This task required participants to make judgments about a series of visually presented body stimuli: they determined whether any of a series of cued, body-part positions matched the same body-part position from the primary task. If mirror neurons (Rizzolatti et al., 1996) were contributing to the facilitation effect, then the same relative facilitation effect would have been found for the body-relevant task that did not require participant movement. Despite the possibility that mirror neurons could have generated the visual-proprioceptive memory facilitation, no such facilitation was found. In addition, subsequent experiments found that sufficient motor activity needed to be generated by the participant for the facilitation effect to be found reliably. These studies document that body representations are multimodal in that they incorporate both visual and proprioceptive inputs. Body representations can also use information about both self and other.

Other multimodal, dual-task studies that introduce conflicts between seen and felt body-part positions also illustrate the intimate connection between multimodal body representations and human movement (see chapters 3, 4, and 8). A typical paradigm uses experimental situations in which people can confuse the sight of hands that are not their own with their own hands through mismatched visual, proprioceptive, and tactile inputs. Visual stimuli presented near a false limb can also interfere with tactile perception (e.g., Farnè & Làdavas, 2000; chapter 5). As long as false limbs are viewed in postures that are biomechanically compatible with the real limbs, the position information from the false limb can be incorporated into a person's body representation so that the felt position of the false limb can be mistaken for that of the real limb. More important, when one views false limbs that move or are touched concurrently with one's real limbs, it increases the sensation that the false limbs are one's own (e.g., Armel & Ramachandran, 2003; Botvinick & Cohen, 1998).

The neuropsychological literature also highlights the importance of multisensory inputs and hierarchical structural body representations for the perception of one's own and others' bodies. The *body schema* has been defined as a long-term representation of the spatial organization of body parts in the context of the whole body (e.g., Buxbaum & Coslett, 2001; Ogden, 1985; Reed, 2002). The finding that configural recognition of both static and dynamic bodies depends on sufficient information about the relation of parts to the structural hierarchy of the whole body point to the importance of the body schema for recognizing movement and posture. The neurological syndrome of autotopagnosia clarifies the nature of the body schema. Patients with autotopagnosia make body-part localization errors, that is, they are unable to point to a wrist when the whole body is present, even though they can point to it when body parts are presented in isolation. Further, these errors tend to be within the general region of the correct body-part location (e.g., identifying a wrist as an elbow). It seems as if these patients cannot integrate their sensory inputs of body-part location with the hierarchical structural body representation.

This syndrome suggests that body parts are precisely organized within the body representation and that such a representation contains information regarding the specific structural hierarchy of body parts.

In addition, other neurological disorders can create a discrepancy between the physical body and its sensory inputs and the perceptions of the body and its actions (see chapter 9). For example, *phantom-limb syndrome* refers to the perception of an intact and moving limb that has been amputated and no longer provides sensory or motoric inputs. These illusory limb perceptions include more than just the perception of limb presence; they also include illusory perceptions of limb posture and actions. Phantom limbs suggest that the neural network for integrating body posture, body structure, and motoric action continues to be activated without actual sensory input. *Supernumerary phantom-limb syndrome* refers to the sensation of having multiple body parts or a reduplication of body parts. Supernumerary phantom-limb phenomena suggest that the structure of the body representation is disrupted. In other words, a body representation with more than two arms is accepted as normal body structure.

Last, we turn to neuroimaging experiments using neurologically intact individuals to consider how the brain integrates body representation with visual motion and configural processing. To date, no studies have investigated the neural bases underlying the configural processing of static body *postures.* However, Grossman (see chapter 16; Grossman & Blake, 2000, 2001, 2002) has investigated the neural bases of biological motion and the neural systems that change with inversion. If configural processing is involved in the perception of biological motion, then the viewing of biological motion should activate neural regions implicated in the configural processing of faces and other classes of objects for which the viewers are experts. This is just what Grossman and Blake (2002) found. Faces and objects viewed by experts activate the fusiform face area (FFA) and the occipital face area (OFA) (Gauthier, Skudlarski, Gore, & Anderson, 2000; Gauthier & Tarr, 1997). Grossman and Blake (2002) found that the FFA and OFA were able to distinguish biological from nonbiological motion. Regions associated with the detection of human form, including the lateral occipital complex (LOC) and extrastriate body area (EBA), were not differentially activated by biological motion. Biological motion also activates neural regions associated with motion (medial temporal lobe, or MT) and body processing (posterior superior temporal sulcus, or STSp) (Grossman, Donnelly, Price, Pickens, Morgan, Neighbor, & Blake, 2000).

What areas are involved when humans view inverted biological-motion displays? When Grossman and colleagues examined the neurological consequences of inversion on biological-motion perception directly, they found that the activity in the STSp was most sensitive to inversion effects (Grossman & Blake, 2001). The STSp was most active during the perception of upright point-light walker animations, less active for inverted point-light walkers, and least active for scrambled biological-motion displays. Together, this work provides insight into the similarities and differences in configural processing for faces and bodies. Some aspects of face and dynamic body stimuli evoke common configural-processing mechanisms in the OFA and FFA. However, other aspects of configural processing specific to the actions of the human body appear to be processed selectively in the STSp.

Thus, body representations are not purely visual, neither in the inputs that activate the representations nor in the information contained in the representations. Both visual form and motion inputs appear to differentially activate body representations. Further, in addition to structural information about body parts, the body schema seems to include information about the human body's biomechanical constraints that allow it to perform actions and functions in the environment.

Consistent with these ideas, Wilson (chapter 10) has proposed that our interactions with others are based on an intimate relationship between body representations and the motor system. She hypothesizes that we perform covert mental simulations in the form of an *emulator* that draws on body-schematic knowledge derived from the representation of one's own body. These simulations facilitate the exquisite timing that occurs between interacting partners in functional activities, such as conversation. By adding biomechanical knowledge based on one's body schema to the process of emulating others' movements, the simulations can be more accurate. Supporting this idea, perceptual prediction for human movement is best when one views oneself since the visual perception of body movement is maximally similar to one's own motor movement. For example, when viewing a videotape of an action, participants are more accurate at predicting the endpoint of that action when they view themselves compared to when they view another person (Knoblich & Flach, 2001; Knoblich, Seigerschmidt, Flach, & Prinz, 2002).

Action Makes the Body Different From Other Objects

When we see a body in a particular posture or when it is in motion, we can instantly recognize it as human. Across a wide range of perceptual conditions, the experience of recognizing a human body as human depends not so much on identifying particular body parts as it does on identifying those parts in relation to one another. That is, the human body forms a particular spatial configuration among its parts, which when they are properly arranged makes it easily recognizable as a whole. Consequently, our perceptual systems have an exquisite sensitivity to the form and dynamics of the human body (Shiffrar, 2001; Slaughter et al., 2004). Here we have proposed that the visual system recognizes the human body via configural-processing mechanisms that take into account knowledge about how the body moves and how its parts are connected as well as its overall visual structure.

Bodies may be unique because of their capacity to convey action. If we need to process and recognize another person's body posture or action quickly and accurately, we may need special processing mechanisms in the visual system as well as body representations, to process and coordinate personal actions with those of another. Specialized processing appears to depend on several types of configural information, meaning that the spatial relations among parts are processed together for more rapid and accurate recognition. Why is such configural processing used for the human body? Specific actions require the identification of all body parts in particular positions. Configural processing is used for static body postures in which action is implicit as well as for biological-motion displays in which structure is implicit. This suggests that we have a common system for representing the body and its actions.

In this chapter, we have provided evidence that configural processing is important for body recognition by reviewing paradigms and experiments that manipulate the spatial relations among body parts. Further, this configural processing has been shown to apply not only to static body postures in which action is inferred, but also to point-light displays in which only the relative action among parts is visible and body structure is inferred. Thus, the human body conveys information about both function and action. It tells us about the current state of ourselves and others, what actions someone else is performing, and how we in turn should respond to those actions. As Kinsbourne (1995) argues, the human body is indeed "referenced for action."

Acknowledgments   We would like to thank Virginia Slaughter as well as Maggie Shiffrar, Emily Grossman, and Meg Wilson for their helpful comments on this chapter.

References

Armel, K. C., & Ramachandran, V. S. (2003). Disownership of the left hand and objects related to it in a patient with right brain damage. *Neuroreport, 8,* 293–296.

Baenninger, M. (1994). The development of face recognition: Featural or configurational processing? *Journal of Experimental Child Psychology, 57,* 377–396.

Bertenthal, B. I., & Pinto, J. (1994). Global processing of biological motions. *Psychological Science, 5,* 221–225.

Biederman, I. (1987). Recognition-by-components: A theory of human image understanding. *Psychological Review, 94,* 115–147.

Blanke, O., Landis, T., Spinelli, L., & Seeck, M. (2004). Out-of-body experience and autoscopy of neurological origin. *Brain, 127,* 243–258.

Botvinick, M., & Cohen, J. (1998). Rubber hands "feel" touch that eyes see. *Nature, 391,* 756.

Buxbaum, L., & Coslett, H. B. (2001). Specialized structural descriptions for human body parts: Evidence from autotopagnosia. *Cognitive Neuropsychology, 18,* 289–306.

Caramazza, A., & Shelton, J. R. (1998). Domain-specific knowledge systems in the brain: The animate-inanimate distinction. *Journal of Cognitive Neuroscience, 10,* 1–34.

Carey, S. (1992). Becoming a face expert. *Philosophical Transactions of the Royal Society of London: Biological Science, 335,* 95–103

Cohen, L. R. (2002). The role of experience in the perception of biological motion. *Dissertation Abstracts International, Section B: Sciences & Engineering, 63,* 3049.

Colby, C. L., & Duhamel, J. R. (1996). Spatial representations for action in parietal cortex. *Cognition and Brain Research, 5,* 105–115.

Damasio, A. R., Damasio, H., & Van Hoesen, G. W. (1982). Prosopagnosia: Anatomic basis and behavioral mechanisms. *Neurology, 32,* 331–341.

Diamond, R., & Carey, S. (1986). Why faces are and are not special: An effect of expertise. *Journal of Experimental Psychology: General, 115,* 107–117.

Donnelly N., Humphreys, G. W., & Sawyer, J. (1994). Stimulus factors affecting the categorisation of faces and scrambled faces. *Acta Psychologica, 85,* 219–34.

Downing, P. E., Jiang, Y., Shuman, M., & Kanwisher, N. (2001). A cortical area selective for visual processing of the human body. *Science, 293,* 2470–2473.

Ehrsson, H. H., Geyer, S., & Naito, E. (2003). Imagery of voluntary movement of fingers, toes, and tongue activates corresponding body-part-specific motor representations. *Journal of Neurophysiology, 90,* 3304–3316.

Farah, M. J. (1990). *Visual agnosia: Disorders of object recognition and what they tell us about normal vision.* Cambridge, MA: MIT Press.

Farah, M. J., Wilson, K. D., Drain, M., & Tanaka, J. N. (1998). What is "special" about face perception? *Psychological Review, 105,* 452–498.

Farnè, A., & Làdavas, E. (2000). Dynamic size change of dynamic hand peripersonal space following tool use. *Neuroreport, 11,* 1645–1649.

Freire, A., Lee, K., & Symons, L. A. (2000). The face-inversion effect as a deficit in the encoding of configural information: Direct evidence. *Perception, 29,* 159–170.

Gallese, V., & Goldman, A. (1998). Mirror neurons and the simulation theory of mind-reading. *Trends in Cognitive Sciences, 2,* 493–501.

Gauthier, I., Curran, T., Curby, K. M., & Collins, D. (2003). Perceptual interference supports a non-modular account of face processing. *Nature Neuroscience, 6,* 428–432.

Gauthier, I., Skudlarski, P., Gore, J., & Anderson, A. W. (2000). Expertise for cars and birds recruits brain areas involved in face recognition. *Nature Neuroscience, 3,* 191–197.

Gauthier, I., & Tarr, M. J. (1997). Becoming a "Greeble" expert: Exploring mechanisms for face recognition. *Vision Research, 37,* 1673–1682.

Gauthier, I., & Tarr, M. J. (2002). Unraveling mechanisms for expert object recognition: Bridging brain activity and behavior. *Journal of Experimental Psychology: Human Perception & Performance, 28,* 431–446.

Grossman, E. D., & Blake, R. (2001). Brain activity evoked by inverted and imagined biological motion. *Vision Research, 41,* 1475–1482.

Grossman, E. D., & Blake, R. (2002). Brain areas actual during visual perception of biological motion. *Neuron, 35,* 1167–1175.

Grossman, E., Donnelly, M., Price, R. Pickens, D., Morgan, V., Neighbor, G., & Blake, R. (2000). Brain areas involved in the perception of biological motion. *Journal of Cognitive Neuroscience, 12,* 711–720.

Hlushchuk, Y., Forss, N., & Hari, R. (2004). Distal-to-proximal representation of volar index finger in human area 3b. *Neuroimage, 21,* 696–700.

Johansson, G. (1973). Visual perception of biological motion and a model for its analysis. *Perception & Psychophysics, 14,* 201–211.

Johansson, G. (1976). Spatio-temporal differentiation and integration in visual motion perception. *Psychological Review, 38,* 379–393.

Kanwisher, N., Downing, P., Epstein, R., & Kourtzi, Z. (2001). Functional neuroimaging of visual recognition. In R. Cabeza & A. Kingstone (Eds.), *Handbook of functional neuroimaging of cognition* (pp. 109–152). Cambridge, MA: MIT Press.

Kinsbourne, M. (1995). Awareness of one's own body: An attentional theory of its nature, development, and brain basis. In J. L. Bermudez, A. Marcel, & N. Eilan (Eds.), *The body and the self* (pp. 205–224). Cambridge, MA: MIT Press.

Knoblich, G., & Flach, R. (2001). Predicting the effects of actions: Interactions of perception and action. *Psychological Science, 12*, 467–472.

Knoblich, G., Seigerschmidt, E., Flach, R., & Prinz, W. (2002). Authorship effects in the prediction of handwriting strokes: Evidence for action simulation during action perception. *Quarterly Journal of Experimental Psychology: Human Experimental Psychology, 55A*, 1027–1046.

Kourtzi, Z., & Kanwisher, N. (2000a). Activation in human MT/MST by static images with implied motion. *Journal of Cognitive Neuroscience, 12*, 48–55.

Kourtzi, Z., & Kanwisher, N. (2000b). Implied motion activates extrastriate motion-processing: Response to David and Senior (2000). *Trends in the Cognitive Sciences, 4*, 295–296.

Kourtzi, Z., & Shiffrar, M. (1999). Dynamic representations of human body movement. *Perception, 28*, 49–62.

Leder, H., & Bruce, V. (2000). When inverted faces are recognized: The role of configural information in face recognition. *Quarterly Journal of Experimental Psychology, 53*, 513–536.

Marr, D. (1982). *Vision: A computational investigation into the human representation and processing of visual information.* San Francisco: Freeman.

McBeath, M. K., Morikawa, K., & Kaiser, M. K. (1992). Perceptual bias for forward-facing motion. *Psychological Science, 3*, 362–367.

McGoldrick, J. E. (2004). *The configural processing of human body postures. Dissertation Abstracts International, 64*(07B), 3553 (University Microfilms No. AAT 3097884).

Ogden, J. A. (1985). Autotopagnosia: Occurrence in a patient without nominal aphasia and with an intact ability to point to parts of animals and objects. *Brain, 108*, 1009–1022.

Oram, M. W., & Perrett, D. I. (1996). Integration of form and motion in the anterior superior temporal polysensory area (STPa) of the macaque monkey. *Neurophysiology, 76*, 109–129.

Pavani, F., Spence, C., & Driver, J. (2000). Visual capture of touch: Out-of-the-body experiences with rubber gloves. *Psychological Science, 11*, 353–359.

Pavlova, M., & Sokolov, A. (2000). Orientation specificity in biological motion perception. *Perception & Psychophysics, 62*, 889–899.

Pavlova, M., & Sokolov, A. (2003). Prior knowledge about display inversion in biological motion perception. *Perception, 32*, 937–946.

Penfield, W., & Jasper, H. (1954). *Epilepsy and the functional anatomy of the human brain.* Boston: Little, Brown.

Pinto, J., & Shiffrar, M. (1999). Subconfigurations of the human form in the perception of biological motion displays. *Acta Psychologica, 102*, 293–318.

Prinz, W. (1997). Perception and action planning. *European Journal of Cognitive Psychology, 38*, 784–791.

Reed, C. L. (2002). What is the body schema? In W. Prinz and A. Meltzoff (Eds.), *The imitative mind: Development, evolution, and brain bases* (pp. 233–243). Cambridge: Cambridge University Press.

Reed, C. L., & Farah, M. J. (1995). The psychological reality of the body schema: A test with normal participants. *Journal of Experimental Psychology: Human Perception and Performance, 21,* 334–343.

Reed, C. L., & McGoldrick, J. E. (2005). Action during perception affects memory: Changing interference to facilitation via processing time. Manuscript in preparation.

Reed, C. L., McGoldrick, J. E., Shackelford, R., & Fidopiastis, C. (2004). Are human bodies represented differently from other animate and inanimate objects? *Visual Cognition, 11,* 523–550.

Reed, C. L., Nyberg, A., Stone, V. E., & Grubb, J. (2005). The embodiment of perceptual expertise and configural processing. Manuscript in preparation.

Reed, C. L., Stone, V., Bozova, S., & Tanaka, J. (2003). The body inversion effect. *Psychological Science, 14,* 302–308.

Reed, C. L., Stone, V. E., Grubb, J., & McGoldrick, J. E. (in press). Turning configural processing upside down: Part- and whole body postures. *Journal of Experimental Psychology: Human Perception and Performance.*

Rhodes, G., Brennan, S., & Carey, S. (1987). Identification and ratings of caricatures: Implications for mental representations of faces. *Cognitive Psychology, 19,* 473–497.

Rhodes, G., Byatt, G., Tremewan, T., & Kennedy, A. (1997). Facial distinctiveness and the power of caricatures. *Perception, 2,* 207–223.

Rizzolatti, G., Fadiga, L., Gallese, V., & Fogassi, L. (1996). Premotor cortex and the recognition of motor actions. *Cognitive Brain Research, 3,* 131–141.

Rosch, E., Mervis, C. B., Gray, W. D., Johnson, D. M., and Boyes-Braem, P. (1976). Basic objects in natural categories. *Cognitive Psychology, 8,* 382–439.

Scapinello, K. F., & Yarmey, A. (1970). The role of familiarity and orientation in immediate and delayed recognition of pictorial stimuli. *Psychonomic Science, 21,* 329–331.

Seitz, K. (2002). Parts and wholes in person recognition: Developmental trends. *Journal of Experimental Child Psychology, 82,* 367–381.

Shiffrar, M. (1994). When what meets where. *Current Directions in Psychological Science, 3,* 96–100.

Shiffrar, M. (2001). The visual interpretation of object and human movement. In T. F. Shipley & P. J. Kellman (Eds.), *From fragments to objects: Segmentation and grouping in vision* (pp. 483–507). New York: Elsevier Science.

Shiffrar, M., & Freyd, J. J. (1993). Timing and apparent motion path choice with human body photographs. *Psychological Science, 4,* 379–384.

Shiffrar, M., Lichtey, L., & Heptulla Chatterjee, S. (1997). The perception of biological motion cross apertures. *Perception & Psychophysics, 59,* 51–59.

Shipley, T. F. (2003). The effect of object and event orientation on perception of biological motion. *Psychological Science, 14,* 377–380.

Slaughter, V., & Heron, M. (2004). Origins and early development of human body knowledge. *Monographs of the Society for Research in Child Development, 69.*

Slaughter, V., Stone, V. E., & Reed, C. L. (2004). Perception of faces and bodies: Similar or different? *Current Directions in Psychological Science, 13,* 219–223.

Sumi, S. (1984). Upside-down presentation of the Johansson moving light-spot pattern. *Perception, 13,* 283–286.

Tanaka, J. W., & Farah, M. J. (1993). Parts and wholes in face recognition. *Quarterly Journal of Experimental Psychology, 46A,* 225–245.

Tanaka, J. W., & Gauthier, I. (1997). Expertise in object and face recognition. In R. L. Goldstone, P. G. Schyns, & D. L. Medin (Eds.), *Psychology of Learning and*

Motivation Series, Special Volume: Vol. 36: Perceptual Mechanisms of Learning, Vol. 36 (pp. 83–125). San Diego, CA: Academic Press.

Tanaka, J. W., & Sengco, J. A. (1997). Features and their configuration in face recognition. *Memory and Cognition, 25*, 583–592.

Taylor-Clarke, M., Jacobsen, P., & Haggard, P. (2004). Keeping the world a constant size: Object constancy in human touch. *Nature Neuroscience, 7*, 219–220.

Wachsmuth, E., Oram, M. W., & Perrett, D. I. (1994). Recognition of objects and their component parts: Responses of single units in the temporal cortex of the macaque. *Cerebral Cortex, 4*, 509–522.

Wilson, M. (2001). Perceiving imitatible stimuli: Consequences of isomorphism between input and output. *Psychological Bulletin, 127*, 543–553.

Yin, R. K. (1969). Looking at upside down faces. *Journal of Experimental Psychology, 81*, 141–145.

Young, A. W., Hellawell, D., & Hay, D. C. (1987). Configurational information in face perception. *Perception, 16*, 747–759.

SECTION III

Perception of Biological Motion

12

Of Bodies, Brains, and Models
*Studying the Perception
of Biological Motion*

Ian M. Thornton

1. Overview

As the title of this volume suggests, the human body is a unique object. It is unique in the sense that related processing can make use of both internal and external sources of information. We each possess a body; we feel it, see it, and control it. We are also frequently in close proximity to other bodies, observing, imitating, interacting with, and predicting their movements. Much of the work reported in this book is concerned with understanding the precise relationship between these two sources of information.

Section I discussed how the body serves as a framework for integrating information across multiple senses, a process which is thought to require and encourage the development of multiple body representations, or schemas, the topic of section II. The four chapters in the current section of the book all relate to the visual perception of the human body in motion. Finally, section IV explores the notion that our bodies are the fundamental tool through which we act on the world, an idea that has important consequences for understanding the relationship between our intentions, actions, and perceptions.

In this introduction to section III, I will briefly introduce the research area from which the four chapters are drawn, known as *biological-motion perception*, discuss some general themes from this domain, and then outline the main thrust of each individual contribution. Finally, I have included a brief connections and future directions section, as an attempt to position biological-motion processing within the wider framework of this book—an understanding of the ways in which we represent the human body.

2. Biological Motion

In its most general sense, *biological motion* could refer to any characteristic movement pattern purposefully generated by a biological entity, for example, flowers slowly opening in the light, amoebae swimming in the ooze, a lion stalking its prey, or a person running for a bus. Waves breaking on the shore, a felled tree crashing to the ground, or a sleeping person falling out of bed, while clearly involving movement of natural or biological entities, lack the active or intentional aspects of the previous examples. They would not typically be of interest in the context of biological-motion research, except perhaps as control stimuli.

In practice, the vast majority of research on biological motion has been concerned with the visual perception of human patterns of movement by human observers. Thus, studies typically ask observers to interpret some visual depiction of an action, such as walking, running, jumping, dancing, bicycle riding, etc., etc. (e.g., Dittrich, 1993; Johansson, 1973, 1975). There have been a number of studies in which human observers interpret the movement of nonhuman animals (e.g., Bellefeuille & Faubert, 1998; Jacobs, Chouchourelou, & Shiffrar, 2005; Mather & West, 1993). Similarly, a few studies have explored the ability of other species, including cats (Blake, 1993), pigeons (Omori, 1996), chickens (Regolin et al., 2000), quail (Yamaguchi & Fujita, 1999), monkeys (Oram & Perrett, 1994), and dolphins (Herman et al., 1990), to perceive the biological motion of their own or other species. In general, the concentration on human motion probably reflects a number of factors, including the social relevance, availability, and complexity of such movements. Clearly, our unique experience of the human body from both the inside and the outside, the theme of this book, also plays an important role in elevating the significance of studying human motion.

Not only have the vast majority of biological-motion studies concerned themselves with the perception of human movement by human observers, but almost all of them have also used a single type of display, known as *point-light stimuli* (Johansson, 1973, 1975; Marey, 1972). As discussed in detail in the next chapter, point-light stimuli are moving objects in which the form cues (i.e., color, texture, shape) have been reduced to a limited number of uniform markers or dots. The classic example of point-light stimuli—the Johansson point-light walker (Johansson, 1973)—is a depiction of a human in which the head and each of the major joints (specifically, the shoulders, elbows, wrists, hips, knees, and ankles) have been replaced by single points of light. When presented statically, such displays are very hard to interpret. However, when placed in motion, the points trace the position of each body part in time, providing a clear and compelling depiction of the underlying action.

3. Research Themes

In the 30 years since Johansson popularized the point-light technique, there has been an ever-increasing output of studies, with a current total of around 500 publications which refer to biological motion. Clearly, it is beyond the scope of this chapter to produce an exhaustive review of all of this literature. Here, I will simply outline three major themes that have emerged, using them as a framework for organizing the wider body of research, providing example citations for each, and also providing specific links to other chapters in this book.

The first main issue, and the one that motivated Johansson's original work, concerns the nature of the motion mechanisms that support the perception of biological motion. That is, how do we detect and integrate the complex local motions underlying our global percepts of human action? Johansson suggested that the speed and efficiency with which such processing takes place had to reflect the "spontaneous" and "automatic" extraction of "mathematically lawful spatio-temporal relations" in early visual patterns of stimulation (Johansson, 1973, 1975). There is now considerable evidence to suggest that such low-level, local-to-global mechanisms do play an important role in biological-motion processing (e.g., Giese & Poggio, 2003; Mather, Radford, & West, 1992; Thornton & Vuong, 2004). However, it has become equally clear that stored representations of our bodies in action can also play an important role, constraining motion solutions in a top-down, global-to-local manner (e.g., Bertenthal & Pinto, 1994; Shiffrar & Freyd, 1990, 1993; Shiffrar et al., 1997; Thornton et al., 1998). Recent studies have also explored the possible role of attention in our ability to explicitly interpret biological-motion displays (Cavanagh et al., 2001; Chandrasekaran et al., 2004; Thornton et al., 2002).

A second major theme has been to determine the full range of information that can be extracted from such dynamic patterns. As already mentioned, observers can easily recognize a range of different action categories (Dittrich, 1993; Johansson, 1973, 1975). Adult (e.g., Bertenthal & Pinto, 1994; Mather et al., 1992; Verfaillie, 1993) and even infant (e.g., Bertenthal, Proffitt, & Kramer, 1987; Booth, Pinto, & Bertenthal, 2002; Fox & McDaniel, 1982; see chapter 14) human observers can distinguish coherent figures from those that have been spatiotemporally manipulated in some way (see chapter 13). Given a small set of highly familiar or familiarized individuals, identity can also be extracted from motion patterns (Cutting & Kozlowski, 1977; Troje et al., in press). Additionally, there is now growing evidence that implicit perception of one's own point-light movements can facilitate performance on a number of tasks (e.g., Loula et al., 2005; see section IV in this volume). Other types of information that can be extracted from point-light displays include the gender of the moving figure (e.g., Kozlowski & Cutting, 1977, 1978; Mather & Murdoch, 1994; Troje, 2002; see Pollick et al., 2004, for a review), an indication of the emotion being portrayed (Dittrich et al., 1996; Pollick et al., 2001), and an estimate of the weight or effort involved in interacting with other objects (e.g., Runeson, & Frykholm, 1981; Shim et al., 2004).

The final theme, and the one most closely related to the topic of this book, is the question of whether the perception of human motion is in any way different from the perception of other types of complex motion. Is biological motion special? As outlined at the beginning of this chapter, there are good reasons to suspect that our perception of the human form in motion may be unique in that our experience of the world is always mediated through our own body (see sections II and IV). Thus, during the perception of moving bodies, particularly our own (Knoblich, 2002; Loula et al., 2005; Repp & Knoblich, 2004; see section IV), we may be able to recruit mechanisms or representations not available during the perception of other types of object motion.

With traditional psychophysical techniques, the special nature of biological motion has been addressed by trying to find situations in which detection or discrimination performance is markedly different from other types of natural or artificial moving stimuli (e.g., Bertenthal & Pinto, 1994; Neri et al., 1998; Shiffrar et al., 1997). Another approach has been to adapt techniques from face and object recognition to assess whether our representations of bodies appear to differ in qualitative ways from other classes of stimuli (Reed et al., 2003, 2004; see chapter 11).

In chapter 14, Jeannine Pinto reviews developmental studies in which one of the questions has been the lower limits of infant sensitivity to biological motion. An innate preference for such patterns, the existence of which has yet to be established, would clearly provide strong evidence for their special status. Finally, in chapter 16, Emily Grossman reviews the evidence from a number of perspectives, including electrophysiology, neuropsychology, and human-imaging studies, which point to the existence of an integrated network of brain areas, specialized for the perception of biological motion.

4. Current Contributions

The four chapters in this section all deal with different aspects of the visual interpretation of human motion. Here, I briefly summarize the main issues of each contribution. In chapter 13, I provide a review of Johansson's point-light technique. I have purposely taken a very stimulus-based approach—describing the various creation methods, manipulation techniques, and task contexts—but my goal is also to shed some light on the general types of research question that have been asked in the psychophysical approach to biological motion. I have also attempted to evaluate the strengths and weaknesses of point-light stimuli within the broader context of research on the human body. As will be seen, techniques that attempt to completely isolate the movement of the body from its form, while useful for some purposes, may also need to be complemented by techniques in which the form and context are present and/or directly manipulated. Similarly, the ability to capture truly "natural" motions in the laboratory will be questioned.

In chapter 14, Jeannine Pinto explores the early development of the human response to biological-motion displays. By mapping the time course of the human infant's processing of biological motion, we may gain important insights into the nature of the mechanisms that underlie this ability. In addition to introducing the main experimental techniques and research questions from this area of study, Pinto also explores possible connections between the time course of biological-motion processing and the development of action-based representations of our own bodies.

In chapter 15, Martin Giese considers the computational tasks that the human visual system must solve in order to support the perception of biological motion. The general theme of this chapter is the idea that quantitative computational models can be useful tools to integrate and even go beyond the rapidly accumulating empirical findings. After outlining a range of constraints, from behavioral, neurophysiological, and computational perspectives, Giese describes and evaluates a neurally plausible implementation of a feature-based model that accounts for many of the current psychophysical results.

In chapter 16, Emily Grossman provides an overview of existing knowledge about the brain mechanisms underlying the perception of biological motion. Evidence from brain-imaging studies, animal physiology, and patient data all shed light on the nature of the motion mechanisms used to process point-light stimuli and help to determine whether such mechanisms are unique or uniquely organized for the processing of biological motion. Considering the findings as a whole, Grossman argues that the human brain may have developed a network of interconnecting regions specifically tuned for the visual interpretation of biological motion.

5. Connections and Future Directions

In this final portion of my introduction, I want to take the opportunity to speculate on several ways in which the study of biological motion could make productive future connections with other areas of research, both within this book and more generally.

As can be seen by this introduction and by the content of chapters 13–16, research in the area of biological motion is almost completely focused on vision. However, as discussed in section I of this book, understanding and controlling our bodies in space involves the integration of sensory information from many channels. Can nonvisual experience impact our interpretation of the typical dynamic patterns used to study biological motion? Several recent studies have begun to suggest that this may be the case. Using static stimuli, Reed and Farah (1995) found that judgments about limb posture could be improved by asking observers to move their own limbs while making the judgments (see also section II). Similarly, Jacobs and Shiffrar (2005), using dynamic stimuli, asked observers to make judgments while walking on a treadmill and found interactions between executed and observed actions. Troje (2003) examined orientation effects in the perception of biological motion (see chapter 13) by also physically varying observer posture from seated to prone. He found that the advantage for an upright figure seems to rely on an ego-centric rather than an environmental reference frame.

Perhaps the most compelling example of nonvisual influences comes from a recent study by Casile and Giese (2004) in which they taught blindfolded participants to perform novel periodic movements. After this nonvisual training, observers showed specific performance advantages for point-light displays moving in ways that corresponded to the learned motor patterns. No advantage was seen for comparable visual patterns that were unrelated to the training movements. In general, these studies all suggest that nonvisual cues about body posture or action can influence our perception of motion patterns. In my own lab, we are also beginning to explore the interaction between audition and vision by using synchronized and unsynchronized soundtracks accompanying visual stimuli. It seems likely that incorporating multimodal perceptions of the body within the context of biological-motion processing will be a useful future direction.

In addition to demonstrating that multimodal information *can* influence the perception of biological motion, it is also necessary to consider *how* such in-formation might be integrated or represented, which is the theme of section II of this book. A link between such body representations or body schema and the perception of biological motion can easily be made through existing lines of research focusing on top-down influences (e.g., Thornton et al., 2002). One common feature of such research is the idea that stored patterns of informa-tion can be used to help interpret incoming sensory information. Increasing knowledge about how body representations are stored (e.g., action-related groupings of body parts; see Reed et al., 2004) could lead to specific pre-dictions about the cognitive strategies that observers adopt during demanding search or judgment tasks (Cavanagh et al., 2001; Chandrasekaran et al., 2004; also see chapter 13).

In my own work, I have also been exploring the notion that the use of top-down strategies is cognitively or attentionally demanding (e.g., Thornton et al., 1998, 2002). Central to this line of research has been the development of experimental paradigms in which the effectiveness of low-level versus high-level processing can be systematically manipulated, to the point where one or the other mode can be essentially "knocked out." Using such paradigms, it might be interesting to explore whether the influence of action planning or action observation, issues dealt with in section IV, varies as a function of processing mode. For example, such effects may only be observed when the perception of target motion is being mediated via putative top-down processing mechanisms (Cavanagh et al., 2001).

The neural mechanisms that support the perception of the human body, particularly when it is in motion, are discussed in detail in chapters 15 and 16. In both modeling and imaging studies, there are already strong links between the representation of the human form and the representation of human motion. In both domains it may be interesting to explore how form and motion interact as the nature of the task (e.g., visual search) and the complexity of the displays (e.g., multiple walkers) are varied to modulate the expected level of processing (i.e., bottom-up or top-down).

Another issue that may lead to fruitful connections is the question of biological-motion processing in special populations. As Grossman points out in chapter 16, there have already been a number of studies of patients with specific lesions to form- or motion-related areas (e.g., Schenk & Zihl, 1997a, 1997b; Vaina et al., 1990). Recently, individuals with more general deficits, for example, patients with parietal damage (Battelli et al., 2003) or children with autism (Blake et al., 2003) or Williams syndrome (Atkinson et al., 2001) have been the subject of research. It seems likely that exploring the perception of biological motion in individuals (e.g., Brugger et al., 2000; see chapter 11) or populations (e.g., Pavlova et al., 2003) with specific body or motor-related deficits will be an interesting avenue for future research.

Finally, an issue that is not really addressed in any detail elsewhere in this volume is the impact that new developments in computer animation and computer graphics may have on the study of the human body. Although many of the studies reported here make use of computer displays in one way or another, we are, as yet, far from pushing the limits of this technology. To take biological-motion research as an example, nearly all studies have presented a single motion pattern completely devoid of the influence of environmental or action-related context.

While justifications in terms of experimental control and simplification can of course be made, it is my strong belief that embedding dynamic human figures into complex but controllable virtual environments will be a positive step forward in our quest to understand the body in action. In chapter 13, I discuss one specific advantage of using computer models rather than point-light figures: the ability to independently vary the strength of form and motion cues. I believe that other factors, such as the ability to interact in real time with virtual characters or the opportunity to manipulate scene/action congruency, will be equally advantageous.

References

Atkinson, J., Anker, S., Braddick, O., Nokes, L., Mason, A., & Braddick, F. (2001). Visual and visuospatial development in young children with Williams syndrome. *Developmental and Medical Child Neurology, 43*, 330–337.

Battelli, L., Cavanagh, P., & Thornton, I. M. (2003). Perception of biological motion in parietal patients. *Neuropsychologia, 41*, 1808–1816.

Bellefeuille, A., & Faubert, J. (1998). Independence of contour and biological-motion cues for motion-defined animal shapes. *Perception, 27*, 225–235.

Bertenthal, B. I., & Pinto, J. (1994). Global processing of biological motions. *Psychological Science, 5*, 221–225.

Bertenthal, B. I., Proffitt, D. R., & Kramer, S. J. (1987). Perception of biomechanical motions by infants: Implementation of various processing constraints. *Journal of Experimental Psychology: Human Perception and Performance, 13*, 577–585.

Booth, A., Pinto, J., & Bertenthal, B. I. (2002). Perception of the symmetrical patterning of human gait by infants. *Developmental Psychology, 38*, 554–563.

Blake, R. (1993). Cats perceive biological motion. *Psychological Science, 4*, 54–47.

Blake, R., Turner, L. M., Smoski, M. J., Pozdol, S. L., & Stone, W. L. (2003). Visual recognition of biological motion is impaired in children with autism. *Psychological Science, 14*, 151–157.

Brugger, P., Kollias, S. S., Müri, R. M., Crelier, G., Hepp-Reymond, M.-C., & Regard, M. (2000). Beyond re-membering: Phantom sensations of congenitally absent limbs. *Proceedings of the National Academy of Sciences, USA, 97*, 6167–6172.

Casile, A., & Giese, M. A. (2004). Possible influences of motor learning on perception of biological motion [Abstract]. *Journal of Vision, 4*, 221a.

Cavanagh, P., Labianca, A., & Thornton, I. M. (2001). Attention-based visual routines: Sprites. *Cognition, 80*, 47–60.

Chandrasekaran, C., Thornton, I. M., & Bülthoff, H. H. (2005). Selective attention to biological motion. *Technical Report 139*. Max Planck Institute for Biological Cybernetics, Tuebingen, Germany. http://www.kyb.mpg.de/publication.html?publ=3371.

Cutting, J. E., & Kozlowski, L. T. (1977). Recognition of friends by their walk: Gait perception without familiarity cues. *Bulletin of the Psychonomic Society, 9*, 353–356.

Dittrich, W. H. (1993). Action categories and the perception of biological motion. *Perception, 22*, 15–22.

Dittrich, W. H., Troscianko, T., Lea, S. E. G., & Morgan, D. (1996). Perception of emotion from dynamic point-light displays represented in dance. *Perception, 25*, 727–738.

Fox, R., & McDaniel, C. (1982). The perception of biological motion by human infants. *Science, 218*, 486–487.

Giese, M. A., & Poggio, T. (2003). Neural mechanisms for the recognition of biological movements. *Nature Reviews Neuroscience, 4*, 179–192.

Herman, L. M., Morrelsamuels, P., & Pack, A. A. (1990). Bottle-nosed-dolphin and human recognition of veridical and degraded video displays of an artificial gestural language. *Journal of Experimental Psychology: General, 119*, 215–230.

Jacobs, A., Chouchourelou, A., & Shiffrar, M. (2005). Is it "biological" motion? Manuscript under review.

Jacobs, A., & Shiffrar, M. (2005). Walking perception by walking observers. *Journal of Experimental Psychology: Human Perception & Performance, 31*, 157–169.

Johansson, G. (1973). Visual perception of biological motion and a model for its analysis. *Perception & Psychophysics, 14,* 201–211.

Johansson, G. (1975). Visual motion perception. *Scientific American, 232,* 76–88.

Knoblich, G. (2002). Self-recognition: Body and action. *Trends in Cognitive Science, 6,* 447–449.

Kozlowski, L. T., & Cutting, J. E. (1977). Recognizing the sex of a walker from a dynamic point-light display. *Perception & Psychophysics, 21,* 575–580.

Kozlowski, L. T., & Cutting, J. E. (1978). Recognizing the sex of a walker from point-lights mounted on ankles: Some second thoughts. *Perception & Psychophysics, 23,* 459.

Loula, F., Prasad, S., Harber, K., & Shiffrar, M. (2004). Recognizing people from their movements. *Journal of Experimental Psychology: Human Perception & Performance, 31,* 210–220.

Marey, E. J. (1972). *Movement.* New York: Arno. (Original work published 1895).

Mather, G., & Murdoch, L. (1994). Gender discrimination in biological motion displays based on dynamic cues. *Proceedings of the Royal Society of London, Series B, 258,* 273–279.

Mather, G., Radford, K., & West, S. (1992). Low level visual processing of biological motion. *Proceedings of the Royal Society of London, Series B, 249,* 149–155.

Mather, G., & West, S. (1993). Recognition of animal locomotion from dynamic point-light displays. *Perception, 22,* 759–766.

Neri, P., Morrone, M. C., & Burr, D. C. (1998). Seeing biological motion. *Nature, 394,* 894–896.

Omori, E. W. S. (1996). Discrimination of Johansson's stimuli in pigeons. *International Journal of Comparative Psychology, 9,* 92.

Oram, M., & Perrett, D. (1994). Responses of anterior superior temporal polysensory (STPa) neurons to "biological motion" stimuli. *Journal of Cognitive Neuroscience, 6,* 99–116.

Pavlova, M., Staudt, M., Sokolov, A., Birbaumer, N., & Krageloh-Mann, I. (2003). Perception and production of biological movement in patients with early periventricular brain lesions. *Brain, 126,* 692–701.

Pollick, F. E., Kay, J., Heim, K., & Stringer, R. (2004). Gender recognition from point-light walkers. Manuscript in preparation.

Pollick, F. E., Paterson, H. M., Bruderlin, A., & Sanford, A. J. (2001). Perceiving affect from arm movement. *Cognition, 82,* B51–B61.

Reed, C. L., & Farah, M. J. (1995). The psychological reality of the body schema: A test with normal participants. *Journal of Experimental Psychology: Human Perception and Performance, 21,* 334–343.

Reed, C. L., McGoldrick, J. E., Shackelford, R., & Fidopiastis, C. (2004). Are human bodies represented differently from other animate and inanimate objects? *Visual Cognition, 11,* 523–550.

Reed, C. L., Stone, V., Bozova, S., & Tanaka, J. (2003). The body inversion effect. *Psychological Science, 14,* 302–308.

Regolin, L., Tommasi, L., & Vallortigara, G. (2000). Visual perception of biological motion in newly hatched chicks as revealed by an imprinting procedure. *Animal Cognition, 3,* 53–60.

Repp, B. H., & Knoblich, G. (2004). Perceiving action identity: How pianists recognize their own performances. *Psychological Science, 15,* 604–609.

Runeson, S., & Frykholm, G. (1981). Visual perception of lifted weights. *Journal of Experimental Psychology: Human Perception and Performance, 7,* 733–740.

Schenk, T., & Zihl, J. (1997a). Visual motion perception after brain damage. I: Deficits in global motion perception. *Neuropsychologia, 35*, 1289–1297.

Schenk, T., & Zihl, J. (1997b). Visual motion perception after brain damage. II: Deficits in form-from-motion perception. *Neuropsychologia, 35*, 1299–1310.

Shiffrar, M., & Freyd, J. J. (1990). Apparent motion of the human body. *Psychological Science, 1*, 257–264.

Shiffrar, M., & Freyd, J. J. (1993). Timing and apparent motion path choice with human body photographs. *Psychological Science, 4*, 379–384.

Shiffrar, M., Lichtey, L., & Heptulla Chatterjee, S. (1997). The perception of biological motion across apertures. *Perception & Psychophysics, 59*, 51–59.

Shim, J., Carlton, L. G., & Kim, J. (2004). Estimation of lifted weight and produced effort through perception of point-light display. *Perception, 33*, 277–291.

Thornton, I. M., Pinto, J., & Shiffrar, M. (1998). The visual perception of human locomotion. *Cognitive Neuropsychology, 15*, 535–552.

Thornton, I. M., Rensink, R. A., & Shiffrar, M. (2002). Active versus passive processing of biological motion. *Perception, 31*, 837–853.

Thornton, I. M., & Vuong, Q. C. (2004). Incidental processing of biological motion. *Current Biology, 14*, 1084–1089.

Troje, N. F. (2002). Decomposing biological motion: A framework for analysis and synthesis of human gait patterns. *Journal of Vision, 2*, 371–387.

Troje, N. F. (2003). Reference frames for orientation anisotropies in face recognition and biological-motion perception. *Perception, 32*, 201–210.

Troje, N. F., Westhoff, C., & Lavrov, M. (in press). Person identification from biological motion: Effects of structural and kinematic cues. *Perception & Psychophysics*.

Vaina, L. M., Lemay, M., Bienfang, D. C., Choi, A. Y., & Nakayama, K. (1990). Intact "biological motion" and "structure from motion" perception in a patient with impaired motion mechanisms: A case study. *Visual Neuroscience, 5*, 353–369.

Verfaillie, K. (1993). Orientation-dependent priming effects in the perception of biological motion. *Journal of Experimental Psychology: Human Perception & Performance, 19*, 992–1013.

Yamaguchi, M. K., & Fujita, K. (1999). Perception of biological motion by newly hatched chicks and quail. *Perception, 28*, 23.

13

Biological Motion
Point-Light Walkers and Beyond

Ian M. Thornton

1. Overview

The purpose of this chapter is to review the role that Johansson's (1973) point-light stimuli have played in the study of biological motion. I begin by describing this type of stimuli and the techniques used to create them and then discuss the various reasons why I believe they have proven to be such a popular and powerful research tool. I will then consider two possible limitations with this technique and introduce additional methods that are becoming available for the study of biological motion. In the final sections I also take one general research theme from the area of biological-motion processing—the question of determining gender from motion—and discuss some preliminary findings on how techniques other than point-light stimuli can be exploited.

2. What Are Point-Light Stimuli?

While in its most general sense, "biological motion" could refer to any characteristic movement pattern of a biological entity (see chapter 12), the vast majority of research in this area has focused on the visual perception of human patterns of movement by human observers. Furthermore, almost all of this work—certainly that presented in chapters 14–16 of the current volume—have used a particular type of display, known as point-light stimuli.

Point-light stimuli are moving objects in which the form cues (i.e., color, texture, shape) have been reduced to a limited number of uniform markers or dots. Compared to full body images, point-light techniques also reduce the overall motion energy, although it is the form reduction that is most obvious (see chapter 15). The term *point-light* derives from one of the original techniques

271

used to create such stimuli. This involved attaching physical lights or reflective markers to the target figure or object and filming or editing so that all other aspects of the display were at such low contrast as to be invisible (e.g., Johansson, 1973; Marey, 1895/1972). Section 4, below, discusses this and other methods of creation in more detail.

In point-light displays, the markers or dots are so sparsely placed that the identity of the object can rarely be spontaneously recovered unless they are seen in motion. The additional information arising from their change in position over time then allows the visual system to recover information about the identity of the object and the event that is taking place. Point-light stimuli are thus an example of a more general class of *structure-from-motion* displays (e.g., Ullman, 1979; Wallach & O'Connell, 1953). Typically, the term *point-light* is associated with displays in which the underlying objects are dynamic (e.g., humans and other animals) rather than static (e.g., cubes or spheres).

3. The Point-Light Walker

The classic example of point-light stimuli—and the theme of the remaining chapters in this section—is the Johansson point-light walker (Johansson, 1973). The nature of this stimulus is shown in Figure 13.1. In a point-light walker, the head and each of the major joints (specifically, the shoulders, elbows, wrists, hips, knees, and ankles) have been replaced by single dots which trace out the position of each body part in time as the relevant action unfolds.

Johansson (1973) found that dynamic displays showing only the movement of such dots could quickly and easily be interpreted by observers. This was true not only for walking, but also for many other kinds of human action, such as running, jumping, dancing, and riding a bike. While a similar technique had previously been used by Marey (1885/1972) to explore human movement, it was Johansson's work that initiated the modern study of biological motion (see Verfaillie, 2000, for a more detailed historical overview).

To date, there have been more than 500 published articles inspired by Johansson's (1973) original study. The exact nature of the point-light figures they have employed vary almost as much as the research questions they have been used to address (see chapter 12). Some have been presented as two-dimensional stimuli, some as three-dimensional (3D). Many have been shown with the figures appearing to move on a treadmill, others with the original global translations intact. Many have presented only a side or sagittal view of the figures; others have explored the impact of view changes; and so on. In the following sections I briefly review some of the reasons for such variety, which typically results from either the method of creation (section 4) or an experimentally motivated manipulation (section 5).

Figure 13.1. Parents with point-light child. The central figure demonstrates the placement of critical dots in a typical point-light figure. It is clear even from this still image that a dynamic human form can easily be recovered from a few points of light when motion is present or implied by the context. Original photograph courtesy of Isabel Arend, artwork by IMT.

4. How Are Point-Light Stimuli Created?

One of the main appeals of point-light stimuli is the range of options available for creating them. The investment involved, in terms of both time and money, and the quality of the final product can vary considerably from technique to technique. At one end of the spectrum, almost anyone with access to a video camera can produce stimuli in a couple of hours. At the other end of the scale, modern motion-capture systems, as used by professional filmmakers and animators, provide maximum quality, but at a cost which can run into the tens if not hundreds of thousands of dollars.

In this section, I briefly review all of the main techniques that have been used to create point-light stimuli, in roughly chronological order, including relevant citations to recent studies that make use of them. For more detailed discussion of most of these techniques see Dekeyser, Verfaillie, and Vanrie (2002).

4.1. Direct Filming

This was the technique pioneered by Marey (1895/1972) and later popularized by Johansson (1973). Active lights or passive reflective markers are placed on the body of an individual, who performs some action. The film is edited or played back so that only the points of light are visible. The advantage of this technique is that a wide range of actions can be captured very quickly. The main disadvantage is that the resulting film or video footage lacks flexibility in terms of experimental manipulation (see section 5.3). Recent studies that have used this technique include Dittrich (1993), Atkinson, Dittrich, Gemmell, and Young (2004), and Shim, Carlton, and Kim (2004). A number of researchers have experimented with ways to subsequently edit out the reflective markers so that natural full-body video footage can also be captured in the same session (e.g., Atkinson et al., 2004; Thomas & Jordan, 2001).

4.2. Synthetic Walkers

At least with periodic actions, such as walking, it is possible to approximate the movement of the limbs by modeling them as a series of interconnected points moving with pendular (arms and legs) or ellipsoidal (shoulders and hips) cycles. Cutting (1978) produced a classic algorithm for the generation of walking patterns, which has formed the basis of a great many experimental studies (e.g., Bertenthal & Pinto, 1994; Cutting, Moore, & Morrison, 1988; Mather, Radford, & West, 1992; Thornton, Pinto, & Shiffrar, 1998; Verfaillie, De Troy, & Van Rensbergen, 1994). The ease with which this algorithm can be implemented and, more important, manipulated (see section 5.3), has made it one of the most important tools in the development of research into biological motion.

While Cutting's algorithm, and its even more sophisticated modern counterparts (e.g., Hodgins, O'Brien, & Tumblin, 1998), provide very compelling impressions of human motion, they still lack some of the naturalness that other techniques, such as direct filming or motion capture, can provide. Thus, synthetic walkers, while useful for a great many purposes, are not typically used when subtle differences in motion are required, for example, to identify individual walkers (e.g., Cutting & Kozlowski, 1977, 1978) or to convey emotion (e.g., Dittrich, 1993; Dittrich et al., 1996; Pollick et al., 2001b). Having said this, such stimuli have been successfully used to study the perception of gender from motion (Kozlowski & Cutting, 1977, 1978; Mather & Murdoch, 1994; see Pollick et al., 2004, for a review).

Interestingly, while other periodic patterns, such as running or riding a bike, could have been generated using the same basic analysis and synthesis technique, to my knowledge it is only synthetic walking patterns that have been studied experimentally in this way. Possibly this is partly due to the arrival of motion capture and associated gait-generation techniques, which are generally more powerful and flexible (see below).

4.3. Manual Assignment

Another method that has proven very popular is a post-production technique where points are added to film footage of human or animal motion, usually on a frame-by-frame basis. That is, on each frame, the position of each joint is recorded or marked in some way so that it can later be animated. The main advantage is that any type of footage can be used. Thus, natural actions can be filmed without having to bring people into the lab, and similarly the movement patterns of animals (e.g., Blake, 1993; Mather & West, 1993) and even famous individuals (Kleiner et al., 2004) can be converted to point-light format. The major disadvantages are that stimulus creation can be a slow, time-consuming process in which it is very easy to introduce local motion artifacts (e.g., point jitter). Typically, some form of automatic smoothing or filtering can be applied to clean up the manually estimated trajectories (see Giese & Lappe, 2002; Pollick et al., 2001a). As yet, the resulting patterns are also strictly two-dimensional, although tools for estimating the three-dimensional properties are being developed (e.g., Kleiner et al., 2004).

4.4. Automatic Tracking

Within the computer vision community, there has been tremendous interest in developing algorithms to automatically segment and track human movement in video footage without the aid of markers (e.g., Black & Jepson, 1998; see Aggarwal & Cai, 1999; Gavrila, 1999; and chapter 15 for reviews). Such algorithms have a number of applications, such as human-computer interfaces, pedestrian detection, and individual identification. As yet, there is no standard solution that has been applied specifically for the generation of point-light stimuli. Clearly, in the future, such tools may greatly facilitate the creation of biological-motion stimuli.

4.5. Animation

While traditional, celluloid animation techniques could have been used to create point-light stimuli, to my knowledge, this has never been done for research purposes. However, the increasing popularity of computer-animated human and animal figures in the film and game industries has led to the appearance of a number of software packages that provide relatively powerful and flexible semi-automatic character animation tools. For example, 3D Studio Max and Poser both include character or walk generators where human figures can be manually posed and animated relatively efficiently (e.g., Daems & Verfaillie, 1999; Dekeyser et al., 2002; Verfaillie & Daems, 2002). Typically, patterns are initially based on motion-capture data (see next section) or built-in prototypes rather than being generated from scratch. Such animations could, in principle, be rendered as point-light figures, although in section 8, I discuss in more detail how solid-body models can be directly used to explore biological-motion processing.

4.6. Motion Capture

The future of stimulus generation for biological-motion research almost certainly lies with motion-capture systems. These techniques have their roots firmly in the work of Marey (1885/1972) and Johansson (1973) in that they involve sets of markers attached to the body. The important difference is that either through active transmission or passive tracking, the 3D position of these markers can be automatically tracked over time by dedicated hardware/software devices. Dekeyser et al. (2002) provide a detailed description of using one motion-capture system for the generation of biological-motion stimuli. Popular commercial systems include Vicon (Oxford Metrics, Oxford, England), MacReflex (Qualisys, Gothenburg, Sweden), Gypsy (Animazoo, Brighton, United Kingdom), and Optotrak (Northern Digital Inc., Ontario, Canada).

Motion-capture techniques make it possible to very accurately track the 3D behavior of markers over time, to edit this information, to manipulate it in both space and time (see below), and to visualize it in many different ways. For example, the behavior of each point can be rendered directly as a 3D point-light figure (e.g., Bülthoff et al., 1998; Troje, 2002; Vanrie et al., 2004) or can be used to animate a solid-body model (Dekeyser et al., 2002; see also section 8). These capabilities make motion-capture systems powerful tools for the study of biological motion. The two main disadvantages are the relatively high cost involved in setting up such systems and, more important, the fact that natural behaviors may be difficult to elicit (see section 6).

4.7. Generation of Novel Patterns

Two recent developments in the field of biological motion have been the establishment of databases containing movement patterns from many different actions or actors (e.g., Atkinson et al., 2004; Troje, 2002; Vanrie & Verfaillie, 2004) and the development of algorithms for morphing (Giese & Poggio, 2000; Troje, 2002) and/or exaggerating patterns of movement (Hill & Pollick, 2000; Pollick, Fidopiastis, & Braden, 2001). Together, these developments have made it possible to generate a wide variety of completely novel movement patterns. This can be achieved by linearly combining (i.e., averaging) movement patterns to produce a composite (e.g., Troje, 2002), by interpolating or extrapolating movements (Hill & Pollick, 2000; Pollick et al., 2001a), or by morphing between two movement patterns (Giese & Lappe, 2002; Giese, Thornton, & Edelman, 2003). In section 5.3.4, I discuss these techniques in more detail.

5. Why Are Point-Light Stimuli Such a Common Research Tool?

Point-light figures clearly provide a compelling demonstration of the visual system's capacity for interpreting movement and change. As noted above and in chapter 12, even in the relative absence of detailed form cues, such displays still allow the processing of sophisticated actions and events. The almost complete dominance of these sorts of stimuli in the modern study of biological motion can thus be partly explained simply by their specificity. That is, they go quite some way toward isolating the dynamic properties of the human body in action (although see Beintema & Lappe, 2002, and chapter 16 for further discussions of this issue).

Point-light figures also provide a complex, ecologically relevant stimulus for those researchers who are interested in the processing of dynamic objects in general, rather than the human body per se. There is a growing interest within fields such as object recognition (e.g., Stone, 1998; Vuong & Tarr, 2004) and face perception (e.g., Knappmeyer et al., 2003; Lander & Bruce, 2000) for exploring the spatiotemporal aspects of object representations. Point-light figures are useful in this context as they are familiar, complex objects, which are relatively easy to manipulate experimentally (see section 5.3) and can be used with a variety of tasks (see section 5.4).

Point-light figures thus combine the specificity needed for exploring detailed questions relating to biological motion with a flexibility that makes them useful in the wider field of dynamic-object perception. Nevertheless, such stimuli are not the only way to approach such issues. Later in this chapter I consider two alternative types of display that are beginning to be applied in similar domains (section 6). First, however, I want to consider some of the more specific characteristics of point-light displays that have made them such a popular research tool for exploring dynamic visual processing.

5.1. Ease of Creation/Availability

As noted above, there are a range of techniques for creating point-light stimuli, varying a great deal in the effort involved and the quality of the final product. In general though, such stimuli are relatively easy to create, making availability an important factor in the popularity of point-light stimuli. Quite recently, a number of laboratories have also begun to make databases of human action—typically via motion-capture systems—available to the research community. This trend will further increase the popularity of such stimuli. Recent articles in which databases are discussed include Atkinson et al. (2004), Troje (2003), and Vanrie and Verfaillie (2004).

5.2. Ease of Masking

Another major factor in the popularity of point-light stimuli is the ease with which they can be experimentally manipulated. In the next section, I discuss some more-general issues, but here I begin with a consideration of concurrent masking techniques. The sparse nature of the spatial layout of a point-light display makes it very easy to mask. Masking in this context simply means surrounding the target figure with a field of dots that are physically identical (i.e., in shape, size, color) to the points making up the walker (Cutting, Moore, & Morrison, 1988). In the absence of motion, this spatial camouflage renders the walker invisible. However, almost as compelling as the general ability of observers to see prototypical point-light displays is the way in which moving masked figures can typically be detected with little apparent effort (Bertenthal & Pinto, 1994; Cutting et al., 1988; Thornton et al., 1998).

The local motion of the masking elements, their global structure, and their global motion can all be manipulated to vary the difficulty of detecting the embedded target figure. The least-effective masks contain elements that simply move at random; the most effective, known as scrambled walker masks, are those in which the local motion mimics that of the individual walker points or limbs. Masking has proven to be useful for exploring a number of issues within the domain of biological motion, such as global versus local processing (Bertenthal & Pinto, 1994), ambiguity (Thornton, Vuong, & Bülthoff, 2003), motion mechanisms (Mather et al., 1992), and the role of attention (Thornton, Rensink, & Shiffrar, 2002). One general finding across all of this work is the extreme difficulty of blocking dynamic target detection even with the most complex forms of mask, suggesting that biological-motion processing is a robust skill that can recruit mechanisms at multiple levels within the visual system.

5.3. Ease of Manipulation

In addition to masking, a wide range of other types of manipulation have also been applied to point-light displays in order to assess the nature of the underlying visual-processing mechanisms. Again, it is the simplicity and sparseness of the basic point-light displays that makes them so flexible in this regard. Such manipulations are particularly useful as they make it possible to create control stimuli when testing specific hypotheses about the processing of biological-motion stimuli (see chapters 14–16 for examples).

Manipulation techniques can broadly be divided into those that primarily alter the spatial aspects of the displays, those that primarily alter temporal aspects of the display, and those that directly manipulate spatiotemporal aspects. However, it should be noted that in a stimulus such as a point-light figure, the boundaries between spatial versus temporal manipulations are not always easy to maintain. Furthermore, given that there are now several hundred papers in which such manipulations have occurred, the following review is not meant to be exhaustive, and I apologize for the necessary omissions in advance.

5.3.1. Spatially Global Manipulations

As with other forms of object, many studies in the spatial domain have explored the impact of global transformations of the whole form. For example, Mather and Murdoch (1994) adapted Cutting's (1978) synthesis algorithm to explore the processing of gender-from-motion. They found that when figures were rotated in depth away from a purely sagittal view, this increased the influence of motion-based cues, such as shoulder and hip sway. Bradshaw et al. (1999) explicitly examined how similar rotations of the whole figure in depth affected recognition performance, finding that the 3/4 view led to the most accurate responses (see also Bülthoff et al., 1998). Verfaillie (1993, 2000) used a priming technique in which the depth rotation of the prime and target figures varied, finding facilitation for both repeated walker orientation and repeated action, depending on the task.

Recently, Thornton et al. (2003) used a chimeric point-light walker—a composite figure with equal local motion in both directions—to demonstrate a preference to perceive rightward versus leftward motion. Vanrie et al. (2004) exploited the depth ambiguity of normal point-light figures to demonstrate that observers have a strong bias to perceive movement toward them rather than away from them. Pavlova et al. (2004) also recently found that the apparent facing direction of animal figures strongly influenced the interpretation of the display.

Rotations in the picture plane have also been used, particularly the technique, borrowed from face perception, of turning the entire figure upside-down (Pavlova & Sokolov, 2000, 2003; Sumi, 1984; Yin, 1969). The logic of such inversion is that the first- and second-order relations between the parts of the figure, the local and global motion, all remain intact but are presented at a novel orientation. Such inverted displays are useful when complex but nonfamiliar control stimuli are required, such as when working with infants (Bertenthal et al., 1985; see chapter 14) or brain-imaging techniques (Grossman & Blake, 2001; chapter 16).

Sumi (1984) reported that when shown an upside-down walker, the majority of his naive observers continued to report an upright biological figure that moved in an unusual way, suggesting an overriding influence of the bottom-up stimulus properties. Generally, as with faces, picture plane inversion seriously reduces the amount of information that can be extracted from point-light displays, for example, the assignment of gender (Barclay et al., 1978), discernment of action category (Dittrich, 1993), and coherence judgments (Tadin et al., 2002; see Pavlova & Sokolov, 2003, for a more detailed review). It is still a matter of some debate as to whether experience and/or prior knowledge of the nature of such manipulations can influence the processing of inverted displays, with some arguing that it can (e.g., Pinto & Shiffrar, 2004) and others that these factors have little effect (Pavlova & Sokolov, 2003).

Recently, Troje (2003) included a condition in which the orientation of the observer could also be either upright or rotated by 90° to explore whether shifts of the environmental or egocentric reference frame are responsible for processing deficits. He found that orientation relative to the observer seems to be what matters, with environmentally upright figures having no advantage if the observer's body is prone. Similarly, Shipley (2003) examined perception of a much less familiar gait pattern—walking on the hands—in which the orientation of the figure is unfamiliar but the natural dynamics, relative to gravity, are intact. When such displays are inverted, so that the orientation of the walker is upright, observers are less sensitive to the presence of the target in noise, suggesting that a mismatch between event dynamics rather than object familiarity is the basis of the inversion effect for point-light walkers.

Another global manipulation is to produce a "scrambled" walker in which the initial spatial position of each point is randomized (e.g., Grossman et al., 2000). As mentioned above, this technique is also used to create complex masking stimuli (Bertenthal & Pinto, 1994; Cutting et al., 1988; see section 5.2). For a scrambled target figure, the head might be below the elbow, the wrist above the ankle, and the knee above the hip. Disrupting the global form/motion in this way but leaving the local motions intact again provides a useful control. A less-extreme manipulation is to produce "incoherent" figures in which the top parts of the walker (head, shoulders, and arms) face in one direction and the bottom parts (hips, legs) in the other (e.g., Mather, Radford, & West, 1992; Verfaillie, 1993). This form of control stimuli is useful when it is necessary to ensure that observers pay attention to the global, rather than the local, structure for distinguishing normal from manipulated displays.

A recent form of global manipulation is to spatially exaggerate the extent of movements relative to some reference pattern. Pollick, Fidopiastis, and Braden (2001) used time-normalized tennis serves to explore the categorization of dynamic patterns. They computed a grand average and three style averages based on the 3D spatial coordinates of points attached to the body of a tennis coach, who produced several repetitions of different serve styles, namely, flat, top spin, and slice. Vector differences between the grand average and the style averages could then be used to spatially interpolate or extrapolate the position of points in each frame of the animated serve. As with facial caricaturing (Calder et al., 1996; Rhodes et al., 1987), the general finding was that as distance from the grand average increased, serves became more distinctive and categorization performance became more accurate.

Finally, it should be noted that across studies, the size and/or position of the walking figure within the visual field has often varied quite dramatically. This variation, however, more typically reflects the constraints of stimulus creation or presentation mode rather than being a direct experimental manipulation (for exceptions, see Jokisch & Troje, 2003; Thornton & Vuong, 2004; Verfaillie et al., 1994).

5.3.2. Spatially Local Manipulations

As might be expected from the nature of the point-light stimuli, a common manipulation technique has been to alter some aspect of the constituent dots themselves. One simple manipulation is simply to remove specific points as a means of exploring their relative contribution to the perception of biological motion. For example, this technique was used by Mather, Radford, and West (1992), who found that removal of the wrist and ankle dots was most detrimental to performance (see also Beintema & Lappe, 2002; and chapter 15). With some creation techniques (e.g., motion capture, synthetic walkers), the presence or absence of occlusion cues—whether the points on the limbs farthest from the camera appear and disappear when the closer limbs move in front—can also easily be manipulated. Such cues can help to convey a sense of the 3D form, but can also locally attract attention, which may interfere with some tasks (e.g., detection of a global form in masked displays).

Another manipulation has been to alter the spatial position of the dots on the underlying body model. Bertenthal and Pinto (1994) shifted the position of the dots a constant distance up or down on the respective limbs, finding little influence on performance. A related manipulation is to dynamically "jitter" the position of the dots on the limbs on a frame-by-frame basis. This manipulation is a useful technique for discouraging the use of local relations between dots, rather than the global configuration, as a way of solving certain tasks, for example, the recognition of novel actions (e.g., Giese et al., 2002).

A less-common manipulation has been to present point-light walkers as binocular, fully 3D stimuli, using either mirror stereoscopes (Ahlström et al., 1997) or Liquid Crystal Display (LCD) glasses (Bülthoff et al., 1998). By altering the depth relations between individual dots, this technique makes it possible to explore the relationship between global (whole walker) and local (individual dot) percepts of the walker. Bülthoff et al. (1998) found that depth-scrambled walkers continued to be perceived as normal, coherent figures, suggesting a strong influence of top-down processing. Ahlström et al. (1997) found that conflicts between the local (disparity) and global (motion) position of the limbs still gave rise to an easily recognizable global pattern. However, they also noted that local paths of motion did seem unnatural, for example, the wrist in the foreground seemed to swing through the body (cf. Shiffrar & Freyd, 1990, 1993).

Finally, a number of studies have directly manipulated the nature of the individual walker dots, typically as a means of exploring underlying motion mechanisms. One example is to randomly switch the contrast polarity of each dot on each frame, that is, from black to white on a gray background, as this should severely disrupt low-level, luminance-based motion detection. Consistent with this notion, Mather et al. (1992) found chance-level performance for contrast-modulated dots when they were briefly presented in randomly modulating noise. When such displays were presented unmasked and for longer durations, little deficit was observed (Ahlström et al., 1997), suggesting that higher-level motion processing can compensate for degraded local motion (Thornton et al., 1998). Similarly, other forms of local manipulation, such as using texture-defined dots (Ahlström et al., 1997; Bellefeuille & Faubert, 1998) or spatial frequency filtering (Ahlström et al., 1997) also have little impact on performance under conditions where active, top-down processing of the stimulus is also possible (Thornton et al., 2002).

5.3.3. Temporal Manipulations

In the temporal domain, there have also been many forms of manipulation. Perhaps the simplest has been to vary the overall duration for which displays are visible. Johansson (1976) reported that even with very brief presentations, of around 200 ms, naive observers could still report the nature of a depicted action. A number of studies have experimentally varied display duration to assess its impact on task performance (e.g., Cutting et al., 1988; Thornton et al., 1998). In general, it seems that very short durations are adopted in experiments when the focus is on understanding putative low-level motion mechanisms (e.g., Mather et al., 1992) and longer durations when the focus is on higher-level, top-down effects (Thornton et al., 1998). Most typically, overall duration is computed in terms of fractions or multiples of step-cycles, which in turn depends on walking speed.

Natural walking speed varies considerably among individuals, with Inman, Ralston, and Todd (1981) reporting a range between 30 and 70 strides per minute for human walking under normal conditions. One stride would be the sequence of movements that occurs between two consecutive repetitions of a body configuration. When point-light walkers are created from movie clips or motion capture, this natural variation will need to be taken into account when creating or comparing experimental stimuli. With synthetic stimuli, frame duration must be specifically chosen to fall within the natural range. Recently, researchers have begun to experimentally manipulate walking speed as a means to vary familiarity with a given gait pattern (Jacobs, Pinto, & Shiffrar, 2004). As walking speeds toward either end of the natural range are likely to be less common, this may affect performance on tasks that rely on familiarity. Consistent with this notion, Jacobs et al. (2004) found no influence of gait speed in an explicit speed-discrimination task, but did find that it influenced walker identity judgments.

Another form of temporal manipulation is to vary the smoothness of motion by inserting blank frames for various interstimulus intervals (ISIs) to create apparent motion displays. As ISI increases, the low-level motion energy in the display drops proportionally. Mather et al. (1992) first used this technique to demonstrate that with very short overall display durations (e.g., half of a stride) performance very quickly drops to chance for ISIs greater than 40 ms. This demonstrates a strong reliance on low-level motion cues when stimuli are briefly presented. Using the same technique, Thornton et al. (1998) showed that ISIs of up to 120 ms could still be tolerated when overall display duration was increased (e.g., two full steps). They suggested that this difference reflects the additional recruitment of top-down processing mechanisms (see also Thornton et al., 2002).

One form of local manipulation in the temporal domain has been to randomly vary the duration for which individual dots are visible (e.g., Neri, Morrone, & Burr, 1998). For example, in the first two frames of an animation, the head, right elbow, left wrist, and both knee joints may be visible, then the shoulder, right ankle, hip, and left elbow, and so on. Neri et al. (1998) varied several parameters, such as the number of dots visible in each frame, display duration, and number of masking elements, to compare the integration of these "limited-lifetime" biological-motion stimuli with that of simple translation. Finding more robustness to noise and much higher temporal-integration windows for biological motion, they concluded that biological motion is probably processed by general, flexible mechanisms, rather than specialized, simple detectors.

The final form of temporal manipulation has been to directly modify the temporal profile of dot trajectories. Hill and Pollick (2000) used the example of actors raising, drinking from, and replacing a glass to explore the impact of increasing or decreasing the duration of movement segments relative to an average profile. Similar to the spatial studies mentioned in section 5.3.2, Hill and Pollick (2000) used both time-varying and time-normalized novel patterns to show that the ability to recognize individuals from learned drinking patterns increased as a function of the level of exaggeration. As the spatial path was held constant and the overall duration did not influence the outcome, these results suggest that observers can use relative temporal profiles as a cue to identity.

5.3.4. Spatiotemporal Manipulations

The most common form of spatiotemporal manipulation has been to shift the phase of each dot of the figure relative to a standard gait cycle (Bertenthal & Pinto, 1993; Cavanagh et al., 2001; Pollick et al., 2001a). Small phase shifts maintain the impression of a gait, but with very relaxed, fluid movement (Cavanagh et al., 2001); larger shifts can abolish the global percept of a coherent figure altogether (e.g., Bertenthal, Proffitt, & Kramer, 1987). These latter stimuli are useful controls as they maintain the local motion and the first-order spatial arrangement (i.e., head above shoulder, above hip, etc.) of the figure while disrupting the global motion.

An extreme form of spatiotemporal manipulation was recently introduced by Beintema and Lappe (2002). They combined two techniques already discussed—local spatial offsets of the dots along the limb (Bertenthal & Pinto, 1994) with limited temporal lifetime (Neri et al., 1998)—to assign points to different positions on the skeleton in every frame. Even with such highly perturbed stimuli, observers were still able to perform a number of detection and discrimination tasks, leading Beintema and Lappe (2002) to conclude that high-level form cues must play a crucial role in recovering the global structure of such displays. More recently, however, the continued role of local motion in these displays has also been questioned (Casile & Giese, 2003; see also chapter 15).

The most sophisticated spatiotemporal manipulation is the use of motion morphing. Spatial morphing (e.g., creating an animal that is half dog and half cat) has become a standard technique for exploring static face and object recognition (e.g., Benson & Perrett, 1991; Blanz & Vetter, 1999). It is only recently that advanced computer-graphics techniques for manipulating dynamic patterns (e.g., Amaya et al., 1996; Unuma et al., 1995; Witkin & Popovic, 1995) have also been applied to behavioral experiments (e.g., Giese & Poggio, 2000; Giese & Lappe, 2002; Pollick et al., 2001; Troje, 2002). As mentioned in section 4.7, such techniques are particularly powerful ways to generate novel stimuli. Examples would include a spatiotemporal pattern midway between walking and running (Giese & Lappe, 2002; Giese, Thornton, & Edelman, 2003) or an extreme male or female gait pattern created by extrapolating along the relevant dimension relative to an average or prototypical pattern (e.g., Troje, 2002).

As with purely spatial morphs, a crucial step in generating spatiotemporal morphs is aligning the target patterns so as to put them into correspondence with each other. This can be achieved, for example, by directly aligning the target feature trajectories, for instance, by minimizing the spatial and temporal offsets between two patterns (e.g., Giese & Poggio, 2000) or by first applying data-reduction techniques, such as principle components analysis, to produce a multidimensional vector space in which the individual dimensions can be directly aligned (Troje, 2002). Whichever technique is used, once the target patterns have been space-time aligned, they can then be directly manipulated to produce blends, averages, caricatures, anticaricatures, and so on. The ability to alter the spatiotemporal characteristics of stimuli in this way provides new opportunities to probe perceptual sensitivity to certain dimensions (e.g., Hill & Pollick, 2000) and to explore the nature of internal representational spaces (Giese & Lappe, 2002; Giese, Thornton, & Edelman, 2003).

5.4. Task Flexibility

Another factor that has helped to make point-light stimuli so popular is the ease with which they can be integrated into different experimental contexts. Traditionally, biological-motion studies have involved direct, explicit judgment on a display that potentially contained a single point-light figure. For example, observers might be asked to interpret what they saw (e.g., Johansson, 1973; Sumi, 1984), to judge the coherence of the display (Bertenthal & Pinto, 1994; Mather, Radford, & West, 1992), to judge the direction in which the figure faces (e.g., Cutting et al., 1988; Thornton et al., 2003), or to assess whether a figure is present or absent in a mask (e.g., Beintema & Lappe, 2002; Cutting et al., 1988).

In chapter 14, Jeannine Pinto describes a number of developmental studies in which point-light displays have been adapted for use with infants (e.g., the infant-control habituation paradigm with a partial-lag design; Bertenthal, Haith, & Campos, 1983). In chapter 16, Emily Grossman describes how such stimuli have been used with imaging techniques to explore the neural substrates of biological-motion processing. More generally, a number of researchers have also begun to use a range of other, less-direct tasks and techniques with point-light stimuli to explore biological motion.

For example, Verfaillie (1993, 2000) used priming to explore the orientation specificity of both object and action recognition. Observers were shown sequences of trials in which either a coherent walker or a figure with the top and bottom halves facing in opposite directions could be presented. The direction of facing (left-right) and of articulation (forward-backward) varied across trials. Observers either made speeded human-nonhuman decisions (object recognition; Verfaillie, 1993) or speeded forward-backward decisions (action recognition; Verfaillie, 2000). In both studies, repeated left-right direction of facing led to significantly faster responses compared to a neutral baseline, suggesting that orientation-dependent representations may play an important role in biological-motion processing.

Cavanagh, Labianca, and Thornton (2001) used visual search (see Wolfe, 1998, for a review) to explore the attentional demands of a range of dynamic stimuli, including point-light walkers. Interestingly, they found that the ability to explicitly detect dynamic targets that differed quite considerably from distractors (e.g., left-facing walker among right-facing walkers, possible versus impossible gaits) always required attention, with search slopes in excess of 100 ms/item. Thornton, Rensink, and Shiffrar (2002) used a dual-task paradigm in which observers were simultaneously presented with a visual change-detection task (Rensink, O'Regan, & Clarke, 1997) and a masked point-light direction-discrimination task. Under dual-task conditions, the ability to process the walking figure depended on the availability of low-level cues to motion, with long-range apparent motion and scrambled walker masks severely disrupting performance. Together the results of visual search and dual-task studies suggest that explicit awareness of biological motion may be less spontaneous and automatic than previously assumed.

Two recent studies have also explored the processing of biological motion under conditions where the critical point-light figures are not the main focus of response, that is, by using indirect or incidental tasks. Bosbach, Prinz, and Kerzel (2004) used a centrally presented, nontranslating point-light walker to examine stimulus-response compatibility (Fitts & Deininger, 1954; Simon, 1969) with dynamic stimuli. In their task, the walker dots could change color from black to blue or red, and observers were instructed to respond as quickly as possible to this color change, with blue responses mapped to the right hand and red to the left (or vice versa). Even though the left-right orientation of the walker was irrelevant to the task, it had a clear effect on performance. For example, a blue response mapped to the right hand gave rise to faster responses when the figure also faced and moved to the right, versus when the figure faced and moved to the left. This dynamic "Simon effect" was not observed when the figure was presented upside-down or as a static image, indicating that the global direction of the centrally presented walker was being processed to a level where it could influence responses.

Similarly, Thornton and Vuong (2004) adapted the flanker-interference paradigm (Eriksen & Eriksen, 1974) to explore the incidental processing of peripherally presented walkers. Here, observers made speeded left-right direction decisions to a centrally presented, nontranslating walker that could be surrounded by up to four flanking walkers. These flankers, which the observers were told to ignore, were equally likely to face and move in the same direction as the target as in the direction opposite to the target. Despite being uninformative with respect to the main task and being placed up to 5° away, the flanking figures had a clear impact on performance, with responses being consistently slower when the target and flanker conflicted, compared to when they were consistent. This was not the case for statically presented or globally incoherent walkers.

6. Beyond Point-Light Walkers

Having reviewed the creation and manipulation of point-light displays and their use in various task contexts, in the remainder of this chapter I want to consider two ways in which such stimuli may be limited. The goal here is not to be overly critical—clearly my view is that point-light figures are, and will remain, a powerful research tool—but rather to acknowledge that in order to answer some questions about the processing of biological motion, we may also need to consider additional approaches.

The first issue concerns the capture of truly "natural" patterns of motion. Here, I am not referring to the quality of the motion data itself—do the stimuli accurately reflect the movement that was performed?—but to the nature of the actions themselves. That is, if a person is being filmed in a laboratory with a collection of markers attached to her body and is told to "walk naturally" or "move naturally," we have to be concerned about her ability to do so. Of course, such an observation issue is not unique to the study of biological motion and is a general problem in the social sciences. Interestingly, it is likely that of the techniques reviewed in section 4, those that provide the highest quality motion data are most prone to this problem. In section 7, I discuss one approach to overcoming this concern.

The second issue concerns the very nature of point-light stimuli. There are several reasons why it might be of interest to attempt to isolate motion cues from form cues. One is simply that the contribution of each can be better assessed if they are studied in isolation. Another might be the existence of physiological data suggesting separate visual pathways for processing these two types of information (e.g., Felleman & van Essen, 1991; Goodale & Milner, 1992; Ungerleider & Mishkin, 1982; see also chapters 15 and 16). However, in the real world, form and motion clearly interact. If we are interested in exploring this interaction, we must look beyond point-light walkers. In section 8, I discuss how animated solid-body models may be the ideal type of stimulus for this purpose.

7. Using Video Footage

As mentioned in section 4, one common technique for creating point-light stimuli is to manually mark the position of each joint on consecutive frames of movie or video footage. This technique has the advantage that a wide range of natural movement patterns can be captured outside of the laboratory, for example, from animals (e.g., Mather & West, 1993) or famous individuals (Kleiner et al., 2004). However, the advantage of capturing movements that are not posed or constrained is offset by the time cost of extracting the point-light figures, the likelihood of errors during manual coding, and the fact that the resulting patterns are not easily manipulated.

However, greater availability of high-quality digital video cameras and the ease with which movie sequences can be imported and displayed on personal computers continues to make the use of video-based stimuli very appealing. As the technology for automatic tracking of movement patterns within video sequences (see section 4.4) and video composite techniques (e.g., Ezzat, Geiger, & Poggio, 2002) become more efficient and robust, it seems likely that filming natural scenes will become a more standard initial step in acquiring biological-motion stimuli.

In the current section, I want to describe some work from my lab in which we have attempted to use digital video sequences to explore biological motion without manually tagging individual frames to create point-light stimuli. Such an idea is not new. For example, Burton et al. (1999) used low-quality video recordings to explore the contribution of face recognition and gait in explicit identity tasks. In this study, walking patterns were taken from the low-quality grayscale video of a commercial closed-circuit surveillance system. The main finding was that gait patterns alone were very weak cues to identity compared to isolated views of the face or the face and body together.

In general, the challenge of trying to more directly use video sequences is to reduce the influence of the static form cues that are likely to dominate responses in most tasks. In my lab we have experimented with two techniques for reducing form cues: blending and degradation. In the first technique, two video sequences are superimposed on top of each other, resulting in a composite movie of, for example, human motion and machine motion. The strength of the two video streams can be parametrically varied to find conditions in which the presence of the target content (e.g., human walker) cannot be detected from still images alone (Vuong, Hof, Bülthoff, & Thornton, 2005).

Here, however, I want to report the findings of a preliminary study in which we used a much simpler technique to explore biological motion. This technique involved the global degradation of form cues by adding visual noise. Recently, techniques such as photographic negation (Knight & Johnston, 1997; Lander et al., 1999), thresholding (Lander & Bruce, 2000; Lander et al., 1999), pixelating, and blurring video sequences (Lander, Bruce, & Hill, 2001) have become standard tools for isolating facial motion.

In the current study, a combination of edge enhancement and blurring was used to transform standard video footage, such as that shown in Figure 13.2, into the degraded form shown in Figure 13.3. This manipulation was carried out manually using Adobe Photoshop. Each frame of the video sequence was first reduced to a grayscale image and was then embossed with a depth of 9 pixels and strength of 244% and then blurred using a Gaussian filter with a pixel radius of 2.5 pixels. The embossing and blurring steps were applied twice recursively to the same image. Such manipulations could also be efficiently applied automatically using image-processing algorithms.

While it is still possible to detect the presence of a form at the center of these images, it is only when they are moving that more detailed information becomes available and it is obvious that a human walker is present. Our goal was to use this method of degradation to explore sensitivity to gender from motion with video sequences of people walking in a natural environment. As mentioned in chapter 12, gender from motion is one of the textbook examples of the type of information that observers can extract from point-light stimuli. First reported by Kozlowski and Cutting (1977, 1978), in a recent review paper, Frank Pollick and colleagues analyzed more than 20 other papers that report above-chance performance at this task (Pollick et al., 2004). Importantly, all of the papers reviewed used either synthetic walkers (e.g., Mather & Murdoch, 1994), film (e.g., Runeson & Frykholm, 1983), or motion-capture data (e.g., Troje, 2002) taken in the laboratory. Our question was whether this

Figure 13.2. A still shot of a male walker taken from the video sequence used in the video-based gender-from-motion study. This shot was specifically selected as it obscures the identity of the individual.

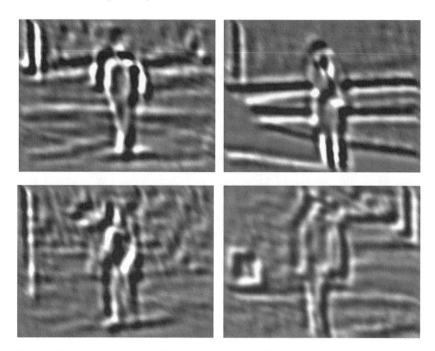

Figure 13.3. Four degraded still shots of different individuals walking in the park. The *upper right* and *lower left* images are female, the others male. While some sense of body shape can still be obtained from these images, it was only when in motion that gender categorization was above chance. *See color insert.*

ability to detect gender from motion would also generalize to everyday patterns of walking.

For this study, our basic video sequences consisted of 40 walking clips that were filmed using a distant camera in a city park. A zoom lens was used to capture several steps from 20 male and 20 female walkers as they made their way along a narrow pathway from a distance of around 60 meters. As the path was curved, the perspective on each walker included both frontal views and deviations of up to 30° to the left and right. Each clip lasted 3 seconds and contained multiple step cycles. While we had no control over walking speed, clothing, or extraneous activities (e.g., talking on a mobile phone, swinging a bag), we can be fairly certain that we were filming natural gait patterns as the majority of the walkers were never aware they were being filmed.

The video sequences were degraded as described above and then shown at the center of a standard computer monitor to 10 male and 10 female observers. The image area subtended 10 × 8 degrees of visual angle (DVA), with the main figure subtending approximately 3 × 7 DVA. Half of the male videos and half of the female videos were shown in motion for the full 3 seconds, while for the remaining clips, a random single frame was displayed as a static image for 3 seconds. The order of presentation and the assignment of clips to the movement or still condition were randomized separately for each observer. After each 3-second presentation, the observers were simply asked to assess the gender of the central figure.

The results from this experiment are shown in Figure 13.4. The upper panel shows accuracy in terms of d-prime, a measure which takes into account both

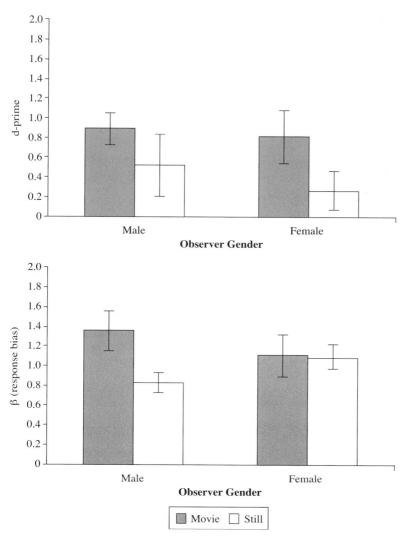

Figure 13.4. The *upper panel* shows d-prime values (sensitivity) for categorizing the gender of walkers shown as degraded movie or still images. A d-prime of zero would reflect chance performance. The *lower panel* shows estimates of observer bias in this same task. In this context, a beta value of 1 is unbiased, 2 reflects a male response bias, 0 a female bias.

the correct responses and false alarms (Green & Swets, 1966). In this context, a d-prime of zero would indicate no ability to distinguish between male and female. A 2 (observer gender) × 2 (stimulus type) repeated-measures ANOVA revealed only a main effect of stimulus type, with video sequences ($M = 0.87$, $SE = 0.14$) giving rise to more accurate responses than did static images ($M = 0.4$, $SE = 0.17$), $F(1, 18) = 4.5$, $MSE = 0.47$, $p < 0.05$. Furthermore, post-hoc analysis indicated that for both male and female observers, video sequences gave rise to responses that were reliably greater than zero, ($ts > 3$, $ps < 0.01$), while static images did not ($ts < 2$, $ps > 0.05$).

The lower panel shows the bias (beta) associated with responses, that is, the tendency to favor male or female responses. In this figure an unbiased observer would have a beta of 1.0, with increasing values indicating a male-response bias, and decreasing values indicating a female-response bias. While female observers appear to be completely unbiased, male observers appear to have a tendency to respond "male" to video sequences and "female" to static images. It is unclear why there should be such a bias only for male observers. We should note, however, that both the observer gender × stimulus type interaction and subsequent post-hoc analysis indicated that these trends were only marginally significant ($ps < 0.08$).

The results from this preliminary study suggest that even when using relatively complex and noisy real-world patterns, observers can use the additional information presented in the moving patterns to establish the gender of the target figure. While the d-prime measures indicate that performance was not very far above chance, this level of performance is consistent with other studies in the literature that have used point-light stimuli (see Pollick et al., 2004, for a summary). This suggests that degraded video stimuli might provide a useful alternative to point-light stimuli when filming under natural conditions is a priority.

8. Using Animated Solid-Body Models

As mentioned in section 6, by their very nature, point-light figures are not suitable for exploring the relationship between the details of human form and human motion. Clearly, some cues to form do remain even in such reduced stimuli, however, it seems unlikely that such cues would be strong enough to support systematic experimental manipulation. A possible alternative to removing form cues is simply to include them but to carefully control the extent to which they provide relevant information, given a specific task. This can easily be achieved using animated solid-body models, or avatars, such as those shown in Figure 13.5.

In the field of face perception, such techniques for combining form and motion have already been used to great effect. For example, going beyond

Figure 13.5. Caricatured male and female walk patterns were used to animate two solid-body models, one male and one female. Here, all four possible target items from the visual search study, run in separate blocks, are depicted as still images (all trials were animated). The two left figures have consistent form and motion (i.e., male form, male motion; female form, female motion). The two right figures have inconsistent form and motion (i.e., male form, female motion; female form, male motion). Distractor items would always have the same form, but the opposite motion.

early attempts that used point-light faces (Bassili, 1978, 1979; Bruce & Valentine, 1988), Hill and Johnston (2001) used motion-capture data from the facial movements of various individuals and applied this to a single average head model. They were interested in a range of measures, such as our ability to assess gender and identity from rigid and nonrigid movements. Importantly, for every stimulus presentation, form information was present but did not vary and was thus uninformative. A similar approach was taken by Pollick, Fidopiastis, and Braden (2001), who examined the categorization of tennis serves by displaying normal and spatially exaggerated movement patterns on the same generic solid-body model of a tennis player (see section 5.3.1).

Knappmeyer et al. (2003) took this approach a step further by explicitly examining how form and motion cues might interact. Again, within the domain of face perception, they familiarized observers with two different head models animated with the characteristic facial movements from two different actors. During testing, the assignment of a motion pattern to a head model could be swapped. The resulting drop in performance for this manipulation across a number of tasks suggests that both the form and the motion were being incorporated into the representation of individual identity.

A number of researchers have already begun to use solid-body models to explore various actions and events (e.g., Daems & Verfaillie, 1999; Pollick et al., 2001a; Reed et al., 2003). However, it is really this ability—to perform manipulations such as swapping form and motion cues, or rendering one or another cue uninformative—that promises to make animated body models such a useful tool for studying biological motion. More sophisticated manipulations, such as morphing between different body shapes or motions (see section 4.7) or changing clothing or context can also easily be achieved. Here, I want to report some preliminary data on a project in which we explored the interaction between form and motion processing when observers were trying to detect the presence of caricatured male and female walking patterns. To do this, we used a visual-search paradigm (Cavanagh et al., 2001; see Wolfe, 1998, for a review) to assess how efficiently a walking style could be detected as a function of form/motion compatibility. That is, would the efficiency of detecting a particular movement pattern be affected by whether the form was consistent (e.g., female walk and female model) or inconsistent (e.g., female walk and male model)?

The stimuli for this task are shown in Figure 13.5. The form information came from body models supplied with the animation package Poser 4.0. For this preliminary study, we also used the exaggerated male and female gait patterns supplied with Poser. As our goal was to assess the impact of form on motion decisions, we were not overly concerned with using completely natural walking patterns, so we chose caricatured motion to reduce the overall difficulty of the task. That is, we purposely chose two motion patterns that were very easy to discriminate from each other and that unambiguously signaled a specific gender. Clearly, in future studies it would be better to use motion-capture data derived from natural walking patterns to animate the solid-body models (e.g., Troje, 2002).

In separate blocks of trials, observers (8 male, 8 female) were asked to search for a given motion pattern (e.g., male walk pattern) in the presence of a variable number of distractor motions (e.g., female walk pattern). Note that in any block of trials all items always had the same form. Thus, in some blocks, the target would be consistent (male walk, male form), and in others it would be inconsistent (e.g., female walk, male form). For example, in the top right of Figure 13.5, the target would be a male figure with a male gait, and the distractor items would be male figures with female gaits. The items were presented in random position around a central virtual clock face (diameter, 5.7 DVA), each figure subtending approximately 1.9×6.7 DVA. There were between one and four items per trial, with the target present on 50% of trials. Displays remained visible, walking in place until a response was made. A block of trials consisted of 80 trials, in a 2 (present/absent) $\times$ 4 (set size) $\times$ 10 (repetition) design. Block order was counterbalanced across observers.

Accuracy on this task was very high, remaining above 90% in all conditions, thus only response-time data will be discussed. Figure 13.6 presents the target-present and target-absent search data as a function of target type. The first thing to notice is how extremely inefficient this search process is, with target-present search slopes in excess of 300 ms/item in all cases (see Figure 13.7). This inefficiency replicates previous findings using visual search with point-light stimuli (Battelli et al., 2003; Cavanagh, et al., 2001). The difficulty in detecting the walking pattern would appear to reflect the need to sample such dynamic stimuli over time, rather than being an indication that the male and female gaits were particularly difficult to discriminate.

Of more interest in the current context is the question of whether the form had any impact on the detection of the target motion pattern. As can be seen in Figure 13.7, this is clearly the case. While the female gait pattern was generally detected more efficiently than the male gait, possibly reflecting low-level differences in motion energy, this difference was dramatically enhanced for the male figures. These slope data were analyzed using a 2 (observer gender) $\times$ 2 (figure gender) $\times$ 2 (figure motion) mixed-factor repeated measures ANOVA. The only significant factor was the figure gender $\times$ figure motion interaction, $F(1, 14) = 6.8$, $MSE = 30167$, $p < 0.05$. While this interaction does not reflect a general advantage for targets with inconsistent form/motion mapping—the pattern was much stronger for the male figures—it does clearly indicate an influence of the form on the detection of motion.

One final interesting pattern in these data is shown in the lower panel of Figure 13.7. Male observers take longer while searching through arrays of female figures, regardless of the motion, while female observers show the opposite pattern. This opposite-gender effect gave rise to a significant observer gender $\times$ figure gender interaction when the search-intercept data were analyzed using the same model as the search slopes above, $F(1, 14) = 6.1$, $MSE = 79044$, $p < 0.05$. Further research would be needed to establish whether this pattern generalizes to other forms of gender-specific displays and/or whether it reflects a benefit for same-gender forms or a deficit, possibly related to increased interest, for opposite-gender forms.

The purpose of this study was to demonstrate the way in which computer-animated solid-body models could be used to explore the interaction between form and motion processing in the context of biological motion. While the current results are far from definitive, they do suggest that such cues are not

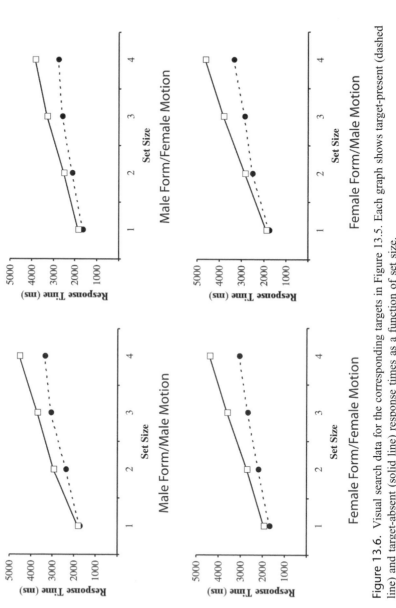

Figure 13.6. Visual search data for the corresponding targets in Figure 13.5. Each graph shows target-present (dashed line) and target-absent (solid line) response times as a function of set size.

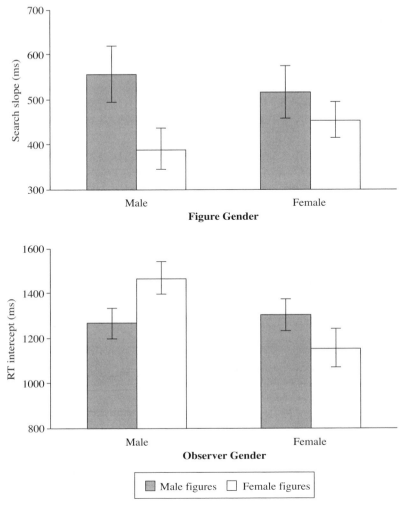

Figure 13.7. Summary of visual search data. (*top panel*) Average search slopes for target-present data displayed as a function of target form and target motion. (*bottom panel*) Average search intercepts for target-present data as a function of figure and observer gender.

processed independently and that solid-body models may prove a useful tool in this area of research.

9. Conclusions

The visual system is highly tuned for the perception of human bodies in motion. Johansson's (1973) point-light technique remains the most common method used for studying such biological motion. In this chapter I have explored the possible reasons for this dominance, suggesting that the specificity, ease of creation, and flexibility of such stimuli are the most likely factors. Another goal of this chapter has been to acknowledge that, for some questions, researchers may need to go beyond this technique, and I have suggested that degraded video and computer-animated models may also prove useful.

Acknowledgments Many thanks to Nils Aguilar for filming and editing the stimuli used in the gender-from-motion study. Thanks also to Quoc Vuong for useful discussions and data analysis. Martin Giese and Jan Vanrie were also kind enough to provide helpful comments on an earlier version of this chapter.

References

Aggarwal, J. K., & Cai, Q. (1999). Human motion analysis: A review. *Computer Vision and Image Understanding, 73*, 428–440.

Ahlström, V., Blake, R., & Ahlström, U. (1997). Perception of biological motion. *Perception, 26*, 1539–1548.

Amaya, K., Bruderlin, A., & Calvert, T. (1996). Emotion from motion. In W. A. Davis & R. Bartels (Eds.), *Graphics interface '96* (pp. 222–229). Toronto, Ontario: Canadian Human-Computer Communications Society.

Atkinson, A. P., Dittrich, W. H., Gemmell, A. J., & Young, A. J. (2004). Emotion perception from dynamic and static body expressions in point-light and full-light displays. *Perception, 33*, 717–746.

Barclay, C., Cutting, J., & Kozlowski, L. (1978). Temporal and spatial factors in gait perception that influence gender recognition. *Perception & Psychophysics, 23*, 145–152.

Bassili, J. N. (1978). Facial motion in the perception of faces and in emotional expression. *Journal of Experimental Psychology: Human Perception and Performance, 4*, 373–379.

Bassili, J. N. (1979). Emotion recognition: The role of facial movement and the relative importance of upper and lower areas of the face. *Journal of Personality and Social Psychology, 37*, 2049–2058.

Battelli, L., Cavanagh, P., & Thornton, I. M. (2003). Perception of biological motion in parietal patients. *Neuropsychologica, 41*, 1808–1816.

Beintema, J. P., & Lappe, M. (2002). Perception of biological motion without local image motion. *Proceedings of the National Academy of Sciences, USA, 99*, 5661–5663.

Bellefeuille, A., & Faubert, J. (1998). Independence of contour and biological-motion cues for motion-defined animal shapes. *Perception, 27*, 225–235.

Benson, P., & Perrett, D. (1991). Perception and recognition of photographic quality facial caricatures: Implications for the recognition of natural images. *Journal of Cognitive Psychology, 3*, 105–135.

Bertenthal, B. I., Haith, M. M., & Campos, J. J. (1983). The partial-lag design: A method for controlling spontaneous regression in the infant-control habituation paradigm. *Infant Behavior & Development, 6*, 331–338.

Bertenthal, B. I., & Pinto, J. (1994). Global processing of biological motions. *Psychological Science, 5*, 221–225.

Bertenthal, B. I., Proffitt, D. R., & Kramer, S. J. (1987). Perception of biomechanical motions by infants: Implementation of various processing constraints. *Journal of Experimental Psychology: Human Perception and Performance, 13*, 577–585.

Bertenthal, B. I., Proffitt, D. R., Spetner, N. B., & Thomas, M. A. (1985). The development of infants sensitivity to biomechanical displays. *Child Development, 56*, 531–543.

Black, M. J., & Jepson, A. D. (1998). Eigen tracking: Robust matching and tracking of articulated objects using a view-based representation. *International Journal of Computer Vision, 26*, 63–84.

Blake, R. (1993). Cats perceive biological motion. *Psychological Science, 4*, 54–47.

Blanz, V., & Vetter, T. (1999). A morphable model for the synthesis of 3D faces. *Proceedings of the 26th Annual Conference on Computer Graphics and Interactive Techniques, ACM Special Interest Group on Computer Graphics and Interactive Techniques (SIGGRAPH)* (pp. 187–194). New York: ACM Press.

Bosbach, S., Prinz, W., & Kerzel, D. (2004). A Simon-effect with stationary moving stimuli. *Journal of Experimental Psychology: Human Perception and Performance, 30*, 39–55.

Bradshaw, M. F., Leach, R., Hibbard, P. B., van der Willigen, R., & Rushton, S. K. (1999). The walker's direction affects the perception of biological motion. In M. A. Grealy & J. A. Thomson (Eds.), *Studies in perception & action V* (pp. 3–6). London: Lawrence Erlbaum Associates.

Bruce, V., & Valentine, T. (1988). When a nod's as good as a wink: The role of dynamic information in facial recognition. In P. E. Morris, M. M. Gruneberg, & R. N. Sykes (Eds.), *Practical aspects of memory: Current research and issues, Vol. 1* (pp. 164–174). Chichester: Wiley.

Bülthoff, I., Bülthoff, H. H., & Sinha, P. (1998). Top-down influences on stereoscopic depth-perception. *Nature Neuroscience, 1*, 254–257.

Burton, A. M., Wilson, S., Cowan, M., & Bruce, V. (1999). Face recognition in poor-quality video: Evidence from security surveillance. *Psychological Science, 10*, 243–248.

Calder, A. J., Young, A. W., Perrett, D. I., Etcoff, N. L., & Rowland, D. (1996). Categorical perception of morphed facial expressions. *Visual Cognition, 3*, 81–117.

Casile, A., & Giese, M. (2003). Roles of motion and form in biological motion recognition. In O. Kaynak, E. Alpaydin, E. Oja, & L. Xu (Eds.), *Artificial networks and neural information processing* (pp. 854–862). Lecture Notes in Computer Science 2714. Berlin: Springer.

Cavanagh, P., Labianca, A., & Thornton, I. M. (2001). Attention-based visual routines: Sprites. *Cognition, 80*, 47–60.

Cutting, J. E. (1978). A program to generate synthetic walkers as dynamic point-light displays. *Behavior Research Methods & Instrumentation, 10*, 91–94.

Cutting, J. E., & Kozlowski, L. T. (1977). Recognition of friends by their walk: Gait perception without familiarity cues. *Bulletin of the Psychonomic Society, 9*, 353–356.

Cutting, J. E., Moore, C., & Morrison, R. (1988). Masking the motions of human gait. *Perception & Psychophysics, 44*, 339–347.

Daems, A., & Verfaillie, K. (1999). Viewpoint-dependent priming effects in the perception of human actions and body postures. *Visual Cognition, 6*, 665–693.

Dekeyser, M., Verfaillie, K., & Vanrie, J. (2002). Creating stimuli for the study of biological-motion perception. *Behavior Research Methods, Instruments, & Computers, 34*, 375–382.

Dittrich, W. H. (1993). Action categories and the perception of biological motion. *Perception, 22,* 15–22.

Dittrich, W. H., Troscianko, T., Lea, S. E. G., & Morgan, D. (1996). Perception of emotion from dynamic point-light displays represented in dance. *Perception, 25,* 727–738.

Eriksen, B. A., and Eriksen, C. W. (1974). Effects of noise letters upon the identification of a target letter in a non-search task. *Perception & Psychophysics, 16,* 143–149.

Ezzat, T., Geiger, G., & Poggio, T. (2002). Trainable videorealistic speech animation. *Proceedings of the 29th Annual Conference on Computer Graphics and Interactive Techniques, ACM Special Interest Group on Computer Graphics and Interactive Techniques (SIGGRAPH)* (pp. 388–396). New York: ACM Press.

Felleman, D. J., & van Essen, D. C. (1991). Distributed hierarchical processing in the primate visual cortex. *Cerebral Cortex, 1,* 1–49.

Fitts, P. M., & Deininger, R. L. (1994). S-R compatibility: Correspondence among paired elements with stimulus and response codes. *Journal of Experimental Psychology, 48,* 483–491.

Gavrila, D. M. (1999). The visual analysis of human movement: A survey. *Computer Vision and Image Understanding, 73,* 82–98.

Giese, M. A., Jastorff, J., & Kourtzi, Z. (2002). Learning of the discrimination of artificial complex biological motion. *Perception, 31*(Suppl.), 117.

Giese, M. A., & Lappe, M. (2002). Measuring generalization fields for the recognition of biological motion. *Vision Research, 42,* 1847–1858.

Giese, M. A., & Poggio, T. (2000). Morphable models for the analysis and synthesis of complex motion patterns. *International Journal of Computer Vision, 38,* 59–73.

Giese, M. A., Thornton, I. M., & Edelman, S. (2003). Metric category spaces of biological motion. *Journal of Vision, 3,* 83a.

Goodale, M. A., & Milner, A. D. (1992). Separate visual pathways for perception and action. *Trends in Neurosciences, 15,* 97–112.

Green, D. M., & Swets, J. (1966). *Signal detection theory and psychophysics.* New York: Wiley.

Grossman, E. D., & Blake, R. (2001). Brain activity evoked by inverted and imagined biological motion. *Vision Research, 41,* 1475–1482.

Grossman, E., Donnelly, M., Price, R., Pickens, D., Morgan, V., Neighbor, G., & Blake, R. (2000). Brain areas involved in perception of biological motion. *Journal of Cognitive Neuroscience, 12,* 711–720.

Hill, H., & Johnston, A. (2001). Categorizing sex and identity from the biological motion of faces. *Current Biology, 11,* 880–885.

Hill, H. H., & Pollick, F. E. (2000). Exaggerating temporal differences enhances recognition of individual from point light displays. *Psychological Science, 11,* 223–228.

Hodgins, J. K., O'Brien, J. F., & Tumblin, J. (1998). Perception of human motion with different geometrical models. *IEEE Transactions on Visualization and Computer Graphics, 4,* 307–317.

Inman, V. T., Ralston, H., & Todd, F. (1981). *Human walking.* Baltimore, MD: Williams & Wilkins.

Jacobs, A., Pinto, J., & Shiffrar, M. (2005). Experience, context, and the visual perception of human movement. *Journal of Experimental Psychology: Human Perception & Performance, 30,* 822–835.

Johansson, G. (1973). Visual perception of biological motion and a model for its analysis. *Perception & Psychophysics, 14,* 201–211.

Johansson, G. (1976). Spatio-temporal differentiation and integration in visual motion perception. *Psychological Review, 38*, 379–393.

Jokisch, D., & Troje, N. F. (2003). Biological motion as a cue for the perception of size. *Journal of Vision, 3*, 252–264.

Kleiner, M., Vuong, Q. C., Bülthoff, H. H., & Thornton, I. M. (2004). Recognising famous gaits. *Perception, S33*, 99.

Knappmeyer, B., Thornton, I. M., & Bülthoff, H. H. (2003). Facial motion can bias the perception of facial identity. *Vision Research, 43*, 1921–1936.

Knight, B., & Johnston, A. (1997). The role of movement in face recognition. *Visual Cognition, 4*, 265–273.

Kozlowski, L. T., & Cutting, J. E. (1977). Recognizing the sex of a walker from a dynamic point-light display. *Perception & Psychophysics, 21*, 575–580.

Kozlowski, L. T., & Cutting, J. E. (1978). Recognizing the sex of a walker from point-lights mounted on ankles: Some second thoughts. *Perception & Psychophysics, 23*, 459.

Lander, K., & Bruce, V. (2000). Recognizing famous faces: Exploring the benefits of facial motion. *Ecological Psychology, 12*, 259–272.

Lander, K., Bruce, V., & Hill, H. (2001). Evaluating the effectiveness of pixelation and blurring on masking the identity of familiar faces. *Applied Cognitive Psychology, 15*, 101–116.

Lander, K., Christie, F., & Bruce, V. (1999). The role of movement in the recognition of famous faces. *Memory and Cognition, 27*, 974–985.

Marey, E. J. (1972). *Movement.* New York: Arno. (Original work published 1895.)

Mather, G., & Murdoch, L. (1994). Gender discrimination in biological motion displays based on dynamic cues. *Proceedings of the Royal Society of London, Series B, 258*, 273–279.

Mather, G., Radford, K., & West, S. (1992). Low level visual processing of biological motion. *Proceedings of the Royal Society of London, Series B, 249*, 149–155.

Mather, G., & West, S. (1993). Recognition of animal locomotion from dynamic point-light displays. *Perception, 22*, 759–766.

Neri, P., Morrone, M. C., & Burr, D. C. (1998). Seeing biological motion. *Nature, 394*, 894–896.

Pavlova, M., Krägeloh-Mann, I., Birbaumer, N., & Sokolov, A. (2004). Biological motion shown backwards: The apparent-facing effect. *Perception, 31*, 435–443.

Pavlova, M., & Sokolov, A. (2000). Orientation specificity in biological motion perception. *Perception & Psychophysics, 62*, 889–899.

Pavlova, M., & Sokolov, A. (2003). Prior knowledge about display inversion in biological motion perception. *Perception, 32*, 937–946.

Pinto, J., & Shiffrar, M. (2004). *The visual analysis of biological motion: Insights from comparisons of the perception of human and animal motion.* Manuscript submitted for publication.

Pollick, F. E., Fidopiastis, C. M., & Braden, V. (2001a). Recognizing the style of spatially exaggerated tennis serves. *Perception, 30*, 323–338.

Pollick, F. E., Kay, J., Heim, K., & Stringer, R. (2004). Gender recognition from point-light walkers. Manuscript in preparation.

Pollick, F. E., Paterson, H. M., Bruderlin, A., & Sanford, A. J. (2001b). Perceiving affect from arm movement. *Cognition, 82*, B51–B61.

Reed, C. L., Stone, V., Bozova, S., & Tanaka, J. (2003). The body inversion effect. *Psychological Science, 14*, 302–308.

Rensink, R. A., O'Regan, K., & Clark, J. J. (1997). To see or not to see: The need for attention to perceive changes in scenes. *Psychological Science, 8*, 368–373.

Rhodes, G., Brennan S., & Carey S. (1987). Identification and ratings of caricatures: Implications for learning the mental representations of faces. *Cognitive Psychology, 19*, 473–497.

Runeson, S., & Frykholm, G. (1983). Kinematic specification of dynamics as an informational basis for person-and-action perception: Expectation, gender recognition, and deceptive intention. *Journal of Experimental Psychology: General, 112*, 585–615.

Shiffrar, M., & Freyd, J. J. (1990). Apparent motion of the human body. *Psychological Science, 1*, 257–264.

Shiffrar, M., & Freyd, J. J. (1993). Timing and apparent motion path choice with human body photographs. *Psychological Science, 4*, 379–384.

Shim, J., Carlton, L. G., & Kim, J. (2004). Estimation of lifted weight and produced effort through perception of point-light display. *Perception, 33*, 277–291.

Shipley, T. F. (2003). The effect of object and event orientation on perception of biological motion. *Psychological Science, 14*, 377–380.

Simon, J. R. (1969). Reactions toward the source of stimulation. *Journal of Experimental Psychology, 81*, 174–176.

Stone, J. V. (1998). Object recognition using spatio-temporal signatures. *Vision Research, 38*, 947–951.

Sumi, S. (1984). Upside-down presentation of the Johansson moving light-spot pattern. *Perception, 13*, 283–286.

Tadin, D., Lappin J. S., Blake R., & Grossman E. D. (2002). What constitutes an efficient reference frame for vision? *Nature Neuroscience, 5*, 1010–1015.

Thomas, S., M., & Jordan, T. R. (2001). Techniques for the production of point-light and fully illuminated video displays from identical recordings. *Behavior Research Methods, Instruments, & Computers, 33*, 59–64.

Thornton, I. M., Pinto, J., & Shiffrar, M. (1998). The visual perception of human locomotion. *Cognitive Neuropsychology, 15*, 535–552.

Thornton, I. M., Rensink, R. A., & Shiffrar, M. (2002). Active versus passive processing of biological motion. *Perception, 31*, 837–853.

Thornton, I. M., & Vuong, Q. C. (2004). Incidental processing of biological motion. *Current Biology, 14*, 1084–1089.

Thornton, I. M., Vuong, Q. C., & Bülthoff, H. H. (2003). A chimeric point-light walker, *Perception, 32*, 377–383.

Troje, N. F. (2002). Decomposing biological motion: A framework for analysis and synthesis of human gait patterns. *Journal of Vision, 2*, 371–387.

Troje, N. F. (2003). Reference frames for orientation anisotropies in face recognition and biological-motion perception. *Perception, 32*, 201–210.

Ullman, S. (1979). *The interpretation of visual motion.* Cambridge, MA: MIT Press.

Ungerleider, L. G., & Mishkin, M. (1982). Two cortical visual systems. In D. J. Ingle, M. A. Goodale, & R. J. W. Mansfield (Eds.), *Analysis of visual behavior* (pp. 549–586). Cambridge, MA: MIT Press.

Unuma, M., Anjyo, K., & Takeuchi, R. (1995). Fourier principles for emotion-based human figure animation. *Proceedings of the 22nd Annual Conference on Computer Graphics and Interactive Techniques, ACM Special Interest Group on Computer Graphics and Interactive Techniques (SIGGRAPH)* (pp. 91–96). New York: ACM Press.

Vanrie, J., Dekeyser, M., & Verfaillie, K. (2004). Bistability and biasing effects in the perception of ambiguous point-light walkers. Manuscript submitted for publication.

Vanrie, J., & Verfaillie, K. (2004). Perception of biological motion: A stimulus set of human point-light actions. *Behavior Research Methods, Instruments, & Computers, 36*, 625–629.

Verfaillie, K. (1993). Orientation-dependent priming effects in the perception of biological motion. *Journal of Experimental Psychology: Human Perception & Performance, 19*, 992–1013.

Verfaillie, K. (2000). Perceiving human locomotion: Priming effects in direction discrimination, *Brain & Cognition, 44*, 192–213.

Verfaillie, K., & Daems, A. (2002). Representing and anticipating human actions in vision. *Visual Cognition, 9*, 217–232.

Verfaillie, K., De Troy, A., & Van Rensbergen, J. (1994). Transsaccadic integration of biological motion. *Journal of Experimental Psychology: Learning, Memory, and Cognition, 20*, 649–670.

Vuong, Q. C., Hof, A., Bülthoff, H. H., & Thornton, I. M. (2005). An advantage for detecting dynamic targets in natural scenes. *Journal of Vision*, under review.

Vuong, Q. C., & Tarr, M. J. (2004). Rotation direction affects object recognition. *Vision Research, 44*, 1717–1730.

Wallach, H., & O'Connell, D. N. (1953). The kinetic depth effect. *Journal of Experimental Psychology, 45*, 205–217.

Witkin, A., & Popovic, Z. (1995). Motion warping. *Proceedings of the 22nd Annual Conference on Computer Graphics and Interactive Techniques, ACM Special Interest Group on Computer Graphics and Interactive Techniques (SIGGRAPH)* (pp. 105–108). New York: ACM Press.

Wolfe, J. M. (1998). Visual search. In H. Pashler (Ed.), *Attention* (pp. 13–73). Hove, England: Psychology Press.

Yin, R. K. (1969). Looking at upside-down faces. *Journal of Experimental Psychology, 81*, 141–145.

14

Developing Body Representations

A Review of Infants' Responses to Biological-Motion Displays

Jeannine Pinto

Most adults are adept interpreters of others' bodily postures and movements. Indeed, observers can perceive and recognize human form and movement from highly reduced displays, typically referred to as *point-light* or *biological-motion* displays. As illustrated in Figure 14.1, point-light displays of biological motion are composed of a small set of discrete elements moving as though they are attached to the head and major joints of an otherwise invisible person (Johansson, 1973, 1975; see also chapter 13). Despite the impoverished nature of these stimulus displays, observers are able to rapidly recognize complex activities, such as dancing or boxing (Dittrich, 1993) and manual sign language (Poizner, Bellugi, & Lutes-Driscoll, 1981) rendered in point-lights. Adult observers also detect subtle socially relevant information, such as emotional state and gender in such displays (Brownlow, Dixon, Egbert, & Radcliffe, 1997; Dittrich, Troscianko, Lea, & Morgan, 1996; Kozlowski & Cutting, 1977, 1978; MacArthur & Baron, 1983).

In this chapter, I will discuss the early development of our recognition of human form from biological-motion displays. I will argue that infants acquire an internal representation of human form during the first year of life. From this foundation, I will propose several possible connections between early changes in the visual perception of biological motion and motor experiences that occur during the same period of development. Such motor experiences may contribute to the emerging internal representation of the human body. To place the developmental research in context, however, I will begin with a review of the visual analyses underlying the perception of point-light displays and the role of internal representations in those analyses.

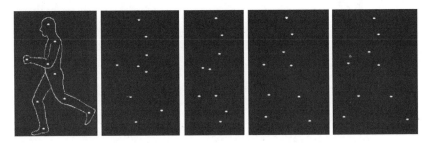

Figure 14.1. Static "snapshots" of point-light displays of a walking human figure. Each of the major joints of the human form has been demarcated with a discrete oscillating element. In the actual displays, the outline of a person does not appear. It is included here to illustrate the structure of the figure, which quickly becomes apparent when the elements move.

Visual Analyses of Biological-Motion Displays

Naïve observers rapidly recognize human form in point-light displays (Johansson, 1973), despite the many possible groupings into which the elements could be organized. Many accounts of this capacity suggest that the visual system employs general processing constraints to limit the number of possible organizations evaluated (Cutting, 1981; Proffitt & Bertenthal, 1988). According to constraint-based accounts, the visual system analyzes the structure contained in relatively small, local areas of the visual field and passes the product of those local analyses to higher-level processes. The higher-level processes apply constraints to those inputs thereby recovering structure from a larger, more-global spatial scope of the visual field. Consistent with such accounts, several researchers have shown that perturbing spatial or temporal properties of the displays disrupts the visual analysis of the display (Mather, Radford, & West, 1992; Thornton, Pinto, & Shiffrar, 1998).

While models that rely on local analyses are able to recover the structure of many point-light figures, several findings suggest that local analyses alone cannot account for human perceptual performance. Research has demonstrated that our perception of human movement in biological-motion displays is tolerant of substantial degradation across space (Pinto & Shiffrar, 1999), time (Thornton, Pinto, & Shiffrar, 1998), and luminance contrast (Ahlström, Blake, & Ahlström, 1997). Analyses grounded solely on local features should fail under conditions of degradation. Furthermore, local analyses should function without regard to the orientation of the figure. However, when biological-motion displays are spatially inverted, observers' perception (Bertenthal & Pinto, 1994; Pavlova & Sokolov, 2000; Pinto & Shiffrar, 1999) and recognition (Ahlström et al., 1997; Pavlova & Sokolov, 2000; Sumi, 1984) are markedly impaired. (For further discussion of the insufficiency of local analyses, see, e.g., Proffitt & Bertenthal, 1988, 1990; Thornton et al., 1998). Given these findings, recent investigations have sought to shed light on the higher level mechanism(s) involved in the visual perception of human movement and the internal representations implicit in those mechanisms (e.g., see chapter 15; Heptulla Chatterjee, Freyd, & Shiffrar, 1996; Pinto & Shiffrar, 2004; Shiffrar & Freyd, 1993; Thornton, Vuong, & Bülthoff, 2003).

Internal Representations of Biological Motion

Evidence for and about internal representations of the human body and bodily movements has been accumulating independently in several areas of research. A growing body of neuropsychological evidence suggests that adults possess a dedicated representation of the spatial organization of body parts (Denes, Cappelletti, Zilli, Porta, & Gallana, 2000; Felician, Ceccaldi, Didic, Thinus-Blanc, & Poncet, 2003; Guariglia, Piccardi, Puglisi Allegra, & Traballesi, 2002; Ogden, 1996; Reed, 2002; Sirigu, Grafman, Bressler, & Sunderland, 1991). For example, Ogden (1996) described a patient with autotopagnosia coincident with a parietal lobe tumor. Though the patient was able to identify individual isolated body parts, he was unable to locate parts of his own or of the experimenter's body on verbal command without systematically searching for it. His difficulty was specific to the body; he was able to identify and locate parts of objects. Further evidence for a cortical representation of the body can be derived from patients' accounts of "phantom" limb sensations (see chapter 9; Brugger, Kollias, Müri, Crelier, Hepp-Reymond, & Regard, 2000; Melzack, Israel, Lacroix, & Schultz, 1997; Ramachandran & Blakeslee, 1998). Patients with phantom limbs describe tactile and proprioceptive sensations in limbs that have been missing from birth or have been amputated. Ramachandran and Blakeslee (1998) argue that these sensations arise from the stimulation of cortical areas that once represented the missing limb. Similarly, Brugger (chapter 9) and Melzack et al. (1997) suggest that the nervous system is equipped with an intact representation of the body. Though neither studies of autotopagnosia nor of phantom limbs directly address questions about the perception of biological motion, they provide evidence for a cortical representation of the organization of the body.

Origins of Internal Representations of the Body

The origins of such body representations are unclear. Some researchers (chapter 9; Brugger et al., 2000; Melzack, Israel, Lacroix, & Schultz, 1997) have cited the experience of phantom limbs in individuals with aplasia as evidence for the existence of primitive motoric body representations, possibly in the form of a neural predisposition toward an organization of sensory inputs across several modalities. However, they have not yet been able to rule out the possibility that adult aplasic patients acquire phantom sensations through visual experience of others' limb movements.

Several studies of motor behavior in early infancy are consistent with the hypothesis that body representations are part of the primitive organization of the nervous system. For example, both fetuses and neonates frequently locate their mouths with their hands (DeVries, Visser, & Prechtl, 1984; Gallagher, Butterworth, Lew, & Cole, 1998; Lew & Butterworth, 1995). The trajectory of the hand varies with the hand's initial location and so cannot be understood as a result of simple reflexive muscle activity. Instead, hand-mouth coordination implies that the movements are guided by some representation of the body organization. Drawing on another domain of research, Meltzoff (1990; Meltzoff & Moore, 1989) has argued that neonates possess a bimodal representation of the body. Meltzoff and Moore (1983, 1989) found that neonates, within their limited motor capacities, could imitate facial gestures produced by an adult model. For example, if the model repeatedly protruded her tongue, the infant protruded his own tongue more frequently than he had during a baseline period. Meltzoff and Moore have speculated that the infant's visual experience of the model's facial action is somehow mapped onto the infant's own face, implying a link between visual and motor representations of the face. Both studies of hand-mouth coordination and neonatal imitation are suggestive. Unfortunately, they each rely on increases in otherwise spontaneous behaviors. Moreover, these findings could reflect a limited representation of the face and hands, rather than a complete representation of the body. Further studies are clearly needed.

How do we come to have an internal representation of the whole body? Is the nervous system predisposed to representing the organization of the body, given typical sensory experiences, as Brugger suggests? What experience contributes to the formation of a body representation? In this chapter, I will review studies of the early development of visual sensitivity to the structure of human bodies rendered in point-light displays. As argued above, an internal representation of the body influences adults' perception and recognition of biological-motion displays. In the next section, I will argue that an adultlike representation of the body does not appear to contribute to infants' perception until about 5 to 7 months of age. Subsequently, I will describe motor developments that typically occur during the same period and that may contribute to infants' emerging representation of the body.

Infants' Sensitivity to Visuospatial Relations of the Human Body

Several researchers have investigated infants' responses to biological-motion displays (e.g., Bertenthal, Proffitt, & Kramer, 1987a; Bertenthal, Proffitt,

Kramer, & Spetner, 1987; Booth, Pinto, & Bertenthal, 2002; Fox & McDaniel, 1982; Proffitt & Bertenthal, 1990). Across many studies of infants during the first year of life, a pattern of responsiveness emerges: infants gradually exhibit evidence of visual sensitivity to the spatial arrangements of the human body. By 5 to 7 months of age, but not by 3 months, infants respond to the spatiotemporal patterning of human limb movements only within the context of a figure that resembles the global, hierarchical structure of a human body. I will argue that this change suggests that infants acquire a representation of the spatial organization of the human body.

Each of the studies described below used an infant-control habituation paradigm with a partial-lag design (Bertenthal, Haith, & Campos, 1983) to determine whether infants could distinguish two biological motion displays. For example, Bertenthal and colleagues (see Bertenthal, 1993; Bertenthal, Proffitt, & Kramer, 1987a) investigated 3-, 5-, and 7-month-old infants' sensitivity to phase relations among the joints of a human body. To do so, they examined whether infants would discriminate an ordinary walking form (or *canonical* figure; see Figure 14.2, left panel) from a form in which the phase relations among the elements had been altered (or *phase-perturbed* figure; see Figure 14.2, right panel). Half of the infants in each age group were familiarized to the canonical figure over repeated presentations (the other half were familiarized to the phase-perturbed figure). Looking time to the display was measured. Over trials, looking time declined. When looking time fell below a criterion value, infants were presented the phase-perturbed figure (or the canonical figure) for two trials. Discrimination of the canonical and phase-perturbed forms was indicated by an increase in looking time to the novel figure. In this study, each group of infants increased looking time to the novel test stimulus, showing sensitivity to the phase relations among the joints.

In itself, this study does not demonstrate sensitivity to human form. Infants' discrimination could be based simply on relatively local differences. For example, infants might stochastically attend to a single element in each display. If that element differed between familiarization and test, then infants could discriminate the two displays. Alternatively, they might attend to a pair of adjacent elements moving in synchrony in the canonical form. In the phase-perturbed form, the distance between these elements would not be constant, and changes in their trajectories would be asynchronous. Such differences might provide a basis for discrimination regardless of the human figure in which they are embedded. In short, infants' discrimination of these displays does not imply that they are sensitive to the same structure that adults perceive.

To examine infants' sensitivity to the human structure per se, Bertenthal et al. (1987a) rotated both of the figures 180° in the picture plane, creating spatially inverted displays. In inverted displays, the global structure remains unchanged, as does the local motion information. However, inversion of the displays impairs the correct and rapid perception of the figures (Bertenthal &

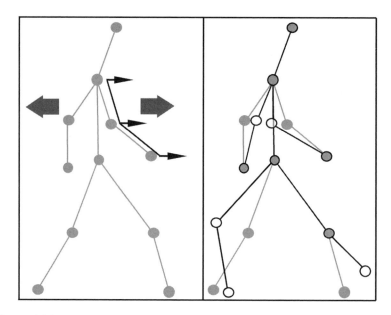

Figure 14.2. Static illustrations of canonical and phase-perturbed human figures walking. The *left panel* represents a canonical human figure. The movements of the major joints of a walking figure can be described as a set of hierarchically nested pendula. (The connecting lines did not appear in the actual displays.) Biomechanical and physical principles constrain the trajectories of the joints. For example, the elements representing the wrist, elbow, and shoulder move simultaneously in the same direction (indicated by the small black arrows) in accord with the rigidity of the bones and the limitations of the joints. When a person walks, adjacent limbs, such as the two arms, move in opposition to one another (indicated by the large arrows) to assist balance. The *right panel* shows a phase-perturbed figure (depicted in black) superimposed over a canonical figure (depicted in gray) for comparison. In this phase-perturbed display, the absolute motion of each element is identical to that in the canonical display, but the onset of the cycle of each element is randomly delayed or advanced. The resulting intralimb phase patterns violate the biomechanical constraints of the joints and appear double-jointed. The interlimb phase perturbations result in an unstable gait.

Pinto, 1994; Pavlova & Sokolov, 2000; Pinto & Shiffrar, 1999; Sumi, 1984). If infants' response reflects familiarity with the (upright) human figure, they may not discriminate the two inverted displays. If infants respond instead to local differences between the canonical and phase-perturbed displays, without regard to the global figure, they should discriminate the inverted figures just as they do the upright figures.

Interestingly, when the figures were rotated, only 3-month-old infants showed discrimination of the inverted displays. Though they were capable of discriminating differing spatiotemporal patterns in the upright figures, neither 5- nor 7-month-old infants discriminated those same patterns when the figures were inverted. A similar loss of responsiveness has been well documented in speech perception (for reviews of this literature, see Best, 1994; Werker, 1989). As infants become more familiar with the language of their community, their ability or willingness to discriminate nonnative speech contrasts declines (Aslin & Pisoni, 1980; Best & McRoberts, 2003; Burnham, 1986; Eilers, Gavin, & Oller, 1982; Eilers, Gavin, & Wilson, 1979). By analogy, the difference in infants' responses to upright and inverted biological-motion displays suggests that, by 5 months of age, infants' responses reflect the familiarity of the upright forms.

The findings described above reveal sensitivity to the global form insofar as the global form provides a context in which other features of the displays are salient and thus discriminable. However, they provide little information about what that global structure is, subjectively, for infants. To probe further, Bertenthal, Proffitt, and Kramer (1987b) presented infants with a global structure that resembled a biological figure different from, but similar to, a human form—a fictitious spider figure. The spider was composed of four compound limbs radiating from a single point (see Figure 14.3A). Like the joints of a human limb, all of the elements comprising a single limb oscillated in synchrony (i.e., in phase). Adjacent limbs oscillated in opposition (i.e., antiphase), simulating a human diagonal gait pattern. Thus, the spider and the human form differed primarily in the global hierarchical organization of their four limbs. Adults perceived the structure and biological nature of the spider figure. Would infants too perceive structure in the displays? To address this question, Bertenthal et al. examined infants' sensitivity to phase relations

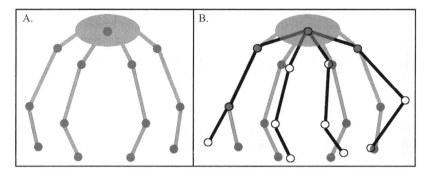

Figure 14.3. Static illustrations of canonical and phase-perturbed "spider" figures. (A) A fictitious spider figure created from four jointed limbs radiating around a single point. Like the canonical human figure, elements representing a single limb moved in phase with one another, while elements representing adjacent limbs moved in opposition to one another. (B) The phase-perturbed display (black elements and lines) was analogous to the phase-perturbed human figure. For comparison, the phase-perturbed figure has been superimposed over the canonical figure (gray elements and lines). The gray bodies and the lines connecting the elements did not appear in the actual displays.

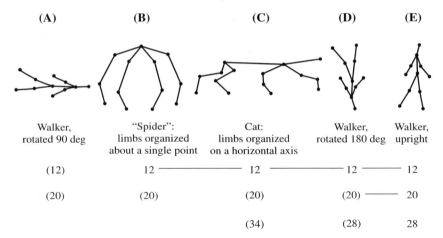

(A)   **(B)**   **(C)**   **(D)**   **(E)**

Walker, rotated 90 deg	"Spider": limbs organized about a single point	Cat: limbs organized on a horizontal axis	Walker, rotated 180 deg	Walker, upright
(12)	12 ——————— 12 ——————— 12 ——— 12			
(20)	(20)	(20)	(20) ——— 20	
		(34)	(28)	28

Figure 14.4. A summary of selected studies of infants' sensitivity to phase patterning. In the *top row*, the figures indicate the global structure and orientation of the canonical forms presented to infants. Each canonical figure was paired with a phase-perturbed rendition in each of the studies included here. Below the figures appear the ages (in weeks) of the infants tested. Parentheses indicate that infants did not discriminate the canonical and phase-perturbed figures at the age indicated. In addition to the studies described in the text, this figure includes (A), a study in which the walking figure was rotated 90°, for comparison.

among the spider's limb elements. They presented 3- and 5-month-old infants with a spider figure and a phase-perturbed counterpart (Figure 14.3B). Despite the similarity of the human and spider figures, only 3-month-old infants discriminated the canonical and phase-perturbed spiders. Five-month-old infants did not. Taken together, these results suggest that, while infants are capable of detecting differences in phase relations at 3 and 5 months, they do not respond to those phase relations in every context. It is possible that the fictitious spider figures looked biologically realistic to 3-month-old infants but not to 5-month-old infants. To assess this possibility, Pinto (1994) conducted another study, this time using a point-light cat (Blake, 1993; see Figure 14.4C). Like the human and the fictitious spider, the cat possessed four limbs, which oscillated in a dynamic gait pattern. The elements attached to a single limb moved in synchrony consistent with the pairwise rigid relations created by the long bones. A phase-perturbed cat figure was created as a foil. Once again, the same pattern emerged: 3-month-old infants discriminated the canonical and phase-perturbed cat displays while 5- and 8-month-old infants did not.

Figure 14.4 summarizes the findings discussed above. These findings provide evidence that suggests that infants as young as 3 months of age are capable of discriminating point-light displays that differ in phase relations. We also see evidence that they do not always respond to phase differences, despite their capacity to do so. Indeed, discrimination of the displays in a visual-habituation paradigm implies not just that infants perceive differences between the displays but also that those differences are salient or interesting enough to elicit attention. As Figure 14.4 suggests, by 5 months of age, infants respond to phase differences in upright human figures and only in upright human figures. I would like to argue that the emergence of an internal representation of the human body provides an explanation for this pattern. An internal representation may mediate 5-month-old infants' discriminatory response by facilitating the encoding of the global structure and of the salient features of the form. The phase relations among the elements of the canonical figure are characteristic of human beings. The phase relations among the elements of the phase-perturbed forms are not. By 20 weeks, infants may better encode a normal human form in motion and discriminate by comparison to that pattern. Though they are similarly organized, the nonhuman figures may not make contact with infants' internal representation of human form. The lack of a matching internal representation may lead to a failure to discriminate.

At 12 weeks, however, infants may be responding to the figures on a lower level of organization. They may not possess an internal representation of human form or they may possess an internal representation that does not include the hierarchical structure of the body.

This interpretation of the behavior of 5- to 8-month-old infants is based on null results and thus problematic on methodological grounds. In another series of studies, therefore, Pinto and Bertenthal examined infants' responses to violations of a global human form. Given the prominence of an object's principal axis of organization in theories of visual object recognition (Ling & Sanocki, 1995; Marr & Nishihara, 1978), we chose to examine infants' perceptions of the principal axis of human form (Pinto, 1996). In a human figure, the principal axis represents a nonaccidental feature of the form, which is created by the head and torso. In order to probe infants' sensitivity to the unity of this axis (manifest in the head, shoulder, and hip of the canonical, or *unitary-axis* display; Figure 14.5A), we constructed a display in which the principal axis was divided at the midriff and the two halves were offset horizontally (a *divided-axis* display; Figure 14.5B). The divided-axis display maintained most of the local spatial and temporal patterns of the human figure, but altered a key element of its global structure.

In the first experiment, we examined whether and when infants show sensitivity to the unity of the principal axis of organization of a sagittal view of a walking point-light person. This study involved two manipulations. To probe infants' sensitivity to the principal axis of organization of human form, we presented unitary- and divided-axis walking figures translating across the video monitor. In addition, half of the infants were presented these displays in an upright orientation; the others were presented the same displays in an inverted orientation. By comparing infants' responses to the stimuli in the two different

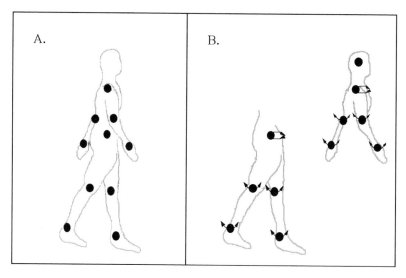

Figure 14.5. Divided walker displays. (A) The canonical (unitary-axis) display with limbs organized about the single principal axis created by the head and torso. (B) The divided-axis display created by offsetting horizontally the upper and lower halves of the body. The outline did not appear in the actual displays.

orientations, we could determine whether infants' responses to the principal axis reflect general processing heuristics or processes especially attuned to human form. If infants are sensitive to the global structure of the human body, then they should be sensitive to the unity of the principal axis of organization and should discriminate the unitary- and divided-axis displays. Moreover, if infants' sensitivity reflects a specific response to human form, then they should discriminate these displays when the displays are presented upright, but not inverted. As we predicted from our studies of infants' sensitivity to phase relations, 5- and 7-month-old infants were sensitive to the global structure of human form. They discriminated the unitary- and divided-axis displays when they were presented upright.

Contrary to our expectations, however, 3-month-old infants did not discriminate the displays in either orientation, despite the availability of local spatial differences between the two displays. Though 3-month-old infants had repeatedly discriminated displays that differed in local spatiotemporal relationships among the elements, they did not respond to the marked spatial differences in these displays. To confirm this response, we conducted two additional studies. We eliminated the translatory motion, creating figures that moved as though walking on a treadmill, and we added lines to make the organization of the elements explicit. Nonetheless, 3-month-old infants continued to fail to discriminate the unitary- and divided-axis displays. It appears that infants do not respond to the organization of limbs at 3 months of age.

Consistent with this assessment, in a subsequent study (Booth, Pinto, & Bertenthal, 2002), 3-month-old infants, but not 5-month-old infants, discriminated a walking from a running figure. Walking and running both generate a diagonal gait pattern with adjacent limbs moving in antiphase. The gaits differ, however, at a local level of organization, the intralimb spatiotemporal patterns. The younger infants responded to those intralimb differences; the older infants did not. However, consistent with the hypothesis that older infants are sensitive to the relations among the limbs, when the interlimb phase relations of the running figure were perturbed, the 5-month-old infants discriminated the phase-perturbed running figure and the canonical walking figure.

Taken together, the studies reviewed above suggest that, between 3 and 7 months of age, infants become sensitive to the global structure of the human body. In particular, they come to respond to the organization of limbs around an upright vertical principal axis, a feature that distinguishes the human form from other animals. At 3 months, however, infants appear to be impervious to the organization among limbs. Instead, they respond to the organization of elements within the limbs.

Infants' increasing responsiveness to the global structure of point-light displays probably does not reflect (only) a change in attention from local to global levels of stimulus organization. Were the change general, 5-month-old, and older, infants would discriminate spatiotemporal differences in point-light displays when the figures reflect nonhuman as well as human forms. In previous studies, we found that they do not. Infants' increasing responsiveness to the global structure of the displays probably does not reflect (only) a change in information-processing capacity, though Younger (1992) provides evidence that, with age, the number of correlated features to which infants can attend increases. Again, such a change alone cannot account for the pattern of findings since, were this the case, 5-month-old infants would extract correlated configural features from point-light displays regardless of their global structure. They do not appear to do so. Instead, changes in infants' responsiveness to the principal axis of organization and the spatiotemporal patterning among the limbs resembles perceptual learning, as described, for example, by Eleanor Gibson (1969).

In Gibson's account, learning involves the apprehension of features that increasingly differentiate between kinds of objects. Gibson's account focuses on features and suggests that configural information supplants feature information over the course of learning. The studies reported above are consistent with the proposal that infants come to differentiate the human form from other similarly limbed structures, possibly by identifying the principal axis as a distinguishing feature of humans. It is also possible that changes in infants' sensitivity to the visuospatial form of a human figure take place entirely within the visual domain. By such an account, one might argue that changes in visual field size, the ability to integrate information over space and time, and the availability of visual invariants in human movement eventually lead infants to attend to the diagnostic features of the human form.

An alternative possibility is that changes in infants' motor activities drive detection of and attention to information within the visual array (Anderson, Campos, Anderson, Thomas, Witherington, Uchiyama, & Barbu-Roth, 2001; Needham, 2000; Needham, Barrett, & Peterman, 2002). Anderson et al. (2001) argue that locomotor experience may cause improvements in infants' use of peripheral optic-flow information. Similarly, Needham (2000; Needham, Barrett, & Peterman, 2002) reports that manual exploration of objects results in greater sensitivity to visual cues about object segmentation. Young infants explore their own bodies and capacities for action (Rochat & Striano, 1999). In fact, several advances in their motor skills may be contemporaneous with advances in their sensitivity to features of human form and movement. Is this mere coincidence? Or might infants' explorations of their own bodies and movements drive their perception of others' bodies?

Motor Development in the First Year of Life

From birth through the first 18 months of life, infants acquire a basic repertoire of motor skills. They learn to reach, grasp an object, and bring it to their faces between approximately 3 and 5 months. They learn to hold their heads erect (3–4 months), sit upright (7 months), and balance their bodies while displacing their weight as they reach (8 months). They learn to stand (8–12 months), walk with the support of furniture (12–15 months), and walk independently (about 18 months). It is difficult to determine a connection between infants' motor experience and development and their sensitivity to biological-motion displays within the available literature. The age estimates provided above are drawn from the classic works of Gesell (Gesell, Halverson, Thomson, Ilg, Castner, Ames, & Amatruda, 1940) and McGraw (1940). These skills emerge gradually, often erratically (Biu, Young, Pethkongkathon, Kanani, & Adolph, 2003). Assessments of an infant on any given day and according to any given operationalization of a skill may vary. Given these observations as a caveat, I would like to suggest that contemporaneous motor experiences may contribute to infants' sensitivity to biological-motion displays.

Possible Motor Contributions to Infants' Visual Sensitivity to Limb Structure

While newborn infants demonstrate a keen ability to bring hand to mouth (Lew & Butterworth, 1995), other early attempts at goal-directed hand movements are less skilled. At 2 months of age, infants typically wave their arms at the appearance of a desirable object. In order to reach successfully, an infant must learn to control the many "degrees of freedom" (Bernstein, 1967) available within the limb. More specifically, reaching infants must command their upper arm around the shoulder joint and lower arm around the elbow joint. Between 3 and 5 months, they can do so sufficiently to bring their hands into contact with an object reliably (Thelen, Corbetta, Kamm, Spencer, Schneider, & Zernicke, 1993). They can control their leg movements sufficiently to contact an object with their feet at 3 months, possibly because the hips require control of fewer degrees of freedom (Galloway & Thelen, 2004). During this same period of development, as infants are attempting to master the joints in their limbs, studies of the perception of biological motion (as reviewed above) suggest that they are attending to the intralimb joint angles in biological-motion displays.

Might signals from the muscles and joints (i.e., proprioceptive information) serve, perhaps indirectly, to guide infants' attention to intralimb joint angles? Studies of infants' sensitivity to corresponding visual-proprioceptive information adds credence to the hypothesized role of motor activity in the perception of limbs in point-light displays. Using a preferential looking procedure to assess infants' sensitivity to visual-proprioceptive congruence, Rochat and Morgan (1995; Morgan & Rochat, 1997) found that, by 3 months, infants are able to detect the relationship between proprioceptive information and a visual display of their own leg movements. While preventing seated infants from viewing their legs, Rochat and Morgan trained a video camera on the children's legs. By looking reliably more at a novel, incongruent video display, 3- to 5-month-old infants suggest that they distinguish between simultaneous videos in which legs move appropriately toward and away from the midline and those in which they do not. Interestingly, they distinguish these displays only when the contours of the legs are available to specify their asymmetrical structure. When the asymmetrical shape of the legs is hidden within a puffy sock, the infants showed no recognition of their own moving legs. These findings suggest that 3-month-old infants are able to encode visual and proprioceptive information about the shape and movements of their own limbs. Such a capacity would presumably support the representation of the limbs of other people.

Possible Motor Contributions to Infants' Visual Sensitivity to the Position and Orientation of the Torso

If motor activity and proprioceptive information contribute to infants' sensitivity to structures of the human body, one might well expect that infants would attend to the principal axis of organization at around the time they begin to control their own head and torso. Between 3 and 4 months, infants are able to sit with assistance and hold their own heads steady (Bertenthal & Von Hofsten, 1998; Gesell et al., 1940). Infants require assistance sitting until about 7 months. Between the time they begin to sit with assistance and the time they can sit independently, infants exercise their trunks in several ways. They may begin to creep, pushing their prone bodies with their legs and arms, and they may begin to stabilize the thorax above the pelvis to maintain postural control while seated upright (Adolph, Vereijken, & Denny, 1998). These achievements might contribute to a multimodal body representation by establishing or reinforcing a cortical representation of the organization among limbs or by adding a structural component in the form of a torso to such a representation. Such a multimodal representation, available then to visual processes, may contribute to infants' perception of biological-motion displays. Indeed, as infants learn to control their head and trunk, they also appear to attend to the principal axis of a human Figure depicted in point-lights.

The timing of these motor and visual changes has prompted these speculations. It appears possible that infants' visuoproprioceptive experience of their own limbs and torso might contribute to the creation of a body representation either directly, by encoding proprioceptive information, or indirectly, by making elements of visible bodies more salient. Of course, one must regard these speculations with particular care. The age at which children acquire motor skills varies considerably. The duration of the period of acquisition—from first attempts to mastery—vary as well. In this chapter, I have had to rely on published averages. Later research will have to determine whether actual individual developments in motor activity correspond with developments in responses to biological-motion displays.

There is increasing evidence that motor production and visual perception contribute to some of the same cortical representations of the body (see chapter 19; Gallese, Fadiga, Fogassi, & Rizzolatti, 1996; Reed & Farah, 1995; Van den Bos & Jeannerod, 2002) and that the motor system may tutor the visual system (Bertenthal & Pinto, 1993; Bülthoff, Bülthoff, & Sinha, 1998; Shiffrar & Freyd, 1993; Viviani, Baud-Bovy, & Redolfi, 1997; Viviani & Stucchi, 1992). Such tutelage might not end at tuning the visual system to motor capacities and constraints; it may include creating a conduit through which visible actions are linked to invisible goals or intentions (see chapters 10, 18, and 20). The developmental course of such representations offers a unique perspective. By virtue of the natural motor limitations of the infant, we are able to examine the relative roles of visual experience and of emerging motor skill in the construction of a body representation. Given the possible importance of body representations for the perception of action and of other people (Blakemore & Decety, 2001; Gallese & Goldman, 1998; Meltzoff & Moore, 1983, 1989), an understanding of their development promises both theoretical and practical rewards.

References

Adolph, K. E., Vereijken, B., & Denny, M. (1998). Learning to crawl. *Child Development, 69,* 1299–1312.

Ahlström, V., Blake, R., & Ahlström, U. (1997). Perception of biological motion. *Perception, 26,* 1539–1548.

Anderson, D. I., Campos, J. J., Anderson, D. E., Thomas, T. D., Witherington, D. C., Uchiyama, I., & Barbu-Roth, M. A. (2001). The flip side of perception-action coupling: Locomotor experience and the ontogeny of visual-postural coupling. *Human Movement Science, 20,* 461–487.

Aslin, R. N., & Pisoni, D. B. (1980). Some developmental processes in speech perception. In G. H. Yeni-Komshian, J. E. Kavanaugh, & C. A. Ferguson (Eds.), *Child Phonology. Vol. 2: Perception* (pp. 67–96). New York: Academic Press.

Bernstein, N. (1967). *The coordination and regulation of movements.* Oxford: Pergamon.

Bertenthal, B. I. (1993). Infants' perception of biomechanical motions: Intrinsic image and knowledge-based constraints. In C. Granrud (Ed.), *Visual perception and cognition in infancy: Carnegie Mellon symposia on cognition* (pp. 175–214). Hillsdale, NJ: Erlbaum.

Bertenthal, B. I., Haith, M. M., & Campos, J. J. (1983). The partial-lag design: A method for controlling spontaneous regression in the infant-control habituation paradigm. *Infant Behavior & Development, 6,* 331–338.

Bertenthal, B. I., & Pinto, J. (1993). Complementary processes in the perception and production of human movements. In L. B. Smith & E. Thelen (Eds.), *A dynamic systems approach to development: Applications* (pp. 209–239). Cambridge, MA: MIT Press.

Bertenthal, B. I., & Pinto, J. (1994). Global processing of biological motions. *Psychological Science, 5,* 221–225.

Bertenthal, B. I., Proffitt, D. R., & Kramer, S. J. (1987a). Perception of biomechanical motions by infants: Implementation of various processing constraints. *Journal of Experimental Psychology: Human Perception and Performance, 13,* 577–585.

Bertenthal, B. I., Proffitt, D. R., & Kramer, S. J. (1987b). *Orientation specificity in the perception of biomechanical motions by infants.* Unpublished manuscript.

Bertenthal, B. I., Proffitt, D. R., Kramer, S. J., & Spetner, N. B. (1987). Infants' encoding of kinetic displays varying in relative coherence. *Developmental Psychology, 23,* 171–178.

Bertenthal, B. I., & Von Hofsten, C. (1998). Eye, head and trunk control: The foundation for manual development. *Neuroscience and Biobehavioral Reviews, 22,* 515–520.

Best, C. C., & McRoberts, G. W. (2003). Infant perception of non-native consonant contrasts that adults assimilate in different ways. *Language & Speech, 46,* 183–216.

Best, C. T. (1994). Learning to perceive the sound pattern of English. In C. Rovee-Collier & L. Lipsitt (Eds.), *Advances in infancy research, Vol. 8* (pp. 217–304). Hillsdale, NJ: Ablex.

Biu, O., Young, J. W., Pethkongkathon, J., Kanani, P., & Adolph, K. E. (2003). *A microgenetic analysis of the trajectory of motor development.* Tampa, FL: Society for Research in Child Development.

Blake, R. (1993). Cats perceive biological motion. *Psychological Science, 4,* 54–57.

Blakemore, S.-J., & Decety, J. (2001). From the perception of action to the understanding of intention. *Nature Reviews Neuroscience, 2,* 561–567.

Booth, A., Pinto, J., & Bertenthal, B. I. (2002). Perception of the symmetrical patterning of human gait by infants. *Developmental Psychology, 38,* 554–563.

Brownlow, S., Dixon, A. R., Egbert, C. A., & Radcliffe, R. D. (1997). Perception of movement and dancer characteristics from point-light displays of dance. *Psychological Record, 47*, 411–421.

Brugger, P., Kollias, S., Müri, R., Crelier, G., Hepp-Reymond, M.-C., & Regard, M. (2000). Beyond re-membering: Phantom sensations of congenitally absent limbs. *Proceedings of the National Academy of Sciences, 97*, 6167–6172.

Bülthoff, I., Bülthoff, H., & Sinha, P. (1998). Top-down influence on stereoscopic depth-perception. *Nature Neuroscience, 1*, 254–257.

Burnham, D. K. (1986). Developmental loss of speech perception: Exposure to and experience with a first language. *Applied Psycholinguistics, 7*, 207–240.

Cutting, J. E. (1981). Coding theory adapted to gait perception. *Journal of Experimental Psychology: Human Perception and Performance, 7*, 71–87.

Denes, G., Cappelletti, J. Y., Zilli, T., Porta, F. D., & Gallana, A. (2000). A category-specific deficit of spatial representation: The case of autotopagnosia. *Neuropsychologia, 38*, 345–350.

DeVries, J. I. P., Visser, G. H. A., & Prechtl, H. F. R. (1984). Fetal motility in the first half of pregnancy. In H. F. R. Prechtl (Ed.), *Continuity of neural functions from prenatal to postnatal life* (pp. 46–64). London: Spastics International Medical Publications.

Dittrich, W. H. (1993). Action categories and the perception of biological motion. *Perception, 22*, 15–22.

Dittrich, W. H., Troscianko, T., Lea, S., & Morgan, D. (1996). Perception of emotion from dynamic point-light displays represented in dance. *Perception, 25*, 727–738.

Eilers, R. E., Gavin, W. J., & Oller, D. K. (1982). Cross linguistic perception in infancy: The role of linguistic experience. *Journal of Child Language, 9*, 289–302.

Eilers, R. E., Gavin, W., & Wilson, W. R. (1979). Linguistic experience and phonemic perception in infancy: A cross-linguistic study. *Child Development, 50*, 14–18.

Felician, O., Ceccaldi, M., Didic, M., Thinus-Blanc, C., & Poncet, M. (2003). Pointing to body parts: A double dissociation study. *Neuropsychologia, 41*, 1307–1316.

Fox, R., & McDaniel, C. (1982). The perception of biological motion by human infants. *Science, 218*, 486–487.

Gallagher, S., Butterworth, G. E., Lew, A., & Cole, J. (1998). Hand-mouth coordination, congenital absence of limb, and evidence for innate body schemas. *Brain and Cognition, 38*, 53–65.

Gallese, V., Fadiga, L., Fogassi, L., & Rizzolatti, G. (1996). Action recognition in the premotor cortex. *Brain, 119*, 593–609.

Gallese, V., & Goldman, A. (1998). Mirror neurons and the simulation theory of mind-reading. *Trends in Cognitive Sciences, 2*, 493–501.

Galloway, J. C., & Thelen, E. (2004). Feet first: Object exploration in young infants. *Infant Behavior & Development, 27*, 107–112.

Gesell, A., Halverson, H. M., Thomson, H., Ilg, F. L., Castner, B. M., Ames, L. B., & Amatruda, C. S. (1940). *The first five years of life: The preschool years.* Oxford: Harpers.

Gibson, E. J. (1969). *Principles of perceptual learning and development.* Englewood Cliffs, NJ: Prentice-Hall.

Guariglia, C., Piccardi, L., Puglisi Allegra, M. C., & Traballesi, M. (2002). Is autotopoagnosia [*sic*] real? EC says yes: A case study. *Neuropsychologia, 40*, 1744–1749.

Heptulla Chatterjee, S., Freyd, J. J., & Shiffrar, M. (1996). Configural processing in the perception of apparent biological motion. *Journal of Experimental Psychology: Human Perception and Performance, 22*, 916–929.

Johansson, G. (1973). Visual perception of biological motion and a model for its analysis. *Perception & Psychophysics, 14*, 201–211.

Johansson, G. (1975). Visual motion perception. *Scientific American, 232*, 76–88.

Kozlowski, L. T., & Cutting, J. E. (1977). Recognizing the sex of a walker from a dynamic point-light display. *Perception & Psychophysics, 21*, 575–580.

Kozlowski, L. T., & Cutting, J. E. (1978). Recognizing the gender of walkers from point-lights mounted on ankles: Some second thoughts. *Perception & Psychophysics, 23*, 459.

Lew, A., & Butterworth, G. E. (1995). Hand-mouth contact in newborn babies before and after feeding. *Developmental Psychology, 31*, 456–463.

Ling, X., & Sanocki, T. (1995). Major axes as a moderately abstract model for object recognition. *Psychological Science, 6*, 370–375.

MacArthur, L. Z., & Baron, M. K. (1983). Toward an ecological theory of social perception. *Psychological Review, 90*, 215–238.

Marr, D., & Nishihara, H. K. (1978). Representation and recognition of the spatial organization of three-dimensional shapes. *Proceedings of the Royal Society of London, Series B, 200*, 269–294.

Mather, G., Radford, K., & West, S. (1992). Low-level visual processing of biological motion. *Proceedings of the Royal Society of London, Series B, 249*, 149–155.

McGraw, M. B. (1940). Neuromuscular development of the human infant as exemplified in the achievement of erect locomotion. *Journal of Pediatrics, 17*, 747–771.

Meltzoff, A. N. (1990). Towards a developmental cognitive science: The implications of cross-modal matching and imitation for the development of representation and memory in infancy. *Annals of the New York Academy of Sciences, 608*, 1–37.

Meltzoff, A. N., & Moore, M. K. (1983). Newborn infants imitate adult facial gestures. *Child Development, 54*, 702–709.

Meltzoff, A. N., & Moore, M. K. (1989). Imitation in newborn infants: Exploring the range of gestures imitated and the underlying mechanisms. *Developmental Psychology, 25*, 954–962.

Melzack, R., Israel, R., Lacroix, R., & Schultz, G. (1997). Phantom limbs in people with congenital limb deficiency or amputation in early childhood. *Brain, 120*, 1603–1620.

Morgan, R., & Rochat, P. (1997). Intermodal calibration of the body in early infancy. *Ecological Psychology, 9*, 1–23.

Needham, A. (2000). Improvements in object exploration skills may facilitate the development of object segregation in early infancy. *Journal of Cognition & Development, 1*, 131–156.

Needham, A., Barrett, T., & Peterman, K. (2002). A pick me up for infants' exploratory skills: Early simulated experiences reaching for objects using "sticky" mittens enhances young infants' object exploration skills. *Infant Behavior & Development, 25*, 279–295.

Ogden, J. A. (1996). *Fractured minds: A case-study approach to clinical neuropsychology.* New York: Oxford University Press.

Pavlova, M., & Sokolov, A. (2000). Orientation specificity in biological motion perception. *Perception & Psychophysics, 62*, 889–899.

Pinto, J. (1994). Human infants' sensitivity to biological motion in point-light cats. *Infant Behavior and Development, 17*, 871.

Pinto, J. (1996). *Developmental changes in infants' perceptions of point-light displays of human gait.* Unpublished doctoral dissertation, University of Virginia, Charlottesville.

Pinto, J., & Shiffrar, M. (1999). Subconfigurations of the human form in the perception of biological motion displays. *Acta Psychologica, 102*, 293–318.

Pinto, J., & Shiffrar, M. (2004). *The visual analysis of biological motion: Insights from comparisons of the perception of human and animal motion.* Manuscript submitted for publication.

Poizner, H., Bellugi, U., & Lutes-Driscoll, V. (1981). Perception of American Sign Language in dynamic point-light displays. *Journal of Experimental Psychology: Human Perception and Performance, 7*, 430–440.

Proffitt, D. R., & Berthenthal, B. I. (1988). Recovering connectivity from moving point-light displays. In W. N. Martin & J. K. Aggarwal (Eds.), *Motion understanding: Robot and human vision* (pp. 297–328). Hingman, MA: Kluwer.

Proffitt, D. R., & Berthenthal, B. I. (1990). Converging operations revisited: Assessing what infants perceive using discrimination measures. *Perception & Psychophysics, 47*, 1–11.

Ramachandran, V. S., & Blakeslee, S. (1998). *Phantoms in the brain.* New York: Harper Collins.

Reed, C. (2002). What is the body schema? In W. Prinz and A. Meltzoff (Eds.), *The imitative mind: Development, evolution, and brain bases* (pp. 233–243). Cambridge: Cambridge University Press.

Reed, C. L., & Farah, M. J. (1995). The psychological reality of the body schema: A test with normal participants. *Journal of Experimental Psychology: Human Perception and Performance, 21*, 334–343.

Rochat, P., & Morgan, R. (1995). Spatial determinants in the perception of self-produced leg movements in 3- to 5-month-old infants. *Developmental Psychology, 31*, 626–636.

Rochat, P., & Striano, T. (1999). Emerging self-exploration by 2-month-old infants. *Developmental Science, 2*, 206–218.

Shiffrar, M., & Freyd, J. J. (1993). Timing and apparent motion path choice with human body photographs. *Psychological Science, 4*, 379–384.

Sirigu, A., Grafman, J., Bressler, K., & Sunderland, T. (1991). Multiple representations contribute to body knowledge processing. *Brain, 114*, 629–642.

Sumi, S. (1984). Upside-down presentation of the Johansson moving light-spot pattern. *Perception, 13*, 283–286.

Thelen, E., Corbetta, D., Kamm, K., Spencer, J. P., Schneider, K., & Zernicke, R. F. (1993). The transition to reaching: Mapping intention and intrinsic dynamics. *Child Development, 64*, 1058–1098.

Thornton, I., Pinto, J., & Shiffrar, M. (1998). The visual perception of human locomotion. *Cognitive Neuropsychology, 15*, 535–552.

Thornton, I. M., Vuong, Q. C., & Bülthoff, H. H. (2003). Last but not least: A chimeric point-light walker. *Perception, 32*, 377–383.

Van den Bos, E., & Jeannerod, M. (2002). Sense of body and sense of action both contribute to self-recognition. *Cognition, 85*, 177–187.

Viviani, P., Baud-Bovy, G., & Redolfi, M. (1997). Perceiving and tracking kinesthetic stimuli: Further evidence of motor-perceptual interactions. *Journal of Experimental Psychology: Human Perception and Performance, 23*, 1232–1252.

Viviani, P., & Stucchi, N. (1992). Motor-perceptual interactions. In G. E. Stelmach & J. Requin (Eds.), *Tutorials in motor behavior, Vol. 2* (pp. 229–248). Oxford: North-Holland.

Werker, J. F. (1989). Becoming a native listener. *American Scientist, 77*, 54–59.

Younger, B. A. (1992). Developmental change in infant categorization: The perception of correlations among facial features. *Child Development, 63*, 1526–1535.

15

Computational Principles for the Recognition of Biological Movements

Model-Based Versus Feature-Based Approaches

Martin A. Giese

1. Introduction

The recognition of body movements is a complex computational problem. Multiple theories about possible underlying computational mechanisms have been discussed in the psychological literature, and in computer vision a variety of technical algorithms for body tracking and human movement recognition have been proposed. However, models for neural processes in the visual cortex must fulfill additional constraints. We discuss two opposing explanations for the recognition of complex body movements: the fitting of kinematic models and an analysis in terms of simple dynamic motion and form features. We present a physiologically plausible neural model that accounts for biological-motion recognition by the analysis of simple form and motion features, which accounts for many known experimental results. We discuss advantages and limitations of the two approaches as models for the cortical processing of biological-movement stimuli. Also we provide some ideas about how the neural model can be extended to account for an influence of motor planning on visual perception.

Biological movements are defined here as the movements of living beings, such as humans and animals. They form a highly important class of visual stimuli and their recognition is crucial for survival and for social interaction in higher species. The recognition of biological movements is a robust capability of the human visual system. This has been demonstrated in classical experiments using strongly impoverished visual stimuli, for example, point-light walkers (Johansson, 1973). *Point-light stimuli* consist of a small number of illuminated dots that move like the joints of a human or an animal. They induce the vivid perceptual impression of human or animal actions (e.g., Dittrich, 1993; Kozlowski & Cutting, 1977; Mather, Radford, & West, 1992). Their perception is sufficiently accurate for the recognition of subtle details like the gender and the identity of walkers (e.g., Beardsworth & Buckner, 1981; Cutting & Kozlowski, 1977). Recognition is possible even from point-light stimuli that are further degraded, for example, by displacing the dots on the skeleton (e.g., Beintema & Lappe, 2002; Dittrich, 1993), by masking with substantial amounts of moving noise dots (Bertenthal & Pinto, 1994; Cutting, Moore, & Morrison, 1988; Thornton, Pinto, & Shiffrar, 1998), or by switching contrast polarity (Ahlström, Blake, & Ahlström, 1997). Even the elimination of individual joints (Mather, Radford, & West, 1992; Pinto & Shiffrar, 1999) or the limitation of the lifetime of the individual dots (Beintema & Lappe, 2002; Neri, Morrone, & Burr, 1998) often does not abolish perception (see chapter 13).

The recognition of normal biological-movement stimuli likely integrates form and motion cues. For instance, subjects can recognize gait patterns from static key frames that show a stick figure in characteristic body postures (Todd, 1983). On the other hand, the recognition of point-light displays seems to suggest that low-level motion information might play an important role in the recognition of such impoverished displays (e.g., Mather, Radford, & West, 1992). However the relevance of form versus motion information for the recognition of point-light stimuli is still a matter of dispute (e.g., Beintema & Lappe, 2002; Giese & Poggio, 2003; Mather, Radford, & West, 1992). Some brain-imaging studies have demonstrated selective activation in specific form-selective areas, like the *fusiform face area* (FFA), during the perception of point-light walkers (Grossman & Blake, 2002), whereas other form-selective areas, for example, the *lateral occipital complex* or the *exstrastriate body area* (EBA) seem not to be selectively activated (Downing et al., 2001; Grossman & Blake, 2002; also see chapter 16 for a more detailed discussion of fMRI results).

The question arises: how does the visual system accomplish the robust recognition of complex movement stimuli, even if they are strongly impoverished? In spite of the growing body of experimental results, the underlying computational principles remain largely unclear. The goal of this chapter is to review different computational explanations and to discuss their relevance with respect to neural implementations in the visual cortex. We will in particular focus on one approach that explains the recognition of biological movements by the analysis of simple form and motion features. A concrete implementation of this computational principle will be given in terms of a physiologically inspired neural model. This model is based on neurally represented learned templates for temporal sequences of complex shapes and optic flow patterns. This suggests a central role of learning in biological-movement recognition.

Finally, it will be discussed how the feature-based approach might be extended in order to account for complex phenomena in the recognition of biological movements, like the influence of attention or internal motor models on motion recognition.

Section 2 in this chapter gives a short overview of computational problems that have to be solved in the context of motion recognition. Section 3 gives a review of different computational solutions that have been proposed in the literature as models for biological systems or in technical applications. Section 4 discusses a number of constraints for biologically plausible implementations. Such constraints can be derived from psychophysical and in particular from neurophysiological experiments. Section 5 sketches a learning-based physio-logically plausible neural model for the recognition of biological movements that is based on the analysis of simple motion and form features. A few example simulations that illustrate the computational performance of this model in comparison with experimental data are presented in section 6. Section 7 dis-cusses limitations of the model and presents some ideas about how this ap-proach might be extended in order to account for top-down effects, like attentional modulation or the influence of motor programs. Concluding remarks can be found in section 8.

2. Computational Problems

The recognition of complex body movements requires the solution of multiple nontrivial computational problems. In order to recognize, for example, a walking human in a natural scene, the following basic problems have to be solved si-multaneously:

a. separating the walker ("figure") from the background scene;
b. determining the position and pose of the walker at a given point in time;
c. determining the movement vectors of individual points of the walker;
d. potentially, recovering the three-dimensional (3D) structure, or at least the depth order of the individual parts of the walker;
e. predicting the movements and positions for future frames of the se-quence. This is particularly important for adding information that is missing because of (self-)occlusion, clutter, or bad quality of the visual images; and
f. classifying the action and estimating the style parameters of the move-ment (e.g., to find out the identity, emotional affect, gender, or speed of the walker).

In contrast to the human brain, none of the existing technical algorithms and theoretical models for motion recognition is suitable for solving all of these problems in a satisfying way. The following section gives an overview of existing technical approaches that provide a solution for at least a subset of these computational problems. This review will be followed by a discussion of the specific constraints of cortical processing that must be taken into account if such algorithms are interpreted as models for explaining motion recognition in the visual cortex.

3. Existing Computational Approaches

Since the 1990s, motion recognition and tracking have been popular topics in computer vision. Accordingly, a large variety of algorithms have been proposed. In this chapter only some key approaches can be briefly sketched (for more extended reviews, see Aggarwal & Cai, 1999; Gavrila, 1999; Moeslund & Granum, 2001). Most existing proposals for computational mechanisms underlying motion recognition can be subsumed under three basic approaches: (1) methods exploiting simple invariants, (2) methods based on explicit body models, and (3) methods based on learned templates for form and motion patterns.

3.1. Exploiting Simple Invariants

A number of early studies tried to recover the link structure or even the 3D shape of walkers from the two-dimensional movements in point-light displays exploiting different types of invariants of articulated movements (e.g., Chen & Lee, 1992; Hoffman & Flinchbaugh, 1982; Rashid, 1980; Webb & Aggarwal, 1982). A simple invariant is given by the distances between points on the same limb, which typically varies less than the distances between dots on different limbs. More accurate approaches try to model specific constraints of the 3D movements of rigidly connected pairs of dots over multiple frames, for example, assuming that the motion is planar, or a rotation around a single axis. Graph optimization algorithms have been successfully applied in order to find a consistent connectivity graph for individual frames or over the whole image sequence. The major problem with these methods is that they assume that a number of trajectories of joints or control points are already known to the system, without specifying how they can be extracted or tracked from real video sequences. The robust extraction of such control points is computationally very difficult, in particular in the presence of clutter.

3.2. Model-Based Approaches

Since the classical work by Marr and Vaina (1982), a large number of methods for the tracking and recognition of biological movements have been proposed that are based on two- or three-dimensional human body models. Marr originally proposed the use of kinematic 3D models that consist of cylindrical primitives (Marr & Vaina, 1982; Vaina & Bennour, 1985) as an intermediate level of representation. The final goal was the extraction of a symbolic description of human body movements. Other approaches model the human body with different 3D form primitives, for example, spheres or superquadrics (e.g., O'Rourke & Badler, 1980) and 2D patch models (e.g., Cham & Rehg, 1999; Ju, Black, & Yacoob, 1996). The parameters of these body models are optimized for an optimal fitting of the original image sequence. Different optimization algorithms have been proposed, for example, the propagation of constraints between different body parts and nonlinear optimization techniques. A large class of approaches combines articulated 2D or 3D models of the human body with dynamic predictive filtering techniques (e.g., Kalman filters) for the estimation of the model parameters (e.g., Rehg & Kanade, 1995; Rohr, 1997; Wachter & Nagel, 1999). A more recent advance is the use of predictive filtering techniques (particle filters), which provide a more appropriate statistical modeling of multiple hypotheses and ambiguities during the tracking process (e.g., Blake & Isard, 1998; Cham & Rehg, 1999).

A few approaches for the tracking of facial movements and facial expression recognition even use physical models, including muscles that are fitted to video sequences (e.g., Essa & Pentland, 1997; Terzopoulos & Waters, 1993). It has also been discussed that the recognition of actions in general might exploit internal control models that realize an internal simulation of the action, potentially providing a basis for imitation learning (e.g., Schaal, 1999; Wolpert, Doya, & Kawato, 2003). The determination of the relevant dynamic variables of such control models (e.g., joint angles) requires typically the reconstruction of the 3D configuration of the human body from image sequences. The robust solution of this computational problem is quite difficult for articulated objects, like the human body.

3.3. Learned Templates for Form and Motion Patterns

Another class of approaches for the analysis of complex body movements exploits simple motion and form features, which can be easily extracted from video sequences. One class of approaches uses simple motion templates. For example, walkers can be localized by detecting periodic motion (e.g., Allmen & Dyer, 1993; Polana & Nelson, 1994). More elaborate approaches use more specific learned templates for the spatial or temporal characteristics of movements (Niyogi & Adelson, 1994; Shavit & Jepson, 1993). Another possibility is to model complex movements in phase space by estimating functions that characterize mutual dependency between the positions of different points on the human body (Campbell & Bobick, 1995).

Other approaches exploit optic flow patterns. For example, facial expressions induce very characteristic optic flow patterns, which can be easily classified using different techniques (Essa & Pentland, 1997; Rosenblum, Yacoob, & Davis, 1996). It has been shown that the required motion templates need not be very accurate. For example, the reliable classification of full-body actions is possible by just matching the spatial shape of the regions in the image sequences where local motion is present or changes over time (Davis & Bobick, 1997).

To associate information over multiple frames, different techniques have been proposed. Hidden Markov models (HMMs) are a widely applied standard technique to define spatiotemporal templates. Temporal sequences of form or motion features are modeled as random variables that depend on nonobservable dynamic hidden state variables (e.g., Bobick, 1997; Bregler, 1997; Starner & Pentland, 1995). The statistics of these variables and the transition probabilities between different states can be learned from training examples. Another class of efficient technical solutions combines learned shape models (e.g., splines) with predictive filtering techniques, like Kalman or particle filters (Ahmad et al., 1997; Black & Jepson, 1998; Blake & Isard, 1998; Wren et al., 1997).

More recent work combines feature tracking with Bayesian inference on graph models using dynamic programming techniques. It was demonstrated that this technique is suitable for the labeling of the joints of human bodies in video sequences with clutter (Song et al., 2001). The behavior of certain classes of Bayesian networks, including predictive filters and hidden Markov models, has been related to recurrent neural networks (Rao, 2004; Rao & Ballard, 1997). This raises the question of whether methods that are based on Bayesian inference can be implemented with real cortical neurons (Lee & Mumford, 2003).

Probably most similar to motion recognition in biological systems are approaches based on neural networks. Neural networks have been used for the recognition of facial expressions (e.g., Rosenblum, Yacoob, & Davis, 1996) as well as the recognition of whole body movements (e.g., Goddard, 1992). Temporal order can be encoded in laterally connected neural networks with and without delays (Goddard, 1992; Lin et al., 1999; Xie & Giese, 2002). Different computational principles in technical neural network models for motion recognition might also be relevant for the biological systems.

4. Constraints of Cortical Processing

This broad spectrum of technical solutions shows that many algorithms exist for solving computational problems that are associated with motion recognition. Models for motion recognition in the brain must fulfill additional constraints that result from the anatomical and physiological properties of cortical neurons. Only algorithms that have a plausible implementation in terms of real neurons are finally suitable as explanation for the information processing in the brain. Instead of just assuming that the brain solves the relevant computational problems "in some way," a serious computational theory has also to take such constraints into account. Several constraints that follow from experimental results on biological-motion recognition and cortical neurons are discussed next.

4.1. Limited Cortical Processing Speed

Cortical neurons in the visual cortex respond to visual stimuli typically with a delay of between 30 and more than 100 ms (e.g., Nowak & Bullier, 1998; Schmolesky et al., 1998). Maximum information about complex form stimuli is conveyed by the responses of IT neurons between 100 and 200 ms after stimulus presentation (Rolls & Tovée, 1995). Such delays limit the processing speed and by this the amount of possible "iterations" of possible computational mechanisms before recognition of movement patterns is achieved. Given the relatively short recognition times for biological movements (see below), this makes methods that require complex recursive search or optimization algorithms very unlikely as explanations of movement recognition in the brain.

4.2. Short Latency of Selective Responses

In spite of the apparent complexity of biological-movement stimuli, recognition is possible with very short presentation times of below 300 ms (Johansson, 1976). This is consistent with electrophysiological data in monkeys, which show selective responses of some biological motion–selective neurons in the superior temporal sulcus (STS) after less than 200 ms (Oram & Perrett, 1996). Fast processing of biological movements is also suggested by MEG studies that show selective activity differences in relevant areas, like the superior temporal sulcus, less than 200 ms after stimulus presentation (Nishitani & Hari, 2002; Pavlova et al., 2004). This result parallels similar observations for the recognition of complex static pictures. For very short presentation times (e.g., 20 ms), selective neural responses arise in the temporal cortex in about 150 ms after stimulus presentation, not substantially exceeding the sum of synaptic delays from the retina to the inferotemporal cortex (Keysers et al., 2001; Thorpe, Fize, & Marlot, 1996). This result has been interpreted as support for a fast computational mechanism for the processing of shapes that is predominantly based on feed-forward connectivity, since this fast processing time does not leave much time for the relaxation of sophisticated feedback mechanisms (e.g., Riesenhuber & Poggio, 1999; Thorpe, Delorme, & van Rullen, 2001). It has however been argued that this low-latency response might reflect a response to salient low-level properties of the stimulus rather than a response that reflects detailed discrimination between complex shapes (Johnson & Olshausen, 2003).

The fact that the visual system responds selectively to biological-motion stimuli within short presentation times (much shorter than a full period of a gait cycle) rules out mechanisms that detect periodic patterns or those that are based on Fourier analyses of cyclic patterns, like gaits. The short response times also make it unlikely that the generic mechanism of visual motion recognition is the fitting or alignment of complex kinematic or dynamic internal models with the visual stimulus. Such alignment requires not only the accurate estimation of scaling and projection parameters between the model and the retinal coordinate frame, but also the determination of the correct initial condition (or posture) for the alignment with the image. Methods that are suitable for an automatic initialization of such models have been proposed (e.g., Rosales et al., 2001). However initial pose estimation is quite difficult in clutter. The coupled estimation of the alignment transformation and initial body posture requires a complex closed-loop optimization for two parameter sets. At least in technical systems, so far this problem has never been solved without many iterations. This computational constraint seems to be difficult to reconcile with the neural response delays in the STS, which are of the order of magnitude of the synaptic delays from the retina to this structure (Oram & Perrett, 1996).

4.3. Hierarchical Structure of the Visual Cortex With Two Pathways

It is a well-established neuroanatomical result that the visual pathway is organized within (at least) two hierarchically processing streams, which process predominantly shape information and position and motion information (Felleman & van Essen, 1991; Goodale & Milner, 1992; Ungerleider & Mishkin, 1982). Both pathways are organized hierarchically, and the complexity of the stimuli that are adequate for eliciting neural responses increases gradually toward higher visual areas (Felleman & van Essen, 1991; Saito, 1993). At the same time, the size of the receptive fields of the neurons increases from less than 1 deg to large parts of the visual field. Neurons in some higher levels of the hierarchy are also characterized by gradual invariance against stimulus position and scale (e.g., Logothetis, Pauls, & Poggio, 1995; Orban et al., 1992).

Many technical algorithms for the analysis of complex form or motion features are based on similar hierarchical architectures. Starting with simple features that can be easily derived from images, for example, by filtering, more complex features are derived by combination. Such architectures underlie in particular many neural and Bayesian network models for the analysis of biological motion and static shapes.

4.4. View Dependence

Biological-motion recognition is strongly dependent on stimulus view and orientation. Point-light walkers are, for example, much more difficult to recognize when they are rotated in the image plane (e.g., Pavlova & Sokolov, 2000; Sumi 1984; Troje, 2003; Verfaillie, 2000; Verfaillie, de Troy, & van Rensbergen, 1994) or in depth (e.g., Bülthoff, Bülthoff, & Sinha, 1998). Dependence of activity in biological motion–sensitive areas on display orientation has also been found in fMRI experiments (Grossman & Blake, 2001). View dependence is also a well-established property of the representation of complex static shapes (e.g., Logothetis, Pauls, & Poggio, 1995; Tarr & Bülthoff, 1998).

View dependence points against algorithms that are based on a three-dimensional kinematic or physical model that is matched to the visual stimulus by undoing the projection transformation. There is no a priori reason that such alignment mechanisms should fail for unfamiliar views of biological movements. Algorithms that are based on the learning of motion and form features predict view-dependent responses (cf. Tarr & Bülthoff, 1998). An analysis in terms of motion and form features in a retinal frame of reference also seems compatible with the psychophysical result that view dependence in biological-motion recognition seems to be dependent on egocentric rather than external coordinates (Troje, 2003).

4.5. Lack of Dependency on Available 3D Information

Interestingly, biological-movement recognition seems not to exploit all available 3D structure information. This was demonstrated in an experiment by Bülthoff, Bülthoff, and Sinha (1998), who brought the stereoscopically suggested veridical depth information of point-light stimuli in conflict with the 3D structure that was suggested by the 2D projection of the stimulus dots. Systematically, their subjects ignored the veridical depth information in favor of interpretations that were compatible with familiar body postures during walking, which matched the 2D projections in the stimuli.

This result seems incompatible with a recognition mechanism that is based on the reconstruction of the true 3D structure, in the sense of a structure-from-motion problem. Rather, this result points toward recognition in terms of familiar, potentially learned two-dimensional patterns (Verfaillie, 2000).

4.6. The Visual Cortex Works on Real Movies or Image Sequences

The primary input of the visual system is given in the form of continuously varying brightness distributions or image sequences. Theories that claim to be biologically relevant need to account for the question of how potentially relevant features can be extracted from real image sequences. This implies that theories that are based on features, like 3D joint trajectories, which are very difficult to extract from real image sequences might have no biological relevance—even if they are quantitatively consistent with psychophysical data sets. The brain might just not be able to estimate the 3D positions of joints with sufficient accuracy.

5. Physiologically Plausible Neural Model

The following sections describe a neural model that tries to take the constraints discussed above into account. In addition, this model reproduces a variety of experimental facts about the recognition of biological movements. More detailed descriptions of the model and additional simulations are described in Giese (2000), Giese and Poggio (2003), and Giese (2004). The model is based only on computational mechanisms with an obvious implementation in terms of real cortical neurons and is meant as proof of plausibility, showing that a variety of results in biological-motion recognition can be accounted for in a quantitatively consistent manner by the same neural architecture. The model was tested with normal full-body human action stimuli, point-light walkers, and a variety of other degraded stimuli from the experimental literature. We tried as far as possible to match the receptive field sizes and tuning properties with real physiological results. However, the model in its present form is not detailed enough for a very precise fitting of individual physiological data sets. The model makes a variety of simplifications and has a number of shortcomings, some of which are discussed in section 7.

   The model is based on a small number of key assumptions that match well-established neurophysiological facts:

   a. Analysis occurs within two pathways that are specialized for the processing of form and motion information.
   b. Each pathway consists of a hierarchy of neural detectors that are selective for features with increasing complexity along the hierarchy. Together with the complexity of the extracted features, the invariance of the detectors against translation and scaling increases along the hierarchy.
   c. Complex movement patterns are represented in terms of learned prototypical example patterns. These patterns are encoded by neural units that are selective for instantaneous complex shapes ("snapshots") and optic flow patterns that are characteristic for biological movements.
   d. Biological-movement perception is sequence selective. Both pathways of the model contain a simple neural mechanism that makes them selective for the temporal order of the stimulus frames.

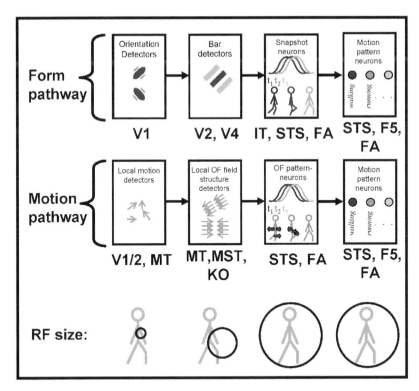

Figure 15.1. Overview of the model with two pathways for the processing of form and optic flow information. Abbreviations indicate potentially corresponding areas in the monkey and human cortex. Approximate sizes of the receptive fields compared to a walker stimulus are indicated below. In the cortex, the two pathways converge at the level of the superior temporal sulcus (STS) (further abbreviations: IT: inferotemporal cortex; FA: fusiform and occipital face area; F5: premotor cortex). Modified from Giese (2004) with kind permission of Springer Science and Business Media. *See color insert.*

Figure 15.1 illustrates the basic architecture of the model, which mimics the functional division of the visual cortex into a ventral and a dorsal processing stream (Felleman & van Essen, 1991; Goodale & Milner, 1992; Ungerleider & Mishkin, 1982). The model consists of two parallel processing streams that are specialized for the analysis of form and optic flow information. Consistent with electrophysiological data (Morel & Bullier, 1990; Saleem et al., 2000), these two pathways converge at the level that corresponds to the superior temporal sulcus. In the monkey and the human brain, the two processing streams are connected at multiple levels (e.g., Felleman & van Essen, 1991; Kourtzi & Kanwisher, 2000; Sereno et al., 2002).

For evaluating the contributions of form and motion information separately, in some simulations we duplicated the highest hierarchy level of the model, resulting in two completely separated pathways for the processing of motion and form information. In this way, we tested if certain perceptual tasks could be accomplished exploiting form or motion information alone.

5.1. Form Pathway

The form pathway in the model analyzes biological movements by the recognition of sequences of body shapes. The neural architecture for the recognition of shapes resembles many other physiologically plausible models for the recognition of static shapes (e.g., Perrett & Oram, 1993; Riesenhuber & Poggio, 1999; Rolls & Milward, 2000). The form pathway comprises four hierarchy levels with form features of increasing complexity. Receptive field sizes are indicated in Figure 15.1. More details about the individual detectors and their motivation by physiological results can be found in Giese and Poggio (2003).

The first level of the form pathway consists of local *orientation detectors* that are modeled by Gabor filters with two different spatial scales and eight different orientations. Gabor filters are a well-established model for simple cells in the primary visual cortex (area V1) (Hubel & Wiesel, 1962; Jones & Palmer, 1987).

The second hierarchy level of the model consists of orientation detectors that are partially position- and scale-invariant (invariant *bar detectors*). Such invariance has been reported for complex cells in the primary visual cortex (Hubel & Wiesel, 1962) and for neurons in areas V2 and V4 (Gallant et al., 1996; Hegdé & van Essen, 2000).

A simple neural implementation of position and scale invariance is the pooling of the responses of neural detectors with the same preferred orientation but different receptive field positions and spatial scales (e.g., Fukushima, 1980; Perrett & Oram, 1993). Recent theoretical studies show that it is critical that pooling is accomplished by a maximum-like operation rather than by simple summation in order to achieve high degrees of feature selectivity and invariance for the pooled responses (e.g., Mel & Fieser, 2000; Riesenhuber & Poggio, 1999). Maximum computation has been found in V4 neurons in macaques (Gawne & Martin, 2002) and in cat visual cortex (Lampl et al., 2004) and can be implemented with several simple physiologically plausible circuits (Yu, Giese, & Poggio, 2002).

The third hierarchy level of the form pathway contains detectors that are selective for complex shapes, which correspond to body configurations that are characteristic for snapshots from biological-movement sequences. It is assumed that these *snapshot neurons* are similar to view-tuned neurons, which have been described in area IT of monkeys and which respond selectively for natural and artificial complex shapes (Logothetis & Sheinberg, 1996; Tanaka, 1996). Consistent with earlier models for stationary object recognition (Riesenhuber & Poggio, 1999), the snapshot neurons are modeled by radial basis functions (e.g.,

Girosi, Jones, & Poggio, 1995) that are trained with the output vectors from the previous level for snapshots from training sequences showing biological movements. Each training sequence was represented by 21 snapshots. The snapshot neurons were embedded in a recurrent neural network that makes their responses sequence selective (see section 5.3).

Neurons that are selective for body configurations have been described in the STS of monkeys (e.g., Oram & Perrett, 1996). In fMRI studies, selective activation for human bodies has been found in the STS (e.g., Bonda et al., 1996; Grossman & Blake, 2002; Vaina et al., 2001), the extrastriate body area (EBA) (Downing et al., 2001), and the occipital and fusiform face area (abbreviated FA in Figure 15.1) (Grossman & Blake, 2002).

The highest hierarchy level of the model is formed by *motion pattern neurons* that temporally smooth and summate the activity of all snapshot neurons that represent the same movement pattern (for the model version with a fusion of pathways, the motion pattern neurons integrate also signals from the motion pathway; see section 5.2). Temporal smoothing is accomplished by a leaky integrator with a time constant of 150 ms. Each motion pattern neuron encodes a complete motion sequence or action: "walking," "dancing," "boxing," etc. Such "grandmother cells" are certainly an oversimplification, and it seems more likely that biological movements are encoded in terms of a sparse population code.

Neurons encoding complete biological movements and actions have been found in different parts of the STS of monkeys (e.g., Oram & Perrett, 1996; Perrett et al., 1985). Functional-imaging studies suggest that in humans similar neurons might exist in the STS (e.g., Bonda et al., 1996; Pelphrey et al., 2003; Vaina et al., 2001) and in the fusiform and the occipital face area (Grossman & Blake, 2002). Another possible site for neurons encoding whole actions is the premotor cortex (area F5) in monkeys and homologous areas in humans (Rizzolatti, Fogassi, & Gallese, 2001).

5.2. Motion Pathway

The motion pathway of the model also has a hierarchical structure (cf. Saito, 1993). It consists of neural detectors that are specialized for the analysis of optic flow information. The first level of the motion pathway consists of *local motion (energy) detectors*. Many neurophysiologically plausible models for such detectors have been proposed in the literature (e.g., Simoncelli & Heeger, 1998; Smith & Snowden, 1994). To save simulation time, the optic flow for the stimuli discussed in this chapter was directly computed from the stimulus geometry in subsequent frames. The optic flow was then converted into motion energy signals assuming receptive fields with physiologically realistic parameters. Additionally, we ran tests showing that the model works also with optic flow fields derived from gray-level pictures using a gradient-based optic flow algorithm. Local motion extraction in the cortex is accomplished by direction-selective neurons in the primary visual cortex (in particular, areas V1 and V3) and component motion–selective neurons in area MT (see Smith & Snowden, 1994, for a review).

The second level of the motion pathway consists of neural detectors with medium-sized receptive fields that analyze the local structure of the optic flow patterns that are generated by biological movements. Two types of such *local optic flow detectors* are included in the model. One class is selective for *translation flow* with different directions and slow and fast speeds. Their responses are computed by summation of the responses of local motion detectors with similar direction and speed selectivity. Neurons with similar properties have been found in area MT of monkeys. The tuning properties of the model neurons are in the range that is typical for MT neurons (Smith & Snowden, 1994).

The second class of local optic flow detectors is selective for *motion edges* (horizontal and vertical). Their output signals are computed by combining the responses of two adjacent subfields with opposite direction preference in a multiplicative way. Neurons with such opponent motion selectivity have been found in multiple areas in the dorsal-processing stream, including area MT (e.g., Allman, Miezin, & McGuinness, 1985; Born, 2000; Xiao et al., 1995), area MSTd (e.g., Saito, 1993; Tanaka, Fukuda, & Saito, 1989), and area MSTl (e.g., Eifuku & Wurtz, 1998). Likely they are also present in the *kinetic occipital area* (KO; by other authors also classified as V3B or part of LO) in humans (Orban et al., 1995). The receptive field size of the motion edge detectors was in the range that is typical for neurons in areas MT and MSTl.

The third level of the motion pathway consists of *optic flow pattern neurons* that are equivalent to the snapshot neurons in the form pathway. They are selective for complex optic flow patterns that arise during biological movements, like the characteristic opponent movements of opposite arms and legs during walking. The receptive fields of these neurons are large (about 8 deg), and they integrate information over the whole biological-movement stimulus. Like the snapshot neurons, the motion pattern neurons are modeled by Gaussian radial basis functions that receive their inputs from the previous level. Their centers are trained with optic flow patterns from example movement sequences (21 centers per stored pattern). The motion pattern neurons are also laterally connected, resulting in sequence selectivity (see following section). Real neurons with similar properties might be found in the STS, in the fusiform and occipital face area (e.g., Bonda et al., 1996; Grossman & Blake, 2002; Vaina et al., 2001). For the model with a fusion of the pathways on the highest hierarchy level, the output signals of the snapshot and the optic flow pattern neurons are summed and temporally smoothed by common motion pattern neurons (see previous section). For the model with separate pathways, a separate set of motion pattern neurons for the motion pathway was introduced.

5.3. Sequence Selectivity

Biological-movement recognition is strongly sequence selective. If, for example, the frames of a movie showing a person walking are scrambled in time, a stimulus results that is not perceived as walking any more. This is true even though the new movie contains the same snapshots or body shapes as the original one.

In the model, sequence selectivity is implemented at the level of the snapshot neurons and the optic flow pattern neurons. These neurons are embedded in networks with asymmetric lateral connections. Each neuron excites other neurons in the network that encode temporally immediate subsequent stimulus configurations (Figure 15.2) and inhibit the other neurons. For an adequate profile and strength of the lateral connections, significant activity arises only when the feed-forward input signals of the neurons arise in the right temporal order. In this case, the network stabilizes a propagating activation pulse with high amplitude, since its feed-forward input and the recurrent activation interact in a synergistic way. If the input signals arise in the wrong temporal order, competition arises between the feed-forward inputs and the recurrent signals in the network, resulting in a solution with very small amplitude (Mineiro & Zipser, 1998; Xie & Giese, 2002). The appropriate connection strength for the lateral connections can be learned by a simple, physiologically plausible, time-dependent Hebbian learning rule (Jastorff & Giese, 2004; Rao, 2004).

This mechanism is only one of many possible physiologically plausible implementations of sequence selectivity. The proposed recurrent mechanism leads to short response latencies (less than 200 ms), consistent with electrophysiological data from neurons in the STS (Oram & Perrett, 1996), and is suitable for recognition with small presentation times, matching psychophysical observations (Johansson, 1976).

6. Selected Simulation Results

In the following, a selection of simulation results is presented that illustrates how some of the computational problems described in section 2 can be solved using the physiologically plausible model described in the preceding section. The results are selected from a much larger set of simulations that demonstrate the consistency of the model with a number of key results from psychophysical, electrophysiological, and imaging studies (see Giese, 2004; Giese & Poggio,

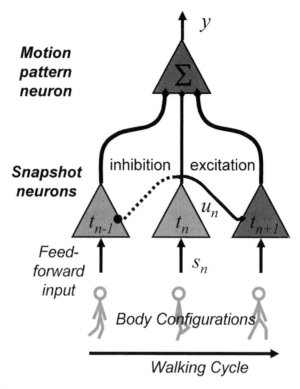

Figure 15.2. Asymmetric recurrent connections between the neurons result in responses that are strongly sequence-selective. The snapshot neurons that encode the body shape at time t_n activate neurons encoding immediately subsequent configurations (e.g., at t_{n+1}) and inhibit the other snapshot neurons. The outputs of the snapshot neurons (and the optic flow pattern neurons) encoding the same motion patterns are summed and temporally smoothed by the corresponding motion pattern neurons. Modified from Giese (2004) with kind permission of Springer Science and Business Media. *See color insert.*

2003, for further details). Similar to the existing technical solutions, the proposed neural model also does not provide a complete solution of all of the discussed computational problems.

6.1. High Pattern Selectivity

Biological-motion recognition is highly selective and allows not only the coarse categorization of different actions, but also the extraction of subtle details. Subjects can recognize familiar people, gender, and emotional affects from moving point-light stimuli (e.g., Cutting & Kozlowski, 1977; Dittrich et al., 1996; Hill, Jinno, & Johnston, 2003; Kozlowski & Cutting, 1977; Pollick et al.,

2002). In computer vision, it has been shown that the analysis of simple image features can be sufficient to recognize people from gait (e.g., Huang, Harris, & Nixon, 1998; Little & Boyd, 1998). In a similar way, the motion and form features extracted by the proposed physiologically inspired model are sufficient for recognition of identity from gait.

Interestingly, this selectivity can be accomplished with either pathway (form or motion) alone. This is illustrated in Figure 15.3, which shows simulations of the model with separate motion and form pathways. The model was trained with the locomotion pattern "walking" of different actors presented as stick figures (M, X, A, and C, two males and two females). The model was then tested with multiple other recordings of walking from the same actors. Only the patterns M1, . . . , and C1, . . . , were used for training. The different line styles correspond to the activities of motion pattern neurons trained with different actors. For both pathways, the motion pattern neurons show excellent discrimination between the gaits of different actors. For this training set, each neuron is active for only one actor. However, the neurons generalize over the multiple repetitions of the gait executed by the same actor. This illustrates that the model, in spite of its simple structure, achieves a substantial level of selectivity.

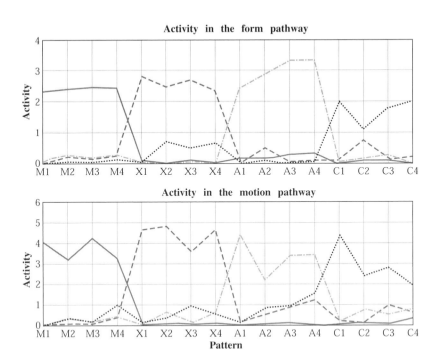

Figure 15.3. Activity of motion pattern neurons of the two pathways (motion and form) after training with the gaits of four actors (M, X, A, and C). Different line styles indicate different motion pattern neurons. *See color insert.*

Additional simulations, reported in Giese and Poggio (2003) and Giese (2004), show that the model, after appropriate training, can also robustly categorize different actions, with sufficiently broad tuning also abstracting from the identity of the actor. Using stimuli generated by motion morphing (Giese & Poggio, 2002), it is possible to measure quantitatively the generalization regimes of different movement categories in psychophysical experiments (Giese & Lappe, 2002). Comparing these experimental results with the model, we found that the size of the generalization fields of individual categories of gaits are matched even quantitatively by the model (Giese & Poggio, 2003).

These results imply that an analysis of form and motion features in image sequences using rather simple neural detectors can account for the psychophysically observed selectivity of biological-movement recognition from image sequences. In particular, this simulation shows that motion or form features alone are sufficient to achieve a high degree of selectivity. This implies that relatively subtle details of biological movements can be extracted from image sequences without the explicit estimation of 3D trajectories, or even the fitting of kinematic or dynamic models. The visual system might thus not have to solve this hard computational problem.

6.2. View Dependence

View dependence is a natural consequence of the representation used by the model, which is based on two-dimensional templates for body shapes and optic flow patterns. As described in section 5, the model contains neural mechanisms that achieve scale and position invariance by nonlinear pooling. It contains no such mechanisms for making responses invariant against 2D rotations of the stimuli in the image plane. Therefore, the responses of the motion pattern neurons in the model are view dependent and vary with rotations of the stimulus in the image plane and in depth.

This view dependence is illustrated in Figure 15.4, which shows the activity of a motion pattern neuron that has been trained with a stick figure walking rightward. Activities are shown for the same stimulus rotated in the image plane (Figure 15.4a) and for the same stimulus rotated in depth (Figure 15.4b). In both cases, the activity of the model neuron decays gradually with the angle between training and test view. In panel a, the dark bars indicate the maximum response of the neuron for a number of distractor stimuli. Gray bars indicate the response to the (rotated) walker stimulus. The range of 2D rotations for which recognition of the walker is still possible matches about the range observed in psychophysical experiments (Pavlova & Sokolov, 2000). The tuning with respect to rotations in depth matches quantitatively the electrophysiological recordings by Perrett et al. (1985) as shown in panel b. For the

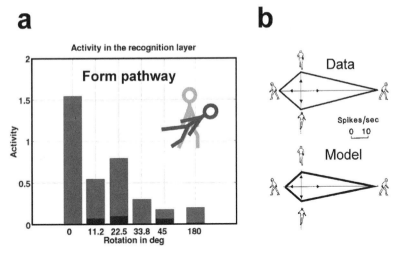

Figure 15.4. View dependence of the neural activity of motion pattern neurons in the form pathway. (a) Activation of a motion pattern neuron trained with walking strongly decreases when the test view (gray stick figure) is rotated against the training view (dark stick figure). (b) Similar view dependence is observed if walkers are rotated in depth. The *upper panel* shows the activity of a biological movement–selective neuron in area TPO in the STS for different directions of walking (adapted from Perrett et al., 1985). The *lower panel* shows the dependence of the (normalized) activity of a motion pattern neuron (form pathway). *See color insert.*

motion pattern neurons in the motion pathway, very similar results are obtained. The view tuning observed in biological motion–selective neurons resembles the view dependence that has been described for shape-selective neurons in area IT (Logothetis, Pauls, & Poggio, 1995; Tarr & Bülthoff, 1998).

6.3. Processing of Strongly Degraded Stimuli

An astonishing property of the recognition of biological movements is its high robustness against degradation of the stimuli. This is impressively shown by the classical experiments by Johansson (1973), who demonstrated that robust action recognition is possible with point-light stimuli that consist only of a small number of dots that move like the joints of a moving person. In a number of subsequent studies, experimenters degraded point-light stimuli even further, for example, by displacing the dots from the joints (e.g., Cutting, 1981; Dittrich, 1993), removing individual dots (Mather, Radford, & West, 1992; Pinto & Shiffrar, 1999), limiting the lifetime of individual dots (Neri, Morrone, & Burr, 1998), or even by reassigning the dots to new positions on the skeleton in every frame (Beintema & Lappe, 2002). Even strong degradations of the stimuli often do not abolish recognition. This fact has led to a variety of speculations about how the visual system might reconstruct the missing information, for example, by collecting position information over many frames or by fitting kinematic models.

The pattern-matching mechanisms of the proposed model are much simpler, and one might ask if it is possible to account for the recognition of point-light stimuli with these simple mechanisms at all. In particular, our learning-based model would have to account for the fact that completely naïve subjects recognize point-light stimuli without any prior training. If recognition of biological motion is really based on learned templates, this implies that the representation would have to generalize spontaneously from trained, normal, full-body stimuli to point-light stimuli, without additional training.

The time courses in Figure 15.5a show the activities of the motion pattern neurons of the form and motion pathways of the model (with separated pathways) after training with a full-body stick figure walking (solid curves). The dashed curves indicate the responses of the same neurons for a point-light walker, and the dashed-dotted curves show the responses for full-body distractor stimuli. The model makes an interesting prediction: the neural model can recognize point-light stimuli, but substantial activation arises only in the motion pathway. This activity is selective for the motion patterns, as shown by the fact that the responses to the distractor stimuli are much smaller. This predicts the lack of selective activation in predominantly form-selective neural structures for point-light stimuli. This prediction seems consistent with a number of fMRI studies that failed to find selectivity for the holistic structure of biological motion patterns for point-light stimuli in form-selective areas, like the lateral occipital complex (LOC) and the extrastriate body part area (EBA) (Downing et al., 2001; Grossman & Blake, 2002). Activation differences between normal and scrambled point-light walkers have been found in the form-selective fusiform and occipital face areas (Grossman & Blake, 2002). More detailed fMRI adaptation studies, however, failed to show pattern-specific adaptation in this area (Jastorff, Giese, & Kourtzi, in press). More experimental work will be required to clarify the precise role of this area in biological-motion perception.

Additional simulations show that the recognition performance of the model is only weakly reduced when the dots of the walker are displaced from the joints. Also, with a limited lifetime of the dots, the model achieves a certain level of performance. A particularly difficult test stimulus for the prediction above was developed by Beintema and Lappe (2002). For their point-light stimulus, new positions on the skeleton were assigned to the dots of the walker in every frame. Subjects still were able to recognize biological movements and to determine the walking direction from these strongly degraded stimuli. By the reassignment of dot positions, the local motion information of the dots is perturbed, making it questionable whether such stimuli can be recognized on the basis of first-order motion mechanisms at all.

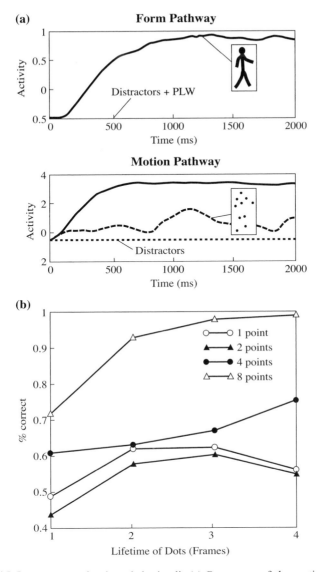

Figure 15.5. Responses for degraded stimuli. (a) Responses of the motion pattern neurons in the form pathway (*top panel*) and the motion pathway (*bottom panel*) for full-body stimuli (solid lines) and for point-light walker (PLW) stimuli (dashed lines). The maximum response for distractors is indicated by the dashed-dotted line (modified from Giese & Poggio, 2003). (b) Correct responses for the discrimination between rightward and leftward walking based on the responses in the motion pathway for strongly degraded point-light walker stimuli. The stimulus dots have limited lifetimes, and their positions are reassigned randomly on the skeleton after their lifetimes have expired. Even though this manipulation reduces the local motion information in the stimulus, a substantial amount of correct detections can be accomplished purely based on local motion information (adapted from Casile & Giese, 2003).

Quantitative simulations using only the motion pathway of our model show, however, that local motion information is sufficient. Figure 15.5b shows the probability of correct responses obtained with our model for the discrimination between rightward and leftward walking. The number of stimulus dots and the lifetime of the dots were varied (Casile & Giese, 2003). In this case, the model was trained with point-light walkers in order to simulate well-trained observers (as in the corresponding experiment by Beintema & Lappe, 2002). Slightly lower correct response rates were obtained when the model was trained with full-body stimuli, simulating observers who are naïve with respect to point-light stimuli. For stimuli with at least four dots the simulation with the model even reaches the performance levels of real human subjects (Casile & Giese, 2005).

The simulation shows that, in spite of the degradation of the motion information by the random update of the point positions, recognition of walking direction is possible based on simple motion-based mechanisms. This explanation is computationally much simpler than the fitting of complex articulated models to the random point positions. Skeleton fitting requires the solution of a nontrivial correspondence problem: points of the stimulus have to be assigned to a priori unknown positions on the skeleton. In particular, in the presence of clutter, this requires a search over a very large hypothesis space, since neither the position nor the posture of the skeleton is a priori known. In technical systems, such search problems have been solved using techniques like *dynamic programming*, which have no obvious neural implementation (Sigal et al., 2003; Song, Goncalves, & Perrona, 2003).

6.4. Fast Processing

The time courses in Figure 15.5a show also that selective activation of the motion pattern neurons rises very fast, in less than 300 ms. The model reproduces thus the experimental observation in psychophysical experiments (Johansson, 1976) that very short stimulus presentation times, below 300 ms, are sufficient for recognition of biological motion. This is also consistent with the electrophysiological observation that the responses of some biological motion–selective neurons in the STS have latencies of less than 200 ms (Oram & Perrett, 1996). In the model, this fast recognition is explained by the fact that the activity wave in the recurrent neural networks of the snapshot and optic flow pattern neurons is formed even when only a small sub-sequence from a full walking cycle is presented. The quantitative simulation shows that, with the given parameters of the nonlinear recurrent network, fast responses to stimuli can be obtained without abolishing the sequence selectivity of the responses. For many explanations that are based on a closed-loop optimization of complex internal models with many degrees of freedom, such fast response times are difficult to achieve, because the search of the configuration space of the model requires sufficient time for optimization of the model parameters.

6.5. Robustness in Clutter

Biological-movement recognition is not only highly robust against substantial degradation of the stimuli, but also against motion clutter, that is, background motion that is not related to the action. This has been shown in masking studies that tested subjects with point-light walkers that were embedded in moving background dots (e.g., Cutting, Moore, & Morrison, 1988; Thornton, Pinto, & Shiffrar, 1998). Subjects are able to detect point-light walkers in substantial amounts of noise dots. This is even true for scrambled walker noise, that is, when the noise dots move like points of the walker, but have random position offsets. This raises the question of how the dots of the walker can be separated from the moving background dots, potentially resulting in a segmentation of the walker (as a figure) from the background. Computer vision algorithms have been proposed that accomplish such segmentation by a stochastic search over different possible groupings of the dots into walker figure and background. Since the set of possible groupings is extremely large, this search has to be restricted by additional constraints (e.g., Rashid, 1980). The proposed model has no such segmentation mechanism. This raises the question of whether it can recognize masked point-light stimuli at all.

Interestingly, the model is quite robust against moving noise dots in the background. This is illustrated in Figure 15.6, which shows the activity of two motion pattern neurons that have been trained with (full-body) walking rightward and walking leftward stimuli, and tested with point-light walkers that were embedded in different numbers of randomly moving background dots. Up to almost 30 background dots, the activities of the two neurons are still substantially different, implying that a discrimination of walking direction would be possible based on the neuron responses. Psychophysical results are even better since subjects can use attentional mechanisms to narrow down the region in which they search for the walker, or for specific subconfigurations of dots (Cavanagh, Labianca, & Thornton, 2001). Such top-down mechanisms are not implemented in the present form of the model (cf. section 7). However, it seems nontrivial that without segmentation, such a high robustness against background clutter can be achieved. The reason for this robustness is that the optic flow features that are extracted by the optic flow pattern neurons are extremely specific, so that it is very unlikely that they arise by chance through randomly moving background dots. Clutter is a fundamental problem for many classical approaches that are based on tracking high-level models driven by low-level image features.

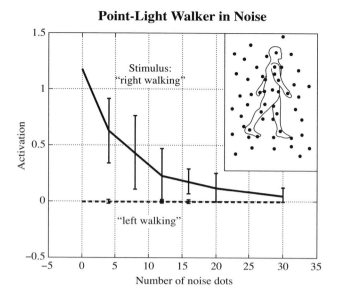

Figure 15.6. Activity of two motion pattern neurons trained with rightward walking (solid line) and leftward walking (dashed line) for a point-light walker walking right-ward and embedded in a variable amount of randomly moving background dots. Error bars indicate standard deviations over 20 repeated simulations. Adapted from Giese & Poggio, 2003.

7. Limitations of the Model

The proposed model is based on many strong simplifications. This section discusses some important shortcomings of the proposed theory, which are particularly relevant with respect to aspects discussed in other chapters in this book. Some approaches to addressing these shortcomings will be briefly discussed.

7.1. Lack of Top-Down Connections

The proposed model has a feed-forward architecture. Form and motion path-ways consist of hierarchies of neural detectors that are connected unidirec-tionally in a bottom-up fashion. Anatomical and neurophysiological studies show that the visual cortex is characterized by strong feedback connectivity between different cortical areas (Felleman & van Essen, 1991; Salin & Bullier, 1995). This type of reciprocal connectivity has motivated different computa-tional hypotheses about how such connections might be exploited for realizing a bottom-up and top-down processing of information in the visual pathway (e.g., Rao & Ballard, 1997; Rolls & Deco, 2002; Ullman, 1996).

Several psychophysical experiments on biological-motion recognition demonstrate significant top-down effects in the processing of biological movements. An example is an experiment by Shiffrar and Freyd (1990) that shows that the perception of motion paths that are induced by apparent motion stimuli can be influenced by the recognition of biomechanically plausible or implausible actions. Two photographs showing different human body postures were presented in sequence with varying interstimulus intervals (ISIs). For short ISIs, subjects perceived the shortest possible paths between corresponding body points in the two photographs. This result would also be predicted by many classical theories for low-level motion processing. For longer ISIs, however, subjects tended to perceive a biomechanically possible path that avoided, for instance, self-collision. This result suggests that the visual system exploits an intrinsic representation of frequently occurring or biomechanically compatible human movements.

In the model, biomechanically possible movements are represented by the neurally encoded sequences of body shapes and optic flow sequences in the two pathways. One possible explanation for the psychophysical experiment by Shiffrar and Freyd is that this information becomes accessible only after the stimulus has been recognized in the feed-forward path. The dependence on the ISI might be explained by the fact that the activation of the relevant high-level representations requires a certain minimum time. Another possible explanation is that the perceived path is generated by a higher-level representation, which integrates low-level motion information and intrinsic knowledge about bio-mechanically possible paths. However, top-down influences of biological-motion recognition on the perceptual organization of low-level motion stimuli are also suggested by a recent psychophysical study that shows that recognition of a point-light walker can disambiguate the perceptual organization of simple ambiguous motion displays (Fujimoto, 2003).

In the model, an influence of motion recognition on low-level motion perception could be implemented by adding modulatory top-down feedback connections from the higher levels of the motion pathway (optic flow pattern neurons, local optic flow detectors) to the lower levels (in particular the local motion energy detectors). Such feedback would have to increase selectively the gain of neurons on lower levels that support the present higher-level interpretation. Additionally, if the feature detectors within the same hierarchy level compete on the lower levels, a bias can be introduced that favors optic flow estimates that are consistent with the learned neurally represented biological-movement patterns on the highest hierarchy level. Similar architectures have been applied successfully to model the influence of task and attention on the processing of lower-level form features (Hamker, 2004; Rolls & Deco, 2002; Tsotsos et al., 1995). It remains to be shown by quantitative simulations if such architectures are suitable for a robust implementation of top-down effects.

Evidence for a massive top-down modulation of the processing of biological motion has also been found in fMRI experiments. Vaina et al. (2001) presented the same biological-motion stimulus, a point-light walker, with two different tasks. The first task was to discriminate between normal and scrambled point-light stimuli. The second task was just to report the average direction of the dots in the display (which showed only a fraction of a full walking cycle). Only for the first task, selective activation was found in biological motion–selective areas, like the STS and area KO. This implies that for identical stimuli the task critically determines whether biological motion–selective areas are involved in the processing.

7.2. Lack of Attentional Modulation

Biological-motion processing is strongly influenced by attention. This has been demonstrated in a number of experiments that have combined biological-motion perception with attentionally demanding tasks, like visual search or execution of a secondary competing task requiring divided attention (e.g., Cavanagh, Labianca, & Thornton, 2001; Thornton, Rensink, & Shiffrar, 2002). These experiments demonstrate that attention often plays a role in the processing of biological motion, with explicit recognition becoming strongly impaired when insufficient attentional resources are available (Thornton & Vuong, 2004). A modulation of the processing by attention is also desirable for computational reasons. It can, for example, help to suppress uninteresting parts of the visual scene, simplifying the detection of biological-motion clutter.

For the recognition of static objects, a number of models have been proposed that implement attentional modulation using physiologically plausible neural mechanisms. Some of these models assume the existence of an explicit saliency map (Itti & Koch, 2000; Koch & Ullman, 1985). Others realize attentional modulation without a separate representation of stimulus saliency (Hamker 2004; Rolls & Deco, 2002). These models comprise similar detector hierarchies as the form pathway of the model discussed in this chapter. The same dynamic mechanisms might therefore be suitable for realizing attentional modulation in motion recognition. An additional challenge is the integration of the multiple relevant time scales for attentional modulation and motion recognition, since in contrast to static pictures, motion patterns are inherently dynamic.

7.3. Missing Influence of Motor Programs

Several experiments (cf. chapters 7, 10, 14, and 18) provide evidence that visual movement recognition might be influenced by internal representations of motor programs for the execution of actions. The observation of goal-directed actions has been shown to induce activity in premotor areas (Buccino, Binkofski, & Riggio, 2004), and the motor responses induced by magnetic stimulation in these regions seem to be influenced by motion recognition (Fadiga et al., 1995). Also it has sometimes been speculated that the *mirror neuron system*, described in the premotor cortex of monkeys (Rizzolatti et al., 2001), might be involved in the visual recognition of goal-directed actions. Mirror neurons are characterized by the property that they fire when the monkey plans a certain motor action, but also when the animal sees the same action. This tight coupling between action recognition and action planning might be important for the learning of movements by imitation (Rizzolatti & Arbib, 1998). A coupling between action planning and action recognition is also predicted by the common coding theory (Prinz, 1997; chapter 18), which assumes a common representation for action planning and action recognition. Top-down influences of recognized imitable motor actions (Wilson, 2001; chapter 10) on visual recognition seem very plausible.

A possible influence of motor programs on visual motion recognition is suggested by an experiment in our own laboratory that shows that nonvisual motor training seems to influence the visual recognition of biological-motion stimuli (Casile & Giese, 2004). For this purpose, subjects were blindfolded and trained with arm movements realizing unnatural coordination patterns. For a purely visual recognition task using point-light stimuli, the performance of the subjects improved selectively only for the stimulus that corresponded to the learned motor pattern. A similar experiment by Hecht, Vogt, and Prinz (2001) also suggests that the motor execution of specific arm movements influences their visual recognition.

In the model, a top-down influence of motor programs on motion recognition might be implemented by extending the hierarchy by a layer that represents goal-directed motor acts. Physiological data from neurons in area F5 suggest that action-selective neurons on this level might show substantial invariance against the style and direction with which an action is executed (Rizzolatti et al., 2001). As on the earlier levels of the model, such invariances can be modeled by pooling over motion pattern neurons that encode different execution styles of the same action. A further challenge is the implementation of a dependence on the goal object, accounting for the fact that most mirror neurons do not fire in the absence of an appropriate goal object (Rizzolatti et al., 2001). In principle, the form pathway of the model can be used for the recognition of goal objects. The neural responses of object recognition neurons in the form pathway would have to be integrated with the responses of the motion pattern neurons appropriately in the highest hierarchy level that represents goal-directed motor acts. Only an implementation of this idea will allow us to decide if the proposed neural mechanisms are sufficiently robust. Neural models for mirror neurons have been proposed by other groups (e.g., Oztop & Arbib, 2002), but they do not focus on detailed physiologically plausible modeling for the visual pathway.

8. Discussion

The recognition of complex movements is biologically a highly important perceptual function. The visual system realizes this function with an amazing degree of robustness and efficiency. The computational-modeling literature and research in computer vision have proposed many algorithms that solve computational problems which are important in the context of movement recognition. Most existing algorithms have no obvious implementation in terms of real cortical neurons. Exceptions are neural network models and potentially also Bayesian approaches that can be linked to neural interpretations (Lee & Mumford, 2003; Rao, 2004). In this chapter, some important computational approaches have been reviewed, and their potential relevance for real cortical neural circuits has been discussed.

In addition, a physiologically inspired neural model was presented. Its computational properties have been illustrated with a number of example simulations. The proposed model accounts for a variety of experimental results exploiting relatively simple and physiologically plausible mechanisms, while avoiding expensive computational problems, like closed-loop optimization of complex models with many parameters or the solution of high-dimensional search problems. In spite of the lack of such sophisticated algorithms, the neural model was found to be suitable for the recognition of normal human action stimuli, point-light walkers, and even strongly degraded point-light stimuli, even in the presence of clutter. This shows that at least a part of the relevant computational problems can be solved using physiologically plausible mechanisms.

Certainly, the proposed model has many limitations, and like the known technical systems, it solves only a part of the relevant computational problems with a limited degree of accuracy. Most important, the model lacks top-down influences and mechanisms for attentional control. Such mechanisms might improve substantially the recognition performance and robustness of the model. Also they are necessary to account for the full spectrum of experimental results on biological-motion recognition. Another important domain of future theoretical research is the study of neural mechanisms that implement top-down influences from motor representations on biological-motion recognition. In spite of a growing body of experimental evidence demonstrating such influences (see e.g., chapters 10, 18, and 19), the knowledge about possible underlying neural circuits is extremely limited. Even though the brain might not use metric geometrical 3D body models, as proposed in the classical work by Marr and Vaina (1982), it seems plausible that visual motion recognition is supported and primed by top-down modulation from neural structures that are involved in the planning of motor actions, like the premotor cortex (Rizzolatti et al., 2001; Saygin et al., 2004). The exact nature and implementation of such top-down influences remains to be explored by future experimental and theoretical studies.

We think that theoretical models will be of crucial importance to gain a complete understanding of the interaction between body representation and action recognition. A first role of theoretical approaches is to define precise and solvable computational problems and to explore the computational feasibility of algorithms for their solution. Much of the ambiguity of the interpretation of data in cognitive science results from incomplete definitions of the underlying computational problems. Since possible explanations are often not concretely implemented, neither their underlying concepts nor the proposed computational solutions are sufficiently accessible for falsification. However, our review of technical solutions shows that there is a vast amount of successful computational approaches that solve individual problems that are relevant in the context of action recognition. To gain a more profound understanding of the computational processes in the visual cortex, it seems important that possible computational principles are linked to multiple levels of empirical research. A specific computational model, which cannot be implemented with real neurons but fits accurately a set of psychophysical data curves, might finally be completely irrelevant for the understanding of biological systems. Instead, it seems important to develop models that link possible neural implementations with electrophysiological, behavioral, and fMRI data. Such models have the advantage that they can be falsified on multiple levels. Additionally, they formulate precise quantitative hypotheses that can be used to guide experimental research in electrophysiology and functional imaging, methods that provide information about the behavior of the cortical neurons. A final clarification of the neural mechanisms underlying the recognition of biological movements might be achieved by electrophysiological studies asking the right empirical questions, potentially guided by precisely formulated computational hypotheses that are derived from theoretical research.

Acknowledgments I am grateful to I. M. Thornton and two anonymous reviewers for providing helpful comments on this chapter. Thanks to T. Poggio and the Center for Biological and Computational Learning, MIT, for supporting the development of the model, and for many interesting comments and discussions. A. Benali, Z. Kourtzi, and C. Curio helped with the data acquisition. The Laboratory of Action Recognition and Learning is supported by the Volkswagen Stiftung, the Deutsche Forschungsgemeinschaft (DFG), and the Human Frontier Science Program (HFSP). Additional support by the Max Planck Institute for Biological Cybernetics in Tübingen is gratefully acknowledged.

References

Aggarwal, J. K., & Cai, Q. (1999). Human motion analysis: A review. *Computer Vision and Image Understanding, 73*, 428–440.

Ahlström, V., Blake, R., & Ahlström, U. (1997). Perception of biological motion. *Perception, 26*, 1539–1548.

Ahmad, T., Taylor, C. J., Lanitis, A., & Cootes, T. F. (1997). Tracking and recognizing hand gestures using statistical shape models. *Image and Vision Computing, 15*, 345–352.

Allman, J., Miezin, F., & McGuinness, E. (1985). Direction- and velocity-specific responses from beyond the classical receptive field in the middle temporal visual area (MT). *Perception, 14*, 105–126.

Allmen, M., & Dyer, C. R. (1993). Computing spatiotemporal relations for dynamic perceptual organization. *Computer Vision Graphics and Image Understanding, 58*, 338–351.

Beardsworth, T., & Buckner, T. (1981). The ability to recognize oneself from a video recording of one's movements without seeing one's body. *Bulletin of the Psychonomic Society, 18*, 19–22.

Beintema, J. P., & Lappe, M. (2002). Perception of biological motion without local image motion. *Proceedings of the National Academy of Sciences, USA, 99*, 5661–5663.

Bertenthal, B. I., & Pinto, J. (1994). Global processing of biological motions. *Psychological Science, 5*, 221–225.

Black, M. J., & Jepson, A. D. (1998). Eigen tracking: Robust matching and tracking of articulated objects using a view-based representation. *International Journal of Computer Vision, 26*, 63–84.

Blake, A., & Isard, M. (1998). *Active contours.* Berlin: Springer.

Bobick, A. (1997). Movement, activity, and action: The role of knowledge in the perception of motion. *Philosophical Transactions of the Royal Society of London, B, 352*, 1257–1265.

Bregler, C. (1997). Learning and recognizing human dynamics. In *Proceedings of the IEEE Conference on Computer Vision and Pattern Recognition (CVPR'97)* (pp. 568–574). Los Alamitos: IEEE Computer Society Press.

Bonda, E., Petrides, M., Ostry, D., & Evans, A. (1996). Specific involvement of human parietal systems and the amygdala in the perception of biological motion. *Journal of Neuroscience, 16*, 3737–3744.

Born, R. T. (2000). Center-surround interactions in the middle temporal visual area of the owl monkey. *Journal of Neurophysiology, 84*, 2658–2669.

Buccino, G., Binkofski, F., & Riggio L. (2004). The mirror neuron system and action recognition. *Brain and Language, 89*, 370–376.

Bülthoff, I., Bülthoff, H. H., & Sinha, P. (1998). Top-down influences on stereoscopic depth-perception. *Nature Neuroscience, 1*, 254–257.

Campbell, L., & Bobick, A. (1995). Recognition of human body motion using phase space constraints. *Proceedings of the International Conference on Computer Vision* (pp. 624–630). Washington: IEEE Computer Society.

Casile, A., & Giese, M. (2003). Roles of motion and form in biological motion recognition. In O. Kaynak, E. Alpaydin, E. Oja, & L. Xu (Eds.), *Artificial networks and neural information processing.* Springer, Berlin (pp. 854–862).

Casile, A., & Giese, M. A. (2004). Possible influences of motor learning on perception of biological motion. *Journal of Vision, 4*, 221a.

Casile, A. & Giese, M. A. (2005). Critical features for the recognition of biological motion. *Journal of Vision, 5*, 348–360.

Cavanagh, P., Labianca, A. P., & Thornton, I. M. (2001). Attention-based visual routines: Sprites. *Cognition, 80*, 47–60.

Cham, T., & Rehg, J. (1999). A multiple hypothesis approach to figure tracking. *Proceedings of the IEEE Conference on Computer Vision and Pattern Recognition.* Los Alamitos: IEEE Computer Society Press.

Chen, Z., & Lee, H. (1992). Knowledge-guided visual perception of 3-D human gait from a single image sequence. *IEEE Transactions on Systems, Man Cyberneticst, 22*, 336–342.

Cutting, J. E. (1981). Coding theory adapted to gait perception. *Journal of Experimental Psychology: Human Perception & Performance, 7*, 71–87.

Cutting, J. E., & Kozlowski, L. T. (1977). Recognizing friends by their walk: Gait perception without familiarity cues. *Bulletin of the Psychonomics Society, 9*, 353–356.

Cutting, J. E., Moore, C., & Morrison, R. (1988). Masking the motions of human gait. *Perception & Psychophysics, 44*, 339–347.

Davis, J., & Bobick, A. (1997). The representation and recognition of action using temporal templates. *IEEE Conference on Computer Vision and Pattern Recognition (CVPR '97)* (pp. 928–934). Los Alamitos: IEEE Computer Society Press.

Dittrich, W. H. (1993). Action categories and the perception of biological motion. *Perception, 22*, 15–22.

Dittrich, W. H., Troscianko, T., Lea, S. E., & Morgan, D. (1996). Perception of emotion from dynamic point-light displays represented in dance. *Perception, 25*, 727–738

Downing, P., Jiang, Y., Shuman, M., & Kanwisher, N. (2001). A cortical area selective for visual processing of the human body. *Science, 293*, 2470–2473.

Eifuku, S., & Wurtz, R. H. (1998). Response to motion in extrastriate area MSTl: Center-surround interactions. *Journal of Neurophysiology, 80*, 282–296.

Essa, I., & Pentland, A. (1997). Coding, analysis, interpretation, and recognition of facial expressions. *IEEE Transactions on Pattern Analysis and Machine Intelligence, 19*, 757–763.

Fadiga, L., Fogassi, L., Pavesi, G., & Rizzolatti, G. (1995). Motor facilitation during action observation: A magnetic stimulation study. *Journal of Neurophysiology, 73*, 2608–2611.

Felleman, D. J., & van Essen, D. C. (1991). Distributed hierarchical processing in the primate visual cortex. *Cerebral Cortex, 1*, 1–49.

Fujimoto, K. (2003). Motion induction from biological motion. *Perception, 32*, 1273–1277.

Fukushima, K. (1980). Neocognitron: A self-organizing neural network model for a mechanism of pattern recognition unaffected by shift in position. *Biological Cybernetics, 36*, 193–202.

Gallant, J. L., Connor, C. E., Rakshit, S., Lewis, J. W., & van Essen, D. C. (1996). Neural responses to polar, hyperbolic, and Cartesian gratings in area V4 of the macaque monkey. *Journal of Neurophysiology, 76*, 2718–2739.

Gavrila, D. M. (1999). The visual analysis of human movement: A survey. *Computer Vision and Image Understanding, 73*, 82–98.

Gawne, T. J., & Martin, J. (2002). Response of primate visual cortical V4 neurons to two simultaneously presented stimuli. *Journal of Neurophysiology, 88*, 1128–1135.

Giese, M. A. (2000). Neural model for the recognition of biological motion. In G. Baratoff and H. Neumann (Eds.), *Dynamische Perzeption* (pp. 105–110). Berlin: Infix-Verlag.

Giese, M. A. (2004). Neural model for biological movement recognition. In L. M. Vaina, S. A. Beardsley, & S. Rushton (Eds.), *Optic flow and beyond* (pp. 443–470). Dordrecht: Kluwer.

Giese, M. A., & Lappe, M. (2002). Measuring generalization fields for the recognition of biological motion. *Vision Research, 42*, 1847–1858.

Giese, M. A., & Poggio, T. (2000). Morphable models for the analysis and synthesis of complex motion patterns. *International Journal of Computer Vision, 38*, 59–73.

Giese, M. A., & Poggio, T. (2003). Neural mechanisms for the recognition of biological movements. *Nature Reviews Neuroscience, 4*, 179–192.

Girosi, F., Jones, M., & Poggio, T. (1995). Regularization theory and neural networks architectures. *Neural Computation, 7*, 219–269.

Goddard, N. H. (1992). *The perception of articulated motion: Recognizing moving light displays.* Unpublished thesis, University of Rochester.

Goodale, M. A., & Milner, A. D. (1992). Separate visual pathways for perception and action. *Trends in Neuroscience, 15*, 97–112.

Grossman, E. D., & Blake, R. (2001). Brain activity evoked by inverted and imagined biological motion. *Vision Research, 41*, 1475–1482.

Grossman, E. D., & Blake, R. (2002). Brain areas active during visual perception of biological motion. *Neuron, 35*, 1167–1175.

Hamker, F. G. (2004). A dynamic model of how feature cues guide spatial attention. *Vision Research, 44*, 501–521.

Hecht, H., Vogt, S., & Prinz, W. (2001). Motor learning enhances perceptual judgment: A case for action-perception transfer. *Psychological Research, 65*, 3–14.

Hegdé, J., & van Essen, D. C. (2000). Selectivity for complex shapes in primate visual area V2. *Journal of Neuroscience, 20*, RC61–66.

Hill, H., Jinno, Y., & Johnston, A. (2003). Comparing solid-body with point-light animations. *Perception, 32*, 561–566.

Hoffman, D. D., & Flinchbaugh, B. E. (1982). The interpretation of biological motion. *Biological Cybernetics, 42*, 195–204.

Huang, P. S., Harris, C. J., & Nixon, M. S. (1998). Comparing different template features for recognizing people by their gait. *Proceedings of Ninth British Machine Vision Conference, 2*, 639–648.

Hubel, D. H., & Wiesel, T. N. (1962). Receptive fields, binocular interaction and functional architecture in the cat's visual cortex. *Journal of Physiology, 160*, 106–154.

Itti, L., & Koch, C. (2000). A saliency-based search mechanism for overt and covert shifts of visual attention. *Vision Research, 40*, 1489–1506.

Jastorff, J., & Giese, M. A. (2004). Time-dependent Hebbian rules for the learning of templates for motion recognition. In U. Ilg, H. H. Bülthoff, & H. A. M. Mallot (Eds.), *Dynamic perception* (pp. 151–156). Berlin: Infix-Verlag.

Jastorff, J., Giese, M. A., & Kourtzi, Z. (in press). Perceptual learning of novel biological movements in the human visual brain. *34th Annual Meeting of the Society for Neuroscience, San Diego.*

Johansson, G. (1973). Visual perception of biological motion and a model for its analysis. *Perception & Psychophysics, 14*, 201–211.

Johansson, G. (1976). Spatio-temporal differentiation and integration in visual motion perception: An experimental and theoretical analysis of calculus-like functions in visual data processing. *Psychological Research, 38*, 379–393.

Johnson, J. S., & Olshausen, B. A. (2003). Timecourse of neural signatures of object recognition. *Journal of Vision, 3*, 499–512.

Jones, J. P., & Palmer, L. A. (1987). An evaluation of the two-dimensional Gabor filter model of simple receptive fields in cat striate cortex. *Journal of Neurophysiology, 58*, 1233–1258.

Ju, S., Black, M., & Yacoob, Y. (1996). Cardboard people: A parametrized model of articulated image motion. *Proceedings of IEEE International Conference on Automatic Face and Gesture Recognition, Killington* (pp. 38–44).

Keysers, C., Xiao, D. K., Foldiak, P., & Perrett, D. I. (2001). The speed of sight. *Journal of Cognitive Neuroscience, 13*, 90–101.

Koch, C., & Ullman, S. (1985). Shifts in selective visual attention: Towards the underlying neural circuitry. *Human Neurobiology, 4*, 219–227.

Kourtzi, Z., & Kanwisher, N. (2000). Activation in human MT/MST by static images with implied motion. *Journal of Cognitive Neuroscience, 2*, 48–55.

Kozlowski, L. T., & Cutting, J. E. (1977). Recognizing the sex of a walker from a dynamic point light display. *Perception & Psychophysics, 21*, 575–580.

Lampl, I., Ferster, D., Poggio, T., & Riesenhuber, M. (2004). Intracellular measurements of spatial integration and the max operation in complex cells of the cat primary visual cortex. *Journal of Neurophysiology, 92*, 2704–2713.

Lee, T. S., & Mumford, D. (2003). Hierarchical Bayesian inference in the visual cortex. *Journal of Optical Society of America, A20*, 1434–1448.

Lin, C. T., Nein, H. W., & Lin, W. C. (1999). A space-time delay neural network for motion recognition and its application to lipreading. *International Journal Neural Systems, 9*, 311–334.

Little, J., & Boyd, J. (1998). Recognizing people by their gait: The shape of motion. *Videre, 1*, 1–32.

Logothetis, N. K., Pauls, J., & Poggio, T. (1995). Shape representation in the inferior temporal cortex of monkeys. *Current Biology, 5*, 552–563.

Logothetis, N. K., & Sheinberg, D. L. (1996). Visual object vision. *Annual Review of Neuroscience, 19*, 577–621.

Marr, D., & Vaina, L. M. V. (1982). Representation and recognition of the movements of shapes. *Proceedings of the Royal Society of London, B, 214*, 501–524.

Mather, G., Radford, K., & West, S. (1992). Low-level visual processing of biological motion. *Proceedings of the Royal Society of London, B, Biological Sciences, 249*, 149–155.

Mel, B., & Fieser, J. (2000). Minimizing binding errors using learned conjunctive features. *Neural Computation, 9*, 779–796.

Mineiro, P., & Zipser, D. (1998). Analysis of direction selectivity arising from recurrent cortical interactions. *Neural Computation, 10*, 353–371.

Moeslund, T. B., & Granum, G. (2001). A survey of computer vision-based human motion capture. *Computer Vision and Image Understanding, 81*, 231–268.

Morel, A., & Bullier, J. (1990). Anatomical segregation of two cortical visual pathways in the macaque monkey. *Visual Neuroscience, 4*, 555–578.

Neri, P., Morrone, M. C., & Burr, D. C. (1998). Seeing biological motion. *Nature, 394*, 894–896.

Nishitani, N., & Hari, R. (2002). Viewing lip forms: Cortical dynamics. *Neuron, 36*, 1211–1220.

Niyogi, S. A., & Adelson, E. H. (1994). Analyzing and recognizing walking Figures in XYT. *Proceedings of the IEEE conference on computer vision and pattern recognition (CVPR '94)* (pp. 469–474). Los Alamitos: IEEE Computer Society Press.

Nowak, L., & Bullier, J. (1998). The timing of information transfer in the visual system. In J. H. Kaas, K. Rockland, & A. Peters (Eds.), *Cerebral cortex* (pp. 205–241). New York: Plenum.

Oram, M. W., & Perrett, D. I. (1996). Integration of form and motion in the anterior temporal polysensory area (STPa) of the macaque monkey. *Journal of Neurophysiology, 76*, 109–129.

Orban, G., Dupont, P., De Bruyn, B., Vogels, R., Vandenberghe, R., & Mortelmans, L. (1995). A motion area in human visual cortex. *Proceedings of the National Academy of Sciences, USA, 92*, 993–997.

Orban, G. A., Lagae, L., Verri, A., Raiguel, S., Xiao, D., Maes, H., & Torre, V. (1992). First-order analysis of optical flow in monkey brain. *Proceedings of the National Academy of Sciences, USA, 89*, 2595–2599.

O'Rourke, J., & Badler, N. (1980). Model-based image analysis of human motion using constraint propagation. *IEEE Transactions on Pattern Analysis and Machine Intelligence, 2*, 522–536.

Oztop, E., & Arbib, M. A. (2002). Schema design and implementation of the grasp-related mirror neuron system. *Biol Cybern., 87*, 116–140.

Pavlova, M., Lützenberger, W., Sokolov, A., & Birbaumer, N. (2004). Dissociable cortical processing of recognizable and non-recognizable biological movement: Analysing gamma MEG activity. *Cerebral Cortex, 14*, 181–188.

Pavlova, M., & Sokolov, A. (2000). Orientation specificity in biological motion perception. *Perception & Psychophysics, 62*, 889–899.

Pelphrey, K. A., Mitchell, T. V., McKeown, M. J., Goldstein, J., Allison, T., & McCarthy, G. (2003). Brain activity evoked by the perception of human walking: Controlling for meaningful coherent motion. *Journal of Neuroscience, 23*, 6819–6825.

Perrett, D. I., & Oram, M. W. (1993). Neurophysiology of shape processing. *Image and Vision Computing, 11*, 317–333.

Perrett, D. I., Smith, P. A., Mistlin, A. J., Chitty, A. J., Head, A. S., Potter, D. D., Broennimann, R., Milner, A. D., & Jeeves, M. A. (1985). Visual analysis of body movements by neurons in the temporal cortex in the macaque monkey: A preliminary report. *Behavioral Brain Research, 16*, 153–170.

Pinto, J., & Shiffrar, M. (1999). Subconfigurations of the human form in the perception of biological motion displays. *Acta Psychologica, 102*, 293–318.

Polana, R., & Nelson, R. (1994). Low level recognition of human motion. *Proceedings of the IEEE CS workshop on motion of non-rigid and articulated objects*, Austin, TX (pp. 77–82).

Pollick, F. E., Lestou, V., Ryu, J., & Cho, S. B. (2002). Estimating the efficiency of recognizing gender and affect from biological motion. *Vision Research, 42*, 2345–2355.

Prinz, W. (1997). Perception and action planning. *European Journal of Cognitive Psychology, 9*, 129–154.

Rao, R. P. N. (2004). Bayesian computation in recurrent neural circuits. *Neural Computation, 16*, 1–38.

Rao, R. P. N., & Ballard, D. H. (1997). Dynamic model of visual recognition predicts neural response properties in the visual cortex. *Neural Computation, 9*, 721–763.

Rashid, R. (1980). Towards a system for the interpretation of moving light displays. *IEEE Transactions on Pattern Analysis and Machine Intelligence, 2*, 574–581.

Rehg, J., & Kanade, T. (1995). Model-based tracking of self-occluding articulated objects. *Proceedings of International Conference on Computer Vision*, Cambridge (pp. 612–617).

Riesenhuber, M., & Poggio, T. (1999). Hierarchical models of object recognition. *Nature Neuroscience, 2*, 1019–1025.

Rizzolatti, G., & Arbib, M. A. (1998). Language within our grasp. *Trends in Neuroscience, 21*, 188–194.

Rizzolatti, G., Fogassi, L., & Gallese, V. (2001). Neurophysiological mechanisms underlying the understanding and imitation of action. *Nature Reviews Neuroscience, 2*, 661–670.

Rohr, K. (1997). Human movement analysis based on explicit motion models. In M. Shah and R. Jain (Eds.), *Motion-based recognition* (pp. 171–198). Dordrecht: Kluwer.

Rolls, E. T., & Deco, G. (2002). *Computational neuroscience of vision.* Oxford: Oxford University Press.

Rolls, E. T., & Milward, T. (2000). A model of invariant object recognition in the visual system: Learning rules, activation functions, lateral inhibition, and information-based performance measures. *Neural Computation, 12*, 2547–2572.

Rolls, E. T., & Tovée, M. J. (1995). Sparseness of the neuronal representation of stimuli in the primate temporal visual cortex. *Journal of Neurophysiology, 73*, 713–726.

Rosales, R., Athitsos, V., Sigal, L., & Sclaroff, S. (2001). 3D hand pose reconstruction using specialized mappings. *Proceedings of the International Conference on Computer Vision (ICCV), 1*, 378–385.

Rosenblum, M., Yacoob, Y., & Davis, L. (1996). Human emotion recognition from motion using a radial basis function network architecture. *IEEE Transactions on Neural Networks, 7*, 1121–1138.

Saito, H. (1993). Hierarchical neural analysis of optical flow in the macaque visual pathway. In T. Ono, L. R. Squire, M. E. Raichle, D. I. Perrett, & M. Fukuda (Eds.), *Brain mechanisms of perception and memory* (pp. 121–140). Oxford: Oxford University Press.

Saleem, K. S., Suzuki, W., Tanaka, K., & Hashikawa, T. (2000). Connections between anterior inferotemporal cortex and superior temporal sulcus regions in the macaque monkey. *Journal of Neuroscience, 20*, 5083–5101.

Salin, P. A., & Bullier, J. (1995). Corticocortical connections in the visual system: Structure and function. *Physiological Review, 75*, 107–154.

Saygin, A. P., Wilson, S. M., Hagler, D. J., Bates, E., & Sereno, M. I. (2004). Point-light biological motion perception activates human premotor cortex. *Journal of Neuroscience, 24*, 6181–6188.

Schaal, S. (1999). Is imitation learning the route to humanoid robots? *Trends in Cognitive Sciences, 3*, 233–242.

Schmolesky, M. T., Wang, Y., Hanes, D. P., Thompson, K. G., Leutgeb, S., Schall, J. D., & Leventhal, A. G. (1998). Signal timing across the macaque visual system. *Journal of Neurophysiology, 79*, 3272–3278.

Sereno, M. E., Trinath, T., Augath, M., & Logothetis, N. K. (2002). Three-dimensional shape representation in monkey cortex. *Neuron, 33*, 635–652.

Shavit, E., & Jepson, A. (1993). Motion understanding using phase portraits. *IJCAI workshop: Looking at people*, Chambéry, France, August 1993.

Shiffrar, M., & Freyd, J. J. (1990). Apparent motion of the human body. *Psychological Science, 1*, 257–264.

Sigal, L., Isard, M. I., Sigelman, B. H., & Black, M. J. (2003). *Advances in neural information processing systems, 16*, 1539–1546.

Simoncelli, E. P., & Heeger, D. J. (1998). A model of neuronal responses in visual area MT. *Vision Research, 38*, 743–761.

Smith, A. T., & Snowden, R. J. (1994). *Visual detection of motion.* London: Academic.

Song, Y., Goncalves, L., Di Bernardo, E., & Perona, P. (2001). Monocular perception of biological motion in Johansson displays. *Computer Vision and Image Understanding, 81*, 303–327.

Song, Y., Goncalves, L., & Perona, P. (2003). Unsupervised learning of human motion. *IEEE Transactions on Pattern Analysis and Machine Intelligence, 25*, 1–14.

Starner, T., & Pentland, A. (1995). Visual recognition of American Sign Language using hidden Markov models. *Proceedings of the International Workshop on Automatic Face and Gesture Recognition*, Zürich, Switzerland, pp. 189–194.

Sumi, S. (1984). Upside-down presentation of the Johansson moving light-spot pattern. *Perception, 13*, 283–302.

Tanaka, K. (1996). Inferotemporal cortex and object vision. *Annual Review of Neuroscience, 19*, 109–139.

Tanaka, K., Fukuda, Y., & Saito, H. (1989). Analysis of motion of the visual field by direction, expansion/contraction, and rotation cells clustered in the dorsal part of the medial superior temporal area of the macaque monkey. *Journal of Neurophysiology, 62*, 626–641.

Tarr, M. J., & Bülthoff, H. H. (1998). Image-based object recognition in man, monkey and machine. *Cognition, 67*, 1–20.

Terzopoulos, D., & Waters, K. (1993). Analysis and synthesis of facial image sequences using physical and anatomical models. *IEEE Transactions on Pattern Analysis and Machine Intelligence, 15*, 569–579.

Thornton, I. M., Pinto, J., & Shiffrar, M. (1998). The visual perception of human locomotion. *Cognitive Neuropsychology, 15*, 535–552.

Thornton, I. M., Rensink, R. A., & Shiffrar, M. (2002). Active versus passive processing of biological motion. *Perception, 31*, 837–853.

Thornton, I. M., & Vuong, Q. C. (2004). Incidental processing of biological motion. *Current Biology, 14*, 1084–1089.

Thorpe, S., Delorme, A., & van Rullen R. (2001). Spike-based strategies for rapid processing. *Neural Networks, 14*, 715–725.

Thorpe, S., Fize, D., & Marlot, C. (1996). Speed of processing in the human visual system. *Nature, 381*, 520–522.

Todd, J. T. (1983). Perception of gait. *Journal of Experimental Psychology: Human Perception & Performance, 9*, 31–42.

Troje, N. F. (2003). Reference frames for orientation anisotropies in face recognition and biological-motion perception. *Perception, 32*, 201–210.

Tsotsos, J., Culhane, S., Wai, W., Lai, Y., Davis, N., & Nuflo, F. (1995). Modelling visual attention via selective tuning. *Artificial Intelligence, 78*, 507–547.

Ullman, S. (1996). *High-level vision.* Cambridge, MA: MIT Press.

Ungerleider, L. G., & Mishkin, M. (1982). Two cortical visual systems. In D. J. Ingle, M. A. Goodale, & R. J. W. Mansfield (Eds.), *Analysis of visual behavior* (pp. 549–586). Cambridge, MA: MIT Press.

Vaina, L., & Bennour, Y. (1985). A computational approach to visual recognition of arm movements. *Perceptual and Motor Skills, 60*, 203–228.

Vaina, L. M., Solomon, J., Chowdhury, S., Sinha, P., & Belliveau, J. W. (2001). Functional neuroanatomy of biological motion perception in humans. *Proceedings of the National Academy of Sciences, USA, 98*, 11656–11661.

Verfaillie, K. (2000). Perceiving human locomotion: Priming effects in direction discrimination. *Brain Cognition, 44*, 192–213.

Verfaillie, K., de Troy, A., & van Rensbergen, J. (1994). Transsaccadic integration of biological motion. *Journal of Experimental Psychology: Learning, Memory, Cognition, 20*, 649–670.

Wachter, S., & Nagel, H.-H. (1999). Tracking of persons in monocular image sequences. *Computer Vision and Image Understanding, 74*, 174–192.

Webb, J. A., & Aggarwal, J. K. (1982). Structure from motion of rigid and jointed objects. *Artificial Intelligence, 19*, 107–130.

Wilson, M. (2001). Perceiving imitable stimuli: Consequences of isomorphism between input and output. *Psychological Bulletin, 127*, 543–553.

Wolpert, D. M., Doya, K., & Kawato, M. (2003). A unifying computational framework for motor control and social interaction. *Philosophical Transactions of the Royal Society, 358*, 593–602.

Wren, C., Azarbayejani, A., Darrell, T., & Pentland, A. (1997). Pfinder: Real-time tracking of the human body. *IEEE Transactions on Pattern Analysis and Machine Intelligence, 19*, 780–785.

Xiao, D. K., Raiguel, S., Marcar, V., Koenderink, J., & Orban, G. A. (1995). Spatial heterogeneity of inhibitory surrounds in the middle temporal visual area. *Proceedings of the National Academy of Sciences, USA, 92*, 11303–11306.

Xie, X., & Giese, M. A. (2002). Nonlinear dynamics of direction-selective nonlinear neural media. *Physical Review E (Statistical, Nonlinear and Soft Matter Physics), 65*, 051904.

Yu, A. J., Giese, M. A., & Poggio, T. (2002). Biophysiologically plausible implementations of the maximum operation. *Neural Computation, 14*, 2857–2881.

16

Evidence for a Network of Brain Areas Involved in Perception of Biological Motion

Emily D. Grossman

Of the images that we encounter on a daily basis, perhaps the most interesting are visions of other people. Much cognitive and psychological research has focused attention on the perception of faces, obviously a very important task in social perception. But another line of research has clearly shown that humans are remarkably sensitive to the kinematics of body motion. *Biological motion perception* refers to the recognition of people and animals in motion. Using a technique in which bodies are depicted solely by the motion of the joints, we can study biological motion perception in isolation from other visual cues, such as form, texture, and colors that naturally occur when we see bodies (described in more depth in chapter 13). Amazingly, human movement is readily recognized on the basis of the movement patterns of the joints, an indication of the robust and highly sensitive nature of our visual system for biological motion. It is natural, then, to wonder whether our brains have developed specialized machinery for the perception of events involving bodies, such as face, body, and hand movements.

In this chapter, I will discuss the neural correlates of biological motion perception, a special class of body perception. This chapter will briefly summarize some of the behavioral findings related to biological motion perception and will detail the current state of knowledge of the underlying neural mechanisms. The literature on biological motion perception provides (1) psychophysical studies that isolate the perceptual computations required for the perception of body movements, (2) case studies of patient populations with unusual perception of biological motion but in which other types of specialized vision are spared, (3) single-unit recordings in monkeys that confirm the existence of cells that fire when body movements are viewed, and (4) neuro-imaging and neural-stimulation experiments on specific brain areas that demonstrate the existence in humans of regions involved in biological motion perception.

Together, the findings support the proposal for the existence of specialized neural machinery for biological motion perception that operates in cooperation with neural mechanisms specialized for other perceptual, cognitive, and motor tasks. This specialized machinery, thought to exist primarily within the human superior temporal sulcus (STS), likely is strongly interconnected with brain areas involved in motion computations and attention (such as extrastriate MT+ and parietal attention areas), form and face perception (ventral temporal cortex), action imitation (premotor cortex), and social perception (many cortical areas, including the amygdala and orbitofrontal cortex).

Seeing Biological Motion

The study of body movement has a rich history going back more than 100 years. In the late 19th century, Etienne-Jules Marey, an inventor, scientist, and artist, developed techniques to measure movements generated from biological sources (Merlin, 1985). Among his inventions are the early cardiograph, which measured movement of the heart, and the sphygmograph, a device used to measure the pulse. He also developed "movement traces," a technique of visualizing human movement without the body using stroboscopic photography. In the early 1970s, Gunnar Johansson modernized Marey's movement traces into cinematic animations. His "point-light" displays of biological motion were created by attaching small lamps to the joints of an actor wearing dark clothing and recording him moving about in a dark room. By adjusting the brightness and contrast of the television screen, Johansson was able to erase any trace of the human form and leave only the lights on the joints visible. Like the motion streaks created with still photography, these point-light animations depict human movement without explicitly representing body shape. Point-light animations are now created through a variety of techniques (discussed in more detail in chapter 13), including videotaping actors with markers on their bodies (Johansson, 1973), computer simulations of movement (i.e., Cutting, 1978), and the use of motion-capture systems (e.g., Giese & Poggio, 2003; Pollick, Lestou, Ryu, & Cho, 2002; Troje, 2002).

Using point-light displays, perceptual sensitivity to the movement patterns of humans and animals can be measured apart from the colors and textures of the body. The interpretation of point-light displays as human movement is immediate and unambiguous. The following is from Johansson's description in his initial report: "The observer has the freedom neither to combine the moving points in other groupings by an act of concentration nor to see these elements just as a series of unrelated points in motion" (Johansson, 1973, p. 203). Seemingly without the directed will of the observer, though mediated by attentional resources (discussed in more detail in chapter 13; Cavanagh, Labianca, & Thornton, 2001), the moving joints are linked into a human form through spatial and temporal integration of the dots (Ahlström, Blake, & Ahlström, 1997).

Observers organize point-light displays into biological movements after exposures lasting only a fraction of a second, but point-light animations convey much more information than just a person in action. Despite the absence of information about height or body shape, observers accurately identify the specific individuals in point-light displays (Cutting & Kozlowski, 1977) and the gender of the actors (Cutting, Proffitt, & Kozlowski, 1978; Sumi, 2000). Observers can easily recognize a cloud of point-light dots as people dancing together (Dittrich, Troscianko, Lea, & Morgan, 1996) or can identify point-light animals (Bellefeuille & Faubert, 1998). Subjects can even make fine judgments about invisible objects manipulated by the point-light actor (e.g., the distance a sandbag is thrown or the weight of an invisible box being lifted; Runeson & Frykholm, 1981, 1983).

Perhaps our expertise shouldn't be surprising considering the amount of practice we have seeing body motion. Research has shown that 4-month-old infants preferentially view upright biological motion displays over upside-down biological motion displays (which are not recognized as biological by adults; Fox & McDaniel, 1982; Pavlova & Sokolov, 2000). By 9 months of age, infants preferentially view biological motion displays with the natural occlusions created by the body over displays without the natural occlusions, implying sensitivity to implied body contours (Bertenthal, Proffitt, & Cutting, 1984; Bertenthal, Proffitt, & Kramer, 1987). By the time children reach preschool age, they are able to accurately identify different animals depicted with point-lights (Pavlova, Krageloh-Mann, Sokolov, & Birbaumer, 2001; Richardson & Webster, 1996). Infants' and children's perception of biological motion is discussed in more detail in chapter 14, however, suffice it to say that these studies illustrate the amazing sensitivity to movement kinematics quite early in development.

I would also like to note that recognizing biological motion is not a selectively human ability. Cats can discriminate point-light animations of cats (Blake, 1993); pigeons can discriminate point-light animations of pigeons (Dittrich, Lea, Barrett, & Gurr, 1998) and bottle-nosed dolphins trained to perform actions as commanded by hand movements follow the same commands when shown point-light videos of the commands (Herman, Morrel-Samuels, & Pack, 1990). Monkeys can also see point-light displays, and studies measuring neuronal firing during biological motion perception will be discussed later in this chapter.

Thus the ability to recognize biological motion from the kinematics of bodies alone is not unique to humans, which suggests that movement patterns capture the essential ingredients needed to detect other living beings. The ability of infants to make fine discriminations between point-light displays suggests that recognizing movement is an important neural function. Together, these psychophysical studies highlight the importance of biological motion perception and suggest the possibility of a brain mechanism specialized for its recognition.

Neuropsychology and Biological Motion Perception

From a historical perspective, lesion studies were among the first to motivate the concept of functional localization in the human brain. Neuropsychological studies document specialization in neural machinery through dissociations in behavior following localized brain injury. Several studies of individuals with brain lesions have demonstrated that damage to some areas of cortex results in difficulty in recognizing biological motion while leaving other kinds of motion perception intact. In contrast, individuals with damage to other areas of cortex have difficulty seeing simple motion patterns, but no difficulty recognizing biological motion. Consider the following examples.

Patient A. L. suffered two strokes that affected her temporal lobe and posterior parietal cortex (Cowey & Vaina, 2000). Immediately following her stroke, A. L. was unable to recognize friends and family by their faces or gaits, though she could identify them by their voices. She shortly regained her ability to recognize familiar faces if the individual remained still, but complained that she could not recognize people when they were moving. During psychophysical testing, A. L. was unable to identify any human movements depicted in point-light animations, even after having been told that the display showed human action. A. L. was also unable to recognize objects defined by flicker, motion direction, or velocity. For example, she was unable to discriminate a rotating cylinder constructed from moving dots from an unstructured display of the same dots. She had no problems with shape recognition per se, because when the objects were defined by luminance instead of by motion, A. L. had no difficulty recognizing them.

Biological motion perception was examined in two individuals with damage to the right parietal cortex as a result of stroke (Battelli, Cavanagh, & Thornton, 2003). These individuals were able to see biological motion in point-light animations when they were displayed alone, but had great difficulty when required to make seemingly simple judgments about the display. For example, when presented simultaneously with four walkers, one of which was "jumbled" to appear disjointed and limping, the patients required much more time than normal observers and made many mistakes in identifying the different walker. Previous studies of patients with parietal lesions have demonstrated a wide range of high-level motion tasks that specifically require engaging attentional mechanisms and are impaired in these individuals (Battelli et al., 2001). Thus it is unclear whether biological motion perception per se is impaired or if biological motion perception suffers as a result of a disabled attentional system (Cavanagh et al., 2001).

Schenk and Zihl (1997a, 1997b) measured motion and form perception in two patients with bilateral lesions in the parietal lobe and extensive damage to the underlying white matter. These patients had normal motion coherence detection thresholds and were able to segregate sketches of objects super-imposed on top of each other. These patients also recognized human activities depicted in point-light animations when the figures were presented alone; however when the biological motion figures were embedded in a field of static or random dots, the patients were unable to detect them. These are conditions that would not effectively mask biological motion for normal observers (Bertenthal & Pinto, 1994). So while the patients were able to detect motion signals and initially seemed to have intact biological motion perception, in fact their perceptual abilities were quite different from that of normal observers.

Patient A. F. is an individual with bilateral lesions of the temporal-parietal-occipital junction extending into the posterior parietal cortex of the left hemi-sphere. A. F. was able to discriminate images based on shape and color, but he was unable to see shapes defined by stereopsis or motion and had elevated thresholds for detecting coherent motion signals in random-dot cinematograms (Vaina, Lemay, Bienfang, Choi, & Nakayama, 1990). Despite these difficul-ties, A. F. could easily identify biological motion in Johansson's point-light displays. He readily described animations of a man climbing the stairs or riding a bicycle and details such as the direction of the walker. Despite ob-vious difficulties in tasks designed to measure basic motion perception abili-ties, A. F.'s ability to see human movement was quite intact.

The evidence from these examples suggests that there may be brain areas recruited for biological motion perception in addition to those needed for simple shape discrimination or motion detection. Based on the location of the lesions, the brain areas near the occipito-parietal junction, possibly extending into the parietal lobe, seem to be implicated in biological motion perception.

It is interesting to note, also, that some individuals without localized brain lesions have difficulty recognizing biological motion. For example, individuals with schizophrenia and children with autism have difficulty discriminating point-light biological motion from motion-matched control stimuli (Blake, Turner, Smoski, Pozdol, & Stone, 2003; Kim, Doop, Blake, & Park, 2003). Despite these difficulties, neither group has difficulty detecting a stationary global form made of smaller parts. In contrast, children with Williams Syndrome, a disorder characterized by moderate mental retardation and highly social behavior, perform *better* than mental age–matched children in dis-criminating point-light biological motion (Jordan, Reiss, Hoffman, & Landau, 2002). This is perhaps even more surprising because these children have difficulty making global motion discriminations on non-biological patterns (Atkinson et al., 2001). Again, these findings provide further evidence that biological motion perception is unique from other, more general kinds of motion and form perception.

Physiology and Biological Motion Perception

The third piece in the puzzle of identifying brain areas involved in biological motion perception can be found in research measuring the tuning properties of single neurons in monkeys. Like humans, monkeys (and pigeons, cats, and dolphins) can recognize biological movement from point-light animations. The following outlines some of the findings from these investigations.

STPa

When one discusses the neural correlates of motion perception, it is natural to begin with the middle temporal area (MT, also known as V5). Hierarchically speaking, MT is the first brain area specialized for the encoding of motion. While cells in earlier brain areas (such as V1) respond to motion in the visual world, it is the neurons in MT that are tuned to speed, direction, and depth of motion. Thus, in a model of brain areas, each of which performs some unique computation based on the inputs from earlier areas, MT is the first to be specialized for motion computations. However, while the characteristics of MT cells make this neural area excellent for encoding motion, there is no evidence that neurons in this visual area are specialized for biological motion. It is in an area anatomically situated anterior to MT, in the anterior superior temporal polysensory region (STPa) that cells have been identified as tuned to biological motion.

Cells in STPa are characterized by their multisensory responses—this region receives connections from visual, auditory, and somatosensory cortex, though the most dominant modality is vision (Desimone & Gross, 1979). Receptive fields of the visually responsive neurons cover a large extent of both the contralateral and ipsilateral visual field, and nearly all cells prefer moving visual stimuli over stationary patterns (Bruce, Desimone, & Gross, 1981). While most STPa cells have no size or shape preferences for the object, or for the direction of motion, many prefer particular patterns of motion, such as movement in depth, radial motion, or optic flow (Andersen & Siegel, 1999).

Cells in STPa, which appear to be uninterested in form but very interested in movement, are also sensitive to viewing body movement. Using full-illumination animations, researchers have shown that many of the cells in STPa fire when a monkey views a full-figure human body walking across the field of view, rotating in space, and moving in and out of occlusion (Perrett et al., 1985). In some instances, cells fire most robustly to the movement of the entire body, while other cells may fire when the monkey views isolated body parts in motion (Oram & Perrett, 1994). One of the ways in which these cells are most interesting to the study of biological motion is in how the proper combination of form and motion are required to induce firing. While cells in STPa are selective for particular types of body motion, such as walking to the left or toward the viewer, cells in this region are also selective for particular views of bodies or body parts (Wachsmuth, Oram, & Perrett, 1994). Thus a cell that fires when viewing someone walking to the left may not fire when the walker is facing the right or walking backward (Perrett et al., 1985).

A small population of STPa cells also responds to body movement as depicted in point-light animations (Oram & Perrett, 1994). Like the findings using whole-body images, many of these cells are selective for direction of gait, viewpoint, or both. The cells do not respond well to jumbled motion, which has the same component motion vectors as biological motion but their spatial positions are scrambled. Some cells that responded when the figure showed articulation did not fire when the figure was a rigid human form rotating in depth. The researchers noted that cells with similar response selectivity (such as a preference for head rotations toward the animal) tended to be found in proximity to each other, such that the cells were clustered according to motion and viewpoint preference.

The evidence for body-selective responses on the superior temporal sulcus of the monkey in combination with the neuropsychological literature suggests the possibility of selective body responses in human brains. However, because of the gross anatomical differences between the monkey and human brains, the candidate brain area for a human homologue of STPa is difficult to determine. Even the anatomical position of possible landmarks, such as MT and MST, vary greatly between monkeys and humans. As will be discussed later in the chapter, researchers have measured neural correlates of body-motion perception in humans using positron emission tomography (PET) and functional magnetic resonance imaging (fMRI). The results of these studies suggest an area on the human STS, anterior to human MT+, which may have some functional response properties in common with the monkey STPa, particularly the neural responses to biological motion.

F5 Mirror Cells

It is important at this point to note the existence of a related class of neurons found in the frontal lobe of awake and behaving monkeys (also discussed in chapters 4 and 19). A region known as premotor cortex (or F5) contains neurons that fire when a monkey makes some kind of action, such as grasping, tearing, or manipulating an object (Kurata & Tanji, 1986; Rizzolatti et al., 1988). The neurons tend to be tuned such that specific actions drive the neuronal response, as opposed to the specific movements that generate that action. For example, a premotor neuron may fire when the monkey grasps food, regardless of whether the thumb and forefinger are used for the action or other fingers are used. Thus the responses of F5 neurons are action category specific.

In addition to action execution, a subset of premotor neurons will also fire during action observation (Gallese, Fadiga, Fogassi, & Rizzolatti, 1996). These neurons have been dubbed mirror neurons, because seeing and executing a motor behavior can drive the cell response. Like the premotor cells that are tuned for specific action categories, the observation response of mirror neurons is also tuned to specific actions. Typically the optimal executed action that drives a mirror neuron is the kind of action that optimally drives the cell when viewed (Rizzolatti, Fadiga, Gallese, & Fogassi, 1996).

Thus it appears that this subset of neurons in the frontal lobe of monkeys combine action representations across the motor and visual systems. It has been proposed that the primary function of this mirror system is for learning motor behaviors through imitation and for understanding the actions of others (Gallese et al., 1996). The mirror cells have been identified in monkeys, but later in this chapter and in chapter 19 evidence will be presented to support the existence of the mirror system in the frontal lobe of humans.

Neuroimaging and Biological Motion Perception

In recent years, the fastest growing branch of psychology has been in the area of cognitive neuroscience. This growth seems to be largely a result of the widespread use of neuroimaging to identify brain areas involved in cognitive performances. Both PET and fMRI have been used extensively to study the neural correlates of body perception, particularly with regard to biological motion. The findings suggest that no single brain area is responsible for body recognition, but that many brain areas subserve body perception. These brain areas include the human MT+, STS, ventral temporal cortex, and premotor cortex.

Extrastriate Visual Cortex

The striate and extrastriate cortex in humans have been mapped in great detail, and no fewer than 10 functional regions have been identified within Brodmann's areas 17, 18, and 19 (Press, Brewer, Dougherty, Wade, & Wandell, 2001). Among these is the human homologue to monkey MT, usually referenced as MT+ in humans because measurement resolution used in imaging studies typically precludes delineating MT proper from its satellites. This region is recognized as a general motion processing region, similar to that found in monkeys, and is strongly activated whenever an observer reports seeing motion (Huk & Heeger, 2002; Orban et al., 1995; Tootell et al., 1995; Watson et al., 1993).

In some cases, MT+ may activate when observers are not seeing movement, but are viewing a stationary image that implies some kind of movement. For example, Peigneux et al. (2000) found activation in the lateral occipital region overlapping with MT+ when the subjects saw the images of people in the midst of arm or torso gestures. Similarly, Kourtzi and Kanwisher (2000) found MT+ to be more activated when subjects viewed stationary images of body postures that implied motion (e.g., a person with the arm poised to throw a ball) than similar images that depicted stationary postures (such as sitting). The authors concluded that observers are in some way mentalizing the completed action in the instances of implied kinetic postures, and as a result MT+ is more activated.

MT+ activation during point-light biological motion perception was reported in a study by Howard et al. (1996). In this study observers viewed three types of motion: a field of translating dots, optic flow patterns, and biological motion. All three types of motion activated MT+, and the patterns of activation were mostly, but not completely overlapping. The authors interpreted this lack of overlap as evidence of subcompartments within the MT+ complex that respond preferentially to different types of motion. Because of the many small satellites surrounding MT+, it is possible that the nonoverlapping response patterns may reflect neural regions outside of MT proper.

Superior Temporal Sulcus

In the human brain, the region most commonly reported to have biological motion selective neural signals can be found on the posterior extent of the superior temporal sulcus (posterior STS). The STS in humans is a large sulcus that extends from the most anterior aspects of the temporal lobe to the most posterior extent of parieto-occipital cortex. Many functional modalities, including speech, hearing, and visual perception, have been shown to activate discrete cortical areas on this large expanse of cortex. The perception of bodies, faces, and hands have all been found to activate regions on the posterior extent of the STS, near where the inferior temporal sulcus (ITS) and STS converge (Allison, Puce, & McCarthy, 2000). Overall, the STS appears to be most activated when the bodies or body parts being viewed are articulating in a manner that is natural to our body structures. It is worth noting that it is as yet unclear whether the human STS is the homologue to the monkey STPa, the region that contains cells tuned to biological motion. Aside from the unique sulcal patterns in humans as compared to monkeys, the location of other sensory areas that could be used as landmarks, such as motion sensitive region MT, are variable between the two species (MT+ in humans is located on the ITS, while in monkeys it is located on the STS). Undoubtedly, future work will attempt to address the possibility of a homology between the two regions.

Selectivity

Whenever a person performs any kind of perceptual or cognitive task, such as viewing a group of dots that combine to depict biological motion, many parts of the brain are activated. For example, the primary visual cortex would be activated during all visual tasks, and motion area MT+ would be activated whenever the display contained motion. But it is unlikely that the computations being performed within these brain areas are specialized in any way for biological motion perception.

Therefore, to identify brain areas that are selective for biological motion, Grossman et al. (2000) showed observers two types of motion (biological and motion-matched non-biological control animations) and looked for brain areas that responded more when biological motion was being shown. They found a region on the posterior extent of the STS (posterior STS) that responded most to biological motion and less to the motion-matched control stimulus. In contrast, MT+ responded equally well to the two types of motion. They also found that posterior STS is not preferentially activated by coherent motion over stationary patterns, or by kinetic boundaries versus coherent motion. Thus simple motion patterns are not sufficient to activate this region.

Similarly, biological motion, when inverted, can serve as a control stimulus for itself. Behavioral studies have shown that recognizing upside-down biological motion is much more difficult than recognizing upright biological motion (Pavlova & Sokolov, 2000). The inversion effect for biological motion is similar to that found for faces (Yin, 1969) and full images of body postures (Reed, Stone, Bozova, & Tanaka, 2003; also see chapter 11), which is thought to reflect configural processing—perception of the whole mediated by the relative position of the parts. Like the discrimination of faces, discrimination of biological motion is more difficult when the animations are inverted (Sumi, 1984), until they are recognized as biological and can then be identified more quickly (Pavlova & Sokolov, 2003). Grossman and Blake (2001) found that inverting the animations results in approximately half of the neural activity on posterior STS, but still more neural response than non-biological animations.

What is it about biological motion, then, that is driving the neural response in the posterior STS? It seems that the posterior STS is selective for the articulation that naturally occurs in human movement. For example, when a human figure is rotated rigidly instead of articulating, brain activity is much lower within the posterior STS (Beauchamp, Lee, Haxby, & Martin, 2002). The same result was demonstrated using full-body biological motion instead of point-light videos (Pelphrey et al., 2003). In this study, neural activity was measured while observers viewed four objects: a robot, a grandfather clock, a complex but meaningless mechanical object, and a person. All objects were visible to the observer at all times, but on a given trial only one of the four objects moved. Many brain areas were activated by the motion of the visual stimuli, including MT+, the posterior STS, the left premotor cortex, the intraparietal cortex, and the fusiform gyri. They also found that MT+ responded best to the mechanical movement and equally well to all of the other objects in motion. In contrast, the STS was most active when the person or robot moved, but not when the grandfather clock or the articulating mechanical object moved. Thus the authors concluded that, unlike MT+, which activated to the motion of all of the objects, the STS was preferentially activated when the object articulated in the same manner as a human body.

One could argue that the posterior STS would respond to any class of stimuli for which the class has a characteristic movement pattern. To test this argument, Beauchamp et al. (2003) compared neural activity during biological motion perception to tool perception, an entirely different class of stimuli, the members of which have characteristic motions that define their function (e.g., twisting for a screwdriver, and swinging for a hammer) and are easily recognized as tools when depicted in point-light animations. The researchers found more activity on the posterior STS during body movement as compared to tool movement (though there was more activity in the middle temporal gyrus and inferior temporal sulcus to tool movement). The STS had an even larger response to the full videos of the moving bodies than for the point-light biological motion, suggesting that the richer visual displays more effectively drive the STS.

Neural activity on the STS is also modulated depending on whether observers recognize the animations as biological or not. Grossman et al. (2004) showed subjects point-light animations of people performing various activities with the figures embedded in an array of noise dots designed to mask the actor and render the biological motion animation nearly impossible to discriminate from the non-biological control stimulus. Not surprisingly, brain imaging revealed little difference in neural activity within the posterior STS to the biological and non-biological controls embedded in noise. The observers then practiced the discrimination task with the animations embedded in noise until they were able to accurately discriminate biological from non-biological motion. In contrast to the findings before practice, after the training brain imaging revealed neural signals within the posterior STS that discriminated between the biological and nonbiological controls (still embedded in noise). Thus the neural mechanism involved in detecting biological motion is plastic and can become more sensitive with training, and the brain activity associated with the same visual stimulus, namely, noisy biological motion animations, depends strongly on the experience of the observer.

Recent computational modeling has supported the notion that biological motion perception is achieved through a flexible neural system. Giese and Poggio (2003) developed a neural-based hierarchical model that is able to discriminate different actions depicted in biological motion animations (described in more detail in chapter 15). Briefly, special care was taken in developing this model such that units within each level of the network would simulate the response-tuning properties of different cortical areas, such as V1, V4, MT, STS, the ventral temporal cortex, and the premotor cortex. The model was trained to discriminate between different exemplars of the same kind of action, such as walking, running, or limping. Following training, the model was able to generalize the discriminations to new exemplars of the same types of activities.

The posterior STS has also been identified as critical for biological motion perception in a study using transcranial magnetic stimulation (TMS). This technique delivers strong magnetic pulses to localized brain areas, temporarily disrupting the local patterns of neuronal firing within the local region. TMS has been shown to impair behavioral measures on a variety of perceptual and cognitive tasks (for review, see Pascual-Leone, Walsh, & Rothwell, 2000). In the case of biological motion perception, TMS stimulation over the posterior STS results in a significant decrease in sensitivity to point-light displays (Grossman, Battelli, & Pascual-Leone, 2005). Stimulation only affects biological motion perception if the animations are viewed in the upright, canonical orientation: sensitivity to inverted animations is unchanged. There is no change in sensitivity to biological motion (either upright or inverted) following stimulation over MT+. These results again demonstrate the importance of the STS in biological motion perception, the lack of specialized computations in MT for biological motion, and the dependence of biological motion and simple motion detection on dissociated neural mechanisms.

The neural response to biological motion on the STS is quite general and not specific to whole-body movements depicted in movies or point-light animations. Point-light animations of body parts have also been shown to activate regions along the posterior extent of the STS. Bonda, Petrides, Ostry, and Evans (1996) compared neural activity while observers viewed point-light displays of goal-oriented hand actions (e.g., reaching for a glass) or viewed whole-body movements (e.g., a walker traveling in different directions). The goal-directed hand movements resulted in higher activity levels on the posterior STS, a region in the superior parietal cortex, and the intraparietal sulcus.

It has also been demonstrated that individuals who are literate in American Sign Language (ASL) can "read" signs that are portrayed through point-light animations in which the fingers and arms are represented (Poizner, Bellugi, & Lutes-Driscoll, 1981). The corresponding neural activity when literate readers are viewing these signs can be found on the posterior STS (Neville et al., 1997). Brain activity is dependent, however, on whether the individual is literate in ASL, suggesting a stronger link with language processing on the STS than with visual perception of body movement.

It is also important to note that the STS is involved in the perception of faces, particularly when the parts of the face are moving. Researchers have found viewing very small face movements, such as shifting eye gaze or opening and closing the mouth, is sufficient to activate the posterior STS (Hoffman & Haxby, 2000; Puce, Allison, Bentin, Gore, & McCarthy, 1998). The researchers compared activation levels to stimuli in which the eyes and mouth were replaced with low contrast checkerboards randomly shuffling the luminance of the checks to give the impression of motion. Brain activity on the STS was higher for the more natural stimuli in which the eyes and mouth were visible, than for the faces with the moving checkerboards.

Ventral Temporal Cortex

Based on its anatomical location and preference for moving bodies over stationary bodies, the posterior STS could be considered part of the dorsal or motion pathway of human visual processing. In addition to the superior temporal sulcus, some studies have identified brain areas in the ventral pathway, sometimes referred to as the form pathway, that are selective for biological motion perception.

Vaina et al. (2001) measured neural activity while subjects viewed point-light animations of whole-body movements. In addition to regions on the STS, they found brain areas on the ventral surface of the temporal lobe to be activated by the biological motion. Beauchamp et al. (2002) found regions on the lateral fusiform gyrus that are more responsive to body movement than to tool movement. Grossman and Blake (2002) showed that the fusiform face area and occipital face area, two regions previously identified as selective for faces (but see Gauthier, Tarr, Anderson, Skudlarski, & Gore, 1999; Kanwisher, McDermott, & Chun, 1997; Puce, Allison, Gore, & McCarthy, 1995), to also contain neural signals that differentiate between biological and non-biological motion.

It is perhaps not surprising to find brain activation selective for biological motion in ventral temporal cortex. Biological motion perception is the global integration of local motion signals into a coherent form. When motion signals are scrambled in simple ways, such as placing the dots between the joints instead of on the joints, or by limiting the amount of movement by any given dot (limited-lifetime displays) individuals have little difficulty recognizing biological motion (Beintema & Lappe, 2002; Bertenthal & Pinto, 1994; Neri, Morrone, & Burr, 1998). However, when the canonical form is altered, such as by turning the animation upside-down, recognizing the biological motion becomes difficult or impossible (Pavlova & Sokolov, 2000; Sumi, 1984). The importance of form information over motion information in biological motion perception is also evident in the neuropsychological literature discussed above. Patients with lesions in the motion pathway have little difficulty recognizing point-light biological motion, while those with lesions in form areas have great difficulty recognizing the animations.

Premotor Cortex

Brain-imaging studies have also discovered activity in the frontal lobe associated with viewing human movement. Premotor cortex, located on the inferior frontal gyrus, is thought to be the human homologue to monkey area F5, the region in which mirror cells were identified (Gallese et al., 1996). Because the hand is one of the major motor representations within the premotor cortex, it is perhaps not surprising that studies which have identified neural activity in the human premotor cortex have typically used images or animations of hands.

Grezes et al. (1998), for example, showed observers animations (not point-light) of hand movements that depicted either meaningful or meaningless pantomimes. Observers were either given no instruction, or asked to take note of the gestures because they would be asked to imitate the pantomimes later. These researchers found the same cortical network of activity to be activated for the two types of hand motion (meaningful or meaningless) when no particular instructions were given. The network includes the MT region and the superior temporal sulcus. However, when subjects were instructed that they would be required to imitate the hand movements, viewing meaningful hand actions also activated the premotor cortex.

In another neuroimaging study, Rizzolatti et al. (1996) examined the neural activity associated with viewing a movie of a hand grasping an object, actively grasping an object, and passively observing the object. They found that simply observing hands grasping objects as compared to passively viewing the objects resulted in increased activation of the MT+ region, the posterior STS, and the premotor cortex.

Most recently, Saygin et al. (2004) have found premotor activation selective for biological motion when subjects view point-light animations of actors walking. The authors interpret their findings in the context of action-observation networks, that is, viewed action shares a common representation with those brain areas involved in producing action. The idea that viewing an action and performing the action may be subserved by a common neural representation has some support from psychophysical findings. A detailed discussion of these findings can be found in chapter 18. As an example, however, consider the experiment of Shiffrar and Freyd (1990), in which they demonstrated that the perceived path of a body limb in an apparent motion sequence can follow body constraints imposed by limb structure. In this study, subjects were shown two stationary images of a body posture in which a limb was positioned either in front or behind another body part. For example, an arm was shown in front of the torso in one image and behind the torso in the other image. If sufficient time was allowed between presentation of the two images, observers reported seeing smooth apparent motion of the arm around the torso, a motion path possible with the constraints of the body. However, this visual interpretation was reported less when the images were presented in rapid succession, and instead observers reported seeing the impossible motion of the arm through the torso. In a subsequent imaging study, experimenters found higher neural activity levels in the superior temporal gyrus and the primary motor and premotor cortices in the trials with long interframe intervals, which favored the impression of possible body movement, than in those trials favoring impossible biological motion (Stevens, Fonlupt, Shiffrar, & Decety, 2000).

Another piece of evidence supporting the shared representation of executed and observed actions, at least within the frontal lobe, comes from a brain-stimulation study. Using TMS, Fadiga et al. (1995) stimulated the hand representation of motor regions while recording the motor evoked potential (MEP) of various muscles in the hand and arm. They found that the amplitude of the MEPs increased if during stimulation the observers viewed the experimenter grasping various objects or making complex arm movements, such as tracing a shape in space. There was no change in MEP amplitude when observers viewed the objects without the experimenter manipulating them or when observers had to perform a luminance detection task on a small dot. The authors interpreted their results as evidence for the automatic recruitment of muscles that would be used during action execution during the observation of those actions.

Conclusions

We live in a dynamic visual world and one of the most biologically salient events is human movement. People are remarkably adept at recognizing the actions performed by others, even when the kinematic patterns of their movements are portrayed by nothing more than a handful of light points attached to the head and major joints of the body. Recently, evidence has accumulated to suggest that the STS is a "hot spot" for the early registration of sensory events related to socially relevant experiences (Allison et al., 2000).

Case studies of individuals with lesions and selective behavioral deficits have indicated a strong dissociation between the neural regions involved in simple motion perception and those underlying biological motion perception.

Those individuals with lesions of early motion areas have little difficulty recognizing biological motion in point-light animations despite having severe difficulty making simple motion judgments, such as velocity discrimination. In contrast, individuals with lesions covering the posterior parietal cortex, including the STS, have great difficulty recognizing biological motion and little difficulty with low-level motion tasks. These individuals also demonstrate that the role of the motion pathway in the perception of biological motion is unclear and that other neural computations, such as the recognition of the human form, may play a larger role in biological motion perception.

Single-unit recording studies in the macaque STPa have reported cells that respond selectively during visual perception of body movements, including the movement of body parts. These findings include cells selective for mouth movements, head movements, hand movements, and movements of the whole body, either depicted by the entire body or by point-lights. Although the homology between the macaque STPa and human STS has not been clearly established, the two species share remarkable similarities, particularly in regard to the stimulus properties which elicit neural responses in these regions.

Many brain-imaging studies have investigated brain areas active during perception of bodies and biological motion. Results vary across studies, but the most robust finding is that of biological motion selective neural activity on the posterior extent of the STS (Beauchamp et al., 2003; Bonda et al., 1996; Grossman & Blake, 2002; Grossman et al., 2000; Howard et al., 1996; Pelphrey et al., 2003; Saygin et al., 2004; Vaina et al., 1990). The STS responds to a number of different body stimuli, but neural selectivity shows preference for natural body movements, such as articulating, grasping, and in some cases, changes in eye gaze and mouth movements. Other simple motion patterns (such as coherent motion, kinetic boundaries, and 3D nonbiological structure from motion) and more-complex motions with non-biological interpretations (such as tool motion) do not effectively activate this region.

In addition to the posterior STS, the ventral temporal and premotor brain areas have also been found to be activated by the perception of biological motion in a number of studies. The ventral temporal pathway is clearly involved in the recognition of objects, shapes, letters, and faces. Point-light animations depict a shape (the body shape) in action, and so one could logically posit that these brain areas are recruited as part of the form recognition that goes along with biological motion perception. One piece of evidence for this is the inversion effect, which is common to biological motion perception and the recognition of other object categories (e.g., faces) that are known to recruit ventral temporal brain areas. The premotor cortex is clearly involved in motor planning and execution. The premotor cortex is most commonly activated when observers view intentional arm movements (such as grasping) and are given the task viewing the actions with the intent to later imitate those actions.

The existence of at least three brain areas with neural signals selective for biological motion introduces the question of why multiple areas would exist. One explanation is that multiple brain areas are required to perform different neural computations. This proposal has most clearly and successfully been demonstrated in the early sensory cortex, which contains multiple representations of the same physical stimulus in interconnected brain areas. For example, in the occipital cortex, V1, V2, V3, V3A, V4, and MT (to name a few) are all retinotopic and interconnected in a predictable and organized way. Though visual space is repeated across the brain areas, a unique neural computation is thought to be resolved within each one. A slight modification of this explanation is that the brain areas recruited during perception may depend on the task of the observer. For example, brain areas selective for faces have been found in ventral temporal areas and on the STS of humans. It has been proposed that ventral temporal brain areas are recruited when the task is to individuate (or identify) the person, while STS regions are recruited during perception of changeable aspects of the face, such as emotional expression (Haxby, Hoffman, & Gobbini, 2002).

Thus the finding of multiple brain areas with neural signals selective for biological motion may be indicative of a network of brain areas, interconnected in some predictable way, the components of which may be recruited depending on task requirements (see Figure 16.1). In this scheme, each individual brain area performs a unique computation. At this stage in our understanding of biological motion perception, the details of this scheme are

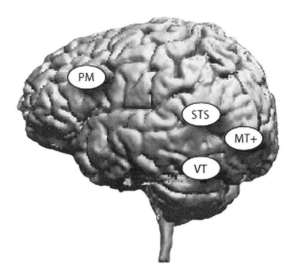

Figure 16.1. Schematic of brain areas involved in perception of biological motion. STS: superior temporal sulcus; MT+: human middle temporal area (MT); VT: ventral temporal cortex; PM: premotor cortex.

largely unclear, however, one can generate some reasonable hypotheses. For example, the exact nature of these neural computations within STSp have yet to be fully revealed, but it appears that the STS is involved in the earliest aspects of the neural response, is recruited regardless of the task, and may be a necessary node in the network for normal biological motion perception. In contrast, based on the findings from other areas of research, the primary function of the ventral temporal and premotor areas is not likely for perception of biological motion. Yet viewing biological events recruits these specialized neural mechanisms. The ventral temporal cortex is likely related to extracting biological form, while the premotor cortex may be responsible for encoding action. It is important to note that the connectivity between these regions (and other involved brain areas yet to be determined) is largely unclear at this point in time.

What Is It For?

It is worth noting some of the implications of our brains containing neural circuitry specialized for biological motion perception. The posterior STS in particular seems to serve as the front end of a much more complicated circuit, which may serve many purposes in social perception. One can argue the importance of biological motion perception in many aspects of human life, including action imitation in learning (chapters 7, 10 and 14), the recognition of intentional action in social situations (chapters 18, 19, and 20), and the quick recognition of changeable aspects of personality, such as emotion (e.g., Atkinson, Dittrich, Gemmell, & Young, 2004). A brief discussion of these tasks is outlined below, though a much more detailed discussion can be found in the references just mentioned.

   One likely consequence of spending so much time watching biological motion is that we learn how to create these behaviors ourselves. Infants as young as 2–3 weeks old (and possibly as early as 2 days old) can imitate facial movements, such as mouth openings and tongue protrusions (Meltzoff & Moore, 1977, 1983). How is it that we are able to imitate motor behaviors that we are viewing? Meltzoff and Moore (1977) propose that imitation is possible because we are able to directly compare production of our own movements with those body movements that we see. This suggests, at some level of neural computation, a shared representation of the actions we see with those that we generate. It is through the comparison of these representations that we are able to learn motor behaviors from others. Single-unit physiology certainly supports the idea of a shared neural substrate for the visual perception of action and the production of action in the mirror cells of monkey F5 (Rizzolatti, Fadiga, Gallese, & Fogassi, 1996). The human homologue to F5 can be found on the inferior frontal gyrus of the premotor cortex. Like the mirror cells in monkeys, producing or viewing actions activates this brain area. These regions serve exactly the kind of computation that Meltzoff and Moore have suggested.

Some researchers have proposed that when we see biological motion, we automatically attribute complex social behaviors, such as intentions and desires, to that person (Adolphs, 2001; Blakemore & Decety, 2001; Frith & Frith, 1999). It has been suggested that the perception of biological motion provides the building blocks for this type of mental inference. While only beginning to be tested directly, some evidence in the literature supports such a model of social perception. For example, extensive single-unit recordings from cells in STPa of monkeys suggest that the response properties of the biological motion–selective neurons are best characterized as selective to attention or intention (intention of the biological motion actor, not the monkey). For example, neurons which fire robustly when the experimenter reaches toward the monkey will not fire when the experimenter is reaching toward but looking away from the monkey, or when the experimenter reaches away and looks away from the monkey (Jellema, Baker, Wicker, & Perrett, 2000). There is also evidence from neuroimaging studies in humans that the STS is involved in the attribution of intent to inanimate objects. Castelli et al. (2000) showed that the STS is activated when individuals infer purposeful or goal-directed intent onto moving geometric shapes, but is not activated when the animations appear to be moving randomly. It is also interesting to note that individuals with schizophrenia and autism have difficulty attributing mental states to other individuals and have difficulty recognizing biological motion. It remains to be seen whether these findings are coincidental or reflect impairment of some common neural mechanism.

Lastly, it's worth mentioning that the extent to which humans use body kinematics to extract subtle social cues is a relatively unexplored domain. We know, for example, that individuals can identify emotions and personalities from point-light walkers (Heberlein, Adolphs, Tranel, & Damasio, 2004), discriminate emotions portrayed by point-light dancers (Dittrich et al., 1996), infer affect from point-light arm movements (Pollick, Fidopiastis, & Braden, 2001; Pollick, Paterson, Bruderlin, & Sanford, 2001), and estimate vulnerability from body movements (Gunns, Johnston, & Hudson, 2002). Some researchers are trying to map, in multidimensional kinetic space, the social and personality cues that individuals infer from point-light animations (Troje, 2002). The results from these studies and others like them will help future work in the role of biological motion perception in everyday social activities.

References

Adolphs, R. (2001). The neurobiology of social cognition. *Current Opinion in Neurobiology, 11*, 231–239.

Ahlström, V., Blake, R., & Ahlström, U. (1997). Perception of biological motion. *Perception, 26*, 1539–1548.

Allison, T., Puce, A., & McCarthy, G. (2000). Social perception from visual cues: Role of the STS region. *Trends in Cognitive Science, 4*, 267–278.

Andersen, K. C., & Siegel, R. M. (1999). Optic flow selectivity in the anterior superior temporal polysensory area, STPa, of the behaving monkey. *Journal of Neuroscience, 19*, 2681–2692.

Atkinson, A. P., Dittrich, W. H., Gemmell, A. J., & Young, A. W. (2004). Emotion perception from dynamic and static body expressions in point-light and full-light displays. *Perception, 33*, 717–746.

Atkinson, J., Anker, S., Braddick, O., Nokes, L., Mason, A., & Braddick, F. (2001). Visual and visuospatial development in young children with Williams syndrome. *Developmental and Medical Child Neurology, 43*, 330–337.

Battelli, L., Cavanagh, P., Intriligator, J., Tramo, M. J., Henaff, M. A., Michel, F., & Barton, J. J. (2001). Unilateral right parietal damage leads to bilateral deficit for high-level motion. *Neuron, 32*, 985–995.

Battelli, L., Cavanagh, P., & Thornton, I. M. (2003). Perception of biological motion in parietal patients. *Neuropsychologia, 41*, 1808–1816.

Beauchamp, M. S., Lee, K. E., Haxby, J. V., & Martin, A. (2002). Parallel visual motion processing streams for manipulable objects and human movements. *Neuron, 34*, 149–159.

Beauchamp, M. S., Lee, K. E., Haxby, J. V., & Martin, A. (2003). fMRI responses to video and point-light displays of moving humans and manipulable objects. *Journal of Cognitive Neuroscience, 15*, 991–1001.

Beintema, J. A., & Lappe, M. (2002). Perception of biological motion without local image motion. *Proceedings of the National Academy of Sciences, USA, 99*, 5661–5663.

Bellefeuille, A., & Faubert, J. (1998). Independence of contour and biological-motion cues for motion-defined animal shapes. *Perception, 27*, 225–235.

Bertenthal, B., & Pinto, J. (1994). Global processing of biological motion. *Psychological Science, 5*, 221–225.

Bertenthal, B. I., Proffitt, D. R., & Cutting, J. E. (1984). Infant sensitivity to figural coherence in biomechanical motions. *Journal of Experimental Child Psychology, 37*, 213–230.

Bertenthal, B. I., Proffitt, D. R., & Kramer, S. J. (1987). Perception of biomechanical motions by infants: Implementation of various processing constraints. *Journal of Experimental Psychology: Human Perception and Performance, 13*, 577–585.

Blake, R. (1993). Cats perceive biological motion. *Psychological Science, 4*, 54–57.

Blake, R., Turner, L. M., Smoski, M. J., Pozdol, S. L., & Stone, W. L. (2003). Visual recognition of biological motion is impaired in children with autism. *Psychological Science, 14*, 151–157.

Blakemore, S.-J., & Decety, J. (2001). From the perception of action to the understanding of intention. *Nature Reviews Neuroscience, 2*, 561–566.

Bonda, E., Petrides, M., Ostry, D., & Evans, A. (1996). Specific involvement of human parietal systems and the amygdala in the perception of biological motion. *Journal of Neuroscience, 16*, 3737–3744.

Bruce, C., Desimone, R., & Gross, C. G. (1981). Visual properties of neurons in a polysensory area in superior temporal sulcus of the macaque. *Journal of Neurophysiology, 46*, 369–384.

Castelli, F., Happe, F., Frith, U., & Frith, C. (2000). Movement and mind: A functional imaging study of perception and interpretation of complex intentional movement patterns. *NeuroImage, 12*, 314–325.

Cavanagh, P., Labianca, A. T., & Thornton, I. M. (2001). Attention-based visual routines: Sprites. *Cognition, 80*, 47–60.

Cowey, A., & Vaina, L. M. (2000). Blindness to form from motion despite intact static form perception and motion detection. *Neuropsychologia, 38*, 566–578.

Cutting, J. E. (1978). Generation of synthetic male and female walkers through manipulation of a biomechanical invariant. *Perception, 7*, 393–405.

Cutting, J. E., & Kozlowski, L. T. (1977). Recognition of friends by their walk. *Bulletin of the Psychonomic Society, 9*, 353–356.

Cutting, J. E., Proffitt, D. R., & Kozlowski, L. T. (1978). A biomechanical invariant for gait perception. *Journal of Experimental Psychology: Human Perception and Performance, 4*, 357–372.

Desimone, R., & Gross, C. G. (1979). Visual areas in the temporal cortex of the macaque. *Brain Research, 178*, 363–380.

Dittrich, W. H., Lea, S. E. G., Barrett, J., & Gurr, P. R. (1998). Categorization of natural movements by pigeons: Visual concept discrimination and biological motion. *Journal of the Experimental Analysis of Behavior, 70*, 281–299.

Dittrich, W. H., Troscianko, T., Lea, S. E., & Morgan, D. (1996). Perception of emotion from dynamic point-light displays represented in dance. *Perception, 25*, 727–738.

Fadiga, L., Fogassi, L., Pavesi, G., & Rizzolatti, G. (1995). Motor facilitation during action observation: A magnetic stimulation study. *Journal of Neurophysiology, 73*, 2608–2611.

Fox, R., & McDaniel, C. (1982). The perception of biological motion by human infants. *Science, 218*, 486–487.

Frith, C. D., & Frith, U. (1999). Interacting minds: A biological basis. *Science, 286*, 1692–1695.

Gallese, V., Fadiga, L., Fogassi, L., & Rizzolatti, G. (1996). Action recognition in the premotor cortex. *Brain, 119*, 593–609.

Gauthier, I., Tarr, M. J., Anderson, A. W., Skudlarski, P., & Gore, J. C. (1999). Activation of the middle fusiform "face area" increases with expertise in recognizing novel objects. *Nature Neuroscience, 2*, 568–573.

Giese, M. A., & Poggio, T. (2003). Neural mechanisms for the recognition of biological movements. *Nature Reviews Neuroscience, 4*, 179–192.

Grezes, J., Costes, N., & Decety, J. (1998). Top-down effect of strategy on the perception of human biological motion: A PET investigation. *Cognitive Neuropsychology, 15*, 553–582.

Grossman, E., Battelli, L., & Pascual-Leone, A. (2005). TMS over STSp disrupts perception of biological motion. *Vision Research*.

Grossman, E., & Blake, R. (2002). Brain areas active during visual perception of biological motion. *Neuron, 35*, 1157–1165.

Grossman, E., Donnelly, M., Price, R., Pickens, D., Morgan, V., Neighbor, G., & Blake, R. (2000). Brain areas involved in perception of biological motion. *Journal of Cognitive Neuroscience, 12*, 711–720.

Grossman, E. D., & Blake, R. (2001). Brain activity evoked by inverted and imagined biological motion. *Vision Research, 41*, 1475–1482.

Grossman, E. D., Kim, C. Y., & Blake, R. (2004). Learning to see biological motion: Brain activity parallels behavior. *Journal of Cognitive Neuroscience, 16*, 1–11.

Gunns, R. E., Johnston, L., & Hudson, S. M. (2002). Victim selection and kinematics: A point-light investigation of vulnerability to attack. *Journal of Nonverbal Behavior, 26*, 129–158.

Haxby, J. V., Hoffman, E. A., & Gobbini, M. I. (2002). Human neural systems for face recognition and social communication. *Biological Psychiatry, 51*, 59–67.

Heberlein, A. S., Adolphs, R., Tranel, D., & Damasio, H. (2004). Cortical regions for judgments of emotions and personality traits from point-light walkers. *Journal of Cognitive Neuroscience, 16*, 1143–1158.

Herman, L. M., Morrel-Samuels, P., & Pack, A. A. (1990). Bottlenosed dolphin and human recognition of veridical and degraded video displays of an artificial gestural language. *Journal of Experimental Psychology: General, 119*, 215–230.

Hoffman, E. A., & Haxby, J. V. (2000). Distinct representations of eye gaze and identity in the distributed human neural system for face perception. *Nature Neuroscience, 3*, 80–84.

Howard, R. J., Brammer, M., Wright, I., Woodruff, P. W., Bullmore, E. T., & Zeki, S. (1996). A direct demonstration of functional specialization within motion-related visual and auditory cortex of the human brain. *Current Biology, 6*, 1015–1019.

Huk, A. C., & Heeger, D. J. (2002). Pattern-motion responses in human visual cortex. *Nature Neuroscience, 5*, 72–75.

Jellema, T., Baker, C. I., Wicker, B., & Perrett, D. I. (2000). Neural representation for the perception of the intentionality of actions. *Brain and Cognition, 44*, 280–302.

Johansson, G. (1973). Visual perception of biological motion and a model for its analysis. *Perception and Psychophysics, 14*, 195–204.

Jordan, H., Reiss, J. E., Hoffman, J. E., & Landau, B. (2002). Intact perception of biological motion in the face of profound spatial deficits: Williams syndrome. *Psychological Science, 13*, 162–167.

Kanwisher, N., McDermott, J., & Chun, M. M. (1997). The fusiform face area: A module in human extrastriate cortex specialized for face perception. *Journal of Neuroscience, 17*, 4302–4311.

Kim, J., Doop, M. L., Blake, R., & Park, S. (2003). *Impaired recognition of biological motion in schizophrenia.* Paper presented at the International Congress on Schizophrenia Research.

Kourtzi, Z., & Kanwisher, N. (2000). Activation in human MT/MST by static images with implied motion. *Journal of Cognitive Neuroscience, 12*, 48–55.

Kurata, K., & Tanji, J. (1986). Premotor cortex neurons in macaques: Activity before distal and proximal forelimb movements. *Journal of Neuroscience, 6*, 403–411.

Meltzoff, A. N., & Moore, M. K. (1977). Imitation of facial and manual gestures by human neonates. *Science, 198*, 75–78.

Meltzoff, A. N., & Moore, M. K. (1983). Newborn infants imitate adult facial gestures. *Child Development, 54*, 702–709.

Merlin, J. S. (1985). Entienne-Jules Marey. *Journal des maladies vasculaires, 10*(Suppl. A), 3.

Neri, P., Morrone, M. C., & Burr, D. C. (1998). Seeing biological motion. *Nature, 395*, 894–896.

Neville, H. J., Coffey, S. A., Lawson, D. S., Fischer, A., Emmorey, K., & Bellugi, U. (1997). Neural systems mediating American sign language: Effects of sensory experience and age of acquisition. *Brain Language, 57*, 285–308.

Oram, M. W., & Perrett, D. I. (1994). Responses of anterior superior temporal polysensory (STPa) neurons to "biological motion" stimuli. *Journal of Cognitive Neuroscience, 6*, 99–116.

Orban, G. A., Dupont, P., De Bruyn, B., Vogels, R., Vandenberghe, R., & Mortelmans, L. (1995). A motion area in human visual cortex. *Proceedings of the National Academy of Sciences, USA, 92*, 993–997.

Pascual-Leone, A., Walsh, V., & Rothwell, J. (2000). Transcranial magnetic stimulation in cognitive neuroscience: Virtual lesion, chronometry, and functional connectivity. *Current Opinion in Neurobiology, 10*, 232–237.

Pavlova, M., Krageloh-Mann, I., Sokolov, A., & Birbaumer, N. (2001). Recognition of point-light biological motion displays by young children. *Perception, 30*, 925–933.

Pavlova, M., & Sokolov, A. (2000). Orientation specificity in biological motion perception. *Perception and Psychophysics, 62*, 889–898.

Pavlova, M., & Sokolov, A. (2003). Prior knowledge about display inversion in biological motion perception. *Perception, 32*, 937–946.

Peigneux, P., Salmon, E., van der Linden, M., Garraux, G., Aerts, J., Delfiore, G., Degueldre, C., Luxen, A., Orban, G., & Franck, G. (2000). The role of lateral occipitotemporal junction and area MT/V5 in the visual analysis of upper-limb postures. *Neuroimage, 11*, 644–655.

Pelphrey, K. A., Mitchell, T. V., McKeown, M. J., Goldstein, J., Allison, T., & McCarthy, G. (2003). Brain activity evoked by the perception of human walking: Controlling for meaningful coherent motion. *Journal of Neuroscience, 23*, 6819–6825.

Perrett, D. I., Smith, P. A., Mistlin, A. J., Chitty, A. J., Head, A. S., Potter, D. D., Broennimann, R., Milner, A. D., & Jeeves, M. A. (1985). Visual analysis of body movements by neurons in the temporal cortex of the macaque monkey: A preliminary report. *Behavioral Brain Research, 16*, 153–170.

Poizner, H., Bellugi, U., & Lutes-Driscoll, V. (1981). Perception of American Sign Language in dynamic point-light displays. *Journal of Experimental Psychology: Human Perception and Performance, 7*, 430–440.

Pollick, F. E., Fidopiastis, C., & Braden, V. (2001). Recognising the style of spatially exaggerated tennis serves. *Perception, 30*, 323–338.

Pollick, F. E., Lestou, V., Ryu, J., & Cho, S. B. (2002). Estimating the efficiency of recognizing gender and affect from biological motion. *Vision Research, 42*, 2345–2355.

Pollick, F. E., Paterson, H. M., Bruderlin, A., & Sanford, A. J. (2001). Perceiving affect from arm movement. *Cognition, 82*, B51–61.

Press, W. A., Brewer, A. A., Dougherty, R. F., Wade, A. R., & Wandell, B. A. (2001). Visual areas and spatial summation in human visual cortex. *Vision Research, 41*, 1321–1332.

Puce, A., Allison, T., Bentin, S., Gore, J. C., & McCarthy, G. (1998). Temporal cortex activation in humans viewing eye and mouth movements. *Journal of Neuroscience, 18*, 2188–2199.

Puce, A., Allison, T., Gore, J. C., & McCarthy, G. (1995). Face-sensitive regions in human extrastriate cortex studied by functional MRI. *Journal of Neurophysiology, 74*, 1192–1199.

Reed, C. L., Stone, V. E., Bozova, S., & Tanaka, J. (2003). The body inversion effect. *Psychological Science, 14*, 302–308.

Richardson, K., & Webster, D. S. (1996). Object recognition from point-light stimuli: Evidence of covariation structures in conceptual representation. *British Journal of Psychology, 87*, 567–591.

Rizzolatti, G., Camarda, R., Fogassi, L., Gentilucci, M., Luppino, G., & Matelli, M. (1988). Functional organization of inferior area 6 in the macaque monkey. II: Area F5 and the control of distal movements. *Experimental Brain Research, 71*, 491–507.

Rizzolatti, G., Fadiga, L., Gallese, V., & Fogassi, L. (1996). Premotor cortex and the recognition of motor actions. *Brain Research Cognitive Brain Research, 3*, 131–141.

Rizzolatti, G., Fadiga, L., Matelli, M., Bettinardi, V., Paulesu, E., Perani, D., & Fazio, F. (1996). Localization of grasp representations in humans by PET. 1: Observation versus execution. *Experimental Brain Research, 111,* 246–252.

Runeson, S., & Frykholm, G. (1981). Visual perception of lifted weight. *Journal of Experimental Psychology: Human Perception and Performance, 7,* 733–740.

Runeson, S., & Frykholm, G. (1983). Kinematic specification of dynamics as an informational basis for person-and-action perception: Expectation, gender recognition, and deceptive intention. *Journal of Experimental Psychology: General, 112,* 585–615.

Saygin, A. P., Wilson, S. M., Hagler, Jr., D. J., Bates, E., & Sereno, M. I. (2004). Point-light biological motion perception activates human premotor cortex. *Journal of Neuroscience, 24,* 6181–6188.

Schenk, T., & Zihl, J. (1997a). Visual motion perception after brain damage. I: Deficits in global motion perception. *Neuropsychologia, 35,* 1289–1297.

Schenk, T., & Zihl, J. (1997b). Visual motion perception after brain damage. II: Deficits in form-from-motion perception. *Neuropsychologia, 35,* 1299–1310.

Shiffrar, M., & Freyd, J. J. (1990). Apparent motion of the human body. *Psychological Science, 1,* 257–264.

Stevens, J. A., Fonlupt, P., Shiffrar, M., & Decety, J. (2000). New aspects of motion perception: Selective neural encoding of apparent human movements. *Neuroreport, 11,* 109–115.

Sumi, S. (1984). Upside-down presentation of the Johansson moving light-spot pattern. *Perception, 13,* 283–286.

Sumi, S. (2000). Perception of point-light walker produced by eight lights attached to the back of the walker. *Swiss Journal of Psychology, 59,* 126–132.

Tootell, R. B., Reppas, J. B., Dale, A. M., Look, R. B., Sereno, M. I., Malach, R., Brady, T. J., & Rosen, B. R. (1995). Visual motion aftereffect in human cortical area MT revealed by functional magnetic resonance imaging. *Nature, 375,* 139–141.

Troje, N. F. (2002). Decomposing biological motion: A framework for analysis and synthesis of human gait patterns. *Journal of Vision, 2,* 371–387.

Vaina, L. M., Lemay, M., Bienfang, D. C., Choi, A. Y., & Nakayama, K. (1990). Intact "biological motion" and "structure from motion" perception in a patient with impaired motion mechanisms: A case study. *Visual Neuroscience, 5,* 353–369.

Vaina, L. M., Solomon, J., Chowdhury, S., Sinha, P., & Belliveau, J. W. (2001). Functional neuroanatomy of biological motion perception in humans. *Proceedings of the National Academy of Sciences, USA, 98,* 11656–11661.

Wachsmuth, E., Oram, M. W., & Perrett, D. I. (1994). Recognition of objects and their component parts: Responses of single units in the temporal cortex of the macaque. *Cerebral Cortex, 5,* 509–522.

Watson, J. D., Myers, R., Frackowiak, R. S., Hajnal, J. V., Woods, R. P., Mazziotta, J. C., Shipp, S., & Zeki, S. (1993). Area V5 of the human brain: Evidence from a combined study using positron emission tomography and magnetic resonance imaging. *Cerebral Cortex, 3,* 79–94.

Yin, R. K. (1969). Looking at upside-down faces. *Journal of Experimental Psychology, 81,* 141–145.

SECTION IV

Intention and Action in Body Perception

17

An Introduction to Intention and Action in Body Perception

The Body as the Actor's Tool

Günther Knoblich

The three previous sections provided compelling evidence that the body is a special object of perception. This is most obvious for one's own body where additional sensory channels provide tactile and kinesthetic information that can be multimodally integrated with visual information (see chapter 2). These and other sources result in structural descriptions of the body, or body representations, that serve to organize bodily information (chapter 7). Because of their unique structure, others' bodies are also special objects of perception (chapter 12). Hard-wired brain circuits capture specific body configurations and body postures.

So, can the body get any more special? The answer provided by the three contributions in this last section is yes. A fundamental fact that has not yet been highlighted is that our bodies are the only interface through which we can intentionally act upon the external world that surrounds us. In a sense, our bodies are the central tools of our minds. Even the most sophisticated artificial tools (cf. chapters 3, 4, and 5) are mere extensions of this basic tool. If one loses the ability to control one's body, one also loses one's ability to control artificial tools, except maybe in a few cases, where individuals control their brain activity in order to manipulate external events (Hinterberger et al., 2004). This implies being completely isolated from the world, as "locked-in" patients are. They cannot perform goal-directed actions, but they seem to be able to perform basic perceptual and cognitive operations (Laureys, Owen, & Schiff, 2004).

But what is the exact role of actions and intentions in body perception? Recent research suggests that actions and intentions affect the perception of one's own body as well as the perception of others' bodies.

Let us first turn to the perception of one's own body. Sarah-Jayne Blakemore and her colleagues have investigated the phenomenon that it is impossible to tickle oneself (Blakemore, Frith, & Wolpert, 1999; Blakemore, Wolpert, & Frith, 1998). Their results show that one generally experiences physically equivalent, tactile stimulations as less intense when they are a consequence of one's own actions, as when one touches oneself (individuals with schizophrenia seem to be an exception; see Blakemore, Smith, Steel, Johnstone, & Frith, 2000). Their explanation for this result is that forward models, predictive mechanisms in the action system, generate signals attenuating the flow of information from the sensory receptors to the brain areas that underlie conscious perception. Similar attenuation mechanisms seem to be at work in visual movement perception (Knoblich & Kircher, 2004; Leube et al., 2003).

Recent work by Manos Tsakiris and Patrick Haggard (2003) demonstrates that the perceived time of bodily stimulation changes depending on whether it results from an action that was carried out voluntarily (intentionally) or involuntarily. In one experiment, participants either voluntarily moved the left index finger to push a button or their finger was moved by a robot to push the same button (involuntary condition). The button press resulted in a magnetic pulse applied to their motor cortex (by transcranial magnetic stimulation, TMS) that made their right index finger twitch. Although the intensity of this pulse was exactly the same in the voluntary and the involuntary condition, the twitch was perceived as occurring earlier and the button-press action was perceived as occurring later in the voluntary condition. Thus, the intention to carry out an action affected the perceived timing of the action, as well as the perceived timing of its consequences, so that they were perceived as being closer together in time. This *intentional binding effect* (Haggard, Clark, & Kalogeras, 2002) illustrates the immediate influence that intentional action has on the perception of one's own body.

Shifts in perceived intensity and perceived timing of bodily sensations provide signals that allow one to determine whether these sensations are the result of one's own or somebody else's action (Frith et al., 2000; Tsakiris & Haggard, 2003). Nicolas Georgieff and Marc Jeannerod (1998; see also Jeannerod, 1999, 2003) postulated that this ability is also supported by a "who-system" for action identification that integrates visual and proprioceptive information. This system is assumed to determine whether currently perceived events correspond to one's intention to perform a particular action. A recent study conducted by Esther van den Bos and Marc Jeannerod (2002) suggests that this system is not only sensitive to spatial and temporal action cues, but also makes use of body representations (see chapters 7 and 9). In this study, participants performed simple hand actions while they concurrently observed a display that showed their own hand or the experimenter's hand performing the same movement. Also, the display was either aligned with their actual hand orientation or rotated. The results showed that the participants less often confused the experimenter's hand with their own hand when the display was aligned with their own hand. This supports the assumption that the body image contributes to identifying self-produced actions.

Let us now turn to the role of actions and intentions in perceiving others' bodily movements and their outcomes, which is the focus of the three chapters in this section. The core assumption here is that the same representations that govern action control and action production are also involved in the perception of actions performed by others (Prinz, 1997, 2002; chapter 18).

At first glance, this assumption seems to be very similar to the functional duality of body representations posited in several chapters (chapters 4, 7, 10, 11 and 12). However, the earlier contributions mainly focused on structural aspects in the representation of body parts that are relatively invariant across self and other. The focus of this section is on invariants that are not necessarily bound to structural aspects of body representations, but arise from the temporal dynamics of actions (Knoblich & Flach, 2003; Knoblich & Prinz, 2001; Loula, Prasad, Harber, & Shiffrar, 2005), their underlying goals (Bekkering & Wohlschläger, 2002), and their relation to the objects they are about to manipulate (Barresi & Moore, 1996; Metzinger & Gallese, 2003). Consequently, the body is mainly viewed as an instrument or frame that serves actors to achieve their goals.

In the first chapter of this section, Wolfgang Prinz outlines a functional foundation for the equivalence of representations involved in action production and action perception, which revives and extends William James's traditional ideomotor theory (compare also the action simulation perspective taken by Dokic & Proust, 2002; Jeannerod, 2003). The chapter by Sarah-Jayne Blakemore extends this picture by reviewing a number of recent results, mainly from brain imagining studies, which suggest that certain brain circuits, for example, the so-called mirror system, support at the same time action perception and action production (see also Decety & Sommerville, 2003; Rizzolatti & Craighero, 2004). Finally, Chris Moore points out that it is important not to forget the objects at which bodily actions are directed. Adding a developmental perspective to the discussion, he argues that intentional relations, that is, relations between actors and the objects at which their actions are directed, are important invariants bridging the gap between perceived and performed actions. The construct of "intentional relations" also creates a link to the higher-level representations that are central to theory-of-mind research.

References

Barresi, J., & Moore, C. (1996). Intentional relations and social understanding. *Behavioral & Brain Sciences, 19*, 107–154.

Bekkering, H., & Wohlschläger, A. (2002). Action perception and imitation. In W. Prinz & B. Hommel (Eds.), *Attention and performance. Vol. 19: Common mechanisms in perception and action* (pp. 294–314). Oxford: Oxford University Press.

Blakemore, S.-J., Frith, C. D., & Wolpert, D. M. (1999). Spatio-temporal prediction modulates the perception of self-produced stimuli. *Journal of Cognitive Neuroscience, 11*, 551–559.

Blakemore, S.-J., Smith, J., Steel, R., Johnstone, E. C., & Frith, C. D. (2000). The perception of self-produced sensory stimuli in patients with auditory hallucinations and passivity experiences: Evidence for a breakdown in self-monitoring. *Psychological Medicine, 30*, 1131–1139.

Blakemore, S.-J., Wolpert, D. M., & Frith, C. D. (1998). Central cancellation of self-produced tickle sensation. *Nature Neuroscience, 1*, 635–640.

Decety, J., & Sommerville, J. A. (2003). Shared representations between self and other: A social cognitive neuroscience view. *Trends in Cognitive Sciences, 7*, 527–533.

Dokic, J., & Proust, J. (2002). *Simulation and understanding of action.* Amsterdam: Benjamins.

Frith, C. D., Blakemore, S.-J., & Wolpert, D. M. (2000). Abnormalities in the awareness and control of action. *Philosophical Transactions of the Royal Society of London, Series B, Biological Sciences, 355*, 1771–1788.

Georgieff, N., & Jeannerod, M. (1998). Beyond consciousness of external reality: A "who-system" for consciousness of action and self-consciousness. *Consciousness and Cognition, 7*, 465–477.

Haggard, P., Clark, S., & Kalogeras, J. (2002). Voluntary action and conscious awareness. *Nature Neuroscience, 5*, 382–385.

Hinterberger, T., Neumann, N., Pham, M., Kubler, A., Grether, A., Hofmayer, N., Wilhelm, B., Flor, H., & Birbaumer, N. (2004). A multimodal brain-based feedback and communication system. *Experimental Brain Research, 154*, 521–526.

Jeannerod, M. (1999). The 25th Bartlett lecture: To act or not to act: Perspectives on the representation of actions. *Quarterly Journal of Experimental Psychology: Human Experimental Psychology, 52A*, 1–29.

Jeannerod, M. (2003). The mechanism of self-recognition in humans. *Behavioural Brain Research, 142*, 1–15.

Knoblich, G., & Flach, R. (2003). Action identity: Evidence from self-recognition, prediction, and coordination. *Consciousness and Cognition, 12*, 620–632.

Knoblich, G., & Kircher, T. T. J. (2004). Deceiving oneself about being in control: Conscious detection of changes in visuo-motor coupling. *Journal of Experimental Psychology: Human Perception and Performance, 30*, 657–666.

Knoblich, G., & Prinz, W. (2001). Recognition of self-generated actions from kinematic displays of drawing. *Journal of Experimental Psychology: Human Perception and Performance, 27*, 456–465.

Laureys, S., Owen, A. M., & Schiff, N. D. (2004). Brain function in coma, vegetative state, and related disorders. *Lancet Neurology, 3*, 537–546.

Leube, D., Knoblich, G., Erb, M., Grodd, W., Bartels, M., & Kircher, T. T. J. (2003). The neural correlates of perceiving one's own movements. *Neuroimage, 20*, 2084–2090.

Loula, F., Prasad, S., Harber, K., & Shiffrar, M. (2005). Recognizing people from their movements. *Journal of Experimental Psychology: Human Perception and Performance, 31*, 210–220.

Metzinger, T., & Gallese, V. (2003). The emergence of a shared action ontology: Building blocks for a theory. *Consciousness and Cognition, 12*, 549–571.

Prinz, W. (1997). Perception and action planning. *European Journal of Cognitive Psychology, 9*, 129–154.

Prinz, W. (2002). Experimental approaches to imitation. In A. Meltzoff & W. Prinz (Eds.), *The imitative mind: Development, evolution, and brain bases* (pp. 143–162). New York: Cambridge University Press.

Rizzolatti, G., & Craighero, L. (2004). The mirror-neuron system. *Annual Review of Neuroscience, 27,* 169–192.

Tsakiris, M., & Haggard, P. (2003). Awareness of somatic events associated with a voluntary action. *Experimental Brain Research, 149,* 439–446.

van den Bos, E., & Jeannerod, M. (2002). Sense of body and sense of action both contribute to self-recognition. *Cognition, 85,* 177–187.

18

Representational Foundations of Intentional Action

Wolfgang Prinz

1. Intentional Action

We speak of intentions from both a first- and a third-person perspective. From the external, third-person perspective, we speak of somebody (or perhaps an animal) entertaining a certain intention (1) when we believe that s/he is pursuing a certain goal, and (2) when we perceive him/her trying to perform certain actions suited to attain that goal. The same applies to the internal, first-person perspective. We speak of ourselves as entertaining an intention when we want to attain a particular goal (say, eat a hamburger) and, at the same time, plan for certain actions to reach this goal (say, head toward a McDonald's restaurant). An important difference is that, when described from a first-person perspective, intentions always go along with conscious awareness (e.g., awareness of the goal being pursued and/or the action to be planned), whereas when ascribed to other persons, they may or may not be considered to imply conscious awareness. Often, when we speak of some other person entertaining an intention, we think of that intention in terms of both a functional and a phenomenal state. Yet, we may also think of others' (or animals') intentions in purely functional terms, that is, without any implications regarding phenomenal awareness.

Accordingly, intentions always imply both ends and means—wanting something and taking measures to get there. Just wanting or just acting is not enough; it is the coupling of means and ends that makes up full-blown intentions. Speaking in representational terms, intentions must couple goal representations with representations of body movements.[1]

What counts as a goal, and what counts as a movement? *Goals* are, by definition, intended or desired states of affairs. This sounds like a precise definition, but it in fact leaves open which of the various states of affairs that follow from a particular action should qualify as the action's goal. Consider, for instance, a participant in a reaction-time experiment, pressing a particular key in response to a particular stimulus. Even for a simple action like this, goals can be defined at various levels. For example, intended states of affairs could refer to (1) feeling the finger moving downward, (2) feeling and/or seeing the finger pushing the key, (3) hearing the noise arising from the key's mechanical operation, (4) hearing a tone triggered by the key press, or even (5) conveying through the key press a particular message to another participant in the experiment. The same applies to movements. *Movements* are segments of bodily activity. They can be specified at various levels, too, such as (1) the efferent pattern of muscle activity required for pushing the finger down, (2) the afferent pattern of kinesthetic proprioception arising from that muscle activity, (3) the afferent pattern arising from seeing the finger going down, (4) the afferent pattern arising from feeling the finger touch the key, and so on.

However, in this chapter, I will not address these subtle differences. Instead I will adopt a less fine-grained perspective and concentrate on the workings of intentions in action from a more general perspective. More specifically, I will focus on how means and ends are related to each other in intentional action. I will pursue this question in two domains of study: action perception and action production. *Action perception* proceeds from movements to goals. Here the main issue is how intention follows from action, that is, how observers recover the underlying goals, or intentions, from the movements they perceive. *Action production* proceeds from goals to movements. Here the main issue is how action follows from intention, that is, how actors generate movements on the basis of (and in the service of) given goals.

How are the two faces of intentions organized? Are goals and movements represented independently and in parallel? Or should we think of one leading to the other—either from means to ends or from ends to means? This issue has been variously addressed in the literature on action perception and action planning (e.g., Hommel, Müsseler, Aschersleben, & Prinz, 2001; Jeannerod, 1994, 1999; Prinz, 1987, 1992). Not surprisingly, it is also a recurrent theme in a number of contributions to this volume (cf., e.g., chapters 3, 4, and 5 on tool use in action production and chapters 10 and 20 on motor coding and mind reading in action perception).

As we know since William James's classical treatise on "the will" (James, 1890), two conflicting requirements are entailed in the functional relationship between movements and goals: distal representation and proximal specification. On the one hand, people perform most of their actions for the sake of goals that lie beyond the movements themselves. In instrumental actions, they perform certain body movements in order to alter certain states of affairs in the environment.[2] Accordingly, we should anticipate that representations of those intended environmental effects play an important role in the control of these movements (distal representation). Yet, on the other hand, in order to be efficient, intentions also need to specify appropriate body movements. Therefore, we should likewise expect them to refer to the proximal movements suited to bring forth those intended distal effects (proximal specification).

How is the conflict between the two competing requirements resolved? This is the issue I will address in the following pages. Of course one may argue that voluntary actions are, by definition, patterns of movements that are selected in the service of given goals (and not vice versa), suggesting that goals should take the lead over movements and implying a functional hierarchy between the two. Likewise, according to the testimony of introspection and its major historical advocates, intentions focus on distal goals in the environment, not on proximal movements of the body (e.g., James, 1890; Lotze, 1852). Still, in order to get a clearer picture, we need to go beyond the testimony of conceptual explications and introspective analyses. Here I will review some experimental evidence from our lab, which speaks to the relative roles of distal representation and proximal specification. The evidence will address both action perception and production. Basically, it will converge on confirming, in more functional terms, the introspective intuition that distal representation leads over (and leads to) proximal specification: goals come first and only then and thereby can appropriate movements be specified.

2. Action Perception

This is the miracle of action perception: when we watch other people's actions and/or their outcomes, we capture not only the physical surface of the ongoing events, that is, the movements in space and time, but also what may be called their underlying intentional subtext—what they are aiming at, whether they fail or succeed, and so on. In other words, we do not see just bodies and objects in motion, but rather intentional agents in action. Hence, what we perceive goes far beyond the information provided by the stimulus. Going beyond the information given is, of course, not peculiar to action perception but rather applies to perception in general (Bruner, 1957; cf. Prinz, 2003). Still, in this particular domain, the subtext is often more salient and conspicuous than the surface from which it is derived. This raises the question how the two are related.

Regular Bowling

We studied the relative roles of physical surface and intentional subtext in an action-induction paradigm. Typically, the notion of *action induction* applies to situations in which people watch other people's actions, closely following their course and their outcome. Under these conditions, it is often the case that observers start moving themselves—often spontaneously, sometimes even countervoluntarily. One of the classical anecdotal examples, which has been running through the literature for more than a century (e.g., Lotze, 1852), refers to people watching a bowling game. In that situation, many people, while they are watching the course of the ball, can hardly prevent themselves from moving their hands or twisting their bodies, as if to exert some magical impact on the ball. Notably, such induced movements occur not only in players who have bowled the ball themselves, but in spectators as well.

In the late 19th century and early 20th century, such induced movements were classified among the so-called ideomotor phenomena (Carpenter, 1874; James, 1890). At that time they were vividly discussed but never really examined (cf. Prinz, 1987). We developed a paradigm that allows us to study how the pattern of induced movements is related to the pattern of events that induces them. More specifically, following the lead of Chevreul (1833), we reasoned that induced movements might reflect either the physical surface of observed events or their intentional subtext, or both. For instance, would observers while watching a bowling ball spontaneously move in accordance with the spatiotemporal characteristics of (i) the movement they see (movement-based, perceptual induction), (ii) the movement they would like to see (goal-based, intentional induction), or (iii) both of these movements?

In our paradigm we studied people's induced movements in a laboratory simulation of the bowling task (de Maeght & Prinz, 2004; Knuf, Aschersleben, & Prinz, 2001; see Prinz, de Maeght, & Knuf, 2004, for an overview). On a computer screen, participants watched a ball (B) traveling toward a target (T), either hitting or missing it. At the beginning of a trial, the ball was shown at its starting position at the bottom, while the target position was shown at the top. The ball's travel was divided into two periods: instrumental and induction. At the onset of the instrumental period, the ball first started traveling on a straight trajectory on which, if continued, it would miss the target. However, during that period, players could intervene by correction movements. These correction movements were performed with a joystick and resulted in pushing the ball to the left or to the right, without affecting the direction of its further travel. Correction movements were aimed at pushing the ball such that it would eventually hit the target (see Figure 18.1).

During the subsequent induction period, in which their hands were still holding the joystick, such intervention was no longer possible. Instead, observers now watched the outcome of the agent's prior intervention, that is, the ball as it continued traveling on a straight line—either hitting or missing the target. Right from the beginning of the induction period, observers could easily tell upcoming hits from upcoming misses (on the left or the right side of the target). During this period, in which they had nothing else to do but watch the outcome of the preceding intervention, we recorded induced movement activity arising in two effectors: hands and heads. We reasoned that this activity should reflect contributions from perceptual induction, intentional induction, or both (Figure 18.2). If people while watching actions or their outcomes

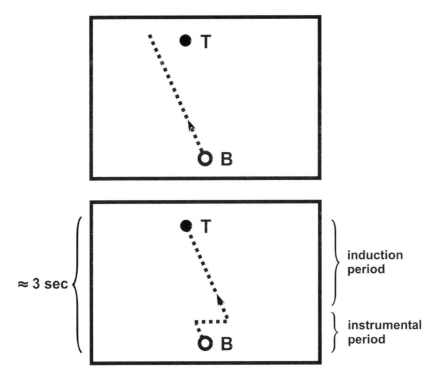

Figure 18.1. A typical event configuration from the action-induction paradigm applied by Knuf et al. (2001) and De Maeght and Prinz (2002). Initially the ball (B) starts traveling toward the target (T) without hitting it (*upper panel*). Then, during the instrumental period, a correction movement is performed to the effect that B may eventually hit T (*lower panel*).

cannot help but move in accordance with what they perceive (e.g., Greenwald, 1970; Hommel et al., 2001; James, 1890; Prinz, 1990, 2002, 2004), their induced movements should reveal what exactly they perceive—just physical surface (i.e., ball movements in themselves), intentional subtext (i.e., ball movements taken with reference to their goal), or both. Moreover, our paradigm should allow us to examine associations and dissociations between the patterns of induced movements in different effectors (i.e., hands versus heads). Associations might suggest that the body tends to act as a whole, whereas dissociations might suggest that it acts as an articulated structure.

Self-Generated Action

Consider first the case of watching the outcome of one's own instrumental actions.[3] This happens in our paradigm when the same participant plays the roles of the player, who performs initial correction movements, and the observer, who then watches their outcomes. For this situation, spontaneous movement

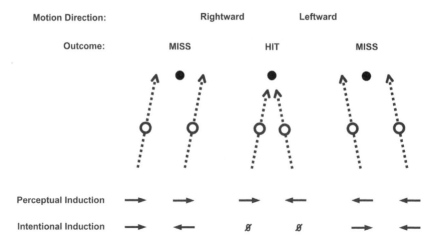

Figure 18.2. Predicted patterns of perceptual and intentional induction for various combinations of motion direction (rightward versus leftward) and trial outcome (miss versus hit). Horizontal arrows indicate the expected directions of induced movements. Perceptual induction: induced movements should reflect the direction of ball motion only (right- versus leftward). Intentional induction: induced movements should only occur with misses, not with hits. Their direction should depend on the side of the upcoming miss (rightward in case of left misses, leftward in case of right misses).

activity during the induction period exhibited both perceptual induction and intentional induction (for details, see de Maeght & Prinz, 2004, Experiment 1; Knuf et al., 2001, Experiment 3).

Perceptual induction predicts movements in accordance with the direction toward which the ball travels on the screen (left- versus rightward). Remarkably, in our experiments, perceptual induction was observed in head movements but not in hand movements. Heads tended to move in accordance with the ball's traveling direction, but hands were not affected by the ball's physical trajectory at all.

This was different for *intentional induction*. Both effectors tended to move in accordance with ball-related intentions, as is illustrated in Figure 18.2: they moved to the right with upcoming left misses, to the left with upcoming right misses, and they did not move at all with upcoming hits. Hence, assuming that players/observers want and intend to achieve as many hits as possible, both effectors moved in accordance with those intentions. With upcoming misses, they moved as if to push the ball toward the target, and with upcoming hits they did not move at all.[4]

In sum, it seems that perceptual and intentional induction are, in principle, both effective, with different results for the two effectors, though. This difference may be related to the different roles played by the two effectors: hands are instrumentally active (performing correction movements in the instrumental period), whereas no such instrumental role applies to heads.

Other-Generated Action

Some of the experiments discussed so far had a second part, in which partici-pants—rather than watching their own actions—watched the outcome of some-body else's actions (de Maeght & Prinz, 2004, Experiments 1 and 2). Hence, the two roles of player and observer, which had been taken by the same individual in the first part, were divided between two individuals in the second part.

In this part of the experiment, participants acted as mere observers. They were also exposed to the ball's full trajectory, including initial correction movements performed on it. This time, however, they believed that correction movements were performed by an invisible player (for details, see de Maeght & Prinz, 2004). Accordingly, during the induction period, observers watched the outcome of that player's instrumental action. Obviously, with this setting, aftereffects resulting from their own preceding intentions and actions could play no role.

Two findings were remarkable. First, perceptual induction was now obtained in both effectors, that is, not only in heads but in hands as well. This seems to suggest that perceptual induction can, in principle, capture both effectors but may perhaps become suppressed when one of them is instrumentally active (or was active right before). Second, intentional induction was again obtained in both hand and head movements. Once more, hands and heads tended to move in accordance with observers' intentions. With upcoming hits, they did not move at all, but with upcoming misses, they moved as if to push the ball toward the target, thus replicating the pattern of results from the first part of the experiment.

These findings suggest two tentative conclusions. First, there is a strong role for intentional subtext in action perception, as shown by intentional induction. Second, there is a role for physical surface too, as shown by perceptual induction. Yet, perceptual induction seems to be absent when the effector is instrumentally active immediately before. In this case, previous intentions may persist and, possibly, act to suppress perceptual induction.

Inverted Bowling

In a further experiment, we examined intentional induction more closely. To what do the intentions actually refer? Do they refer to objects in the environ-ment (ball-on-screen) or to effectors in the body (hand-on-joystick)? In the experiments reported so far, joystick movements and ball movements were always directly coupled. Hence, there was no way to disentangle the two pos-sible levels of intentional reference. In a further experiment, we arranged for a setting in which proximal body movements (hands) could be dissociated from their distal movement effects (ball). Would induced movements reflect intended body movements or their desired environmental effects?

In this experiment, we inverted the relationship between joystick movements and the shifts of the ball effectuated by these movements—to the effect that, in the instrumental period, leftward joystick movements would now lead to rightward ball shifts and vice versa. Again the experiment had two parts, watching self-generated action first and other-generated action second.

Inverting the relationship between proximal movements and distal effects should leave the resulting pattern of perceptual (i.e., movement-based) induction unaffected. In fact, as concerns perceptual induction, we replicated the previous pattern of findings. While watching self-generated action, perceptual induction was obtained in (noninstrumental) heads, but not in (instrumental) hands, whereas, while watching other-generated action, it was obtained in both effectors. Once more it seems that the aftereffects of immediately preceding intentional action render a given effector unsusceptible to perceptual induction for a while.

Even more interesting in this regard were the results for intentional induction. In the first part of the experiment, in which participants watched the outcome of self-generated actions, the pattern of intentional induction also exhibited a dissociation between hand and head movements. Hand movements reflected proximal intentions (referring to movements of the hand-on-joystick), whereas head movements reflected distal intentions (referring to movements of the ball-on-screen). In other words, in cases of upcoming misses, both effectors acted as if to push the ball toward the target—through appropriate (i.e., noninverted) head movements referring to the distal ball and through appropriate (i.e., inverted) hand movements referring to the proximal joystick, respectively. This dissociation seems to suggest that intentions referring to body movements and intentions referring to environmental effects may coexist and both be functional in different effectors at the same time.

No such dissociation was obtained in the second part of the experiment, when participants watched other-generated actions. Under this condition, intentional induction was observed in both hands and heads, too, but in both effectors it was related to the ball-on-screen and not to the hand-on-joystick. In other words, both effectors were now governed by intentions referring to the events on the screen, and intentions referring to body movements played no further role.

Conclusions

Taken together, these observations suggest three major conclusions regarding the relationship between physical surface and intentional subtext in action perception. First, intentional (goal-based) movement induction is at least as ubiquitous as perceptual (movement-based) induction, suggesting that intentions are mandatory ingredients of perceived actions throughout. Second, these intentions refer to desired events in the environment rather than to the body movements required to realize them. Third, a special situation seems to apply to instrumental effectors. They show two (perhaps interrelated) aftereffects of intentional action: persistence of movement-related intentions and suppression of perceptual induction.

3. Action Production

Action production implies the specification of body movements for the realization of given goals. Accordingly, for the selection and planning of goal-directed actions, goals and movements need to get in touch with each other. How do they come together? How do representations of distal goals and representations of proximal movements get assigned to each other? Introspection yields the answer: goals come first and movements second. Consider, for example, what our intuitions have to say about how we operate a screwdriver to drive a screw into a wood beam. What both our attention and intention explicitly refer to in this situation is the distal goal—that is, the motion of the screw as it is driven into the beam by the tip of the screwdriver. Yet, our proximal movements—that is, the movements of our hands and arms operating the tool—are virtually out of focus. In a way, we do not know what our limbs are doing; we just rely on their doing all of the things necessary to gradually turn the screw into the wood beam. Distal goals lead to proximal movements, as it appears. This is what introspection suggests.

In more theoretical language, we can think of three basic options of how goals and movements can come together in action production: backward planning, forward planning, and concurrent planning. According to *backward planning*, action production proceeds from goals to movements, implying that goals are selected first and only then and thereby are appropriate movements selected. According to backward planning, action selection is tantamount to goal selection, and movement specification comes for free as a by-product of goal selection. This is exactly what our commonsense intuitions about operating a screwdriver suggest. The second option is *forward planning*. According to forward planning, action production proceeds from movements to goals, implying that movements are selected first, and only then and thereby are appropriate goals selected (i.e., computed as anticipations of end states to which those movements lead). Hence, according to forward planning, action selection is tantamount to movement selection, and goals come for free as by-products of movement selection. The third option is *concurrent planning*. According to concurrent planning, goals and movements are both selected in parallel. Then, in a second step, appropriate assignments between goals and movements are selected in a multiple-constraint satisfaction procedure. Thus, according to concurrent planning, action selection is tantamount to optimizing assignments between goals and movements.

How can the relative roles of goals and movements be assessed in a way that exceeds the testimony of introspection? The strong impact of distal goals on proximal movement performance has been demonstrated in a number of studies addressing motor performance and motor learning. For instance, it has been shown that action effects and action goals play an important role in generating various types of compatibility effects (e.g., Hommel, 1993; Kunde, 2001; Kunde, Koch, & Hoffmann, 2004). The same applies to evidence from imitation tasks, suggesting that imitators copy goals rather than gestures (Bekkering & Wohlschläger, 2002; Wohlschläger, Gattis, & Bekkering, 2003). In the same vein, it has been shown that the initiation and selection of actions can be modulated by concurrent irrelevant stimuli addressing same versus different goal states (Brass, Bekkering, & Prinz, 2001; Brass, Bekkering, Wohlschläger, & Prinz, 2000; Drost, Rieger, Brass, Gunter, & Prinz, in press; Stürmer, Aschersleben, & Prinz, 2000). Also, motor learning may be enhanced when learners' attention is directed to features of distal movement effects rather than to features of proximal movements (Wulf, Höss, & Prinz, 1998; Wulf, McNevin, Fuchs, Ritter, & Toole, 2000; Wulf & Prinz, 2001).

Yet, rather than reviewing the evidence from these and related paradigms (cf., e.g., Prinz, 1997, 2002, 2004), I will in the following address a different family of paradigms, which require the planning of two coordinated, concurrent actions rather than an individual one. One of the attractive features of these paradigms is that the two concurrent actions can be the same or different in terms of distal goals, proximal movements, or both. This renders them a perfect means for studying the relative roles of goals and movements on the production side.

Bimanual Reaching

In the bimanual coordination task illustrated in Figure 18.3 (Weigelt et al., in prep.), a stimulus panel with two columns of four stimulus boxes each was presented on a screen. The stimulus panel mirrored an analogue response panel mounted on a table in front of the participants. On this panel, they performed simultaneous bimanual reaching movements. On each trial, the pair of movements to be performed was specified in two steps. First, a pair of positions in the lower half of the stimulus panel was highlighted, indicating the starting positions for the two hands on the response panel. Starting positions could be the same or different (AA/BB or AB/BA). After the hands were set, the imperative stimulus was presented. Imperative stimuli consisted of pairs of letters, indicating the landing positions for the two hands. Landing positions could be the same or different as well (e.g., BB/CC/DD, BC/CD/DB, and so on). Starting positions were blocked, whereas landing positions were randomized.

The pairs of reaches resulting from given combinations of starting and landing positions could show either the same amplitude (both one step or both

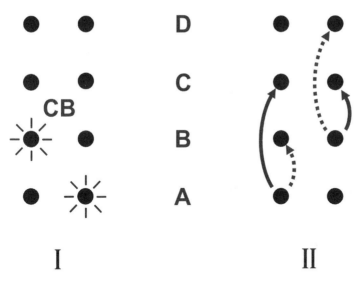

I   II

Figure 18.3. Bimanual reaching paradigm (Weigelt et al., subm.). I: stimulus panel with sample starting positions highlighted (BA) and target positions cued by sample imperative stimulus (CB). II: example of reaching for the same versus different target positions (solid versus dashed arrows), while starting positions and movement amplitudes are both different.

two steps) or two different amplitudes (one step for one hand and two steps for the other hand). Thus, in order to study the impact of the same versus different goals, we need to study trials on which goal specification was manipulated while starting positions and amplitudes were kept constant. Consider trials on which starting positions and movement amplitudes are both different for the two hands. For instance, when the hands start at positions A and B, two cases can be distinguished, depending on the mapping of amplitudes to starting positions—one where the landing positions are the same (CC) and another one where the landing positions are different (BD; see Figure 18.3, panel II). Hence, on these trials, the impact of the same versus different goals can be separated from any effects of the same versus different starting positions or amplitudes. Results indicated a remarkable difference. There was a 62 ms reaction-time advantage for the same over different landing positions. This finding suggests that information about the landing positions of concurrent movements contributes to the speed at which they get started. Hence, the advantage for the same over different targets suggests a functional role for goal representations and goal-related intentions for the initiation of the two con-current, coordinated movements.

In this paradigm, the landing positions for the two hands could be the same or different on two correlated dimensions: spatial (positions on the response panel) and symbolic (cue letters on the stimulus panel). In a further experiment, we tried to dissociate the impact of these two dimensions (Weigelt,

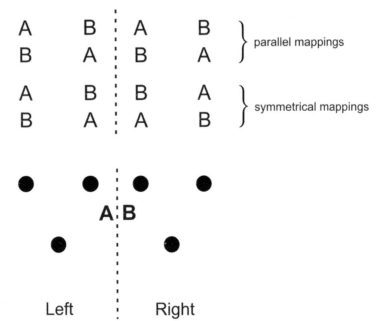

Figure 18.4. Bimanual reaching paradigm (Weigelt et al., subm.). On a response panel mounted in front of them, participants reached from starting positions (*bottom*) to target positions (*top line*). Target positions were cued by a pair of letters flashed on a stimulus panel that matched the response panel (e.g., AB). Participants responded depending on mapping instructions (i.e., symmetrical versus parallel mapping of letters to target positions). Note: Mapping instructions were shown on the screen during an initial practice period only. They were removed when the experiment started.

Mechsner, Rieger, & Prinz, subm.). Again, there was a stimulus panel on the screen and an analogue response panel on the table (Figure 18.4). This time, starting positions for the two hands were fixed. Upon presentation of the imperative stimulus, the two hands moved upward, targeting one of the two landing positions assigned to them. As a result, the movements performed on a given trial could either form a symmetrical pattern (inward or outward) or a parallel pattern (leftward or rightward). As before, the imperative stimulus was a pair of letters, which could be the same or different (AA, BB, AB, BA), specifying the target positions of the two hands. The mapping of letters to target positions could be symmetrical or parallel. In symmetrical mappings, letters were assigned to target positions in a symmetrical fashion (BAAB or ABBA). In parallel mappings, that assignment was repetitive (ABAB or BABA). Thus, physically identical pairs of reaches could be cued by two identical letters in one mapping and by two different letters in the other. For instance, a symmetrical movement pair led to the same (i.e., symbolically equivalent) target positions when the mapping was symmetrical, but to different (nonequivalent) target positions when the mapping was parallel.

Results indicated two major effects. First, as expected, response times (RTs) were much faster (97 ms) with symmetrical than with parallel mappings. Second, and more important, with both mappings, movements were faster when participants targeted equivalent as compared to nonequivalent locations. This seems to imply that the speed at which a given pair of reaches can be generated is dependent on whether the two movements aim at the same versus different targets. We may therefore conclude that the planning of two coordinated movements is more efficient with the same than with different goals—even under conditions when sameness and difference is defined by arbitrary equivalence rules.

Bimanual Circling

An even stronger conclusion is suggested by findings from a bimanual circling task studied by Mechsner and colleagues (Mechsner, Kerzel, Knoblich, & Prinz, 2001; Mechsner & Prinz, 2003). It is well known that when humans circle both hands simultaneously in a horizontal plane they tend to home in on a small number of coordination patterns that are stable over time. For instance, there is a strong tendency toward synchronization and, in particular, toward symmetrical movements of the two hands. More complex patterns are less stable and often impossible to do. For example, for untrained participants, it is virtually impossible to have the two hands circle separately with unequal frequencies (i.e., frequency ratios like 2:1, 3:2, and so on).

In an experiment run by Mechsner et al. (2001), participants circled two flags on top of a table by operating two cranks mounted under the table. On each trial they started circling at a slow pace and were then required to speed up over a period of some 20 seconds. We studied two coordination modes: symmetry and antiphase (inward circling in both cases; see Figure 18.5b, c). As is known from

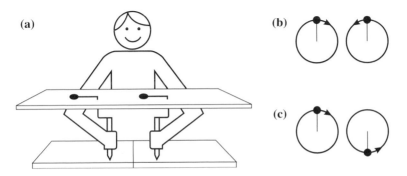

Figure 18.5. (a) Bimanual circling task with two flags above the table and two hand-operated cranks beneath the table; (b) symmetrical coordination; (c) antiphase coordination. From Mechsner et al., 2001. Reprinted with permission.

previous studies (Carson, Thomas, Summers, Walters, & Semjen, 1997; Semjen, Summers, & Cattaert, 1995), symmetrical coordination is more stable and easier to perform than antiphase coordination. This was also observed in our experiment. Symmetrical coordination was, on average, more accurate and could be driven to higher speeds than antiphase coordination. Further, particularly at high speeds, antiphase coordination tended to switch into symmetry, whereas no such switches were observed in the reverse direction.

In further experiments, we wanted to study whether the symmetry bias arises from movements and/or from movement effects. In principle, the bias could emerge from both hand movements beneath the table (i.e., proximal intentions involved in the planning) and flag movements above the table (i.e., distal intentions involved in the planning at that level). Hence, in order to separate contributions from these two sources, we took measures to alter—partially, at least—the relationship between movements and their associated effects.

Consider first the case of altering phase relations. This was attained by introducing two different phase relationships between hand movements and flag movements for the two hands. For the left crank, the flag was always exactly above the hand, whereas for the right crank, the flag position was shifted by 180° relative to hand position. Notably, this simple manipulation earns us a full dissociation between the coordination patterns for hands and flags: symmetry in flags now requires an antiphase pattern in hands and vice versa. Therefore, this task should help us to localize the source of the symmetry bias. Does it arise in symmetrical movements or in symmetrical effects?

Quite to the surprise of the majority of researchers in the field, we found that the symmetry bias does not originate in proximal movements, but rather in their distal goals. Symmetry of flag movements was the preferred coordination mode—and this was the case despite the fact that symmetry in flags required antiphase in hands. We may therefore conclude that task-specific coordination patterns are first established at the level of desired (distal) movement effects, before the required (proximal) body movements are specified on demand—either symmetrical or antiphase, depending on the particular transformation rule for the ongoing task. Obviously, this finding is in clear support of backward planning, that is, the view that representations of distal goals take the lead over the specification of proximal movements.

If it is true that action planning is mainly dependent on the ease with which distal intentions can be implemented, one should perhaps even expect to see participants capable of implementing complex and unstable coordination patterns in their hands if one takes measures to couple these movements with simple and stable coordination patterns in the flags. This was in fact shown in a further experiment, in which different frequency ratios between hand and flag movements applied to the two hands. As before, the left flag always circled directly above the left hand, implying a frequency ratio of 1:1. However, due to a gear system, the right flag circled in a 4:3 ratio relative to the right hand. Accordingly, when the task required the establishment of a synchronous, isofrequent pattern in the flags, the hands needed to move in a frequency ratio of 3:4 relative to each other. As mentioned above, a frequency ratio like this is extremely difficult and, under normal circumstances, virtually impossible to establish and maintain for untrained participants.

Yet, our results indicated that the impossible pattern could easily be established in the hands if it was coupled with an isofrequent pattern in flags (exhibiting, e.g., symmetrical or parallel movements). Obviously, then, what makes a given coordination pattern easy or difficult is the complexity of the intended distal movement effects—and not the complexity of the proximal movements themselves. At least for the bimanual circling task, we have to conclude that distal representation is a prerequisite for proximal specification. Action production relies on backward planning: goals come first and only then and thereby can appropriate movements be specified. Proximal specification appears to depend on distal representation.

4. Action Planning and Perception

To sum up, intentions are representational structures underlying the planning of voluntary actions. Their chief functional role is to link environmental goal states to body movements suited to realize them. Therefore, intentional structures need to refer to both distal goals and proximal movements (distal representation and proximal specification). We discussed three basic options about how the two sides of intentional reference may be combined: goals lead over movements, movements lead over goals, or goals and movements are effective in parallel.

The goals-over-movements view has traditionally been supported by introspection. In more functional terms, it implies a hierarchy proceeding from distal representation to proximal specification—to the effect that movement specification comes for free as a by-product of goal representation. Conversely, the movements-over-goals view implies a hierarchy proceeding from proximal specification to distal representation. With this view, goal representation comes for free as a by-product of movement specification. Finally, the parallel-representation view invokes heterarchical intentional structures, with equal roles for distal goals and proximal movements.

Our review of pertinent experimental evidence has provided strong support for the goals-over-movements view. As regards action perception, we reviewed evidence from action induction. Here it was shown that intentional (goal-based) induction is no less ubiquitous than perceptual (movement-based) induction, suggesting that intentions are mandatory ingredients of perceived action. As regards action production, we reviewed evidence from bimanual coordination. Here it was shown that the efficiency and stability with which concurrent bimanual movements can be coordinated is mainly determined by the ease of coordinating their (distal) goals—and is virtually unaffected by the complexity of their (proximal) movements. Hence, evidence from both domains rules out the movements-over-goals view and supports the goals-over-movements view. Goal representation leads to movement specification, that is, goals come first and only then and thereby can appropriate movements be specified.

While drawing this conclusion we have to acknowledge that William James, as always, knew it all along. He opened his chapter on the will with a sophisticated discussion of intentional reference from an introspective point of view. In his words, the chief issue to be resolved was to what "ideas of movements" actually refer. He concluded his discussion as follows:

> I trust that I have now made clear what that "idea of a movement" is which must precede it in order that it be voluntary. It is not the thought of innervation which the movement requires. It is the anticipation of the movement's sensible effects, resident or remote, and sometimes very remote indeed. Such anticipations, to say the least, determine what our movements shall be." (James, 1890, vol. I, p. 521)

James knew it all along, but it is always nice to see the testimony of introspective intuition corroborated by experimental facts—nice and certainly not trivial.

To conclude, I would like to address a functional feature that action planning shares with perception. It refers to what Brunswik (1952, 1956) addressed under the notion of distal focusing in perception and action. The claim that this notion applies to both perception and action can be understood in two ways: weak and strong. The weak claim is to invoke an analogy: like the machinery for perception, the machinery for action planning and control focuses on the distal world in which the perceiver/actor lives. The difference is that the perception machinery starts with proximal information originating in the body and ends up with distal representations of events in the world, whereas the action machinery starts with distal representations of (desired) events in the world and ends up with proximal specifications of body movements. The strong claim is to invoke a homology: perception and action planning make use of one and the same machinery for distal representation. This machinery is the meeting place for late products of perceptual construction (originating in proximal/sensory information at receptors) and early ingredients of action planning (ending up in proximal/motor information in effectors). This is the claim I would like to endorse (cf. Prinz, 1990, 1997).

Notes

1. It is often argued that a further component needs to be taken into account, referring to the environmental conditions suited, or required, to realize the action. This

component, which is often addressed under notions like context or occasion (e.g., Ach, 1905; Gollwitzer, 1996; Hoffmann, 1993; Lewin, 1926) must certainly also be included in full-fledged theories of intentional action (i.e., explaining under which conditions given intentions are realized). Yet, for the present discussion, it can be disregarded since these triggering conditions are kept constant across experimental conditions.

2. There are, of course, exceptions—cases in which the goal of performing a particular gesture lies either in the gesture itself (i.e., in attaining a particular spatiotemporal pattern) or in the posture achieved through the gesture (i.e., a particular spatial pattern in the resulting end state). Yet, even for these cases, in which the desired state of affairs refers to states of the body rather than the environment, it has been shown that representations of these bodily goal states play a critical role in the production and perception of those gestures (cf., e.g., Bekkering & Wohlschläger, 2002; Bekkering, Wohlschläger, & Gattis, 2000; Brass et al., 2000; Brass et al., 2001; Stürmer et al., 2000).

3. The present review of experimental findings is highly selective. Neither does it give a full account of the theoretical motivation behind the experiments nor a full analysis of their major results. Technically speaking, it will only address the ball condition (and not the target condition; cf. de Maeght & Prinz, 2004; Knuf et al., 2001).

4. In a further condition of the same experiment, in which participants had initially performed correction movements on the target (target condition), the pattern of induced movements was exactly reversed, that is, induced movements acted as if to push the target toward the ball (Knuf et al., 2001, Experiment 3).

References

Ach, N. (1905). *Über die Willenstätigkeit und das Denken.* Göttingen: Vandenhoeck & Ruprecht.

Bekkering, H., & Wohlschläger, A. (2002). Action perception and imitation. In W. Prinz & B. Hommel (Eds.), *Attention and performance. Vol. 19: Common mechanisms in perception and action* (pp. 294–314). Oxford: Oxford University Press.

Bekkering, H., Wohlschläger, A., & Gattis, M. (2000). Imitation of gestures in children is goal-directed. *Quarterly Journal of Experimental Psychology, 53,* 153–164.

Brass, M., Bekkering, H., & Prinz, W. (2001). Movement observation affects movement execution in a simple response task. *Acta Psychologica, 106,* 3–22.

Brass, M., Bekkering, H., Wohlschläger, A., & Prinz, W. (2000). Compatibility between observed and executed finger movements: Comparing symbolic, spatial, and imitative cues. *Brain and Cognition, 44,* 124–143.

Bruner, J. S. (1957). On perceptual readiness. *Psychological Review, 64,* 123–152.

Brunswik, E. (1952). The conceptual framework of psychology. *International Encyclopedia of Unified Sciences, 1*(10). Chicago: University of Chicago Press.

Brunswik, E. (1956). *Perception and the representative design of psychological experiments.* Berkeley: University of California Press.

Carpenter, W. B. (1874). *Principles of mental physiology, with their applications to the training and discipline of the mind and the study of its morbid conditions.* New York: Appleton.

Carson, R. G., Thomas, J., Summers, J. J., Walters, M. R., & Semjen, A. (1997). The dynamics of bimanual circle drawing. *Quarterly Journal of Experimental Psychology, 50,* 664–683.

Chevreul, M. E. (1833). Lettre à M. Ampère sur une classe particulière de mouvements musculaires. *Revue des Deux Mondes, série II, 258*–266.

De Maeght, S., & Prinz, W. (2004). Action induction through action observation. *Psychological Research, 68*, 97–114.

Drost, U., Rieger, M., Brass, M., Gunter, T., & Prinz, W. (in press). Action-effect coupling in pianists. *Psychological Research.*

Greenwald, A. G. (1970). Sensory feedback mechanism in performance control: With special reference to the ideomotor mechanism. *Psychological Review, 77*, 73–99.

Gollwitzer, P. M. (1996). The volitional benefits of planning. In P. M. Gollwitzer & J. A. Bargh (Eds.), *The psychology of action: Linking cognition and motivation to behavior* (pp. 287–312). New York: Guilford.

Hoffmann, J. (1993). *Vorhersage und Erkenntnis.* Göttingen: Hogrefe.

Hommel, B. (1993). Inverting the Simon effect by intention: Determinants of direction and extent of effects of irrelevant spatial information. *Psychological Research, 55*, 270–279.

Hommel, B., Müsseler, J., Aschersleben, G., & Prinz, W. (2001). The theory of event coding (TEC): A framework for perception and action. *Behavioral and Brain Sciences, 24*, 849–937.

James, W. (1890). *The principles of psychology.* New York: Holt.

Jeannerod, M. (1994). The representing brain: Neural correlates of motor intention and imagery. *Behavioral and Brain Sciences, 17*, 187–245.

Jeannerod, M. (1999). To act or not to act: Perspectives on the representation of actions: The 25th Bartlett lecture. *Quarterly Journal of Experimental Psychology, 52*, 1–29.

Knuf, L., Aschersleben, G., & Prinz, W. (2001). An analysis of ideomotor action. *Journal of Experimental Psychology: General, 130*, 779–798.

Kunde, W. (2001). Response-effect compatibility in manual choice-reaction tasks. *Journal of Experimental Psychology: Human Perception and Performance, 27*, 387–394.

Kunde, W., Koch, I., & Hoffmann, J. (2004). Anticipated action effects affect the selection, initiation, and execution of actions. *Quarterly Journal of Experimental Psychology, Section A, Human Experimental Psychology, 57A*, 87–106.

Lewin, K. (1926). Vorsatz, Wille und Bedürfnis. *Psychologische Forschung, 7*, 330–385.

Lotze, R. H. (1852). *Medicinische Psychologie oder Physiologie der Seele.* Leipzig: Weidmann.

Mechsner, F., Kerzel, D., Knoblich, G., & Prinz, W. (2001). Perceptual basis of bimanual coordination. *Nature, 414*, 69–72.

Mechsner, F., & Prinz, W. (2003). What is coordinated in bimanual coordination? In W. Tschacher & J.-P. Dauwalder (Eds.), *The dynamical systems approach to cognition: Studies of nonlinear phenomena in life science, Vol. 10* (pp. 71–93). Singapore: World Scientific.

Prinz, W. (1987). Ideomotor action. In H. Heuer & A. F. Sanders (Eds.), *Perspectives on perception and action* (pp. 47–76). Hillsdale, NJ: Erlbaum.

Prinz, W. (1990). A common-coding approach to perception and action. In O. Neumann & W. Prinz (Eds.), *Relationships between perception and action: Current approaches* (pp. 167–201). New York: Springer-Verlag.

Prinz, W. (1992). Why don't we perceive our brain states? *European Journal of Cognitive Psychology, 4*, 1–20.

Prinz, W. (1997). Perception and action planning. *European Journal of Cognitive Psychology, 9*, 129–154.

Prinz, W. (2002). Experimental approaches to imitation. In A. N. Meltzoff & W. Prinz (Eds.), *The imitative mind: Development, evolution, and brain bases* (pp. 143–162). Cambridge: Cambridge University Press.

Prinz, W. (2003). How do we know about our own actions? In S. Maasen, W. Prinz, & G. Roth (Eds.), *Voluntary action: Brains, minds, and sociality* (pp. 21–33). Oxford: Oxford University Press.

Prinz, W. (2005). An ideomotor approach to imitation. In S. Hurley & N. Chater (Eds.), *Perspectives on imitation: From cognitive neuroscience to social science* (pp. 141–156). Cambridge, MA: MIT Press.

Prinz, W., de Maeght, S., & Knuf, L. (2004). Intention in action. In G. Humphreys & J. Riddoch (Eds.), *Attention in action: Advances from cognitive neuroscience* (pp. 93–107). Hove, UK: Psychology Press.

Semjen, A., Summers, J. J., & Cattaert, D. (1995). The coordination of the hands in bimanual circle drawing. *Journal of Experimental Psychology: Human Perception and Performance, 21*, 1139–1157.

Stürmer, B., Aschersleben, G., & Prinz, W. (2000). Correspondence effects with manual gestures and postures: A study on imitation. *Journal of Experimental Psychology: Human Perception and Performance, 26*, 1746–1759.

Weigelt, M., Mechsner, F., Rieger, M., & Prinz, W. (2005). *Target-related coordination of bimanual reaching movements.* Manuscript submitted for publication.

Weigelt, M., Töllner, T., Mechsner, F., Rieger, M., & Prinz, W. (2005). *Target cueing affects the preparation of bimanual movements.* Manuscript in preparation.

Wohlschläger, A., Gattis, M., & Bekkering, H. (2003). Action generation and action perception in imitation: An instance of the ideomotor principle. *Philosophical Transactions of the Royal Society of London, B, 358*, 501–515.

Wulf, G., Höss, M., & Prinz, W. (1998). Instructions for motor learning: Differential effects of internal versus external focus of attention. *Journal of Motor Behavior, 30*, 169–179.

Wulf, G., McNevin, N. H., Fuchs, T., Ritter, F., & Toole, T. (2000). Attentional focus in complex motor skill learning. *Research Quarterly for Exercise & Sport, 71*, 229–239.

Wulf, G., & Prinz, W. (2001). Directing attention to movement effects enhances learning: A review. *Psychonomic Bulletin and Review, 8*, 648–660.

19

When the Other Influences the Self

Interference Between Perception and Action

Sarah-Jayne Blakemore

Overlapping Neural Networks Associated with Perception and Action

The notion that actions are intrinsically linked to perception goes back to the 19th century when William Carpenter developed the principle of "ideomotor action," in which simply thinking about an action is sufficient to lead to the performance of an action (Carpenter, 1888). Similarly, William James claimed, "[E]very mental representation of a movement awakens to some degree the actual movement which is its object" (James, 1890, p. 293). The implication is that observing, imagining, or in any way representing an action excites the motor programs used to execute that same action (Jeannerod, 1994; Prinz, 1997). Interest in this idea has grown since the 1990s due in part to the neurophysiological discovery of mirror neurons in the monkey ventral premotor cortex. These neurons discharge both when the monkey performs certain hand movements and when it observes another monkey or human performing the same movements (Gallese et al., 1996; Rizzolatti, Fadiga, Fogassi, & Gallese, 1996).

There are several notable properties of the mirror system. First, mirror neurons respond to the sight of goal-directed actions only: they respond only when the monkey observes a hand grasping an object, and not to the sight of the hand or the object alone (Rizzolatti et al., 2001). Second, mirror neurons respond as long as a goal is achieved, even if the end of the action is out of the monkey's sight (Umilta et al., 2001). In this experiment, the monkey observed the experimenter reach for a peanut, and in some trials the end portion of the action, in which the peanut was grasped, was occluded from the monkey's vision. The neuron fired even if the actual grasp of the peanut could not be seen, as long as the peanut was present (the same neuron did not fire when the grasping action was "mimed" in the absence of a graspable object). Third, recent evidence suggests that mirror neurons respond to the sound of an action, firing to the sound of a stick being dropped or paper being torn (Kohler et al., 2002). These observations suggest that mirror neurons represent some general aspect of actions, such as the overall goal, rather than some other, more-elementary property of movement, such as specific motor commands, movement velocity, movement direction, or muscle activity.

One condition required for mirror neurons to fire is that the observed goal-directed action is performed by an agent. Premotor mirror neurons appear to distinguish between biological and nonbiological motion, responding only to the observation of hand-object interactions and not to the same action performed by a mechanical tool, such as a pair of pliers (Rizzolatti et al., 2001). How do premotor neurons gain information about this aspect of an observed action? One possibility, proposed by Rizzolatti and his colleagues, is that the premotor cortex receives information about biological motion from the superior temporal sulcus (STS). Single-cell studies in the macaque monkey have revealed that STSa cells selectively respond to depictions of the face and the body, either in action or represented by a static image (Jellema & Perrett, 2002; Oram & Perrett, 1994; Perrett et al., 1992; Perrett, Smith, Mistlin, et al., 1985, Perrett, Smith, Potter, et al., 1985). STSa neurons continue to respond to biological actions even when part of the action is occluded (Jellema & Perrett, 2002). The response properties of neurons in STSa have been interpreted as demonstrating the contribution of the STS to the visual recognition and understanding of others' actions (Emery & Perrett, 1994; Jellema et al., 2000). This area receives information from both dorsal and ventral visual streams (involved in vision for action and vision for identification, respectively), rendering it an interface between perception for identification and perception for action. This combination of visual information would be useful for recognizing the movements of other animate beings and categorizing them as threatening or enticing, in order to predict their future actions and make an appropriate response.

It is possible that premotor cortex neurons receive information about the source of the action—whether it is biological or nonbiological—from the visual analysis performed by STS cells. The STS and the premotor cortex are connected via the parietal cortex (Rizzolatti et al., 2001). Intriguingly, recent results suggest that the parietal cortex might also contain neurons with mirror properties, responding to both movement execution and movement observation (Rizzolatti et al., 2001).

Human STS Responds to Biological Motion

The ability to distinguish between biological and nonbiological movement develops early: 3-month-old babies can discriminate between displays of moving dots that depict biological motion and displays in which the same dots move randomly (Bertenthal, 1993). This suggests that the detection of biological motion becomes hard-wired in the human brain at an early age (see chapters 14 and 15).

Several brain-imaging studies have investigated the neural processing of the perception of biological motion in humans. One such study used fMRI to compare brain regions activated by dot displays showing biological motion and regions activated by dot displays showing coherent motion in which all of the dots moved at equal velocity in the same direction (Grossman et al., 2000). They found a specific area responsive to biological motion located within the ventral bank of the occipital extent of the STS. This activation was more pronounced in the right hemisphere than in the left hemisphere. A second fMRI study compared dot displays showing biological motion and dot displays showing rigid object motion, in which an object appears to rotate (Grèzes et al., 2001). Activation specific to seeing biological motion was detected in the posterior portion of STS, more prominently in the right hemisphere, and in the left intraparietal cortex. A third fMRI study demonstrated that imagining biological motion also activates the STS (Grossman & Blake, 2001). Other neuroimaging studies have detected activation in the right posterior STS in response to seeing hand, eye, and mouth movements (Puce et al., 1998; Rizzolatti, Fadiga, Matelli, et al., 1996; Wicker et al., 1998). The STS, especially in the right hemisphere, clearly plays an important role in the perception of biological motion (Allison et al., 2000; Frith & Frith, 1999).

The Human Mirror System

There is a large body of evidence that in humans several brain regions are activated both during action generation and during the observation of others' actions (Decety et al., 1997; Grafton et al., 1996; Hari et al., 1998; Rizzolatti, Fadiga, Matelli, et al., 1996). Premotor and parietal cortices are activated both by the perception of action and by the execution of action. Furthermore, premotor and parietal cortices are activated to a greater extent when subjects observe movements with the intention to imitate them compared with the intention simply to recognize them (Grèzes et al., 1999).

In some brain regions, the overlap between action observation and action execution is highly specific. Action observation activates the premotor cortex in a somatotopic manner (Buccino et al., 2001). In this fMRI experiment, subjects observed actions performed by the mouth, hand, and foot that were either performed in isolation (mimicking chewing, grasping, and kicking) or with an object (chewing food, grasping a cup, and kicking a ball). The results demonstrated that watching mouth, hand, and foot movements alone (without objects) activates the same functionally specific regions of the premotor cortex as making those respective movements. Furthermore, when actions were directed toward objects, the parietal cortex became activated. Again, functionally specific regions of the parietal cortex were activated according to the object-directed action being performed.

It has been argued that the mirror system facilitates action understanding and that we understand other people's actions by mapping observed actions onto our own motor representations of the same actions (Jeannerod, 2001; Rizzolatti et al., 2001). However, there is evidence that the motor system also is geared up for making actions it observes. This suggests that another role of the mirror system is to prepare the observer's motor system to make the observed actions even in cases when the observer has no intention to imitate the observed action.

Observing a movement has measurable consequences on the peripheral motor system (Fadiga et al., 1995). Fadiga and colleagues stimulated the left primary motor cortex of human subjects using transcranial magnetic stimulation (TMS) while the subjects observed meaningless actions and grasping movements (and other visual control tasks). Motor evoked potentials (MEPs) were recorded from the subjects' hand muscles. It was found that during action observation, there was a decrease in the threshold needed to evoke MEPs in the hand muscles that would be used for the observed movements. This was not the case for MEP thresholds from other muscles, which would not have been used in the observed movement. Thus, the peripheral motor system seems to prepare to execute observed movements.

Interactions Between Action Observation and Action Execution

Recently, several experiments have been performed which provide evidence for an interference effect between observed and executed actions. In one psychophysical study, subjects were instructed to perform a finger movement (tapping or lifting) in response to a visual "go" signal. The go signal was a photograph of a finger movement that was either the same (compatible) or the alternative (incompatible) finger movement to that being prepared by the subject. The results showed that the reaction time to initiate the prepared finger movement was significantly slowed down when the go stimulus was a visual representation of a different finger movement (Brass et al., 2001). In addition to this interference effect, when the go stimulus was congruent with the prepared finger movement, performance was facilitated relative to the baseline reaction time. The authors interpreted their finding as a facilitation effect in terms of the reaction time to carry out the action when there is high ideomotor compatibility between a prepared and an observed action.

In another psychophysical study, subjects prepared to grasp one of two bars that differed in orientation, being positioned clockwise or counterclockwise (Craighero et al., 2002). The go signal to grasp the bar was a photograph of the final hand posture necessary for the grasping action, which was either in the same orientation as (congruent) or a different orientation from (incongruent) the prepared grasping response. Reaction times to initiate the grasping action were measured, and it was demonstrated that there was a facilitation when there was a similarity between the hand position in the go stimulus and the final grasping-hand position. This result was interpreted as demonstrating the close link between observed hand positions and specific motor actions. These results support the notion that, during observation of action, the specific neural networks subserving that particular movement are already tuned for action (Jeannerod, 1994; Prinz, 1997).

If the motor system is geared up to execute observed movements, this might result in interference when the observed movement is qualitatively different from the *simultaneously* executed movement. To investigate this hypothesis, an experiment was performed in which subjects made sinusoidal movements with their right arm at the same time as they observed arm movements that were either congruent or incongruent with their own movements (Kilner et al., 2003). The subject made arm movements while observing arm movements made either by another human or by a robot, which were either in the same direction (congruent) or tangential (incongruent) to the subject's own movements (Figure 19.1). In addition, there were two baseline conditions in which the subjects moved their arms without observing anything.

Arm movements were recorded using an Optotrak recording system, and variance in the movement was used as a measure of interference to the movement (Figure 19.2). The results of this experiment revealed that there was a significant interaction effect between the observed effector (human or robot) and movement congruency (congruent or incongruent with executed movements) on the variance of the subjects' arm movements. The significant interaction between observed effector and movement congruency was due to there being more interference in subjects' arm movements when they watched human arm movements that were incongruent with their own movements than in any other condition (Figure 19.3). Executed movements in all of the conditions in which subjects observed movements were compared with the baseline condition in which subjects executed the same movements without observing any movements. The only condition that differed significantly from

	Congruent	Incongruent
Robot	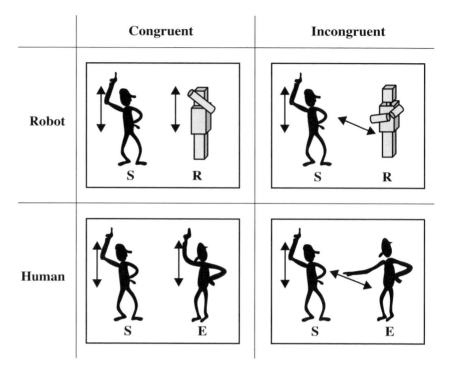	
Human		

Figure 19.1. Experimental design. In each condition, the subjects (S) were instructed to make sinusoidal movements of their right arms from the shoulder, which were either vertical or horizontal at a rate of 0.5 Hz. While making these arm movements, the subjects observed movements made by another effector situated facing the subjects, either the right arm of the experimenter (E) or a robotic arm (R), which were either congruent or incongruent with the executed movements. In addition, there were two baseline conditions in which the subjects moved their arms either horizontally or vertically without watching anything. Reprinted from Kilner et al., 2003, with permission from Elsevier.

the baseline movement condition in terms of movement variance was the condition in which subjects watched the experimenter making incongruent arm movements.

These results demonstrate that observing human arm movements significantly interferes with ongoing executed movements if the observed movements are qualitatively different from the movements being made. There was no significant interference to ongoing movements during the observation of a human making similar movements. Neither were ongoing movements significantly interfered with during the observation of a robot making either congruent or incongruent movements. Only the observation of another human making incongruent arm movements significantly interfered with the execution of arm movements (Figure 19.3).

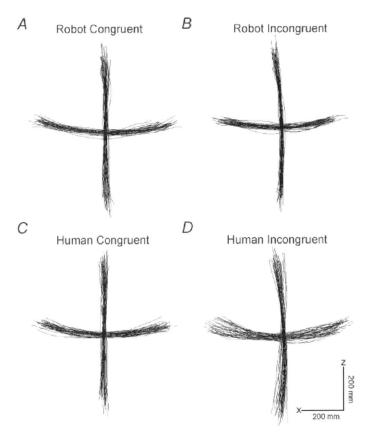

Figure 19.2. Arm movement data from a single subject. A–D show the individual movements in the XZ plane made by a single subject during four of the conditions. The plots show horizontal and vertical movements made by the subject while observing the robot making congruent movements (A), observing the robot making incongruent movements (B), observing the experimenter making congruent movements (C), and observing the experimenter making incongruent movements (D). The scale of all four plots is in the lower right corner. Reprinted from Kilner et al., 2003, with permission from Elsevier.

Interference Occurs When Observing Biological Motion

The finding that observing a robot making incongruent movements had no significant effect on executed movement demonstrates that the interference effect is not simply due to increased attentional demands, task complexity, or any other artifactual effect of observing an incongruent movement. Rather, it suggests that the brain processes biological and nonbiological movements differently. This is perhaps not surprising given the large body of evidence

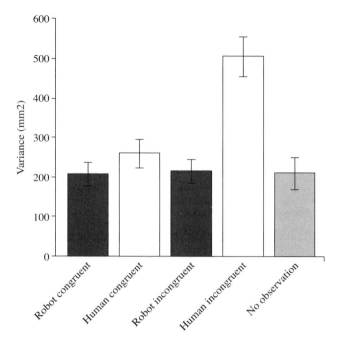

Figure 19.3. Interference effect of observing biological movement on executed movements. For each segmented movement, the variance in the movement orthogonal to the dominant dimension of movement and in the dominant dimension of the incongruent movement was calculated. The mean of the movement variances was calculated across all trials for each condition. Mean variances (and standard error bars) are shown for five conditions: observing the robot making congruent movements (robot congruent); observing the experimenter making congruent movements (human congruent); observing the robot making incongruent movements (robot incongruent); observing the experimenter making incongruent movements (human incongruent); and the baseline condition (no observation). The only condition that differed significantly from the baseline movement condition was the condition in which subjects watched the experimenter making incongruent arm movements ($P < 0.0005$). The other three comparisons were not significantly different ($P > 0.1$). Reprinted from Kilner et al., 2003, with permission from Elsevier.

showing that distinct neural processing systems exist for these two types of movement, in particular in the STS (Allison et al., 2000; Frith & Frith, 1999; Oram & Perrett, 1994). Our results are in line with the proposal that observed movements are classified as biological (human) or nonbiological (robot) and treated differently accordingly. Only the observation of biological movement interfered with executed movements. Observing a robot, whose movement was nonbiological, making incongruent movements had no significant interference effect on ongoing movements. The aspect of biological motion which is the trigger for interference, and which is absent in robotic movements, remains unknown. Whether the interference is caused by a characteristic component of biological motion (non-Newtonian motion, nonconstant velocity, nonlinear trajectory and acceleration, for example), or the presence of human features, such as limbs or eyes, or some other nonspecific factor, such as attention, needs exploring.

Although the presence of observed biological movement was necessary for the interference effects demonstrated in the Kilner et al. study over and above stimulus-response incompatibility effects, other studies have shown that a mere representation of the biological motion will interfere with motion (Stürmer et al., 2000). The interference effect obtained between observed and performed hand movements also occurred when subjects observed a static picture of a hand in the final position of the movement (Stürmer et al., 2000). In other words, observation of the actual movement was not necessary to elicit an interference effect. Instead a representation (albeit static) of biological movement was sufficient to interfere with the movement.

It is interesting to note that observing a congruent movement had no significant facilitation effect on executed movements relative to the baseline condition in our study (Kilner et al., 2003). This is in contrast to the facilitation effect found in previous studies measuring response time to make a movement in which the presentation of a go signal that was congruent with the prepared movement significantly speeded it up (Brass et al., 2001; Craighero et al., 2002). Possible explanations for this difference in results are the stimuli used and measures taken in the different studies: in the Brass et al. and Craighero et al. studies, stimuli were presented prior to the movement, whereas in the Kilner et al. study, the observed movement and executed movement occurred simultaneously. In addition, this latter study measured movement variance rather than reaction times.

An Interference Effect of the Mirror System

Although the STS is activated by the observation of biological movements, it is not activated by the execution of action. Therefore it is unlikely that the interference effect of observing biological motion on action demonstrated in the aforementioned psychophysical studies (Brass et al., 2001; Craighero et al., 2002; Kilner et al., 2003) occurs at the level of the STS.

A number of other brain regions, including the premotor and parietal cortex, are activated both by the observation and the execution of action in humans (Decety et al., 1997; Hari et al., 1998; Rizzolatti, Fadiga, Matelli, et al., 1996) and monkeys (Gallese et al., 1996; Rizzolatti, Fadiga, Fogassi, & Gallese, 1996). If the interference effect between observed hand postures (Brass et al., 2001; Craighero et al., 2002) or observed movements (Kilner et al., 2003) and executed movements is due to interference within a common neural network that encodes both observed and executed movements, then it seems likely that this could occur within the premotor cortex and/or the parietal cortex. Furthermore, there is evidence that mirror neurons in the premotor cortex distinguish between biological and nonbiological actions, responding only to a hand movement and not to the same movement performed using a pair of pliers (Rizzolatti et al., 2001). This is likely to be due to the forward connections between the STS (which rapidly distinguishes between biological and nonbiological movement) and the premotor cortex. This distinction between the observation of biological and mechanical movement in terms of the mirror responses in the premotor cortex might explain the finding that interference effects seem to be specific to the observation of incongruent human movements and do not occur when observing nonbiological incongruent movements.

There is, however, another important distinction that needs to be considered, that is, between movements and goal-directed actions. The mirror neurons in the premotor cortex make this distinction (Rizzolatti et al., 2001) since they respond only to goal-directed actions (a hand grasping an object) and not to movements (a hand moving in the absence of an object to grasp). In the case of mirror neurons, goal-directed implies object-directed actions. In contrast, thresholds are reduced in the motor cortex during observation of meaningless movements as well as non-object-directed actions (Fadiga et al., 1995). Likewise, in the various demonstrations of interference between observation and action discussed above, the subjects were observing pictures of hands or movements with no obvious goal or object (Brass et al., 2001; Craighero et al., 2002; Kilner et al., 2003). It is possible that, for humans, movements not directed toward objects can nevertheless be goal-directed, for example, gesturing, dancing, or moving one's leg to reduce pain. The finding that the interference arises from any kind of movement and is not restricted to object-directed actions (Brass et al., 2001; Craighero et al., 2002; Kilner et al., 2003) suggests either that the interference originates from a different system than the mirror system proper, or that there is a striking difference between the human and monkey mirror system. One possibility is that the human mirror system cares less about the object-related nature of movements than does the monkey mirror system. It appears that simply observing movements causes a form of "motor contagion," which interferes with the execution of movements if these are different from those being observed.

Interference presumably occurs because two operations draw on the same system at the same time. Historically, perception and action have been presumed to draw on separate representational systems and resources. That interference is obtained between concurrent perception and production of action suggests that perception and action draw on common representational resources. Where the interference effect occurs requires further investigation.

It has been proposed that the mirror system might have evolved to facilitate communication, empathy, and the understanding of other people's minds (Gallese & Goldman, 1998). Simulating other people's actions would trigger action representations from which the underlying goals and intentions could be inferred on the basis of what our own goals and intentions would be for the same actions (Goldman, 1992). The mirror system is a possible neural mechanism for simulation of other people's actions (Gallese & Goldman, 1998).

Perception and action have classically been thought to rely on separate representational systems and resources. The studies showing that significant interactions occur between observed and executed actions (Brass et al., 2001; Craighero et al., 2002; Kilner et al., 2003) support the notion that perception and action draw on common neural systems.

Acknowledgments   The research described in this chapter was carried out with J. Kilner and Y. Paulignan and was supported by the Wellcome Trust UK and the CNRS, France. The author is supported by the Royal Society, London.

References

Allison, T., Puce, A., & McCarthy, G. (2000). Social perception from visual cues: Role of the STS region. *Trends in Cognitive Sciences, 4,* 267–278.

Bertenthal, B. I. (1993). Infants' perception of biomechanical motions: Intrinsic image and knowledge-based constraints. In C. Granrud (Ed.), *Visual perception and cognition in infancy* (pp. 175–214). Hillsdale, NJ: Erlbaum.

Brass, M., Bekkering, H., & Prinz W. (2001). Movement observation affects movement execution in a simple response task. *Acta Psychologica, 106,* 3–22.

Buccino, G., Binkofski, F., Fink, G. R., Fadiga, L., & Fogassi, L. (2001). Action observation activates premotor and parietal areas in somatotopic manner: An f MRI study. *European Journal of Neuroscience, 13,* 400–404.

Carpenter, W. (1888). *Principles of mental physiology.* United Kingdom: Appleton.

Craighero, L., Bello, A., Fadiga, L., & Rizzolatti G. (2002). Hand action preparation influences the responses to hand pictures. *Neuropsychologia, 40,* 492–502.

Decety, J., Grèzes, J., Costes, N., Perani, D., & Jeannerod, M. (1997). Brain activity during observation of actions: Influence of action content and subject's strategy. *Brain, 120,* 1763–1777.

Emery, N. J., & Perrett, D. I. (1994). Understanding the intentions of others from visual signals: Neurophysiological evidence. *Current Psychology, 13,* 683–694.

Fadiga, L., Fogassi, L., Pavesi, G., & Rizzolatti, G. (1995). Motor facilitation during action observation: A magnetic stimulation study. *Journal of Neurophysiology, 73,* 2608–2611.

Frith, C. D., & Frith, U. (1999). Interacting minds: A biological basis. *Science, 286,* 1692–1695.

Gallese, V., Fadiga, L., Fogassi, L., & Rizzolatti, G. (1996). Action recognition in the premotor cortex. *Brain, 119,* 593–609.

Gallese, V., & Goldman, A. (1998). Mirror neurons and the simulation theory of mind reading. *Trends in Cognitive Science, 2,* 493–501.

Goldman, A. I. (1992). In defense of simulation theory. *Mind and Language, 7,* 104–119.

Grafton, S. T., Arbib, M. A., Fadiga, L., & Rizzolatti, G. (1996). Localization of grasp representations in humans by positron emission tomography: Observation compared with imagination. *Experimental Brain Research, 112,* 103–111.

Grèzes, J., Costes, N., & Decety, J. (1999). The effects of learning and intention on the neural network involved in the perception of meaningless actions. *Brain, 122,* 1875–1887.

Grèzes, J., Fonlupt, P., Bertenthal, B. I., Delon-Martin, C., Segebarth, C., & Decety, J. (2001). Does perception of biological motion rely on specific brain regions? *Neuroimage, 13,* 775–785.

Grossman, E., & Blake, R. (2001). Brain activity evoked by inverted and imagined motion. *Vision Research, 41,* 1475–1482.

Grossman, E., Donnelly, M., Price, R., Pickens, D., & Morgan, V. (2000). Brain areas involved in perception of biological motion. *Journal of Cognitive Neuroscience, 12,* 711–720.

Hari, R., Fross, N., Avikainen, E., Kirveskari, E., Salenius, S., & Rizzolatti, G. (1998). Activation of human primary motor cortex during action observation: A neuromagnetic study. *Proceedings of the National Academy of Sciences, 95,* 15061–15065.

James, W. (1890). *Principles of psychology.* New York: Holt.

Jeannerod, M. (1994). The representing brain: Neural correlates of motor intention and imagery. *Behavioural and Brain Sciences, 17,* 187–202.

Jeannerod, M. (2001). Neural simulation of action: A unifying mechanism for motor cognition. *Neuroimage, 14,* S103–S109.

Jellema, T., & Perrett, D. I. (2002). Neural coding for visible and hidden objects. *Attention & Performance, 19,* 356–380.

Jellema, T., Baker, C. I., Wicker, B., & Perrett, D. I. (2000). Neural representation for the perception of the intentionality of actions. *Brain and Cognition, 44,* 280–302.

Kilner, J. M., Paulignan, Y., & Blakemore, S.-J. (2003). An interference effect of observed biological movement on action. *Current Biology, 13,* 522–525.

Kohler, E., Keysers, C., Umilta, M. A., Fogassi, L., Gallese, V., & Rizzolatti, G. (2002). Hearing sounds, understanding actions: Action representation in mirror neurons. *Science, 297*(5582), 846–848.

Oram, M. W., & Perrett, D. I. (1994). Responses of anterior superior temporal polysensory (STPa) neurons to "biological motion" stimuli. *Journal of Cognitive Neuroscience, 6,* 99–116.

Perrett, D. I., Hietanen J. K., Oram, M. W., & Benson, P. J. (1992). Organization and functions of cells responsive to faces in the temporal cortex. *Philosophical Transactions of the Royal Society of London, Series B, 335,* 23–30.

Perrett, D. I., Smith, P. A. J., Mistlin, A. J., Chitty, A. J., Head, A. S., Potter, D. D., Broennimann, R., Milner, A. D., & Jeeves, M. A. (1985). Visual analysis of body movements by neurons in the temporal cortex of the macaque monkey: A preliminary report. *Behavioural Brain Research, 16,* 153–170.

Perrett, D. I., Smith, P. A. J., Potter, D. D., Mistlin, A. J., Head, A. S., Milner, A. D., & Jeeves, M. A. (1985). Visual cells in the temporal cortex sensitive to face view and gaze direction. *Proceedings of the Royal Society of London, Series B, 223,* 293–317.

Prinz, W. (1997). Perception and action planning. *European Journal of Cognitive Psychology, 9,* 129–154.

Puce, A., Allison, T., Bentin, S., Gore, J. C., & McCarthy, G. (1998). Temporal cortex activation in humans viewing eye and mouth movements. *Journal of Neuroscience, 18,* 2188–2199.

Rizzolatti, G., Fadiga, L., Fogassi, L., & Gallese, V. (1996). Premotor cortex and the recognition of motor actions. *Cognitive Brain Research, 3,* 131–141.

Rizzolatti, G., Fadiga, L., Matelli, M., Bettinardi, V., & Paulesu, E. (1996). Localization of grasp representations in humans by PET: Observation versus execution. *Experimental Brain Research, 111*, 246–52.

Rizzolatti, G., Fogassi, L., & Gallese, V. (2001). Neurophysiological mechanisms underlying the understanding and imitation of action. *Nature Reviews Neuroscience, 2*, 661–670.

Stürmer, B., Aschersleben, G., & Prinz, W. (2000). Correspondence effects with manual gestures and postures: A study of imitation. *Journal of Experimental Psychology: Human Perception & Performance, 26*, 1746–1759.

Umilta, M. A., Kohler, E., Gallese, V., Fogassi, L., Fadiga, L., Keysers, C., Rizzolatti, G. (2001). I know what you are doing: A neurophysiological study. *Neuron, 31*, 155–165.

Wicker, B., Michel, F., Henaff, M. A., & Decety, J. (1998). Brain regions associated with mutual gaze: A PET study. *Neuroimage, 8*, 221–227.

20

Representing Intentional Relations and Acting Intentionally in Infancy
Current Insights and Open Questions

Chris Moore

Humans are natural psychologists par excellence. They interpret the activity of their conspecifics as caused by psychological states—perceptions, beliefs, emotions, intentions, and so on. These psychological categories are used both to explain past action and to predict future action. The idea of "theory of mind," which took the field of developmental psychology by storm from the mid-1980s to the mid-1990s has now left few areas of the psychological sciences untouched. A keyword search on *theory of mind* picks up articles not only in developmental psychology, but also in comparative psychology, adult social psychology, psychopathology, both developmental and adult, and cognitive neuroscience. Two rather broad theoretical approaches to theory of mind dominated thinking through the 1980s and 1990s. One was *theory theory* (e.g., Gopnik & Wellman, 1992), which essentially said that social understanding was a purely conceptual matter, with concepts of mental states constructed by observation of the behavior of others and the self and by abstracting out the principles governing the contexts and causes of those behaviors. In opposition to theory theory, others (e.g., Goldman, 1992; Harris, 1991) proposed that social understanding proceeds through simulation of others' psychological states and also one's own noncurrent psychological states by using the current psychological states of the self as a model and then adjusting various default settings appropriately to model the different circumstances of the other person or the self at another time. More recently, a third approach to social understanding, which can be regarded as taking the middle ground between theory theory and simulation theory, has started to gain increasing attention (e.g., Barresi & Moore, 1996; Hommel, Müsseler, Aschersleben, & Prinz, 2001;

Meltzoff & Prinz, 2002; Sebanz, Knoblich, & Prinz, 2003). This third approach argues, with simulation theory, that social understanding is grounded in experiences of psychological activity but, unlike simulation theory, does not prioritize the self. Rather it argues that observation of the psychological activity of both self and others is critical. These observations are integrated through some form of common representational code. The primary representations of psychological activity may then be further elaborated through conceptual activity as theory theory suggests. In this chapter, I summarize some of the main elements of one of this new breed of theoretical account, called *intentional relations theory* (Barresi & Moore, 1996), and then examine some recent evidence from one area of developmental psychology that has added important new insights requiring a refinement of the original position. I end by pointing to the questions in this area of developmental psychology that are most pressingly in need of answers.

1. Intentional Relations Theory

Although much of the research on theory of mind has focused on how people conceptualize mental states—in particular, beliefs and desires—a full account of the origins, both phylogenetic and ontogenetic, of theory of mind requires that the understanding of such representational mental states be seen as evolving out of simpler forms of psychological concepts. A broader characterization of social understanding reveals that a key feature of all psychological activity is that such activity is directed at, or about, something. Another way to put this is that psychological activity has a relational structure whereby an agent is linked to an object through the psychological activity. Some examples ranging from simple to more complex are listed below. In all of these cases, there is an agent (Columbus, the baby, etc.), an object (land, the rattle, etc.), and a form of psychological activity linking them (sees, wants, etc.). We refer to these structures as *intentional relations* (Barresi & Moore, 1996).

1. Columbus sees land.
2. The baby wants the rattle.
3. I'm thinking of a purple cow.
4. Chris thinks the chapter will be finished by March.
5. Günther wants the chapter to be finished by March.

In order to understand how humans acquire a theory of mind that has this relational structure, we need to say a bit more about each of the three components of the structure: agents, objects, and the psychological acts that connect them. Where relevant, the potential role of the body will be indicated.

1.1. Agents and Self-Other Equivalence

Intentional relations are attributed first and foremost to animate entities, most importantly to people, in virtue of their sensorimotor, cognitive, and emotional capacities. Now, we certainly have no trouble attributing intentional relations to other animals and even to some apparently purposeful inanimate objects; however, the further we go from people, the more the range of psychological activities that we might attribute to these nonhuman agents becomes restricted. For example, we may be perfectly comfortable saying that the family dog *saw* the ball and *wanted* to play, or that he *heard* the can opener and *thought* he was going to get something to eat. With an organism significantly less "human," such as a fly buzzing around a pot of jam, we may be willing to attribute certain simpler psychological states, such as the fly *wanted* the jam. But we would probably not go so far as to say that it had any thoughts about the matter. Clearly the difference between flies and dogs is that the latter have physical forms that are closer to humans and, more important, display more complex behavior, which makes considerably more sense to us in the context of our interactions with them. Along the same lines, while they may not display "behavior" in the usual sense of the word, the fact that we can have quite complex interactions with certain artifacts, such as computers, leads quite naturally to a willingness to interpret these artifacts with reference to intentional categories. However, it is people to whom we naturally apply the full range of intentional relations.

It is important to note that the category of agents to whom we attribute intentional relations includes ourselves. Thus I can talk about my own feelings and thoughts in the same way as I can talk about yours. This is an obvious but nevertheless remarkable fact. The perceptual experience we have of our own agentive activity (first-person experience) is quite different from the experience we have observing others as agents (third-person experience). First-person experience tends to emphasize the object of our experience and involves subjective information about our attitude toward the object as well as proprioceptive information about our action. In contrast, third-person information tends to be primarily about the agent and her behavior, especially in cases where the object of the other person's intentional relation cannot be directly observed (such as when it is a mental representation or at some distance spatially). Nevertheless, as mature natural psychologists, we have no difficulty recognizing that self and other are equivalent in their status as agents of a range of intentional relations. Thus, for example, I know that the experience I have when I shift my eyes in response to a movement in the periphery of my visual field and spy an animal off to my right is actually the same kind of event as when I observe a change in the sclera-iris configurations of another person's eyes. Given the qualitative difference in the raw information available about the intentional relations of self and other, there has to be some way for the equivalence of self and other to be constructed. This we call the problem of *self-other equivalence*, and it stands as one significant challenge for the comprehension of the nature of human social understanding.

In concert with the theme of this volume, it is interesting to consider to what extent the possession of a particular kind of body helps to establish the equivalence between self and other. The overlap in direct experience between self and other for certain kinds of intentional relations would seem to be essentially nonexistent. For example, as noted, my own act of looking at and seeing an object presents little or no information to me that is common to my observation of your looking at and seeing the same object. However, for other kinds of intentional relation, there clearly is an overlap in direct experience. Thus, if I reach for an object in front of me, I can see my own arm movements in essentially the same way that I can see the arm movements of another person as he reaches for that object. The fact that we possess bodies with similar form may well play some role in the initial establishment of the equivalence between our own and others' action on objects. Nevertheless, it is important to recognize that there remain differences across the perception of one's own and of others' actions. Not only are there inevitable perspectival differences, but also it is clear that one's own action is essentially processed intermodally (see chapter 3). As a result, even for the most clear-cut cases of object-directed action, the raw perceptual experience would appear to be different for actions of self and actions of others.

1.2. Objects and Object-Directedness

Psychological activity is generally directed at some object. By *object* here, we do not mean necessarily a real, concrete object, although such items can be involved. We use the term *object* in a generic sense to mean anything toward which a psychological relation is directed. Objects can be real physical things (e.g., 1 and 2 above), or they can be imaginary things (e.g., 3), including various representations and even propositions (e.g., 4, 5). Propositional representations may be assumed to reflect the way the world actually is or could be (as in beliefs) or reflective of the way the agent would like the world to be (as in desires or intentions). Although it is the understanding of intentional relations to such propositional representations that has attracted most study to date, our interest in this chapter will be on intentional relations to real objects.

Clearly, intentional relations to mental representations will present a challenge to a naïve observer of human activity. If the object of an intentional relation is not directly observable, then presumably it must be inferred from patterns of activity. Less obvious is the fact that the same must be true for a range of intentional relations to real objects. Take the example of the first sentence above: "Columbus sees land." The land is real, but it is also spatially distant from the agent. Therefore, the observer of Columbus may take note of his head and eye orientation but may not also be able to observe the object of his gaze: the land. Yet when someone exhibits looking activity, we assume that there is an object to which that looking is directed. The second challenge for a theory of social understanding is determining how we come to understand that intentional activity is object-directed.

1.3. Psychological Acts

Humans are entities that have various systems of the body, including the brain or mind, which enable the variety of intentional relations. We typically distinguish three broad categories of psychological acts. First, *epistemic* acts are those in which the acquisition, maintenance, or manipulation of knowledge occurs. Humans are able to perceive objects in the immediate environment, remember objects from the past, and imagine objects that may be fictional or anticipated. Such acts are usually referred to using perceptual terms (e.g., see, hear) and cognitive terms (think, know, remember, imagine). Second, humans also have *emotional* orientations to objects. They like things, fear things, are proud of things, and so on. Finally, *conative* acts capture the fact that humans are purposeful: they produce actions directed at objects and intended to achieve desired goals.

Of course, agents do other things as well. Sometimes, agents act like any other solid objects: they fall out of trees or bump against chairs. In such cases, we do not attribute intentional relations. We say the event occurred "accidentally" as opposed to "on purpose." Part of developing social understanding is learning to distinguish activity that occurs in intentional relation to objects from activity that reflects mere mechanical relations. Other acts do occur in virtue of agents' animacy—people breathe, blink, and pump blood throughout their bodies—however, these acts are also not within the domain of intentional relations theory because they are not relational or directed at objects.

To what extent is the body a necessary prerequisite for the variety of intentional relations? Bodies enable object-directed activity, and they are the source of both first-person and third-person information about intentional relations. To take a simple example, a reach for a desired apple involves a directed arm movement, and this movement yields both visual information and proprioceptive information, which in the case of the self are coordinated intermodally. However, bodies also are inevitably involved in nonintentional action. So having a body does not determine intentionality. Nevertheless, certain kinds of activity that are the result of biological motion may well be processed from early in life independently from other kinds of motion (see, for example, chapter 14) and thereby allow some bootstrapping of the detection of intentional action.

1.4. The Intentional Schema

We have identified self-other equivalence and object-directedness as two properties of human social understanding that may not be immediately evident in the information available through observation of the activity of human agents. Barresi and Moore (1996) proposed that the dual challenge of understanding self-other equivalence and object-directedness could be solved if (a) the individual were able to interact regularly with others in such a way that they shared intentional relations to an object or event; and (b) while in such interactions, the individual were able to integrate, through an *intentional schema*, the available first-person information from the self's activity and third-person information from the other's activity into a set of representations that retained the qualities of both. They suggested that just such conditions exist in human development by the end of the first year.

The behavioral evidence is quite clear on the first part of the claim (e.g., Carpenter, Nagell, & Tomasello, 1998). By 12 months, infants are able to participate in a range of object-focused (or triadic) interactions with others. They engage in object exchange; they follow gaze to objects distally located; they direct others' attention toward objects that are the current focus of their attention; they use others' emotional expressions to guide their own reactions to novel objects; and they imitate actions on objects that others perform. In these object-focused interactions, infants share intentional relations, including epistemic, emotional, and conative ones, with others. There is no doubt, then, that by 12 months, infants are regularly in situations in which they have available both first-person information about their own object-directed activity and third-person information about others' equivalent object-directed activity.

In the remainder of this chapter, we consider the extent to which the second, and more controversial, part of the claim is supported. Is there evidence for an intentional schema that can integrate first- and third-person information about intentional activity? It is worth noting that the discovery of mirror neurons some 10 years ago has provided circumstantial support (e.g., Gallese, Fadiga, Fogassi, & Rizzolatti, 1996) even if the mirror neurons have been interpreted to date as evidence for simulation theory (e.g., Gallese & Goldman, 1998). Mirror neurons may be seen as at least a partial neural implementation of Barresi and Moore's (1996) proposed intentional schema in that they code object-directed activity from both a first- and third-person perspective. Of course, there is no direct evidence yet that mirror neurons exist in human infants, and indeed the ontogenetic tuning of such neurons in unknown. At the same time, there is growing evidence in favor of the idea that adult human perception of action and production of action rely upon a common representational code (e.g., Hommel et al., 2001; chapter 18).

What might behavioral evidence for the intentional schema look like in infancy? Moore and Corkum (1994) suggested that a habituation approach to the issue might allow some traction. Because the intentional schema would be important for understanding the object-directedness of intentional activity, they suggested examining infants' representations of the object-directedness of intentional actions of others. The suggested approach was as follows. Infants would first be habituated to an intentional event involving an agent engaged in some intentional activity directed at an object. After habituation, the infant would be presented with test events that either maintained the intentional structure of the original event while changing the action or maintained the same form of the action but disrupted the intentional structure of the event by changing the object. Greater recovery of looking to the event that disrupted the intention structure would be taken as evidence that infants represented the original event in terms of its intentional structure.

Independently, Woodward (1995) hit on the same empirical strategy, although it was not in the context of intentional relations theory. She had become interested in the question of whether infants recognized that others had goals or intentions when they acted, and she conducted the first study using what has become known as the *switch paradigm*. Since then, Woodward has produced by far the most comprehensive body of evidence relevant both to her original interest in goal-directed activity and to intentional relations more generally. Some other research groups have provided additional evidence for infants' representation of the object-directed nature of human activity (e.g., Király et al., 2003; Moore, 1999b; Phillips, Wellman, & Spelke, 2002; Thoermer & Sodian, 2001). It is to a review of this evidence that we now turn.

2. Infants' Representations of Intentional Relations

The logic of the switch paradigm for examining infants' representations of intentional relations is shown in Figure 20.1. In the first, habituation, phase, the infant is repeatedly shown a live event involving an intentional relation. The event is displayed on each trial until the infant has looked away for at least 2 seconds. In between trials, the display is hidden for 2 seconds. Two objects are present in the display, and the intentional activity is directed at one of them. As a result, the intentional relation is established with a particular spatiotemporal form. After the infant has habituated, which usually entails a decrement of 50% or more in looking time over three habituation trials compared to the first three habituation trials, the two test displays are presented in alternation, typically for three trials with order counterbalanced across participants. Infant looking time to the test displays is measured and compared. In the compatible, or *old intention*, test event, the form of the action has changed but the intentional relation is still the same because the action is directed at the same object as in the habituation display. In the incompatible, or *new intention*, test event, the form of the action is still the same as in the habituation display, but the action is

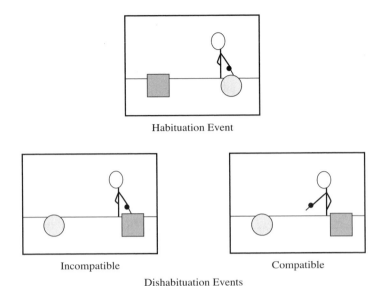

Figure 20.1. Schematic representation of habituation and dishabituation events for the switch paradigm for examining infants' representation of the object-directedness of psychological acts.

now directed at a different object, and so the intentional relation is changed. Therefore, greater recovery of looking to the new intention test event is taken to mean that the infant has represented the event in terms of the intentional relation.

2.1. Conative Acts

Using the switch paradigm, Woodward (1998) first demonstrated that infants as young as 5–6 months represent a reach and grasp by a human arm to be object-directed. In these displays, only the arm and hand were shown reaching for the object and grasping it. Performance on displays involving a human reach and grasp was compared to similar displays in which a rod, a flat occluder, or a mechanical claw extended and touched or grasped objects. Infants showed greater dishabituation to the new intention test event only for the human reach and grasp. In a subsequent study (Woodward, 1999), performance of 5- and 9-month-old infants was examined for displays in which the human arm reached and grasped an object or extended toward the object and touched it with the back of the hand without grasping. The latter action was used as an example of an act that was human but not purposeful. In this study, infants at both ages again showed evidence of representing the reach and grasp as object-directed. However, the infants did not differentiate between the old intention and new intention test trials for the back-of-the-hand touch. Interestingly, if infants are shown during habituation that the back-of-the-hand action can be used in an apparently goal-directed way, for example, to sweep an object from one place to another, then 8- and 10-month-olds and perhaps even 6-month-olds appear to represent the action as goal-directed (Király et al., 2003). Together, these results show that by the middle of the first year, infants have a fairly well differentiated representation of the familiar action of reaching and grasping as object-directed. Interestingly, of course, infants themselves are capable of visually guided reaching by 5 months, and so it appears that representing others' reaching and grasping as intentional develops at about the same time as infants are capable of producing similar conative acts. Before long, they appear to be able to generalize such object-directedness to more unfamiliar actions.

The studies reviewed above all used only the human arm and hand in the stimulus events. Studies on reaching and grasping that have shown infants the whole of the upper body, including the face, have yielded a slightly more mixed picture. Woodward (2003) found that both 7- and 9-month-olds showed the response pattern characteristic of representing the events in terms of intentional relations. However, Thoermer and Sodian (2001) found that infants at 12 but not 10 months appeared to represent grasping as object-directed. Of possible interest here is that these studies differed in terms of how the manual reach was enacted. In Woodward's (2003) studies, the actor performed a contralateral reach, thereby to some extent twisting the whole torso. In contrast, Thoermer and Sodian (2001) presented displays in which the actor reached ipsilaterally, and as a result there was less overall bodily orientation toward the target. If this difference were replicable, it would have important implications for the extent to which infants' understanding of intentional relations is tied to the form of the actions at different ages.

2.2. Epistemic Acts

Studies using the switch paradigm to investigate infants' representations of epistemic acts, such as looking and pointing, have found that representing such acts as object-directed comes rather later than for reaching and grasping. Woodward (2003) reported experiments in which infants were shown displays of an actor looking toward one of two toys. For dishabituation trials, the position of the toys was switched, and the actor gazed at the same toy as in the habituation trials or at the other toy. The results showed that when gaze was the only cue, 12-month-olds but not 7- or 9-month-olds dishabituated more to the gaze at the new toy than to the gaze at the old toy. This result supports the idea that by 12 months, infants represent gaze as object-directed, although it should be recognized that one study has failed to replicate this effect for 12-month-olds (Thoermer & Sodian, 2001).

It is important to note that the positive result of Woodward (2003) occurred despite the fact that infants at all ages in the study followed the actor's gaze during both habituation and test events and spent more time looking at the same toy as the actor. So the representation of others' gaze as object-directed appears to coincide developmentally neither with infants' own looking behavior (obviously, infants have been looking at things since birth) nor with infants' ability to follow the gaze of others.

The attention-directing act of pointing has also been examined using the switch habituation paradigm. Woodward and Guajardo (2002) tested infants of 9 and 12 months on the grounds that infants often start to point themselves between these ages. Because infants often do not follow points at this age (e.g., Carpenter, Nagell, & Tomasello, 1998), the pointing gesture demonstrated was one in which the pointing finger actually contacted the target object. Displays in which only the arm was visible and in which the person from the waist up was visible were used, although this variable did not influence the results. The results showed that only the 12-month-olds dishabituated to the new intention events during the test trials. In a follow-up experiment, Woodward and Guajardo (2002) showed that for infants between 8 and 11 months, whether the infants were already pointing themselves was a strong predictor of their tendency to represent pointing as object-directed.

Using essentially the same approach as Woodward and colleagues, other researchers have examined infants' representation of pointing when the gesture does not contact the target object. Thoermer and Sodian (2001) tested a group of children at 10 and 12 months of age and found that at neither age did they recover more to the new intention event. Indeed, in their study, at 12 months, the infants showed greater recovery of looking to the test event in which the form of the pointing gesture changed even though it was directed at the same toy as in the habituation event. This result was found despite the fact that when tested for their ability to follow pointing, the large majority of the infants participating in the study succeeded by 12 months.

Working with slightly older infants of 12–14 months, Moore (1999b) also used the switch paradigm to examine the representation of the object-directedness of distal pointing. In his studies, the displays showed an adult from the waist up producing a pointing gesture that did not contact the target object. In line with Woodward and Guajardo (2002), infants showed greater recovery of looking to the new intention display in the test phase than to the old intention, supporting the idea that by 14 months, infants represent pointing that does not contact a target to be object-directed.

It should be noted that in all of these studies of pointing in which the model's head is visible, the gaze has been congruent with the direction of pointing, so strictly speaking it is not possible to say that infants are attending to the pointing gesture. However, other related evidence does imply that in the pointing studies, the infants are attending to the manual gesture. In particular,

Woodward and Wilson-Brune (2003) reported that when 9–12-month-old infants were tested in separate habituation sessions for whether they represented both gaze and pointing as object-directed, there was no correlation between performances on the two types of attentional act. Some infants appeared to represent gaze but not pointing as object-directed, whereas others seemed to have the reverse pattern of representation. It is interesting, therefore, that despite the similarity of gaze and pointing in terms of their manifesting an epistemic psychological relation of attention, the evidence implies that infants do not appreciate this similarity.

2.3. Emotional Acts

Emotional expressions are not by themselves obviously directed at a particular object. However, when seen in combination with gaze direction, they provide information to the observer about the affective orientation of the agent toward the gazed-at object. Such information may be used to predict how the agent will behave subsequently to the object. For example, an agent who looks and smiles at one of two toys is more likely to subsequently reach for that toy than for the other one. This kind of understanding has also been examined in infants (e.g., Phillips, Wellman, & Spelke, 2002) although the displays are necessarily a bit more complex than when simply assessing the object-directedness of reaching, gaze, and pointing.

Phillips et al. (2002) reported a number of experiments examining infants' representation of emotion. In their most stringent experiments, they first presented infants with an event in which an adult smiled and looked at one of two similar toys. They then presented test events involving a sequence of two actions separated by a curtain being closed and opened. In the first part of the test events, the adult was shown emoting toward one of the toys. The curtain then closed briefly and opened to reveal the adult either holding the toy toward which she had previously emoted (consistent event) or holding the other toy (inconsistent event). They found that 14-month-olds but not 12-month-olds discriminated the two test events and looked longer at the inconsistent event.

3. Implications for Intentional Relations Theory

How are these findings relevant to the issues in intentional relations theory broached at the outset of this chapter? First, they inform our knowledge of the origins of understanding object-directedness. What they show is that the understanding of the object-directedness of psychological activity starts to develop in the first year but is not an all-or-none achievement. It appears first for behaviorally implemented conative acts, for example, reaching and grasping, as early as 5 months of age. By 9–10 months, it is evident for epistemic actions that involve direct object contact, such as pointing. Finally, by the beginning of the second year, infants represent epistemic and emotional acts as object-directed even when the target object is more distally located.

Second, these results provide evidence on the issue of self-other equivalence. Infants' representations of others' actions as object-directed sometimes but not always coincides with their own ability to produce equivalent object-directed actions. A working summary to date is that for those actions that directly contact objects—reaching and grasping, contact pointing—infants appear to represent the actions of others as object-directed at about the same time as they start to produce similar object-directed actions themselves. It is possible but, of course, by no means proven that this congruence is mediated by an early developing mirror neuron system. However, for psychological acts that do not contact objects—gaze, distal pointing, emotions—there appears to be no clear developmental correspondence between representing others' acts and being able to produce these acts. For example, as noted, infants look at objects well before they represent gaze as object-directed and indeed are able to follow gaze before they represent it as object-directed (Woodward, 2003). Therefore, the development of self-other equivalence for action at a distance is more protracted.

The absence of self-other equivalence for actions at a distance need not impair the infant's ability to act appropriately in response to such actions. Other mechanisms apart from the use of a common code for action and perception can mediate successful interaction (see e.g., Moore & Corkum, 1994). For example, gaze following may be, at first, the result of a relatively low-level attentional cueing mechanism whereby the observation of another person's head or eye turn cues the infant's attention in the same direction (Moore, 1999a). Indeed there is even evidence for such a mechanism in both young infants and adults (Friesen & Kingstone, 1998; Hood, Willen, & Driver, 1998). Such processes will allow the infant to interact regularly with others in such a way that they share intentional relations to objects and events. Subsequent integration of the available information pertaining to the intentional relations of both self and other would then allow the construction of representations of those intentional relations.

Together, these findings argue against the idea that representing intentional relations to real objects is a one-step developmental achievement late in the first year. Thus, the notions that there is a single intentional schema of general applicability (Barresi & Moore, 1996) or that there is a single conceptual insight (e.g., Tomasello, 1999) are almost certainly oversimplified. Infants develop an understanding of object-directedness for different kinds of psychological relations at different times over the final 6 months of the first year. They also seem initially to have little recognition of the correspondence between self and other for certain psychological relations. A more likely model of development during this time is that infants' understanding of psychological activity is constructed in a relatively piecemeal way (Woodward & Wilson-Brune, 2003). As infants attempt to make sense of their object-centered interactive experiences, they will detect the patterns of first- and third-person information corresponding to different types of intentional relations in an initially case-by-case way. The first- and third-person informational components would still be integrated in a manner consistent with intentional relations theory, but the resulting intentional representations would not necessarily be linked up as part of a more general conceptual understanding. One might say that infants' initial entry into social understanding is through islands of intentional understanding just as their later entry into linguistic constructions is characterized by verb islands rather than grammatical categories (e.g., Tomasello, 2003).

If intentional understanding is initially piecemeal, this also has implications for whether infants understand intentional relations at the personal or subpersonal level. According to some accounts (e.g., Tomasello, 1999), infants represent people as intentional agents, and so it is people that are intentional. An islands approach to early intentional understanding would characterize infants' earliest attributions of intention to psychological acts rather than to persons. Only as infants started to detect the correspondences among the variety of intentional acts that individual people perform would infants move to attributing intentions to people independently of the particular acts they perform. Understanding intentional relations at the subpersonal rather than personal level also means that the representations generated by integrating first- and third-person information for particular intentional acts are not attributable independently to agents such as self or other. Nevertheless, these representations can guide behavior in social interactive situations, such as object-centered play. Essentially, the infant is capable of determining when intentional relations are or are not shared and of behaving proactively to facilitate such sharing.

The habituation approach to investigating infants' representations of intentional relations has been of considerable value to date. There is good reason to believe that it can be further exploited to explore infants' intentional representations. First, on the issue of intentional islands, one might examine the extent to which infants generalize their intentional construals across similar intentional actions. For example, using the switch paradigm, one might habituate infants to someone gazing at one of the two objects and then use a different but related epistemic act, such as pointing, in the test trials. If infants construe both gaze and pointing in terms of a more abstract category such as "attention," then they should show more recovery to the new intention test trials even though the particular act is different. Indeed, the intentional islands account proposed earlier would predict that initially in their development, infants would not generalize across related acts, but later in development, they would.

Second, one can examine the extent to which intentional relations are seen by infants to be properties of persons or of particular actions. The key question here is whether infants will transfer intentional relations across individuals from habituation to dishabituation trials. Preliminary evidence on this issue is available, and it is mixed. Moore (1999b) habituated 13-month-olds to one woman pointing at one of two objects and then showed another woman pointing in the test trials. Infants showed the same pattern of recovery of looking as when the same woman had been present in both habituation and test trials. These results are consistent with the idea that the infants represented the pointing action as object-directed but not that the pointing action reflected the intention of the person doing the pointing (because different people were doing the pointing in the habituation and test trials). However, Sootsman et al. (2003) found that, for a grasping action, 13-month-old infants did not recover looking after habituation when a new and quite distinctive actor was used in the test trials, but they did recover looking to the new intention trials when a similar-looking actor was used. At present it is not clear whether the discrepancy between these two sets of results reflects real differences in how infants construe different object-directed actions or methodological differences between the studies.

4. Conclusion

Considerable progress has been made in the last few years in our understanding of the earliest phase of intentional representation in infants. The last half of the first year witnesses a profound change in the scope of infants' representations of intentional relations. From object-contacting purposeful acts at 6 months to epistemic action at a distance at 12 months, infants gradually construct representations of the range of intentional relations—conative, epistemic, emotional—that characterize humans. It is likely that a variety of aspects of experience go into the construction of these representations. First, infants observe both their own and others' purposeful acts in a similar way, e.g., as arms reaching for, grasping, and otherwise transforming the arrangements of objects in the world. Second, different intentional relations show regular co-occurrences: people reach for the objects they look and smile at; people look at the objects they point at; and so on. Third, infants are regular participants in object-centered interactions during which they share intentional relations with others—they both look at the same object; they smile at the same object; and they otherwise communicate about the object. It is during these interactive experiences that they experience both the first-person characteristics of intentional relations and the third-person characteristics in recognizable patterns. And it is the representation of these patterns that ultimately allows the infant to bridge the epistemic gap between self and other for the full range of intentional relations.

Acknowledgments   This chapter was prepared with support from a grant from the Natural Sciences and Engineering Council of Canada. I am very grateful to the organizers of the conference Body Perception From the Inside Out and, in particular, Günther Knoblich. Günther Knoblich, Petra Hauf, Frederique de Vignemont, and Patrick Haggard provided valuable feedback on the first draft. My thanks also go to John Barresi for his continuing intellectual collaboration.

References

Barresi, J., & Moore, C. (1996). Intentional relations and social understanding. *Behavioral and Brain Sciences, 19*, 107–122.

Carpenter, M., Nagell, K., & Tomasello, M. (1998). Social cognition, joint attention, and communicative competence from 9 to 15 months of age. *Monographs of the Society for Research in Child Development, 63*, No. 255.

Friesen, C., & Kingstone, A. (1998). The eyes have it! Reflexive orienting is triggered by nonpredictive gaze. *Psychonomic Bulletin and Review, 5*, 490–495.

Gallese, V., Fadiga, L., Fogassi, L., & Rizzolatti, G. (1996). Action recognition in the premotor cortex. *Brain, 119*, 593–609.

Gallese, V., & Goldman, A. (1998). Mirror neurons and the simulation theory of mind-reading. *Trends in Cognitive Sciences, 12*, 493–501.

Goldman, A. (1992). In defense of simulation theory. *Mind and Language, 7*, 104–119.

Gopnik, A., & Wellman, H. (1992). Why the child's theory of mind really *is* a theory. *Mind and Language, 7*, 145–171.

Harris, P. (1991). The work of the imagination. In A. Whiten (Ed.), *Natural theories of mind: Evolution, development, and simulation of everyday mindreading* (pp. 283–304). Oxford: Blackwell.

Hommel, B., Müsseler, J., Aschersleben, G., & Prinz, W. (2001). The theory of event coding (TEC): A framework for perception and action planning. *Behavioral and Brain Sciences, 24*, 849–937.

Hood, B., Willen, J., & Driver, J. (1998). Adults' eyes trigger shifts of visual attention in human infants. *Psychological Science, 9*, 53–56.

Király, I., Jovanovic, B., Prinz, W., Aschersleben, G., & Gergely, G. (2003). The early origins of goal attribution in infancy. *Consciousness and Cognition, 12*, 752–769.

Meltzoff, A., & Prinz, W. (Eds.). (2002). *The imitative mind: Development, evolution and brain bases.* New York: Cambridge University Press.

Moore, C. (1999a). Gaze following and control of attention. In P. Rochat (Ed.), *Early social cognition: Understanding others in the first months of life* (pp. 241–256). Mahwah, NJ: Erlbaum.

Moore, C. (1999b). Intentional relations and triadic interactions. In P. Zelazo, J. Astington, & D. Olson (Eds.), *Theories of mind in action: Development and evolution of social understanding and self control* (pp. 43–62). Mahwah, NJ: Erlbaum.

Moore, C., & Corkum, V. (1994). Social understanding at the end of the first year of life. *Developmental Review, 14*, 349–372.

Phillips, A., Wellman, H., & Spelke, E. (2002). Infants' ability to connect gaze and emotional expressions to intentional action. *Cognition, 85*, 53–78.

Sebanz, N., Knoblich, G., & Prinz, W. (2003). Representing others' actions: Just like one's own? *Cognition, 88*, B11–B21.

Sootsman, J., Morgante, J., Wilson-Brune, C., & Woodward, A. (2003). *Eyes on the prize: Twelve-month-old infants track the goals of individual agents.* Paper presented at Cognitive Development Society, Park City, UT.

Thoermer, C., & Sodian, B. (2001). Preverbal infants' understanding of referential gestures. *First Language, 21*, 245–264.

Tomasello, M. (1999). *The cultural origins of human cognition.* Cambridge, MA: Harvard University Press.

Tomasello, M. (2003). *Constructing a language: A usage-based theory of language acquisition.* Cambridge, MA: Harvard University Press.

Woodward, A. L. (1995). *Infants' reasoning about the goals of a human actor.* Presented at the Biennial Meetings of the Society for Research in Child Development, Indianapolis, IN.

Woodward, A. L. (1998). Infants selectively encode the goal object of an actor's reach. *Cognition, 69*, 1–34.

Woodward, A. L. (1999). Infants' ability to distinguish between purposeful and non-purposeful behaviors. *Infant Behavior and Development, 22*, 145–160.

Woodward, A. L. (2003). Infants' developing understanding of the link between looker and object. *Developmental Science, 6*, 297–311.

Woodward, A. L., & Guajardo, J. (2002). Infants' understanding of the point gesture as an object-directed action. *Cognitive Development, 17*, 1061–1084.

Woodward, A. L., & Wilson-Brune, C. (2003). *Gaze-following and gaze comprehension in the first year of life.* Paper presented at Cognitive Development Society, Park City, UT.

Name Index

Italicized page numbers refer to figures.

Abbatucci, J., 174, 197
Abramson, A. S., 184, 197
Ach, N., 408–409n1, 409
Ackroyd, K., 99, 101
Adams, W. J., 117, 122, 130
Adelson, E. H., 122, 131, 327, 355
Adler, T., 209
Adolph, K. E., 316, 318–319
Adolphs, R., 213, 224, 379, 382
Aerts, J., 383
Aggarwal, J. K., 275, 298, 322, 326, 352, 358
Aglioti, S. A., 16, 35, 54, 57, 67–68, 73, 83, 157, 168, 173, 186, 197–198
Agosti, R., 143, 199
Aguilar, N., 298n
Ahlström, U., 298, 306, 319, 324, 352, 363, 379
Ahlström, V., 282, 298, 306, 319, 324, 352, 363, 379
Ahmad, T., 328, 352
Aimard, G., 207
Akimotot, H., 203
Akiyama, I., 205
Al-Aboudi, M., 206
Alais, D., 19, 57, 109, 122, 130
Alexander, G. E., 33, 58
Ali, J., 81, 85
Alisharan, S. E., 35, 59
Alkadhi, H., 178, 198, 200
Allison, T., 356, 369, 373, 375, 380, 383, 415, 420, 423–424
Allman, J., 336, 352
Allmen, M., 327, 352
Allport, A., 50, 57
Alpaydin, E., 299, 352
Altschuler, E. L., 28, 63, 175, 198, 206
Amatruda, C. S., 316, 320
Amaya, K., 284, 298
Ames, L. B., 316, 320
Amorim, M.-A., 196, 198
Andersen, K. C., 366, 380
Anderson, A. W., 252, 255, 373, 381
Anderson, D. E., 316, 319
Anderson, D. I., 316, 319
André, J. M., 20, 61
Anjyo, K., 302
Anker, S., 268, 380
Annoni, J. M., 87, 104

Anscombe, G. E. M., 159, 168
Arbib, M. A., 72, 85, 216, 224, 349–350, 356, 423
Arend, I., 273
Aristotle, 159
Armel, K. C., 39, 57, 69, 78, 83, 160–162, 167–168, 251, 254
Aschersleben, G., 216, 226, 394, 396, 402, 410–411, 425, 427, 441
Aslin, R. N., 57, 311, 319
Assal, G., 200, 208
Athitsos, V., 357
Atkinson, A. P., 274, 277–278, 298, 378, 380
Atkinson, J., 267–268, 366, 380
Atzei, A., 197
Augath, M., 357
Austen, E. L., 38, 57, 69, 83
Avikainen, E., 424
Avikainen, S., 29, 61, 212, 225
Azarbayejani, A., 359

Babinski, M. J., 185, 198
Bach-y-Rita, P., 36, 58
Badler, N., 327, 356
Baenninger, M., 231, 235, 254
Baker, C. I., 379, 382, 424
Baldissera, F., 215, 224
Ballard, D. H., 328, 346, 356
Balslev, D., 49, 57
Banks, M. S., 13–14, 19, 58, 109–110, 109, 112, 112–113, 114, 117–118, 119, 122, 129–131
Baratoff, G., 353
Barbu-Roth, M. A., 316, 319
Barclay, C., 280, 298
Bargh, J. A., 213–214, 216, 224, 228, 410
Barnes, J., 227
Baron, M. K., 305, 321
Barresi, J., 389, 427–428, 432, 438, 441, 441n
Barrett, J., 363, 381
Barrett, T., 316, 321
Bartels, M., 203, 390
Bartels, R., 298
Bartenstein, P., 200
Barton, J. J., 380
Baselitz, Georg, 229, 230
Bassili, J. N., 293, 298
Bates, E., 357, 384

Battaglia, P. W., 18–19, 57
Battelli, L., 267–268, 295, 298, 364–365, 372, 380–381
Baud-Bovy, G., 318, 322
Bavelas, J. B., 213, 224
Beardsley, S. A., 353
Beardsworth, T., 324, 352
Beauchamp, M. S., 371, 373, 376, 380
Beck, B. B., 43–44, 50, 57, 57n6
Beck, P. D., 56, 64
Becker, H., 176, 198
Beevers, L., 180, 209
Beintema, J. A., 277, 281, 284–285, 298, 324, 341–342, 344, 352, 373, 380
Beis, L., 20, 61
Bekkering, H., 214, 216, 224, 226, 389, 402, 409, 409n2, 411, 423
Bellefeuille, A., 262, 268, 282, 298, 380
Belliveau, J. W., 358, 384
Bello, A., 423
Bellugi, U., 305, 322, 372, 382–383
Benali, A., 351n
Bender, M. B., 207
Benedek, L., 185, 198
BenHamed, S., 168
Bennour, Y., 327, 358
Bense, S., 200
Benson, D. F., 178, 204
Benson, P. J., 203, 284, 298, 424
Bentin, S., 373, 383, 424
Berlucchi, G., 16, 35, 57, 67–68, 73, 83, 168, 186, 197–198
Bermúdez, J. L., 58–59, 61, 72, 83–84, 100–101, 152, 159, 161–162, 168–169, 203
Bernieri, F., 213–214, 224
Bernstein, N., 317, 319
Berrios, G. E., 189, 200
Berry, I., 207
Bertelson, P., 120, 130–131
Bertenthal, B. I., 243–244, 254, 263–264, 268, 274, 278, 280–281, 284–285, 298–299, 306–309, 311, 313, 315, 318–319, 322, 324, 352, 363, 365, 373, 380, 415, 423–424
Berti, A., 47, 50, 57, 74, 75, 76, 82–83, 98, 101
Beschin, N., 27, 62, 103
Best, C. C., 319
Best, C. T., 311, 319
Bettinardi, V., 384, 425
Biederman, I., 229, 236, 254
Bienfang, D. C., 270, 365, 384
Biggs, S. J., 56, 64
Bilikiewicz, T., 193, 198
Binkofski, F., 28, 57, 199, 349, 352, 423
Birbaumer, N., 168, 170, 201, 204–205, 269, 301, 356, 363, 383, 390
Bisiach, E., 42, 57, 74, 81–84, 168, 198
Biu, O., 316, 319
Black, A., 213, 224
Black, M. J., 275, 299, 327–328, 352, 355, 357
Blake, A., 327–328, 352
Blake, R., 233, 243, 252, 255, 262, 267–268, 275, 280, 298–300, 302, 306, 312, 319, 324, 331, 335–336, 342, 352, 354, 363, 365, 370, 373, 376, 379–382, 415, 424

Blakemore, S.-J., 96, 101, 180, 196, 198, 216, 224, 318–319, 379–380, 387–390, 424
Blakeslee, S., 307, 322
Blandin, Y., 216, 224
Blanke, O., 68, 84, 189, 190, 191, 193, 195, 198, 230, 254
Blankenburg, F., 150–151, 168
Blanz, V., 284, 299
Block, N., 149, 168
Bobick, A., 327–328, 352–353
Boisson, D., 157, 168, 185, 198
Boker, S. M., 213, 224, 227
Boldrey, E., 150, 169
Boller, F., 84
Bonda, E., 335–336, 352, 372, 376, 380
Bonicalzi, V., 200
Bonifazi, S., 99, 102
Bonnier, P., 15, 57, 65, 84, 88, 180, 198
Booth, A., 263, 268, 309, 315, 319
Bordeaud'hui, M., 30, 60
Born, R. T., 336, 352
Boronat, C., 83, 87
Bors, E., 176–178, 198
Bosbach, S., 286, 299
Bossum, J., 32, 57
Bottini, G., 42, 57, 81–84, 156, 168, 186–187, 198
Botvinick, M. M., 37, 39–40, 54, 55, 57, 69, 71, 77–78, 84–85, 137, 143, 160–162, 167–168, 197n5, 198, 251, 254
Bouyer, G., 128, 130
Boyd, J., 339, 355
Boyes-Braem, P., 231, 257
Bozova, S., 142, 144, 170, 233, 237, 269, 301, 370, 383
Braddick, F., 268, 380
Braddick, O., 268, 380
Braden, V., 277, 281, 293, 301, 379, 383
Bradshaw, J. L., 42, 58, 279
Bradshaw, M. F., 299
Brady, T. J., 384
Brammer, M. J., 168, 227, 382
Brandt, T., 200
Brasil-Neto, J. P., 196, 198
Brass, M., 214–216, 224, 226, 402, 409, 409n2, 410, 416, 421–423
Braun, C., 150, 168, 170, 205
Bregler, C., 328, 352
Bremmer, F., 89, 101, 168
Brennan, S., 235, 257, 302
Bresciani, J.-P., 128, 130
Bressler, K., 170, 307, 322
Brewer, A. A., 368, 383
Brissaud, E., 65, 84
Broennimann, R., 356, 383, 424
Bromage, P. R., 196, 205
Bromfield, E., 200
Brooks, D. J., 203, 208
Browman, C. P., 212, 224
Brown, J. M., 212, 214, 225
Brownlow, S., 305, 320
Bruce, C., 366, 380
Bruce, R., 193, 199
Bruce, V., 232, 234, 236, 239, 256, 277, 288, 293, 299, 301

Brücke, H., 173, *173*, 199
Brückner, L., 209
Bruderlin, A., 269, 298, 301, 379, 383
Bruehlmeier, M., 178, 199
Brugger, P., 67, 83n, 84, 137–139, 143, 180–184,
   184, 188–189, 191, 195, 197n2, 198–199, 201,
   267–268, 307–308, 320
Bruner, J. S., 395, 409
Brunswik, E., 408–409
Bruyn, G. W., 199
Buccino, G., 28, 57, 184, 199, 213, 225, 349,
   352, 415, 423
Buckner, T., 324, 352
Budriesi, C., 209
Bullier, J., 329, 333, 346, 355, 357
Bullmore, E. T., 203, 227, 382
Bülthoff, H. H., 106, *110*, 111, *112*, 122, *123*,
   130–131, 268, 276, 278–279, 282, 288, 299,
   301–303, 307, 318, 320, 322, 331, 341,
   352, 358
Bülthoff, I., 299, 318, 320, 331, 352
Burchard, J. M., 182, 199
Burge, J., 129–130, 130n
Burke, D. C., 177, 199
Burnett, C. T., 23, *53*, 58
Burnham, D. K., 311, 320
Burr, D. C., 19, 57, 109, 122, 130, 269, 283, 301,
   324, 341, 355, 373, 382
Burrowes, K., 200
Burton, A. M., 288, 299
Butler, S., 44, 58
Butner, S. E., 29, 62
Butterworth, G. E., 201, 308, 316, 320–321
Buxbaum, L., 251, 254
Byatt, G., 235, 257
Bychowski, G., 189, 199

Cabeza, R., 256
Cacace, A. T., 174, 199
Cacioppo, J. T., 202, 213, 225
Cai, Q., 275, 298, 326, 352
Caldara-Schnetzer, A. S., 50, 63, 87, 104
Calder, A. J., 281, 299
Calvert, G. A., 45, 47, 60, 71, 86, 89, 101,
   160, 168
Calvert, T., 298
Camarda, R., 383
Campbell, J., 16, 58
Campbell, L., 327, 352
Campos, J. J., 285, 298, 309, 316, 319
Camus, P., 65, 81, 84
Canavero, S., 178, 200
Cappa, S. F., 198
Cappelletti, J. Y., 307, 320
Caramazza, A., 229, 254
Carey, S., 234–236, 255, 257, 302
Carlen, P. L., 172, 200
Carlton, L. G., 270, 274, 302
Carmena, J. M., *54*, 56, 58
Carp, E., 191–192, 200
Carpenter, M., 441
Carpenter, W. B., 396, 409, 413, 423,
   432. 436
Carr, L., 136, 140, 143
Carson, R. G., 406, 409

Casile, A., 266, 268, 284, 299, *343*, 344,
   349, 352
Cassol, E., 207
Castellanos, F., 200, 214
Castelli, F., 379–380
Castiello, U., 21, *22*, 63, 78, 87, 148, 168
Castner, B. M., 316, 320
Cattaert, D., 406, 411
Cavallari, P., 215, 224
Cavanagh, P., 263, 266–268, 284, 286, 294–295,
   298–299, 345, 348, 353, 363–365, 380–381
Ceccaldi, M., 307, 320
Cham, T., 327, 353
Chandrasekaran, C., 263, 266, 268
Chapin, J. K., 56, 64
Charles, N., 207
Chartrand, T. L., 213–214, 216, 224, 226
Chater, N., 411
Chen, Z., 326, 353
Cheng, J. L., 219, 225
Chevreul, M. E., 396, 409
Chitty, A. J., 356, 383, 424
Cho, S. B., 356, 362, 383
Choi, A. Y., 270, 365, 384
Chouchourelou, A., 141, 144, 262, 268
Chowdhury, S., 358, 384
Christie, F., 301
Christmann, C., 202
Chun, M. M., 373, 382
Clark, J. J., 301
Clark, M. S., 228
Clark, S., 212, 224, 388, 390
Clarke, K., 27, 46, 61–62, 75, *75*, 76, 78, 86, 103,
   169, 204, 286
Clarke, S., 174, 200
Clower, D. M., 32, 58
Cobb, S., 24, 63, 206
Cochran, W. G., 108, 130
Code, C., 88
Coeytaux, A., 198
Coffey, S. A., 382
Cohen, D., 214, 225
Cohen, J., 37, 39–40, *54*, 55, 57, 69, 77–78, 84,
   137, 143, 160–162, 167–168, 197n5, 198,
   251, 254
Cohen, L. G., 198
Cohen, L. R., 248, 255
Cohen, M. J., 208
Colby, C. L., 70–72, 84, 102, 230, 255
Cole, J., 137, 143, 201, 308, 320
Collins, D., 246, 255
Connor, C. E., 353
Conomy, J. P., 176–177, *177*, 200
Conrad, K., 195, 200
Cook, E., 18, 61
Cooke, D. F., 40, 59, 70, 72, 84–85, 96, 101–102,
   159, 165, 168
Cooper, G., 224
Cooper, S., 195, 207, 213
Cootes, T. F., 352
Corbetta, D., 317, 322
Corkin, S., 205
Corkum, V., 432, 438, 441
Coslett, H. B., 67, 81, 83–84, 87, 251, 254
Costes, N., 143, 381, 423–424

Cousins, J. P., 199
Cowan, M., 299
Cowey, A., 364, 381
Craighero, L., 212–213, 215–216, 224–225, 227, 389, 391, 417, 421–423
Crammond, D. J., 93, 96, 103
Craske, B., 196, 200
Creem, S. H., 45, 58
Crelier, G., 84, 143, 198–200, 268, 307, 320
Crist, R. E., 56, 58
Critchley, M., 67, 73, 76, 81, 84, 171, 181, 188, 197n4, 200
Cronholm, B., 172–173, 200
Cronly-Dillon, J., 202
Crozier, G., 23–24, 60
Culhane, S., 358
Cumming, W. J., 67, 84
Curby, K. M., 246, 255
Curio, C., 351n
Curran, T., 246, 255
Curt, A., 178, 198–200
Cutting, J. E., 263, 268–269, 274, 278–280, 282, 285, 289, 298–299, 301, 305–306, 320–321, 324, 338, 341, 345, 353, 355, 362–363, 380–381
Cynader, M. S., 169

Daems, A., 221, 228, 276, 294, 299, 303
Dale, A. M., 384
Daléry, J., 29, 31, 58, 84
Damasio, A. R., 213, 224, 231, 255
Damasio, H., 213, 224, 231, 255, 379
d'Amato, T., 31, 58
Dancer, C., 29–30, 64, 87
Daprati, E., 29–30, 32, *53*, 58, 64, 80, 84, 186, 200
Darrell, T., 359
Dauwalder, J.-P., 410
Davenport, C., 199
Davey, J., 202
David, A. S., 203, 219, 227
Davis, A., 176, 200
Davis, J., 328, 353
Davis, K. D., 203
Davis, L., 328, 357
Davis, N., 358
Davis, W. A., 298
de Ajuriaguerra, J., 178, 202
De Bruyn, B., 356, 382
De Gelder, B., 120, 130–131
de Maeght, S., 396, *397*, 398–399, 409n3, 410–411
De Renzi, E., 66, 84
de Tribolet, N., 200
De Troy, A., 141, 145, 220, 228, 274, 303, 331, 358
de Vignemont, F., 11, 136–138, 242–243, 441n
Decety, J., 140, 143–144, 192, 196, 198, 207, 216, 221, 224, 227, 318–319, 375, 379–381, 384, 389–390, 415, 421, 423–425
Deco, G., 346–348, 357
Degueldre, C., 383
Deininger, R. L., 286, 300
Dekeyser, M., 274, 276, 299, 302
Delfiore, G., 383

Della Salla, S., 180, 204
Delon-Martin, C., 424
Delorme, A., 329, 358
Demasio, H., 382
Demattè, M. L., *95*, 102
Denes, G., 307, 320
Denier van der Gon, J. J., 14, 19, 64, 109, 131
Dening, T. R., 189, 200
Dennett, D. C., 56, 58
Denny, M., 318–319
Denny-Brown, D., 96, 102
Deny, G., 65, 81, 84
Derrfuss, J., 215, 224
Desimone, R., 366, 380–381
Desmurget, M., 218, 225
Despland, P. A., 191, 208
Devinsky, O., 189, 200
DeVries, J. I. P., 308, 320
Dewhurst, K., 181, 193, 208
Di Bernardo, E., 357
Di Cesare, G., 202
di Pellegrino, G., 27, 58, 74, 78, 84, 90–92, 102–103, 212, 225
Diamond, R., 234–236, 255
Didic, M., 307, 320
Dieterich, M., 186, 200
Dietz, V., 199
Dimberg, U., 213, 225
Dimitrov, D. F., 56, 58
Dittrich, W. H., 262–264, 268, 274, 280, 298, 300, 305, 320, 324, 338, 341, 353, 363, 378–381
Dixon, A. R., 305, 320
Dohle, C., 28, 57
Dokic, J., 389–390
Dolan, R., 144
Donnelly, M., 252, 255, 300, 381, 424
Donnelly, N., 231, 235, 255
Donnet, A., 178, 200
Doop, M. L., 365, 382
Dougherty, R. F., 368, 383
Downing, P. E., 68, 84, 190, 200, 231, 233, 255–256, 324, 335, 342, 353
Downs, J. H., 144, 227
Doya, K., 327, 359
Drain, M., 239, 255
Drewing, K., 128, 130, 130n
Driver, J., 11–12, 14, 24, 27, 38, 45–47, *46*, *53–54*, 61–63, 67, 69, 71, 73–75, *75*, 76, 78, *79*, 86–87, 89, 99, 103–104, 120, 130, 159–160, 165, 168–169, 204, 206, 256, 438, 441
Drost, U., 402, 410
Drzezga, A., 200
Dubeau, M. C., 143
Duhamel, J.-R., 70–71, 84, 89, 101–102, 159, 168, 230, 255
Dunbar, C., 205
Dupont, P., 356, 382
Durlach, N., 51, *54*, 60
Dyer, C. R., 327, 352

Eddy, T. J., 33, 58
Edelman, S., 277, 284–285, 300
Eder, Sl, 208

Egbert, C. A., 305, 320
Egyd, B., 176, 200
Ehrenwald, H., 180, 200
Ehrenwald, J., 192, 200
Ehrsson, H. H., 230, 255
Eifuku, S., 336, 353
Eilan, N., 58–59, 61, 100–101, 169, 203
Eilers, R. E., 311, 320
Elbert, T., 168, 201, 203
Elian, N., 72, 83–86
Ellis, R., 45, 64
Ellis, S. R., 60
Elmehed, K., 213, 225
Emery, N. J., 414, 423
Emmorey, K., 382
Enns, J. T., 38, 57
Epstein, R., 231, 256
Epstein, W., 18, 36, 58, 61
Erb, M., 204, 390
Eriksen, B. A., 286, 300
Eriksen, C. W., 286, 300
Erminio, F., 198
Ernst, M. O., 12–14, 19, 58, 106, 109–112,
    109–110, 112–113, 114, 118, 119, 122, 123,
    128–131
Ersland, L., 174, 183, 201
Essa, I., 327–328, 353
Etcoff, N. L., 299
Ettlin, T. M., 177, 201
Evans, A., 352, 372, 380
Ezzat, T., 288, 300

Faber, T. L., 32, 58
Fadiga, L., 28, 63, 71, 85, 87, 102, 199, 212–213,
    215–216, 224–225, 227–228, 246, 257, 318,
    320, 349, 353, 368, 375, 378, 381, 383–384,
    413, 415–416, 421–425, 432, 441
Faglioni, P., 66, 84
Farah, M. J., 28, 63, 135, 144, 195, 206, 231,
    233, 235–237, 239, 241–242, 246, 250, 255,
    257, 266, 269, 318, 322
Farnè, A., 12–14, 24, 27, 41, 46, 58, 63, 69, 74,
    76, 84–85, 91, 93–94, 95, 97, 98, 99, 99,
    101–103, 129, 157, 168, 197n5, 201, 251, 255
Farrer, C., 31–32, 58, 196, 201
Faubert, J., 262, 268, 282, 298, 380
Faulk, M. E., Jr., 66, 87
Fazio, F., 143, 384
Fechner, G. T., 44
Feibel, A., 184, 197
Feinberg, T. E., 81, 83, 85
Feldmann, E., 200
Felician, O., 307, 320
Felleman, D. J., 287, 300, 330, 333, 346, 353
Féré, C., 189, 201
Ferguson, C. A., 319
Ferster, D., 355
Fidopiastis, C. M., 248, 257, 269, 277, 281, 293,
    301, 379, 383
Field, T., 214, 225
Fieser, J., 334, 355
Finger, S., 172, 201
Fink, G. R., 101, 104, 192, 199, 208, 423
Fink, M., 207
Finke, R. A., 218, 225

Fischer, A., 382
Fiske, S. T., 228
Fitts, P. M., 286, 300
Fize, D., 329, 358
Flaccus, L. W., 34, 36, 58
Flach, R., 141, 144, 222, 226, 253, 256, 389–390
Flanagan, J. R., 218, 228
Flinchbaugh, B. E., 326, 354
Flor, H., 173, 181, 201–205, 390
Flügel, J. C., 34, 36, 58
Fogassi, L., 28, 63, 70–72, 85, 87, 96, 102, 199,
    207, 212, 216, 225–228, 246, 257, 318, 320,
    335, 353, 356, 368, 378, 381, 383, 413, 421,
    423–425, 432, 441
Foldiak, P., 355
Fonlupt, P., 144, 221, 227, 375, 384, 424
Forss, N., 59, 169, 202, 212, 225, 230, 255
Foster, C., 198
Fourneret, P., 148, 168
Fowler, C. A., 212–214, 225, 227
Fox, P. T., 144, 224, 227, 263, 363
Fox, R., 268, 309, 320, 381
Frackowiak, R. S. J., 169, 198, 204, 384
Frak, V., 56, 61
Franck, G., 383
Franck, N., 29, 31–32, 58, 64, 80, 84, 170, 200
Franz, E. A., 23, 58, 174, 201
Franzen, M. D., 20, 63, 178, 207
Frassinetti, F., 47, 50, 54, 57, 59, 74, 75, 76, 83,
    98, 101
Freire, A., 235, 237, 255
Freund, H.-J., 28, 57, 199
Freund, S., 203
Freyd, J. J., 194, 194, 207, 218–219, 221, 225,
    227, 233, 257, 263, 270, 282, 302, 307, 318,
    320, 322, 347, 357, 374, 384
Friesen, C., 438, 441
Frith, C. D., 71, 86, 89, 101, 103, 160, 169,
    196, 198, 201, 204, 379–381, 388, 390, 415,
    420, 423
Frith, R. J., 144
Frith, U., 379–381, 415, 420, 423
Fromm, C., 170
Fross, N., 424
Frykholm, G., 264, 269, 289, 302, 363, 384
Fuchs, T., 402, 411
Fujii, T., 44, 60
Fujimoto, K., 347, 353
Fujita, K., 262, 270
Fukuda, M., 357
Fukuda, Y., 336, 358
Fukushima, K., 334, 353
Funk, M., 183, 184, 185, 201

Gagner, M., 29, 62
Galasko, D., 198
Gallagher, S., 16, 33, 38, 59, 67, 82, 85, 100,
    102, 183, 201, 308, 320
Gallana, A., 307, 320
Gallant, J. L., 334, 353
Gallese, V., 28, 63, 71, 85, 87, 102, 192, 195,
    199, 201, 207, 212, 216, 224–228, 246, 255,
    257, 318, 320, 335, 356, 368, 374, 378, 381,
    383, 389–390, 413, 421–425, 432, 441
Gallinek, A., 172, 195, 201

Galloway, J. C., 317, 320
Gallup, G. G., 28, 33, 58–59, 203
Gandevia, S. C., 55, 59, 153, 168
Garbelotto, S., 206
Garraghty, P. E., 206
Garraux, B., 383
Gatenby, J. C., 219, 226
Gattis, M., 402, 409, 409n2, 411
Gauthier, I., 143–144, 231, 234–235, 237, 246,
    252, 255, 257, 373, 381
Gavin, W. J., 311, 320
Gavrila, D. M., 275, 300, 326, 353
Gawne, T. J., 334, 353
Gawryszewski, L. D. G., 45, 63
Gazzaniga, M. S., 45, 59, 85, 102, 131
Geary, J., 56, 59
Gehi, A., 205
Geiger, G., 288, 300
Gemmell, A. J., 274, 298, 378, 380
Genner, T., 195, 201
Gentilucci, M., 71, 85, 87, 104, 383
Georgieff, N., 29, 31, 58, 84, 388, 390
Gepshtein, S., 129–130
Gergely, G., 441
Gerstmann, J., 185, 201
Gesell, A., 316, 318, 320
Geyer, S., 230, 255
Giampietro, V., 227
Gibson, E. J., 315, 320
Gibson, J. J., 36, 59
Giese, M. A., 263, 265–266, 268, 275, 277, 281,
    284–285, 298n, 299–300, 324, 328, 332, *333*,
    334, 337, *338*, 340, 342, *343*, 344, *346*, 349,
    352–354, 359, 362, 372, 381
Giraux, P., 178, 201
Girosi, F., 335, 354
Glass, T., 144, 227
Gloning, I., 189, 196, 201
Gloning, K., 189, 201
Gobbini, M. I., 377, 382
Goddard, N. H., 328, 354
Goethe, 192–193
Goldberg, M. E., 70–71, 84, 102
Goldenberg, G., 44, 59, 193, 202
Goldinger, S. D., 213, 225
Goldman, A., 195, 201, 216, 225, 246, 255, 318,
    320, 422–423, 427, 441
Goldstein, J., 356, 383
Goldstein, L., 212, 224
Goldstone, R. L., 144, 257
Gollwitzer, P. M., 408–409n1, 410
Goncalves, L., 344, 357
Goodale, M. A., 287, 300, 302, 330, 333,
    354, 358
Goodglass, H., 66, 87
Gopnik, A., 427, 441
Gore, J. C., 219, 226, 252, 255, 373, 381,
    383, 424
Graf, E. W., 122, 130
Graf, W., 101, 168
Grafman, J., 84, 170, 307, 322
Grafton, S. T., 44–45, 59, 61, 218, 225,
    415, 423
Granrud, C., 319, 423
Granum, G., 326, 355

Grasby, P. M., 208
Grassi, F., 143
Gray, W. D., 231, 257
Graziano, M. S. A., 29, 33, 35–36, 40, *54*, 57n5,
    59, 70–72, 84–85, 89, 93, 96, 101–102, 159,
    165, 168, 200
Grealy, M. A., 299
Green, D. M., 106, 130, 292, 300
Greenberg, R., 214, 225
Greenfield, E., 41, 63, 170, 207
Greenspan, A. I., 28, 63
Greenwald, A. G., 397, 410
Gregory, R. L., 23, 59, 77, 85
Grether, A., 390
Greyson, B., 192, 202
Grèzes, J., 143, 374, 381, 415, 423–424
Grisoli, F., 200
Grodd, W., 204–205, 390
Gross, C. G., 29, 59, 70–71, 85, 89, 102, 366,
    380–381
Gross, Y., 20, 35, 59, 67, 72, 85, 196, 202
Grossi, D., 180, 202
Grossman, E. D., 233, 243, 252, 254n, 255,
    264–265, 267, 280, 285, 300, 302, 324,
    331, 335–336, 342, 354, 370–373, 376, 381,
    415, 424
Grossman, E. M., 186, 202
Grotstein, J. S., 191, 202
Grouios, G., 182, 197n3, 202
Grubb, J., 142, 144, 234, 236, 257
Gruneberg, M. M., 299
Grunwald, A. J., 60
Grush, R., 218, 225
Grüsser, O.-J., 202
Grüsser, S. M., 174, 189, 202
Guajardo, J., 436, 442
Guariglia, C., 307, 320
Gullapalli, R. P., 169
Gunns, R. E., 379, 381
Gunter, T., 402, 410
Gur, S., 20, 62, 205
Gurewitsch, M., 192, 202
Gurr, P. R., 363, 381
Gurwitsch, A., 148, 168
Guthrie, T. C., 186, 202

Hagedorn, J. C., 24, 63
Haggard, P., 11, 22, 55, 61, 64, 136, 158,
    160, 162, 168, 170, 230, 258, 388,
    390–391, 441n
Hagler, D. J., 357, 384
Hagmann, S., 44, 59
Haith, M. M., 285, 298, 309, 319
Hajnal, J. V., 384
Hallett, M., 187, 198, 203
Halligan, P. W., 20, 41–42, 47, 49, *54*, 59, 159,
    169, 172, 174, 178, 181, 202–203
Halverson, H. M., 316, 320
Hamker, F. G., 347–348, 354
Hand, W. D., 206
Handy, T. C., 45, 47, 59
Hanes, D. P., 357
Hänninen, R., 20, 59, 169, 202, 204
Happe, F., 380
Harber, K., 144, 269, 389–390

Hari, R., 20, 29, 59, 61, 157, 169, 178, 180, 189, 193, 202, 204, 212, 225, 230, 255, 329, 355, 415, 421, 424
Harrington, J., 19, 64
Harris, C. J., 339, 354
Harris, C. S., 18, 59
Harris, P., 427, 441
Hashikawa, T., 357
Hatfield, E., 192, 202, 213, 225
Haueisen, J., 213, 225
Hauf, P., 441n
Haxby, J. V., 371, 373, 377, 380, 382
Hay, D. C., 237, 258
Hay, J. C., 12, 14, 18, *53*, 60
Hayakawa, Y., 44, 60
Hayashi, M., 205
Head, A. S., 356, 383, 424
Head, H., 15–16, 34, 44, 60, 65–66, 73, 76, 82–83, 85, 100, 102
Heberlein, A. S., 379, 382
Hécaen, H., 178, 202
Hecht, H., 349, 354
Heeger, D. J., 335, 357, 369, 382
Hegdé, J., 334, 354
Heim, K., 269, 301
Held, R., 51, *54*, 60
Hellawell, D., 237, 258
Helmholtz, H. von, 117, 131
Henaff, M. A., 380, 425
Henderson, W. F., 173, 202
Hennigsen, H., 203
Henriquez, C. S., 56, 58
Hepp-Reymond, M. C., 84, 143, 198–200, 268, 307, 320
Heptulla Chatterjee, S., 140, 144, 244, 257, 270, 307, 320
Herman, L. M., 262, 268, 363, 382
Heron, M., 231, 250, 257
Hesslow, G., 216, 225
Heuer, H., 227, 410
Heutink, J., 41, 63, 170, 207
Heyes, C., 214, 225
Hibbard, L. S., 151, 170
Hibbard, P. B., 299
Hietanen, J. K., 213, 228, 424
Hift, S., 196, 201
Hihara, S., 73, 85
Hikosaka, O., 36, 61
Hill, H. H., 277, 283–285, 288, 293, 300–301, 338, 354
Hillis, J. M., 109, 114–115, *116*, 122, 131
Hillyer, S., 28, 63
Hindle, J. V., 205
Hinterberger, T., 387, 390
Hirsch, S. R., 208
Hirsch, T. B., 144, 227
Hirstein, W., 67, 87, 138, 144, 155, 169, 173, 206
Hlushchuk, Y., 230, 255
Hlustik, P., 151, 169
Hodgins, J. K., 274, 300
Hof, A., 288, 303
Hoff, H., 189, 201
Hoffman, D. D., 326, 354
Hoffman, E. A., 373, 377, 382
Hoffman, J. E., 365, 382

Hoffman, J. M., 32, 58
Hoffmann, J., 402, 408–409n1, 410
Hoffmann, K. P., 101
Hofmayer, N., 390
Höhling, C., 203
Holmes, G., 15–16, 34, 44, 60, 65–66, 73, 76, 82–83, 85, 100, 102
Holmes, N. P., 11–14, 23–24, *25*, 33, 37, 39, 45, *46*, 47, *53–54*, 55, 60, 69, 73, 83n, 85, 87
Holmes, T., 199
Holtz Boendermaker, S., 200
Hommel, B., 85, 144, 216, 226, 389, 394, 397, 402, 409–410, 427, 432, 441
Honoré, J., 30, 60
Hood, B., 438, 441
Hoogenraad, T. U., 96, 103
Horenstein, S., 102
Höss, M., 402, 411
Hotz Boendermaker, S., 198
Houghton, A. D., 176, 202
Houghton, A. L., 202
Howard, L. A., 29–30, 64, 87
Howard, R. J., 369, 376, 382
Hu, X. T., 29, 35, 59, 102
Huang, P. S., 339, 354
Hubel, D. H., 334, 354
Hudson, S. M., 379, 381
Hugdahl, K., 201
Hughes, B., 36, 58
Huk, A. C., 369, 382
Hume, D., 167
Humphreys, G. W., 101, 231, 235, 255, 411
Hunt, M., 41, 59, 169
Hunter, J. P., 203
Hurley, S., 411
Husain, M., 27, 46–47, 61–62, 75, *75*, 76, 78, 86, 103, 169, 204
Huse, E., 204–205
Hustwit, M. P., 172, 201
Hyvarinen, J., 70, 86, 89, 103

Iacoboni, M., 143, 216, 226
Ibrahim, S., 196, 208
Ichihara, S., 21, 60
Igarashi, Y., 21, 60
Ikeda, K., 12, 14, 18, 60
Ilg, F. L., 316, 320
Imamizu, H., 48–49, *54*, 60, 62, 64
Ingle, D. J., 87, 302, 358
Inman, V. T., 283, 300
Intriligator, J., 380
Iriki, A., 12, 14, 32–33, 45–47, 60–61, 73, 75–77, 80, 82, 85–86, 97–99, 102–104, 157, 169, 180, 203
Isard, M. I., 327–328, 352, 357
Ishibashi, H., 73, 85
Israel, R., 67, 86, 205, 307, 321
Itakura, S., 28, 60
Itti, L., 348, 354
Iversen, S. D., 168
Iwamura, Y., 32, 36, 45, 60–61, 73, 76, 80, 85, 97, 103, 169, 203

Jabir, F. K., 198
Jackson, C. V., 23, *53*, 55, 61

Jackson, S. R., 205
Jacobs, A., 136, 141, 144, 262, 266, 268, 283, 300
Jacobs, R. A., 57
Jacobsen, P., 55, 64, 170, 230, 258
Jalavisto, E., 174, 203
James, W., 44, 61, 148, 169, 389, 394–397, 408, 410, 413, 424
Janke, M., 176, 200
Janzer, R. C., 200
Jarvelainen, J., 29, 61
Jasper, H., 230, 256
Jaspers, K., 188, 203
Jastorff, J., 300, 337, 342
Jeannerod, M., 29, 31–32, *53*, 56, 58, 61, 64, 72, 80, 84–85, 143, 148, 168–169, 200, 213–214, 227, 318, 322, 388–391, 394, 410, 413, 416–417, 423–424
Jeeves, M. A., 356, 383, 424
Jellema, T., 379, 382, 414, 424
Jenkinson, M., 19, 62, 205
Jepson, A. D., 275, 299, 327–328, 352, 357
Jerabek, P. A., 144, 227
Jiang, Y., 68, 84, 200, 233, 255, 353
Jinno, Y., 338, 354
Joannette, A., 88
Johansson, G., 243, 255, 262–264, 269, 271–272, 274, 276, 282, 285, 297, 300–301, 305–306, 321, 324, 329, 337, 341, 344, 354, 362–363, 365, 382
Johnson, D. M., 231, 257
Johnson, J. S., 330, 354
Johnson, S. H., 44, 61
Johnson-Frey, S. H., 47, 61, 99, 103
Johnston, A., 288, 293, 300–301, 338, 354
Johnston, E. B., 131
Johnston, L., 379, 381
Johnstone, E. C., 388, 390
Jokisch, D., 281, 301
Jones, J. P., 354
Jones, L. A., 196, 203
Jones, M., 335, 354
Jordan, H., 365, 382
Jordan, J. S., 216, 218, 226
Jordan, T. R., 274, 302
Jostorff, J., 354
Jousmäki, V., 20, 59, 169, 202
Jovanovic, B., 441
Ju, S., 327, 355
Juba, A., 185, 197n4, 203

Kaas, J. H., 67, 85, 173, 203, 206, 355
Kaeser, H. E., 201
Kahn, R. L., 208
Kaiser, M. K., 60, 229, 256
Kallio, K. E., 173, 203
Kalogeras, J., 388, 390
Kamiya, S., 191, 203
Kamm, K., 317, 322
Kanade, T., 327, 356
Kanani, P., 316, 319
Kant, 167
Kanwisher, N., 68, 84, 142, 144, 200, 219, 226, 231, 233, 243, 255–256, 333, 353, 355, 369, 373, 382

Karni, A., 55, 61
Karp, B. I., 187, 203
Katz, D., 203
Katz, J., 172, 174, 203
Kaube, H., 144
Kavanaugh, J. E., 319
Kawato, M. I., 23, 48–49, 60, 64, 215, 228, 327, 359
Kay, J., 269, 301
Kaynak, O., 299, 352
Kazamatsuri, H., 203
Keenan, J. P., 190, 203
Kellman, P. J., 257
Kelso, J. A. S., 18, 61
Kennedy, A., 235, 257
Kennett, S., 22, 45, *46*, *54*, 61–62, 73–74, 76, 86, 159–160, 168–170
Kersten, D., 122, 131
Kerzel, D., 218–220, 226, 286, 299, 405, 410
Ketay, S., 45, 59
Kew, J. J. M., 174, 203
Keysers, C., 216, 226, 228, 329, 355, 424–425
Khateb, A. S., 50, 63, 87, 104
Kheddar, A., 128, 130
Killakey, H. P., 203
Kilner, J. M., 417, *418–420*, 421–424
Kim, C. Y., 381
Kim, J., 56, 64, 270, 274, 302, 365, 382
Kingstone, A. F., 38, 57, 69, 83, 256, 438, 441
Kinsbourne, M., 16, 43, 61, 69, 81, 83, 86, 150, 169, 197n3, 203, 254, 256
Kipling, R., 192, 203
Király, I., 433, 435, 441
Kircher, T. T. J., 190, 203, 388, 390
Kirveskari, E., 212, 225, 424
Kitagawa, N., 21, 60
Kitazawa, S., 45, 64, 73, 88
Kleiner, M., 275, 288, 301
Kleiner-Fisman, G., 212, 226
Knappmeyer, B., 277, 294, 301
Knecht, S., 174, 201, 203
Knight, B., 288, 301
Knill, D. C., 109, 122, 131
Knoblich, G., 31, 61, 141, 144, 196, 204, 216, 222, 226, 253, 256, 263–264, 269, 388–390, 405, 410, 428, 441, 441n
Knösche, T. R., 213, 225
Knuf, L., 396, *397*, 398, 409nn3–4, 410–411
Koch, C., 348, 354–355
Koch, I., 402, 410
Koehler, K., 188, 204
Koenderink, J., 359
Koeppe, C., 202
Kohler, E., 216, 226, 228, 414, 424–425
Kojima, H., 111, 131
Kolb, L. C., 176, 204
Kollias, S. S., 84, 143, 198–200, 268, 307, 320
Komiya, K., 205
Körding, K. P., 122, 131
Kostyk, S. K., 205
Kourtzi, Z., 141, 144, 219, 226, 231, 243, 256, 300, 333, 342, 351n, 354–355, 369, 382
Kozlowski, L. T., 263, 268–269, 274, 289, 298–299, 301, 305, 321, 324, 338, 353, 355, 363, 381

Krageloh-Mann, I., 269, 363, 383
Krägeloh-Mann, I., 301
Kralik, J. D., 56, 64
Kramer, S. J., 263, 268, 284, 299, 308–309, 311, 319, 363, 380
Kubischik, M., 101
Kubler, A., 390
Kunde, W., 402, 410
Kurata, K., 368, 382
Kuroda, T., 49, 60

Labianca, A. T., 268, 286, 299, 345, 348, 353, 363, 381
Labrecque, R., 20, 63, 207
Lackner, J. R., 55, 61, 70, 86, 154, *155*, 169, 196, 204
Lacroix, R., 67, 86, 182, 204–205, 307, 321
Làdavas, E., 12–14, 27, 41, 43, 46–47, 58–59, 61, 69, 74–76, 84–86, 89, 91–93, *95*, 97, *98*, 99, *99*, 101–103, 129, 157, 168, 191, 201, 204, 251, 255
Lagae, L., 356
Lai, Y., 358
Lakin, J. L., 216, 226
Lampl, I., 334, 355
Lancaster, J. L., 144, 227
Landau, B., 365, 382
Lander, K., 277, 288, 301
Landis, T., 20, 50, 63–64, 68, 84, 87, 104, 143, 189, 198–199, 202, 208, 230, 254
Landy, M. S., 108–109, 111, 114, 122, 130n, 131
Lanitis, A., 352
Lappe, M., 275, 277, 281, 284–285, 298, 300, 324, 340–342, 344, 352, 354, 373, 380
Lappin, J. S., 302
Lapresle, J., 186, 208
Larbig, W., 201, 204–205
Laubach, M., 56, 64
Laureys, S., 387, 390
Lavrov, M., 270
Law, I., 49, 57
Lawson, D. S., 382
Lawson, J., 33, 62
Lazeyras, F., 87
Lazorthes, Y., 207
Le Chapelain, L., 20, 61
Lea, S. E. G., 268, 300, 305, 320, 353, 363, 381
Leach, R., 299
Leaning, F. E., 193, 197n6, 204
Lebedev, M. A., 56, 58
LeBorgne, Y., 204
Lecours, A. Roch, 88
Leder, H., 232, 234, 236, 239, 256
Lee, H., 326, 353
Lee, J. S., 208
Lee, K. E., 235, 237, 255, 371, 380
Lee, T. S., 328, 350, 355
Leenders, K. L., 199
Leinonen, L., 70, 86
Leischner, A., 189, 204
Leker, R. R., 55, 61
Lemay, M., 270, 365, 384
Lemery, C. R., 213, 224
Lemon, R., 151, 169

Lempert, H., 69, 86
Lenzi, G. L., 143
Leroy, J., 29, 62
Lestou, V., 356, 362, 383
Letailleur, M., 191, 204
Leube, D., 388, 390
Leung, H.-C., 219, 226
Leutgeb, S., 357
Leventhal, A. G., 357
Lew, A., 201, 308, 316, 320–321
Lewicki, M. S., 131
Lewin, K., 408–409n1, 410
Lewis, J. W., 353
Ley, H., 186, 204
Lhuisset, L., 216, 224
Lichtey, L., 140, 144, 244, 257, 270
Liddle, P. F., 208
Liepmann, H. M. O., 44, 61
Lin, C. T., 328, 355
Lin, W. C., 355
Ling, X., 313, 321
Linnankoski, I., 70, 86
Lippman, C. W., 188, 204
Lipsitt, L., 319
Little, J., 339, 355
Llewellyn D. M. E., 198
Lloyd, D. M., 29–30, 64, 68, 71, 86–87
Loeser, J. D., 176, 205
Logothetis, N. K., 330–331, 334, 341, 355, 357
Look, R. B., 384
Loomis, J. M., 36, 51, 61, 77, 86
Lotterie, J.-A., 207
Lotze, M., 204
Lotze, R. H., 34, 36, 44, 61, 174, 180, 395–396, 410
Loula, F., 141, 144, 263–264, 269, 389–390
Lovely, T. J., 199
Luanté, J., 157, 168, 185, 198
Lubker, J., 214, 227
Lundervold, A., 201
Lunn, V., 191, 204
Luppino, G., 72, 85, 87, 102, 104, 216, 227, 383
Lutes-Driscoll, V., 305, 322, 372, 383
Lutz, S., 200
Lützenberger, W., 205, 356
Luxen, A., 383

Maack, L. H., 192, 204
Maasen, S., 411
Macaluso, E., 71, 86, 89, 103, 160, 169
MacArthur, L. Z., 305, 321
MacKay, W. A., 93, 96, 103
Maeda, F., 212, 226
Maes, H., 356
Mainy, N., 170
Mäkinen, T., 20, 59, 169, 202
Malach, R., 384
Malitz, S., 208
Maloney, L. T., 122, 131
Maloney, T. M., 109, 131
Mamassian, P., 122, 130–131
Manfredi, M., 35, 57, 73, 83, 168, 197
Mansfield, R. J. W., 302, 358

Maravita, A., 11–14, 24, 27, 45–47, *46*, *53–54*, 61–62, 67, 69, 71, 73–75, *75*, 76–78, *79*, 82, 86–87, 98–99, 103, 157, 169, 180, 204
Marcar, V., 359
Marcel, A. J., 58–59, 61, 72, 83–84, 100–101, 169, 203
Marchetti, C., 180, 204
Marescaux, J., 29, 51, *54*, 62
Marey, E. J., 262, 269, 272, 274, 276, 301, 362
Marie-Cardine, M., 31, 58
Marlot, C., 329, 358
Marr, D., 229, 256, 313, 321, 326–327, 351, 355
Marsden, C. D., 203
Marshall, J. C., 20, 41–42, 47, 49, *54*, 59, 104, 169, 174, 178, 181, 202–203
Martin, A., 371, 380
Martin, C. C., 144, 227
Martin, J., 334, 353
Martin, W. N., 322
Martinez, O., 208
Martory, M. D., 198
Mason, A., 268, 380
Massa-Micon, B., 200
Matelli, M., 71–72, 85, 87, 102, 104, 383–384, 415, 421, 425
Mather, G., 262–263, 269, 274–275, 278–283, 285, 288–289, 301, 306, 321, 324, 341, 355
Matthes-von Cramon, G., 215, 224
Mattingley, J. B., 27, 42, 58, 62, 90, 103
Maury, V., 128, 130
Maximov, K., 190, 204
Mayer-Gross, W., 176, 204
Mayeux, R., 178, 204
Mazziotta, J. C., 143, 216, 226, 384
McBeath, M. K., 229, 256
McCarthy, G., 356, 369, 373, 380, 383, 423–424
McClelland, J., 177, 207
McColl, L., 202
McCutcheon, B., 203
McDaniel, C., 263, 268, 309, 320, 363, 381
McDermott, J., 373, 382
McFarland, D. H., 213–214, 226
McFarland, D. J., 199
McGlone, F. P., 29–30, 64, 87
McGoldrick, J. E., 141–142, 144, 236, 241–242, 248, 250, 256–257, 269
McGonigle, D. J., 157, 169, 180, 204
McGraw, M. B., 316, 321
McGuinness, E., 336, 352
McKeown, M. J., 356, 383
McLuhan, M., 34, 44, 62
McNevin, N. H., 402, 411
McRoberts, G. W., 311, 319
Mechsner, F., *404*, 405, *405*, 410–411
Medin, D. L., 144, 257
Medlin, A. L., 208
Meehan, J., 208
Mel, B., 334, 355
Meltzoff, A. N., 143–144, 214, 226–227, 256, 308, 318, 321, 378–379, 382, 410, 428, 441
Melzack, R., 20, 33, 35, 59, 62, 67–68, 85–86, 176, 182, 184, 196, 202, 204–205, 207, 307, 321
Meneghello, F., 41, 58, 102, 201
Menninger-Lerchenthal, E., 181, 191–193, 205

Menz, R., 192, 205
Menzel, E. W., 33, 62
Merleau-Ponty, M., 147, 149, 159, 169
Merlin, J. S., 362, 382
Mervis, C. B., 231, 257
Merzenich, M. M., 156, 169, 203
Metzinger, T., 193, 205, 389–390
Meyer, R., 168
Meyers, J. S., 102
Miall, R. C., 23, 49, *54*, 62, 64, 218, 226
Michel, F., 380, 425
Miezin, F., 336, 352
Miklósi, A., 217, 226
Mikorey, M., 184, 193, 205
Miles, T. R., 15, 62
Milner, A. D., 287, 300, 330, 333, 354, 356, 383, 424
Miltner, W. H. R., 209
Milward, T., 334, 357
Mineiro, P., 337, 355
Minsky, M., 51, 62
Mishkin, M., 206, 287, 302, 330, 333, 358
Missimer, J., 199
Mistlin, A. J., 356, 383, 414, 424
Mitchell, N., 204
Mitchell, S. W., 67, 86, 175, 205
Mitchell, T. V., 356, 383
Miyauchi, S., 48–49, 60, 62, 64
Miyazawa, N., 178, 181, 205
Moeslund, T. B., 326, 355
Money, J., 37, 62
Monroe, R. A., 193, 205
Montoya, R., 181, 205
Mon-Williams, M., 19, 37, *53*, 62, 196, 205
Moore, C., 178, 205, 274, 278, 299, 324, 345, 353, 389, 427–428, 432–433, 436, 438, 440–441
Moore, M. K., 143–144, 214, 226, 308, 318, 321, 378–379, 382
Moore, T., 35, 59, 72, 84, 101–102
Morel, A., 333, 355
Morgan, D., 268, 300, 305, 320, 353, 363, 381
Morgan, R., 317, 321–322
Morgan, V., 252, 255, 300, 381, 424
Morgante, J., 441
Mori, E., 96, 104
Morikawa, K., 229, 256
Morin, J., 204
Morrel-Samuels, P., 268, 363, 382
Morris, P. E., 299
Morrison, D., 202
Morrison, R., 274, 278, 299, 324, 345, 353
Morrone, M. C., 269, 283, 301, 324, 341, 355, 373, 382
Mortelmans, L., 356, 382
Moss, A. D., 42, 62
Mühlnickel, W., 201–202
Müllbacher, W., 202
Mullen, P. E., 192, 204
Mullett, J., 213, 224
Mumford, D., 328, 350, 355
Münk, H., 15, 65, 86
Murdoch, L., 263, 269, 274, 279, 289, 301
Müri, R. M., 84, 143, 199, 268, 307, 320
Murray, D. J., 64

Müsseler, J., 216, 218, 226, 394, 410, 427, 441
Mutter, D., 29, 62
Myers, R., 384

Nadu, T., 208
Nadvorna, H., 200
Nagel, H.-H., 327, 358
Nagell, K., 432, 436, 441
Naito, E., 230, 255
Nakayama, K., 270, 365, 384
Nathan, P. W., 178, 205
Needham, A., 316, 321
Neighbor, G., 252, 255, 300, 381
Nein, H. W., 355
Nelson, R. J., 169, 327, 356
Neri, P., 264, 269, 283–284, 301, 324, 341, 355, 373, 382
Neumann, H., 353
Neumann, N., 390
Neumann, O., 410
Neumann, R., 213, 226
Neville, H. J., 373, 382
Newport, R., 196, 205
Nichelli, P., 209
Nicolelis, M. A. L., *54*, 56, 58, 62, 64
Nicolls, G., 202
Nielsen, F. Å., 49, 57
Nielsen, T. I., 24–25, *26*, 31, *53*, 62
Nightingale, S., 42, 62, 101
Nishihara, H. K., 313, 321
Nishitani, N., 329, 355
Nixon, M. S., 339, 354
Niyogi, S. A., 327, 355
Nokes, L., 268, 380
Noll, D. C., 169
Nouet, H., 189, 205
Novalis, 4
Nowak, A., 202
Nowak, L., 329, 355
Nuflo, F., 358
Nyberg, A., 234, 247–248, 257
Nyman, G., 70, 86

Obayashi, S., 32, 60, 77, 80, 85–86, 93, 97, 103–104
O'Brien, J. F., 274, 300
O'Connell, D. N., 272, 303
O'Doherty, J. E., 56, 58, 144
Oelz, O., 199
Ogden, J. A., 150, 169, 233, 251, 256, 307, 321
Ohry, A., 20, 62, 176, 205
Oja, E., 299, 352
Okamoto, S., 191, 203
Oki, K., *179*
Oldfield, R. C., 15, 62
Oller, D. K., 311, 320
Olshausen, B. A., 131, 330, 354
Olson, I. R., 219, 226
Olson, M. E., 18, 61
Ommaya, A. K., 206
Omori, E. W. S., 262, 269
Ono, T., 357
O'Rahilly, R., 181, 205

Oram, M. W., 230, 233, 256, 258, 262, 269, 329–330, 334–335, 337, 344, 355, 367, 382, 384, 414, 420, 424
Orban, G. A., 330, 336, 356, 359, 369, 382–383
O'Regan, K., 286, 301
Orgass, B., 16, 43, 63, 65, 87
Orne, M. T., 38, 62
O'Rourke, J., 327, 356
Ortigue, S., 198
Oruç, I., 109, *124*, 131
O'Shaughnessy, B., 82, 86, 148, 169
Ostry, D., 352, 372, 380
Owen, A. M., 387, 390
Oztop, E., 350, 356

Paccalin, C., 213–214, 227
Pacherie, E., 29, 58, 84
Pack, A. A., 268, 363, 382
Packman, T., 23, 58
Paillard, J., 32, 58, 87, 102
Palmer, L. A., 354
Pantev, C., 201, 203
Pantzer, T. M., 219, 225
Papagno, C., 65, 67, 88
Park, S., 365, 382
Parker, L., 207
Parnes, S. M., 199
Parsons, L. M., 81, 86, 139, 144, 183, 206, 224, 227
Pascual-Leone, A., 198, 203, 212, 226, 372, 381, 383
Passingham, R. E., 198, 203
Pateisky, K., 201
Paterson, H. M., 269, 301, 379, 383
Patil, P. G., 56, 58
Paulesu, E., 198, 384, 425
Paulig, M., 185, 206
Paulignan, Y., 148, 168, 424
Pauls, J., 330–331, 341, 355
Paulson, O. B., 49, 57
Paus, T., 213, 228
Pavani, F., 11, 14, 21, *22*, 38, *39*, 41, *54*, 58, 63, 69, 78, 87, 102, 165, 169, 197n5, 201, 206
Pavesi, G., 212, 225, 353, 381, 423
Pavlova, M., 243–244, 256, 267, 269, 279–280, 301, 306, 310, 321, 329, 331, 340, 356, 363, 370, 374, 383
Paysant, J., 20, 61
Pegna, A. J., 50, 63, 74, 87, 98, 104
Peigneux, P., 369, 383
Pelphrey, K. A., 335, 356, 371, 376, 383
Penfield, W., 66, 87, 150, *152*, 169, 230, 256
Pentland, A., 327–328, 353, 358–359
Perani, D., 82–83, 143, 384, 423
Perenin, M.-T., 207
Perkowitz, S., 52, 63
Perona, P., 344, 357
Perozzo, P., 200
Perreault, M. C., 195, 208
Perrett, D. I., 230, 233, 256, 258, 262, 269, 284, 298–299, 329–330, 334–335, 337, 340, *341*, 344, 355–357, 367, 379, 382–384, 414, 420, 423–424

Peterman, K., 316, 321
Peters, A., 355
Pethkongkathon, J., 316, 319
Petit, L., 50, 63, 87, 104
Petrides, M., 352, 372, 380
Pham, M., 390
Phegan, C. M. L., 55, 59, 153, 168
Phillips, A., 433, 437, 441
Phillips, M. L., 203
Phillips, N., 29, 64, 87
Piccardi, L., 307, 320
Pick, A., 181, 206
Pick, H. L., 12, 14, 18, 60
Pickens, D., 252, 255, 300, 381, 424
Pienkos, E., 24, 63
Pietromonaco, P., 213, 228
Pigarev, I. N., 71, 85
Pinel, J. P. J., 69, 83
Pinto, J., 141–142, 144, 231, 243–244, 254, 256,
    263–265, 268, 270, 274, 278, 280–281,
    283–285, 298, 300–301, 306–307, 309–310,
    312–313, 315, 318–319, 321–322, 324, 341,
    345, 352, 356, 358, 365, 373, 380
Pisoni, D. B., 311, 319
Plato, 4
Podoll, K., 55, 63, 188, 206
Poeck, K., 16, 43, 63, 65, 87, 174–175, 182,
    184, 206
Poggio, T., 263, 268, 277, 284–285, 288, 300,
    324, 329–332, 334–335, 337, 340–341, *343*,
    346, 351n, 354–356, 359, 362, 372, 381
Poizner, H., 305, 322, 372, 383
Polana, R., 327, 356
Polanyi, M., 44, 63
Pollick, F. E., 264, 269, 274–275, 277, 281,
    283–285, 289, 292–294, 300–301, 338, 356,
    362, 379, 383
Poncet, M., 200, 307, 320
Pons, T. P., 173, 206
Popovic, Z., 284, 303
Poranen, A., 89, 103
Porta, F. D., 307, 320
Porter, R., 214, 227
Potter, D. D., 356, 383, 414, 424
Povinelli, D. J., 33, 58
Pozdol, S. L., 268, 365, 380
Pradat-Diehl, P., 32, 64, 80, 84, 200
Prasad, S., 144, 269, 389–390
Pravani, F., 256
Prechtl, H. F. R., 308, 320
Press, W. A., 368, 383
Price, D. B., 172, 181, 206
Price, R., 252, 255, 300, 381, 424
Prinz, W., 8, 144, 214, 216, 222, 224, 226–227,
    246, 253, 256, 286, 299, 349, 354, 356,
    389–391, 394–399, *397*, 402, 404–405,
    408–409, 409n3, 410–411, 413, 417, 423–425,
    427–428, 441
Procyk, E., 143
Proffitt, D. R., 45, 58, 263, 268, 284, 299,
    306–309, 311, 319, 322, 363, 380–381
Proteau, L., 216, 224
Proust, J., 29, 58, 84, 389–390
Proust, M., 4
Puce, A., 369, 373, 380, 383, 415, 423–424

Puglisi Allegra, M. C., 307, 320
Pütz, B., 49, 60

Rabe-Hesketh, S., 203
Rabischong, P., 33, 63
Radcliffe, R. D., 305, 320
Radford, K., 263, 269, 274, 280–281, 285, 301,
    306, 321, 324, 341, 355
Raichle, M. E., 357
Raiguel, S., 356, 359
Rakshit, S., 353
Ralston, H., 283, 300
Ramachandran, V. S., 24, 28, 39, 57, 63, 67, 69,
    78, 83, 87, 138, 144, 155, 160–162, 167–170,
    173–175, 185–186, 196, 198, 201, 206, 208,
    251, 254, 307, 322
Ramos, L. M. P., 96, 103
Rao, R. P. N., 131, 328, 337, 346, 350, 356
Rapson, R. L., 202, 213, 225
Rashid, R., 326, 345, 356
Rasmussen, T., 150, *152*, 169
Reckless, G. Z., 218, 226
Redolfi, M., 318, 322
Reed, C. L., 28, 63, 135, 137, 141–144, 150, 170,
    195, 206, 219, 227, 231, 233–234, 236–237,
    239, 246–248, 250–251, 256–257, 264, 266,
    269, 294, 301, 307, 318, 322, 370, 383
Regard, M., 84, 143, 199, 268, 307, 320
Regli, F., 208
Regli, L., 200
Regolin, L., 262, 269
Rehg, J., 327, 353, 356
Reichert, K., 177, 206
Reiss, J. E., 365, 382
Renaseau-Leclerc, C., 20, 63, 207
Rensink, R. A., 270, 278, 286, 301–302,
    348, 358
Reny, F.-A., 181, 206
Repp, B. H., 263–264, 269
Reppas, J. B., 384
Requin, J., 322
Reverdin, A., 20, 64, 178, 208
Rheingold, H., 196, 206
Rhodes, G., 235, 257, 281, 302
Richards, W., 122, 131
Richardson, K., 363, 383
Ridding, M. C., 203
Riddoch, G., 33, 36, 63, 172, 176, 178, 206
Riddoch, M. J., 101, 411
Riechert, T., 174, 207
Rieger, M., 402, 404, 410–411
Riesenhuber, M., 329, 334, 355–356
Riggio, L., 45, 63, 349, 352
Ring, K., 195, 207
Ritter, F., 402, 411
Ritter, K., 205
River, Y., 55, 61
Rizzolatti, G., 28–29, 63, 71–72, 85, 87,
    89, 96, 102, 104, 184, 195, 199, 207, 212–213,
    216, 224–228, 246, 251, 257, 318, 320,
    335, 349, 351, 353, 356, 368, 374, 378, 381,
    383–384, 389, 391, 413–416, 421–425,
    432, 441
Ro, T., 24, 63
Roane, D. M., 81, 85

Robertson, I. H., 27, 41, 62–63, 103, 170, 207
Robinson, D., 55, 63, 188, 206
Rochat, P., 167, 170, 316–317, 321–322
Rockland, K., 355
Rode, G., 186, 207
Roelcke, U., 199
Rogers, M. J. C., 20, 63, 178, 207
Rogers-Ramachandran, D., 24, 63, 155, 170, 175, 206, 208
Rohr, K., 327, 357
Roll, P., 69, 87
Roll, R., 69, 87
Rolls, E. T., 329, 334, 346–348, 357
Rorden, C. R., 41, 63, 165, 170, 197n5, 207
Rosales, R., 330, 357
Rosch, E., 231, 257
Rosen, B. R., 384
Rosen, G., 201
Rosenblum, M., 328, 357
Rosenthal, R., 38, 63
Ross, H. E., 64
Rossi, M., 47, 59
Roth, G., 411
Roth, N., 180, 187, 207
Roth, Peter, *184*
Rothwell, J. C., 203, 372, 383
Rotondo, J. L., 213, 224, 227
Roux, F.-E., 174, 207
Rovee-Collier, C., 319
Rowland, D., 299
Rozanski, J., 208
Ruben, J., 168
Rubino, F., 29, 62
Ruby, P., 192, 196, 207
Runeson, S., 264, 269, 289, 302, 363, 384
Rusconi, M., 81, 84
Rushton, K., 19, 62, 205
Rushton, S. K., 299, 353
Ryle, G., 44, 63
Ryu, J., 356, 362, 383

Saadah, E. S. M., 182, 202, 207
Sabadini, L., 212, 214, 225
Sacks, O., 42, 63
Saito, H., 335–336, 357–358
Sakamoto, M., 36, 61
Sakata, H., 72, 85
Saleem, K. S., 333, 357
Salenius, S., 169, 204, 212, 225, 424
Salin, P. A., 346, 357
Salmon, E., 383
Salonen, O., 20, 59, 169, 202
Sanabria, D., 45, 60
Sanders, A. F., 227, 410
Sanders, G., 203
Sandifer, P. H., 197n4, 207
Sanford, A. J., 269, 301, 379, 383
Sanocki, T., 313, 321
Santana, M.-V., 213, 227
Santucci, D. M., 56, 58
Sasaki, K., 49, 60
Sathian, K., 28, 63
Sauer, H., 188, 204

Saunders, J. A., 109, 122, 131
Savage-Rumbaugh, E. S., 33, 62
Sawyer, J., 231, 235, 255
Saygin, A. P., 351, 357, 374, 376, 384
Scandolara, C., 71, 85, 87, 104
Scapinello, K. F., 231, 237, 257
Scatena, P., 182, 207
Schaal, S., 327, 357
Schaefer, M., 202
Schall, J. D., 357
Schandler, S. L., 208
Schenk, T., 267, 270, 365, 384
Schieber, M. H., 151, 170
Schiff, N. D., 387, 390
Schilder, P., 67, 87, 196, 207
Schlack, A., 89, 101
Schmitt, A., 200
Schmitt, T. L., 18, 64
Schmolesky, M. T., 329, 357
Schneider, K., 317, 322
Schneider, S., 36, 58
Scholl, B. J., 160, 170
Schoppmann, A., 169
Schrater, P. R., 122, 131
Schultz, G., 67, 86, 205, 307, 321
Schürmann, M., 29, 61
Schwartz, E., 206
Schwartz, S., 87
Schweizer, R., 150, 168, 170
Schwiemann, J., 168
Schwoebel, J., 83, 87
Schyns, P. G., 144, 257
Sclaroff, S., 357
Sebanz, N., 428, 441
Seeck, M., 68, 84, 198, 230, 254
Segebarth, C., 424
Seghier, M. L., 87
Seigerschmidt, E., 222, 226, 253, 256
Seiler, W., 201
Seino, M., 203
Seitz, K., 241, 257
Seitz, R. J., 28, 57, 199
Sellal, F., 20, 63, 178, 207
Semenoff, D., 199
Semenza, C., 66, 87, 150, 170
Semjen, A., 406, 409, 411
Sengco, J. A., 258
Senior, C., 219, 227
Seppä, M., 20, 59, 169, 202
Sereno, M. E., 333, 357
Sereno, M. I., 357, 384
Seresen, E. A., 67, 88
Sergent, C., 12, 14, 24, *53*, 62, 78, *79*, 86
Sersen, E. A., 182, 184, 209
Sewekow, K., 177, 206
Seymour, B., 144
Shackelford, R., 248, 257, 269
Shah, N. J. Z. O., 89, 101
Shapiro, M. F., 187, 207
Shavit, E., 327, 357
Sheinberg, D. L., 334, 355
Shelton, J. R., 229, 254
Shepard, R. N., 219, 227
Sherman, C. J., 207
Sherman, R. A., 176, 207

Shiffrar, M., 136, 140–141, 144, 194, *194*, 199, 201, 207, 221, 227, 231, 233, 243–244, 253, 254n, 256–257, 262–264, 266, 268–270, 274, 278, 280, 282–283, 286, 300–302, 306–307, 310, 318, 320, 322, 324, 341, 345, 347–348, 356–358, 374–375, 384, 389–390
Shim, J., 264, 270, 274, 302
Shimojo, S., 18, 20, 22, *53*, 64
Shipley, T. F., 244, 257, 280, 302
Shipp, S., 384
Shockley, K., 213, 227
Shore, D. I., 71, 86
Shorland, B., 30, 64, 87
Shroff, N. M., 45, 59
Shuman, M., 68, 84, 200, 233, 255, 353
Siddall, P. J., 177, 207
Siegel, R. M., 366, 380
Sigal, L., 344, 357
Sigelman, B. H., 357
Simmel, M. L., 67, 87, 174, 182–183, 207
Simmons, A., 203, 227
Simon, J. R., 286, 302
Simoncelli, E. P., 122, 131, 335, 357
Singer, T., 136, 144
Sinha, P., 299, 318, 320, 331, 352, 358, 384
Sirigu, A., 32, 64, 80, 84, 149–150, 170, 178, 200–201, 307, 322
Sitti, R., 208
Sittig, A. C., 14, 19, 64, 109, 131
Siva, N., 206
Skoyles, J. R., 181, 207
Skudlarski, P., 219, 226, 252, 255, 373, 381
Skworzoff, K., 193, 207
Slaughter, V., 231, 250, 253, 254n, 257
Small, S. L., 169
Smania, N., 35, 50, 57, 73, 83, 168, 197
Smievoll, A. I., 201
Smith, A. T., 335–336, 357
Smith, D., 204
Smith, J., 388, 390
Smith, L. B., 319
Smith, M. K., 29, 62
Smith, P. A., 356, 383, 414, 424
Smoski, M. J., 268, 365, 380
Smyth, G. E., 173, 202
Smythe, F. S., 189, 208
Snijders, H. J., 24, 55, 60
Snowden, R. J., 335–336, 357
Sodian, B., 433, 435–436, 442
Sokolov, A., 243–244, 256, 269, 279–280, 301, 306, 310, 321, 331, 340, 356, 363, 370, 374, 383
Sol, J.-C., 207
Sollier, P., 189, 191, 208
Sollod, R., 37, 62
Solodkin, A., 169
Solomon, J., 358, 384
Sommerville, J. A., 389–390
Song, Y., 328, 344, 357
Sootsman, J., 440–441
Soto-Faraco, S., 38, 57, 69, 83
Sparrow, L., 30, 60
Spelke, E., 433, 437, 441
Spence, C., 11–14, 23–24, *25*, 27, 33, 38, 45, *46*, 47, *53–54*, 55, 60, 62–63, 67, 69, 71, 73–74,

76, 78–79, *79*, 83n, 85–87, 89, 98, 101, 103–104, 159, 165, 168–169, 180, 206, 208, 256
Spencer, J. P., 317, 322
Spetner, N. B., 299, 309, 319
Spinelli, L., 68, 84, 198, 230, 254
Squire, R., 357
Srinivasan, A. V., 208
Srinivasan, M. A., 56, 64, 178
Stambaugh, C. R., 56, 64
Stamenov, M. I., 224–228
Starner, T., 328, 358
Stauder, K. H., 186, 204
Staudt, M., 269
Steel, R., 388, 390
Stegbauer, K., 199
Stein, B., 89, 101
Steinbach, T., 200
Stelarc, 56, *179*, 180, 208
Stelmach, G. E., 322
Ste-Marie, D., 212, 224
Stephan, T., 200
Stern, C. E., 205
Sterzi, R., 42, 57, 81, 84, 168, 198
Stevens, J. A., 140, 144, 221, 227, 375, 384
Stewart, M., 206
Stip, E., 195, 208
Stone, J. V., 277, 302
Stone, L., 198, 206
Stone, V. E., 141–142, 144, 170, 231, 233–234, 236–237, 239, 257, 269, 301, 370, 383
Stone, W. L., 268, 365, 380
Strack, F., 213, 226
Strafella, A. P., 213, 228
Stratton, G. M., 196, 208
Stremmel, C., 176, 208
Striano, T., 316, 322
Stringer, R., 269, 301
Stryker, M. P., 169
Stucchi, N., 318, 322
Studdart-Kennedy, M., 212, 217, 228
Stürmer, B., 402, 409n2, 411, 421, 425
Sullivan, R., 26, 64
Sumi, S., 244, 257, 279–280, 285, 302, 306, 310, 322, 331, 358, 363, 384
Summers, J. J., 406, 409, 411
Sundberg, H., 201
Sunderland, T., 170, 307, 322
Surakka, V., 213, 228
Suzuki, K., 44, 60
Suzuki, W., 357
Swets, J. A., 106, 130, 292, 300
Sykes, R. N., 299
Symons, L. A., 235, 237, 255
Sztajzel, R., 50, 63, 87, 104

Tadin, D., 280, 302
Takeuchi, R., 302
Takino, R., 49, 60
Tamada, T., 48–49, 60, 64
Tamburro, R. P., 202
Tanaka, J., 144, 170, 231, 233–237, 239, 241, 246, 255, 257–258, 269, 301, 370, 383
Tanaka, K., 334, 336, 357–358

Tanaka, M., 32, 36, 45, 60–61, 73, 76–77, 80, 85–86, 97, 103–104, 142–144, 169, 203
Tanji, J., 368, 382
Tarr, M. J., 234, 252, 255, 277, 303, 331, 341, 358, 373, 381
Tastevin, J., 37, *54*, 64
Taub, E., 168, 201, 203, 206, 209
Taylor, C. J., 352
Taylor, C. S. R., 35, 40, 59, 70, 72, 84–85, 101–102, 159, 165, 168
Taylor-Clarke, M., 22, 55, 61, 64, 154, 160, 168, 170, 230, 258
Terzopoulos, D., 327, 358
Thelen, E., 317, 319–320, 322
Thinus-Blanc, C., 307, 320
Thoermer, C., 433, 435–436, 442
Thomas, J., 406, 409
Thomas, M. A., 299
Thomas, S. M., 274, 302
Thomas, T. D., 316, 319
Thompson, C., 188, 208
Thompson, K. G., 357
Thomson, H., 316, 320
Thomson, J. A., 299
Thornton, I. M., 263, 266, 268, 270, 274, 277–279, 281–283, 285–286, 288, 298–303, 306–307, 322, 324, 345, 348, 351n, 353, 358, 363–364, 380–381
Thorpe, S., 329, 358
Thunberg, M., 213, 225
Tillung, T., 201
Tipper, S. P., 29–30, *53*, 64, 80, 87
Tobita, M., 44, 60
Todd, F., 283, 300
Todd, J. T., 181, 193, 208, 324, 358
Töllner, T., 411
Tomasello, M., 432, 436, 438–439, 441–442
Tommasi, L., 269
Toole, T., 402, 411
Tootell, R. B., 369, 384
Töpfner, S., 205
Torre, V., 356
Tovée, M. J., 329, 357
Townsend, S., 101
Traballesi, M., 307, 320
Tramo, M. J., 380
Tranel, D., 213, 224, 379, 382
Treisman, A., 160, 170
Tremblay, F., 212, 224
Tremewan, T., 235, 257
Trillet, M., 207
Trinath, T., 357
Troje, N. F., 263–264, 266, 270, 276–278, 280–281, 284–285, 289, 294, 301–302, 331, 358, 362, 379, 384
Trommershäuser, 122
Troscianko, T., 268, 300, 305, 320, 353, 363, 381
Tsakiris, M., 11, 136, 162, 165, 170, 388, 391
Tschabitscher, H., 201
Tschacher, W., 410
Tsotsos, J., 347, 358
Tucker, M., 45, 64
Tumblin, J., 274, 300
Turnbull, O. H., 42, 62
Turner, J. A., 178, 208

Turner, L. M., 268, 365, 380
Twombly, S. J., 172, 206

Uchiyama, I., 316, 319
Ullman, S., 272, 302, 346, 348, 355, 358
Umiltà, C., 45, 63
Umiltà, M. A., 216, 221, 226, 228, 413, 424–425
Ungerleider, L. G., 287, 302, 330, 333, 358
Uno, Y., 49, 60
Unuma, M., 284, 302

Vaina, L. M. V., 267, 270, 326–327, 335–336, 348, 351, 353, 355, 358, 364–365, 373, 376, 381, 384
Valentin, G., 182, 208
Valentine, T., 293, 299
Valenza, N., 68, 87
Vallar, G., 42, 57, 65, 67, 74, 81–84, 88, 168, 198
Vallortigara, G., 269
van Beers, R. J., 14, 19, 64, 109, 131
van den Bos, E., 31, *53*, 64, 318, 322, 388, 391
van der Linden, M., 383
van der Willigen, R., 299
van Ee, R., 117, 130
van Essen, D. C., 287, 300, 330, 333–334, 346, 353–354
van Gijn, J., 96, 103
Van Hoesen, G. W., 231, 255
Van Rensbergen, J., 141, 145, 220, 228, 274, 303, 331, 358
van Rullen, R., 329, 358
Vandenberghe, R., 356, 382
Vanrie, J., 274, 276–279, 298n, 299, 302–303
Velay, J.-L., 69, 87
Velmurugendran, U. C., 208
Vereijken, B., 318–319
Verfaillie, K., 141, 145, 220–221, 228, 263, 270, 272, 274, 276–281, 285–286, 294, 299, 302–303, 331, 358
Verret, J. M., 186, 208
Verri, A., 356
Vetter, R. J., 182, 208, 284
Vetter, T., 299
Vieira, W., *194*, 208
Vighetto, A., 207
Villringer, A., 168
Villringer, K., 202
Vinken, P. J., 199
Vinson, N. G., 219, 227
Visser, G. H. A., 308, 320
Viviani, P., 318, 322
Vix, M., 29, 62
Vogeley, K., 192, 208
Vogels, R., 356, 382
Vogt, S., 349, 354
von Angyal, L., 185, 198
von Cramon, D. Y., 215, 224
Von Hofsten, C., 318–319
von Stockert, F.-G., 186, 208
Votaw, J. R., 32, 58
Vroomen, J., 120, 130–131
Vuilleumier, P., 20, 64, 87, 178, 185, 191, 208
Vuong, Q. C., 263, 270, 277–278, 281, 286, 288, 298n, 301–303, 307, 322, 348, 358

Wachsmuth, E., 233, 258, 367, 384
Wachter, S., 327, 358
Wade, A. R., 368, 383
Wade, D. T., 20, 41–42, 59, 169, 174, 178,
    181, 202
Wai, W., 358
Wall, P. D., 200
Wall, R. T., 198
Wallace, R., 24, 63
Wallach, H., 272, 303
Wallbott, H. G., 140, 145, 213, 228
Wallesch, C. W., 88
Walsh, V., 372, 383
Walters, M. R., 406, 409
Wandell, B. A., 368, 383
Wang, Y., 357
Wann, J. P., 19, 62, 196, 205, 208
Ward, A., 203
Ward, J., 219, 227
Warren, D. H., 18–19, 64
Warrington, E., 150, 169
Waters, K., 327, 358
Watkins, K. E., 213, 228
Watson, J. D., 369, 384
Watt, S., 109, 131
Webb, J. A., 326, 358
Webb, R., 67, 85
Weber, E. H., 36, 44, 64
Weber, M., 206
Webster, D. S., 363, 383
Wegner, D. M., 196, 208
Weigelt, M., 402–403, 403, *404*, 411
Weihing, J., 212, 214, 225
Weinstein, E. A., 178, 180, 208
Weinstein, S., 67, 88, 182, 184, 208–209
Weiss, P., 89, 104
Weiss, T., 180, 209
Weiss, Y., 122, 131
Welch, R. B., 19, 37, 64, 117, 131
Wellman, H., 427, 433, 437, 441
Werker, J. F., 311, 322
Wernicke, C., 185, 209
Wessberg, J., 56, 64
West, S., 262–263, 269, 274–275,
    280–281, 285, 288, 301, 306, 321, 324,
    341, 355
Westhoff, C., 270
Wicker, B., 379, 382, 415, 424–425
Widawski, M. H., 19, 64
Wienbruch, C., 201
Wiesel, T. N., 334, 354
Wieser, H.-G., 143, 199
Wigan, A. L., 192, 209
Wiggins, D., 147, 170
Wilhelm, B., 390
Willen, J., 438, 441
Wilms, A., 170
Wilson, K. D., 239, 255
Wilson, M., 137, 139–141, 143, 212, 217, 228,
    243, 246, 253, 254n, 258, 349, 359

Wilson, S. M., 299, 357, 384
Wilson, T. P., 223, 228
Wilson, W. R., 311, 320
Wilson-Brune, C., 437, 439, 441–442
Wisdom, J. O., 193, 209
Wisdom, S. B., 198
Witherington, D. C., 316, 319
Witkin, A., 284, 303
Wohlschläger, A., 214, 224, 389, 402, 409,
    409n2, 411
Wolf, S. L., 28, 63
Wolfe, J. M., 286, 294, 303
Wolpert, D. M., 23, 64, 101, 122, 131,
    198, 215, 218, 228, 327, 359, 388, 390
Woodruff, P. W., 382
Woods, R. P., 32, 58, 216, 226, 384
Woodson, R., 214, 225
Woodward, A. L., 433–439, 441–442
Woodward, J. M., 177, 199
Worthington, A., 180, 209
Wren, C., 328, 359
Wright, I., 382
Wulf, G., 402, 411
Wurtz, R. H., 336, 353

Xiao, D. K., 336, 355–356, 359
Xie, X., 328, 337, 359
Xu, L., 299, 352

Yacoob, Y., 327–328, 355, 357
Yamadori, A., 44, 60, 96, 104
Yamaguchi, M. K., 262, 270
Yamamoto, S., 45, 64, 73, 88
Yap, G. S., 71, 85, 102
Yarmey, A., 231, 237, 257
Yeni-Komshian, G. H., 319
Yin, R. K., 231, 237, 258, 279, 303, 370, 384
Yoshioka, T., 48–49, 60, 64
Young, A. J., 274, 298
Young, A. W., 237, 258, 299, 378, 380
Young, J. W., 316, 319
Young, M. J., 131
Younger, B. A., 315, 322
Yu, A. J., 334, 359
Yuille, A. L., 122, 131

Zajonc, R. B., 213, 228
Zamboni, G., 189, 209
Zangwill, O. L., 15, 23, *53*, 55, 61–62
Zeilig, G., 20, 62, 205
Zeki, S., 382, 384
Zeloni, G., 91, 103
Zernicke, R. F., 317, 322
Zihl, J., 267, 270, 365, 384
Zilles, K., 101, 104, 199
Zilli, T., 307, 320
Zimmerman, D. H., 223, 228
Zipser, D., 337, 355
Zook, J. M., 169
Zurfluh, W., 191, 209

Subject Index

Italicized page numbers refer to figures.

abstract knowledge, 12, 68, 77–81, *79*
action and intention. *See* intentional action
action induction, 395–99, 397, *398*
action perception, 7, 395–401, 397, *398*, 407–8,
    409n2, 413–23
  and biological-motion perception, 415, 419–21
  and human mirror system, 184, 415–16,
    421–23
  and interference effect, 416–23, *418*, 419, *420*
  and neural networks, 413–14
action planning, 140, 267, 394, 407–8
action production, 32, 389, 394–95, 401–7, 409n2
  and bimanual circling, 405–7, *405*
  and bimanual reaching, 402–5, 403, *404*
  and tools, 44–45, 394
action recognition, 253–54, 285–86, 349
agents, 428–31, 433, 437
alien body parts, 42, 156, 180, 189
American Sign Language (ASL), 372–73
amodal completion, 219
amputation, 35, 67, 138, 155–56, 172–76, *173*,
    175, 180–81, 197n1
anesthesia, 55, 153–54
animations, 267, 275–76, 283, 362–67, 370–74.
    See also point-light walkers
  and solid-body models, 276, 292–97, *293*,
    296, *297*
anorexia, 55
anosognosia, 42, 157, 180, 185–87
antiphase coordination, 405–6, *405*
aplasic phantom limb, 67, 138–39, 156, 181–85,
    184, 197n3, 307–8
apparent motion, 219, 221, 233
apraxia, 32, 44–46
artificial body parts, 17, 33–42
  and clothing effect, 34–37
  and televisual display of body parts, 30
  and virtual body effect, 37–42, *39*, 57n5
aschematia, 65, 180
asomatognosic patients, 156
attended modality, 18–19
attention, 263, 325, 439
attentional modulation, 345, 348
auditory system
  and action perception, 414
  and biological-motion perception, 266,
    366, 369

and body representations, 74
  and covert imitation, 212
  and multimodal cue integration, 109
  and peripersonal space, 89–91, 93
  and phantom sensations, 189, 193
  and televisual display of body parts, 29
autism, 267, 365
automatic tracking, 275, 288
autoscopic hallucinations, 187, 189–90, *190*, 192
autoscopic phenomena, 68, 172, 187–90, *190*,
    191–92, 195–96
autotopagnosia, 66, 150, 233, 251–52, 307
avatars, 292–97, *293*, 296, *297*

backward planning, 401
bar detectors, 334
Bayesian decision theory (BDT)
  and biological-motion perception, 328
  and body mereology, 159, 161–65
  and multimodal cue integration, 14, 118–27,
    119, *121*, *123*, *125*, 129
behavioral studies
  of action perception, 395–400, 397, *398*
  of biological-motion perception, 370
  of body representations, 73–81
  of body shadows, 21–23
  of configural processing, 231, 233
  of mirror reflections and self-recognition,
    24–27
  of phantom sensations, 174, 183–85, *184*
  of prismatic visual displacement, 18–19
  of prosthetic manipulations, 33, 36
  of televisual display of body parts, 29–31, 33
  of tools, 45–46, 48–49
  of virtual body effect, 37–40, *39*, 57n5
bimanual circling, 405–7, *405*
bimanual reaching, 402–5, 403, *404*
biological motion, 262, 323
biological-motion displays, 4, 6, 261–67, 271–98
  and animated solid-body models, 292–97, *293*,
    296, *297*
  and computational principles, 265, 323–51, 361
    cortical processing, constraints of, 323,
      328–32
    existing approaches to, 326–28
    neural model, 323, 332–50, *333*, 338, *339*,
      341, *343*, *346*

biological-motion displays (*continued*)
  problems of, 325–26
  and configural processing, 243–45, 248, 250,
      252–54 (*see also* configural processing)
  early-development responses to, 265
  infant responses to, 305–18, *306*
    motor development, 316–18
    network of brain areas, 363–64
    visuospatial relations, 308–16, 310, *311*,
        312, *314*
  and internal representations, 307–8
  and point-light walkers (*see* point-light
      walkers)
  and video footage, 287–92, 289, *290*, 291
  visual analyses of, 306–7
biological-motion perception, 261–67
  and action perception, 414–15, 419–21
  and network of brain areas, 361–79, *377*
    neuroimaging, 368–75
    neurophysiology, 366–68
    neuropsychology, 364–66
    point-light walkers, 362–64
body image, 15–17, 38, 40, 55–56, 67, 81, 171
body mereology, 136–37, 147–68
  and addition of body parts, 156–58
  and deletion of body parts, 155–56
  and differentiation of body parts, 149–54
    motor mereology, 151–52, *152–53*
    size of body parts, 152–54, *155*
    somatosensory mereology, 149–50, *152–53*
  and multisensory integration, 158–66
    "common sensible," 159–60
    rubber hand illusion, 160–66, *162*, *164*
body perception, 15–56, *53–54*
  historical concept of, 15–17
  introduction to, 11–14
  and prosthetic manipulations, 33–42
    clothing effect, 34–37
    virtual body effect, 37–42, *39*, 57n5
  and tools, 42–51, *46*, 57n6
    detached tools, 50–51, 52
    as physical intermediaries, 43–48
    pointing tools, 48–50, 52
  and visual manipulations, 17–33
    mirror reflections and self-recognition,
        23–28, *25*, 26, 56–57n4
    prismatic visual displacement, 18–20
    shadows of body, 20–23, *22*, 56n3
    televisual display of body parts, 28–33
body representations, 4, 5–7, 12–13, 135–43
  and biological-motion perception, 266
  and body mereology, 136–37, 147–68
    addition of body parts, 156–58
    deletion of body parts, 155–56
    motor mereology, 151–52, *152–53*
    multisensory body mereology, 158–66
    size of body parts, 152–54, *155*
    somatosensory mereology, 149–50,
        152–53
  and configural processing, 229–58, *230*
    action perception, 253–54
    for biological motion displays, 243–45
    embodied representations, 245–49, *247*, *249*
    exact distances between features, 235
    expertise, 245–49, *247*, *249*

holistic representations, 235–43, *236*,
    238, *240*
  relative position of parts/features, 235
  spatial body representations, 250–53
  "special" objects, 231–34
and covert imitation, 211–24
  imitable stimuli, 212–15
  perceptual prediction for human movements,
      220–22
  real time simulation, 217–20
  turn-taking, 222–23
and intentional action, 388–90
and other people's bodies, 140–43
and own physical body, 136–38
and phantom sensations, 55, 67, 138–39,
    171–97
  after spinal-cord injury, 176–78, *177*, 181
  amputation phantoms, 172–76, *173*, *175*,
      180–81, 197n1, 252
  congenital phantom limb, 181–85, *184*,
      197n3
  half-body phantoms, 185–87, 197nn4-5
  out-of-body experiences, 190–93, *190*
  phantom bodies, 188–89
  research perspectives, 193–96
  supernumerary phantoms, 55, 137, 178–81,
      179, 185, 187, 189, 193, 197n2, 252
  visual doppelgänger, 189–90, *190*
  whole body phantoms, 139, 187–88
sensory and intentional components of, 65–83
  abstract knowledge, 77–81, *79*
  intentional aspects, 71–77, *75*
  multisensory aspects, 69–71
  self-awareness, 77–81, *79*
body schema, 15–17
  and body mereology, 154
  and body representations, 55–56, 65–67, 71,
      73, 76, 81, 135
  and configural processing, 250–51, 253
  and covert imitation, 211–24
    imitable stimuli, 212–15
    perceptual prediction for human movements,
        220–22
    real-time simulation, 217–20
    turn-taking, 222–23
  and mirror reflections and self-recognition, 28
  and peripersonal space, 100
  and phantom sensations, 139, 171
  and tools, 42–43, 49
  and virtual body effect, 38
body sense. *See* proprioception
body space, 149–59, 165
bottom-up control, 96, 159, 161, 165–66, 218,
    267, 346
boundary extension, 219
bowling, 395–400
  inverted, 399–400
  regular, 395–99, 397, *398*
    other-generated action, 399
    self-generated action, 397–98, 409nn3-4
brain areas, network of, 361–79, *377*
  and neuroimaging, 368–75
    extrastriate visual cortex, 362, 368–69
    premotor cortex, 362, 367–68, 374–75
    selectivity, 370–73

superior temporal sulcus, 362, 367, 369–70, 374
  ventral temporal cortex, 362, 373–74
  and neurophysiology, 366–68
  and neuropsychology, 364–66
  and point-light walkers, 362–64
brain-damaged patients. *See also* right-hemisphere brain damage (RBD)
  and biological-motion perception, 267
  and body representations, 66, 73–76, *75*, 78, 80–81
    face/body perception, 142
    phantom sensations, 138, 178–81, 189–92
  and covert imitation, 213
  and network of brain areas, 364–65
  and tools, 44
broadly congruent mirror neurons, 212

canines, 65, 246–48, *247*, 429
canonical figures, 309–13, 310, *311*, 312, 315, 373
caricatures, 235, 285, 294
cat figures, 312, *312*
cats, 262, 334, 363, 366
central factors, 172–73, *173*
chameleon effect, 213
chimeric point-light walker, 279
clothing effect, 17, 33, 34–37, 193, 294
clutter, 345–46, *346*
coaenesthesia, 65, 171
cognitive body representation, 160, 163–66
"common sensible," 159–60
computational principles, 6, 265, 323–51
  cortical processing, constraints of, 323, 328–32
  existing approaches to, 326–28
  neural model, 323, 332–50, *333*
    limitations of, 346–50
    selected simulation results of, 337–46, 338, *339*, *341*, *343*, *346*
  problems of, 325–26
computer mice, 43, 48–50, 52, 77
conative acts, 431, 434–35, 437
concrete awareness, 188
concurrent planning, 401
configural processing, 142–43, 232, 234–49, 370
  for biological motion displays, 243–45
  and embodied representations, 245–49, *247*, *249*
  and exact distances between features, 235
  and expertise, 245–49, *247*, *249*
  and holistic representations, 235–43, *236*, *238*, *240*
  and relative position of parts/features, 235
configuration, 232
congenital phantom limb, 67, 138–39, 156, 181–85, *184*, 197n3
conscious representation, 38, 81–82, 148
conversational turn-taking, 141, 214, 222–23, 253
corporeal awareness
  and covert imitation, 215
  and phantom sensations, 171–77, 181, 184–89, 194–96, *194*
coupling, strength of, 116–17, 118–27, *119*, *121*, *123*, *125*
coupling prior, 124, 126, 129
covert imitation, 140, 211–24

and imitable stimuli, 212–15
perceptual prediction for human movements, 220–22
in real time, 217–20
and turn-taking, 222–23
crossmodal congruency tasks, 74–76, *75*
  and body representations, 73
  and body shadows, 21, *22*
  and mirror reflections and self-recognition, 24, 56–57n4
  and tools, 45
  and virtual body effect, 38, 41–42
crossmodal effects
  and body mereology, 157, 159
  and body representations, 78–79
  and multimodal cue integration, 110, *110*, 111, 115–17
  and phantom sensations, 177, 180–81
crossmodal extinction, 13
  and body representations, 74–75, *75*, 78, *79*
  and mirror reflections and self-recognition, 27
  and peripersonal space, 90–94, 97–98, 98, 99, *99*, 100
  and tools, 46–48
  and virtual body effect, 41–42
cue integration, 105–30
  benefits/costs of, 112–17, 113–14, *116*
  combining redundant signals, 108–12, 109, *110*, *112*
  probability density distribution, 106–7, *107*
  strength of coupling, 118–27, *119*, *121*, *123*, *125*

deafferented patients, 32, 173–74, 176, 178, 181, 195
deefferented patients, 176, 178
degradation, 6, 288–92, *290*, 306, 324, 332, 341–44, *343*
denial of ownership, 31, 35, 55, 81, 156–58, 185–87, 189, 192, 197n4
detached body, 56
detached tools, 50–51, 52
discrimination performance, 113–18, *114*, *116*
dishabituation approach, *434*, 435, 440
disownership. *See* denial of ownership
disparity-texture signals, 115–17, *116*
dissimilar heautoscopy, 191
dissociation, 38, 42, 196, 364, 397, 399–400, 406
"distal attribution," 36
distal representation, 394–95, 399–402, 406–8
distractor stimuli, 38–39, *39*, *46*, 73, 78–79, 342
divided-axis displays, 313–14, *314*
dogs. *See* canines
dolphins, 262, 363, 366
doppelgänger, 188, 189–93, *190*, 196
dual-task paradigm, 250–51
duplicative experience, 187–88
dynamic body perception, 267
  and biological-motion perception, 266
    point-light walkers, 272, 286, 295
  and body mereology, 165
  and configural processing, 244–45, 248, 250–53
  and peripersonal space, 96
  and phantom sensations, 174

dynamic-object perception, 277
dynamic programming, 344
dysmorphophobia, 55

"eccentric projection," 36, 44
edge enhancement, 288
electrophysiological studies, 70, 159
embodied representations, 245–49, *247*, *249*
embodied self, 4, 56, 141, 148
embodiment, 143, 161, 171
emotion, 213, 274
emotional acts, 427, 431, 437–38
empathy, 192, 216, 422
emulator, 218, 220–24, 253
environment, 280, 394, 399–400, 408–9n1,
    409n2
epistemic acts, 431, 435–37, 438
exosomesthesia, 187, 197n5
expertise, 245–49, *247*, *249*
extensions of body
    and body mereology, 157
    and body representations, 55–56, 73
    and peripersonal space, 89, 96–98, *98*, *99*
    and phantom sensations, 187
    and prosthetic manipulations, 34, 187
    and tools, 42–51, *46*, 57n6, 157, 187
extinction. *See* crossmodal extinction;
    visual-tactile extinction
extracorporeal awareness. *See* phantom
    sensations
extracorporeal space, 187–89
extrapersonal space, 5
    and body representations, 68, 70, 72–76, *75*,
        77–78, *79*, 81
    and body shadows, 21
    and mirror reflections and self-recognition, 24
    and phantom sensations, 139, 189, 191
    and tools, 46–47, *46*, 49–50
extrastriate visual cortex, 362, 368–69

F5 mirror cells, 367–68
face perception
    and biological-motion perception
        computational principles, 327
        network of brain areas, 361–62, 370, 373
        point-light walkers, 277, 279, 288,
            292–94
    and body representations, 142–43
    and configural processing, 231–34, *232*,
        235–39, *236*, 241–42, 245, 252–53
"face space," 235, 237
fake-finger illusion, 37
fake limbs, 5, 37–42, *39*, 57n5, 69, *79*,
    93–94, 251
false proximate awareness, 188
fast processing, 344–45
feature-based processing, 234, 325
"feeling of a presence," 187–89
felt location
    and mirror reflections and self-recognition,
        24, 27
    and phantom sensations, 188
    and prismatic visual displacement, 18–20
filming, 274, 287–92
finger agnosia, 150

fingernails, 36–37
first-person perspective, 393, 429, 431–32, 439
flanker-interference paradigm, 286–87
flashlights, 48–50
fMRI (functional magnetic resonance imaging),
    178, 180, 324, 335, 342, 348, 367–68,
    415–16
focality, 44, 148
force-feedback devices, 51, 110, *110*
form cues, 277, 284, 287–88, 292, 294, 324
form pathways, 333–35, *333*, 339, *339*, *341*, *343*,
    346, 349
form patterns, 327–28
forward-model. *See* emulator
forward planning, 401
functional properties, 393–94
fusiform face area (FFA), 252, 324, 335, 342, 373

gait-generation techniques, 275
gait patterns, 288, 290, 294–95, 311–12, 315,
    324, 330, 339
gender-from-motion, 279, 284, 289–92, *289*,
    290, *291*, 293–95, *296*, 297, 363
geometric mereology, 149, 152–54, *155*
goals, 393–403, 406–8, 409n2, 413–14,
    422–23, 433
"grandmother cells," 335

habituation approach, 35–36, 432–36, *434*,
    439–40
half-body phantoms, 42, 81, 172, 185–87,
    197nn4-5
half-stimuli, 239, *240*
hand-mouth coordination, 182–85, 308, 316–17
haptic size stimuli, 108–13, *109*, *110*, 112, *113*,
    115–22, *116*, *119*, *121*, 126. *See also*
    tactile system
heautoscopy, 188, 190–93, *190*
hemianesthesia, 96
hemiphantom, 172, 195
hemiplegia, 96, 185–87
"hemiplegic twin," 185
heterosexual heautoscopy, 191
hidden Markov models (HMMs), 328
holistic processing, 142–43, 159, 236
holistic representations, 235–43, *236*, *238*, *240*
"homunculus," 150
human mirror system, 184, 415–16, 421–23
hypoesthesia, 185

identification
    and biological-motion perception, 263
    and body representations, 55
    with mirror-reflected body, 24–28, *25*, 26
    and prosthetic manipulations, 33
    and televisual display of body parts, 29–32
    and virtual body effect, 38
ideomotor theory, 389, 396, 413
illusions, 55, 70, 138, 154–55, 178, 181, 219,
    252. *See also* autoscopic hallucinations;
    rubber hand illusion
imitation, 28, 140–41, 192, 212–15, 308, 327,
    349, 378, 402
incorporation phenomenon
    and body representations, 55

and phantom sensations, 186, 193
and prosthetic manipulations, 35–37
and tools, 45, 49, 52, 76
and virtual body effect, 40
induced movements, 395–99, 397, 398, 409n4
infant responses, 305–18, 306
and action perception, 415
and intentional relations theory, 432,
433–37, 434
and motor development, 316–18
and network of brain areas, 363–64
and visuospatial relations, 308–16, 310, 311,
312, 314
intentional action, 4, 6–7, 387–89, 393–409,
408–9n1
and body mereology, 151
and body representations, 12, 68–69,
71–77, 75
intentional binding effect, 388
intentional induction, 398–400, 398, 407
intentional relations theory, 427–41
and agents, 428–31, 433, 437
implications for, 437–40
infant representations of, 432, 433–37, 434
and intentional schema, 432–33
and objects/object-directedness, 428, 430–38,
434, 440
and psychological acts, 428–31, 434, 437–39
and self-other equivalence, 429–30,
432, 438
intentional schema, 432–33
interference effect, 416–23, 418, 419, 420
and biological-motion perception, 419–21
and human mirror system, 421–23
internal prostheses, 37
internal representations, 307–8, 313
interstimulus intervals (ISIs), 241, 283, 347
introspection, 395, 401–2, 407–8
"intuitive physics," 194
inversion effects
and action perception, 399–400
and biological-motion perception, 306
infant responses to, 309–11, 313–14
network of brain areas, 370, 373
point-light walkers, 279–80, 286
and body mereology, 150
and configural processing, 142, 229–31,
230, 233, 236–39, 238, 241–44,
246–48, 252
islands approach, 439

jewelry, 35, 73, 158, 186, 197n4
Johansson point-light figures. See point-light
walkers

kinematic studies, 323, 327, 340, 342, 361,
363, 379
kinesthetic information, 7, 139, 143, 181
Krukenberg hand, 173

laser pointers, 43, 47, 48–50, 74, 75
learned templates, 324, 327–28, 342
limb dysplasia, 182
line bisection tasks, 47, 50, 74, 75
line drawings, 30, 31

localization tasks, 18, 189, 251–52
local optic flow detectors, 336

manipulation, ease of (point-light walkers), 274,
279–85
spatially global manipulations, 279–81
spatially local manipulations, 281–82
spatiotemporal manipulations, 284–85
temporal manipulations, 282–84
manual coding, 275, 288
masking, 142, 242, 244, 278, 280, 281, 324, 345
maximum-likelihood estimation (MLE), 14,
108–9, 109, 111, 114, 115, 124, 129
mereologies. See body mereology
metameric behavior, 113–16, 114, 116
migraine illusions, 55, 188
mimicry, 213–14
mirror agnosia, 28
mirror ataxia, 28
mirror-box techniques, 24–27, 25, 26
"mirror hallucinations," 189
mirror neurons, 28, 29
and action perception, 413–14, 422
and body representations, 140
and computational principles, 349
and configural processing, 246, 251
and covert imitation, 212–13, 217, 221
and intentional relations theory, 432
and network of brain areas, 350, 367–68, 374
mirror reflections, 12–13
and body representations, 55, 77–78, 79, 80
and peripersonal space, 98
and phantom sensations, 175, 186, 189, 196
and self-recognition, 23–28, 25, 26, 56–57n4
and tools, 43–44
mirror system, human, 184, 415–16, 421–23
misoplegia, 42
modeling, 216, 267
monkeys, 12
and action perception, 413–14, 422
and biological-motion perception, 262, 334
computational principles, 329, 333–36, 349
network of brain areas, 361–63, 366–69,
374, 379
and body mereology, 157, 159, 165
and body representations, 56, 70, 72–73, 80
and configural processing, 233, 246
and covert imitation, 212, 217
and mirror reflections and self-recognition, 28
and peripersonal space, 89–90, 93, 95–97
and prosthetic manipulations, 35–36
and televisual display of body parts, 29, 32
and tools, 45
and virtual body effect, 40–41, 57n5
morphing, 277, 284–85, 294
motion capture, 273, 275, 276, 278, 281, 283,
288–89, 293, 362
motion clutter, 345–46, 346
motion cues, 287, 294, 324
motion edges, 336
motion pathways, 333, 333, 335–37, 339, 339,
342, 343, 344, 346–47
motion pattern neurons, 335, 338, 339, 342,
344–45, 346, 349
motion patterns, 327–28, 342

motor computations, 361–62, 366, 370, 378–79.
  See also computational principles
"motor contagion," 422
motor evoked potential (MEP), 375, 416
motor mereology, 151–52, *152–53*, 167
motor systems
  and action perception, 402, 413, 417
  and biological-motion perception
    computational principles, 323, 325,
      348–50
    infant responses, 305, 308, 316–18
  and body representations, 56, 68, 72–73
  and configural processing, 143, 223, 243,
    246, 253
  and covert imitation, 213
  and tools, 47
movements, 394–408, 414, 422
"movement traces," 362
multimodal perception, 4–5, 8, 15–56, *53–54*.
  See also multisensory representation
  and biological-motion perception, 265–66
  and body representations, 65–88, 137
    and abstract knowledge, 77–81, *79*
    and configural processing, 251
    intentional aspects of, 71–77, *75*
    multisensory aspects of, 69–71
    and self-awareness, 77–81, *79*
  historical concept of, 15–17
  introduction to, 11–14
  and multimodal cue integration, 105–30
    Bayesian decision theory, 118–27, *119, 121,*
      123, 125
    benefits/costs of, 112–17, 113–14, *116*
    combining redundant signals, 108–12, 109,
      110, 112
    probability density distribution, 106–7, *107*
    strength of coupling, 118–27, *119, 121,*
      123, 125
  of peripersonal space, 89–101
    automatic processing, 94–96, *95*
    extension, 96–98, *98, 99*
    functional properties, 93–94
    neuropsychological evidence, 90–93, *92*
    plasticity determinants, 98–100
  and prosthetic manipulations, 33–42
    clothing effect, 34–37
    virtual body effect, 37–42, *39*, 57n5
  and tools, 42–51, *46*, 57n6
    detached tools, 50–51, 52
    as physical intermediaries, 43–48
    pointing tools, 48–50, 52
  and visual manipulations, 17–33
    body shadows, 20–23
    mirror reflections and self-recognition,
      23–28, *25*, 26, 56–57n4
    prismatic displacement, 18–20
    televisual display of body parts, 28–33
multisensory body mereology, 154, 158–66
  "common sensible," 159–60
  rubber hand illusion, 160–66, *162, 164*
multisensory representation, 5, 7, 11–14. *See also*
    multimodal perception
  of body representations, 69–71
  of peripersonal space, 89–101
    automatic processing, 94–96, *95*

extension, 96–98, *98, 99*
functional properties, 93–94
neuropsychological evidence, 90–93, *92*
plasticity determinants, 98–100

near-death experience, 192
neglect disorders
  and body mereology, 156
  and body representations, 55, 74, *75*,
    81–82, 137
  and phantom sensations, 185–86, 197n4
  and prosthetic manipulations, 35
  and tools, 47–48, 50
  and virtual body effect, 42
neural control of machines, 56
neural model, 323–24, 332–50, *333*, 372
  limitations of, 346–50
  selected simulation results of, 337–46, 338
    degraded stimuli, processing of,
      341–44, *343*
    fast processing, 344–45
    high pattern selectivity, 338–40, *339*
    motion clutter, robustness against,
      345–46, *346*
    view dependence, 340–41, *341*
neural networks
  and action perception, 413–14, 421
  and biological-motion perception, 328, 335,
    337, 344
  and body representations, 67, 70–71
  and phantom sensations, 184
neural representations, 17, 55, 56n2
  and action perception, 415
  and biological-motion perception, 264–65, 267
    computational principles, 328–29 (*see also*
      neural model)
    infant responses, 307
  and body mereology, 149–51, 153–57, 159, 165
  and body representations, 73, 80
    face/body perception, 142
    imitable stimuli, 140
  and body shadows, 21, 22
  and configural processing, 231, 233, 246,
    250–52
  and covert imitation, 212–13, 215
  and mirror reflections and self-recognition,
    27–28
  and peripersonal space, 89, 90–93, *92*,
    95–97
  and phantom sensations, 172–74, 183, 188,
    192, 195
  and prismatic visual displacement, 19–20
  and prosthetic manipulations, 33, 35–37
  and televisual display of body parts, 32–33
  and tools, 42–43, 45, 46–48
    pointing tools, 49–50
  and virtual body effect, 40–42
neural transmission time, 217–18
neuroimaging, 6
  and action perception, 415
  and biological-motion perception, 362,
    368–75, 379
    extrastriate visual cortex, 362, 368–69
    premotor cortex, 362, 367–68, 374–75
    selectivity, 370–73

superior temporal sulcus, 362, 367, 369–70, 374
ventral temporal cortex, 362, 373–74
and configural processing, 231, 233, 252
and phantom sensations, 173–74, 177–78, 180, 183
neuromatrix, 68, 184
neurophysiology, 6, 55
and action perception, 413
and biological-motion perception, 265, 366–68 (*see also* neural model)
and configural processing, 246
and mirror reflections and self-recognition, 27–28
and peripersonal space, 89–90
and phantom sensations, 174, 192
and prismatic visual displacement, 19–20
and prosthetic manipulations, 33, 35–37
and televisual display of body parts, 32–33
and tools, 44, 46–48
pointing tools, 49–50
and virtual body effect, 40–42
neuropsychology, 6, 55
and biological-motion perception, 264, 307, 364–66, 373
and body mereology, 150, 157
and configural processing, 233, 250–52
and covert imitation, 212
and mirror reflections and self-recognition, 27–28
and peripersonal space, 89, 90–93, *92*, 97–98
and phantom sensations, 172, 181, 188, 192
and prismatic visual displacement, 19–20
and prosthetic manipulations, 33, 35–37
and televisual display of body parts, 32–33
and tools, 44, 46–48
pointing tools, 49–50
and virtual body effect, 40–42
new intention, 433
nociception, 159
nonvisual influences, 266
novel movement patterns, 276–77, 281, 284

object mereology, 137
object recognition, 277, 285, 349
objects and object-directedness, 428, 430–38, *434*, 440
object space, 237
obstacle shunning, 138, 174–75, 177, 193–94, *194*, 195, 197n6
occipital face area, 252, 324, 335, 342, 373
occluders, *25*, 32, *39*, 56–57n4, 218, 221, 281, 363, 367, 414
optic flow pattern neurons, 336–37, 344–45, 347
optic flow patterns, 328, 333–36
orientation detectors, 334
orientation effects. *See also* inversion effects
and action perception, 417
and biological-motion perception, 306
computational principles, 334
infant responses to, 313–14, 317–18
network of brain areas, 372
point-light walkers, 266, 280, 285–86
and configural processing, 142
and intentional action, 388

and virtual body effect, 38, 40–41
out-of-body experience (OBE), 68, 139, 188, 190–93, *190*, *194*, 197n6
overt imitation, 214–16
ownership of body, 39, 42. *See also* denial of ownership

pain
and action perception, 422
and body mereology, 149
and phantom sensations, 173, 175–76, *175*, 177–78, 197n1
and prosthetic manipulations, 36
and virtual body effect, 40
paraplegic patients, 20, 176, *177*, 178, 181, 196
parapsychology, 188, 191, 193, 195
paresthesias, 177
parietal cortex, 414–15, 421–22
part masks, 242
pattern masks, 242
pattern selectivity, 338–40
perceived action. *See* action perception
perceptual analyses, 140–43
perceptual expertise, 246–47, *247*
perceptual induction, 398–401, *398*, 407
perceptual learning, 315
perceptual prediction, 219–23
peripersonal space, 5, 12–13
and body representations, 69–79, *75*, *79*
and body shadows, 21, 23
multisensory representation of, 89–101
automatic processing, 94–96, *95*
extension, 96–98, *98*, *99*
functional properties, 93–94
neuropsychological evidence, 90–93, *92*
plasticity determinants, 98–100
and phantom sensations, 139, 187
and prosthetic manipulations, 36
and televisual display of body parts, 33
and tools, 42–43, 45–48, 50
peripheral factors, 172–73, *173*
personal beliefs, 68, 81
personification anosognosia, 185–87, 189
PET (positron emission tomography), 367–68
phantom bodies, 188–89
phantom half-body, 42, 81, 172, 185–87, 197nn4-5
phantom sensations, 5, 7
and biological-motion perception, 307–8
and body mereology, 155–56
and body representations, 55, 67, 137–39, 171–97
after spinal-cord injury, 176–78, *177*, 181
amputation phantoms, 172–76, *173*, *175*, 180–81, 197n1, 252
congenital phantom limb, 181–85, *184*, 197n3
half-body phantoms, 185–87, 197nn4-5
out-of-body experiences, 190–93, *190*
phantom bodies, 188–89
research perspectives, 193–96
supernumerary phantoms, 55, 137, 178–81, *179*, 185, 187, 189, 193, 197n2, 252
visual doppelgänger, 189–90, *190*
whole body phantoms, 139, 187–88

phantom sensations (*continued*)
and prismatic visual displacement, 19–20
and prosthetic manipulations, 35
phase-perturbed figures, 309–13, 310, *311*,
312, 315
phenomenology
of body mereology, 147–48, 160, 166
of intentional action, 393
of phantom sensations, 171, *179*, 180, 187–88,
193, 195
pigeons, 262, 363, 366
Pinocchio illusion, 70, 154, *155*, 196
plasticity, 39, 67–68, 76, 98–100, 138, 157, 214
pointing tools, 48–50, 52, 76–77
point-light stimuli, 262, 271–72, 287, 324
point-light walker displays. *See* biological-motion
displays
point-light walkers, 6–7, 262–67, 271–98
and body representations, 141
as common research tool, 277–87
availability, 278
ease of creation, 278
ease of manipulation, 279–85
ease of masking, 278
task flexibility, 285–87
and computational principles, 323–27, 331–32,
339–49, *341*, *346*
and configural processing, 243–45, 248,
252, 254
creation of, 273–77
animation, 275–76
automatic tracking, 275
direct filming, 274
generation of novel patterns, 276–77
manual assignment, 275
motion capture, 276
synthetic walkers, 274–75
description of, 272–73, *273*
going beyond, 287–97
using animated solid-body models, 292–97,
293, 296, *297*
using video footage, 287–92, 289, *290*, 291
infant responses to, 305, *306*, 309–15, 311,
312, *314*, 317
and network of brain areas, 362–67,
369–74, 379
and perceptual prediction, 220–21
point of subjective equality (PSE), 111, *112*, 118
postural schema, 15–16
postures and movements, 214, 229–54, *230*
and action perception, 253–54
and configural processing, 234–49
for biological motion displays, 243–45
embodied representations, 245–49, *247*, *249*
exact distances between features, 235
expertise, 245–49, *247*, *249*
holistic representations, 235–43, *236*,
238, *240*
relative position of parts/features, 235
and spatial body representations, 250–53
and "special" objects, 231–34
prediction devices, 8
and biological-motion perception, 327–28, 342
and covert imitation, 211–24
imitable stimuli, 212–15

perceptual prediction for human movements,
220–22
real-time simulation, 217–20
turn-taking, 222–23
and intentional action, 388
premotor cortex (PM), 362, 367–68, 374–75,
377, 414–16, 421–22
prior knowledge, 14, 122–24, 126, 129
prismatic displacement, 18–20, 55
probability density distributions, 106–8, *107*, *109*
proprioception, 4, 8, 16
and biological-motion perception, 317
and body mereology, 148, 153–54, 156,
158–65
and body representations, 65–66, 69–70,
81–82, 137, 143
and configural processing, 250–51
and intentional action, 388, 394
and intentional relations theory, 429
and mirror reflections and self-recognition, 24,
25, 27
and multimodal cue integration, 109
and peripersonal space, 93–94
and phantom sensations, 139, 191, 196
and prismatic visual displacement, 18–20
and prosthetic manipulations, 33
and televisual display of body parts, 29–30,
32–33
and virtual body effect, 40
prosthetic manipulations, 33–42
and body representations, 81
and clothing effect, 34–37
and supernumerary phantoms, *179*, 180
and virtual body effect, 37–42, *39*, 57n5
proximal specification, 394–95, 400–402, 406–8
psychological acts, 428–31, *434*, 437–39
psychophysical studies, 264, 347, 361–64,
374–75, 416–18, *418*, 419, *420*

real-time simulation, 217–20
redundant information, 13–14, 105–6, 108–12,
109, *110*, *112*
reduplications, autoscopic, 191–93, 195
referred sensations, 173–74
rehabilitation, 33, 99
remapping
and body representations, 78
and multimodal cue integration, 117,
123–24, 128
and peripersonal space, 97–98
and phantom sensations, 174
and tools, 47
remote manipulation, 51, 56
reorganizational processes, 173, 177–78
representational foundations, 393–409, 432.
See also body representations
and action perception, 395–401, 397, *398*,
407–8
and action planning, 407–8
and action production, 401–7
and intentional action, 393–95
representational momentum, 218–21
right-hemisphere brain damage (RBD), 13
and body mereology, 158
and body representations, 74–76, *75*, 78

and mirror reflections and self-recognition, 27
and peripersonal space, 90, 94, 97
and phantom sensations, 180
and prismatic visual displacement, 20
and prosthetic manipulations, 35
and tools, 46–47
and virtual body effect, 41
rings, 35, 73, 158, 186, 197n4
robotic devices, 50–51
rubber hand illusion, 160–66, *162*, *164*
and body mereology, 157, 159, 160–66, *162*, *164*
and body representations, 137
and peripersonal space, 93–94
and phantom sensations, 197n5
and virtual body effect, 37–42, *39*, 57n5

schema. *See* body schema
schizophrenia, 30–32, 80, 365, 388
scrambling
and biological-motion perception
computational principles, 337, 342, 345, 348
network of brain areas, 367
point-light walkers, 278, 280, 282
and configural processing, 231, 235, 239, *240*, 242, 244–45, 252
selectivity, 370–73
self-attribution, 32, 159, 160–66, *162*, *164*, 167
self-awareness, 12, 68, 77–81, *79*
self-generated action, 397–98, 400, 409n3
self-other equivalence, 429–30, 432, 438
self-recognition, 33, 55, 165, 186
and mirror reflections, 22, 23–28, *25*, 26, 56–57n4
sensorimotor perception/behavior
and mirror reflections and self-recognition, 23–24, 27–28
and phantom sensations, 178
and prosthetic manipulations, 33–34, 37
and tools, 42, 50–51
and virtual body effect, 38
sensory conflicts, 37, 77, 160
sensory estimation, 105–10, *107, 109–10*, 112–13, 112, 117, 122, 126
"sensory ghost," 175
sequence selectivity, 337, *338*
shadows, 17, 20–23, *22*, 55, 56n3
and body representations, 78–79
and televisual display of body parts, 30
shunning behavior. *See* obstacle shunning
signal detection theory, 106
"Simon effect," 286
simulation theory, 422–23, 427, 432
single-neuron recordings, 70–72, 361, 366, 378–79, 414
skin conductance response (SCR), 40, 161
snapshot neurons, 334–37, *338*, 344
somatognosia, 171
somatoparaphrenia, 42, 81, 157, 180, 185–87, 195, 197nn4-5
somatosensory information
and biological-motion perception, 366
and body mereology, 158
and body representations, 69–71, 77
and mirror reflections and self-recognition, 24
and multimodal cue integration, 105–6

and peripersonal space, 91
and prosthetic manipulations, 36
and televisual display of body parts, 30, 32–33
and tools, 45, 52
and virtual body effect, 40
somatosensory mereology, 137, 149–50, *152–53*, 153–56, 167
somatotopic organization, 90, 173–74
somesthesis, 147–48, 159, 171, 187–89
spared representation of contralateral intact limb, 182, 197n3
"spare" limb, 180
spatial body representations, 250–53
spatial localization, 18, 188–89
spatial perspective, *190*, 191–92, 195
spatial proximity, 70, 74, 94
"special" objects, 231–34
speech perception, 212, 311
spider figures, 311–12, 311, *312*
spinal-cord injuries, 20, 176–78, *177*, 181
"spinal phantoms," 176–78, *177*, 181
static body perception, 244–45, 248, 250–54, 266, 286
STPa, 366–67, 379
strictly congruent mirror neurons, 212
structure-from-motion displays, 272
STS. *See* superior temporal sulcus
stump characteristics, 181–82
subjective impressions, 38–39, 69–70, 74, 155
subsidiary awareness, 44
superficial schema, 15–16
superior temporal sulcus (STS), 362, 367, 369–70, 374, *377*, 414–15, 421–22
supernumerary phantoms, 252
and body mereology, 157
and body representations, 55, 137, 185, 187, 189, 193
after brain damage, 178–81, *179*, 197n2
and body shadows, 22
and prismatic visual displacement, 19–20
switch habituation paradigm, 436
switching strategies, 111
switch paradigm, 433–36, *434*
symmetrical coordination, 405–6, *405*
synthetic walkers, 274–75, 281, 289

tactile system, 7. *See also* haptic size stimuli
and biological-motion perception, 307
and body mereology, 149–50, 154–65, *162, 164*
and body representations, 69–71, 73–74, 77–78, 80–81, 137
and body shadows, 21–22
and configural processing, 251
and intentional action, 388
and mirror reflections and self-recognition, 24
and peripersonal space, 89–92, *92*, 93–95, *95*, 98, *99*
and phantom sensations, 139, 173, 178, 185, 187, 191
and prosthetic manipulations, 35–36
and televisual display of body parts, 29–30, 32
and tools, 45–47, *46*, 52
and virtual body effect, 37–39, *39*, 41–42
target motion, 267, 285, 288, 295, *296*

task flexibility, 285–87
teeth, 36–37
telesurgical devices, 43, 50–51, 52, 77
televisual display of body parts, 28–33, 51, 55.
    See also video monitors
template matching, 236, 239, 241
tetraplegia, 176
theory of mind, 216, 389, 427–28
theory theory, 427–28
"Third Hand, The," *179*, 180
third-person perspective, 393, 429, 431–32, 439
three-dimensional visual stimuli, 29, 40
    and biological-motion perception
        computational principles, 325–27,
            331–32, 340
        point-light walkers, 272, 275–76, 281–82
    and body representations, 72, 81
    and covert imitation, 212
tickling, 387–88
TMS (transcranial magnetic stimulation),
    372, 416
tools, 5, 12–13, 17, 34, 42–51, *46*, 57n6
    and action perception, 401, 414
    and biological-motion perception, 370
    and body mereology, 157
    and body representations, 73–77, *75*, 137
    detached tools, 50–51
    and peripersonal space, 97–98, 98, 99, *99*, 100
    and phantom sensations, *179*, 180, 193
    as physical intermediaries, 43–48
    pointing tools, 48–50, 52
tool use, 43, 57n6
tool-use learning tasks, 48–49
top-down influences
    and biological-motion perception, 263, 266–67
        computational principles, 345, 346–48, 349
        point-light walkers, 282–83
    and body mereology, 159, 164, 166
    and covert imitation, 217–18
    and peripersonal space, 94–96
    and phantom sensations, 138, 181, 187
topological mereology, 149–52
transcranial magnetic stimulation (TMS),
    183, 388
transitivism, 185–86, 189, 192, 196
translation flow, 336
transparent screens, 94, *95*
turn-taking in conversation, 141, 214,
    222–23, 253
two-dimensional visual stimuli, 29, 33, 48, 272,
    275, 326–27, 331, 340

unconscious body schema, 38
unilateral limb aplasia, 182, 197n3
unitary-axis displays, 313–14, *314*

ventral temporal cortex (VT), 362, 373–74, *377*
vibrotactile stimuli, 21, 24, 38, *39*, 45, *46*, 70–71,
    73, *79*, 154, *155*, 196
video games, 77
video monitors, 79–80, 98. *See also* televisual
    display of body parts
videotaping, 362
    and configural processing, 253
    and covert imitation, 213, 222

point-light walkers, 273–75, 287–92, 289,
    290, 291
view dependence, 331, 340–41, *341*
virtual body effect
    and body representations, 69
    and prosthetic manipulations, 37–42, *39*, 57n5
virtual movements, 174–75
virtual-reality environments, 77, 196
visual capture, 11–12
    and body representations, 55
    and body shadows, 22
    and mirror reflections and self-recognition,
        24, 27
    and phantom sensations, 196
    and prismatic displacement, 18–20
    and prosthetic manipulations, 33
    and tools, 47
    and virtual body effect, 38
visual distractors, 38–39, *39*, *46*, 73, 78–79, 342
visual doppelgänger, 189–90, *190*, 192
visual manipulation, 17–33
    and body shadows, 20–23, *22*, 56n3
    and mirror reflections and self-recognition,
        23–28, *25*, 26, 56–57n4
    and prismatic displacement, 18–20
    and televisual display of body parts, 28–33
visual search, 286, 294
visual system, 6–8
    and biological-motion perception, 262, 265,
        306–8
        computational principles, 323–24, 330–31,
            333, 342, 347, 349–50
        infant responses to, 305, 308–18, *310*, 311,
            312, *314*
        network of brain areas, 361–64, 366, 369
        point-light walkers, 266, 271, 287
    and body mereology, 154, 157–65, *162*, *164*
    and body representations, 70–76, *75*, 78–79,
        79, 137
    and configural processing, 142, 231, 241,
        244–54, *249*
    and covert imitation, 212
    and intentional action, 388
    and multimodal cue integration, 105, 108–13,
        109, *110*, 112, *113*, 115–22, *116*, *119*,
        121, 126
    and peripersonal space, 89–92, *92*, 93–95, *95*,
        96–97, *98*
    and phantom sensations, 139, 174–75,
        177–78, 181, 184, 186–91, 193, 195–96,
        197n4
    and televisual display of body parts, 29–31
    and tools, 45–47, *46*
    and virtual body effect, 38–39, *39*, 40–42
visual-tactile extinction, 13, 27, 78, 90–94, *95*,
    96–97, 100
visual-tactile integration/interference, 11–12, 21,
    22, 38, *39*, 69, 76, *79*. *See also* tactile
    system; visual system

whole body phantoms, 139, 172, 187–88
whole-body stimuli, 233, 239, 241–43
whole masks, 242
"who-system," 388
Williams syndrome, 267, 365